DEVELOPMENTAL PSYCHOLOGY

DEVELOPMENTAL PSYCHOLOGY

THIRD EDITION

Robert M. Liebert
*State University of New York
at Stony Brook*

Rita Wicks-Nelson
Hennepin County Mental Health Center

PRENTICE-HALL, INC., Englewood Cliffs, New Jersey 07632

Library of Congress Cataloging in Publication Data

LIEBERT, ROBERT M.
    Developmental psychology.

    Bibliography: p.
    Includes index.
    1. Developmental psychology.   I. Wicks-Nelson,
Rita, 1980 joint author.   II. Title.
BF713.L53 1981   155   80-22490
ISBN   0-13-208256-X

DEVELOPMENTAL PSYCHOLOGY third edition
Robert M. Liebert / Rita Wicks-Nelson

Editorial/production supervision: Alison D. Gnerre
Interior design: A Good Thing
Cover design: Lee Cohen
Cover photo: © Michael Philip Manheim 1977, Photo Researchers, Inc.
Photo research: Anita Duncan
Manufacturing buyer: Edmund W. Leone

Printed in the United States of America
10 9 8 7 6 5 4 3 2

Prentice-Hall International, Inc., London
Prentice-Hall of Australia Pty. Limited, Sydney
Prentice-Hall of Canada, Ltd., Toronto
Prentice-Hall of India Private Limited, New Delhi
Prentice-Hall of Japan, Inc., Tokyo
Prentice-Hall of Southeast Asia Pte. Ltd., Singapore
Whitehall Books Limited, Wellington, New Zealand

Contents

4 Sensory and Perceptual Development   86

5 Genetic Determinants of Behavior   109

III Cognitive & Intellectual Development   149

6 Learning Processes   150

Preface

As in the preceding editions, our aim in this third edition is to present a broad but selective introduction to developmental psychology as a branch of science that is at once basic and applied. We continue to believe that there is fundamental continuity among all developmental processes, and that the many practical applications of the field are best appreciated and understood in the light of the theory and research that spawned them.

In accord with this belief, the third edition has undergone a significant reorganization, resulting in five broad sections. In the introductory section we provide an expanded treatment of the history of developmental psychology as a science, explain the vital role of theory in its development, and introduce social learning, cognitive-developmental, psychoanalytic, and maturational theories. The section concludes with a simple but reasonably complete survey of the research methods used by developmentalists. The second section lays out the basic biological foundations on which all development rests, including a reworked treatment of genetic transmission and heredity. The third section then draws on the building blocks of the first two, describing cognitive and intellectual development in all its aspects.

The fourth and longest section, dealing with social development, draws on all that has gone before to present the developing individual in his or her social and cultural context. The section begins with a new chapter on the social and economic environment and also includes a new chapter devoted entirely to sex roles. The organization and treatment of self-control, moral standards, and interpersonal reactions have been completely updated and revised. The concluding section of the book deals with maturity in its many meanings. Evolved from the Road to Maturity chapter of the preceding edition, the section contains an entire chapter devoted to adolescence and another that deals with the years of adulthood and finally with death.

Throughout the book we have continually tried to stress the central importance of solid research in advancing our knowledge and understanding. We have likewise tried to show the pervasive influence of the four major theoretical positions introduced at the outset, and to contrast them wherever possible.

Those familiar with this text will notice that a series of Close-ups has superseded the Selections and Extended Discussions of previous editions. The Close-ups, as their name implies, are brief, highly focused discussions dealing with selected questions and issues in developmental psychology. We are especially grateful to Robert Plomin for contributing his original comments on "Behavioral Genetics and Personality" to the Close-up in Chapter 5.

Previous readers of this text will also notice the absence of our coauthor, Gloria Strauss Marmor. Due to other professional commitments, Dr. Marmor was unable to participate in the new edition, but we would like to acknowledge her past important contributions to *Developmental Psychology*.

We also thank our editor, John Isley, for the invaluable assistance and counsel we received in preparing this edition. Sincere thanks are given to Alison Gnerre of Prentice-Hall for her dedication to the production of the text, as well as to Donna Andrews, Sue Geiss, Marilyn Gobbo, and Jean Steinberg for their various contributions.

Robert M. Liebert   Rita Wicks-Nelson
Stony Brook, New York   Minneapolis, Minnesota

Acknowledgments

We are greatly indebted to those who reviewed the manuscript during its preparation; without their thoughtful input this book would be less complete, less accurate, and less interesting.

Richard Aslin, *Indiana University*

Robert T. Brown, *University of North Carolina at Wilmington*

Janice Westlund Bryan, *Middlesex Community College and Radcliffe Seminars Program*

Sylvia Farnham-Diggory, *University of Delaware*

Beverley Gounard, *State University of New York College at Buffalo*

Mark Grabe, *The University of North Dakota*

Jerald Greenberg, *Ohio State University*

Andrew Hansson, *Grand Rapids Junior College*

Sam L. Hutchinson, *Radford University*

Richard C. Labarba, *University of South Florida*

Suzanne Henry Martorano, *University of Kentucky*

Scott Paris, *The University of Michigan*

Dennis L. Molfese, *Southern Illinois University of Carbondale*

Victoria J. Molfese, *Southern Illinois University of Carbondale*

Edward K. Morris, *The University of Kansas*

Lizette Peterson, *University of Missouri-Columbia*

Charlotte Petterson, *University of Virginia*

Michael Pressley, *The University of Western Ontario*

Colleen F. Surber, *University of Wisconsin-Madison*

Michael Walraven, *Jackson Community College*

M. Virginia Wyly, *State University College at Buffalo*

Introduction

Developmental psychology is the branch of science concerned with the origin and change of behavior and related mental and bodily events. The field sweeps widely across philosophy, sociology, biology, anthropology, and education. Moreover, every branch of traditional academic psychology (e.g., learning, memory, perception) and applied psychology (e.g., clinical psychology, engineering psychology, personnel management, professional consulting) draws on developmental psychology and contributes to it. Then, too, as a science, developmental psychology relies heavily on research guided by theory, and thus involves the input of those involved in designing and analyzing social science research.

The first two chapters introduce developmental psychology as a field of study and specialization, and explain the role played by theory and research throughout the study of development.

We have given a good deal of emphasis to research; chapter 2 is devoted almost entirely to research design and to explaining the complications and pitfalls that arise in developmental research. As the reader will see, many significant questions remain unsolved in our understanding of human development. Progress will be most swift and sure if the research underlying claims about development becomes more accessible to evaluation by the layperson.

1 Some Developmental Viewpoints

WHAT IS DEVELOPMENTAL PSYCHOLOGY?

From the moment we are conceived, each of us is changing, and we continue to change all the time. Some of the bigger, physical changes are easy to see, as when the almost helpless human baby is transformed into a vigorous toddler, a strapping child, an active adolescent, and then a full-grown adult, following a sequence that is characteristic of every human being. Other developments, more difficult to describe or explain, also go on continuously. The infant's rudimentary ability to solve problems and communicate with others, for example, gives way within a few short years to sophisticated language and intellectual skills that differentiate our species from all other forms of animal life. With changes in physical and mental maturity come a host of gradual changes in social behavior and emotional experiences. The child who used to blush in social situations, commit various faux pas, and struggle openly with feelings of fear, anger, and love often becomes a socially skilled, poised adult with a unique and complex personality that may amaze even those who have seen the transformation take place.

Developmental psychology is that branch of psychology that studies these changes and, in fact, all the changes in physical, mental, and social functioning that occur throughout the life span, from conception to death. Simply put, it is a very broad field.

The Concept of Development

Modern developmental psychology is quite new.* Until at least the 1960s the designation given to psychological research of infants, children, and adolescents was "child psychology." Thus as late as 1968 one prominent writer observed:

> Although, logically, equal emphasis should be placed on development during all stages of life, so far most research has dealt primarily with infants, children, and adolescents. Because of this emphasis the term "developmental psychology" is often used interchangeably with the older terms "child psychology," [and] "adolescent psychology." (Stevenson, 1968, p. 36)

Today's concept of psychological development as a set of interacting, changing processes did not emerge in its present form until the last decade (Goulet and Baltes, 1970), although a few grand theorists, such as Erik Erikson, had insisted for some time that there were meaningful stages of adult development, as well as child development.

The Shift from Description to Explanation

One reason why an integrated concept of development did not emerge earlier was that until the 1950s the field was primarily devoted to describing changes rather than to explaining them. The first developmental psychologists were content to describe the child as completely as possible during its intrauterine existence (i.e., in the womb of its mother before birth), proceed to a similarly detailed description of the first weeks or months of life, and

*The first issue of the American Psychological Association's journal, *Developmental Psychology*, was published in 1969. (The *Journal of Abnormal Psychology*, by contrast, was founded in 1906!)

4

Portraits of Childhood

In medieval times childhood was not regarded as a psychologically distinct period. Children were merely viewed as "ill formed adults at the edges of society" (Kessen, 1965), a notion that is reflected in the art of this period (see Figure 1-1). According to one analysis of medieval society:

> ... the idea of childhood did not exist; this is not to suggest that children were neglected, forsaken, or despised. The idea of childhood is not to be confused with affection for children: it corresponds to an awareness of the particular nature of childhood, that particular nature which distinguishes the child from the adult, even the young adult. In medieval society this awareness was lacking. That is why, as soon as the child could live without the constant solicitude of his mother, his nanny, or his cradle-rocker, he belonged to adult society. [Ariès, 1962, p. 128]

Born in seventeenth- and eighteenth-century philosophy, the idea of childhood as a special period, in which youngsters were seen to have unique psychological, educational, and physical needs, came to hold influence. Philippe Ariès writes of the times: "... fondness for childhood and its special nature no longer found expression in amusement and coddling, but in psychological interest and moral solicitude. The child was no longer regarded as amusing or agreeable, but as in need of help and guidance. [It was realized that] in order to correct the behavior of children people must first understand them" (1962, p. 133). At first it was hoped that philosophy would provide this understanding. As early as the fourth century B.C. Plato articulated the question of whether ability is acquired or innate. The controversy that emerged thereafter utlimately showed that philosophy alone was incapable of illuminating the nature of the child's development. The clash is captured in the differing views of philosophers John Locke (1632–1704) and Jean Jacques Rousseau (1712–1778).

Locke asserted that the human infant is at birth a **tabula rasa**, or blank slate, and that experience, transmitted through the senses, molds each of us into a unique individual. Consistent with this view, Locke enburdened parents with the responsibility of teaching their children self-control and rationality, and of planning their environment and experiences from the moment of birth.

Rousseau, on the other hand, cast the newborn human as a "noble savage," endowed with an innate sense of justice and morality. Rousseau believed that all virtues are inborn and will develop naturally. For Rousseau, planned environments and experiences are detrimental to development; human nobility, he insisted, is imperiled by an interfering society.

BEGINNINGS OF CHILD DEVELOPMENT RESEARCH

By the middle of the nineteenth century a new approach to understanding childhood emerged: Abstract speculation about the child's "nature" was replaced by empirical efforts to record and study the behavior and development of the young. This was the dawn of contemporary developmental psychology. The impetus for the new science came from many sources, but evolutionary biology and its founder, Charles Darwin (1809–1892), played a unique role:

> ... with the publication of Darwin's **Descent of Man**, in 1871, the child became a unique part of the scientific endeavor; ... For nearly half a century after Darwin's shattering of the mirror, the child became the best natural lab-

(a)

(b)

(c)

FIGURE 1-1

Portraits of Childhood. (a) Erasmus Quellin's "Portrait of a Boy with a Dog," painted in the seventeenth century, shows that little distinction was made between childhood and adulthood, for the child is depicted simply as a miniature adult. (b) "Ralph Izard," by Jeremiah Theuss (1753), gives a first hint of childhood. The trend sharpens in "The Wilson Children," (c) by an unknown artist circa 1860, and "A Sunflower for Teacher," (d) by Winslow Homer (1875). (e) Robert Henri's "Forces of Peace" is definitely a little girl in

(d)

(f)

(e)

the modern sense. But only in this Norman Rockwell painting (f) of two boys, do we see the mood of childhood as it has recently emerged,

oratory for the study of evolution, and the idea of **development** dominated the science of man. [Later workers] built child psychology with Darwin's bricks. [Kessen, 1965, p. 6]

Darwin did much to generate the nineteenth century's pervasive interest in development of all sorts, but developmental psychology had a founder more uniquely its own. G. Stanley Hall shared Darwin's general viewpoint, but he focused it in a particular way. Hall administered questionnaires to large groups of children of different ages in order to discern age trends in children's beliefs, knowledge, and feelings as they grew older. In addition to his quest for discovering "the contents of children's minds," Hall, who was founder and first president of the American Psychological Association [APA] also turned to children for the study of such traditional topics as perception, memory, and learning. Meanwhile, Alfred Binet had begun to distinguish between intellectually normal and subnormal children in France, and Sigmund Freud had startled the world with his suggestion that the experiences of early childhood seemed to account for unusual

patterns of behavior in adulthood. There was clearly much to be learned and expansion was in order.

By the 1920s developmental psychology had come into the public eye as the bearer of solutions to practical problems. John Watson, the father of behaviorism, had begun to write and lecture on psychology and child-rearing practices. His impact, along with that of Freud, Binet, Hall, and many others, was felt with the emergence of clinics established for the purpose of assessing children and advising parents. In turn, this interest led to an enormous research investment in child development. Short-term studies were set up in numerous university-based nursery schools, and long-range (or longitudinal) projects were established at such places as Berkeley and Yale in the United States and in several principal European cities.

Thus came the recognition of childhood as the psychological as well as the physical precursor of adulthood. But many years passed before psychologists were to have the profound insight to realize that development is a continuous process, which must be seen in the context of the entire human life span.

then move on to early childhood, middle childhood, and so on. Such studies could be readily justified on practical grounds alone. Consider, for example, Mary Shirley's (1933) study of motor development, based on careful observations of twenty-five children. The data, illustrated in Figure 1–2, were of obvious interest and value to parents, physicians, and psychologists for determining what constituted normal, precocious, and retarded development. Nonetheless, such descriptive information was not alluring enough to continue attracting researchers. While the field of psychology as a whole expanded considerably, developmental research waned sharply. In 1938 approximately five hundred publications concerned with children's development appeared; in 1949 that number had shrunk in half (Stevenson, 1968).

Then, at the beginning of the 1950s, developmental psychology was revitalized. Many factors—a prospering economy and the research funds that came with it, a large new generation of youngsters, the establishment of various government agencies—contributed to this rise, but chief among them was the fact that developmental psychologists had adopted a new approach to their subject. No longer concerned primarily with description for

FETAL POSTURE
0 mo.

CHIN UP
1 mo.

CHEST UP
2 mo.

REACH AND MISS
3 mo.

SIT WITH SUPPORT
4 mo.

SIT ON LAP
GRASP OBJECT
5 mo.

GRASP DANGLING OBJECT
6 mo.

SIT ALONE
7 mo.

SIT ON HIGH CHAIR

STAND WITH HELP
8 mo.

STAND HOLDING FURNITURE
9 mo.

CREEP
10 mo.

WALK WHEN LED
11 mo.

PULL TO STAND BY FURNITURE
12 mo.

CLIMB STAIR STEPS
13 mo.

STAND ALONE
14 mo.

WALK ALONE
15 mo.

FIGURE 1–2
The sequence of motor development during the first fifteen months of life, illustrating the utility of a chronological approach for providing normative information. Adapted from M. M. Shirley, The First Two Years: A Study of Twenty-Five Babies, Vol. II. University of Minnesota Press, Minneapolis. © 1933, University of Minnesota, by permission.

its own sake, their interest had turned to a concern with the processes that underlie the development of behavior.

PLAN OF THIS BOOK

Our aim in this book is to introduce modern developmental psychology, including its theories, research, and practical accomplishments. Developmental psychology, however, is very much at the crossroads of psychology, while also intersecting with other areas such as medicine and education. As a result, there is such an abundance of literature that any effort to recite all findings and viewpoints, even briefly, would result in a truly encyclopedic presentation. Our goal instead is to introduce the underlying processes that are the substance of developmental psychology. We have tried to explain how basic and applied processes operate and develop in the human, ever mindful of the fact that development occurs *over* time but never *because* of time. The idea behind this book is to capture and transmit what is current in developmental psychology in a way that is both interesting and accurate.

The book itself is organized around three major areas of growth: biological, intellectual, and social. After a nontechnical explanation of research methods and functions in chapter 2 we turn to the biological foundations of development, including a description of growth and alternative accounts of the growth process. Cognitive and intellectual development are presented next, relating changes in these processes to their roots in biology and in the environment. A treatment of social development follows, as we endeavor to show how such phenomena as self-control are products of the more basic processes that have already been discussed. At the same time, social development raises some questions not raised when one is limited to the biological or logical sphere, such as in the area of moral development. A description of some of the behavior problems of youth and a summary of available treatments closes the social development section.

The final section of the text is called "The Road to Maturity." (Maturity is best defined as realizing the potential inherent in the human life span.) Beginning with some of the hallmark transitions of adolescence, we take the opportunity to put the development of children and adolescents, to which most of the book is devoted, into a larger perspective that includes adulthood.

We begin each section with a broad summary statement and each chapter with an outline, which serve as road maps to what lies ahead. At the same time, every chapter has a summary to facilitate review of what has already been discussed. In addition to our basic presentation, the pages that follow contain additional "Close-ups," which allow us to take a more detailed look at some issue of special theoretical or practical significance.

RECURRING ISSUES IN DEVELOPMENTAL PSYCHOLOGY

In their search for underlying causes and explanations, modern developmental psychologists repeatedly face a few recurring issues that seem to arise regardless of the aspect of development being studied (e.g., cognitive, or social). We will consider three such issues.

Biological vs. Environmental Determination (The Nature-nurture Issue)

Of all the issues and disputes that appear in the study of development, perhaps none has been as pervasive as the debate regarding the relative contributions of biological and environmental influences to behavior. The problem has been discussed as the *heredity-environment* issue, the *nature-nuture* controversy, and by many other names. Although the question underlying this dichotomy appears to be quite simple (i.e., How much of the individual's behavior is contributed by his or her biological and genetic makeup and how much by social and environmental influences?), the apparent simplicity is deceptive.

As Anastasi (1958) has noted in a careful analysis, the questions "Which one?" and "How much?" simply overlook the fact that an individual's hereditary endowment and the environment to which he or she is exposed must *interact* in order to produce behavior. Because both heredity and environment make an absolutely necessary contribution to behavior, questions that presume that these factors simply differ in quantity or importance, like two bank accounts, are not likely to be fruitful. Instead, we ultimately must

Continuity vs. Discontinuity in Development

ask *how* (i.e., in what manner) biological and social influences combine for various kinds of behavior.

Two types of behavioral change often are identified in the study of human development, those that are gradual or *continuous* and those that are sudden or *discontinuous.*

To understand the nature of this distinction, consider the following example suggested by the work of Jean Piaget (whose theory of cognitive development will be discussed in detail in a later chapter). An experimenter begins by showing a four-year-old child two short, wide glass beakers, each containing the same quantity of milk. The youngster is asked whether both beakers have an equal amount of fluid, and agrees that they do. Then, while the child watches, the experimenter pours the entire contents of one of these beakers into a third beaker—a tall, thin one. When the child is asked to compare the two beakers that now contain milk, he or she often will say that the tall, thin beaker has more milk in it than the original short, wide one. In contrast, older children, like adults, will immediately point out that the two beakers in question must have the same amount of milk, for the volume of the two original beakers was equal at the beginning and no liquid was lost or gained by merely pouring the contents of one of them into a container of a different shape.

How and why does this transition in handling the problem occur? Is there a qualitative change or *discontinuity* from one mode of thinking to another as the child grows older, or would the change, if we were able to watch it more closely, appear to be a gradual, *continuous* process of growing sophistication? The former viewpoint leads to the suggestion that development proceeds in a series of relatively discrete *stages*; it thus compels the theorist to try to identify these stages and analyze their components. As we shall see, this is the conclusion that, with some qualifications, Piaget has reached in examining the child's intellectual development. Likewise, other stage theorists have argued that many aspects of human emotional and social development proceed in a relatively discontinuous, stagewise fashion.

Other theorists, though, have emphasized the possibility that development may only seem discontinuous. Observers who compare children of different ages may be unable to detect gradual changes as they occur, and thus may mistakenly take large or dramatic shifts as evidence of discontinuity. Even if the same children are observed over time, the frequency and nature of the observations can play an important role in determining whether developmental changes will seem gradual or relatively abrupt.

The continuity-discontinuity issue involves much more than measurement. Major questions revolve around the processes through which change occurs. Stage theorists often insist that universal, biologically based factors play a prominent role in development. Relatively uniform structural changes, they argue, occur in the psychological processes of almost all children and give rise to relatively discontinuous changes in behavior.

In contrast, theorists who emphasize continuities often assume that social and experiential factors underlie many developmental changes. Children, they point out, must *learn* to behave as they do; the learning is likely to be a gradual, continuous process that will vary from one child to another depending upon individual differences in socioeconomic, ethnic, and cultural background, as well as other factors.

Although it should be emphasized that all theorists agree that there are both continuities and discontinuities in development, differences in emphasis and vantage point are of sufficient importance to have implications for almost every substantive topic raised in this book.

Behavioral vs. Cognitive Emphasis

Psychology emerged as an independent science in the late nineteenth century and was at first devoted exclusively to understanding the nature of thought and the structure of the human mind. The early psychologists were interested in *cognitive processes* (such as perceiving, knowing, and expecting), and it seemed to them that these processes could be studied only through asking trained subjects to examine their own mental processes—to introspect. As a scientific tool, the method of introspection just didn't work; there was no way to settle disputes when two investigators disagreed. Psychologists searched for the objectivity of science, and a vigorous young psychologist named John Watson attracted a great deal of interest by saying that psychology should not be concerned with cognitive processes at all; rather, it should adopt a behaviorist stance. According to Watson:

FIGURE 1-3
John B. Watson, father
of modern behaviorism.
Culver Pictures.

Psychology as the behaviorist views it is a purely objective experimental branch of natural science. Its theoretical goal is the prediction and control of behavior. Introspection forms no essential part of its methods, nor is the scientific value of its data dependent upon the readiness with which they lend themselves to interpretation in terms of consciousness. [Watson, 1913, p. 158]

During the early part of this century many psychologists joined Watson in adopting a behaviorist stance, and experimental psychology prospered as a result. But Watson certainly erred in equating the study of cognitive processes with the method of introspection. Asking children to analyze the workings of their own minds to find out how they think when they solve problems is not the best method of investigation. European psychologists such as Jean Piaget were the first to see that more objective methods could be applied to the study of mental processes. As illustrated in his previously mentioned work on children's perception of liquid quantity, Piaget showed that mental processes might be inferred from a child's overt behavior. Piaget's inferences led to further predictions, which were tested and confirmed objectively, and the excitement caused by his work and that of a number of other modern cognitive psychologists has made the strictly behavioral stance seem shallow to many developmentalists. Strict behaviorism still thrives in some quarters, however, and modern behaviorists believe they can understand all the phenomena studied by cognitively oriented psychologists (perceptual, intellectual, and language development, for example) without resorting to a discussion of mental processes.

As with the other issues discussed in this section, the distinction between behaviorist and cognitive approaches has become more one of relative emphasis than outright antagonism in the past few years, but the fundamental question of the role of internal mental processes in psychological development remains quite important.

THE ROLE OF THEORY

Even in our brief discussion thus far, it has been impossible to avoid the word "theory." What functions do theories serve in the investigation of development? The answers are many.

Theories always serve an explanatory-descriptive role, providing a basis for organizing and condensing facts that are already known. They also should enable us to predict future events. To do so, a theory must be *testable* and thus potentially *capable of being refuted* or falsified. It must lead to the derivation of specific hypotheses or predictions that can be confirmed or disconfirmed publicly. Related to this predictive function is the manner in which theories guide research into areas that might not otherwise attract interest or that might otherwise seem too complicated to be handled. Like a prospector's map of secret treasure, they lead us to expect substantial yields in areas that would otherwise seem to have little promise.

On the other hand, theories also may turn research away from phenomena that, from the standpoint of other theories, are generally believed to be critical. For example, it is widely held that a child's early toilet-training experiences play a vital role in later social development. However, several learning theory approaches to behavior suggest that these early experiences have little or no important bearing on, say, the behavior of an adolescent. Adherents to the latter view will be guided by their theory to *not* seek, and perhaps eschew, information about lavatory practices in early childhood, which might otherwise occupy their research or clinical efforts.

Although a number of significant developmental studies have been done without the impetus of a full-blown theory, some theoretical notions or coherent hunches about how the processes of development must work are always present. More important, though, is that modern developmental research has for the most part been guided by theory. Anyone who has contact with children will develop her or his own unique view of development, and as someone has quipped, parents are just developmental psychologists who do not publish. But four broad formal theories have strongly influenced those who do publish, and each theory merits a brief introduction here.

Maturational Theory

A scholarly analysis of the impact of theories of child development (Caldwell and Richmond, 1962) refers to "maturational theory" as one of the major theories that has guided developmental psychology. The basic

FIGURE 1–4
Arnold Gesell,
prominent
maturational theorist,
testifies before a
Senate subcommittee
concerned with
mounting juvenile
delinquency,
December
1943.   Wide World
Photos.

FIGURE 1-5
Sigmund Freud in
London in June, 1938,
after being rescued
from Nazi-occupied
Vienna. Wide World
Photos.

idea behind this theory is that most of the changes we see in children over time occur because of a specific and prearranged scheme or plan within the body. Maturation, according to this view, reveals the natural unfolding of the plan, and patterns of growth charted over time are like the trail of a sky-writing plane which shows us only that part of the mission that is already completed.

The view that all development, from infant nursing patterns to the emergence of moral values, is self-regulated by the unfolding of natural processes and biological plans was popularized by Arnold Gesell (1940, 1956). Gesell himself studied primarily children's physical and motor development, work that generated major interest but only minor controversy. Then, as now, almost everyone was willing to agree that, for example, rate of growth is heavily influenced by a simple process of maturation. But the maturational view of intellectual and personality development—that is, of complex social behavior—continues to be vigorously attacked and defended. We will therefore have many occasions to mention it later.

Psychoanalytic
Theory

Psychoanalytic theory, the theory developed by Sigmund Freud, ranks among the most far-reaching and influential views in modern history. Freud too was convinced that the structure of human personality is intrinsic, and that people mature psychologically according to principles that apply universally. But he was also convinced that the functional aspects of each individual personality are shaped by experience in a social context.

Freud's great message to developmentalists was his insistence on the importance of early experience for establishing patterns that will then endure through the entire life span. Those developmentalists who have revised classical psychoanalytic theory, Erik Erikson notable among them, have provided a bridge from which we can view the psychological characteristics of adolescence, middle age, and old age in social terms.

Freud's most important insight, which is rarely seriously challenged, is that humans are not always conscious of their own motives. He attributed great strength, durability, and enormous motivational properties to unconscious impulses and warned that the rational person and the rationalizing person are not easy to tell apart. The influence of Freud's views are covered in detail in the latter chapters of this book.

Social Learning Theory

We already had occasion to note John Locke's idea that the infant's mind is a blank slate for which very little is predetermined but on which experience writes whatever chance or conscious planning might produce. John Watson was among the first psychologists to champion this view; an important tenet of his behaviorist view was that the child *learns to be* what he

FIGURE 1–6
B. F. Skinner, a celebrated learning-oriented psychologist, explained learning on the basis of external reward and punishment.
© Karsh, Ottawa.

FIGURE 1–7
Jean Piaget focused on the development of thought processes and knowledge in his approach to the cognitive-developmental theory. The Bettmann Archive, Inc.

or she becomes, usually in a social context. Since Watson did not have much learning theory to work with, he could only condition infants and children to make simple responses and dream of the day when anything could be taught. And Watson assumed that with correctly selected techniques anything could be learned, by almost anyone.

Several theories of learning were developed after Watson took his stand. Clark Hull believed that all learning was based on drive and drive-reduction, and Neal Miller and John Dollard wrote a social learning theory based on Hull's ideas. B. F. Skinner had no use for Hull's views because the concept of drive seemed to him circular, and so Skinner explained learning on the basis of external reward and punishment, as another learning-oriented psychologist, E. L. Thorndike, had begun to do years before.

A rather different brand of social learning theory was developed by Albert Bandura and Richard Walters in the decade between 1955 and 1965. Bandura and Walters accepted the idea that conditioning, reward, and punishment all contribute to social development, but they questioned whether all (or even most) of what actually goes on during childhood learning could be explained in these terms. Children learn by observation, they argued, and this type of learning can take place without any direct reward or punishment at all. This approach has become extremely influential because it speaks directly to the issue of *processes* of social development, and it has inspired a compelling body of research. Some aspect of social learning theory is mentioned in every chapter of this book.

Cognitive-
Developmental
Theory   Still another possible way to approach psychological development is to focus on the development of thought processes and knowledge. Jean Piaget, whom we have already mentioned, took just such an approach in his cognitive-developmental theory. Piaget postulates four basic periods in cognitive development (the sensorimotor, preoperational, concrete operational, and formal operational stages, which will be explained in detail in chapter 7), each characterized by unique and ever more sophisticated types of reasoning.

Piaget's writings have also suggested that social and emotional adjustment as well as moral development can only be understood with reference to their cognitive underpinnings. Cognitive-developmental theory assumes a dynamic interaction between underlying structure and experience, and thus is responsive to aspects of both maturational and social learning theory. Perhaps for this reason, Piaget's influence has pervaded modern developmental psychology.

At one time it was felt that a single theory of development would prevail over the others, but it has become plain that agreement at this global level is impossible. The four theories just discussed are so broad and all-encompassing that today we think of them more as viewpoints than as rigorous scientific formulations. You will have a better understanding of these theories and the way they interact as you read subsequent chapters.

RESEARCH IN DEVELOPMENTAL PSYCHOLOGY

We have seen that philosophical debate was unable to resolve questions about development and that careful, systematic observation was needed to solidly establish developmental psychology. From the homey but painstaking descriptions of infants in the nineteenth and early twentieth centuries to the elaborate million-dollar studies done to analyze the effects of mass media on cognitive and social development, research has played the major vitalizing role in our advance toward a fuller understanding of human development.

Research is not simply the scientist's version of casual observation. Instead, it is a very special class of activity in which a systematic effort is made to obtain and evaluate information about one or more phenomena according to a set of explicit rules. It is to the various ways in which developmental psychologists have undertaken this task that the next chapter is devoted.

SUMMARY

Developmental psychology studies all the changes in physical, mental, and social functioning that occur throughout the life span from conception to death. *Development* refers to a process of growth and change in capability over time, as a function of both maturation and interaction with the environment.

The idea of childhood as a special period emerged in seventeenth- and eighteenth-century philosophy and did not become scientifically important until the middle of the nineteenth century. Thereafter there was much interest in developmental research and the early twentieth century witnessed emergence of clinics for assessing and advising parents. Interest declined in the 1940s but was revived in the 1950s with a new emphasis on the processes that underlie developmental changes rather than toward describing the changes themselves.

One of the major issues in contemporary psychology involves the relative status of biological and environmental determinants of behavior. It is difficult to determine the contributions of each factor, since an individual's hereditary endowment and the environment interact in order to produce behavior. Another important issue is the behavioral versus the cognitive emphasis. Watson's behaviorism ruled out the study of mental processes because they could not be observed directly, but contemporary psychologists are successfully applying objective methods to the study of cognition. Finally, developmental psychologists differ in the relative emphasis they give to continuous versus discontinuous shifts in development.

Theories serve an important explanatory role in organizing and condensing facts that are already known, and they should enable us to predict future events. Four important theories are related to developmental psychology: maturational theory, psychoanalytic theory, social learning theory, and cognitive-developmental theory. Theories offer predictions that must be scientifically tested by research.

2 Methods of Developmental Research

In chapter 1 we considered the nature of development and examined some of the issues surrounding the concept. The present chapter deals with the methods used in developmental research and explores their strengths and weaknesses.

THREE METHODS OF DEVELOPMENTAL RESEARCH

Every developmental investigation can be characterized in terms of whether its underlying strategy involves the *experimental, correlational,* or *case study* approach. Although all of these methods involve *observation* of one sort or another, they differ in crucial ways.

The *experimental method* involves actual manipulation of various treatments, circumstances, or events to which the person is exposed; it thereby permits explicit inferences as to causal relationships between these manipulations and subsequent behavior. The *correlational method* explores the existing relationship between two or more events or variables but, although it provides a relatively large yield of information, it does not typically permit causal inferences to be drawn directly. The *case study method* involves systematic description of the behavior of a single individual, thus providing a depth of information not typically available, but severely limiting the ability to make general statements about a population of individuals.

The Experimental Method

The experimental method can be illustrated by tracing a specific study done by Coates and Hartup (1969). The point of departure for Coates and Hartup's research was an earlier finding that children's learning of an adult's behavior was greater if they had been asked to describe out loud—i.e., to verbalize—each act as it was observed than if they had been permitted to watch the adult's actions passively. Coates and Hartup wanted to examine the relationship between chronological age and the influence of such verbalizations on observational learning by young children. In their study children of two age groups, four-year-olds and seven-year-olds, observed a film of an adult's performance of some novel tasks. Before watching this film, though, the children were divided into groups that received one of three sets of instructions. Only two need concern us here: In the *induced verbalization* condition, the children were given specific labels to use in describing the model's actions; in the *passive observation* condition, they were given no instructions regarding verbal descriptions.

Coates and Hartup, like most investigators, were guided by a set of theoretical possibilities. Specifically, they believed that younger children do not spontaneously produce relevant verbalizations while learning visually, whereas older children do produce and employ such verbalizations. The investigators also felt that if younger children were helped to produce relevant descriptions or labels, their learning would be improved.

On the basis of these hypotheses, the following predictions were made: (1) seven-year-olds in the *passive observation* condition will show greater observational learning than four-year-olds in the *passive observation* condition; (2) four-year-olds will show greater observational learning in the *induced verbalization* condition than in the *passive observation* condition; and (3) there will be little difference in observational learning in the *induced verbalization* and *passive observation* conditions among the seven-year-olds, for they presumably produce relevant verbalizations spontaneously.

So far, then, the investigators have taken a finding from earlier studies and combined it with theory to generate the three predictions or *experimental hypotheses* stated above. At this point the three predictions are still untested. They are no more than ideas, but the ideas are well formulated as general propositions that can be tested in a *controlled situation*. The controlled situation not only must meet the requirements of the propositions under test but also must exclude or minimize the effect of other factors not hypothesized to be relevant. What are these requirements in the present example? First, a situation must be created in which children have an equal opportunity to be exposed to novel behaviors and are either asked or not asked to verbalize a description of what they see. Their recall (learning) under these two conditions must then be compared. Second, the subjects must differ in age in the manner prescribed by the hypotheses. Finally, precise measurement of the *variable of interest*—in this case the children's reproduction of the model's actions—must be possible.

To meet these requirements, children in the Coates and Hartup experiment were brought individually to a mobile research laboratory by an adult experimenter who introduced them to a second adult. They were told that they were going to watch a movie, after which they would go into another room of the laboratory and "be asked to show what the man in the movie did" (1969, p. 558). Additionally, one of the adults demonstrated two novel behaviors (turning around and marching in place), which illustrated the type of things the child would see. To provide an adequate test of the experimental hypotheses, the film had to display a fairly large number of behaviors that met the dual criteria of being both novel and readily subject to imitation and verbal representation. The production met these qualifications admirably.

> A 7-minute color film . . . was prepared that depicted the behavior of a 25-year-old male model. The model displayed 20 critical behaviors. In order of presentation these were: has his hands over his eyes; puts his hands behind his back; builds a tower of blocks in a unique way; puts a toy on top of the tower; walks backward four steps from the tower; puts a baton in front of him on the floor; kneels down on one knee behind the baton; fires a pop gun at the tower; takes down the tower of blocks in a unique way; sits on a Bobo clown; hits the clown in the nose; hits the clown with a mallet; throws a ball at the clown; tosses a Hoola Hoop around the clown; drags the clown with the hoop to a corner of the room; walks backward four steps from the bean bag target; throws a bean bag between his legs at the bean bag target; walks backward four steps from the target; squats down with his back to the target; walks across the room whirling the Hoola Hoop over his arm. [1969, p. 558]

All of the children who participated in this experiment saw the live demonstration and film described above, but the type of instruction they received before the observational period varied.

In the *induced verbalization* condition, the experimenter indicated that he would describe what the actor was doing while the film was being shown and that the child should repeat his statements. A short practice session then ensued in which the child was asked to imitate a verbal description of the other adult's turning and marching. In the *passive observation* group, no verbalization instructions were given. Thus the condition or manipulation that the experimenter created, the *independent variable,* was the type of instruction.

It is important to note how Coates and Hartup decided which children would receive which type of instruction. Ideally, of course, the investigators would want the two instruction groups to be as similar as possible except for the type of instruction given: Preexisting differences between the groups in overall memory capacity, intelligence, or any number of other factors might easily obscure or confound the effects of the independent variable. While the goal of completely equating the groups of an experiment on all relevant factors is impossible to ensure, experience has shown that assigning people *randomly* to conditions tends to produce maximal similarity between groups in the long run. (Technically, a *random assignment procedure* is one in which each potential subject has an equal chance of being assigned to any of the groups. This may be done by drawing the subjects' names blindly from a hat or by using a random numbers table or similar aid designed for the purpose.) Within each age group, children in the Coates and

FIGURE 2–1
A portion of the results of Coates and Hartup's experiment showing that, as predicted, observational learning by younger but not older children is improved by inducing verbal descriptions of what they see.   Data from Coates and Hartup, 1969. Copyright 1973 by the American Psychological Association. Reprinted by permission.

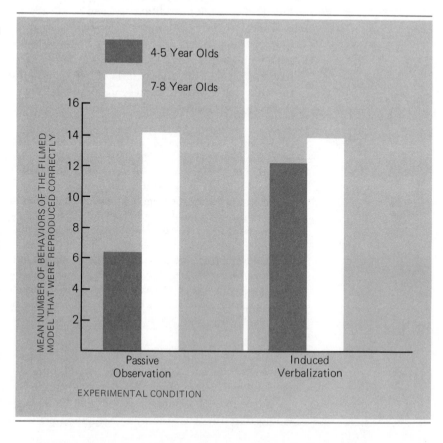

Hartup experiment were assigned randomly to either the induced verbalization or the passive observation group.

A *dependent variable* is a measurable aspect of the subject's behavior that changes as the independent variable changes. The term derives from the fact that these measures *depend upon* or are controlled by the experimental manipulations (which are *in*dependent in the sense that the experimenter can change them at will). In the Coates and Hartup experiment, the major dependent variable was the number of behaviors in the film that were correctly reproduced by the children. This measure was obtained by taking each subject, after he or she had watched the movie, into another room that contained all the objects with which the filmed model had played. The children, tested individually, were then asked to demonstrate what the man in the movie had done. They were first asked to show what the man did before playing with the toys, then what the man did with the blocks, and so on.

A portion of the results of this experiment is shown in Figure 2–1. The three experimental predictions considered here (see p. 22) received clear support. Of particular importance, the study demonstrates that asking young children to verbalize what they have seen can produce or *cause* improvements in learning, since this factor was manipulated directly as part of the experiment (cf. Neale and Liebert, 1980). In correlational research, direct manipulations are not used and thus we can rarely be as confident about cause and effect.

The Correlational Method

Correlation, as the name implies, deals with the relationship between two or more factors or variables. The method involves questions of the general form: "Do variable X and variable Y go together or vary together in some way?" Questions of this type are frequently asked in developmental psychology: Is the child's performance in school related to the socioeconomic status of his or her family? Is there a relationship between late toilet training and compulsiveness in adulthood? Is the frequency of dating behavior during adolescence related to later marital success and happiness?

Rather than manipulating the events or experiences to which the person is exposed, the investigator measures phenomena that already exist. In studying the correlation between variables, researchers often compute a correlation coefficient. One commonly used coefficient, designated by the symbol r,* indicates both the direction and the magnitude of the relationship. It may range from $+1.00$ to -1.00.

The *direction* is shown by the sign of the coefficient. A positive sign means that high scores on one variable, X, tend to be associated with high scores on another variable, Y, and low scores on X tend to go with low scores on Y. For example, a positive correlation is found between children's age and height; older children are likely to be taller. Conversely, a negative sign means that high scores on X tend to be associated with low scores on Y and low scores on X with high scores on Y. Age and the quickness of re-

*There are several types of correlation coefficients of which r, the Pearson product-moment correlation coefficient, is only one. Our comments on correlational techniques also apply to the other types.

flexes are usually found to be negatively correlated in adults; as people grow older, their reflexes become slower.

The *magnitude* or strength of a correlation is indicated by the absolute value of the coefficient (disregarding sign). Correlation coefficients of +.60 and −.60 are equivalent with respect to how strongly the variables under consideration are related. The strongest relationship is indicated when $r = +1.00$ or $r = -1.00$; in both cases the two variables are perfectly correlated so that either can be determined from the other with perfect accuracy. As the coefficient decreases in absolute value, the magnitude of the relationship becomes weaker, and the ability to estimate one variable from the other decreases. A coefficient of 0.00 indicates that the variables are unrelated, in which case knowledge of one does not tell us anything at all about the other.

A word of caution should be introduced here. Because correlation coefficients range in absolute value from 0.00 to 1.00, it is tempting to view them as percentages (i.e., to assume that a correlation of .60 means a "60 percent" correlation). From this faulty assumption one may be tempted to conclude that a correlation of .50 is twice as large as one of .25. This is an error. The appropriate rule of thumb is to compare squared correlation coefficients to get an idea of the relative strengths of each. Thus, in a sense, a correlation of .80 is approximately *four* times as large as a correlation of .40 (i.e., $.80^2 = .64$ and $.40^2 = .16$; .64 is four times .16).

A Comparison of the Experimental and Correlational Methods

The critical issue that distinguishes experimental and correlational research is whether or not we can infer a causal relationship between (or among) the variables under investigation. In a true experiment, when a relationship is found, cause-and-effect is always implied; that is, the independent variable can be said to lead to a change in the dependent variable. Correlational findings, on the other hand, reveal relationships between (or among) variables without *necessarily* implying causality—although some causal relationship may underlie the findings. For example, there is a positive correlation between the amount of ice cream eaten by children in a particular city on summer days and the number of children who drown on those days. But drownings do not cause an increase in ice cream consumption nor, contrary to popular opinion, does eating ice cream markedly increase the likelihood of cramps and subsequent drowning. Rather, it is a third variable—temperature—that is causally related to both of the other variables. Warmer weather makes it more likely that children will be both swimming (and drowning) *and* eating ice cream.

It is, unfortunately, easy to misconstrue some developmental studies as experimental when they are really correlational in character. To illustrate this point, consider the following hypothetical example. A school psychologist notices that the mothers of many of the children who have behavior problems seem particularly impatient in dealing with their children. To check on this observation, a systematic investigation is conducted. Specifically, twelve children with behavior problems and twelve children with no reported school difficulties are asked to work with their mothers on a standardized task that requires an interaction between mother and child. Two independent raters are asked to observe the mothers during the sessions and evaluate their interaction with their children on a seven-point scale (1 = very patient, 7 = very impatient). The raters agree almost perfectly. For each mother and child, the psychologist now has reliable information both as to whether the child is considered a school problem or not and a reliable rating of the mother's patience.

Note that the investigator made no attempt to influence the mother's interaction with her child; this behavior was merely measured as it occurred. When the psychologist in our example proceeds to analyze the findings, they might be arranged in a manner such as that shown in Table 2–1. Then the average ratings of the mothers' patience for both the problem and the no-problem children (6.0 and 4.0, respectively, in our example) can be compared with a statistical test. Finally, the results might reasonably be described by saying: "As predicted, mothers of children with behavior problems were found to be less patient in parent-child interactions than were those of children with no reported behavioral difficulties in the school situation."

When the results are described this way, it might be tempting to conclude that the ability of some children to get along with their peers, please their teachers, and otherwise avoid being labeled "problems" is partially caused by the patience of their mothers, just as the inability of other children in these areas results from maternal impatience. To draw this conclusion may be erroneous, however, for it treats the study as if it involved

TABLE 2–1

Data From a Hypothetical Study Comparing The Rated Patience Of Mothers Of Children With Behavior Problems and Mothers Of Children With No Reported School Problems. Because the study is correlational and simply measured an existing relationship, we cannot be sure whether mothers' impatience caused school problems or whether school problems made mothers more impatient. It is also possible that some third variable caused the relationship.

Children With Behavior Problems		Children With No Reported Problems	
Family	Ratings of Mother	Family	Ratings of Mother
A	7	M	5
B	6	N	2
C	6	O	1
D	7	P	7
E	4	Q	4
F	7	R	3
G	7	S	6
H	7	T	5
I	6	U	3
J	7	V	2
K	5	W	6
L	3	X	4
Total	72		48
Average	6.0		4.0

Note: 1 = very patient; 7 = very impatient.

an experimental manipulation, which it did not. In fact, the study does not necessarily indicate that a mother's impatience can lead to behavior problems for her child.

It is possible that the impatience of the mothers and the problems of their children "go together" because children who are uncooperative or unruly have an adverse effect on their parents' interactions with them—that is to say, "problem" children may produce impatient parents. Or it may be that some third variable, such as the physical health of the families involved, is influencing the behavior of both the mothers and the children. Because the investigator merely obtained measures for each mother-child pair without experimental intervention, there is no solid basis for distinguishing among these alternatives; no causal relationship can be inferred. However, problem children do tend to have impatient parents and thus the presence of one characteristic can be predicted from the presence of the other.

In a sense, then, correlational research compromises the control that is provided by the experimental method for the sake of economically making a broad inspection of a particular problem. By measuring existing characteristics of the subject, it also often permits the natural quality of the situation to remain; the very absence of intervention may bring the researcher closer to "real life" than is typically possible with experimental investigations. Behavior is almost always *multiply determined* (i.e., it is caused by a number of variables operating at the same time and in conjunction with one another), and the correlational approach can easily take this fact into account by studying the relationships among many variables. Although the experimental approach also can deal with multiple determinants of behavior by manipulating a number of different independent variables at once, it is rare in practice for a single experiment to employ more than three or four independent variables, and many experiments have only one.

Generalizing from Representative Samples.   In alliance with some statistical procedures, the correlational and experimental methods both supply the scientist with an important kind of power, the power to make general statements about a population or large group of individuals on the basis of observing only a portion of the individuals in that population. These methods allow the developmental psychologist, for example, to observe a relatively small group of children, sometimes as few as thirty or forty, and draw conclusions about thousands of unobserved children. Can such generalization be done without making serious errors?

Yes, to a remarkable extent, as long as the researcher is careful to observe a group of individuals who accurately reflect the characteristics (sex, age, health, intelligence, and so on) of the population to which they belong. A group that accurately and proportionately displays the characteristics of the population to which generalizations are to be made is called a *representative sample.* A description of development based on the observation of a representative sample of children applies to many more children than were—or ever could have been—observed. On the other hand, descriptions of behavior based on unrepresentative samples are limited in scope to describing the particular individuals observed.

Systematic biographies of children from birth or early childhood constituted the earliest source of data for developmental psychology and are still useful today for some purposes. Case study methods are the most flexible tools we have in the scientific search because they impose the fewest constraints on the way observation is to be undertaken and they can be pursued in nearly any situation. But this latitude has its price. Because one or two children hardly make up a representative sample, we cannot be sure that what is true for them also holds true for any larger group of children.

Case studies are often useful for didactic purposes, to provide a prototypical example of some form of behavior or behavioral development. To illustrate both the remarkable verbal ability of children of very high intelligence and the continuity and growth of this ability over time, Munn (1946) presented the following poem, written by a seven-year-old girl with an IQ of 188:*

> *Oh, Master of fire! Oh, Lord of air,*
> *Oh, God of waters, hear my prayer!*
> *Oh, Lord of ground and of stirring trees,*
> *Oh, God of man and of pleasant breeze,*
> *Dear Father, let me happy be—*
> *As happy as a growing tree!* [p. 418]

Noting that "follow-up studies of children whose IQs were very high when first determined have shown that, in most instances, the promise of early childhood has been fulfilled," Munn then reported a story written by the same child at twelve:

> Now, behold, there was once an Untutored Child of Nature whose abode was in the wildest wilds of Africa, whose name was Itchy-galoop. And he lived in primitive bliss and ate mangosteens and fried pig, and his drink was the limpid waters of the brook. And he wore a neat but not gaudy garment of leaves, and used no hair tonic.
>
> And it came to pass that a Missionary came unto those wilds and when he beheld Itchy-galoop with his incumbrous garments he was aghast and said unto him:
>
> "Untutored Child of Nature, the way thou goest thou wilt inevitably end up in perdition, so come to my tent and be baptized tomorrow at nine A.M."
>
> And Itchy-galoop was awed by the majestic and noble aspect of the Missionary's nose, and consented.
>
> And the Missionary was glad, and said unto him: "I will now proceed to civilize thee." So he got out his second-best pair of pants and a violet shirt and arrayed Itchy-galoop therein.
>
> And it came to pass that when Itchy-galoop had learned to read, the Missionary presented him with a book of the science of medicine and hygiene. And Itchy-galoop looked therein and was dismayed. He saw plainly that it was a miracle he had survived so long, and began industriously to study.
>
> And he boiled the limpid water of the brook before he quaffed thereof, and partook no more of fried pig which is hard to digest, and washed his mangosteens before he ate of them. And he thumped his chest doubtfully and felt of

his pulse, and foresaw that he was dying of tuberculosis and heart disease. And he said, "Yea, it is a certainty that I have every disease in this book from appendicitis on." So he took unto a folding couch that the Missionary had brought and groaned when he thought he ought to.

And when he had survived for a week in this precarious state he awoke one morning with a feeling of unaccountable happiness. And he said unto himself, "This is verily the light-heartedness before the end," and felt his pulse. And suddenly it came to him that the sky was blue and that he was feeling better than ever in his life before. A great conviction dawned on him and he arose and went in search of the Missionary and said to him with menacing aspect, "Get out of here on the double-quick, and if you come into my vision perambulating around in this vicinity again I will immediately examine into the contents of your cranium with my primeval stone hatchet."

And Itchy-galoop stood on a high hill and when the speck of Missionary had faded into the distance he took the book and wrapped his trousers around it and threw it far out into the sea. And he sighed with happiness and went and ate some mangosteens without washing them. [Munn, 1946, p. 418]

The author of this lovely fable, Munn reports, grew up to become "a writer of poetry and fiction which ranks with that of the greatest writers" (p. 418).

With these examples Munn has illustrated (1) the quality of the verbal ability of a child with a superior IQ, and (2) the persistence of achievement in this high IQ individual as she matured. Case study material in this instance clearly serves the purpose of painting a vivid picture of the phenomena it is intended to exemplify. Nonetheless, there is no individual or group introduced directly for purposes of comparison. The reader could better understand the contribution of IQ to literacy if the six-line poem written by a child of superior intelligence had been compared with a six-line poem written by a child of the same age but of average intelligence. Instead Munn (and the author of any case study) depends upon certain rough-and-ready assumptions by the reader, who will inevitably make his or her own comparisons. As far as it goes, there is nothing wrong with this. One does not need much experience with children to recognize that the poem reprinted above is beyond the capacity of most seven-year-olds. But how much beyond? Our guesses based on the seven-year-olds we have known cannot provide this information. In sum, the case study method can provide certain gross discriminations in some clear-cut cases, but for finer discriminations we need comparisons that aren't provided by the case study method.

Case studies are most helpful to the developmentalist when circumstances preclude the use of other methods. Investigations of the development of so-called feral children—human infants who, lost or abandoned by their parents, spent the early years of their lives in the wilderness—have been approached in such a manner (Davis, 1947). Obviously, there are constraints on the experimenter who wishes to study the development of children subsequent to years of social isolation. He or she cannot in good conscience set up a relevant experimental study because it would involve a comparison between two groups of children, one consisting of children reared normally, and a second consisting of children who are banished to the wilderness to fend for themselves or to be reared by wild animals. Nor does the investigator have the opportunity to employ the usual correlational techniques, for there are too few such individuals for any statistical study to be meaningful. The researcher's only alternative is to wait for the discovery of such a child and to fit the pieces of the child's life together into a case study.

The "Clinical" Case Study. Several variations on the case study method increase its scientific utility and information yield. One is the "clinical" method used extensively by Piaget.*

In his early work Piaget observed the development of his own three children at home. He recorded his observations and later published them in two books, *The Origins of Intelligence* and *The Construction of Reality in the Child.* His research was "child-guided" in that his aim was to follow the child's natural way of thinking. For example, when his daughter Jacqueline was between two months and six months of age, Piaget observed, milestone by milestone, the development of the infant's ability to guide her hand with her eyes. He watched and recorded each faltering step and permitted the child's natural development (rather than his own preconvictions) to form the basis for his observations. This is a usual hallmark of case studies.

At the same time, however, Piaget intervened occasionally, as we would expect a skilled clinician to do, in order to clarify for himself the structure and content of the child's thoughts. When another of Piaget's daughters, Lucienne, was two years old, he noted her fledgling success at removing a watch chain from a partially open matchbox. To probe the child's understanding of how the matchbox opened, Piaget altered the situation by virtually concealing the chain in the box so that Lucienne had to slide the box open systematically—or fail in her mission. With older children the clinical probe of thought took on a verbal form. Piaget began to interview not only his own but other children, asking them question after question: "Why do boats float?" "Where does the sun come from?" "What causes the tide?" and followed up on each answer until its full basis and meaning to the child were apparent. From material gathered in this way, Piaget fashioned one of the most important psychological theories of the century.

Single-Subject Experimental Designs

Most versions of the case study method involve only the observation and description of an individual. It is possible, however, to employ the experimental method with a single subject and to demonstrate the controlling influence of certain environmental events upon behavior.

The logic of the single-subject experimental design involves careful measurement of some aspect of the subject's behavior during a given time period (i.e., as a *baseline* or control procedure), the introduction of some environmental modification or treatment during the next (*experimental*) time period, a return to the conditions that prevailed during the control period, and finally a second introduction of the experimental manipulation. The intent of this procedure, sometimes referred to as an *ABAB* design, is

---

*Here the word "clinical" is used in the sense of deeply probing and does *not* refer to clinical-level problems or abnormalities.

straightforward. If behavior changes from *A*, the control period, to *B*, the experimental period, reverses again when the experimentally manipulated conditions are reversed (i.e., returns to *A*), and "re-reverses" when *B* is again introduced, then there is little doubt that it is the manipulation, and not chance or uncontrolled factors, that produced the changes.

The *ABAB* single-subject design may be illustrated by a study conducted by Tate and Baroff (1966) in which methods of reducing the self-injurious behavior of a nine-year-old boy, Sam, were investigated. The lad, who had been diagnosed as psychotic, engaged in a range of self-injurious behaviors including "banging his head forcefully against floors, walls, and other hard objects, slapping his face with his hands, punching his face and head with his fists, hitting his shoulder with his chin, and kicking himself." The investigators also reported that such acts were "a frequent form of behavior observed under a wide variety of situations."

Despite his self-injurious behavior, Sam was not entirely asocial. In fact, it was noted that ". . . he obviously enjoyed and sought bodily contact with others. He would cling to people and try to wrap their arms around him, climb into their laps and mold himself to their contours." It was this observation that gave rise to the experimental treatment. Specifically, the investigators decided to punish Sam's self-injurious outbursts by the immediate withdrawal of physical contact. Their hope, of course, was that this contingent "time-out" from human contact would reduce the frequency of the behaviors that produced it.

The study was run for twenty days and involved a daily walk around the campus for Sam, with two adult experimenters who talked to him and held his hands continuously. During the control days, Sam was simply ignored when he engaged in self-injurious behavior. During the experimental days, the adults responded to any self-injurious actions by immediately jerking their hands away from Sam and maintaining this time-out until three seconds after the last self-injurious act. The results of the systematic reversal of these procedures, shown in Figure 2–2, illustrate the dramatic effects of contingent punishment for reducing undesirable behavior in this case. It is clear that these changes resulted from the punishment rather than chance or accident, for the self-injury disappeared, reappeared, and diminished again according to the manipulation. Moreover, the "side effects" of the punishment procedure appear to be positive rather than negative. Tate and Baroff note that:

> on control days Sam typically whined, cried, hesitated often in his walk, and seemed unresponsive to the environment in general. His behavior on experimental days was completely different—he appeared to attend more to environmental stimuli. . . . There was no crying or whining, and he often smiled. [1966, p. 283]

The Tate and Baroff study shows that the single-subject design can serve as a well-controlled experiment and can demonstrate convincing causal relationships. Rather than illustrating the complexity of an individual case, the design can be used to demonstrate a principle of behavior through

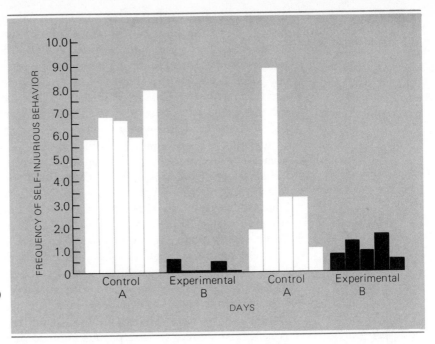

FIGURE 2–2
Effects
of the contingent
punishment
procedure in Tate and
Baroff's study,
illustrating
experimental effects
within a single-subject
design. (The individual
bars are data for each
day of the experiment.)
Adapted from Tate
and Baroff, 1966, by
permission.

the systematic treatment of one individual under controlled conditions. Nevertheless, as with all studies involving only one individual, caution must be exercised in drawing inferences about the population at large.

LONGITUDINAL VERSUS CROSS-SECTIONAL APPROACHES TO DEVELOPMENTAL RESEARCH

Most developmental studies, regardless of whether they employ the experimental, correlational, or case study method, can also be categorized according to whether they take a longitudinal or a cross-sectional approach.

In a *longitudinal study,* the same child or children are observed or tested repeatedly at different points in their lives, and stability or change in their characteristics or behavior is noted over time. Piaget's case study of the development of eye-hand coordination in his daughter Jacqueline is a clear example of the longitudinal approach, spanning with detailed observations a critical four-month period in the life of a single child. In a *cross-sectional study,* on the other hand, there is usually only one observation for each child, but developmental changes are identified by including children of different ages in the plan of the study. Development is charted, not by observing the change in individuals over time, as in the longitudinal method, but rather by noting the differences between children of different ages at the same point in calendar time. The experimental study by Coates and Hartup (1969) cited earlier in the chapter is a cross-sectional investigation in which the development of a learning process was explored by including children of two different ages—four-year-olds and seven-year-olds.

The Logic of Longitudinal Research

As the name implies, the longitudinal approach involves a lengthwise account of development; as such, it has long been recognized as the most obvious and direct way to "see" actual growth occurring. In one of the earliest longitudinal studies on record, Buffon measured the change in height of a single child over the seventeen years between 1759 and 1776. Somewhat later, changes in height as related to age were charted in a larger and more representative sample of children who participated in the first and second Harvard Growth Studies. It was inevitable that the longitudinal method would be applied next to the development of truly psychological characteristics; soon the emergence of emotional and social behavior, along with intellectual functioning, were the subject of longitudinal scrutiny. One such study, begun by Lewis Terman in 1921, focused on children with IQ test scores so high that many would consider them geniuses. Terman's aim was to follow the development of these gifted children to determine what kind of adults they would become and whether extraordinary events would attend their development. In a "Close-up" that appears later in this book, Terman himself describes his findings.

The longitudinal approach is well suited to studying almost any aspect of the course of development. More important, it is the *only* way to answer certain questions about the stability (or instability) of behavior: Will characteristics (such as aggression, dependency, or mistrust) observed in infancy or early childhood persist into adulthood? Will a traumatic event such as being abandoned by one's parents influence later social and intellectual development? How long will the beneficial effects of special academic training in the preschool years last? Such questions can only be explored by using the repeated measurement technique of the longitudinal approach.

The longitudinal approach, however, is plagued by disadvantages that may frequently offset its strengths. An obvious one is cost, inasmuch as the expense of merely keeping up with a large sample of individuals can be staggering. Then, too, there is the related problem of sample constancy over time. Experience has shown how difficult it is to maintain contact with people over several years (as long as thirty years in some longitudinal studies!) in a highly mobile society. And even among those who do not move away, some will lose interest and choose not to continue their participation. These "dropouts" are often significantly different from their more research-minded peers, and this fact may also distort the outcome of longitudinal findings. For example, a group of individuals may *seem* to show intellectual growth between the seventeenth and twenty-fifth year of life. What has actually happened, however, is that those who found earlier testing most difficult are the very ones who have quit the study and thereby spuriously raised the group average on the next round. Fortunately, new statistical techniques can partly remedy the situation (Labouvie, Bartsch, Nesselroade, and Baltes, 1974).

Even if the sample remains constant, though, the fact that children are given the same test many times may make them "test-wise." Improvement over time may be attributed to development when it actually stems from practice with a particular test. Changing the test from year to year would solve the practice problem but would raise the question of how to compare children's responses to different tests.

The Logic of the Cross-Sectional Approach

The cross-sectional approach, with its focus on the behavior of individuals of different ages at the same point in time, avoids almost all the problems associated with repeated testing and avoids costly record keeping and sample loss as well.

The cross-sectional approach, however, is not without problems of its own. The most serious logical tangle is the problem of *cohort effects,* meaning that differences between age groups (cohorts) may result as easily from chance environmental events as from significant developmental processes. Suppose, for example, that a researcher devises a way to measure how imaginative children are and then tests a group of five-year-olds and a group of ten-year-olds as a first step in studying the development of imagination. Let us say that the five-year-olds were found to be more imaginative than the ten-year-olds. Can we then conclude that imagination declines within this period? Not without facing serious objections. If testing were carried out in, say, 1977, a critic might point out that our ten-year-olds were born in 1967 and our five-year-olds in 1972, which means that they differ in "generation" as well as age. Our society may have changed enough between 1967 and 1972 to make the experiences that influence the growth of imagination very different for different generations of children. For example, a new curriculum adopted to nourish the imagination may have been too late for the children born in 1967 but may have benefited the younger children. Alternatively, the country may have been recovering from an economic depression that more severely affected the lives of the

Close-up

Ethical Responsibilities of Developmental Researchers

Until the end of World War II, individual investigators were expected to establish their own ethical standards and safeguards for their subjects. In the past few decades, however, professional organizations, government agencies, and scientists themselves have moved away from allowing the ethics of research to be determined solely by individual researchers. In place of an individualistic system, a number of formalized codes of research ethics have been developed. Such codes have been established by the U.S. National Commission for Protection of Human Subjects of Biomedical and Behavioral Research. This commission conducts hearings and recommends guidelines for safeguarding the rights and safety of research participants. The American Psychological Association expects all of its members to follow a set of ten ethical principles, adopted in 1973. The principles are as follows:

PRINCIPLE 1. In planning a study the investigator has the personal responsibility to make a careful evaluation of its ethical acceptability, taking into account these principles for research with human beings. To the extent that this appraisal, weighing scientific and humane values, suggests a deviation from any principle, the investigator incurs an increasingly serious obligation to seek ethical advice and to observe more stringent safeguards to protect the rights of the human research participant.

PRINCIPLE 2. Responsibility for the establishment and maintenance of acceptable ethical practice in research always remains with the individual investigators. The investigator is also responsible for the ethical treatment of research participants by collaborators, assistants, students, and employees, all of whom, however, incur parallel obligations.

PRINCIPLE 3. Ethical practice requires the investigator to inform the participant of all features of the research that reasonably might be expected to influence willingness to participate, and to explain all other aspects of the research about which the participant inquires. Failure to make full disclosure gives added emphasis to the investigator's responsibility to protect the welfare and dignity of the research participant.

PRINCIPLE 4. Openness and honesty are essential characteristics of the relationship between investigator and research participant. When the methodological requirements of a study necessitate concealment or deception, the investigator is required to ensure the participant's understanding of the reasons for this action and to restore the quality of the relationship with the investigator.

PRINCIPLE 5. Ethical research practice requires the investigator to respect the individual's freedom to decline to participate in research or to discontinue participation at any time. The obligation to protect this freedom requires special vigilance when the investigator is in a position of power over the participant. The decision to limit this freedom increases the investigator's responsibility to protect the participant's dignity and welfare.

PRINCIPLE 6. Ethically acceptable research begins with the establishment of a clear and fair agreement between the investigator and the research participant that clarifies the responsibilities of each. The investigator has the obligation to honor all promises and commitments included in that agreement.

PRINCIPLE 7. The ethical investigator protects participants from physical and mental discomfort, harm and danger. If the risk of such consequences exists, the investigator is required to inform the participant of that fact, secure consent before proceeding, and take all possible measures to minimize distress. A research procedure may not be used if it is likely to cause serious and lasting harm to participants.

PRINCIPLE 8. After the data are collected, ethical practice requires the investigator to provide the participant with a full clarification of the nature of the study and to remove any misconceptions that may have arisen. Where scientific or humane values justify delaying or withholding information, the investigator acquires a special responsibility to assure that there are no damaging consequences for the participant.

PRINCIPLE 9. Where research procedures may result in undesirable consequences for the participant, the investigator has the responsibility to detect and remove or correct these consequences including, where relevant, long-term after effects.

PRINCIPLE 10. Information obtained about the research participants during the course of an investigation is confidential. When the possibility exists that others may obtain access to such information, ethical research practice requires that this possibility, together with the plans for protecting confidentiality, be explained to the participants as a part of the procedure for obtaining informed consent.

It is useful to take a closer look at these principles, especially in the light of their particular implications for developmental research.

The first two principles are straightforward. The investigator has a responsibility to evaluate the ethics of his or her own research, and this responsibility extends to the investigator's research assistants, students, and any other people who come in contact with the subjects during the investigation.

Principle 3 deals with what is called informed consent. Ideally, prospective subjects should be given full disclosure about all of the details of the research so they can make an informed decision concerning whether or not they choose to participate. Implementing this principle is sometimes difficult, however. When potential subjects are infants, young children, or persons disabled in any way, it is necessary to obtain consent from parents or legal guardians as well as from the subjects themselves. In many cases parents and guardians must be told not only about the research, but they must also be advised as to how to explain the research ex-

perience to the subject. The amount of information that can be usefully presented to a young child, for example, must be decided jointly by the investigator and the parent or guardian.

In some cases the results of a study may be seriously biased if the participants know of the purpose of the study in advance. Principle 4 requires that subjects be given complete information at the conclusion of a study, a procedure known as debriefing. Again, special sensitivity is required in handling children and other subjects for whom a straightforward explanation may not be sufficient to satisfy the spirit of the debriefing requirement.

Principle 5 deals with a participant's right to decline or discontinue participation in any investigation at any time and principle 6 with his or her fair treatment in general. Here again there is a special problem with children, who may accede to demands of adult investigators, thinking that they are much more powerful. Investigators themselves are expected to take responsibility for assuring that the rights of every subject are unfailingly maintained.

Principles 7, 8, and 9 deal with the investigator's responsibility to remove any and all harmful effects that might be caused by participation in the research. Some research would simply be forbidden if such effects were anticipated.

Principle 10 concerns confidentiality, which is vital in all types of research with subjects of any age or social condition. It should also be noted, however, that assurances of confidentiality offered by psychologists doing research are often not honored in courts of law, where information gathered in research is typically not considered "privileged communication." In fact, the courts can subpoena the investigator's data and records, in which case the researcher must choose between an ethical responsibility and a legal one.

older children, who were born closer to its lowest point. Since social conditions change, they can be expected to affect different generations differently, rendering in some cases differences between age groups in cross-sectional studies difficult to interpret.

THE IMPORTANCE OF CONVERGING EVIDENCE

Even from our relatively brief discussion it can be seen that each of the research methods employed by developmentalists has both strengths and weaknesses. There is, then, no one best method, and the selection of a specific method usually depends as much on practical considerations as on suitability. For these reasons it is generally recognized that no single investigation can definitely settle a question. Developmental psychologists rarely rely on one study (or even one method) to reach conclusions. They prefer to find converging evidence from as many sources as possible.

A good example of this converging evidence approach is the investigation of the influence of television violence on the young. The earliest studies were simply case reports in which individual youngsters had apparently learned or copied violent or antisocial acts from a television show. Soon correlational studies disclosed a general positive relationship between the amount of aggressive behavior exhibited by children and adolescents and the amount of television violence they viewed at home. And, finally, experimental studies began to demonstrate that the introduction of violent television programming in laboratory or even school settings directly caused an increase in young viewers' willingness to aggress against others. No single study or method could have made a strong case for the contribution of television violence to aggressive behavior, but the combined body of evidence is highly persuasive (Liebert and Poulos, 1976).

Thus ends our foray into issues of the research methods used by developmentalists. We will meet many of these issues again, however, in later chapters.

SUMMARY

Three major methods are used in developmental research: the experimental, the correlational, and the case study approach. The *experimental method* consists of the testing of experimental hypotheses in a controlled situation. This involves the manipulation of something by the experimenter, called the *independent variable,* and the precise measurement of the effects of this manipulation on some form of behavior, called the *dependent variable.* Subjects are divided into two or more groups, which are each exposed to a different form of the independent variable. *Random assignment* is the procedure used to ensure that the groups are basically alike before they are manipulated. If differences in the dependent variable are observed between the groups, one can conclude that the independent variable had a causal effect.

The *correlational method* deals with the joint relationship between two or more factors and can answer questions of the form: "Do variable X and variable Y go together or vary together in some way?" In this method, nothing is manipulated by the experimenter; the situation is measured as it exists and subjects are observed under naturally occurring conditions. A *correlation coefficient*, *r*, is the statistic that indicates the degree of relationship between two sets of data by showing both the direction (positive or negative) and the magnitude (high or low) of the relationship. The correlation may range from a +1.00 (perfect positive relationship) to a −1.00 (perfect negative relationship), with .00 indicating no relationship. A positive sign means that high scores on X (child's age) tend to be associated with high scores on Y (height): The older the child, the taller he or she is likely to be. A negative sign means that high scores on X (adult's age) tend to be associated with low scores on Y (reflex speed): As adults grow older, their reflexes become slower. The higher the numerical value of the *r*, regardless of whether it is in a positive or a negative direction, the stronger and more certain is the relationship.

The case study method involves the detailed description of one subject, a systematic biography. The *"clinical" case study* is a more deeply probing variation, and as used by Piaget in studying his children, involved careful observation and recording, interviewing, and occasional intervention. *The single-subject experimental design (ABAB)* combines the application of the experimental method and the case study's focus on a single individual. This means careful measurement of the subject's behavior for a given period, followed by the introduction of some manipulation, a return to the conditions of the first period, and finally a reintroduction of the manipulation. Tate and Baroff (1966) used this *ABAB* design to study the effect of contingent time-out from human contact on a child's self-injurious behavior.

Each of these three methods has strengths and weaknesses, but the experimental method, when appropriate, is the preferred method of scientists because it provides a controlled situation that allows conclusions to be drawn regarding cause and effect. Correlational research, which does not have these controls, can only reveal the relationship between or among variables but cannot lead to cause-and-effect conclusions. However, correlational studies are important for studying conditions that cannot be manipulated and for measuring characteristics in a natural environment rather than in an artificial situation in a laboratory. Also, the correlational approach can make a broad inspection of a problem by studying the interrelationship of many variables. Both the experimental and the correlational methods may and should use *representative samples*, which allow generalizations to be made about the findings for the larger population. In contrast, the case study method cannot do this because it involves a single subject. Therefore case studies should be used only when circumstances are not appropriate for other methods, or for extensive observation such as that provided by the deeper probing clinical method used by Piaget. Nevertheless, the case study method as used by Piaget and Freud has generated important theories. The single-subject experimental design incorporates the controlling aspects of the experimental method and therefore allows causal inferences to be drawn about the manipulation's effect, but since it does not use a representative sample, this conclusion only applies to the particular subject in the experiment and one cannot generalize, i.e., that the same results would be found for others.

Regardless of the method employed, most developmental studies take either a cross-sectional or a longitudinal approach. In a cross-sectional study, there is usually only one observation for each child, and developmental changes are identified by studying children of different ages. A problem with the method is the potential effect of cohort differences. In a longitudinal study, the same children are observed and tested at different ages, which is the more direct way to actually measure growth, but the method has the problems of repeated testing and potential loss of subjects.

Because every method has some weaknesses, developmental psychologists rarely rely on one study or even one method to reach conclusions. Instead, they find converging evidence from as many sources as possible. A good example of the converging evidence approach is the investigation of viewing violence on television and its effects on children's aggressive behavior.

Biological Foundations

Our size, strength, muscle coordination, and sensory abilities all influence how we will think, feel, and act. Thus, in a fundamental way, biological development underlies psychological development. This section describes the contribution of biological factors to development. In subsequent sections we will refer to these biological processes repeatedly and show how they relate to intellectual and social development.

Chapter 3 begins with conception, development in the womb (prenatal development), and the birth process. The human newborn is then described in terms of its appearance and abilities shortly after birth. The individual's physical growth and expanding motor development is then described with emphasis on the early years. Chapter 4 examines the sensory and perceptual development of the infant and young child. It also explains the fascinating ways in which developmental psychologists have come to understand aspects of the inner experience of those too young to answer questions or follow instructions.

Chapter 5, the last in the section, explains the process of genetic transmission, which controls all of our inherited characteristics, and discusses the role of hereditary factors in intellectual and social development.

3 Early Physical Development

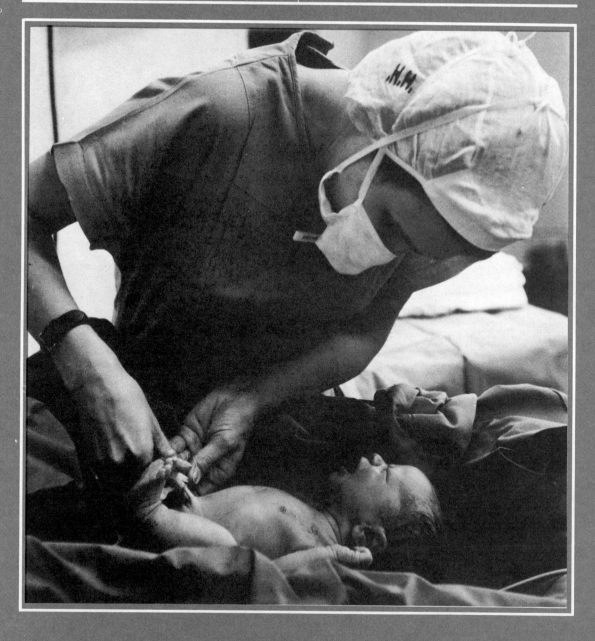

In the introductory chapters we discussed many of the central viewpoints, issues, and methods involved in studying development. We are now prepared to examine the specific course of development, beginning with early physical and motor growth. In this chapter we shall explore the processes and norms of conception, prenatal development, birth, characteristics of the newborn, and physical and motor functioning. Important here is the interplay between biological and environmental factors. While biological factors play a strong role, for example, in determining the sex of a child, we shall learn how the environment, from the earliest days of growth in the uterus, influences the continuous path of development.

CONCEPTION

Five-pound, twelve-ounce Louise Brown, the first living child to be conceived outside of the human body, was born in July, 1978. Discouraged in their attempts to conceive a child, her parents had sought the help of physician Patrick Steptoe and physiologist Robert Edwards. Mrs. Brown was given hormones to promote the ripening of egg cells (*ova*) and these ova were then surgically removed. Sperm cells provided by Mr. Brown were combined with the ova and nutrients in a culture dish, and fertilization occurred within hours. The resulting cell mass, the *zygote*, was inserted into Mrs. Brown's uterus a few days later. The rest of the story is history. Worldwide reaction to the birth ranged from excitement and delight to cautiousness and misgivings ("All about that baby," Newsweek, 1978; Kolata, 1978b). Will the procedure result in a high incidence of abnormality? Will women eventually hire other women to bear their babies? Is a fertilized egg in a culture dish a living being? In short, is our knowledge leading to a dangerous manipulation of nature that has complex ethical and social implications?

There is no doubt that our understanding of conception and prenatal development is now substantial. The belief in Western culture that sexual intercourse is the cause of conception can be traced back more than 2,000 years. The invention of microscopes eventually led to the discovery of the *gametes* (that is, the reproductive cells—the ova and sperm), but development itself was not understood for some time to come. During the late seventeenth and early eighteenth centuries the doctrine of preformation was still widely held (Simpson, Pittendrigh, and Tiffany, 1957). *Preformation* took as its basic assumption that the adult was preformed in the gametes. Some scholars claimed that the ova contained the miniature adult (the *homunculus*) and the sperm merely triggered its growth, whereas others argued that the head of the sperm encapsulated the homunculus and the ova merely nourished it (see Figure 3–1). Among the latter investigators was Anton van Leeuwenhoek, inventor of the compound microscope, who reported that he had observed miniature adults of both sexes in sperm cells under his microscope. In either case, it was said that within the gamete was contained a tiny complete human whose germ cells held other tiny complete humans, whose germ cells held other tiny complete humans, and so on. Speculation and calculation were given to the number of generations that might be packed inside any one gamete and to the size of each homunculus (Grinder, 1967).

FIGURE 3–1
Drawing of a human sperm that contains a homunculus.   From A. Montagu, **Human Heredity** (Cleveland: The World Publishing Co., 1963). Second revised edition, p. 79.

Preformation implied that development was merely an enlargement or swelling of parts that already existed. This view gradually collapsed in face of evidence that *conception* is the union of the ovum and sperm resulting in the creation of the zygote, which proceeds, in ways not yet well understood, to differentiate all body parts during the prenatal months. Although we now look at the doctrine of preformation with surprised disbelief, the facts of conception and prenatal development are, in their own right, just as amazing.

The Gametes as Specialized Cells

All of the cells of the body have a nucleus that contains chromosomes, which are composed of deoxyribonucleic acid (DNA). It is the *DNA* that bears the genetic information passed on from generation to generation and does much of the directing of cell activity. Tiny segments of chromosomes are known as genes and the human being has many thousands of them.

The exact form and number of chromosomes are distinct for each species, with the number ranging from as few as 4 to as many as 254 (Sinnott, Dunn, and Dobzhansky, 1958). In all cells *except the gametes* the chromosomes consist of matching pairs, each member of which influences the same characteristics of the individual as does the other member. Human cells contain twenty-three pairs of chromosomes, twenty-two of which, the autosomes, are common to both sexes and one pair of which, the sex chromosomes, differs sharply in males and females. Figure 3–2 depicts the chromosomal complement of one cell for each sex. Note that the sex

FIGURE 3–2
The chromosome complement in all human cells. Each cell contains 22 pairs of autosomes that are alike for the sexes and 1 pair of sex chromosomes that is different for males and females.   Courtesy M. M. Grumbach, University of California, San Francisco.

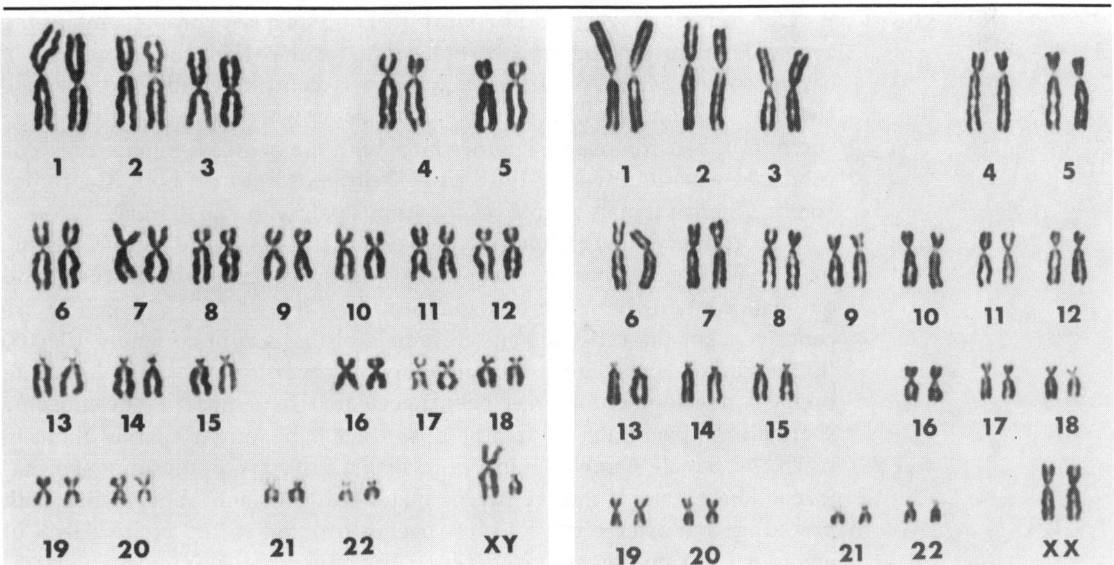

chromosomes in females are alike; they are called X chromosomes. Males, on the other hand, have one X and one Y chromosome, the latter being smaller and lighter and having fewer genes.

The ova and sperm differ from other cells in that during maturation they undergo a specialized cell division, *meiosis,* that results in their carrying only twenty-three single chromosomes (that is, one chromosome from each of the original twenty-three pairs). When conception occurs, the father and mother each thus contribute half of the normal complement of chromosomes to the zygote.

An examination of the processes just described provides some explanation of the enormous variability found in humans. In meiosis, the chromosomes of each pair sort out by chance so that there are 2^{23}, or 8,388,608, possible different combinations of chromosomes for each possible ovum and sperm combination. This means that for each embryo billions of chromosomal combinations are possible because the particular ovum and sperm that form the new individual unite by chance. In addition, other genetic mechanisms (such as crossing over, in which pieces of the chromosomes break off and reattach on different chromosomes), as well as environmental influences, contribute further to produce an almost infinite variety of individuals.

Conception takes place when an ovum is released by an ovary and joins with a sperm in the Fallopian tube leading from the ovary. Usually only one ovum per month is released, about midway through the menstrual cycle. If fertilization is to occur, it must take place within approximately a day following the release of the ovum. As many as 400 million sperm cells may be contained in the semen of one ejaculation, but most do not even reach the Fallopian tube. They are deterred by the acid and the warmth of the female reproductive tract, and probably do not live more than a few days in this environment.

Sex Determination

Due to meiosis, each adult contributes only one sex chromosome to the zygote. Females pass on an X chromosome, for they themselves carry no Y chromosomes. Males, on the other hand, may contribute either an X or a Y chromosome. The sex of the zygote depends on whether an X-chromosome sperm or a Y-chromosome sperm unites with the ovum. A female zygote is produced when the twenty-third pair of chromosomes are both X chromosomes, whereas a male zygote results from a pair with one X and Y.

Theoretically, there should be an equal chance of the zygote's being male or female, inasmuch as one-half of the sperm cells contain the X and one-half contain the Y chromosome. In fact, more males apparently are conceived, for the ratio of male to female births is approximately 106:100 (in the United States) even though a larger proportion of males die during prenatal development. It has been speculated that more Y-chromosome spermatozoa penetrate the ova because their light weight enables them to reach the female gametes more quickly than the X-chromosome spermatozoa. The greater vulnerability of males to death and abnormality both preceding and after birth also has been attributed to the relative lack of genes on the Y chromosomes.

On occasion two or more individuals are conceived, an event that can
occur in two ways. Twins can be produced when two ova are released and
fertilized by two different sperm almost simultaneously. The resulting *dizygotic,* or fraternal, twins may be of the same or different sex and are no more
genetically alike than nontwin siblings. *Monozygotic,* or identical, twins involve fertilization of one ovum by one sperm, and the subsequent division
of the zygote into two units. These twins share an identical genetic make-up
and thus are always of the same sex.

The likelihood of actually bearing twins depends upon many factors
(Scheinfeld, 1973). Dizygotic twinning increases with the woman's age (up
to thirty-five to thirty-nine years), and number of previous children. Racial
background is also related to dizygotic twinning, with black women having
a higher rate than white women who, in turn, have a higher rate than Oriental women. A thirty-eight-year-old black woman who has given birth to
five children would theoretically have a greater chance of producing dizy-

FIGURE 3–3
The chances of
producing dizygotic
twins increases with
age (up to 35–39
years) and number of
previous children.
These factors hardly
influence
monozygotic
twinnings (data for
white women).
Adapted from
Scheinfeld, 1973.

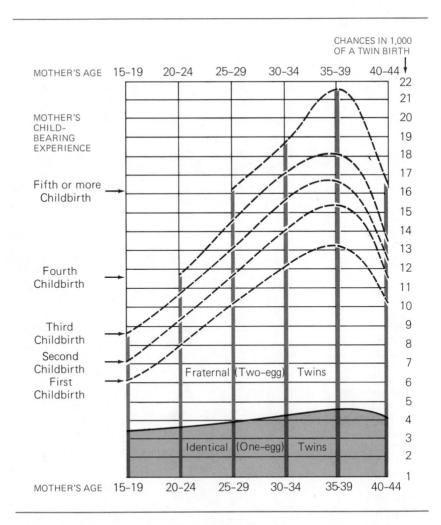

gotic twins than a twenty-year-old oriental woman who is expecting her first child. Monozygotic twinning, rarer overall, is hardly influenced by these factors (see Figure 3–3). In general, if a woman already has twins, has a sister with twins, or is herself a twin, she has a higher than average chance of bearing twin children. It is generally thought that some inherited tendencies for twinning exist that may influence the release of ova, the division of a fertilized zygote, or the uterine environment supportive of carrying twins.

Twins are a subject of fascination and the simultaneous birth of three, four, five, and even six human babies is even more dramatic. Underlying such multiple births are both processes involved in twinning. That is, several ova and sperm may unite at the same time, a fertilized zygote may divide, or both processes may occur simultaneously. The famous Dionne quintuplets, born in Canada in 1934, derived from one zygote and were therefore all identical.

STAGES OF PRENATAL DEVELOPMENT

Period of the Ovum (Germinal Period)

Within a few days after conception the fertilized ovum journeys down the Fallopian tube towards the uterus, with the help of muscular contractions in the wall of the tube and the beating of the hair-like cilia (see Figure 3–4). The zygote has already begun to multiply by *mitosis,* at first slowly and then more rapidly. In mitosis, the chromosomes in each cell double and then the cell divides into two cells, each with a full complement of chromosome pairs. Figure 3–5 illustrates this process. Within the multiplying mass a cavity forms. This hollow ball of perhaps one hundred cells, the *blastocyst,* burrows into the uterine wall. It has an inner mass that is destined to be a new individual and an outer layer that develops into the *chorion* (outer sac), *amnion* (inner sac), *umbilical cord,* and *placenta,* (see Figure 3–6). The developing organism floats freely in the amniotic fluid in the amnion except for the attachment by the umbilical cord to the placenta, which can be seen in Figure 3–7. The umbilical cord is truly a lifeline in that its newly formed arteries and veins serve as a transport system between the devel-

FIGURE 3–4
Diagram of conception and early development. The ovum leaves the ovary and is fertilized by a sperm in the Fallopian tube. The resulting zygote immediately begins to develop and travels to the uterus within a few days.
Adapted from K. L. Moore, **Before We Are Born** (Philadelphia: W. B. Saunders, 1974), p. 25.

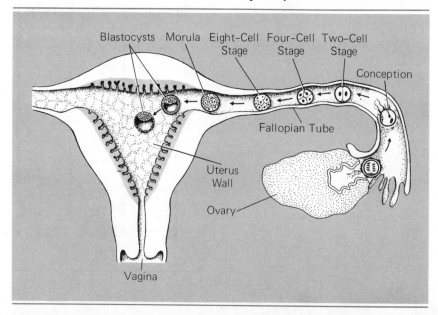

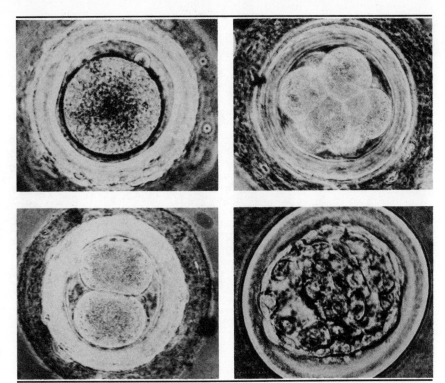

FIGURE 3–5
Photographs of the fertilized ovum and early multiplication into 2, 8, and several cells. The first multiplication takes about 36 hours, but then the rate quickens. From L. Nilsson, **A Child Is Born** (New York: Delacorte Press, 1974).

oping child and the prospective mother. The vessels in the umbilical cord make indirect contact with the adult's system at the placenta. Nutrients, oxygen, some vitamins, drugs, vaccines, and some disease-producing organisms pass to the developing child, whereas waste materials pass in the opposite direction.

FIGURE 3–6
The blastocyst at four and one-half days. The inner cells will develop into the individual, while the outer cells will form supporting tissues. From University of California, Davis.

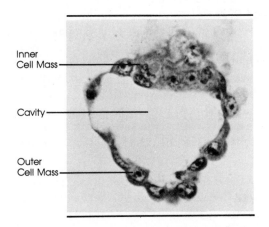

Inner Cell Mass

Cavity

Outer Cell Mass

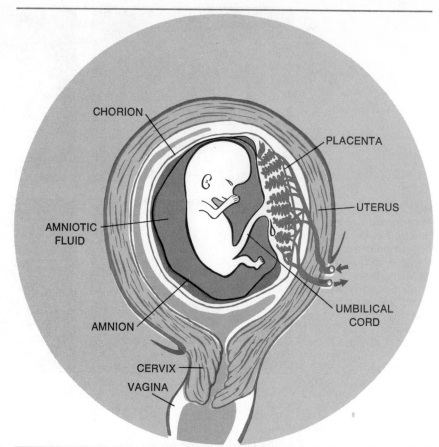

FIGURE 3-7
The developing child floats freely within the amnion, except where it is attached to the placenta by the umbilical cord. From W. A. Kennedy, **Child Psychology,** 2nd ed. (Englewood Cliffs, N.J.: Prentice-Hall, Inc., 1975). © 1975, p. 49. Reprinted by permission of Prentice-Hall, Inc.

CHORION

PLACENTA

UTERUS

AMNIOTIC FLUID

UMBILICAL CORD

AMNION

CERVIX

VAGINA

Period of the Embryo

The embryonic period begins during the second week after implantation in the uterus and lasts until the eighth week. It is a dramatic time in which growth is rapid and cell and organ differentiation occur. The inner mass of cells of the blastocyst lines itself into three layers: the *ectoderm* is the basis for the formation of skin, sense organs, and the nervous system; the *mesoderm* further differentiates into the muscles, blood, and circulatory system; and the *endoderm* gives rise to the digestive system and other internal organs and glands. By two months the embryo is slightly more than one-inch long and roughly resembles a human being. Development proceeds rapidly in the upper region so that the body appears top heavy and the head is bent over. The ears, eyes, mouth, and jaws are clearly recognizable. The limbs, beginning as broad buds, lengthen and begin to form fingers and toes. The spinal cord and other parts of the nervous system take shape. Most organs exist at least in some rudimentary form. The heart, at first disproportionately large, begins to beat (Figure 3-8).

The Period of the Fetus

From the eighth week until birth the developing organism is referred to as the *fetus*. Considerable knowledge of both the physical characteristics and the behavior of the fetus has been obtained from three different sources.

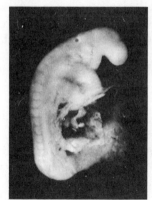

Three and one-half
weeks

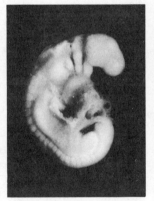

Four
weeks

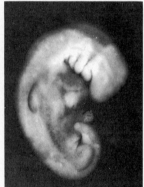

Five
weeks

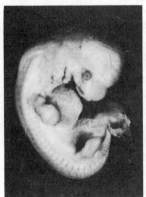

Five and one-half
weeks

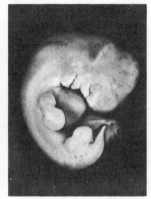

Six
weeks

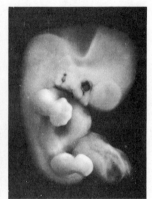

Six and one-half
weeks

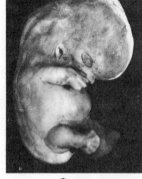

Seven
weeks

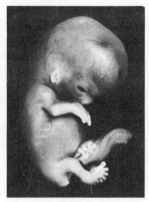

Eight
weeks

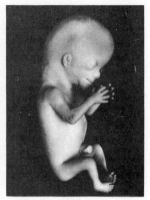

Twelve
weeks

FIGURE 3–8
Development in the uterus during the first three months after conception.
Courtesy Carnegie Laboratories of Embryology. University of California, Davis.

51

First, fetuses must sometimes be operatively removed from the uterus for therapeutic reasons, and their spontaneous behavior and reactions to stimulation have been recorded (Landreth, 1967). Second, studies can be made of premature infants (born between the sixth and eighth month after conception), which presumably reflect their behavioral capacities while in the uterus. Finally, measures of the behavior of the living fetus in the uterus may be obtained, either through the reports of mothers or through the use of specialized instruments.

The rate of growth reaches its peak during the early fetal period and then declines. Development is characterized primarily by further genesis of existing structures, changes in body proportion, and refinement in functions. Only a few parts make their first appearance, namely, the hair, nails, and external sex organs. Other highlights of this period are: ossification of the bones, growth of the lower body region so that the head is no longer quite so dominant, the appearance of fine hair (*lanugo*) that later will mostly disappear, the development of a protective cheeselike substance (*vernix*) to coat the body, and the convolution of the brain.

The beginning of the fetal period has been called the month of initial activity (Rugh and Shettles, 1971). Spontaneous movement begins early and can be felt by the prospective mother at about sixteen weeks. Individual differences emerge in that some fetuses are quiet whereas others kick and squirm a great deal. The arms bend at the wrist and elbow; the hands can form a fist; the fetus can frown, squint, and open its mouth. Reaction to stimulation is global at first but soon becomes specific. For example, if the eyelids are touched at the end of the third month squinting occurs instead of a previous jerking of the entire body. Many reflexes, which are automatic and unlearned responses to specific stimuli appear: swallowing, coughing, and sucking, to name a few.

During the last trimester changes occur that further prepare the fetus for living independently. For example, movements of respiration are practiced even though oxygen is being provided through the placenta. The fetal form of hemoglobin in the blood gradually makes way at thirty-four weeks for an "adult" form (Tanner, 1970). Vital functions for swallowing, urination, and movements of the gastrointestinal tract become refined. Weight gain is noticeable as fatty tissue accumulates. Should the fetus be born after about twenty-eight weeks it stands a good chance of survival, although full-term development of about thirty-eight weeks after conception is normal and optimal.

INFLUENCES ON PRENATAL DEVELOPMENT

The idea that the individual developing in the uterus can be influenced by a variety of sources is an ancient one. Few of us believe today that an evil eye cast upon a pregnant woman brings a deformed child, that a rabbit crossing the path of a prospective mother results in a child with a cleft lip (a hare lip), or that the amount of reading that a mother does during pregnancy influences intelligence. Nevertheless, the mother's body provides the entire fetal environment, interacting with the fetus by way of the placenta. Aside from nutrients, the placenta permits passage of some drugs, chemicals, hormones, and microorganisms. These facts have two implications for prenatal care. First, they emphasize the necessity of adequate diet, rest, exercise, and medical check-ups. Secondly, they indicate the importance of avoiding agents or circumstances that could cause abnormal or less than optimal development for the child.

The study of malformations and other deviations from normal prenatal development is referred to as *teratology*. The term is derived from the Greek *teras*, meaning monster or marvel. Progress in teratology has resulted in a better understanding of the adverse effects of many agents and circumstances on the developing organism. A basic principle of prenatal growth is that structures emerge in a fixed order, with rapid differentiation and growth occurring during the so-called *critical period*. During this time, usually somewhere in the first trimester of pregnancy, susceptibility to influence is particularly high. As Figure 3–9 illustrates, the specific outcome of exposure to a teratogen varies with the exact time and amount of exposure and the body system involved. To further complicate the picture, individuals probably vary in susceptibility to teratogens.

A word of caution is warranted in any review of prenatal influences. Since ethical considerations preclude human experiments in this area, con-

FIGURE 3–9
Illustration of the critical periods in prenatal development. Black denotes highly sensitive periods; white denotes periods that are less sensitive to teratogens.   Adapted from K. L. Moore, **Before We Are Born** (Philadelphia: W. A. Saunders, 1974), p. 96.

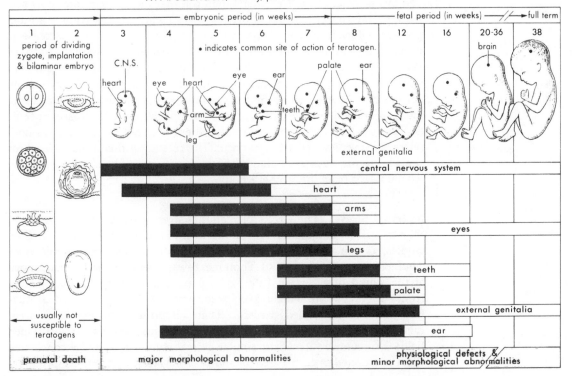

clusions must be drawn from animal experiments and human case studies and correlational investigations. Even so, because the developing child is influenced by innumerable variables, tracing a defect to a specific teratogen is an enormous task in many instances. Finally, research of prenatal influences has had serious methodological problems in the past (Copans, 1974).

Maternal Age.   Women over thirty-five and under twenty years of age have a higher risk for infant defect, prematurity, and infant death (Gordon, 1973; Vital and Health Statistics, 1972). There are several reasons. In older women the ova, which have been present in an immature state from birth, may have been adversely affected by aging or exposure to chemicals, drugs, and other harmful agents. In young women the reproductive system may not be fully developed. Pregnant teenagers also may have generally poor prenatal care.

Maternal Nutrition.   Because the mother-to-be is the sole source of nutrition for the unborn child, a diet providing the proper balance of proteins, fats, carbohydrates, minerals, and vitamins is vital. Many correlational studies of humans indicate a relationship between maternal diet deficiencies and prematurity, low birthweight, stillbirth, growth retardation, and poor mental functioning (Knobloch and Pasamanick, 1958, 1974; Montagu, 1962; Winick, Brasel, and Valasco, 1973). Diet deficiencies during the first trimester of pregnancy are especially deleterious (e.g., Nelson, Asling, and Evans, 1952), but researchers point out that the last trimester may also be important because of rapid brain growth (Lester, 1975). Animal studies provide evidence that inadequate maternal diet may cause a decrease in nerve cells, thereby diminishing nervous system functioning (Dobbing, 1970; Kaplan, 1972). Despite these findings, however, much is still not known about the effects of maternal nutrition. Poor nutrition may simply not meet the diet needs of the fetus, or it may act indirectly by increasing the mother's vulnerability to pregnancy complications and disease. Specific deficiencies may be harmful whereas others may not be, or perhaps only relatively severe deficiency is harmful. The reason for this is that at least for some nutrients, such as calcium, the fetus acts almost like a parasite, taking what it needs from the mother's body.

Maternal Stress.   The effects of maternal stress are even less understood than the effects of maternal nutrition. Much of the research involves animal studies, dating back to Thompson's experiments with rats (Joffe, 1969; Thompson and Grusec, 1970). Thompson's rats were trained to avoid shock at the sound of a buzzer. Later, during pregnancy, they were prevented from engaging in the avoidance behavior when the buzzer sounded, a situation that was presumed stressful. Their offspring, some of which were raised by other mothers, showed more emotionality (low activity in an open field) than control rats. Many similar animal studies lead to the conclusion that conditioned maternal anxiety and physical stress can alter offspring behavior, although the effects are varied and interact with postnatal treatment (Thompson and Grusec, 1970).

Turning to human studies, it seems reasonable that maternal emotions could influence the growing child. The emotions act through the autonomic nervous system that activates the endocrine glands, which, in turn, regulate the secretion of hormones such as adrenalin. Since hormones can pass through the placenta, they may indeed affect the fetus. An early and often cited study by Sontag (1944) did show a relationship between fetal activity and expectant mothers' autonomic functioning. Moreover, babies who were active en utero, presumably as the result of maternal stress, later had high levels of crying, squirming, diarrhea, and eating problems. Other investigations have demonstrated a relationship between maternal anxiety and infant fussiness, vomiting, crying, and sensitivity to sound (Copans, 1974).

Nevertheless, it cannot be concluded at this time that maternal stress affects prenatal development. As Copans (1974) pointed out, studies involving humans have serious methodological shortcomings. Many depend on unreliable retrospective reports of stress. The investigations are correlational, leaving the question of causation open. Perhaps stressed women do not obtain adequate nutrition or rest, and these are the causative factors. Or perhaps the infants' behaviors are reactions to the postnatal handling they receive from their mothers whose lives remain stressful after the birth of their babies (Carey, Lipton, and Myers, 1974). The most that can be said is that maternal stress appears to be related to pregnancy complications (Nuckolls, Cassell, and Kaplan, 1972).

Rh Incompatibility. The *Rh factor,* named after the Rhesus monkey in which it was first discovered, is a protein in the blood that is inherited by 85 percent of the general population. Difficulty arises only when the father carries the factor (Rh positive), the mother does not (Rh negative), and the child develops as Rh positive. If the offspring's blood comes into contact with the mother's, the mother's system may manufacture antibodies to ward off the Rh protein that is foreign to it. The antibodies destroy the child's oxygen-carrying red blood cells, a condition known as *erythroblastosis,* and death or mental retardation can occur.

These effects do not usually show up during the first pregnancy because the Rh factor cannot cross the placenta. However, the mother may receive the Rh factor when the placenta separates at birth. She then begins to manufacture antibodies. Should she become pregnant again, the antibodies, which can cross the placenta, are available to damage the fetus. Fortunately, this process can be prevented by administering to the mother at the birth of her first child a substance, *rhogam,* that deters antibody formation.

Some Specific
Teratogens

Maternal Diseases. Maternal diseases, both infectious and noninfectious, are implicated in fetal defect and death. Table 3–1 lists some of them and their possible effects. Rubella (German measles) and syphilis are among the most potentially dangerous of the infectious diseases.

TABLE 3-1
Some of the Maternal Diseases that can Cause Damage Prenatally

Infectious Diseases

Rubella	death; prematurity; deafness; blindness; heart, liver, pancreas defects; mental retardation
Syphilis	death; blindness; deafness; mental retardation
Influenza A	malformations
Pneumonia	early fetal death
Tuberculosis	fetal death; lowered resistance to tuberculosis
Toxoplasmosis	mental retardation; heart defects; brain defects; fetal death
Mumps	fetal death; malformations; heart disease
Scarlet fever	early fetal death

Noninfectious Diseases

Diabetes mellitus	fetal death; stillbirth; respiratory difficulties; metabolic disturbances
Anemia (iron deficiency)	death; brain impairment

Source: Data from R. Rugh and L. Shettles, From Conception to Birth, pp. 148-153. Copyright © 1971 by Robert Rugh and Landrum P. Shettles. Reprinted by permission of Harper and Row, Publishers, Inc.

In 1942 Australian physicians noted that women who contracted Rubella early in pregnancy had a high incidence of defective babies. Upon crossing the placenta, the Rubella virus can result in miscarriage; stillbirth; prematurity; deafness; blindness; heart, liver, and pancreas defects; and mental retardation. Estimates of defect during the first month are as high as 50 percent, with the incidence dropping off subsequently, so that exposure during the last two trimesters is not considered harmful. Women can thus be most dangerously exposed before they realize they are pregnant. During the 1964 worldwide epidemic of Rubella, an estimated 20 to 30 thousand defective babies were born in the United States (Chess, 1974). A preventive vaccine available for over a decade now promises to dramatically reduce the ravages of Rubella, but it must be administered at least two months before pregnancy (Rugh and Shettles, 1971).

Syphilis is caused by a bacterium, Treponema pallidum, that can gain access to the fetus if the disease is untreated or severe. Unlike the seriousness of Rubella in early pregnancy, syphilitic infection of the fetus occurs after the fifth month of pregnancy and can spread to many organs. Death en utero or soon after birth is common, and babies who survive may be blind, deaf, or mentally retarded. Fortunately, blood tests can identify syphilis in the mother and early treatment with antibiotics is effective in preventing fetal infection.

Of the noninfectious maternal diseases diabetes mellitus can be extremely hazardous. This condition is characterized by insufficient secretion of insulin from the mother's pancreas to metabolize sugar. Along with the possibility of inheriting diabetes, the unborn child is subjected to a generally unhealthy uterine environment. If the mother is not treated, the probability of fetal death and stillbirth is 50 percent. As many as 80 percent of the surviving babies show some anomalies: enlarged pancreases, excessive weight, a puffy appearance, respiratory difficulty, and metabolic disorders such as low blood sugar. With maternal care, however, these difficulties can be prevented. The physician must control the mother's diet, provide insulin, and in extreme cases deliver the infant early to avoid anticipated danger (Rugh and Shettles, 1971).

Drugs, Chemicals, and Hormones. Although suspicion has long existed that drugs taken by the mother may adversely affect the fetus, appropriate caution has not always been taken by the medical profession or by expectant mothers. The best policy for the prospective mother to follow is to avoid all drugs unless they are professionally recommended and monitored. In a culture as drug dependent as ours, however, this policy is not adhered to. Dalby (1978) reported that 42 to 73 percent of all pregnant women smoke tobacco, and that approximately eleven drugs are ingested during pregnancy, including aspirin, antacids, antibiotics, barbituates, and antihistamines. The popular reasons for taking these drugs are for relief of discomfort, as well as for pleasure.

Although our discussion must necessarily be brief, we shall provide a few dramatic examples of prenatal drug effects and comment on some widely used drugs. (Table 3–2 gives a general summary.) One particularly tragic example involved the drug *thalidomide*, a chemical that was synthesized in 1953 and at first appeared to be a harmless, sleep-inducing agent. Late in 1959, however, reports describing the malformed infants of mothers who had taken thalidomide during pregnancy began to mount. In many cases, the drug caused malformation of the arms and legs; often fingers were absent and other internal organic abnormalities occurred (Carmichael, 1970).

TABLE 3-2
Possible Prenatal Effects of Some Drugs and Chemicals

Drugs/Chemicals	Effects
Aspirin (in excess)	bleeding in the newborn; possible circulatory anomalies
Heroin, morphine	convulsions; tremors; newborn death; newborn withdrawal symptoms
Barbituates	depressed breathing; drowsiness during the first week of life
Antihistamines	fetal death; malformations
Quinine	deafness
Tobacco	low birthweight; prematurity; high heart rate; convulsions
Lead	anemia; hemorrhage; miscarriage
Alcohol	growth retardation; microcephaly; disfigurations; cardiac anomalies; behavioral and cognitive deficit
Thalidomide	malformations, especially of the limbs

Recently investigators have begun to document the effects of alcohol on the developing embryo and fetus (Abel, 1980; Claren and Smith, 1978; Dehaene, 1977; Chernoff, 1977). Maternal consumption of three or more drinks per day during pregnancy has been associated with a distinct pattern of congenital malformation termed the *fetal alcohol syndrome*. The syndrome is characterized by permanent growth retardation (postnatally as well as prenatally); microcephaly (abnormally small brain); eye and nose disfiguration; joint, limb and cardiac anomalies; and behavioral/cognitive impairment, such as fine motor dysfunction and mental retardation. The greatest risk for the developing fetus occurs during the twelfth to eighteenth week and the last trimester of gestation, which are periods of rapid growth of the cortical neurons. Alcohol consumption, however, is often associated with other negative influences, such as malnutrition; it thus may only indirectly lead to the anomalies described above. The data on this issue are not conclusive, but it appears that malnutrition alone is not responsible for the characteristics of the fetal alcohol syndrome. The daily consumption of moderate amounts of alcohol may cause permanent pre- and postnatal damage above and beyond the effects of malnutrition.

The potential damage of cigarette smoking during pregnancy had been suspected for several years before a large-scale study by Simpson in 1957 found that smokers had a high risk of delivering prematurely (Ferreira, 1969). Furthermore, risk increased with the number of cigarettes smoked per day. Many later studies confirmed the association of smoking with prematurity and low birthweight (e.g., Frazier, Davis, Goldstein, and Goldberg, 1961; Yerushalmy, 1971, 1972). Nicotine and the byproduct of carbon monoxide are suspect. It appears that smoking prior to pregnancy can harm the fetus even when the mother refrains from smoking during pregnancy, and that the number of years a woman smokes also may be an important variable. Perhaps cigarettes cause progressive damage to the mother's arterial system, including that of the uterus, thereby affecting the transport of oxygen and nutrients to the fetus (Naeye, 1979).

The use of narcotics is associated with prematurity, low birthweight, and fetal death (Ferreira, 1969; Rugh and Shettles, 1971). A high proportion of the neonates of addicted mothers are addicted also and experience the withdrawal symptoms of hyperactivity, tremors, respiratory problems, and gastrointestinal difficulties (Ferreira, 1969). Neonatal addiction has no psychological components at this time of life but it is speculated that it may predispose the child to greater dependence on or craving for the drug at later times. Behavioral disturbance, too, may result from maternal addiction to heroin and methadone (Kolata, 1978a). Such babies are characterized by unusually strong reflex responses, tremors, irritability, excessive crying, disturbed sleep, and a voracious appetite that does not lead to weight gain. They later display short attention spans and hyperactivity. It is generally noted that women who are narcotic users frequently suffer from poor environmental circumstances such as malnutrition, heavy smoking, and inadequate prenatal care. It is thus impossible to identify the narcotics as the specific teratogens. Animal studies provide evidence that rats exposed prenatally to morphine and methadone were hyperactive postnatally. Thus, maternal addiction appears at least to be implicated in hyperactivity.

Angel Dust: Possible Prenatal Damage

Phencyclidine, known as angel dust and PCP, was developed in the late 1950s as an anesthetic, but was not approved for use because of the disorientation, hallucinations, and delirium that it caused. By 1970 its illicit use was common. Although the prenatal influence of angel dust has not been documented to date, Golden, Sokol, and Rubin (1980) have reported a case study that points to its possible teratogenic effects.

A nineteen-year-old woman presented herself for prenatal care when she was in her eleventh week of gestation. Her health and pregnancy appeared normal except for a mild iron deficiency (anemia) and small weight gain. The birth process proceeded normally. However, the neonate was small and had an atypical, triangular-shaped face (see Figure 3–10). He also displayed poor head and eye control and had a dislocated hip. Initial, mild respiratory difficulties abated rapidly but the infant was lethargic and floppy. Even slight auditory and tactile stimulation caused flapping movements of the extremities. Jaundice appeared on the second day of life.

When attempts to discover infection were unsuccessful, maternal drug ingestion became suspect. The mother, who had earlier denied drug use, now stated that throughout the pregnancy she had daily smoked an average of six joints of marijuana dusted with PCP. An extensive medical examination proved negative for other possible determinants of the infant's problems, including infections, thyroid problems, and chromosomal anomalies.

At twenty-six days of age the infant was released from the hospital, only to return shortly due to weight loss, poor eating, jaundice, jitteriness, and respiratory distress. At two months of age the infant displayed poor eye control, tremors, and spastic, tense muscles, suggesting cerebral palsy. The investigators implicated PCP as the teratogen because their examination for other determinants was negative and because angel dust but not marijuana has been reported to cause similar effects in animals. They noted the need for a registry of cases of maternal use of PCP and fetal outcome.

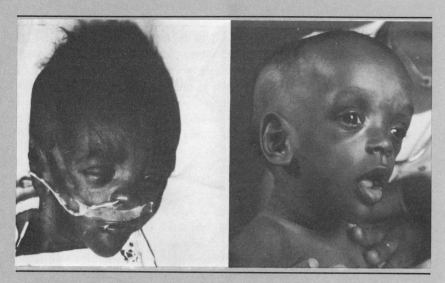

FIGURE 3–10
Facial features of the infant, as a neonate and at seven-and-one-half months, possibly damaged by maternal use of angel dust. From N. L. Golden, R. J. Sokol, and I. L. Rubin. Angel dust: possible effects on the fetus. **Pediatrics**, 1980, **65**, 18–20. Copyright American Academy of Pediatrics, 1980.

Although most drugs are taken knowingly, sometimes they are ingested quite involuntarily. Miller (1974) noted two striking examples of general environmental conditions in Japan adversely affecting infants by way of maternal exposure. In one case, congenital cerebral palsy was associated with expectant mothers who had eaten fish that had been contaminated with methyl mercury from industrial wastes. In the other, the birth of undersized infants exhibiting brown skin discolorations was attributed to maternal intake of cooking oil that had been contaminated with biphenyls during the manufacturing process.

When administered prenatally, hormones are known to alter development. Diethlystilbesterol (DES) is a female sex hormone that was given to pregnant women in the 1950s and early 60s to prevent miscarriages. Tragedy came to light only years later when cancer of the vagina and cervix was discovered in the daughters of these mothers, now young women themselves. An extensive national campaign was recently conducted through television commercials, newspaper ads, and college posters and newspapers to alert as many women as possible to this problem. The administration in the 1950s of progestin, a synthetic substance related to the male sex hormones and given for the same reason as DES, resulted in some female babies being born with abnormal external sex organs (Money and Ehrhardt, 1972).

Radiation. Abnormalities of structure and function can be caused by exposure to radiant energy such as x-rays and radioisotopes. Both animal studies and examination of human children who were en utero during the atomic bombings of Japan indicate that radiation may be responsible for leukemia, microcephaly, cataracts, stunted growth, miscarriages, and stillbirths (Rugh and Shettles, 1971; Thompson and Grusec, 1970). In some cases defects may display themselves only after the passage of time. As with other teratogens, the amount and time of exposure and the stage at which exposure takes place are important variables. The embryonic period, because so many organs are rapidly differentiating, is considered critical; however, the brain and spinal cord are thought to be highly vulnerable to radiation and they begin to develop about three weeks after conception and do not reach maturity until after birth. For the most part, then, radiation of the abdomen of expectant mothers is inadvisable, and many physicians will take pelvic x-rays only on the first ten days following the beginning of the menstrual period, when conception is not possible (Rugh and Shettles, 1971). Dental x-rays, which are weak, are not considered hazardous when an abdominal shield is used. Nevertheless, it is always best to restrict radiation as much as possible.

Paternal Influences. Interest in teratogens is focused, in large part, on their exposure to women, particularly during pregnancy. But according to Kolata (1978a), evidence is growing that birth defects may be higher than usual for the children of males who are exposed to certain substances before their offspring are conceived. Although it is doubtful that such exposure is a major cause of birth defects, it bears investigation.

Most of the research to date has been done with animals. The first demonstration of the effects involved the administration of thalidomide to male rabbits. Significantly higher death rates were found during the fetal and neonatal periods, presumably due to defects in the offspring. During the past fifteen years, administration of lead, narcotics, alcohol, caffeine, and methadone to male animals has resulted in birth defects in their offpsring. An example of the findings is the work of Joffe and Soyka (cited in Kolata, 1978a) in which methadone was given to male rats. The litters produced by mating these males were smaller than average and the offspring were more likely to die before weaning, have low birthweights, and perform abnormally on a behavioral test.

As evidence of the effects in humans Kolata (1978a) cited a study of males who, as operating room personnel, were exposed to anesthetic gases. Wives of these men, compared to those of men not exposed, had significantly higher rates of miscarriages and their offspring were more likely to be born with defects.

How can these teratogenic effects be explained? Joffe and Soyka offer a few possibilities. The sperm cells themselves might be damaged, perhaps during maturation, or the administered substances might act through the semen. Some substances, in fact, (e.g., thalidomide, narcotics, anticonvulsants) are excreted in the semen and enter the female circulation system through the vaginal walls. Thus, perhaps during pregnancy harmful substances contaminate fetal circulation through the placenta.

BIRTH

Approximately thirty-eight weeks after conception the human fetus is sufficiently developed to enter the outside world. Biological preparation for *parturition*, the technical term for birth, begins with *lightening*. Toward the end of gestation, the head of the fetus turns down so that birth occurs with the head first. In turn, the fetus's movement into this position relieves ("lightens") the pressure against the mother's diaphragm so that she can breathe more freely.

Labor, the process by which the fetus is expelled from its mother's uterus, occurs within a few hours to a few weeks after lightening. It is initiated primarily by hormonal changes controlled by the pituitary and adrenal glands. Labor is divided into three stages (see Figure 3–11, p. 64). In stage one the cervix of the uterus dilates and frequently the amnion ruptures, allowing the escape of fluids. The first stage generally takes from seven to twelve hours, but can vary greatly among individual women. The fetus emerges during the second stage, which usually lasts from one-half to two hours. Stage three involves the expulsion of the placental membranes, the so-called *afterbirth*. The average length of labor in the United States is fourteen hours for the first child, with less time for subsequent births. But length of labor and the psychosocial context of birth varies considerably around the world.

Perinatal Complications

Birth is not usually a complicated affair; in fact, it generally proceeds according to expectation. Among the perinatal difficulties that do arise is the abnormal positioning of the infant. The normal fetal position for birth is

Close-up

Variations in the Methods of Childbirth

Anthropological studies in particular have drawn attention to the considerable variations in childbirth that exist across the world. As an example, the following description contrasts the Cuna Indians of Central America with the Siriono Indians of Bolivia, South America.*

Ideally, the Cuna girls did not learn of the existence of either coitus or childbirth until the final stages of the marriage ceremony. Pregnancy was seen by the Cuna as a time of anxiety and rising fear of childbirth. Each day the pregnant woman went to the house of the medicine man, who specialized in prenatal care and childbirth, for a cup of freshly brewed medicine tea. Labor, however, was too "hidden" for the medicine man to attend. Children and men, even husbands and medicine men, were excluded from the labor area. The midwives kept the medicine man informed of the progress of the labor. He chanted and supplied medications in response to the labor progress reports. Labor under these circumstances was frequently prolonged and so extreme that unconsciousness of the laboring woman occurred at times.

In contrast to this, the Siriono patterned birth as an easy, open process, in keeping with their relaxed sexual attitudes. Birth took place in a communal hut and was a public event freely witnessed by men as well as women. The mother labored in a hammock while groups of women gathered, gossiping about their own labors and wondering whether the coming baby would be a boy or a girl. No help, however, was given to the mother during the usual normal labor. She herself tied the childbirth rope over her hammock to pull during contractions. She dug the earth under the hammock to cushion the baby's fall. The grunts and groans of labor did not appear to bother others within earshot. When the baby

was born it slid over the edge of the hammock, dropping a few inches to the ground. This casual treatment of labor had an interesting accompaniment—extremely short labor durations. Seven of the eight labors observed by the recording anthropologist lasted only one to three hours. The eighth one, which took longer, resulted in the birth of twins. (Newton, 1970, p. 86).

Such cultural differences and their implications have not gone unnoticed in the United States. Indeed, the last decades have witnessed growing recognition of the variations in childbirth and increased criticism of the medical methods that have been dominant. The expectant mother journeys to the impersonal atmosphere of the hospital, experiences labor with strangers, is frequently given medications that both dulls the pain and the drama of childbirth, and delivers her baby with a medical staff directing the activities. For the most part, other family members, including the father and siblings, are not permitted to share the event. Notwithstanding that complicated deliveries may best be handled by medical personnel in hospitals, many people have come to question the wisdom of this kind of rigid and impersonal childbirth.

In 1944 Grantly Dick-Read, an English physician, published a book that was to have wide influence on future childbirth methods. In this book, **Childbirth Without Fear**, Dick-Read argued that a medication-free childbirth in which the mother is alert and participating fully is optimal for both the mother and child. He believed that childbirth should be a positive emotional experience for the woman rather than the all too often anxiety-ridden period spent anticipating pain. The expectation of pain creates tension, Dick-Read claimed, that in turn works in opposition to uterine contractions, thereby actually

*Reprinted by permission of the Publisher. Sage Publications, Inc.

causing pain. Dick-Read attempted to change this situation by influencing attitudes toward childbirth and teaching women about the process, particularly training them to recognize contractions and to relax instead of tensing.

Others have been influenced by Dick-Read's work. The Lamaze method, brought from the Soviet Union in 1952 by a French physician, Fernand Lamaze, utilizes some of Dick-Read's suggestions, although it is chiefly based on Pavlov's classical conditioning paradigm (Chabon, 1966; Lamaze, 1970). It offers specific education for both prospective parents. Training for women emphasizes breathing techniques, while the men are encouraged to remain with and act as helpmates to their wives throughout labor and delivery.

More recently, Frederick Leboyer (1975) has focused on the experiences of the newborn rather than those of the adults. Leboyer's concern is that modern medical practice thrusts the child from a serene, dark, warmly protective environment into a cold, noisy, bright world in which it is held upside down, spanked, and cut off from placental oxygen abruptly. He argues that such treatment may be traumatic for the newborn. In the alternative Leboyer method of childbirth the room is dimly lit, the child is laid on the mother's abdomen, cutting of the umbilical cord is delayed, and the newborn is bathed in warm water. In short, an environment similar to the uterine environment is simulated so that birth can be a transition rather than an abrupt trauma.

Another ''new'' approach to childbirth involves a return to midwifery. Although midwives have had a long history of responsibility in childbirth, they all but disappeared in the United States in this century (Brack, 1976). This is in contrast to other Western countries; in Great Britain, for example, midwives still deliver from 60 to 80 percent of babies. Brack notes several historical reasons for this situation: the lack of midwife training in the United States, the need for the newly established profession of medicine to strengthen itself, and the restriction of women from prestigious professions. With the construction of more hospitals and advances in medical procedures in the twentieth century, childbirth came to be viewed as a medical procedure, with the increased use of forceps and anesthesias. Some women and professionals are now simply rejecting this model. Believing that childbirth is a natural event best accomplished with a minimal amount of interference in a supportive environment, they are calling upon midwives to aid them. In turn, there has been an increase in training for the once-forgotten profession of midwifery. All fifty states now license nurse-midwives and some states are permitting lay midwives to practice.

The potential advantages of the approaches just described have not been extensively documented, nor, for that matter, have the possible disadvantages. A few investigations indicate that training in childbirth is associated with reduction in the use of maternal medication (Laird and Hogan, 1956; Earn, 1962). The psychological consequences for the newborn are almost impossible to examine, but many parents describe their own experiences as deeply satisfying.

head first, face down. If the buttocks emerge first, the full *breech position,* or the fetus is in a diagonal position, delivery is more difficult and dangerous. Surgical instruments, forceps, can be helpful but are used more cautiously than in the past, because it has been discovered that they cause brain damage as they are applied to the baby's head. For a variety of reasons (e.g., the fetus is too large for the mother or must be delivered early to ward off the

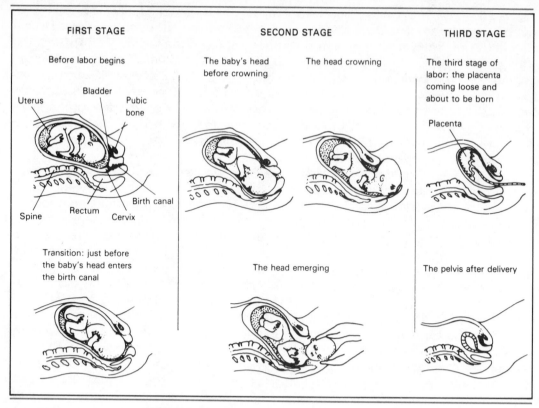

FIRST STAGE

Before labor begins

Uterus
Bladder
Pubic bone
Spine
Rectum
Cervix
Birth canal

Transition: just before the baby's head enters the birth canal

SECOND STAGE

The baby's head before crowning

The head crowning

The head emerging

THIRD STAGE

The third stage of labor: the placenta coming loose and about to be born

Placenta

The pelvis after delivery

FIGURE 3–11
Diagram of childbirth. From D. Schulz and S. Rodgers, **Marriage, the Family, and Personal Fulfillment**, 2nd ed., © 1980, p. 143. Reprinted by permission of Prentice-Hall, Inc., Englewood Cliffs, N.J.

threat of disease), fetuses are sometimes delivered through surgical openings in the uterus and abdominal walls, the so-called *Caesarean section.*

Anoxia. *Anoxia,* lack of oxygen, may occur at birth if the umbilical cord fails in any way to provide oxygen until the newborn begins to use the lungs. This may happen if the cord is damaged, knotted, squeezed shut, or detached too soon, or if the respiratory system does not react properly. The nervous system is especially sensitive to oxygen loss and severe anoxia may result in retardation and cerebral palsy. The effects of mild anoxia are disputed: Some researchers claim a causal relationship to lower IQ scores, learning disability, and hyperactivity, while others fail to find such a relationship (Goldstein, Caputo, and Taub, 1976; Gottfried, 1973; Knobloch and Pasamanick, 1974). There are several possible reasons for the discrepant findings, including difficulty in establishing anoxia in the first place, difficulty in measuring behavioral status, and assessment of various-aged children.

Medication. The use of pain relieving medications during birth is presently of high interest to researchers, and again, there is disagreement about their effects. Increasing evidence indicates at least subtle influences on sucking, nursing, visual attentiveness, motor performance, and sleep (Aleksandrowicz and Aleksandrowicz, 1974; Brazelton, 1970; Kolata, 1978a; Kron, Stein, and Goddard, 1963; Stechler, 1964; Yang, Zweig, Douthitt, and Federman, 1976). The effects vary with the specific drug, the dosage, and the time during delivery it is administered. Earlier administration, it is thought, has a weaker effect because the mother's system is still operating for the child and will metabolize the drug rapidly (Yang et al., 1976). A recent report by Brackbill and Broman is noteworthy (Kolata, 1978a). Data for 3,500 children were examined; the children were healthy and had experienced uncomplicated en utero development and births. Still, medication affected the children's behavior through at least seven years of life. Cognition and motor abilities were most influenced. Babies of highly medicated mothers lagged in sitting, standing, moving about, and in the capacity to inhibit crying and reactions to distracting stimuli. Language and cognition were impaired. There is a possibility that women who take no medication are different than those who do. Yang and his colleagues (1976) found that the number of drugs received by women during delivery was correlated positively with irritability, tension, depression, and fears for themselves during pregnancy. If such behaviors are at all enduring, they might affect children's development through mother-child interaction. At the very least, we must consider this possibility when interpreting correlations between medication at birth and children's behavior.

Prematurity and Low Birthweight

A birth is considered *premature* when it occurs before thirty-seven weeks of gestation. Premature babies are usually small and thus weight is a clue to prematurity. But full-term babies may also be born small. The causes of being small-for-date-of-birth may be different than for prematurity, as may the specific consequences. Nevertheless, *low-birthweight* babies, defined as weighing less than 5½ pounds (2,500 grams), are at high risk during and after birth. In the United States in 1975, 7.4 percent of all attended live births involved low-birthweight babies (U.S. Bureau of the Census, 1977). The consequences of prematurity and low birthweight have become increasingly important from a practical, social viewpoint as recent medical advances have ensured the survival of an increasing number of such infants. These strides have been truly remarkable; one estimate, for example, is that mortality among premature infants was reduced by 55 percent in the United States between 1933 and 1955 (Caputo and Mandell, 1970).

Many studies have shown that low birthweight is associated with an increased likelihood of physical defects and impairments, both at birth and through later life. More than half of the low-birthweight children in one sample had at least one physical or neurological impairment, including 37 percent with visual defects and 12 percent with hearing defects (Drillien, 1961). Interestingly, the incidence of defects was positively related to the year of birth; that is, children born more recently were more likely to display them. This finding presumably is a result of the increased survival rate of very low birthweight babies in recent years. Neurological damage often has been found to be associated with low birthweight (De Hirsch, Jansky, and Langford, 1966; Lubchenco, Horner, Reed, Hix, Metcalf, Cohig, Elliott, and Bourg, 1963; Wiener, Rider, Oppel, Fischer, and Harper, 1965). These findings include evidence of strabismus (a condition in which both eyes cannot be focused on the same point, so that the individual appears to be "cross-eyed"), abnormal EEG recordings, and spastic movement. Defects appear to be associated with very low birthweight rather than with relatively "heavy" prematures (Robinson and Robinson, 1965).

One of the most important longitudinal studies of the relationship between birthweight and later development, initiated at Johns Hopkins University during the early 1950s, is the Baltimore Study. This investigation followed the intellectual development and school performance of almost one thousand infants, including a premature group weighing less than 3.3 pounds at birth and a normal weight group, through their twelfth year of life. The study utilized sophisticated controls for a variety of factors, such as social class, race, season, and hospital of birth. Measures of intelligence taken at forty weeks of age, three to five years, six to seven years, eight to ten years, and twelve to thirteen years showed that the low-birthweight individuals did significantly less well than did the normal-weight ones. There were also differences in the degree of impairment within the premature group as a function of birthweight; heavier infants within the low-birthweight class were less likely to show impairment than were those of very low birthweight. The Baltimore Study was also interested in determining whether children who had been low-birthweight infants were more likely to be in special or below-grade-level school classes than were controls. It was found that while 75 percent of the control group were in an appropriate grade, only 45 percent of the smaller prematures had achieved regular school placement by the age of twelve (Weiner, 1968; Caputo and Mandell, 1970).

A relationship between low birthweight and later adjustment difficulties or problems in social behavior has been established in many correlational studies (Caputo and Mandell, 1970). Caution is needed, however, in interpreting this finding. Consider, for example, a study by Pasamanick, Rogers, and Lilienfeld (1956), in which the frequency of referrals to the Baltimore Board of Education for deviant behavior was significantly higher for low-birthweight children than for matched control children. But when only premature children who were born *without pregnancy complications* were considered, this difference disappeared. Thus the underlying factor may be pregnancy complications or events associated with them. Likewise, Robinson and Robinson (1965) reported that neither low-birthweight nor very low-birthweight children differed from controls in terms of teacher behavior ratings when corrections were made for social class.

Low-birthweight babies are surviving in greater numbers today than in the past partly because of careful prenatal, perinatal, and postnatal care. After birth they are placed into environmentally controlled incubators and are closely observed and monitored (Figure 3–12). Paradoxically though, this medically beneficial treatment may serve as a disadvantage for "preemies" by depriving them, sometimes for many weeks, of sensory stimulation and normal human contact. This kind of separation, it is reasoned, leads to a

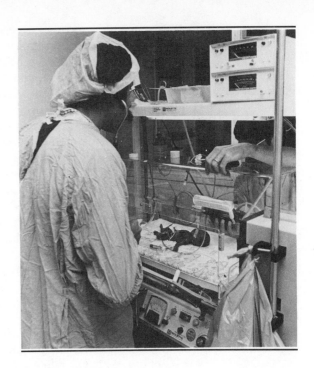

poor mother-child bond that, in turn, has undesirable effects. There is evidence that parents respond differently and less favorably to low-weight infants than to average babies and that later in life "preemies" are more likely to be abused (Frodi, Lamb, Leavitt, Donovan, Neff, and Sherry, 1978; Goldberg, 1978). The reasons for this probably include the physical appearance of the neonates, aversive behaviors (for example, an unpleasant cry), and the high frequency of problems associated with low birthweight.

There have been many attempts to provide these infants with environments that are rich in stimulation and compensate for human isolation (Cornell and Gottfried, 1976; Powell, 1974). Scarr-Salapatek and Williams (1973), for example, compared control preemies who received the usual hospital care with preemies who received rocking, talking, and handling from their mothers and nurses, plus mobiles within their vision. When the infants went home, the mothers were trained to interact with them so as to foster development. As a result, the treated infants showed greater weight gain and obtained higher scores on a standard test of infant development. In reviewing intervention studies such as the one just described, Cornell and Gottfried (1976) concluded that the most pervasive finding is a facilitation in motor development and muscle tone. The findings concerning maternal-child interactions are mixed. Mothers who handle their infants seem to feel closer to their babies and cuddle them more, and feel self-confident. However, these effects wear off quickly and maternal care does not seem to change as a result of the intervention (Goldberg, 1978; Powell, 1974).

Neonate is a term that is applied to the child from birth to about one month of age. At birth, the neonate is approximately twenty inches long and weighs about seven and one-half pounds. Its skin is smooth and covered with vernix. It may also have lanugo on its shoulders and back. In other ways, too, the neonate has a standard appearance. It has a relatively large head, flat nose, high forehead, and receding jaws. These features will swiftly mature and give way to individual characteristics that are usually considered more attractive.

There are many instruments for assessing the neonate. Some are aimed at immediate detection of abnormalities or signs of future problems, whereas others evaluate behavioral capacities and individual differences (St. Clair, 1978). One of the most useful and popular measures of the medical condition of the infant at birth is the Apgar instrument, devised by Virginia Apgar in 1953. The measure is simply a rating of heart rate, respiration, reflex irritability, muscle tone, and color that is made one minute after birth (and sometimes repeated three, five, and ten minutes later). Each of the five dimensions is scored as 0, 1, or 2, with the larger numbers indicating the more superior condition. Table 3–3 illustrates this measuring system. Apgar reported that with regard to neonatal death, babies with total scores of 10, 9, or 8 had excellent prognosis whereas prognosis was poor for total scores of 0, 1, or 2. The rating serves well for the immediate screening of the neonate's medical condition, but its relationship to later development is not clear (St. Clair, 1978).

TABLE 3–3
The Apgar Scoring Method

Dimension	Score		
	0	1	2
Heart rate	absent	slow, below 100 beats per minute	100–140 beats per minute
Respiration	absent	slow, irregular	good, accompanied by crying
Reflex irritability	absent	grimace or cry	cough, sneeze, vigorous cry
Muscle tone	limpness	some flexion	active motion
Color	pale or blue	pinkish body, blue extremities	pinkish

Source: Adapted from "Proposal for a New Method of Evaluating the Newborn Infant" by V. Apgar, Anesthesia and Analgesia, 1953, 32, 260–267.

The Brazelton Neonatal Behavioral Assessment Scale is one of the most widely used scales that taps a variety of infant reactions (Brazelton, 1973). It evaluates, for example, responses to light, noise, and a pin prick; general alertness; cuddliness; motor maturity; and reflex action. This scale is being used extensively in research (as is the Apgar) and evidence is accumulating that it discriminates neonates from different cultures as well as those who are born prematurely, drug addicted, or developmentally disabled (Sostek, 1978).

It is often said that newborns are not very interesting; their lives seem to be taken up with the maintenance tasks of eating, sleeping, and crying. To some degree this is certainly true. The neonate sleeps sixteen to twenty hours a day and obviously is capable of only limited responding. As more neonatal studies are done, however, the complexity of the newborn's existence is increasingly appreciated.

Reflexes.   Neonatal behavior is rich in *reflex action,* comprised of unlearned and automatic specific responses to specific stimulation. Close to one-hundred reflexes have been described at one time or another (Capute, Accardo, Vining, Rubenstein, and Harryman, 1978; Kessen, Haith, and Salapatek, 1970). However, the eliciting stimuli and developmental course of even some of the most studied reflexes are not always agreed upon. Table 3–4 and Figures 3–13 and 11–3 describe and depict just a few of the reflexes. For our purposes, we can recognize at least three different groups.

TABLE 3-4
Some Neonatal Reflexes

Babinski (see Figure 3–13)	Stroking the sole of the foot results in the spreading out of the toes and the upward extension of the big toe.
Babkin	Pressing the neonate's palm causes the mouth to open, the head to turn sideward, and the eyes to close.
Galant	Stroking the neonate's back along the spine results in the trunk arching toward that side.
Moro (See Figure 3–13)	Withdrawal of physical support (dropping, allowing the head to drop, change in position) and a sharp noise results in the arms extending outward and returning to midline.
Palmar grasp (See Figure 11–3)	Touching the palm causes the fingers to grasp the object
Placing	Stroking the top of the foot with an edge, such as a table edge, results in the raising of the foot and placing it on the edge.
Plantar grasp	Touching the balls of the foot results in inward flexion of the toes.
Positive support	Holding the infant around the chest and bouncing it on the balls of its feet results in contractions of the legs so that the legs can support the infant's weight.
Rooting	Stroking the cheek or corner of the mouth causes the head to turn toward the object and movements that look as if the infant is searching for something to suck.
Sucking	Placing an object in the mouth results in sucking.
Walking (See Figure 3–13)	Holding the infant upright and allowing the feet to touch a surface results in stepping movements.

Some reflexes are directly related to vital functions. They include breathing, blinking, sneezing, sucking, swallowing, and rooting. Other reflexes, called postural reflexes, help maintain the orientation of the body in space (Capute et al., 1978). The positive support reflex is an example. A

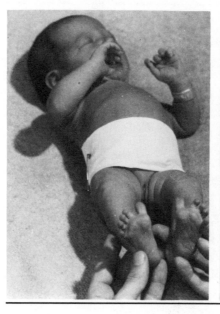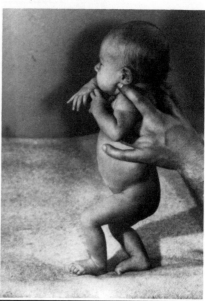

FIGURE 3-13
Three reflexes that are present at birth, but wane during the first year of life in normal infants. From H. F. R. Prechtl, **The Neurological Study of Newborn Infants,** 2nd ed. (London: SIMP/ Heinemann Medical; Philadelphia: Lippincott, 1977).

third varied group of the primitive reflexes seem to be of little advantage, although it is speculated that they may have been adaptive in the evolution of the human species. The Moro, Babinski, and Palmar Grasp reflexes are among these.

A good number of the neonatal reflexes persist into adulthood but many of the postural and primitive reflexes seem to disappear during the first year of life. Their appearance, strength, and disappearance at specific times are taken as signs of nervous system functioning. For example, the absence of the Moro reflex at birth is believed to indicate severe central nervous system damage or depression. On the other hand, persistence beyond the usual four to five months is associated with mental retardation and cerebral palsy (Capute et al., 1978). What processes underlie such patterns? The postural and primitive reflexes are controlled primarily by the "old" brain (that is, the brain stem, cerebellum, etc.), but as the "new" brain, the cerebral cortex, develops in infancy it inhibits or integrates them. Thus, they "disappear." If the cerebrum is not functioning properly, inhibition will not occur and the reflexes will persist (Capute et al., 1978).

Sensory Capacity.   It stands to reason that in order to behave, even reflexively, the neonate must be able to sense the environment. It has been difficult to discover the quality of early sensory abilities because neonates are limited in their overt responses and obviously cannot verbally report their experiences. However, recent improvements in measuring infant responding confirm that all the basic senses are operating at some level at birth. The world is immediately seen, heard, smelled, tasted, and felt, and to some degree, was sensed in utero. Sensory capacity is discussed in detail in chapter 4, but we note here the general consensus that the neonate's abilities are better developed than was once thought.

States of Consciousness.   Neonatal behavior has been successfully categorized according to states of consciousness (Ashton, 1973; Beintema and Prechtl, 1968; Brazelton, 1973; Wolff, 1965, 1966). As illustrated in Table 3–5, these states are based primarily on respiration, muscle tone, motor ac-

---

TABLE 3-5
Seven Infant States as Classified by Wolff

State	Characteristics
Regular Sleep	Full rest; little or no body movement; eyes firmly closed; face in repose; even respiration.
Irregular Sleep	Gentle body movement; facial grimaces; mouthing; eyelids relaxed or pinched; irregular respiration.
Periodic Sleep	Intermediate between regular and irregular sleep, some facial, mouth and body movement; respiration varies from shallow and rapid to deep and slow.
Drowsiness	More active than regular sleep but less so than irregular and periodic sleep; spurts of writhing; eyes open and close intermittently and are glazed and unfocused; respiration variable but usually regular.
Alert Inactivity	Relative inactivity; face relaxed; eyes open with a bright shiny appearance; respiration more variable and faster than regular sleep.
Waking Activity	Spurts of motor activity; eyes open but do not shine; perhaps some moaning or whimpering; face relaxed or pinched; respiration irregular.
Crying	Crying vocalization; diffuse motor activity.

Source: Adapted from Wolff, 1966.

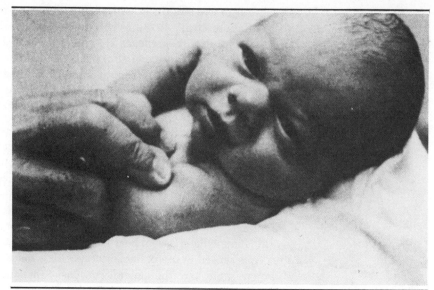

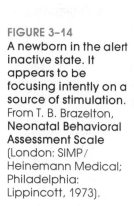

FIGURE 3-14
A newborn in the alert inactive state. It appears to be focusing intently on a source of stimulation. From T. B. Brazelton, **Neonatal Behavioral Assessment Scale** (London: SIMP/ Heinemann Medical; Philadelphia: Lippincott, 1973).

tivity, and alertness. They depend upon physiological variables such as hunger, nutrition, degree of hydration, and time in the wake-sleep cycle, and are relatively independent of the environment (Ashton, 1976; Brazelton, 1973). As might be expected, developmental changes are noticeable. For example, one study showed that the infant is alert for only 11 percent of the time during the first week of life but by the fourth week is alert 21 percent of the time (Wolff, 1965). The alert inactive state has been singled out as important in the development of attention. It is then that neonates appear to deliberately inspect the environment, thereby taking in new information. They are then well on the way to organizing the world (See Figure 3–14).

INDIVIDUAL DIFFERENCES AMONG INFANTS

Our view of infancy has changed during the last few decades. Prechtl expressed the current respect for the infant's repertoire of reflexive behavior with these words:

> I am impressed by the great repertoire of newborns, but you must give them the chance to show it. If you put a newborn baby in a supine position in its cot and cover it with a blanket up to its neck, of course it gives the impression of being a kind of vegetable which just cries and sucks from time to time and that's all. But if, for example, you watch a baby on the skin of its mother, without clothes but at a warm temperature, it shows a lot of things: rooting, crawling, grasping, and numerous anti-gravity postural responses. [cited in Stone, Smith, and Murphy, 1973, p. 240]

Moreover, the view that the world of the infant is nothing more than a buzzing confusion has been replaced by a view of infancy that emphasizes the capability of the young human to organize the world. What led to this change? First, the old assumption that the infant's sensory ability is severely limited has been discarded. Second, considerable evidence now indicates that infants are selective as to the kind of information they take in. Third, it has been shown that even the very young infant can learn from experience.

A new respect for the individuality of infants is also evident. Although parents have long been eager to speculate about differences among babies, scientists, cautious by professional commitment, have collected relevant data slowly. Birns (1965) presented a soft tone, a loud tone, a cold disk applied to the thigh, and a pacifier (rubber nipple) to thirty babies. The babies were tested four times between the ages of two days and five days. Observers recorded the intensity of each infant's response to the stimulation. Birns found that some babies tended to respond vigorously to all stimuli every time they were tested, whereas others gave responses of mild intensity quite consistently. Thus it seems that individuality is apparent within a few days of birth.

Brown (1964) observed six infants during their first week of life on a daily basis for about an hour after feeding. The infants tended to show considerable individuality and consistency in their behavior. One child, Dorothy, slept quite a bit (37 percent of the time), cried a lot (39 percent), and was rarely alert (4 percent). She hardly reacted to the stimulation used by the experimenter to test sensitivity. Ted slept a great deal (56 percent of the time) and cried very little (17 percent). Most of his activity seemed directed at decreasing tension and returning to sleep. Charles was alert, quiet, and receptive (37 percent of the time). He slept a good deal but was able to remain quietly awake for long periods of time.

Fascinating evidence of individuality in infancy has been provided by Schaffer and Emerson (1964) in the course of a longitudinal study of thirty-seven infants from working class families. All thirty-seven were of normal developmental status. The mothers were interviewed when the babies were about one year old and then again when they were eighteen months. The interview was specifically aimed at the infants' behavior in commonly occurring situations such as being held on the lap, cuddled, carried, swung, bounced, and the like. Questions were also asked about the mothers' reactions. Schaffer and Emerson found that whereas some of the children sought contact (being held, kissed, carried), others tried to avoid it. The infants displaying the former behaviors were labeled "cuddlers" and those displaying the latter, "non-cuddlers." The following descriptions are quoted from the reports given by mothers of cuddlers and non-cuddlers.

CUDDLERS	NON-CUDDLERS
"Cuddles you back."	"Gets restless when cuddled, turns face away and begins to struggle."
"Snuggles into you."	
"Holds quite still and puts on a soppy face."	
"Loves it."	"Will not allow it, fights to get away."
"Laps it up."	"Has never liked this since able to struggle, squirms and whimpers."
"Would let me cuddle him for hours on end."	"Gets restless, pushes you away."

"Wriggles and arches back, and
only stops when put down again."

"Restless and whiny until allowed back in cot."

"Will kick and thrash with his
arms, and if you persist will begin to
cry."

The investigators pointed out that the non-cuddlers by no means resisted all contact, nor did they fail to go to their mothers when they were
frightened. It was restriction of movement that caused their avoidance of
contact. They showed marked dislike of being wrapped, changed, or of having clothes put on, and when tucked into bed they struggled free of blankets. They also slept less, on the average, and appeared to be ahead in
motor development. These behaviors were not associated with different
handling techniques by the mothers, and the researchers were inclined to
view them as a general characteristic, akin to restlessness, that could be inherited. Their hunch about inheritance is difficult to test, and in chapter 5
we will further discuss the heritability of behavior. Regardless of the cause
of "cuddliness," however, the Schaffer and Emerson findings demonstrate
that individuality displays itself early in life.

PATTERNS OF PHYSICAL GROWTH

As even casual observation reveals, the first few years of life are a period
of very rapid physical growth for the human organism. For any one system
growth may involve increases in size and number of cells, in further differentiation, and in completion of certain processes such as myelinization of
the nervous system (the laying down of the protective myelin covering).
The remainder of this chapter will concentrate on two tasks that researchers
have set for themselves: (1) to identify general principles that adequately
characterize and summarize growth, and (2) to collect normative data regarding the development of particular body parts and functions.

Major Periods of Growth

Viewed in its larger perspective, bodily growth occurs through approximately the first twenty years of life in humans. It is generally considered
advantageous to divide this overall growth period into three major subdivisions: infancy and early childhood (to about the fifth year of life),
middle and late childhood (to about age twelve), and adolescence (to about
age twenty). Growth is more rapid and more likely to show spurts during
both the infancy-early childhood period and the adolescent period than
during middle childhood.

Growth of Body Systems

Different parts of the body show somewhat different growth patterns
relative to the age of the child. Various organ systems or tissues and their
growth curves are represented in Figure 3–15. The *body size* category, which
includes the skeleton, muscles, and internal organs, shows more rapid
growth during the infancy-early childhood period and the adolescent pe-

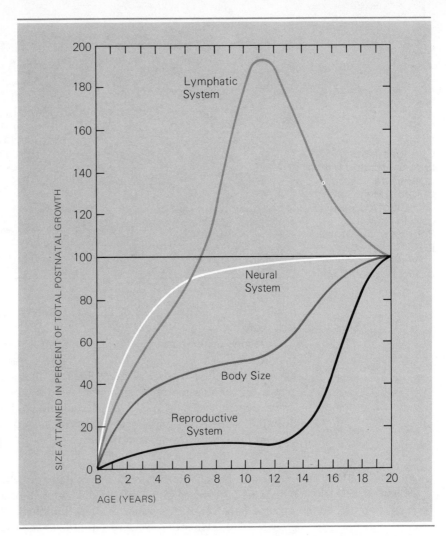

FIGURE 3–15
Varying patterns of development for the four systems of growth. Adapted from J. M. Tanner, Physical growth. In P. H. Mussen, ed., **Carmichael's Manual of Child Psychology,** 3rd ed., Vol. 1. Copyright 1970, reproduced by permission of John Wiley & Sons, Inc.

riod than during middle childhood. The *lymphatic system* (thymus, lymph nodes, and intestinal lymphoid mass) reaches an adult level by seven years of age and is even larger during preadolescence before it declines. Similarly, the *neural system* (head, brain, and spinal cord) is almost fully developed by the age of six. In contrast, the *reproductive organs* grow very slowly until adolescence, at which point they undergo rapid growth.

Principles of Growth

It has often been noted that early development proceeds *cephalocaudally*— that is, from the cephalic or head region to the caudal or tail region. Thus, as seen in Figure 3–16 the appearance of the fetus is remarkably top-heavy and the neonate's less so; not until middle adolescence are the proportions of adulthood fully apparent. The functioning of the organism appears in keeping with this direction of physical growth. Infants are able to lift their

FIGURE 3–16
Changes in body form associated with age. Adapted from C. M. Jackson, Some aspects of form and growth. In W. J. Robbins et al., **Growth** (New Haven: Yale University Press, 1929), p. 118, by permission.

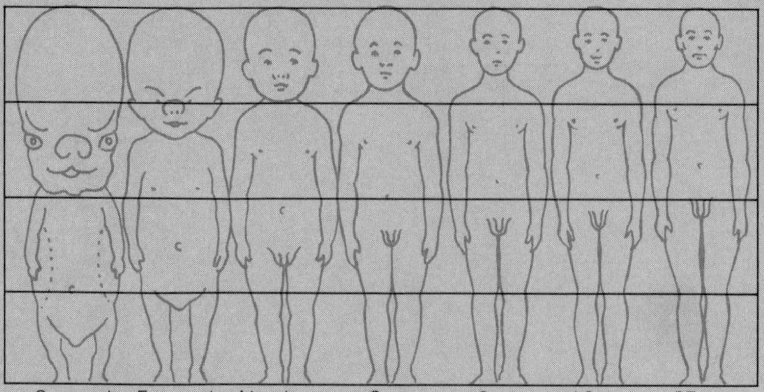

2 month 5 month Newborn   2 yr.   6 yr.   12 yr.   25 yr.
(fetal)

heads within the first weeks of life but cannot stand until the end of the first year.

A second general principle of development is that growth proceeds from the proximal or center axis of the body to the extremities or more distal regions. *Proximodistal* growth is exemplified in prenatal development by the growth of the chest, trunk, and internal organs before the growth of the limbs, fingers, and toes. It is also reflected, although not as clearly, in function; the refined motion of the fingers requires a longer time for development than the movements of the arm.

Individual Rates of Physical Growth

One of the most intriguing facets of body growth is that there are large individual differences in the *rate* at which growth occurs. Tanner (1963) has suggested that each individual displays a biologically determined natural growth curve. Evidence for such an argument comes from a number of different sources. First, the correlation between an individual's body length at two years old and in adulthood is approximately +.80, which, as we saw in chapter 2, is quite high indeed. Second, Tanner notes that when children have been impeded from normal growth for a period of time, they often appear to "catch up" or make up for the loss when the impeding factor is removed.

The most striking and perhaps most fundamental characteristic of the growth of an animal is that it is self-stabilizing, or, to take another analogy, "target-seeking." Children, no less than rockets, have their trajectories, governed by the control systems of their genetical constitution and powered by energy absorbed from the natural environment. Deflect the child from its natural growth trajectory by acute malnutrition or a sudden lack of a hormone and a restoring force develops so that as soon as the missing food or hormone is supplied again the child catches up towards its original curve. When it gets there, it slows down to adjust its path onto the old trajectory once more. [Tanner, 1963, p. 818]

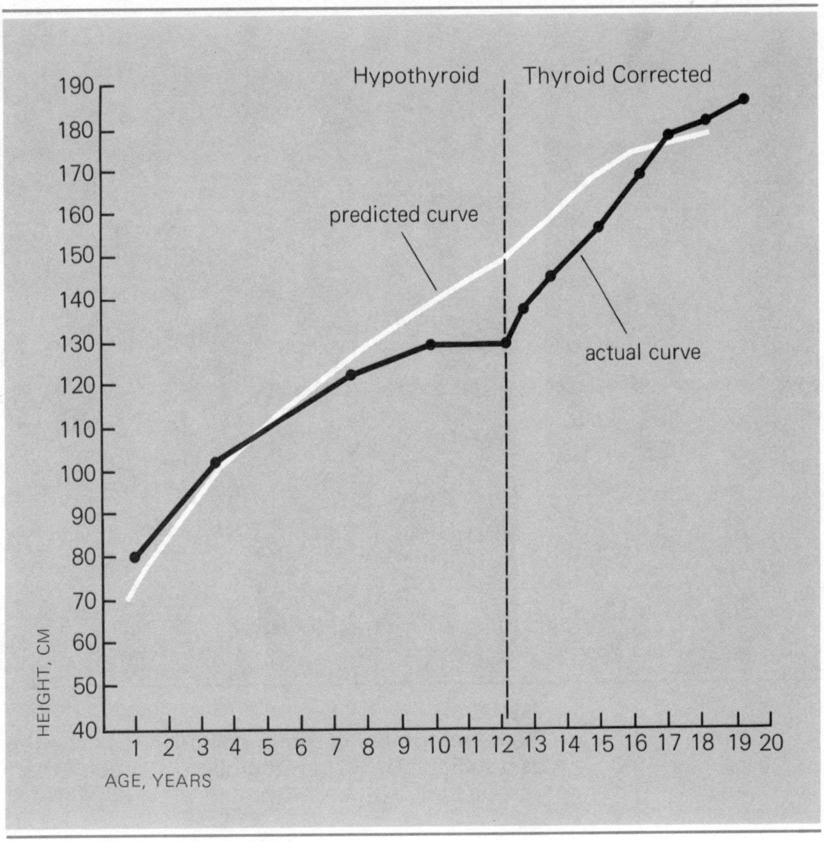

FIGURE 3-17
The rate of growth of a boy suffering from hypothyroidism, both before and after treatment. Note how he "caught up" with the normal growth rate. Adapted from J. M. Tanner, The regulation of human growth. **Child Development**, 1963, **34**, 825, figure 5. Copyright 1963 by the Society for Research in Child Development, Inc. Reproduced by permission.

The evidence for such predetermined growth patterns is illustrated in the case cited by Tanner of a boy suffering from hypothyroidism. (*Hypothyroidism* is a deficiency in the activity of the thyroid gland, which decreases the amount of thyroxine, a growth-regulating hormone produced by the gland.) The boy's growth virtually ceased from the age of eight to the age of twelve, although, as seen in Figure 3-17, he showed a rate of growth that was almost exactly average until then. When appropriate treatment was given for the glandular condition, growth not only resumed but showed an unusually rapid acceleration so that he quickly "caught up" with the growth rate that would have been predicted from his height at ages one through four.

MOTOR DEVELOPMENT

As children grow physically, their ability to move about and manipulate the environment also shows rapid gains. This type of motor accomplishment is often referred to as perceptual-motor because it involves many complex perceptual and cognitive processes, which will be discussed in later chapters. For now, though, we can examine the general course of motor development and some of the established norms.

FIGURE 3–18
The development of motor skills involves experience and practice, as well as a sufficient level of maturation.   © Louis Goldman, Rapho/Photo Researchers, Inc., Ken Kays.

The Course of
Motor
Development

Although motor development relies on changes in the neuromuscular system, the underlying processes are not well understood. Nevertheless, some general principles can be noted.

First, motor functions follow a predictable pattern. Babies cannot walk before they sit, nor write before they grasp voluntarily. As we saw earlier, the pattern generally follows cephalocaudal and proximodistal directions.

Second, gross motor control involving large areas of the body is achieved more easily than fine motor control involving smaller muscle groups. Children can hold their bottles during the latter part of their first year of life, but lack the ability to finely finger a flute. In other words, mass movement becomes specific or *differentiated*. When an infant cries the entire body appears to be involved, but later crying is limited to the upper portion, perhaps only the head.

Third, complex motor skills develop progressively through differentiation and *hierarchic integration* (Werner, 1948). Once specific control (differentiation) is achieved, the many individual actions can be put together or integrated into larger, complex, and more coherent whole units of motor behavior. After gaining greater and greater control over arm, leg, and neck movements (differentiation), the infant will begin to put these differentiated but relatively simple actions together and perform the more complex and integrated act of sitting up without support (hierarchic integration).

Reflexive and Voluntary Movement. Early movement is regulated by the lower centers of the brain and is thus reflexive. Gradually the cortex largely assumes regulatory power and the child displays voluntary motion. As we saw earlier, many of the postural and primitive reflexes seem to disappear entirely or at least become integrated into voluntary movement (Capute et al., 1978). One of the central issues, though, is the exact relationship between reflexive and voluntary movement. The grasp reflex, for example, appears to be related to voluntary grasping. But the two are actually quite different; the reflex involves palm and finger flexion without the thumb being brought into opposition. As the grasp reflex gradually disappears by six months of age, it is replaced by the voluntary grasp that involves thumb opposition and increased control (Eckert, 1973). How the two motor acts are related and whether or not the reflex is the direct foundation for the voluntary grasp remain a mystery.

Zelazo, Zelazo, and Kolb (1972) raised the question of whether the reflexes could and should be strengthened by exercise. One group of male infants received daily active exercise of the walking and placing reflexes during their second to eighth weeks of life. A second group received passive exercise that involved gross motor and social stimulation but did not elicit the reflexes. A no-exercise group was simply tested weekly along with the exercise groups. A fourth group was tested only at the final week of testing. The results of these tests showed that active exercise increased walking responses over time. Babies in the other groups exhibited somewhat fewer walking responses over time. For the placing response infants who had active exercise maintained their base level, whereas the others declined from their base level. Later parental reports indicated that walking occurred earlier for the infants who had been actively exercised. Zelazo and his associates suggested that the walking reflex should be stimulated because it conceivably facilitates mobility and perhaps competence. Moreover, they speculated that the widely held belief in the invariance of motor development reflects more about child-rearing practices than about the infant's capacities. Thus they addressed the old question of the roles of maturation and learning.

Maturation and Learning

To what extent is the type of development described above simply a function of bodily maturation and to what extent does it rely on experience? The question has continually woven itself into the inquiries of developmental psychologists (see chapter 1). Maturation, it will be recalled, refers to those changes that primarily represent an unfolding of the nature of the capacities of the organism (and the species) that are at least relatively independent of special environmental circumstances, training, or experience. One psychological dictionary defines *maturation* as referring to those changes "that take place more or less inevitably in all normal members of the species so long as they are provided with an environment suitable to the species" (English and English, 1958).

A classical experiment demonstrating maturational processes in motor development was conducted by Carmichael in the late 1920s. Working with the salamander *Amblystoma*, he divided the animals into a control group and an experimental group. The latter were placed in water containing an anesthetic; the control animals were allowed to develop in fresh water. In time, the control salamanders began to show vigorous movement, whereas those in the anesthetic were immobile. But when the drugged animals were then placed in fresh water, they immediately began to swim. Within half an hour they were indistinguishable from the controls, who had been swimming for five days (Carmichael, 1970). Although other similar experiments have not shown such clear effects, this study serves to strengthen belief in built-in processes that operate independently of experience.

A few early investigations addressed to the maturation-experience issue involved human infants. Dennis and Dennis (1940) collected information about Hopi Indian children concerning the development of walking. Traditionally reared Hopi infants were secured to cradle boards in such a way that they were unable to move their hands, roll over, or raise their bodies. The babies were removed from the cradle boards only once or twice a day to have their clothes changed. But other Hopi infants, their parents being influenced by European ways, were not restricted in this manner. Dennis and Dennis were thus able to examine the effect of naturally occurring events and found that infants in *both* groups walked at about fifteen months.

Gesell and Thompson (1929) similarly studied stair climbing in a pair of identical twins. One twin (T) was trained to climb stairs at forty-six weeks of age and was provided practice in the activity until she was fifty-two weeks old. At this time she was able to climb the stairs alone in twenty-six seconds. The control twin (C) received no training and at fifty-three weeks could climb the stairs in forty-six seconds, but two weeks later she accomplished the task in ten seconds.

Taken together, these studies provide evidence that maturation is important for the development of motor behaviors. But any conclusion must be assessed carefully. As Bower (1974) has pointed out, we do not actually understand the antecedents of developing behavior and so infants who receive training and practice for a particular behavior may not receive *relevant* training. In the Gesell and Thompson study, for example, twin T was trained by being passively moved up and down the stairs, but perhaps a more reasonable training would have involved crawling on the floor (which, in fact, twin C might have done). But even if maturational processes play a strong role, practice cannot be ruled out. Most, if not all, people are biologically capable of skiing, but without practice they cannot ski. Specific complex motor acts are learned. The opportunity for such learning begins early; for example, during the latter part of the infant's first year, play is characterized by motoric games such as pat-a-cake, peek-a-boo, and clapping (Crawley, Rogers, Friedman, Iacobbo, Criticos, Richardson, and Thompson, 1978). Infants playing any of these games with an adult receive a good deal of feedback about their performances, and feedback is one of the most important variables controlling motor learning. In general, motor learning depends upon physical maturation, the specific task being learned, and the match between feedback and the child's capacity to process information (e.g., Newell and Kennedy, 1978; Singer, 1973). Biological readiness may be a necessity, but it does not ensure the blooming of specific motor abilities.

Motor Milestones

In this final section we will cite norms or averages regarding motor development and, in later chapters, will have occasion to mention norms regarding intellectual and social skills. Although norms help us to understand the approximate rate and nature of human development, it cannot be emphasized too strongly that it is unwise to apply group averages uncritically to any one individual case. Williams (1946) has likened the problem to one of determining the average shoe size in an army. The information would be of enormous value in determining the amount of leather needed to outfit the army. It would be foolish, though, to order the average size shoe for everyone. So too with developmental norms. We do not expect each individual to fit the average, although norms are useful as a general guide for individual assessment.

Upright Position and Locomotion. The child's ability to achieve the upright position and to move through space proceeds in a series of orderly gradations that illustrate the principles already described. Table 3–6 indicates the important milestones and the approximate times at which they are achieved. The table cannot show, of course, the practice, the waverings, and the failures that were the foundation for the successes. Shirley (cited by Eckert, 1973) conceptualized upright locomotion growth as falling into five stages: postural control of the upper body; postural control of the entire trunk; active effort toward locomotion; locomotion by creeping; and pos-

TABLE 3-6
Motor Milestones for the Upright Position and Locomotion,
and When They Are Achieved

Motor Behavior	Average Age in Months	Normal Variation in Months
Lifts head when held at shoulder	.1	
Head erect and steady	1.6	.7–4
Sits with support	2.3	1–5
Sits alone momentarily	5.3	4–8
Rolls from back to stomach	6.4	4–10
Sits alone steadily	6.6	5–9
Pulls to standing position	8.1	5–12
Stands up by furniture	8.6	6–12
Stands alone	11.0	9–16
Walks alone	11.7	9–17
Walks backward	14.6	11–20
Jumps off floor, both feet	23.4	17–30+
Walks upstairs alone, both feet on each step	25.1	18–30+
Walks down stairs alone, both feet on each step	25.8	19–30+
Hops on one foot, two or more hops	30+	30+

Source: From the Bayley Scales of Infant Development, 1969.

tural control and coordination for walking. This suggests that the infant must control its body in new postures in a static position and then undertake movement concerned with the postures (Eckert, 1973).

Manual Skills. Halverson (1931, 1936) identified a sequence of manual growth from film records of neonates and infants. These stages, which are shown in Figure 3–20, range from simply touching and holding objects (at twenty weeks) to the increasingly sophisticated use of the fingers (at twenty-four to thirty-six weeks) and then to the successful coordination of hand, thumb, and fingers in producing highly precise and effective pincer movements (at fifty-two weeks).

Later changes are equally dramatic. By eighteen months, the child can typically fill a cup with cubes, build a tower from three blocks, and turn the pages of a book (Landreth, 1967). Through early childhood these accomplishments continue to advance; a four-year-old typically can fold paper diagonally and produce simple figures like a cross. At five years the youngster can pluck pellets one by one and drop them into a bottle, use a crayon with great assurance, draw a recognizable person, and copy a square and circle, although the diamond is troublesome (Gesell, Halverson, Thompson, Ilg, Castner, Ames, and Amatruda, 1940).

With rare exceptions adults show a preference for the use of one hand over the other. *Handedness* (also called laterality) is not absolutely consistent across activities; that is, some people may write with their left hand and eat with their right. Nonetheless, approximately 90 percent of the adult human

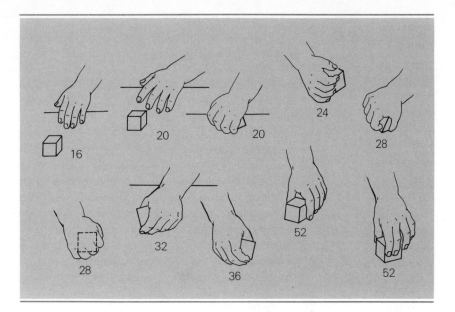

FIGURE 3–20
The development of manual skills during the first year of life. The numbers indicate the age of the child in weeks, while the hands illustrate the growth in manual dexterity that occurs. Adapted from H. M. Halverson, 1931. By permission.

population all over the world shows a preference for the right hand. Developmental norms and patterns are not well established (Hardyck and Petrinovich, 1977). Gesell and Ames (1947) observed a complex shifting back and forth from using both hands (bilaterality) to using either the right or left (unilaterality). It is not until about four years of age that most children stabilize their preference (Gesell and Ames, 1947).

Theories of handedness range from the social psychological (i.e., children simply acquire the habit) to the genetic. Heredity may indeed be involved (Blau, 1977; Hardyck and Petrinovich, 1977), but preference can be affected by specific brain damage, educational practices, and family and cultural values. The influence of cultural tolerance for left-handedness is difficult to assess, but the frequency of left-handedness has been estimated at 10.4 percent, 5.9 percent, and 1.8 percent in cultures that were extremely permissive, permissive, and harsh/restrictive, respectively (Dawson, cited in Hardyck and Petrinovich, 1977).

Being left-handed is a disadvantage in that virtually all environments are set up for right-handed people. There is another disadvantage: Left-handedness has long been associated with evil, corruption, dishonesty, and deficiency. In fact, the French word *gauche* means left and awkward, and the English word *sinister* means toward the left and evil. One analysis of the Bible revealed eighty positive references to right-handedness and only negative references to left-handedness (Hardyck and Petrinovich, 1977). It is widely believed that left-handed children exhibit more than average problems in social behavior, reading, bladder control, schizophrenia, and the like (e.g., Blau, 1977). Hardyck and Petrinovich (1977) argue, however, that although a subset of left-handed individuals may have specific deficits, most do not. If deficits do exist, perhaps many are the result of attitudes and expectations regarding left-handedness.

SUMMARY   *Conception,* the union of ovum and sperm, marks the beginning of development. We have progressed from the seventeenth and eighteenth century
belief that the adult figure as we know it is preformed in the gametes, to the
ability in the twentieth century to remove ova (egg cells) from a woman's
ovary and combine them in a culture dish with sperm cells, producing a
healthy infant nine months later. The doctrine of *preformation* now seems
unbelievable, but our knowledge of conception and prenatal development
is equally amazing.

All body cells except the gametes contain twenty-three pairs of chromosomes; *gametes* (sex cells) contain only twenty-three single chromosomes.
When conception occurs the ovum and sperm each contribute twenty-three
chromosomes to the zygote, creating the necessary pairs. Twenty-two of the
twenty-three pairs are autosomes, common to both the male and female.
The twenty-third pair, the sex chromosomes, is markedly different for
males and females. At conception the female always contributes the X
chromosome, while the male may contribute either an X or a Y. A male zygote is the result of an XY combination, and a female is formed when two
Xs are joined.

Multiple conceptions occasionally happen, generally resulting in the
birth of two children. Cases in which more than two children are conceived
are rare. *Dizygotic* twins are produced when two ova are simultaneously fertilized by two different sperm. A zygote that divides into two units after an
ovum has been fertilized by one sperm results in the birth of *monozygotic*
twins. There are many contributing factors in multiple births.

There are three stages of prenatal development: the periods of the
ovum, the embryo, and the fetus. The *ovum* period begins at conception and
ends during the second week after implantation in the uterus; the second to
eighth week after implantation constitutes the period of the *embryo;* and the
fetal stage lasts from the eighth week to birth. During these three stages the
fetus develops rapidly and in a very orderly fashion. Today we are very
much aware of the many influences on prenatal development. These include diet, rest, exercise, and good health, and the avoidance of specific
teratogens, agents or conditions that contribute to the abnormal development
of the fetus. Teratogens include maternal illnesses such as Rubella, drugs,
chemicals, hormones, and radiation that women may be exposed to during
pregnancy. The stage during which a woman comes in contact with any teratogen greatly influences the effects it will have on the developing fetus.
Attention has been concentrated on teratogens and women, especially during pregnancy, but it should be kept in mind that exposure of men to certain teratogens, such as anesthetic gases, may also cause birth defects.

Birth, or *parturition,* can be expected approximately thirty-eight weeks
after conception. It begins with *lightening,* the repositioning of the fetus.
Within a short time after lightening, labor begins. *Labor* is the process of the
fetus being expelled from the uterus. First labors average approximately
fourteen hours (although length of time varies greatly among individual
women) and occurs in three stages. The birth process is usually predictable
and uncomplicated. Breech birth, anoxia, prematurity, low birthweight, and

pain-relieving or labor-inducing medication can cause serious complications. If problems are foreseen a physician may decide to deliver the fetus through surgical openings in the abdomen and uterus, a procedure called the *Caesarean section.*

Neonates, infants from birth to about age one month, generally look very much alike. As infants move out of this state, however, their appearance will take on individual characteristics.

The Apgar instrument is popular for measuring the medical state of the neonate. The Brazelton Neonatal Behavioral Assessment Scale evaluates infant reactions and reflexes. Neonatal reflexes are many and varied. Those associated with vital functions include breathing and sucking, while postural reflexes help maintain the body's orientation in space. Neonates are aware of the environment through the use of basic, though underdeveloped, senses, and have been categorized according to varied states of consciousness. Studies are now showing that infants exhibit individuality in their behavior even during the very beginnings of their neonatal stage.

Growth is not a haphazard process. Different body systems develop at various stages in an individual's life span. For instance, the neural system is almost fully developed by age six, whereas the reproductive organs mature most rapidly during adolescence. The body also grows in specific directions: *cephalocaudally,* from the cephalic (head) region to the caudal (tail) region, and *proximodistally,* from the proximal (center) axis of the body to the extremities. Individuals have different rates of growth, and one study suggests that everyone has a biologically determined natural growth curve.

As a child grows motor abilities develop in a predictable pattern, becoming more proficient, refined, and complex. Differentiation and hierarchic integration describe the formation and progression of the motor skills. *Differentiation* is the increased control and specificity exhibited by an individual (e.g., an infant first waves the arm when learning "bye-bye," but later can move the hand at the wrist to display the same message). Individually learned actions are then combined, forming more sophisticated behaviors. This process is referred to as *hierarchic integration.* The relationship of reflexive and voluntary motor action is not well understood.

Motor ability requires both maturation and learning. *Maturation* describes changes that are almost inevitable for the majority, providing that conditions are appropriate. *Learning* is not inevitable, but reflects practice and concentration devoted to a particular skill.

"Motor milestones" mark the approximate period when an infant masters certain skills, namely postural control, stages of locomotion, and various manual skills. Of interest, both developmentally, psychologically, and socially is *handedness,* a preference for one hand over the other.

4 Sensory and Perceptual Development

From the moment of birth, stimulation from the environment is constantly bombarding us. Two related processes, sensation and perception, enable us to receive stimulation and help us to organize it.

What exactly do we mean by sensation and perception? The terms often are confusing because they overlap in meaning. *Sensation* involves stimulation of the sensory receptors by physical energies from the internal and external environment. The retina of the eye, for example, reacts to light rays and translates information into electrochemical potentials, which are nerve impulses. The retina thus serves as a sensory receptor. The nerve impulses that the retina creates are transmitted to the brain, which reacts to the stimulation in various ways. It is at this stage of the brain's reaction that sensation and perception are differentiated. If the brain merely transmits the impulses to the response system—the muscles or glands—psychologists are likely to label the process as sensation. However, if the brain first selects, organizes, and then modifies the input, the process will be said to involve perception as well. *Perception* thus involves both the integration of impulses from the different sense organs and the comparison of these impulses with previous input. In a way, then, the processes of sensation and perception are actually names for different points in a complex process of information gathering and evaluation that ultimately leads to "knowing."

Today there is considerable interest in early sensation and perception and they are being studied for at least three reasons: there is a general curiosity about infancy, more knowledge in this area would be helpful in the examination of the nature vs. nurture question, and some investigators believe that the development of basic sensory and perceptual processes is largely completed during infancy (e.g., Bower, 1974). With an emphasis on early development, this chapter presents descriptions of the sensory and perceptual abilities that are present in humans at birth, followed by a discussion of how these "wired-in" abilities develop and become integrated into more complex perceptual processes. Consideration of intersensory perception—that is, perception involving more than one modality—and the effects of environmental modifications on perceptual development complete the chapter.

BASIC SENSORY AND PERCEPTUAL ABILITIES

Taste

Although there have been few investigations of gustatory stimulation and its development over time, research has established that the neonate is able to distinguish at least salt, sugar, lemon juice, and quinine (Nemanova, as cited by Pick, 1961). Interestingly, a liking for sugar is also evident at birth; the neonate relaxes and sucks contentedly when presented with a sweet solution, but reacts to salty, sour, or bitter liquids by grimacing and breathing irregularly (Pratt, 1954). Even when presented with a substance that is more nutritious but less sweet, the neonate prefers the sweeter substance (Bower, 1977).

Almost no attention has been given to the development of taste beyond infancy. It is known that there are definite physical changes in the taste buds as we grow older; for example, children's taste buds are more widely distributed on the tongue than the taste buds of adults. It is not known, though, whether these physical changes affect relative sensitivity and the experience of taste, and if so, how (Pick and Pick, 1970). In one of the few studies that has examined individual differences in children's sensitivity for taste, evidence indicated that children with the lowest sensitivity had the most enthusiasm about and acceptance of food (Korslund and Eppright, 1967).

Touch and Pain

Examination of prematurely delivered infants has shown that humans are able to respond to tactile stimulation early in life. Prematures respond to touch with fanning of the toes, slight motor responses, and waking from a half-sleep (Saint-Anne Dargassies, 1966). In the neonate, touching various areas of the body produces many of the reflexes discussed in chapter 3, including the Babinski reflex, the grasp reflex, and the rooting reflex. We know that sensitivity to painful stimuli is exhibited early, but it probably is not well developed. When a painful stimulus is applied, the newborn will cry and try to withdraw. If the newborn is unable to withdraw, he or she will attempt to push away the stimulus with a hand or foot.

During the first few days after birth, the newborn's sensitivity to touch and pain cues increases noticeably; for example, fewer pinpricks (Sherman and Sherman, 1925) and less electric shock (Lipsitt and Levy, 1959) are required to arouse a five-day-old infant as compared to a neonate.

Tactual stimulation becomes increasingly important as young children develop sufficient motor ability to handle objects and navigate within their surroundings. They then collect information about the world as they feel the hard floor and soft carpet, the rough stones and the smooth sidewalk, or the round ball and the square block. Under usual circumstances, such perception is the result of the combination of touch and vision. But it is possible to examine the effects of touch only by asking children to perform various tasks as they handle objects that are out of sight. The ability to recognize objects tactually increases with age as exploration of the objects becomes more systematic (Gliner, 1967).

There is also reason to believe that the sense of touch can be developed more highly when experience and necessity conspire to sharpen it. Thus the blind are better than the sighted in using such cues (Hunter, 1954). Interestingly, blind persons who were sighted until later in life do best of all in tests of tactual perception.

Smell

The sense of smell, or *olfaction*, appears to be one of the most highly developed senses in the newborn (Rovee, Cohen, and Shlapack, 1975). In a series of investigations infants were placed in a stabilimeter, which registers activity level, with a pneumograph around the abdomen to measure breathing (see Figure 4–1). A cotton swab saturated with an odorant was then placed beneath their nostrils, and changes in activity and breathing were noted. The neonates discriminated the four odors employed, and they showed the usual habituation reaction, that is, repeated presentation of the substances resulted in weaker responses (Engen, Lipsitt, and Kaye, 1963; Lipsitt, Engen, and Kaye, 1963). Very young infants also turn away from the

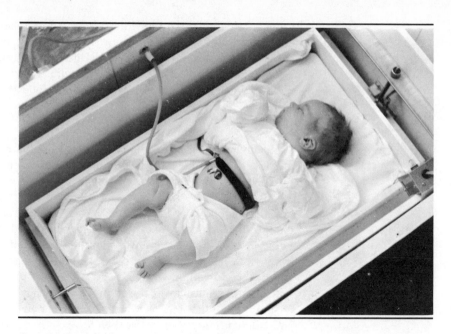

direction in which aversive odors originate, indicating that they can localize odors in space (Bower, 1974). Several European studies show that sensitivity to odors is well developed by age six, continues to improve until middle age, and then declines (McCartney, 1968). Olfactory preferences also exhibit clear-cut changes, and, as might be expected, individuals who have been smokers for over fifteen years have lower sensitivity than nonsmokers.

Hearing   Several reports indicate that the unborn fetus responds to auditory stimulation (Bench and Vass, 1970; Bernard and Sontag, 1947; Forbes and Forbes, 1927; Peiper, 1925). Peiper, for example, reported that many fetuses responded to an automobile horn with movement. Both behavioral and electrophysiological responses to sound have been recorded for premature infants (Schulman, 1970). Although fluidlike substances in the ear of the newborn may somewhat limit the ability to hear in the first few days of life, even very young infants respond to sound with a variety of responses, such as muscle change, breathing disruption, eye blinking, and changes in heart rate and activity level.

Most newborns also possess the ability to discriminate one sound from another on the basis of several acoustic variables (Eisenberg, 1976). Numerous studies indicate that the newborn can discriminate sounds of different duration (Clifton, Graham, and Hatton, 1968; Eisenberg, 1965; Keen, 1964), a function that is critical to the processing of spoken language. Newborns can also discriminate sounds of different frequency or pitch (Birns, Blank, Bridger, and Escalona, 1965; Kasatkin and Levikova, 1935; Levanthal and Lipsitt, 1964), and seem to have clear pitch preferences. Low frequency sounds have a calming effect on newborns (Birns, 1965), whereas high frequencies tend to elicit distress reactions (Eisenberg, 1976). Hutt and Hutt (1970) further defined newborns' pitch preference with the discovery that neonates show differential patterns of responses to signals within the typical frequency range of speech. Similarly, Freedman (1971) found that the sound of a female's voice elicited more response from newborns than did the sound of a bell. Taken together this evidence suggests that human neonates are biologically prepared both to tune into frequencies of sound that are within the range of human speech and to discriminate sounds in a way that is functional for later speech development.

Infants are also able to locate sounds; they have been observed at birth to turn their eyes in the direction of a sound source (Butterworth and Castillo, 1976). However, they seem unable to locate the *exact* position to the right or left (Bower, 1974).

A study of children from ages five to fourteen showed increased sensitivity to sound until the ages of twelve to thirteen years for both sexes and for white and black children (Eagles, Wishik, Doerfler, Melnick, and Levine, as cited by Pick and Pick, 1970). Then, as seen in Figure 4–2, hearing ability decreases progressively through the adult years, especially for the high pitches.

Overall, then, infants and newborns (even those born prematurely) show a remarkable sensory capacity to taste, touch, smell, and hear. But these abilities have been given much less consideration than visual abilities, for a variety of reasons.

VISUAL, SENSORY, AND PERCEPTUAL ABILITIES

In many ways, vision may be considered our most important sense modality. Adults report that they value their eyesight more highly than any of their other senses and use the visual mode to indicate understanding and comprehension that are not, in fact, related to ocular functions (e.g., "I see what you mean!"). It also has been argued that visual stimulation provides

FIGURE 4–2
Audiogram for different age groups, showing hearing loss in higher pitches as people grow older.
Adapted from C. C. Bunch, Age variations in auditory acuity.
Archives of Otolaryngology, 1929, 9, 625–636. Copyright 1929, American Medical Association, by permission.

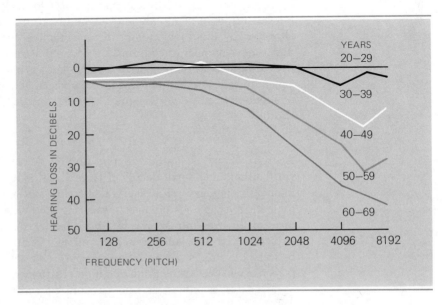

an extremely important source of contact between the infant and his or her environment:

> . . . when he is both awake and contented the young infant's main pre-occupation is looking—either in exploring the environment or in examining particular parts of it more carefully. No reinforcement is needed for this response other than the presence of sufficiently interesting sights. [Fantz, 1969, p. 48]

Perhaps for these reasons considerably more work has been accomplished in this area than in any other.

Basic Visual Abilities

Until a few decades ago the newborn infant was believed to be incapable of processing visual information in a meaningful way. We know now, however, that the infant is born biologically ready to process visual information, although this processing becomes increasingly sophisticated with age.

Brightness and Movement. The simpler dimensions of visual sensitivity, our basic sensory capacities, are present at or soon after birth. The sensitivity of the newborn to *brightness* and *movement* are two such dimensions. Using the pupillary reflex as an index of the infant's response to brightness, Sherman, Sherman, and Flory (1936) found that infants will respond to changes in brightness immediately after birth. Likewise, Haith (1966) presented infants, twenty-four to ninety-six hours old, with either a stationary array of lights or an intermittently moving array. Haith found the infants were more likely to stop sucking on a pacifier and attend when the moving array was presented than when the stationary one was shown.

A few days after birth neonates are able to track some moving objects, but this response is initially uneven, and focus on the objects is easily lost. However, by about two months of age smooth accurate tracking is evident, due to development of coordination of the muscles of the eye and perhaps to development of brain centers that mediate vision (cf. Bronson, 1974). It is generally believed that movement in the visual field is a strong determinant of attention from the very beginning of life, a topic to which we shall return shortly.

Acuity. *Visual acuity*—the relative ability of individuals to detect both small stimuli and small details of large visual patterns—has been tested in infants through several measurement techniques. One method, called "optokinetic nystagmus," involves measuring the involuntary sideways movement of the eyes in response to a horizontally moving stimulus, such as a striped pattern presented above the infant's head. The width of the space between the stripes can be varied to measure visual acuity, inasmuch as the response will occur only if the infant detects the striped pattern.

Neonates as young as one day old possess eyesight approximately

Close-up

How Developmental Psychologists Determine the Visual Experiences of Neonates

In sensation and perception experiments with children, adolescents, and adults, various stimuli are presented and the subjects are asked to respond in some way (for example, with a verbal reply, by pressing a response key, or perhaps by filling out a questionnaire) to indicate their experiences. Plainly, however, it would be fruitless to ask infants to describe their sensory experiences. How, then, can developmental psychologists know what is experienced by the infant, who can neither speak nor voluntarily signal in any direct way?

Actually, various experimental methods have been used by psychologists and physiologists to measure the early visual capacities of the infant and young child (Cohen, DeLoache, and Strauss, 1978). Most of the available procedures involve presenting a stimulus or set of stimuli to an infant and observing and measuring a response, which should appear automatically if a particular sensory ability is present. For instance, investigators wishing to determine whether infants can "see" an object might present the object above each infant's head to determine whether his or her eyes turn in the direction of the object in question. This measure of **visual fixation** can tell us whether infants see the stimulus.

Other methods help us to understand the infant's preference for a certain type of sensory input (e.g., curved lines vs. straight lines). **Preferential looking** is one such method. This method involves presenting the subject with two or more stimuli and recording the amount of time spent looking at each. Providing that certain positional and other biases are controlled, the stimulus garnering the greatest amount of visual attention is assumed to be the preferred stimulus. Notice, however, that even if the infant fails to display a preference, it is not possible to declare absolutely that no preference exists. Also, it is obvious that the situation requires that infants **distinguish** among stimuli—and can therefore see the difference between them. Thus the method is not just a measure of preference, but is also a measure of the ability to see.

A method often used to determine whether infants can discriminate between two stimuli is the **habituation technique.** This method is based on the fact that infants will lose interest in familiar stimuli but still remain potentially quite responsive to novel stimuli. (Habituation is in fact a type of learning, which we will more thoroughly review in Chapter 6.) The use of the habituation technique is straightforward. A stimulus is shown repeatedly to the infant until his or her response (e.g., heart rate, sucking, movement, or visual fixation) gradually drops to a stable level. When the response is thus "habituated," a second stimulus is introduced into the infant's visual field. If the infant responds with renewed vigor to the new stimulus, it can be inferred that the infant is able to visually discriminate the new stimulus from the old one. By varying stimuli on a number of dimensions such as size, shape, color, and so on, the technique can be used to learn a great deal about the sensory capacities of neonates.

The methods described above have been used by developmental psychologists to assess early visual capacities such as acuity, color and brightness sensitivity, and the infant's ability to perceive shapes and faces. We will have occasion to mention the methods briefly in the following discussion of the young human's developing sensory and perceptual skills.

equivalent to 20/300 to 20/400 (Dobson and Davida, 1978; Marg, Freeman, Peltzman, and Goldstein, 1976; Fantz, Ordy, and Udelf, 1962; Sokol, 1978). This means that the infant sees at 20 feet what adults with normal vision can see at 300 to 400 feet. Thus, an infant's visual acuity is considerably poorer than that of a normal adult. However, the development of visual acuity is quite rapid, and between six months and one year of age the typical infant's acuity will approach its final adult limits.

Vision as a
Perceptual Ability

Thus far we have considered vision largely as a set of sensory capacities. We now turn to visual perception, which involves the processing of sensory input into a psychologically meaningful form. As we shall see, perception involves preferences as well as abilities.

Pattern Perception: Fantz's Work. The work of Robert Fantz (1958b, 1961) is historically quite important in that it took to task the earlier assumption that infants lack the ability to distingush pattern and form. Fantz used preferential looking as an indication that a particular pattern is, indeed, being recognized. He began by building a special infant crib, similar to the one shown in Figure 4–3. Above the infant's head was a plain gray ceiling, on which various pairs of target stimuli were placed. An identical pair of figures, such as two triangles, was hung from the ceiling of the looking chamber one foot apart and one foot above the infant's head. By means of a special peephole in the top of the apparatus, Fantz could tell how much time the infant spent fixating on each of the triangles. Not surprisingly, looking time was equivalent for these two identical figures. But when a

FIGURE 4–3
"Looking chamber"
used to test pattern
discrimination in
human infants. An
infant lies on a crib,
looking at objects
hung from the ceiling,
while an observer
records the amount of
fixation time for each
object.   From R. L.
Fantz, The origin of
form perception.
Scientific American,
May 1961, p. 66.
Photograph by David
Linton, by permission.

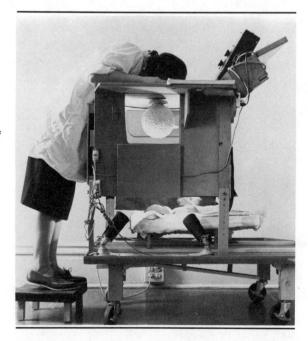

"bull's-eye" and horizontal stripes were introduced together, it was found that infants above the age of eight weeks preferred the bull's-eye to the stripes. Such a finding could be obtained only if the infant was able to visually discriminate one pattern from the other.

Later the procedure was changed somewhat. Under the new rules, only a single stimulus was presented and terminated as soon as the infant looked away. To reduce the likelihood that differences in looking time could be accounted for by very early visual experience and learning, infants under five days of age served as subjects and were compared with older infants. Several other stimulus configurations were also used, including a drawing similar to the human face. Some of the results are shown in Figure 4–4, from which it can be seen that definite preferences exist in the very young. Thus, as Fantz has written:

> The results . . . explode both the myth that the young infant is untestable and the myth that there is little to test. It is now difficult to maintain the earlier views that the world of the neonatal infant is a big blooming buzzing confusion. . . . The young infant has a patterned and organized visual world which he explores discriminatingly with the limited means at his command. [1969, pp. 55–56]

FIGURE 4–4
Fixation time (preference) of very young children to patterned and plain discs. Black bars show the results for those 2 to 3 months old, gray bars for those more than 3 months old.
Adapted from Origin of form perception, by Robert Fantz.
Copyright © 1961 by **Scientific American,** Inc. All rights reserved.

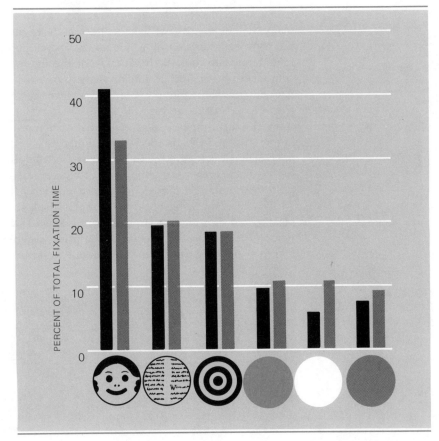

Just as important, though, as the fact that any discrimination was displayed are the findings with regard to particular stimuli. Fantz quickly pointed out that infants looked for longer times at complex rather than simple presentations and at social rather than nonsocial configurations (see again Figure 4–4). Other investigators have confirmed this preference and have set out to explore exactly what aspects of visual stimuli capture and maintain fixation (Cohen, DeLoache, and Pearl, 1977).

Stimulus Complexity. The complexity of a stimulus is usually defined by the number of turns or elements it contains or by the degree of randomness (Figure 4–5). Preference for complexity appears to increase during the first few months of life and is displayed throughout childhood and adulthood (Brennan, Ames, and Moore, 1966; Greenberg and O'Donnell, 1972; Nunnally and Lemond, 1973). Varying complexity, however, often creates differences in the amount of contour (i.e., ouline, border, edge, or black and white contrast), and several investigators suggest that contour is the critical component of *early* preference. The evidence clearly supports this view. The amount of time infants gaze at stimuli has been shown repeatedly to vary with the amount of contour (Karmel, 1969, 1974; McCall and Melson, 1970; Fantz, Fagan, and Miranda, 1975).

The way in which infants scan stimuli also is instructive. In one study, babies were placed in a head-restraining crib in which a visual display—a black triangle on a white field—appeared above their eyes, and scanning of the eyes was recorded by a camera (Salapatek and Kessen, 1966). The infants tended to look at the vertices of the figure, where contrast (that is, contour) is the highest. A similar study uncovered a tendency among three-day-olds to fixate on the border between patches of black and white (Kessen, Salapatek, and Haith, 1965). These results are fascinating because research with animals has revealed that certain retinal cells respond only to border effects. Perhaps specialized human cells are particularly well developed at birth compared with other parts of the visual system and account for the fact that the very young seem almost compelled to gaze at certain aspects of stimuli (e.g., Stechler, Bradford, and Levy, 1966).

In any event, aspects of the stimulus itself—notably movement, complexity, and contour—are strong determinants of early attention, and attraction to them appears to require little prior experience. It is even thought that they underlie the infants' preference for schematics of the human face

FIGURE 4–5
Examples of simple
and complex stimuli.

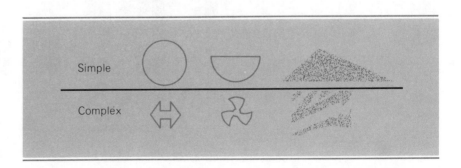

(cf. Maurer and Salapatek, 1976; Bond, 1972; Haaf, 1974; Haaf and Bell, 1967). The influence of experience soon displays itself, however, in memory for images.

Face Perception.   For many years students of human development have asked whether infants possess an innate ability to recognize the human face. John Bowlby (1958) has claimed that the infant is innately predisposed to respond to the human face and that this predisposition forms a major basis for the development of attachment. (We will have more to say about Bowlby's view and about attachment in chapter 11.)

Early investigations by Fantz (1963) and Stechler (1964) seemed to show that infants do have an innate preference for human faces, but these studies were flawed in that Fantz and Stechler did not control for other variables such as stimulus complexity. For example, infants might prefer a picture of a human face to a blank circle because of the many lines appearing in the face, and not simply because it was a human face (Hershenson, 1964; Thomas, 1965). More recently, however, investigators have begun to provide acceptable evidence supporting the innate predisposition hypothesis (Goren, 1975; Thomas and Jones-Molfese, 1977). Goren (1975), for example, presented newborns with facial stimuli differing in the arrangement of features. The results indicated that a regular schematic face elicited greater attention than scrambled or blank faces when the stimulus was slowly moved in a specific pattern in front of the infant.

Changes in Attention Deployment.   Attention to visual stimuli changes as children progressively learn about the world. The role of experience also is indicated in the way in which children come to explore displays. As we previously noted, infants initially fixate on the borders or on specific parts of stimuli. However, over time, they are able to maintain attention for longer periods and their exploration becomes more systematic throughout early and middle childhood (Day, 1975; Maurer and Salapatek, 1976).

What is meant by *systematic*? This term refers to the individual visually scanning a display in some task-appropriate way or with some consistent pattern. Figure 4–6 shows the actual eye movements of children at various age levels; note that the oldest children took in more information and followed the contour of the figure more than did the younger ones (Zaporozhets, 1965). Many other studies show that when the task is to judge the sameness or difference of two visual displays, older children—compared with younger ones—systematically explore the parts of the displays that are most relevant to solving the task (Day, 1975).

In sum, children are born with considerable visual ability that develops rapidly within the first year as the result of both further maturation and experience. Initially, features of the stimulus exert a good deal of control on what is looked at, and limited but somewhat organized information is taken in. Gradually the child becomes less dependent upon the stimulus itself and selects, attends to, and more systematically explores the environment on the basis of previous experience and developing capacities to think and process information.

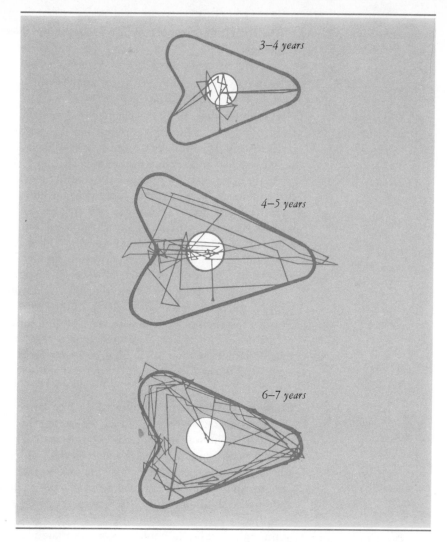

FIGURE 4–6
Patterns of eye movements showing scanning of visual form at three age levels. From A. V. Zaporozhets, The development of perception in the preschool child, in P. H. Mussen, ed., European research in cognitive development, **Monographs of the Society for Research in Child Development,** 1965, 30, 82–101. Copyright 1965 by the Society for Research in Child Development, Inc. Reproduced by permission.

3–4 years

4–5 years

6–7 years

Depth Perception. Many years ago it was determined that perception of depth (which is a form of distance perception) is almost as accurate in four-year-olds as in adults (Updegraff, 1930), and recent work has explored the question of whether the ability to perceive depth is present at birth or soon thereafter. Gibson and Walk provide the following overview of the problem:

Human infants at the creeping and toddling stage are notoriously prone to falls from more or less high places. They must be kept from going over the brink by side panels on their cribs, gates on their stairways and the vigilance of adults. As their muscular coordination matures they begin to avoid such accidents on their own. Common sense might suggest that the child learns to recognize fall-ing-off places by experience—that is, by falling and hurting himself. But is experience really the teacher? Or is the ability to perceive and avoid a brink part of the child's original endowment? [1960, p. 64]

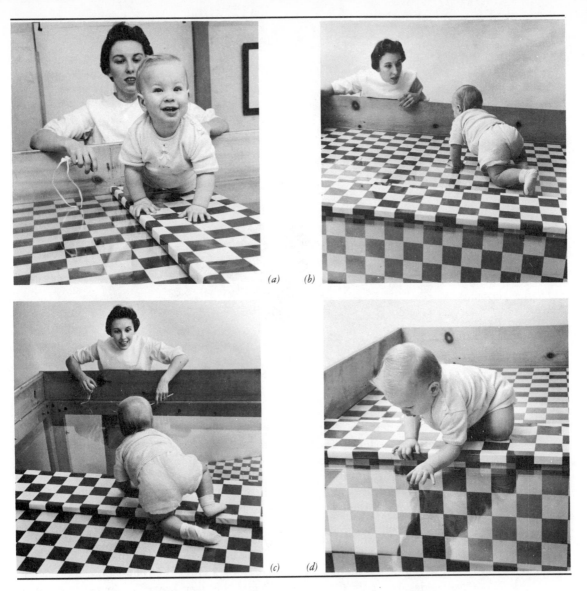

FIGURE 4–7
An infant on the visual cliff (a), crawls to his mother across the shallow side (b), but refuses to do so on the deep side (c), even though he has tactual evidence (d) that the cliff is solid.   From E. J. Gibson and R. D. Walk, The "visual cliff," **Scientific American,** April 1960, p. 65. Photos by William Vandivert, by permission.

To investigate the question, Gibson and Walk developed a special experimental setup, which they referred to as the visual cliff. The "cliff," shown in Figure 4–7, is constructed from a heavy sheet of glass with a platform in the center raised slightly above the surface of the glass. The center platform, covered with a patterned material, is wide enough to hold the

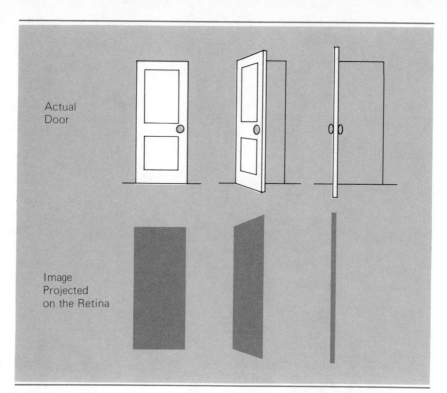

Actual Door

Image Projected on the Retina

baby when it is in creeping position. The "shallow" side of the cliff is created by fastening the same patterned material directly beneath the glass on one side of the platform. The illusion of depth is created on the other side of the platform by placing the material several feet below the glass. The infant's mother stands alternately at either the deep or the shallow side and beckons to the child to come to her (Gibson and Walk, 1960; Walk and Gibson, 1961).

Gibson and Walk began by testing thirty-six infants between 6½ and 14 months of age. The results of this initial study were quite clear. Twenty-seven of the infants were willing to crawl off the center onto the shallow sides, but only three ventured into the deep area. The investigators note that a number of infants actually crawled *away* from their mothers when called from the cliff side; others cried, presumably because it appeared to them that it was not possible to reach their mothers without crossing the brink. Clearly, infants old enough to crawl display perception of depth.

Are younger infants capable of perceiving depth? In a later study, Campos, Langer, and Krowitz (1970) devised a measure that did not require locomotive abilities and thus could be used with younger infants. The investigators simply placed 44- to 115-day-old infants on either the shallow or the deep side of the visual cliff apparatus and measured changes in the infants' heart rates. Using this technique, the Campos study showed that infants as young as two months old experience the perception of depth. Thus, though there is not definitive evidence that depth perception is innate, it is present at a quite young age.

Visual Constancy. *Visual constancy* refers to the phenomenon of seeing certain aspects of the environment as constant despite changes that may occur at the retina. For example, people tend to see objects as having constant shapes despite the fact that images of the objects strike the retina in different ways, depending upon the way in which they are presented (Figure 4–8). The same is true for size of objects. That is, people tend to see objects as being of particular sizes regardless of the distance from which they are viewed, even though objects project smaller retinal images as they are moved farther away. It appears that the retinal image either is not used with regard to constancy or is supplemented with other information. Furthermore, some ability to perceive shape and size constancy is evident very early in life.

Research conducted by Bower (1966) seemed to demonstrate that infants as young as eight weeks of age perceived the constancy of an object's shape even when the orientation of the object was changed. More recent evidence (Caron, Caron, and Carleson, 1977; Cohen, 1977; Ruff, 1978) has refined this conclusion somewhat. In one such study, Cohen (1977) presented eighteen-, twenty-four-, and thirty-week-old infants with photos of a single three-quarter facial profile or multiple three-quarter profiles until their responses to these stimuli had habituated. Subsequently the infants were presented with photos of the front views of the same face (or faces) and of a different face. Thirty-week-old infants in the single-face condition dishabituated to both the familiar face and the different one, but in the multiple-face condition these infants dishabituated only to different faces. These responses indicate both that infants can discriminate between the same face in different orientations and that multiple examples of profiles enable infants of this age to disregard the orientation and respond to the face alone. The eighteen- and twenty-four-week-old infants, however, did not follow this pattern. They dishabituated to the same face in either the single- or multiple-face conditions. Cohen (1977) concludes that shape constancy does exist in infants, but develops at a later age than earlier data have suggested.

Color Perception. In 1671 Isaac Newton conducted a series of experiments with prisms, which led him to the conclusion that there are a few primary colors and "an infinite number of intermediate gradations." What Newton did not realize was that much depends on the process of human color perception. Modern researchers have presented children and adults with various wavelengths of light (the physical dimension of light that varies with the color or hue of the light), simply asking the subjects to name the color of the light that they see. Results accumulated over many sessions have largely confirmed what Newton misunderstood: We do react to the color spectrum in plateaus. For example, as a yellow light's wavelength is increased gradually, it will suddenly be called a shade of red rather than a shade of yellow. (Bornstein, Kessen, and Weiskopf, 1976). Color vision is not simply a response to some wavelength gradations. We naturally tend to see categories.

The habituation technique is really the only available method for investigating the color perception abilities of infants. Bornstein and his associates (1976) used this method; they presented four-month-old infants with various wavelengths of light and found that the infants also responded as if blue, green, yellow, and red were separate colors. An infant repeatedly presented with the light of one wavelength habituates; if a change in wavelength produces renewed attention (dishabituation), we conclude that the infant sees a new color. If dishabituation does not occur, the infant is presumed to be seeing the "old" color. Apart from replicating earlier demonstrations (e.g., Staples, 1937; Fagan, 1974) of color vision in infants, the Bornstein study is important because it shows that human color categorization is not a result of language and naming systems. Rather, it appears that there is an innate tendency to perceive color in terms of a few primary categories and that this tendency gives rise to the categorizations found in our language.

INTERACTION OF THE SENSORY SYSTEMS

In many situations, perception involves the simultaneous use of more than one sense modality. Eye-hand coordination requires interaction of vision, touch, and proprioception (reaction of the muscular system to stimulation), whereas reading involves vision and audition. The interaction of two or more sensory systems is referred to as *intersensory behavior* Intersensory behavior is not well understood, and for that matter, even a general conceptualization of how it develops is not agreed upon. It is often discussed in terms of increasing ability to integrate the different perceptual systems.

Vision-Touch

Bower (1974) provides a fascinating description of the relationship of vision and touch in early life. Newborns, if properly supported, will grasp at tangible objects, indicating that vision and touch are intricately associated. Bower exposed newborns to a "virtual" object; that is, an object that does not actually exist but appears to exist because of a special optical arrangement. The newborns howled when their hands reached the location where the object should have been, although they did not seem disturbed when they simply grasped at empty air in other situations. It is as if they expected something and were upset because there was nothing to grasp. At six months of age this behavior changed in that the babies began to explore. First they looked at their hands and rubbed them together; then they explored the situation visually by moving their heads from side to side; and finally they stopped grasping for the virtual object. According to Bower:

> The older infant knows something is wrong with the visual-tactual coordination and systematically checks the tactual and then the visual halves of it. The responses of older infants are differentiated; they seem to be aware of vision and touch as separate modalities, unlike the younger infants who apparently have a wholistic, unanalyzed awareness of the situation. The younger infants have at their disposal all the behaviors used by the older infants. . . . One must conclude that they have not yet differentiated the visible qualities of an object from its tangible qualities. [1974, p. 116]

But the differentiation of vision and touch leads to another interesting development. At about six months an infant who is grasping a tangible ob-

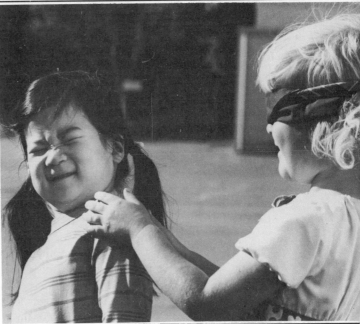

FIGURE 4-9

Intersensory perception involves translating information from one sense modality into another. Left, © Louis Goldman, Rapho/Photo Researchers, Inc.; right, © Alan Caruba, Photo Researchers, Inc.

ject will drop it immediately when its hand is covered by a cloth. Vision has become dominant at the expense of touch and will remain so even though the dropping response will disappear in time. Adults, for example, who are grasping an object while viewing it through a lens that minimizes its actual size, act as if the object is as small as it appears visually. Developmental studies of localization of touch also give evidence of the increasing dominance of vision. They involve stimulating a point on the skin and requesting individuals, who have their eyes closed, to indicate where they have been touched. Children perform better than adults, apparently because adults place greater reliance upon vision (Dunford, 1930; Renshaw, 1930). Older people are more precise when their eyes are open.

The relationship between vision and touch has been investigated by examining children's ability to explore forms in one mode and then to transfer the information they have acquired to another. Such intersensory recognition improves noticeably throughout the first seven years of life (Abravanel, 1967; Birch and Lefford, 1963, 1967; Bryant, Jones, Claxton, and Perkins, 1972; Zaporozhets, 1965). For example, in the Bryant and associates' study it was demonstrated that young infants between six and eleven months of age are capable of transferring information from the sensory modality of touch to that of vision. The investigators' young subjects, who were allowed to explore one member of a pair of objects tactually, subsequently chose that object from an array of similar objects when allowed to explore them visually without touching them.

In another study, three-, four-, five-, and six-year-olds were allowed to touch abstract forms without seeing them, and then they were asked to identify them visually. Children at the younger two ages could recognize only about half as many of the forms as could the two older groups (cf. Zaporozhets, 1965). As noted earlier in our discussion, exploration of objects both visually and tactually becomes more systematic with age, and so one would expect that more information is taken in, leading to better recognition and transfer between modalities.

Vision-Audition

Vision and audition, too, seem to be correlated at birth; when infants hear a sound they orient their eyes in the direction from which it emanates. Aronson and Rosenbloom (1971) conducted an experiment similar to the virtual object study of Bower in that it demonstrated the reactions of three-week-old babies to a situation in which their usual expectations were not met. Mothers and their infants were positioned on opposite sides of a window, and the mothers spoke to the infants through a microphone. Their voices were then displaced so that the sound seemed to come from a few feet to the right or left of the mothers. The infants definitely were disturbed by the situation. Later it was shown that young infants orient midway between the location of the mouth and the sound, whereas older infants look at the mother but turn their heads so as to maximally pick up the sound (Aronson and Dunkel, cited in Bower, 1974). As with Bower's subjects, the older babies appeared to differentiate the two modalities. However, in this case, as visual-auditory perception continues to develop, probably up to the age of ten years, it is the auditory cues that appear to become more prominent (Birch and Belmont, 1965; Rudnick, Sterritt, and Flax, 1967).

A similar demonstration of the vision-audition interaction in infants was performed by Carpenter (1975). Two-week-old infants were presented with either their mother's face or a female stranger's face, accompanied by either their mother's voice or the voice of the stranger. The dissonant face-voice combinations clearly upset the subjects, indicating that by two weeks of age an infant is able to discriminate his or her mother's face and voice from that of a female stranger, and the infant has learned that the mother's face (visual stimulus) and voice (auditory stimulus) occur together.

MODIFYING THE PERCEPTUAL ENVIRONMENT

Many different kinds of investigations have been conducted in an attempt to better understand the influence of the perceptual environment on development. In a general way, they can be categorized into *deprivation* and *enrichment* studies. The former involve examining nonhuman animals or humans after they have experienced an atypical lack of sensory stimulation. Enrichment studies, as the name indicates, involve examination after exposure to a particularly rich sensory environment.

Sensory Deprivation

For ethical reasons, long-term deliberate sensory deprivation is not imposed on humans. Studies have been conducted, however, with those who have had impaired vision, which was subsequently restored or corrected by surgery. For example, recent investigations (Aslin and Banks, 1978; Banks, Aslin, and Letson, 1975; Salapatek and Banks, 1977) have shown that unless children suffering from convergent strabismus (a disorder of the eye muscles) receive corrective surgery prior to the age of three years, binocular vision will remain permanently impaired. Physiological evidence seems to suggest that unless the visual system receives adequate input during the early or "sensitive" years, the appropriate number and organization of cortical neurons fail to develop (Hubel and Wiesel, 1965, 1970). That is, corrective procedures administered after this period of development are ineffective.

Depriving animals of sensory stimulation very early in life provides clues to the necessity of such experience for normal perceptual development. In some cases, deprivation has not had strong consequences. For example, Lashley and Russell (1934) found that rats reared in darkness from birth to one hundred days of age were able to jump from one platform to another as accurately as those reared under normal conditions. Although their experiment met with some criticism, other research has corroborated the findings (Nealey and Edwards, 1960; Walk and Gibson, 1961), and also has shown that depth perception in chicks is not greatly impaired by early deprivation (Fantz, 1958a; Kurke, 1955).

But other perceptual abilities, at least in certain animals, are affected by deprivation. In one famous study, a chimpanzee was subjected to tactual deprivation (Nissen, Chow, and Semmes, 1951) by covering his legs and forearms with cardboard. After thirty months the cardboard was removed and his reactions were compared with those of a normally reared chimp. He was less able to locate the spot where he was pinched, and appeared not to feel a pinprick. Additionally, he required more than two thousand trials to learn to turn his head to the right or left depending on which hand was touched; the control animal took two hundred trials.

In another investigation, two chimps were reared for the first sixteen months of their lives in total darkness except for a few minutes of light each day required for their care. Subsequent tests revealed that they responded to light—their pupils constricted and followed a flashlight—but that they did not respond to objects unless the objects touched their bodies, nor did they blink at motion toward their faces. One of the animals, named Snark, never overcame these deficiencies and even deteriorated after months of a lighted environment. What was the cause of his visual retardation? The investigator, A. H. Riesen, noted:

There had been no previous evidence that stimulation by light is essential for the normal growth of the primate retina or optic nerve. It was a surprise to find that, while the eyes of these chimpanzees remained sensitive to light after 16 months in darkness, the retina and optic disk in both animals did not reflect as much light as normal chimpanzee eyes do. Snark later developed a marked pallor of the optic disk in both eyes. There is other evidence suggesting that fish and amphibians, at least, need light-stimulation for normal eye development. So the physiological effects of the lack of light may be part of the explanation for Snark's loss of visual function. . . . We now have clear evidence from further experiments with chimpanzees that not merely light itself but stimulation by visual patterns is essential to normal visual development. [1965, p. 78]

Taken together, these studies demonstrate that without environmental interaction, perceptual systems may deteriorate or fail to develop properly.

Enriching the Environment

If sensory deprivation sometimes has adverse effects, sensory enrichment has been shown to have a positive influence. One of the first to emphasize the crucial role of the environment, D. O. Hebb (1949), conducted a series of experiments involving a variety of tasks and found that rats reared in a diverse visual setting were superior to those reared with little visual stimulation.

And, as we have seen, if the effects of deprivation sometimes display themselves in the biological systems, so does the influence of enrichment (Rosenzweig, 1966; Rosenzweig, Bennett, and Diamond, 1972). Rats reared in small groups with the opportunity to interact with wheels, ladders, boxes, and the like, along with free exploration and training in mazes, actually showed increases in the weight of the cerebral cortex and changes in the chemistry of the brain.

Working with human infants, White and Held (1966) compared the effects of four kinds of environments on the development of visually directed reaching. Using the hand under the guidance of the eyes, a facility that is said to distinguish human from nonhuman animals, ordinarily is mastered by about the fifth month of life (White, 1975). White and Held found, however, that it may emerge as early as three months under certain conditions. The uniform and somewhat bland surroundings of a typical hospital nursery provided a baseline against which the influence of three modified environments were tested. The first modification involved twenty extra minutes per day of handling by the nurses. Under the second modification plan, numerous forms and colors were displayed above the cribs to heighten interest and increase hand movements. Moreover, extra opportunities for head and neck movements and extra handling were provided. Under the third modification program, pacifiers were mounted on the rails of the cribs just within the infants' sight to encourage grasping (see Figure 4–10). Extra handling was also included in this program. The results showed that the second and third modifications encouraged reaching at an earlier age, a finding that is important because manipulating objects is considered central to the development of intelligent behavior.

Because various investigations have shown that perceptual stimulation is necessary for normal development and that enrichment can lead to optimal growth, educators and parents are now focusing on providing extra toys and objects with which infants and very young children can interact. While probably not harmful, unless perhaps the child is inundated with stimulation, it would seem that this practice requires detailed consideration of the way in which children develop (cf. White, 1975). At the very least, toys must be suitable to the manner in which information is perceptually being taken in.

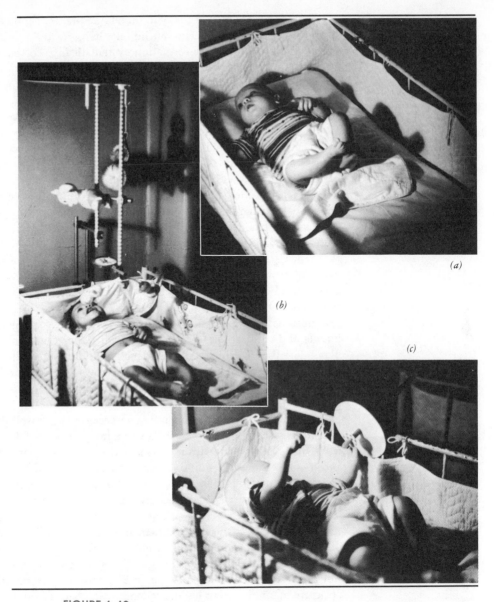

FIGURE 4-10
Three of the different environments for infants employed by White and Held:
(a) the typical nursery, (b) enrichment with brightly colored objects, and
(c) enrichment with pacifiers.   Reprinted by permission from B. L. White and
R. Held, Plasticity of sensorimotor development in the human infant, in J. F.
Rosenblith and W. Allismith, eds., **The Causes of Behavior,** II, pp. 60–70.
Copyright 1966 by Allyn and Bacon, Inc., Boston.

SUMMARY   *Sensation* involves the simple processing of information that comes from
the stimulation of sensory receptors. *Perception* is the complex process of selecting, organizing, and modifying input from sensory receptors. Sensation
and perception are actually names for different points in the elaborate process of gathering and evaluating information.

There is much interest today in understanding sensation and perception in the very young child. Human infants arrive in the world with considerable ability to take in information systematically. For example, they respond to touch, distinguish some tastes, and differentiate and localize odors and sounds. Many of these abilities develop rapidly during the first year, continue to grow at a slower pace during childhood, and then decline at different ages throughout adulthood.

Of all the sensory and perceptual systems, vision has been studied most extensively. Basic visual ability is more sophisticated at birth than was previously thought, and it develops quickly. It is difficult to demonstrate when certain abilities first appear, but the neonate fixates and tracks moving objects, at least to some extent, and responds to form and pattern. Color vision and visual constancy have been demonstrated during the first year of life. The same is true for distance perception. Gibson and Walk's "visual cliff" studies dramatically demonstrate such perception.

With regard to vision, the characteristics of stimuli exert much control over the stimuli on which the young infant will fixate. Movement, complexity, and contour are especially compelling aspects. Infants also are attracted to the human face.

Stimulus control is soon modified, however, by experience. In general, infants and children are attracted by novel rather than familiar visual displays. The way in which children visually explore objects also changes. Examination becomes more extensive and follows systematic patterns that are task appropriate. Clearly, learning and thinking are now intertwined with perception.

The development of intersensory perception is not well understood, although it is thought to primarily involve integration of the perceptual systems. But experiments with infants show that different systems (i.e., vision and touch, vision and sound) are related at birth, and that differentiation may be an important part of the growth of intersensory perception. In any event, one system may become dominant over another, at least for certain tasks.

Modification of the environment has provided striking demonstration that perceptual development is a function of the interaction of biological capacities and experience. Depriving animals of sensory stimulation can result in detrimental biological change and inferior perceptual functioning. Enrichment, on the other hand, can lead to analogous improvement. Applying the principles of these findings to child rearing requires detailed analysis, however.

5 Genetic Determinants of Behavior

That a person's physical characteristics and social dispositions can be passed on "through the blood" from one generation to another is an ancient idea. It was not until quite recently, though, that the fundamentals of genetic transmission were carefully investigated and adequately established. It is to these mechanisms and principles, and to the investigations they have inspired, that the present chapter is devoted. We will consider the nature of hereditary transmission and research methods, turn to the thorny issue of the inheritance of behavioral dispositions, and finally describe some non-inherited genetic defects that influence behavior. We will begin, however, with a broader perspective by briefly considering the theory of evolution.

THE THEORY OF EVOLUTION

Living organisms seem to fall into groups, each having identifiable physical, psychological, and social attributes. Humans share specific interspecies characteristics that separate them from other organisms: They walk upright, possess manual dexterity, have large convoluted cerebrums, and communicate with language. Humans vary with respect to each other as well. They differ in height, weight, eye color and shape, hair texture, and finger prints; some are more outgoing, passive, and altruistic than others. This enormous interspecies and intraspecies variability is at the heart of the theory of evolution.

The theory of evolution was proposed almost simultaneously by two British men, Charles Darwin and Alfred Russel Wallace (1858, in Appleman, 1970), but it is Darwin who won public acclaim for *Origin of Species*, published in 1859. Fascinated from childhood by the varied products of nature (as a boy he avidly collected minerals and insects), Darwin had been struck by the enormous variability he had observed in plants and animals during a five-year voyage aboard the *Beagle*. The question he had dwelled on was uppermost in the minds of many scholars of that day: What caused the formation of new species of life? Happening upon Thomas Malthus's *Essay On Population* provided Darwin with two key concepts: the *struggle for existence* and the *survival of the fittest.* In Darwin's own words:

> In October 1838, that is, fifteen months after I had begun my systematic enquiry, I happened to read for amusement Malthus on *Population,* and being well prepared to appreciate the struggle for existence which everywhere goes on from long-continued observation of the habits of animals and plants, it at once struck me that under these circumstances favourable variations would tend to be preserved and unfavourable ones to be destroyed. The result of this would be the formation of new species. [Darwin, F., 1959, pp. 42–43, as cited in Murphy, 1968]

The following ideas form the skeleton of Darwin's proposal:

1. Animals and plants have excessive numbers of offspring, all of which vary somewhat as individuals. These offspring compete for existence in the environment in which they find themselves.

FIGURE 5-1

Charles Darwin. The Bettmann Archives, Inc.

2. Depending upon the specific environment and the characteristics of the offspring, some will survive and others will not.

3. Those that survive will procreate and pass on their adaptive characteristics. The attributes of the nonsurvivors will not be passed on. Over long periods of time, then, species will change or evolve, or become extinct.

When first proposed the theory of evolution was extremely controversial. It seemed to stand in opposition to the idea of divine creation and it cast humans as animals related to monkeys and apes, albeit superior to them. Despite the controversy, however, the theory has endured because it brings some order to our observations of life. Furthermore, as details of inheritance have been discovered, they have proved to be consistent with the theory.

In observing variability in living forms, Darwin had noted that large and small variations seemed to be passed on from generation to generation (Ashton, 1967). Little was known, though, about the structures and processes that could account for variability and inheritance of characteristics. The discovery of the chromosomes and genes came in the early twentieth century. Since then immense knowledge has been accumulated about their structure and functioning. It is known, for example, that spontaneous changes in the genes (mutation) provide some of the variability that fascinated Darwin. Variability depends on other processes as well: each of the chromosome pairs randomly separating to form ova and sperm cells, random combinations of the gametes at fertilization, and exchange of genes between chromosomes.

THE WORK OF GREGOR MENDEL

Our understanding of these genetic mechanisms had its modern beginning in the work of Johann Gregor Mendel (1828–1884), a monk who conducted his scientific work in the gardens of his monastery. Mendel first published his studies in 1865, not long after Darwin's first publication, but his ideas received little attention. At the turn of the century, however, they were rediscovered almost simultaneously by others—in this case, the Dutch biologist Hugo de Vries, the German botanist Karl Correns, and Austrian Eric Tschermak.

Working with common garden peas, Mendel first identified overt characteristics in which the plants differed and then mated dissimilar ones. For example, he carefully cross-fertilized smooth-seeded and wrinkle-seeded plants to see how this selective breeding would affect the next generation. When the resulting pods were ripe, there was no evidence of the wrinkledness; rather, all the offspring displayed smooth seeds. When these second-generation plants were allowed to self-fertilize, however, the resulting third generation had both smooth and wrinkled seeds, in the ratio of 3:1. A similar pattern was found for several other characteristics, as can be seen in Table 5–1. Mendel's self-appointed task was to explain why some characteristics disappeared in the second generation only to reappear in the third generation in one-fourth of the plants. At the time virtually nothing was known of genetic processes.

TABLE 5–1

Results of Mendel's Experiments With Seven Characteristics of the Pea Plant. Although the first generation involves mating plants with dissimilar characteristics, the overt appearance, or phenotype, of second-generation plants is invariably only one form of the characteristic, the dominant one. Nonetheless, the second-generation plants carry the remaining recessive form of the characteristic and transmit it to the third generation, where it appears in the approximate ratio of 3:1.

First Generation	Second Generation	Third Generation Same as Second Generation	Third Generation Displayed Other Form	Ratio
Smooth vs. wrinkled seeds	smooth	5474	1850	2.96:1
Yellow vs. green seeds	yellow	6022	2001	3.01:1
Violet vs. white flowers	violet	705	224	3.15:1
Inflated vs. constricted pods	inflated	882	229	2.95:1
Green vs. yellow pods	green	428	152	2.82:1
Axial vs. terminal flower position	axial	651	207	3.14:1
Tall vs. dwarf stem length	tall	787	277	2.84:1

Source: The Royal Horticultural Society, London.

Mendel assumed that the parent plants contained two hereditary factors that were forms of the particular characteristic. These factors were later to be called *genes,* and each member of the gene pair, an *allele.* Mendel proposed that the two genes separated in the gametes, each parent passing on only one gene to the offspring. (And, indeed, this assumption was subsequently confirmed, as we learned in chapter 3.) If the offspring received the same form from each parent, it was *homozygous* for the characteristic. If it received the two different forms, it was *heterozygous.* Mendel also proposed that one form was *dominant* over the other, always displaying itself. The *recessive* form displayed itself only in the absence of the dominant form. Thus, Mendel posited that a form not overtly showing itself may still be present, to be passed on to future generations. The distinction was therefore made between the *genotype,* the genetic endowment unique to each individual, and the *phenotype,* the outward manifestation of the genes.

By applying these assumptions Mendel was able to explain his curious findings. In the cross-fertilizations of pea plants that Mendel originally carried out, when both parents are heterozygous there is a 25 percent chance of the offspring having the recessive phenotype. This particular pattern is well recognized in human genetics for such characteristics as straight hair, blue eyes, and albinism. Phenylketonuria and sickle cell anemia are conditions in which this pattern also is displayed. Let us look more closely at sickle cell anemia. (Phenylketonuria will be discussed later.)

When two recessive genes for the sickle cell trait are inherited, they affect the hemoglobin of the blood, making it less soluble (Ashton, 1967). In turn, this causes the red blood cells to become deformed or "sickled" in shape. The sickled cells tend to clump, thereby blocking the blood supply and reducing the amount of oxygen that reaches various body parts. Some of the deformed cells are also destroyed, causing a severe or fatal anemia

FIGURE 5-2
The effects of the mutant recessive genes for sickle cell anemia. Adapted from A. E. H. Emery, Elements of Medical Genetics, 5th ed. (Edinburgh: Churchill Livingstone, 1979).

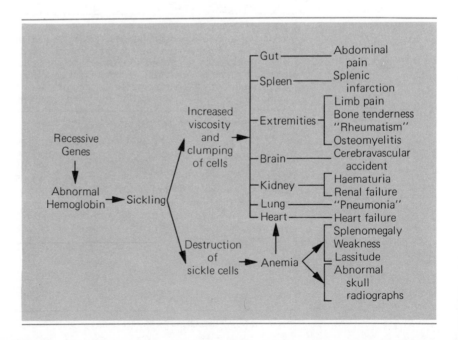

(see Figure 5–2). The genes for sickle cell are particularly prevalent among black people; in the United States 60,000 blacks suffer from the condition and 1 out of 10 are carriers (Marx, 1978). Sickle cell anemia provides an especially interesting example of the workings of genetic processes. The recessive gene is thought to be a mutant—that is, a spontaneous change from the original. Since it is obviously disadvantageous, causing illness and death, the question arises as to why it continues to exist. It appears that the mutant gene, which is most common in Africa, India, and parts of the Mediterranean area, is simultaneously advantageous in that it decreases vulnerability to malaria.

A characteristic can be carried, of course, by a dominant gene and theoretically it will always display itself when passed on to offspring. A well-noted pattern occurs when the dominant gene is carried heterozygously by one parent and not at all by the other. In this case there is a 50 percent chance of the gene being transmitted and displayed in the children. In humans, examples of characteristics carried by dominant genes are curly hair, brown eyes, free ear lobes, extra fingers and toes (polydactyly), and Huntington's chorea (Figure 5–3). Huntington's chorea is a fatal disease that does not usually appear until adulthood, when it causes limb spasms, psychotic behavior, and mental deterioration. The well-known folksinger, Woody Guthrie, died of Huntington's chorea and his biography describes the onset of the disease and the unfortunate deterioration that it brought (Yurchenco, 1970).

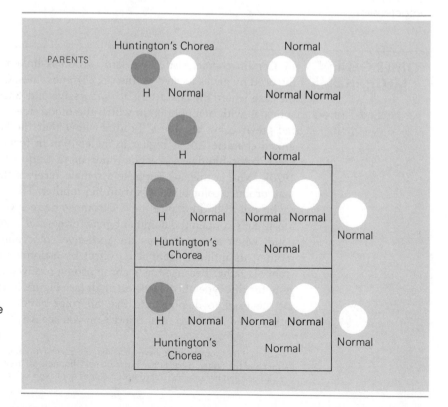

FIGURE 5–3
The probability of inheriting Huntington's chorea when one parent carries the dominant gene heterozygously and the other does not carry it at all. If the dominant gene is inherited, the disease will display itself. There is a 50 percent chance of this occurring.

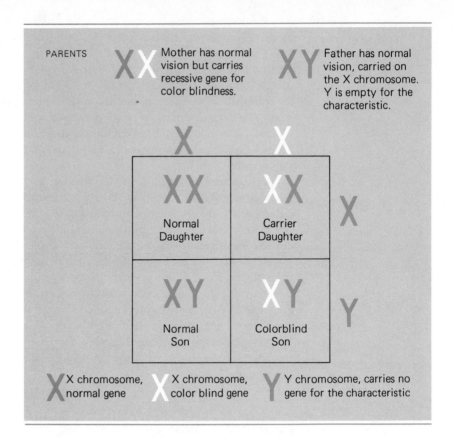

FIGURE 5–4
The inheritance of red-green color blindness when the mother, but not the father, carries the recessive sex-linked gene for the characteristic.

Inside figure:

PARENTS

XX — Mother has normal vision but carries recessive gene for color blindness.

XY — Father has normal vision, carried on the X chromosome. Y is empty for the characteristic.

	X	X
X	XX — Normal Daughter	XX — Carrier Daughter
Y	XY — Normal Son	XY — Colorblind Son

X — X chromosome, normal gene
X — X chromosome, color blind gene
Y — Y chromosome, carries no gene for the characteristic

OTHER GENETIC MECHANISMS

Sex-Linked Inheritance

Certain characteristics are said to be sex-linked because they are influenced by genes located on the sex chromosomes. Of particular interest is the case where the characteristic is recessive and carried on the X chromosome, as with hemophilia, in which the blood does not clot normally, and red-green color blindness. Studies show that the frequency of the sex-linked characteristic is higher in males than in females; for example, red-green color blindness is eight times more frequent in males (McClearn, 1970). Why is this so? Suppose a female receives the recessive gene that may produce color blindness from her mother. The daughter will probably *not* be color blind because the X chromosome received from her father will most likely contain the dominant gene for normal color vision. On the other hand, when a son receives the recessive color blindness gene from his mother, its influence cannot be offset by a dominant normal-vision gene from his father because the Y chromosome received from his father has no gene for this type of color vision at all (see Figure 5–4). The same reasoning can be used to demonstrate that all color-blind women must have had fathers who were also color blind. Can you see why?*

*A color-blind woman must have received the recessive color-blind gene from both her mother and her father. If her father carried color blindness on his X chromosome he must have been color blind because his Y chromosome does not have a color-vision gene.

Polygene Inheritance

As we have seen, Mendel's work was based on characteristics for which there are only a few alternatives. Pea plants have seeds that are either smooth or wrinkled; certain flowers are either violet or white. In humans, albinism does or does not display itself. But many other attributes do not fall into a few categories; they are displayed along a continuum. In the case of intelligence, for example, individuals are not only extremely bright or dull; rather, they fall into the entire range between those extremes. The same is true for height, weight, skin color, and temperament. Such continuous characteristics are influenced by many genes, each of which contributes only a small influence. As the number of genes increases, so does the number of phenotypes until discrete phenotypes cannot be distinguished. Figure 5–5 shows this relationship as well as indicating that characteristics that are polygenic—influenced by many genes—tend to distribute themselves in the recognizable normal curve. In studying polygene inheritance it is not possible to trace the effects of each gene even though each one may follow Mendelian principles. Instead, the distribution of the phenotypes in an entire population must be examined with complex statistical methods.

HOW GENES INFLUENCE DEVELOPMENT AND BEHAVIOR

Genes are composed of deoxyribonucleic acid (DNA), and DNA is centrally involved with protein synthesis, acting as a basic blueprint for development. The picture of how genes are related to physical and behavioral development is far from complete, but biologists suggest at least three different kinds of genes that have specific duties related to development. *Structural genes* determine the specific protein to be synthesized, *operator genes* turn protein synthesis on and off, and *regulator genes* inhibit and activate the other two types (Scarr-Salapatek, 1975). Regulator genes probably account for the timing of development. It appears that at any one time the genes dictate the production of certain enzymes, which are proteins, and that changes in enzyme production are intricately involved in the organism's movement along the life span. Prenatal development and biological changes at puberty are perhaps the most dramatic examples of such genetic timing.

To understand genetic effects on behavior it is first necessary to realize that genes do not directly determine behavior. The pathway from genotype to behavioral phenotype is a complex one involving the production of biochemical substances that enter into many functions of the body. Different phenotypes may stem from one genotype and the same phenotype may be the result of different genotypes.

It is also apparent that genes cannot act in a void. The nature-nurture

FIGURE 5–5
As the number of genes increase, so do the resulting phenotypes. Involvement of many genes results in the characteristic being displayed along a continuum.
Adapted from I. H. Herskowitz, **Genetics** (Boston: Little, Brown and Co., 1965).

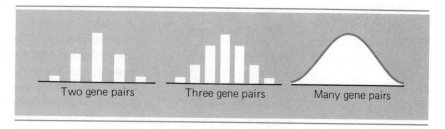

Two gene pairs   Three gene pairs   Many gene pairs

controversy in its simplest form (i.e., is a characteristic determined by genes or environment?) is therefore a meaningless issue. A characteristic cannot exist unless both genes and environment exist. Furthermore, there is an interaction between genes and the environment. To cite a simple example, coat color in rabbits has known genetic determinants but nevertheless varies according to the temperature of the environment in which development occurs. Furthermore, individuals of different genotypes may respond differently to prenatal and postnatal environments (Plomin, DeFries, and Loehlin, 1977). The relationship between genes and the environment might even be better labeled transactional because there is an ongoing process of influence and change.

The *range of reaction* also must be taken into consideration. For any one genotype operating in any one environment the range of reaction is the broadest possible expression (phenotypes) of the genotype. The range of reaction itself may be broad or narrow depending upon the particular genotype and environment, but a one-to-one relationship between genotype and phenotype is virtually nonexistent. Thus, as Davis has summarized:

> . . . even a full set of relevant genes does not fixedly determine the corresponding trait. Rather, most genes contribute to determining a *range of potential* for a given trait in an individual, while his past and present environments determine his phenotype (that is, his actual state) within that range. At a molecular level the explanation is now clear: The structure of a gene determines the structure of a corresponding protein, while the interaction of the gene with subtle regulatory mechanisms, which respond to stimuli from the environment, determines the amount of protein made. [1970, p. 1280]

Finally, an erroneous assumption frequently made with regard to genetic influence is that a characteristic that is known to be genetically controlled cannot be altered. Height is genetically determined, but can be affected by diet and disease. It has been suggested, however, that some characteristics are more strongly *canalized* than others; that is, that the path from genotype to phenotype is not as flexible for some traits as for others (Waddington, 1957; Wilson, 1978). Short of drastic environmental events, most babies babble and walk early in life. These behaviors seem to be strongly canalized. Perhaps behaviors that are critical to survival are the most highly canalized (Wilson, 1978). But in no case should it be assumed that genetically controlled characteristics cannot be altered to some extent.

DETERMINING HEREDITARY INFLUENCE ON HUMANS

Behavior Genetics

Behavior genetics is that branch of science dealing with the influence of an organism's genotype on its behavior. Part of behavior genetics is concerned with explaining differences *between* species. Many species specific behavioral patterns involved in mating, aggression, and territoriality have been shown to be controlled biologically through species-wide genetic endowments that have been shaped by evolutionary pressures (e.g., Eibl-Eibesfeldt, 1970; Gottesman, 1966). The issue becomes more complex, however, when we turn to genetics for a possible explanation of *individual differences within a species*. We know, of course, that such differences do exist. Some organisms are generally more friendly, more aggressive, more intelligent, more excitable, or simply more active than others. The human behavior geneticist tries to determine whether any of these differences are rooted in a person's unique genetic endowment.

The problem is that such a matter is often difficult to investigate. When a child is very similar in intelligence or sociability to one or both biological parents, it is commonly inferred that these characteristics have been inherited. But a youngster with very bright parents may appear to be quite bright because his or her parents provide a relatively rich environment rather than because of the genetic contribution they have made. Argument and intuition alone do not enable us to discriminate between these two alternatives. Instead, a research strategy in which either heredity or environment is varied while the other is held constant is needed if we are to sort out genetic and environmental influences on behavior. Such experimental manipulation is not possible with humans so researchers depend upon experimental manipulations with animals and correlational studies of humans. As is so frequently the case, neither approach is perfect but drawing on both allows us to construct a reasonable picture.

Animal Studies

Genetic experimentation with animals has become increasingly sophisticated, but for our purposes here we need only consider the relatively simple methods of inbreeding of strains and selective breeding.

Inbreeding experiments involve the mating of related animals, such as brothers and sisters. After a number of generations of family matings, often as many as twenty, this process will produce a "pure" strain in which the animals are genetically alike. Many pure strains can thus be produced, each of which will be genetically different than the others. Throughout the entire process the animals, reared in the laboratory, all experience identical environments; therefore any behavioral differences between the strains can be attributed with certainty to genetic factors. This method has demonstrated a genetic component in such diverse behaviors as learning, sexual behavior, alcohol preference, aggression, taste perception, activity level, and seizure susceptibility (DeFries and Plomin, 1978; McClearn, 1970).

Selective breeding is the mating of animals who are extreme on some characteristic (e.g., the fastest with the fastest and the slowest with the slowest) and continuing in this fashion through several generations. For this method, genetic theory predicts an increasing separation in behavior among the groups as they become more genetically dissimilar, despite identical environments. In investigating principles governing learning, for example, experimenters recognized that some rats learned much faster than others to find their way through a complex of unfamiliar corridors to the feeder of a maze. One investigator (Thompson, 1954) then interbred maze "bright" rats and maze "dull" ones for six succeeding generations. As seen in Figure 5–6, the difference in learning ability between the two groups steadily increased as selective breeding continued. Eventually, in the sixth generation, the maze "dull" strain made 100 percent more errors than the maze "bright" strain. Selective breeding studies have also demonstrated the genetic selection of emotionality (Broadhurst, 1958), aggressiveness (Lagerspetz, 1961), and sex drive (Wood-Gush, 1960).

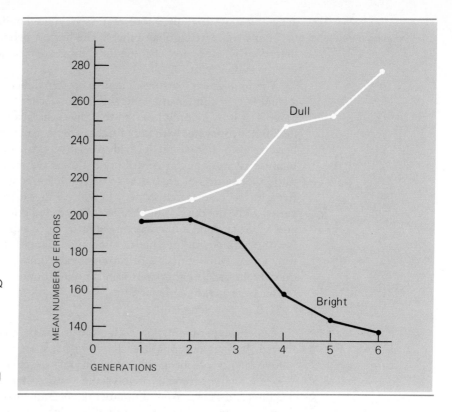

FIGURE 5–6
Errors in maze learning for successive generations of selectively bred "bright" and "dull" strains of rats. From A. R. Jensen, How much can we boost IQ and scholastic achievement? **Harvard Educational Review**, 39, Winter 1969, p. 49. Copyright 1969 by the President and Fellows of Harvard College.

Family Studies

The several kinds of family studies that exist all begin with identifying a representative (called the index case or the proband) of the characteristic of interest. The family is then studied in various ways to determine whether, and possibly how, the characteristic was passed on through hereditary processes.

One type of family study is the *pedigree analysis*. It consists of tracing the characteristic through the family to discover whether any known genetic pattern reveals itself. If so, it not only serves as evidence for genetic transmission but also indicates the specific mechanism involved. For the most part, this method applies to characteristics that are clearly identifiable; that is, that are influenced by a single gene and transmitted according to Mendelian principles.

Figure 5–7 shows a hypothetical pedigree for an X-linked recessive trait. If you recall, males have a greater prevalence of these traits, but females tend to carry them (see p. 116). The pedigree traces four generations, beginning with the mating of a normal male and a carrier female. It is assumed that each subsequent mating was with a normal individual. Thus, when the normal male of the second generation mated, the trait did not appear in his family. However, in the other families it continued to be carried by the females and to display itself in the males.

The *consanguinity study* is based on the belief that as the degree of relationship among individuals increases, so should the frequency of the characteristic. (Consanguinity means of the same blood.) Closely related people

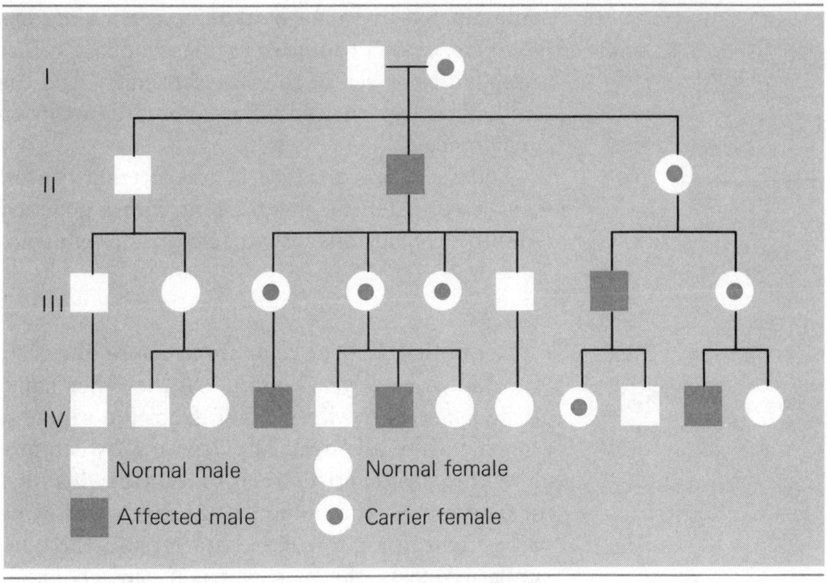

FIGURE 5-7
A hypothetical pedigree for an X-linked recessive trait. Adapted from A. E. H. Emery, **Elements of Medical Genetics, 5th ed.** (Edinburgh: Churchill Livingstone, 1979).

have more genes in common than those not as closely related. For example, a parent and a child share, on the average, one-half of their genes, as do siblings. First cousins, however, share only one-eighth of theirs. A genetic hypothesis would predict, then, that more parents and siblings of index cases would display the characteristic than first cousins. Furthermore, the frequency of the characteristic would be even less among randomly selected, unrelated members of the population at large. Using the latter type of analysis, it has been found, for instance, that whereas only 10 percent of the population at large showed occasional abnormalities in brain wave patterns (EEG), some 60 percent of the nonepileptic relatives of epileptic patients showed them (Lennox, Gibbs, and Gibbs, 1940).

Consanguinity studies have a serious problem in that genetic and environmental effects are often difficult to separate. We would expect close relatives, compared to those less close, to be more alike on the basis of their sharing more similar environments as well as more genes. This confound, or confusion, always exists in family studies, although it has not always been recognized.

One of the most fascinating consanguinity analyses was published by Henry Goddard in 1912, concerning the two distinct family lines of Martin Kallikak. As a Revolutionary War soldier, Kallikak reputedly had an affair with a feeble-minded tavern girl that eventually resulted in 480 descendants. Another line of 496 descendants was produced as the consequence of his later marriage into presumably better stock. Interviews of all family members or persons who knew them revealed a striking difference between the two lines, with Kallikak's first liaison resulting in more mental deficiency, "immorality," alcoholism, and criminality. The difference was attributed to hereditary factors. Goddard concluded that he had separated the effects of nature and nurture, and the study supported the passing of many compulsory sterilization laws (McNeil, 1966). In fact, the investigation was contaminated by many weaknesses, including inability to locate all family members, death of some of the descendants, refusals to be interviewed, and unreliability of verbal reports of friends. And the possibility that the two family lines experienced different environments was evidently not seriously considered.

Today we are cautious in interpreting consanguineous patterns. They may be consistent or inconsistent with a genetic hypothesis, but for more definitive conclusions researchers turn to twin and adoption studies.

Recall that *dizygotic twins* are no more like each other genotypically than are siblings born years apart. On the other hand, the remaining group of *monozygotic* twins, who develop from the same union of ovum and sperm, are genetically identical. The degree to which monozygotic twins are more alike on a characteristic than dizygotic twins (or siblings) provides a basis for determining the influence of genetic endowment. If a person is like his or her twin in a particular characteristic, the twin pair is *concordant;* if dissimilarity exists, the twin pair is *discordant.* The question is then asked: Is there greater concordance among monozygotic twins on a particular measure than among dizygotic twins? For a variety of characteristics and behaviors, as shown in Figure 5–8, the answer appears to be yes.

Twin studies have been faulted on the ground that determination of zygosity has not always been reliable. In the past, identification of monozygotic twins tended to rest on reports that only one chorion and placenta were present at birth, or on global overt appearance of the twins. However, 25 to 30 percent of monozygotic twins have two amnions, chorions, and placentas, presumably because the zygote divided before implantation and thus two implantations occurred (Sheinfeld, 1973). With regard to appearance, monozygotic twins often do look remarkably alike (Figure 5–9), but dizygotic twins may also show significant resemblance. Recent twin studies have thus relied on more sophisticated indices. Among the most widely used are blood typing and a carefully constructed rating of physical characteristics that correlates with blood typing identification.

Another criticism of the twin method is its inherent assumption that the environments of both kinds of twins, reared together, do not substantially differ. Nevertheless, monozygotic twins share more activities, have more friends in common, and dress more alike than dizygotic twins and, of course, are always of the same sex (Loehlin and Nichols, 1976; Smith, 1965). These factors conspire to make others perceive them as more alike and to treat them more alike than they would dizygotic twins. Perhaps, it has been argued, greater similarity of environments thus underlies the greater concordance of monozygotic twins. As plausible as this position is, recent findings have demonstrated that neither environmental treatment nor physical appearance is systematically related to similarity on measures of personality or cognition (Loehlin and Nichols, 1976; Matheny, Wilson, and Dolan, 1976). Summarizing this turn of events, DeFries and Plomin note that, "the burden of proof has shifted to those who claim that the twin method is invalid because identical twins share more similar environments than frater-

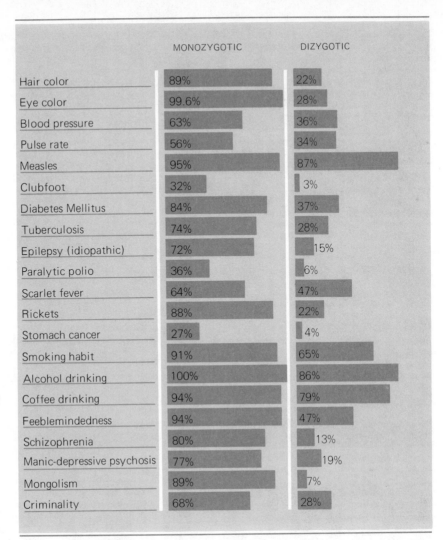

	MONOZYGOTIC	DIZYGOTIC
Hair color	89%	22%
Eye color	99.6%	28%
Blood pressure	63%	36%
Pulse rate	56%	34%
Measles	95%	87%
Clubfoot	32%	3%
Diabetes Mellitus	84%	37%
Tuberculosis	74%	28%
Epilepsy (idiopathic)	72%	15%
Paralytic polio	36%	6%
Scarlet fever	64%	47%
Rickets	88%	22%
Stomach cancer	27%	4%
Smoking habit	91%	65%
Alcohol drinking	100%	86%
Coffee drinking	94%	79%
Feeblemindedness	94%	47%
Schizophrenia	80%	13%
Manic-depressive psychosis	77%	19%
Mongolism	89%	7%
Criminality	68%	28%

FIGURE 5–8
Percentage of concordance or similarity between dizygotic and monozygotic twins for a variety of characteristics and diseases. Reprinted with permission of Macmillan Publishing Co. Inc., from **Genetics** by M. W. Strickberger. Copyright © Monroe W. Strickberger, 1968.

nal twins (1978, p. 480)." Be that as it may, some investigators have most confidence in the adoption method.

Adoption (or Foster Family) Method

When parents rear their own biological children, the source of any parent-child similarities observed later is uncertain. The parents *may* have transmitted their own characteristics genetically, but it is equally plausible that the transmission process is social; children may learn to be like their parents because of the general environment and specific instruction and example these adults provide. On the other hand, parents rearing children they have adopted can only transmit their own characteristics socially. If we therefore compare the resemblance of some characteristic of biological parents and their children with that of adoptive parents and theirs, and if we find greater similarity among the biological pairs, then the characteristic in

FIGURE 5-9
Photographs of a pair of monozygotic twins taken at ages 5, 20, 55, and 86 years. From F. J. Kallman and L. F. Jarvik, Individual differences in constitution and genetic background. In J. E. Birren, ed., **Handbook of Aging and the Individual,** p. 241. Copyright © 1959 The University of Chicago Press. Courtesy Dr. John Rainer.

question is influenced by heredity. This reasoning lies at the heart of the various adoptee methods of genetic research.

We can now turn to some of the substantive aspects of behavior and development in which genetics have been implicated. Any one investigation mentioned may combine the methods discussed in the preceding pages or variations of them in order to obtain maximal information.

INTELLIGENCE

It is extremely difficult to arrive at a totally satisfactory definition of intelligence. Whether the term should designate the ability to learn, rate of learning, the ceiling upon what can be learned, or yet some other human capacity is still undecided. In a later chapter this topic will be discussed in detail, but for the present purposes *intelligence* simply will refer to performance on a variety of tasks or tests which presumably tap mental ability.

The notion that human intelligence is at least in part genetically determined is perhaps a little distasteful to members of a society that cherishes the belief that all people are created equal. Nevertheless, both animal studies and a great deal of research involving humans support the view that at least some of the intellectual variation among people can be traced to differences in genetic endowment. Before discussing the subtle points surrounding this issue, we shall turn to a relatively clear example of how inheritance can be closely related to intelligence.

Phenylketonuria: An Inherited Disorder

The biological basis for phenylketonuria (PKU) is the lack of the enzyme that metabolizes the amino acid phenylalanine to tryosine. As a result, particular substances are produced that are injurious to the nervous system. The defect, which is transmitted by a recessive gene, results in retardation in the majority of untreated individuals. It has been estimated that PKU is responsible for about 1 percent of all institutional retardates and occurs in one case per twenty thousand live babies. Infants born with this defect tend to have blue eyes, fair hair, and light-colored skin. They generally are irritable, hyperactive, and short-tempered. Many have seizures and abnormal EEGs (Rosenthal, 1970).

It is possible to detect PKU within the first two weeks of life with urine or blood tests, and several states of the United States now provide massive screening programs. Early detection is extremely important because it has been found that children placed on low phenylalanine diets within the first few weeks of life show only minimal impairment of intellectual abilities. Unfortunately, if the diet restriction is delayed for very long, a substantial and permanent intellectual deficit will occur. The pattern is shown in Figure 5–10.

Thus the PKU syndrome is an interesting example of how heredity and the external environment conspire to determine behavior. If a child does not have the relevant genetic make-up for this condition he or she can, of course, consume quantities of phenylalanine (found in bread, eggs, cheese, fish, and milk) without experiencing difficulty. On the other hand, noticeable retardation does not appear in children who carry the genetic component if they are provided with a low phenylalanine diet early enough in

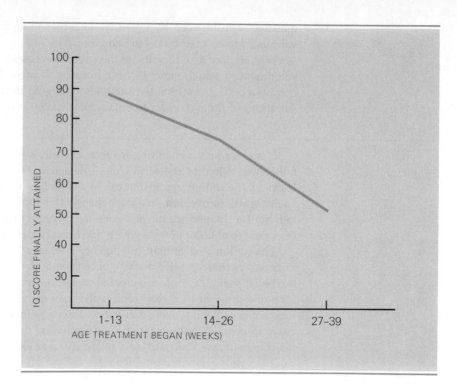

FIGURE 5–10
The effect of dietary
treatment (restricting
certain foods) on the
intellectual
development of
phenylketonuric
(PKU) children. Note
that intellectual
functioning will be
near normal only if
the treatment is
introduced very
early.   Data from
Baumeister, 1967.

the life cycle. But children with the defective genetic endowment *and* an un-controlled diet frequently are retarded.

There are several other inherited disorders that result in retardation, also traceable to a single gene and involving a biochemical disturbance. Thus, we are certain that heredity underlies some extreme deviations in intelligence. But how can we identify hereditary factors when variations in intelligence are not so extreme? In such cases it must be assumed that many genes are involved, and so the task is not an easy one.

The Inheritance
Factor: Research
Findings

Consanguinity Studies.   Sir Francis Galton (1822–1911) was among the first to study the possibility that intelligence might be inherited. Influenced by the work of his half cousin, Charles Darwin, he argued that eminent men tend to be related to one another. He used as evidence the genealogies of families of prominent men active in the fields of law, science, art, and the military, and theorized from this information that greatness ran in certain families. Although Galton set up a proposition that was later tested repeatedly, the analysis that he employed failed to distinguish between the effects of heredity and environment. Galton's work was thus flawed badly by potential bias, but its basic logic was not unsound: If intelligence is inheritable at all, people who are closely related should be more alike in intelligence than those who are not closely related. This proposition has been tested by many researchers and the general findings follow the pattern shown in Figure 5–11. In reviewing the findings, the first point to notice is that arbitrarily picked pairs of people who are unrelated biologically and who do not interact together socially will not be similar in IQ at all—that is, the cor-

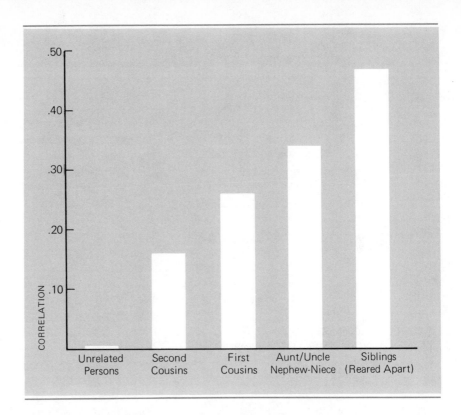

FIGURE 5–11
Portions of the
consanguinity IQ
data summarized by
Jensen (1969) from
over 100 studies in
eight different
countries.

relation between the IQ scores of many such pairs will average to 0. Note also that IQ similarity increases directly with increasingly close biological relationships, a result that is consistent with the genetic hypothesis.

Twin Studies.   Further evidence suggesting the existence of a hereditary factor in IQ is found in several major studies involving twin comparisons. The correlation for IQ scores for dizygotic pairs ranges from .55 to .62, quite different from the .87 correlation between scores for monozygotic twins (Erlenmyer-Kimling and Jarvik, 1963; Plomin and DeFries, 1979). Dissimilar sharing of environments for siblings, dizygotic, and monozygotic twins may partially account for these findings, but research on monozygotic twins reared apart gives support to the genetic theory. In a study by Newman, Freeman, and Holzinger (1937), the Stanford-Binet Intelligence Scale was administered to nineteen pairs of monozygotic twins living in separate homes, revealing an average correlation of .77 between the scores of members of the pairs. A corroborative finding was obtained by Shields (1962) with a different test of intelligence. The high degree of similarity between IQ scores of twins sharing identical genetic constitutions but having different environments, as indicated by these studies, strongly supports the notion that inheritance plays an important role in determining IQ.

Adoption Studies.   Comparison of adoptive or foster children with their biological and adoptive parents or siblings completes the picture of avail-

Racial/Ethnic Differences in IQ

Studies do indicate that intelligence is at least partially inheritable, and more current research has concentrated on specific sociological aspects of this proposition. As we shall see in detail in chapter 9, IQ differences have been observed among various ethnic, racial, and social class groups. For example, whites regularly score higher than blacks on IQ tests. Data suggesting hereditary factors in individual IQ, then, may seem to indicate that racial or ethnic differences are also rooted in genetics. But how valid is this theory?

In 1969 Arthur Jensen published an article in the **Harvard Educational Review** in which, based on analyses of family, twin, and adoption studies, he concluded that heredity is responsible for about 80 percent of the variation seen in IQ scores. He suggested further that the usual fifteen or so points difference in performance by blacks and whites on IQ tests could be due to genetic differences between the racial groups. Many psychologists have challenged Jensen's conclusions. Among the most outspoken is Leon Kamin, who presented his criticisms in **The Science and Politics of IQ** (1974b).

Kamin dismissed the entire body of scientific literature on heritability of IQ as sociopolitically slanted and methodologically unsound. A few of the points he makes will give the flavor of his objections.

Kamin's primary argument is that IQ data of the kind we have reviewed can—and often have—become the "scientific" justification for discriminatory practices. He illustrates the point by reviewing the use of intelligence tests during the early 1900s, when at least some psychologists tried to reduce the number of eastern and southern European immigrants by showing that the great majority were "feeble-minded." One investigator claimed that 83 percent of Jews, 80 percent of Hungarians, 79 percent of Italians, and 87 percent of Russians would fall into the feeble-minded category. It is easy to see how an interest in finding fault with all genetic research on intelligence could be spurred by this dark chapter in the use of IQ tests.

Kamin's arguments are not limited to the use of heritability data alone; he also challenges the procedures and the findings themselves. Here is one example. A major assumption in studies of twins and other siblings reared apart is that their environments are no more similar than would be the case for any two randomly selected, unrelated children; only in this way can similarities in the siblings' IQ scores be attributed to heredity. Kamin points out that this assumption has often not been met, offering these examples of the problem of "separated" twins:

Benjamin and Ronald, separated at 9 months:

'Both brought up in the same fruit-growing village, Ben by the parents, Ron by the grandmother. . . . They were at school together. . . .'

Bertram and Christopher, separated at birth:

'The paternal aunts decided to take one twin each, and they have brought them up amicably, living next door to one another in the same Midlands colliery village. . . . They are constantly in and out of each other's houses. . . .' [Cited in Kamin, 1974, p. 11]

Kamin also questioned the data contributed by Cyril Burt (e.g., 1966, 1972), which has been among the most supportive of the genetic hypothesis. Burt, an Englishman who died several years ago, had been knighted for his contribution to education—the first psychologist so honored. His work included many comparisons of intelligence in family members and in twin pairs. Nevertheless, Kamin suggests that Burt's evidence is suspiciously pat, and others also seriously challenge the veracity of Burt's data (for more on this controversy see Dorfman, 1978; Jensen, 1978; McAskie, 1978).

Do criticisms such as Kamin's completely nullify the research findings we have reviewed? Many feel that they do not. Discounting Burt's data and some of the weaker studies, there is still a considerable amount of research showing that individual intelligence (as defined by test scores) is transmitted genetically, socially, or by some combination of the two. If this were not true, the IQs of parents and children would be no more alike than those of completely unrelated people. Furthermore, the similarity between monozygotic twins and between adopted children and their biological parents probably does not rest exclusively on social transmission. However, this does not mean that **group** differences on IQ can be attributed to genetic influence.

To begin with, IQ scores within a population vary; Jensen claimed that 80 percent of the variability in IQ scores can be accounted for by inheritance. This figure, the heritability estimate, is the amount of variability in phenotypes that is accounted for by genetic factors. If heritability is high, the environment has relatively little influence in creating different phenotypes. Jensen arrived at the 80 percent figure largely by analyzing data from twin and adoption studies; other investigators arrive at considerably lower heritability estimates (e.g., Jencks, Smith, Acland, Bane, Cohen, Gintis, Heynes, and Michelson, 1972; Plomin and DeFries, 1979).

Perhaps even more important, though, heritability applies to variation within a population. It is calculated for a particular population given a particular environment. For example, if one analyzes a twin study, the actual figures used would be derived from a particular racial population of twins who experienced a particular environment. It is unfortunate that almost all of the IQ studies have been conducted on whites because we do not have IQ heritability estimates for blacks, and to generalize the estimate from one population to another can be misleading.

But even if heritability for black and white populations should be about equal, and even if they were quite high, would this mean that group differences in IQ scores are due to genetic factors? We cannot draw this conclusion. As we have seen, even when a characteristic is under known genetic control it is influenced by the environment, and there is reason to believe that the environments of blacks and whites differ in important ways. Many psychologists believe that the fifteen-point difference between blacks and whites on IQ tests may indeed be due to environmental differences. The same is true for differences among various ethnic and socioeconomic classes.

Given this belief, relevant changes in the environment should produce changes in IQ scores. Many programs have been designed specifically to provide an environment that would foster children's intellectual development. Indeed, Jensen's now-famous report opened with the declaration that such programs failed in their purpose. At the time of Jensen's article, however, most of the programs were barely under way and his conclusions were premature. We shall return to a discussion of some of these programs in later chapters, as well as to research that attests to the malleability of IQ scores and to further questions about the meaning of these scores.

able data. These studies substantiate the role of heredity in IQ performance (DeFries and Plomin, 1978; Munsinger, 1975; Scarr and Weinberg, 1976; Skodak and Skeels, 1949). In the main, this research demonstrates a higher correlation between adoptees and their biological parents and siblings than between adoptees and their adoptive parents and siblings. Adoptive parents also tend to be more similiar in IQ to their natural children than to their adopted children.

GENETIC DETERMINANTS OF ABNORMAL BEHAVIOR

Another class of behaviors for which genetic components have been vigorously studied is that customarily labeled abnormal, deviant, or psychotic.* The largest body of research has been directed toward the etiology of the psychosis called schizophrenia. *Schizophrenia* is characterized by disturbances in reality relationships and concept formations, as well as affective, behavioral, and intellectual deficits. Schizophrenics may experience delusions and hallucinations, communicate in a disorganized way, and display inapproprite emotions. There are several subtypes, but they need not concern us here.

Considerable speculation exists about schizophrenia, and three main types of theories have been advanced to explain its occurrence. *Monogenic-biochemical* theory proposes that the presence of one particular gene, which determines abnormal metabolic function, leads to schizophrenia. The *diathesis-stress* model postulates that schizophrenia results from the coexistence of a biological predisposition to develop the illness and a set of environmental stresses to precipitate it. ("Diathesis" means constitutional predisposition toward abnormality.) Such a theory may incorporate models involving either the monogenic or the polygenic inheritance of the disorder. *Life-experience* theory ignores possible genetic determinants of the disorder and is concerned entirely with conditions in the environment that might produce it (Rosenthal, 1970). It is possible, of course, that no one theory is exclusively correct, for the disorder may have more than one etiology.

Empirical Evidence of Genetic Influence on Schizophrenia

Theories that propose a genetic basis for schizophrenia logically predict that the closer the genetic relationship between two individuals, one of whom is schizophrenic, the higher the risk that the other will also display similar tendencies. Considerable evidence has been collected that supports this prediction.

In reviewing sixteen studies conducted from 1928 to 1973, Davison and Neale (1978) note that despite great variability of results, fourteen of the studies show a higher incidence of schizophrenia for parents of a schizophrenic than for the population at large. The expected incidence in the population is usually judged to be 1 percent, but for parents in these fourteen

---

*It should be noted that the adequacy of these labels and the reliability of their usage has been seriously challenged (e.g., Bandura, 1968; Mischel, 1968). Nonetheless, inasmuch as there are undeniable differences between the behavior of most hospitalized persons who have been diagnosed as schizophrenic and that of persons who are functioning more or less adequately in occupational and marital roles, the question of genetic determinants of abnormal behavior remains a meaningful one, despite terminological and even major theoretical disputes.

studies it was found to range from 1.2 to 12 percent. The incidence for siblings of schizophrenic probands ranged from 2.6 to 14.3 percent. The findings from several studies show overall that parents and siblings of schizophrenics have a greater risk of schizophrenia than the general population, that first-degree relatives have a greater risk than second-degree relatives, and that the risk for third-degree relatives is only slightly greater than that for the population at large (Rosenthal, 1970).

Franz Kallmann (1938), a German psychiatrist who was a pioneer researcher in the genetics of schizophrenia, estimated the risk of being labeled a schizophrenic by examining large samples of individuals. Figure 5–12 summarizes some of his results, which are interpreted as supporting a genetic hypothesis. Concordance for schizophrenia is higher for monozygotic than dizygotic twins, and further, Kallmann's data show that concordance is still high when monozygotic twins were reared apart. There have been studies that both support and criticize Kallmann's data. Jackson (1960), for example, pointed out that the twins were not actually apart during their formative years. Rosenthal's (1970) report of sixteen pairs of monozygotic twins reared apart cites concordance for ten of them, however, giving support to Kallmann's findings.

Turning to adoption studies, Heston (1966) investigated forty-seven

FIGURE 5–12
**Schizophrenia among
relatives of the
schizophrenic.**
Adapted from
**Abnormal Psychology
and Modern Life** by
James C. Coleman.
Copyright © 1964 by
Scott, Foresman, and
Company. Reprinted
by permission of the
publisher.

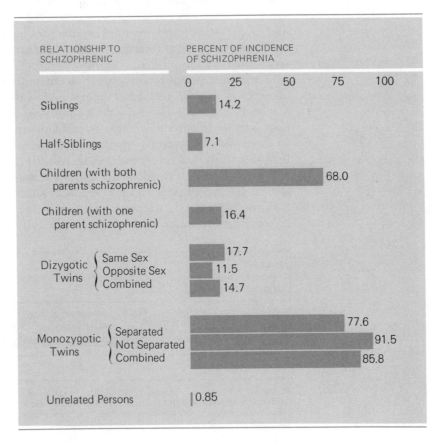

children who had been born to schizophrenic mothers while the mothers were being treated in state psychiatric hospitals. The infants were taken from their mothers shortly after birth and reared by adopted parents or in foundling homes. Fifty infants, also separated from their mothers at birth but for nonpsychiatric reasons, were identified as controls.

Heston performed extensive follow-up assessments on both groups, including a battery of psychological tests and independent ratings by two psychiatrists. The results were clear: 16.6 percent of the children of schizophrenic mothers were themselves diagnosed as schizophrenic, whereas none of the children of control mothers were so diagnosed. Equally impressive for the genetic hypothesis, the children of schizophrenic mothers were also more likely than the controls to be diagnosed as neurotic and on the average had been involved more frequently in criminal activity and had spent more time in penal institutions. Similar results, including a tendency to display psychological disorders other than schizophrenia, were found in a large scale study of adopted children in Denmark (Kety, Rosenthal, Wender, and Schulsinger, 1968; Wender, Rosenthal, Rainer, Greenhill, and Sarlin, 1977).

In an interesting variation of the adoption study, Wender and his colleagues (1974, cited in Davison and Neale, 1978) identified a group of adoptees who had normal biological parents but schizophrenic adoptive parents. The adoptees, who ranged in age from twenty-two to fifty-two years at the time of the study, were diagnosed on the basis of interviews and psychological testing. Various comparisons indicated that having a normal biological parent, regardless of the diagnosis of the adoptive parent, was related to a low incidence of schizophrenia (Table 5–2).

Karlsson's adoption investigation compared eight schizophrenic adoptees with their biological siblings and with their adoptive siblings (Karlsson, as cited in DeFries and Plomin, 1978). None of the adoptive siblings were schizophrenic, whereas 21 percent of the biological siblings were so diagnosed (72 percent of the latter also had one schizophrenic parent). Both this study and the Wender et al. research suggest that being reared with a schizophrenic person is not a strong factor in schizophrenia, and, in general, the overall evidence for a hereditary factor is quite strong.

These studies do not mean that schizophrenia is inherited directly; rather, a predisposition to psychological difficulty is transmitted. Whether

TABLE 5-2
Percentage of Adoptees Rated Schizophrenic According to Biological and Adoptive Parent Diagnosis.

Normal Biological Normal Adoptive	Normal Biological Schizophrenic Adoptive	Schizophrenic Biological Normal Adoptive
10%	11%	19%

Source: From Wender, Rosenthal, Kety, Schulsinger, and Welner, 1974, cited by Davison and Neale (1978) in the **Archives of General Psychiatry, 30**, 121–128. Percentages of Adoptees Rated Schizophrenic According to Biological and Adoptive Parent Diagnosis. Copyright 1974, American Medical Association.

the predisposition is manifested at all and how it is manifested almost certainly depend upon the type and amount of stress created by the environment later in life.

INHERITANCE OF SOCIAL BEHAVIOR

Although much of the investigation into the genetic bases of behavior has focused on intelligence and abnormalities, some interesting work is available on the genetic determinants of "normal" social behavior.

Introversion-extroversion

Several studies suggest that genes play a part in determining *introversion-extroversion* (Eysenck, 1956; Gottesman, 1966; Scarr, 1969; Vandenberg, 1966, 1967). These terms refer to two opposing styles or approaches to the social environment. An extreme introvert is shy and anxious in novel social situations and is always ready to withdraw from people; an extreme extrovert is friendly, at ease among people, and ready to seek out social gatherings. Differences on this dimension may be observed during the first years of life and, moreover, do not change much over time. Friendly infants, for example, tend to become friendly adolescents, whereas unfriendly infants tend to become unfriendly teenagers (Schaefer and Bayley, 1963).

Scarr (1969) gave psychological tests to twenty pairs of female monozygotic and dizygotic twins for whom zygosity had been diagnosed through blood grouping. Monozygotic twins were found to be more similar on measures of introversion-extroversion than were dizygotic twins. In another investigation (Freedman and Keller, 1963), twenty pairs of same-sexed twins, eleven of whom were monozygotic and nine of whom were dizygotic, comprised the sample. Every child was filmed individually in many situations over an eight-month period. At the end of the observation period, the films of one twin in each pair were shown to a group of four judges while the films of the other twin were presented to a comparable group. The judges rated each child's behavior on several dimensions, one of which was social orientation. Comparison of the ratings showed a greater similarity in social behavior between monozygotic twins than between dizygotic twins.

Activity Level

A person's overall activity level seems to be one aspect of personality clearly influenced by hereditary factors. We have noted previously that animals can be selectively bred for high or low activity level, and this finding is of course suggestive. In addition, two studies of clinically hyperactive children have shown that such youngsters are five to ten times more likely to have parents who were themselves hyperactive than are nonhyperactive, control group children (Cantwell, 1972; Morrison and Stewart, 1971).

If activity level is actually heritable in humans, we would expect twin studies to support the clinical studies just cited. And they do. Both Scarr (1966) and Willerman (1973) found significantly greater similarity on activity level among MZ (monozygotic) twins than among DZ (dizygotic) twins. In Willerman's study the correlation for activity level among MZ twins was .90, as compared with a correlation of .57 for DZ twins. A later study, reported by Willerman and Plomin (1973), shows significant correlations between the rated activity levels of normal children and the activity levels of both parents when the parents were themselves children. This last result is made more impressive by the fact that in the same study the parents' attitudes toward child rearing, though quite variable, were generally unrelated to the activity levels of their children. Apparently, activity level is genetically influenced in ways evident from an early age and is not usually altered very much by the normal range of environmental circumstances.

Temperament

We have already mentioned several studies with animals that suggest that emotionality has a hereditary component. Support for the idea that emotionality or *temperament* (a nearly equivalent term) is also genetically influenced in humans comes from a landmark longitudinal study by Thomas, Chess, and Birch (1970). These investigators define temperament by a set of rating scales including such items as level and extent of motor activity, sen-

FIGURE 5–13
Individual children differ considerably in overall activity level, a characteristic that is believed to be influenced, in part, by genetic factors.   Photos by Rocky Weldon, DeWys.

sitivity to stimuli, and response to new objects. They followed the development of 141 children for over a decade by interviewing the parents periodically—every three months during the first year, every six months during years one to five, and annually after age five. The interviews were structured objectively so that parental statements, such as that their baby "couldn't stand" a new food, had to be restated by the parent in terms of specific step-by-step descriptions. In addition, some home observations were conducted by individuals unfamiliar with the child's behavioral history (and who therefore could not have had preconvictions that might bias results). From their data, the authors conclude that children show distinct individuality in temperament in the first weeks of life and that these characteristics persist over time. Acknowledging that they do not have evidence that these differences are "inborn," Thomas and his associates state, nevertheless, that they are inclined toward this view. Support for this hypothesis is forthcoming from studies of newborns which show, for example, individual differences in the intensity of responding to stimuli which are consistent during even the first few days of life (Birns, 1965; Schaffer and Emerson, 1964).

In a study more typical of the behavior genetics approach, Buss, Plomin, and Willerman (1973) obtained extensive questionnaire data on temperament from mothers of twins in eight different locations in the United States. One hundred and twenty-seven pairs of monozygotic and same sex dizygotic twins ranging in age from four months to sixteen years were involved. Correlations for the monozygotic twins were .63 and .73 for boys and girls, respectively; for the dizygotic twins the comparable correlations were only .00 and .20.

Broad-Spectrum
Studies

Gottesman (1963) began his broad spectrum study by locating all of the same-sex twins enrolled in public high schools in the Minneapolis-St. Paul area, drawing his twin sample from a population of over thirty-one thousand children. Voluntary cooperation of more than half of the twin pairs in this sample was secured. Gottesman then identified sixty-eight twin pairs—thirty-four monozygotic pairs and thirty-four dizygotic pairs, and compared concordance rates on several scales. The measures used in the study were derived from three paper-and-pencil tests, a test of intelligence, and two personality measures. IQ scores were more closely related for monozygotic than for dizygotic pairs, and, more importantly for our present interest, six scales of the twenty-four on the personality tests were found to be more closely related for monozygotic than for dizygotic twins. Overall, Gottesman's results seem to suggest *some* hereditary component on *some* measures of personality.

In another investigation, Loehlin and Nichols (1976) selected 514 identical and 336 fraternal twin pairs from a sample of high school students who had taken the National Merit Scholarship Qualifying Test. Several self-report inventories of personality and attitudes were completed by the adolescents. The primary measure of personality, the California Personality Inventory, consists of eighteen scales among which are dominance, responsibility, achievement, tolerance, self-control, and flexibility. In general, the identical-twin correlations were higher than the fraternal-twin correlations. The overall median for the identical-twin correlations was .50; for the fraternal twins it was .32. Moreover, sixty-nine of the seventy-two comparisons showed higher identical-twin correlations. The Loehlin and Nichols data revealed other interesting findings regarding personality, two of which are discussed in the following article, written by Robert Plomin especially for this book.

Plomin, a behavior geneticist, is actively involved in research of the genetic and environmental influences on social and intellectual development. In his article he specifically focuses on social behavior. He also shares his regard for behavior genetics by pointing to the numerous questions that behavior genetic analyses can help answer. Plomin's discussion is a fitting summary of the efforts to understand hereditary determinants of behavior.

Close-up

Behavioral Genetics and Personality, by Robert Plomin

There are two things about human behavioral genetics that particularly appeal to me. The first is a sense of historical continuity going back over a hundred years to the time of Francis Galton, who studied family resemblance and who suggested the use of the twin method. In 1918, R.A. Fisher showed that Mendel's laws of inheritance can be generalized to the important case in which many genes and many environmental factors affect a character. This is the case that is most relevant to the complex characters that interest behavioral scientists. In 1924, the first twin study and the first adoption study collected data on mental ability. The years since 1924 have seen numerous behavioral genetic studies converging on the conclusion that a substantial portion of individual differences in IQ is due to heredity. Although one might hope that it wouldn't take almost 70 years to prove a point, a conclusion such as this one that goes against the grain of our common beliefs demands substantial verification. In fact, wide acceptance of this idea has come only during the past five years, when more behavioral genetic IQ data were collected than in the previous 70 years combined (Plomin and De-

Fries, 1980). Such plodding progress must sound boring to some, but I find the sense of historical continuity exciting, particularly in contrast to the research fads that dominate some areas of psychology.

Behavioral genetics also appeals to me because of the power of its findings. By "power," I mean the amount of variance (individual differences) explained. Behavioral genetic analyses of IQ data from family, twin and adoption studies lead to the conclusion that fully half of the variance of IQ is due to genetic differences among individuals. This is a very powerful result in comparison to other findings in the behavioral sciences. For example, in the last few years, much has been made of the fact that IQ is related to birth order and family size—"dumber by the dozen" was the title of one article on the topic. However, birth order and family size explain less than 2% of the variance of IQ (Grotevant, Scarr, and Weinberg, 1977). In other words, if all you know about someone is birth order and family size, you know very little about the person's IQ. This is not to say that behavioral genetic analyses find heredity to be all important; to the contrary, they provide the best evidence for environmental influence.

For example, in the case of IQ, if 50% of the variance is due to heredity, the other 50% is due to environmental factors. However, there is much to be learned about the specific environmental factors responsible for individual differences in IQ.

Before I turn to the study of personality, I want to emphasize that behavioral geneticists are not out to show that all behavior is due to genes rather than environment. Instead, behavioral genetic methods permit us to untangle genetic and environmental influences without assuming that either one is all important. Most people do not need to be convinced that the environment can have an important effect on behavioral development. However, it is important to note that development can also be affected by genes. We now know that the raw stuff of evolution is genetic variability and that, for mice, fruit flies and human beings, at least a third of all genes differ among members of each species. This genetic variability can lead to behavioral differences as it does to differences in height, hair color and the number of ridges on one's fingerprints. Thus, both genetic and environmental hypotheses are reasonable, and the usefulness of behavioral genetics lies in providing tools to evaluate these hypotheses. Behavioral genetic methods can also be used to go beyond simply describing the relative importance of genetic and environmental influences, as I shall discuss later in this article.

STUDIES OF SELF-REPORT PERSONALITY

During the last 75 years, most research in the area of human behavioral genetics has focused on IQ and schizophrenia. This emphasis has recently shifted to specific cognitive abilities and other areas of psychopathology. However, other domains of psychology, including personality, have been relatively neglected. Nearly all behavioral genetic research on personality has involved administration of self-report questionnaires to adolescents and adults. These

studies have led to some surprisingly counter-intuitive conclusions, two of which have been summarized in a book called **Heredity, Environment and Personality: A Study of 850 Pairs of Twins** (Loehlin and Nichols, 1976). The first is that heredity affects all personality traits to the same moderate degree (about 40% of the variance is attributable to genes). This conclusion is based on the authors' own large study of adolescent twins as well as on other twin studies. Who would have thought that genes would influence dozens of personality traits to the same extent?

The second counterintuitive conclusion is that environmental influences important in the development of personality are not the kind that make family members similar to one another (called "between-family" or "common" or "shared" environmental influences). We have typically assumed that the environment works this way, and most research on environmental influences has examined such "between-family" influences. For example, we look at things such as feeding, weaning, toilet-training and childrearing practices that vary from family to family. We study the extent to which the personality of children in different families differs as a result of differences in such practices. However, the results of behavioral genetic studies reviewed by Loehlin and Nichols strongly suggest that environmental influences on personality operate "within" families, making members of the same family different from one another, rather than between families. Possible examples of such influences are birth order, changes in parenting with an increase in the number of children in the family, and labelling effects within a family. [See Plomin, DeFries, and McClearn (1980) for a discussion of how behavioral genetic analyses can determine the extent to which environmental influences operate between and within families.]

Before we go too far in discussing the implications of these two conclusions, we should note again that they are based solely on the results of self-report questionnaires.

Would more objective measures of personality lead to the same conclusions? Because of the difficulty of assessing behavior objectively as compared to using self-report questionnaires, there are few studies of this type (Plomin and Foch, 1980). It seems likely that genetic and environmental factors affecting objectively assessed behavior may differ from those that influence self-reports. The focus of my recent research has therefore shifted from twin studies of self-reports and general ratings of behavior (e.g., Buss and Plomin 1975; Plomin and Rowe, 1977) to the study of objectively assessed behavior in the domain of personality.

STUDIES OF OBJECTIVELY ASSESSED PERSONALITY

In overview, my studies of objectively assessed behavior in infants and young children suggest a picture that is very different from the self-report conclusions that all personality traits are equally influenced by heredity and that important environmental influences upon personality development operate within rather than between families. To the contrary, my results suggest that few aspects of objectively assessed personality seem to be influenced by heredity and that environmental influences salient to personality tend to operate between families.

For example, in one study of 1- and 2-year-old infant identical and same-sex fraternal twins (Plomin and Rowe, 1979), observers rated the social behavior of the infants in several standardized situations in their homes. The situations included the initial warm-up of the children to me as a stranger in their home, the quality of interactive play, "cuddling" (described elsewhere in this text), and the social behavior of the infants when their mothers left the house for a brief time. During alternating time-sampled observation periods, the raters observed the infants' behavior in relation to the mother and then their behavior directed toward the stranger. This proved to be important. None of the infants' social behavior directed toward the

mother showed evidence of genetic influence, a finding in agreement with the results of a previous study (Lytton, Martin, and Eaves, 1977). However, social behavior directed toward the stranger proved to be substantially influenced by genetic factors. It is particularly interesting that this observation seems to fit with the results of questionnaire studies of adolescents and adults in suggesting that the genetic underpinnings of social behavior may be revealed by reactions to strangers rather than responses to familiar figures (Horn, Plomin, and Rosenman, 1976).

Although the studies by Lytton and his colleagues and by Plomin and Rowe agree that infants' social behavior directed toward their mother shows no genetic influence, the studies provide conflicting evidence concerning the relative influence of between- and within-family environment. However, a study of 5- to 10-year-old twins found that between-family environment is more important than within-family factors for several objectively assessed measures of personality (Plomin and Foch, 1980). In this study, twins were brought to a laboratory by their mother and participated individually in a series of game-like situations which were videotaped through a one-way mirror. The study focused on activity level, selective attention, fidgeting, vigilance and aggressiveness—behaviors commonly considered in diagnosing hyperactivity, which is the most frequently diagnosed behavioral disorder of childhood. Figure 5–14a illustrates our Bobo clown measure of aggressive behavior. The clown is a five-foot-tall, inflated plastic figure with sand in the bottom so that it rocks back to an upright position after it is punched. The experimenter modeled the use of the clown in an aggressive manner, hitting it and saying "Take that." Then the experimenter said, "Now you try it," and we videotaped the child's performance. Ethical considerations deterred us from using more realistic measures of aggressiveness, but it has been shown that the Bobo clown measure is highly related to teacher and peer ratings of aggres-

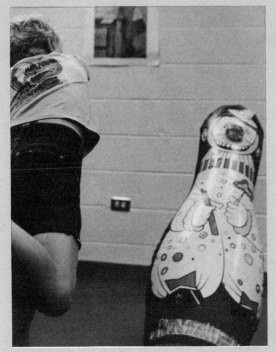

(a)

(b)

(c)

(e)

(d)

FIGURE 5-14
Objective assessment of social behavior in the Plomin and Foch study.

siveness (Johnston, DeLuca, Murtaugh, and Diener, 1977). Even though there are many studies of aggression and many books written about it, this was the first behavioral genetic analysis of aggressive behavior. Its results were clear: There was no evidence for genetic influence, and nearly all of the environmental variance lay between rather than within families (Plomin, Foch, and Rowe, 1980).

Very similar results were obtained for measures of selective attention and vigilance. Selective attention was assessed using a test for which the child wore earphones and pointed to a picture that represented a word heard through the earphones (Figure 5–14b). The task became progressively more difficult as background noise (first "white noise" and then cafeteria sounds) became louder and louder, making it harder to pick out the word from the background noise. We measured vigilance by asking the child to indicate whether a playing card was the same as one presented one second earlier (Figure 3–14c). A series of 160 such trials demanded considerable vigilance from children of this age.

Two other measures, activity level and fidgeting, suggested some genetic influence. After the children participated in our experiment, their mothers returned home with pedometers for the children to wear for a week. A pedometer is an instrument about the size of a wristwatch that registers up-and-down movements and is typically used by runners to record distance (see Figure 5–14d). We measured fidgeting by asking the children to remain quiet while lying in a bean-bag chair for 9 minutes, an interminably long time for children of this age (see Figure 5–14e). A videotape of this session was rated for head, limb and body movements. Both activity and fidgeting showed some genetic influence. Activity level displayed very substantial between-family environmental variance, while fidgeting suggested some influence of within-family environment.

Although more research will be needed to verify these findings, the results of these studies of objectively assessed behavior indicate the determinants of personality development are more complex than suggested by the results of using self-report questionnaires. Some behaviors apparently are influenced by genetic factors (for example, social responding to strangers, activity level and fidgeting), while others (for example, social responding to familiar figures, aggressive behavior, selective attention and vigilance) are not. Furthermore, although between-family environmental influences appear to be predominant when personality is assessed objectively, some behaviors (such as fidgeting) seem to be influenced by within-family factors.

THE USEFULNESS OF BEHAVIOR GENETICS

Results such as these make the point that the methods of behavioral genetics are not designed solely to detect genetic influence. Rather, they permit us to investigate the relative importance of genetic and environmental influences upon individual differences in behavior. This seems to be a reasonable first step in understanding the development of behavior, but it is only a first step. On the genetic side, we can study the number of genes involved in certain behaviors, whether any major single-gene influences can be detected, on what chromosomes such major genes reside, and the physiological pathways from genes to behavior. On the environmental side, we can ask the extent to which salient environmental influences operate between or within families, and we can begin to identify specific environmental factors by using behavioral genetic designs that separate genetic and environmental influences. For example, identical twins (which are identical genetically) may be useful in studying within-family environmental factors because differences within pairs can be caused only by within-family environmental factors. [See Plomin, DeFries, and McClearn (1980) for a more detailed explanation of these procedures.]

Another interesting area of research from both genetic and environmental perspectives is the study of factors influencing the relationship among behaviors, as distinct from the usual focus on one behavior at a time. For example, we know that specific cognitive abilities (such as memory, spatial ability, verbal ability and perceptual speed) are all moderately related to one another. To what extent are genetic factors responsible for this relationship; in other words, do the same gene systems tend to affect different cognitive abilities? To what extent is this relationship due to the influence of the same environmental factors on the various abilities? These questions can be answered by behavioral genetic analyses (e.g., Plomin and DeFries, 1979).

There is also much to be learned about the interface between genetic and environmental influences. For example, we can study **genotype-environment interaction**, which means that individuals of different genotypes respond differently to environmental influences (Plomin, DeFries, and Loehlin, 1977). Studies of genotype-environment interaction may be useful in isolating environmental influences that are potent for certain individuals but not for others.

Finally, much remains to be learned about the developmental interaction between genes and environment. Genes do not exert their full effect at the moment of conception; they turn on and off throughout development. Similarly, we would expect different environmental factors to come into play as the child begins to make its way through the world outside the womb, then outside the crib, and then outside the home. Although much more is unknown than known about this developmental interaction, what is known is quite remarkable. In general, the relative contributions of genetic and environmental factors remain the same from childhood through adulthood. For ex-

ample, for weight, the mixture of genetic and environmental influences is stable after one year of age. For height, the relative contributions of genes and environment remain stable after two years of age. For IQ, this stability is reached by about the age of seven. These data in themselves do not prove that the same genetic or environmental factors affect these characters in childhood and adulthood, but there are other behavioral genetic analyses that can use data from longitudinal studies to answer this question.

There are two large-scale, longitudinal studies of personality and cognitive development that should be introduced here because they will become increasingly well known during the next few years. One is the Louisville Twin Study (Wilson, 1978), which has followed the development of nearly 400 pairs of twins from three months of age through childhood. The other is the Colorado Adoption Project being conducted by my colleagues, J. C. DeFries and Steven Vandenberg, and myself. In 1977, we began a research program which will follow the development of nearly 300 adopted children and 100 unrelated children reared with the adoptees, as well as 300 "control" children reared by their natural parents. The birth parents and adoptive parents of the adopted children and the natural parents of the control children have been tested on a broad battery of personality and cognitive measures. The adopted and control children are being tested and will be observed yearly in their homes.

Such research obviously requires a great deal of time and effort. However, in view of the historical continuity of behavioral genetics and the powerful findings such studies can yield, I have no doubt that these studies are well worthwhile and that they will provide landmark contributions to our knowledge of the development of human behavior.

In this chapter we have discussed evidence for genetic influence on intelligence, schizophrenia, and normal social behavior. Such effects are hereditary because they involve transmission from one generation to the next. But there is a type of genetic effect, chromosomal aberrations, that, for the most part, is not inherited. Chromosomal aberrations fall into two categories, abnormal number and structure, and both lead to problems in development. Abnormality in number occurs during meiosis (maturation of the ovum or sperm) or mitosis, early in development of the fertilized egg. In either case, the chromosome pair does not separate as it should, causing either an extra chromosome or the loss of a chromosome in certain cells. Abnormalities in structure are caused by chromosome breakage and reunion in various patterns that are different than normal. Radiation, chemicals, and virus have been implicated in this process. As many as 22 to 50 percent of early spontaneous abortions are estimated to be due to chromosomal aberrations and 1 in 200 live births involve some kind of gross chromosome abnormality (Reed, 1975). Although it is beyond the scope of this book to fully discuss these disorders, examples of a few of the more commonly known ones will be described.

Down's Syndrome

Approximately 10 to 15 percent of the people institutionalized for mental deficiency suffer from *Down's syndrome,* and the syndrome occurs in about one in every 500 to 600 live births. The afflicted show from moderate to severe retardation and are strikingly alike in physical appearance. They frequently have small skulls, chins, and ears; short, broad necks, hands, and feet; flat nasal bridges; sparse hair; a fissured tongue; and, perhaps most recognizable, a fold over the eyelid, which appears oriental to Westerners and suggested the name *Mongolism.* Such people generally appear good natured and content.

For many years there was considerable speculation about the origins of the syndrome, with both genetic and environmental factors being variously suspected. The fact that concordance was almost perfect for monozygotic twins and extremely low for dizygotic twins strongly supported belief in some genetic basis for the disorder (Carter, 1964). Finally, in 1959, with the improvement of cell preparation techniques, it was discovered that the majority of Down's syndrome cases are caused by an extra, free-floating #21 chromosome (trisomy #21). Other chromosomal aberrations are responsible for about 5 percent of the cases (Holmes, 1978). The condition is not inherited and the risk of a woman bearing a child with Down's syndrome increases markedly with age (Figure 5–15). This suggests damage to the female gametes that interferes with normal meiosis, the risk of damage growing with age. The age of the father does not influence the likelihood of Down's syndrome, perhaps because the male's reproductive cells are continually produced throughout the life span, whereas the female's reproductive cells are partly formed before birth. Nevertheless, the father is increasingly being identified as the carrier of the chromosome abnormality. (Holmes, 1978; Miller and Erbe, 1978; Magenis, Overton, Chamberlin, Brady, and Lovrien, 1977).

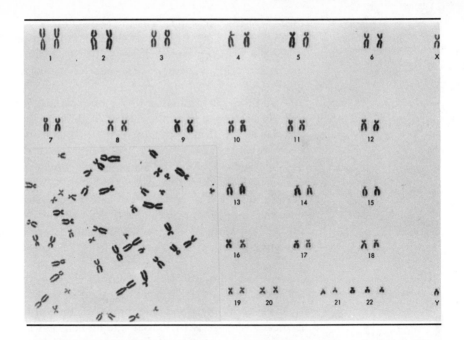

Maternal Age	Risk of Occurrence	Risk of Recurrence
20–30	1:1500	1:500
30–35	1:750	1:250
35–40	1:600	1:200
40–45	1:300	1:100
45–up	1:60	1:20

Sex Chromosome Aberrations

We will now consider three disorders that are representative of a larger group of abnormalities resulting from sex chromosome aberrations.

Klinefelter's syndrome, found in phenotypic males, is the most commonly occurring malady of such origin. Most often individuals suffering from this defect have an additional X chromosome (XXY), although more than two X chromosomes have been reported. As in Down's syndrome, there is an apparent error in meiosis, and the mothers of Klinefelter males tend to be older than those in the general population. About 25 percent of the afflicted exhibit below-normal intelligence and they suffer from atypical sexual development such as small genitals and lack of sperm. In addition, there is some evidence to indicate an increased incidence of antisocial behavior. Klinefelter's syndrome has been treated with male sex hormones with varying degrees of success.

Turner's syndrome, on the other hand, occurs in phenotypic females and is the result of a lack of sex chromosomes. Most frequently there is only a single X chromosome (XO). Mental deficiency occurs in about 20 percent of the cases (Robinson and Robinson, 1965), and appears to involve difficulty in space-form perception. Other abnormalities include a lack of ovarian tissue, failure to develop secondary sex characteristics, short stature, and deformity of the neck and forearm. The syndrome occurs disproportionately among monozygotic twins (Rosenthal, 1970) and some association with maternal age has been reported (Reed, 1975). Treatment with female sex hormones can bring on secondary sexual characteristics and adjustment can be quite good.

The third sex chromosome disorder we will consider, that of the XYY male, has attracted enormous attention since it was first revealed in a report associating it with both mental retardation and aggressive behavior (Jacobs, Brunton, and Melville, 1965). It was soon noted that XYY males were unusually tall and appeared with high frequency among institutionalized criminals. Follow-up data disclosed that the XYY male tended to show behavioral disorders at an early age and to be less likely to have violent siblings than normal control males (Price and Whatmore, 1967). Several case studies appeared to confirm the relationship between the XYY configuration and mental deficiency and aggression. Forssman (1967), for example, described an atypically tall XYY male who had an IQ of 69 at age sixteen and who had become extremely aggressive during adolescence. What was most intriguing was the association of the 2 Y chromosomes and violence, with causation being implied. Later research cast doubt on this interpretation. A study by Witkin and his colleagues (1976) of over 4,000 men in Denmark substantiated the atypical height, low intelligence scores, and high frequency of XYY men in penal institutions. The criminal XYY men had not, however, been involved in violent acts; if anything, their crimes appeared rather mild. Based on extensive analyses these investigators concluded that low intelligence, not extreme aggression, could underlie the criminal behavior and institutionalization of the XYY male.

GENETIC SCREENING AND COUNSELING

There are over 2,000 known genetic diseases and they account wholly or in part for 25 percent of all diseases (Brown, 1978; Karp, 1976). Several of these disorders, due to inheritance or chromosomal aberrations, have already been mentioned. It is not an exaggeration to say that our knowledge of genetic disorders grows daily. Partially as a response to this, there has been a steady increase in genetic screening and counseling. Most states now have a genetic screening program, which is sometimes compulsory. In 1951 there were about 10 genetic counseling centers in the United States; by 1975 this figure had risen to approximately 300 (Karp, 1976). Genetic counseling includes screening, calculating the risk of genetic disorder, discussing the management of individuals suffering from a particular genetic defect, and providing general help with decision making.

One relatively new screening method that is now widely used is amniocentesis. The procedure is simple: A needle is inserted into the amnion sac of the developing fetus to draw out a sample of the amniotic fluid. The fluid and fetal cells floating in it can be examined for over eighty biochemical and chromosomal defects. First used in the late 1950s, amniocentesis has been shown to be safe for both prospective mother and child. It is recommended particularly when a genetic disease is suspected in the family and when the prospective mother is past thirty-five years of age, because these conditions increase the risk of genetic disorders.

The advantages of genetic screening and counseling cannot be denied. The risk of PKU, sickle cell anemia, and countless other diseases can be ascertained. Carriers of many disorders can be recognized. Down's syndrome and other chromosomal aberrations can be diagnosed prenatally, providing couples with the alternative of deciding whether or not to continue with a pregnancy. We have seen that the early identification of PKU neonates allows for their immediate treatment with diet control. A dramatic example of genetic counseling involving an entire family came to light a few years ago (New York Times, 1975). The family began to notice a definite pattern of illness and death, but was unsure of its implications. One member finally sought help from the National Genetics Foundation. After gathering information from as many family members as possible, geneticists were able to determine that a rare disorder was being transmitted by an autosomal dominant gene. The disease is now called Joseph's disease, after the surname of the ancestor to whom it has been traced. Causing severe muscular dysfunction, the fatal disorder does not display itself until early adulthood and, by then, many of the sufferers have had children. An unusual meeting of the eighty-five family members was held in order to diagnose them individually and to educate them about the risk of the disease.

Despite such benefit, though, there is much concern over the potential misuse of screening and identification of people carrying defective genes (Ausubel, Beckwith, and Janssen, 1974; English, 1974; Karp, 1976; Lappé and Morison, 1976). *Eugenics,* the attempt to manipulate genetics to improve the human species, can be dangerous. The word "eugenics," which means wellborn, was coined by Francis Galton in 1883. Galton, you will recall, was interested in the fact that intelligence seemed to run in families, and he suggested that the human species could be improved by encouraging talented people to mate (Karp, 1976). The idea was not a new one, but it became particularly pervasive in the United States during the 1920s, resulting in restriction of "inferior" immigrants and compulsory sterilization laws for the mentally retarded, criminal, and other "socially inadequate" individuals.

Even though sterilization laws are now unconstitutional, our expanded knowledge of genetics raises the possibility of a new eugenics movement.

At one time in the recent past, for example, there was eager discussion about early screening for XYY males, even though the association between this genotype and violent crimes was far from substantial. But suppose an association were found? How would the identification of the genotype be used? Would we treat the XYY male in a certain way? Would he be compelled to attend special schools or programs? Would a next step be prenatal diagnosis with amniocentesis—and recommendation or compulsion of abortion? Similar concerns are expressed with regard to sickle cell anemia, carried mostly by blacks, and Tay-Sachs, a fatal disease carried by a recessive gene that is prevalent almost exclusively among Jewish people. The basic issue is the protection of the individual—or groups of individuals—in face of what is viewed as best for the society or species as a whole. Awareness of this tension is necessary if we are to apply our genetic knowledge wisely.

SUMMARY

The *theory of evolution,* proposed by Darwin in *Origin of Species* in 1859, attempted to explain the formation of new species of life and the enormous variability found in living forms. Darwin postulated that organisms that are the fittest in their environment survive to pass on their characteristics, whereas the unfit do not transmit their characteristics. In this way species change over time. Although Darwin could not specifically describe the causes of variability, our present knowledge of genetic mechanisms allows us to do so. Spontaneous changes in genes, *mutations,* is one way in which variability occurs.

One of the major processes of inheritance explained by Gregor Mendel's experiments with peas is the role of *dominant* and *recessive genes.* Heredity involves receiving pairs of genes (*alleles*). For some characteristics, when the genes in the pair are not alike, the dominant one will always display itself over the other. Because of dominant and recessive genes, Mendel distinguished between *genotype,* the entire genetic endowment, and *phenotype,* the outward appearance or manifestation of the genes. The inheritance of some human characteristics involves recessive, dominant, or sex-linked genes. Still other characteristics, such as intelligence, height, and weight, are influenced by a combination of many genes (*polygene inheritance*).

Genes influence development by controlling the synthesis and operation of biochemical substances. However, genetic effects have ongoing interaction with environmental influences. Thus, there is not a one-to-one relationship between genotypes and phenotypes. Rather, any one genotype operating in any one environment has a *range of reaction* in its phenotypic expression.

Behavior genetics is the study of genetic influences on behavior. Experiments with animals using *inbred strains* and *selective breeding* have demonstrated a genetic component in such behaviors as learning ability, sex drive, emotionality, and aggressiveness. The major methods used to study genetic determinants in humans are: *pedigree analysis, consanguinity studies, the twin study method,* and the *adoptee* or *foster family method.* Each of these methods has interpretative problems in that the effects of the environment are not totally controlled.

Much research supports the view that there is some hereditary component in IQ. The closer the family relationship the more alike is IQ. Monozygotic twins show greater concordance in IQ than do dizygotic twins, and adopted children resemble their biological families more closely than they resemble their adoptee families. Nevertheless, IQ is influenced by the environment. Moreover, the data do not permit firm conclusions about racial/ethnic IQ differences.

Consanguinity, twin, and adoption studies provide evidence for genetic effects on schizophrenia, a relatively serious psychotic disturbance. "Normal" social behavior also may be genetically influenced, although the evidence is not as clear-cut as for IQ and schizophrenia. The genetic hypothesis is supported for introversion-extroversion, activity level, and temperament. Several broad-spectrum studies indicate that at least on some personality dimensions monozygotic twins are more alike than are dizygotic twins.

Genetic processes are implicated in many defects and diseases. Examples of hereditary diseases are PKU, sickle cell anemia, hemophilia, and Huntington's chorea. Some defects are caused by noninheritable chromosome aberrations. Down's, Klinefelter's, Turner's, and the XYY syndromes are examples.

Genetic screening and counseling is helpful in determining the risk of defects, identifying carriers, and identifying prenatally many genetic dysfunctions. *Amniocentesis* is a procedure in which amniotic fluid and cells from the fetus can be examined prenatally for genetic disease and defect. However, genetic screening and counseling hold the potential for abuse of individuals and groups of people, so they must be continuously monitored.

Cognitive and Intellectual Development

The increasing ability to benefit from experience lies at the heart of what is meant by cognitive and intellectual development, which is the focus of this section.

Chapter 6 deals with the basic processes of learning and also begins our discussion of more complex forms of learning and reasoning. Chapter 7 continues this theme by focusing on the development of thought. Jean Piaget's highly influential cognitive-developmental theory is described in this chapter, in the chronological sequence of four periods (sensorimotor, preoperational, concrete operational, and formal operational) identified in his writings. The chapter concludes with a discussion of selective attention and memory, two cognitive processes which have been studied through ingenious experimental research.

Chapter 8 deals with language and the development of the ability to send and receive information efficiently and accurately. Communication skills are linked to the more basic cognitive processes we have already discussed.

Chapter 9 is concerned with the meaning of intelligence, a psychological construct implicated in all aspects of cognitive and intellectual development. We describe the nature of intelligence tests and the rationale that lies behind them, explain the various definitions of intelligence that have been held over the years, and describe the range of human intellectual ability, from severe retardation to great intelligence and creative genius.

Learning Processes

WHAT IS LEARNING?

Learning is a term that does not lend itself to a single definition. Generally, though, we can say that learning refers to *all processes by which an activity originates or is changed through reacting to an encountered situation* (Hilgard and Bower, 1966, p. 2). Learning involves not one but a number of related processes, each influenced by underlying biological dispositions and abilities. It is a complex combination of processes that work separately and jointly in human development. Our discussion of learning begins with habituation, often considered the simplest and most basic type of stimulus-response learning. We will then go on to explore developmental aspects of classical conditioning and operant conditioning, two other stimulus-response processes. Observational learning, which we turn to next, is the process through which an individual learns by observing others. Finally we consider some complex processes in learning, including the acquisition of learning sets and the development of hypothesis testing strategies. These last topics pave the way for our discussion of cognitive development in chapter 7.

HABITUATION

We learned in chapter 3 that the infant makes a number of reflexive responses (e.g., the Moro reflex) to the presentation of various stimuli in its environment. Individuals of all ages exhibit a reflexive startle response to the presentation of intense stimuli, and a reflexive orienting response (e.g., pay attention) to the presentation of new or unusual stimuli. After repeated presentation of the same stimulus, however, the initial reflexive response will diminish and eventually disappear. This process of "getting used to" a stimulus is called *habituation;* it involves learning because responses are changed through reacting to previously encountered situations with the same stimulus. As an example of habituation, consider the newborn infant whose family lives near an airport. When the newborn first arrives home from the hospital, it may startle and begin to cry when an airplane flies over the house. But as time passes, the infant habituates to the loud noise of the airplane, and eventually seems not to notice the noise. It has been discovered also that the reflexive response to the original stimulus will often reappear after a new stimulus has been presented. Such *dishabituation,* as this recovery is technically called, shows clearly that habituation does not derive merely from fatigue. For example, suppose the infant who has habituated to frequent noise from airplanes touches something hot and burns its hand. If, immediately after burning its hand, an airplane flies over the house making a loud noise, the infant is likely to become startled from the airplane noise; that is, its original startle response to the airplane noise has dishabituated or recovered because of the presentation of another strong stimulus.

Developmental Trends in Habituation

Habituation is sometimes called a "primitive" learning process. It is readily demonstrable in newborn infants (Schaffer, 1973), and occurs only for certain responses under certain conditions. It is, in the words of one learning theorist, "A highly prepared form of learning in that only certain connections habituate, typically those between generalized warning signals and arousal, orienting, and startle responses" (Wickelgren, 1977, p. 37).

The fact that even newborn infants show habituation effects has an important practical significance for researchers, providing a tool for studying the ability of infants to perform perceptual discriminations. If an infant habituates to the repeated visual presentation of one stimulus and then is dishabituated after being shown a moderately different looking stimulus, we know the infant can discriminate between the two stimuli and thus we discover something about the infant's perceptual abilities, which the infant could not tell us in any other way. (Recall the Close-up on this technique in chapter 4.)

Although habituation and dishabituation are apparent in newborns, the process undergoes some change over the course of development. For example, with increasing biological maturity, the individual executes an ever more elaborate and organized orienting response to new stimulation (Reese and Porges, 1976). Therefore, though habituation is present from birth, the type of response that can be habituated becomes more complex and more subtle with increasing age and experience.

CLASSICAL CONDITIONING (RESPONDENT CONDITIONING)

Like habituation, *classical conditioning* involves a change in the situations in which a particular reflexive or innate response will occur. The difference is that in habituation the individual stops responding to situations that had previously elicited the response, whereas in classical conditioning the individual begins to respond to situations that had *not* previously elicited the response. Thus, in a fundamental way, respondent conditioning is a more active learning process than is habituation.

Pavlov's Pioneer Studies in Classical Conditioning

The first important studies of classical conditioning were done by the Russian physiologist Ivan Pavlov at the end of the nineteenth century. Pavlov's research primarily entailed a series of investigations on the digestive processes of dogs. His experimental procedure involved introducing meat powder into the mouths of his canine subjects and then measuring the flow of various digestive juices. During the course of his work, Pavlov ran into what at first seemed to him to be an irritating problem. The dogs often appeared to anticipate the food, so that salivary flow began even before any meat powder had been introduced. When earnest efforts to eliminate this troublesome interference failed, the decision was made to study it systematically. Pavlov reasoned that inasmuch as untrained dogs salivated when meat powder was placed on their tongues, salivation was a natural or *unconditioned response* (UCR). But salivation that came to be elicited by the sight of the food had to be acquired by some form of experience and was thus a learned or *conditioned response* (CR).

This reasoning led Pavlov to investigate the manner in which conditioned responses are formed. He presented the dogs with the sound of a metronome (*conditioned stimulus,* or CS) followed in a few seconds by food (*unconditioned stimulus,* or UCS). At first, no salivation occurred until the UCS was presented. Then, after a number of presentations, saliva was secreted during the time interval before the meat powder was presented, apparently in response to the CS. This salivation was the learned or conditioned response. Using this procedure Pavlov taught dogs to salivate to an impressive array of environmental stimuli, including a rotating disk and a light. His investigations went far beyond merely demonstrating the phenomenon, for he was also interested in the specific circumstances under which conditioned responses were formed, modified, and weakened.

Generalization, Discrimination, and Extinction. To develop a conditioned response it is necessary that the conditioned stimulus be followed repeatedly with the unconditioned stimulus; with repeated pairings the conditioned response develops gradually. But conditioning would have few implications for understanding the development of behavior if the particular CS used in training were the only one that could produce the CR. Classical conditioning is not limited in this way, however. Stimuli that are similar to the CS used during training also can produce the conditioned response. This is referred to as *generalization.* The greater the similarity between the new stimulus and the original conditioned stimulus, the greater the degree to which they are substitutable.

Another phenomenon, *discrimination,* can also occur, so that there is a *generalization gradient.* For example, if a dog is conditioned to salivate to a tone of one pitch, it will also salivate to somewhat higher and lower notes than the one used in conditioning, but the further the tone is in pitch from the original CS, the weaker the salivation response will be. Discrimination is the result of the UCS being paired with a particular stimulus but never with others. An experiment by Pavlov illustrates the concepts of generalization and discrimination. Using classical conditioning procedures, he trained dogs to salivate upon presentation of a circle drawn on a card. He found that the dogs would also salivate when presented with an ellipse drawn on a card; that is, the dogs' conditioned response had generalized to a new stimulus that was very similar to the original conditioned stimulus. Next, Pavlov attempted to condition discrimination by giving the dogs meat powder (UCS) only after presentation of a circle but never after presentation of an ellipse. Following this procedure, the dogs learned to discriminate the two stimuli—they would salivate in response to the circle but not the ellipse.

Finally, just as responses can be conditioned to new stimuli, so can they be eliminated by repeated presentation of the CS in the absence of the UCS. This gradual diminution of a conditioned response is called *extinction.*

Watson's
Influence

One of the first psychologists in the United States to take seriously the proposition that classical conditioning may have implications for the development and modification of human behavior was John Watson, the father of modern behaviorism. Watson (1914) was convinced that given certain conditions and stimuli, responses are orderly and predictable. He advocated that learning principles be applied to the development of behavior and, in fact, was enthusiastic about the developmental implications of such an endeavor:

> Give me a dozen healthy infants, well-formed, and my own specified world to bring them up in and I'll guarantee to take any one at random and train him to

become any type of specialist I might select—doctor, lawyer, merchant, chief and yes, even beggar-man and thief, regardless of his talents, penchants, tendencies, abilities, vocations, and race of his ancestors. [Watson, 1914; reprinted 1958, p. 104]

Watson instigated several studies with young children that illustrate the early application of conditioning procedures. The most famous of these is Watson and Rayner's case of "little Albert," published in 1920.

Albert was an eleven-month-old child with no detectable fear except of loud sound, such as that made by striking a steel bar behind him. Assuming that the sound was a UCS that elicited fear, Watson and Rayner tried to show that they could induce or condition the fear of a white rat (a CS) in Albert by systematically pairing exposure to the animal with the sound. After a series of seven such presentations, the rat, which previously had not elicited any fear, produced a fairly sharp avoidance reaction that included crying and attempts to escape from the situation.

In a follow-up study, Mary Cover Jones (1924) showed that fear responses can be partially extinguished by procedures similar to conditioning. Her subject, Peter, was a boy of two years and ten months, who had previously developed a severe fear reaction to furry objects. Jones first arranged for Peter to play, in the presence of a rabbit, with three children who exhibited no fear of the animal. The treatment appeared to be working well when a setback occurred, due to Peter's illness and accidental exposure to a large dog. Jones then decided to treat the boy with a combination of exposure to fearless others and *counterconditioning*. The latter involved moving the animal progressively closer to Peter while he ate some of his favorite foods, thus pairing the feared stimuli with pleasantness. The boy's fear diminished with this treatment until he was able to hold the rabbit by himself.

Developmental Trends in Classical Conditioning

Psychologists have been interested in the demonstration of classical conditioning in infancy in order to determine whether such learning operates as a developmental process early in life. Initial studies provided some positive results, but they were justifiably criticized on the grounds of poor method. In the mid-1950s, valid experiments gradually erased the remaining doubt. A variety of responses—such as blinking, crying, heart rate, head turning, fear responses, eye movement, and sucking—can be classically conditioned during the first few weeks of life (Brackbill and Koltsova, 1967; Fitzgerald and Porges, 1971; Stevenson, 1970). In some cases, however, conditioning required many trials, and it has been suggested that susceptibility to such learning increases with age for at least some responses (Kasatkin, 1972; Reese and Porges, 1976).

Preparedness and the Likelihood of Classical Conditioning. A growing body of evidence has suggested that the conditionability of various associations depends very much on the preparedness of the association. We are biologically *prepared* (presumably through evolution of the species) to learn some things quickly while other things are learned only with difficulty or not at all (Seligman, 1970). Preparedness refers to characteristics of an entire species that allow its members to learn certain things or make certain associations. The first demonstration of such preparedness in classical conditioning was recorded by Garcia and Koelling (1966). These investigators provided a convincing demonstration that rats were highly prepared to associate tastes with subsequent illness and thus to avoid foods that had been associated with illness in the past. By way of sharp contrast, efforts to condition aversion to audio-visual signals by associating them with illness were unsuccessful, although it proved quite easy to associate audio-visual signals with pain such as electric shock. The one general principle that has emerged thus far regarding preparedness in human classical conditioning is consistent with these findings: Visual stimuli are readily conditioned to pain stimuli, whereas olfactory and gustatory stimuli (i.e., those associated with smell and taste) are much more readily conditioned to wretching, nausea, and "sickness" (Whitehurst and Vasta, 1977). If a person, child or adult, is shown a light and then receives a shock, after a number of pairings the light alone will produce a startle-like response. But if a person is given something to taste and then shocked the taste alone will probably not come to produce the response, even after many pairings.

OPERANT CONDITIONING (INSTRUMENTAL LEARNING)

Unlike classical conditioning, in which behavior is elicited by some identifiable stimulus, *operant conditioning* (or instrumental learning) focuses on the consequences (rewards and punishments) that follow behavior. The pioneer investigator in this area was E. L. Thorndike.

In a typical experiment, Thorndike (1898) placed a cat into a slatted cage with food located outside; escape, then, was potentially followed by food reward. The cat had to perform a particular response, such as pulling a cord or pressing a lever, to open the door; by virtue of the creature's high level of activity, sooner or later it "accidentally" performed the act and succeeded in escaping. Thorndike observed that on subsequent trials, "All the other non-successful impulses will be stamped out and the particular impulse leading to the successful act will be stamped in by the resulting pleasure . . ." (1898, p. 11).

From such observations, Thorndike formulated a general law, the *law of effect*, applicable to the behavior of all organisms:

> Any act which in a given situation produces satisfaction becomes associated with that situation, so that when the situation recurs the act is more likely than before to recur also. Conversely, any act which in a given situation produces discomfort becomes disassociated from that situation, so that when the situation recurs the act is less likely than before to recur. [Thorndike, 1905, p. 203]

Thorndike endeavored to apply the law of effect and several other principles derived from his research to a number of practical human problems. He published over five hundred articles and books, among them a fairly complete volume on experimental psychology and several books focusing on educational matters (cf. Joncich, 1962). In one such volume, written for teachers and setting forth his philosophy of educational psychology, Thorndike reflected:

> Human nature does not do something for nothing. The satisfyingness and annoyingness of the states of affairs which follow the making of the connection are the chief forces which remodel man's nature. Education makes changes chiefly by rewarding them. The prime law in all human control is to get the man to make the desired response and to be satisfied thereby.
>
> The Law of Effect is the fundamental law of learning and teaching. . . . By it animals are taught their tricks; by it babies learn to smile at the sight of the bottle or the kind attendant, and to manipulate spoon and fork; by it the player at billiards or golf improves his game; by it the man of science preserves those ideas that satisfy him by their promise, and discards futile fancies. It is the great weapon of all who wish—in industry, trade, government, religion or education— to change man's responses either by reinforcing old and adding new ones, or by getting rid of those that are undesirable. [Cited in Joncich, 1962, pp. 79–80]

Extended and elaborated, the law of effect is central to operant conditioning. Examples of instrumental behaviors (called *operants*) include doing homework, playing chess, driving a car, and dressing oneself. Completion of any one of these acts results in some consequences. For example, driving a car may result in viewing the beautiful countryside, avoiding unpleasant work at home, or getting a speeding ticket. Future behavior, in turn, is influenced by these consequences. Drivers are less likely to speed, at least for awhile, after getting a speeding ticket.

Developmental Trends in Operant Conditioning

Does operant conditioning begin at birth? It would seem that such a prominent process would start early in development. Interestingly, however, until the 1960s it had proven impossible to actually demonstrate operant conditioning in newborn or very young infants. But the breakthrough occurred when researchers successfully came to grips with the problem that the human infant is limited in both the range of responses it can produce and in the range of stimuli its immature sensory system can detect. One major advance involved the use of *conjugate reinforcement*, in which, for example, an attractive visual display is illuminated in direct proportion to the rate with which the infant emits some response well within its repertoire. In one well-known study (Siqueland and DeLucia, 1969) infants were shown attractive colored slides that were illuminated from the rear so that the more the infant sucked on a specially prepared device resembling a nipple, the brighter was the illumination of the slide. In this way, the investigators were able to demonstrate operant conditioning in infants as young as three weeks of age and as old as one year. The accumulated evidence seems to show clearly that with properly selected responses and appropriate reinforcers newborns can, indeed, be operantly conditioned (cf. Hulsebus, 1973).

While it is true that operant conditioning can be demonstrated in newborns, we must keep in mind that readiness is a requirement for the development of operant responses. In other words, to the extent that an operant response entails perceptual, motor, or intellectual skills, it is locked into biological development. It appears, for example, that a majority of newborn infants are biologically incapable of executing the sequence of reaching and grasping as two separate responses (Bower, 1974). Very young infants thus may be unable to learn to reach and grasp effectively, even when the environment is appropriately arranged.

The Nature of Consequences

The consequences that control our actions can take many forms and appear in many different patterns and configurations. One of the significant theoretical accomplishments of the operant conditioning approach is that it has organized these various patterns and combinations of consequences into functionally meaningful groups.

Positive and Negative Consequences: Giving vs. Taking Away. One major distinction that can be drawn between the consequences that we experience is that they may involve either receiving some stimulation or experience, or losing some stimulation or experience. The first type of consequences is traditionally referred to as a *positive consequence*, whereas the second type is traditionally referred to as a *negative consequence*.

Reinforcement and Punishment: Stimuli that are Approached and Avoided. The distinction between positive and negative consequences in-

FIGURE 6–1
Parental affection is a powerful positive reinforcer for most children. Nancy Hays, Monkmeyer Press Photo Service.

volves *only* the question of whether a stimulus is presented or removed, and does not refer to the effects of the consequence. The latter is determined empirically; that is, *a consequence is said to be a reinforcement if it encourages the response that caused it, and a punishment if it discourages the response that caused it.* According to operant terminology there are four different types of consequences: positive reinforcement, negative reinforcement, positive punishment, and negative punishment (cf. Whitehurst and Vasta, 1977).

Positive reinforcers are those consequences that, when presented, tend to increase the likelihood of the responses on which they are contingent. Praise may positively reinforce a child's studying. *Negative reinforcement* also increases the likelihood of the response on which it is contingent, but works in a different way. Negative reinforcement involves the termination of some experience or stimulation that is noxious or unpleasant, as when a restriction is lifted for good performance.

The presentation of a stimulus that will discourage the reoccurrence of a particular response is *positive punishment.* Most organisms will show a decrement in those responses (e.g., touching an exposed electrical wire) that result in an electric shock, an almost universally effective punishment. Finally, *negative punishment* involves the reduction in a response by removing some stimulation or experience contingent upon the occurrence of the response. Not allowing a child to watch television in order to eliminate poor school grades is an example of negative punishment.

It is important to keep in mind that within the operant conditioning framework consequences are judged by their effects and not by their intentions. For example, parents, teachers and even peers may use frowns and various forms of verbal disapproval in order to discourage particular actions. Nevertheless, the research shows that attention, even when it is tinged with criticism, often serves as a positive *reinforcer,* increasing the very behavior it is designed to discourage (e.g., Madsen, Becker, Thomas, Koser and Plager, 1968).

There is evidence, as well, to suggest that many consequences sometimes combine to affect responses. For example, studies show that learning

TABLE 6-1
Types of Consequences and Their Effects

Perceived Nature of the Stimulus	Stimulus Presented (Positive)	Stimulus Taken Away (Negative)
"good"	Positive reinforcement	Negative punishment
"bad"	Positive punishment	Negative reinforcement

tends to occur more quickly when mild punishment for incorrect responses is used to supplement reinforcement for desired responses (Whitehurst, 1969).

A Closer Look at Reinforcement

A great deal is known about the way in which reinforcement works, much more than could be summarized even briefly here. Still, to understand the central role that operant conditioning plays in cognitive and social development, it is useful to further examine the operation of reinforcement and some of its more precise effects on behavior.

Extinction. Extinction in operant conditioning is the weakening of a learned operant due to the lack of reinforcement. If an instrumental response has been acquired by providing reinforcement, and if the reinforcement is then withheld, there is soon a decrement in response rate. The mechanism parallels that found in classical conditioning when the CS is presented alone without the UCS after the conditioned response has been acquired. The degree to which an organism resists extinction is one indication of the strength of the conditioned response.

Quite striking behavioral changes can come about through extinction. Take the hypothetical case of a six-year-old girl whose disruptive behavior in the classroom is being reinforced by the attention it evokes from the teacher. Should the teacher refrain from attending to the child subsequent to her disruptive acts, the behavior would drop off over time.

Chaining and Successive Approximation. Instrumental (or operant) conditioners have addressed themselves to the manner in which sequences of behavior are learned and maintained through reinforcement. They have shown that animals can be taught long chains of behavior leading to reinforcement—this is accomplished by having the reinforcer follow the last act in the sequence, then having it follow only if the last two acts are performed, then the last three, and so on backward down the sequence. Animals have been taught fascinating chains of behavior in this way, such as climbing a ladder, crossing a bridge, descending a ladder, crawling through a tube, and pressing a bar for food (e.g., Pierrel and Sherman, 1963). Although it is not always necessary to use such a chaining procedure with verbal human beings, the technique has proven useful in building behaviors in the very young or in the retarded.

Even so, chaining requires that the desired acts must occur before they can be reinforced. If they do not, they must be shaped by *successive approximation* (shaping). As the name implies, this involves a successively changing reinforcement contingency. At first a large class of responses that has some relevance for the ultimately desired behavior is reinforced. Then the contingency is gradually altered so that reinforcement is given only for closer and closer approximations of the desired behavior. In teaching a pigeon to stand in one small corner of its cage, for example, the investigator might begin by rewarding the bird for standing anywhere on the left-hand side of the cage. After a while, the bird will spend most of its time there, so

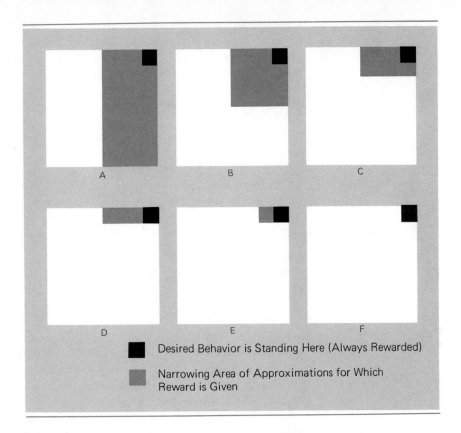

FIGURE 6–2
A diagram
representing the
principle of
successive
approximation.

Desired Behavior is Standing Here (Always Rewarded)

Narrowing Area of Approximations for Which
Reward is Given

the investigator can now safely narrow the contingency down to one quadrant, one-half of the quadrant, and so on. One such progression illustrating the basic principle of successive approximation is shown in Figure 6–2.

Shaping requires the presence of a number of factors. The procedure rests on the fact that most responses show a degree of random variation in their character or intensity. By selectively reinforcing some responses but not other similar responses, one can teach *response differentiation*. Once a particular type of response has been differentiated from the general response class, it, too, will display random variation. Thus a series of response differentiations are possible, and they can be arranged in a sequence or plan so that an individual's behavior is gradually shaped through successive approximations into a complex behavioral routine.

An important variant of successive approximation involves building the components of the behavior that is finally desired. In teaching language to a woman who was a mute psychotic, Neale and Liebert (1969) first rewarded imitation of single syllables (e.g., "Buh," "Mmm"), then words (e.g., "Bread," "Milk"), then abbreviated sentences ("Milk, please"), and finally complete sentences ("May I have some bread, please?"). Such a procedure has often been shown to be highly effective. If the investigators had waited for the patient to produce a full sentence before issuing any reward, little progress would ever have been made.

Generalization in Operant Conditioning. Generalization was mentioned previously, in our discussion of classical conditioning. A very similar phenomenon occurs in operant conditioning: Responses that have been reinforced after the presentation of one stimulus will now be more likely to occur upon the presentation of other, similar stimuli. Consider the pigeon who has been reinforced for pecking on an illuminated response key (a typical operant conditioning experiment set-up in the animal laboratory). In this experiment the light behind the key will be brightened or dimmed. The frequency of pecks will be greatest for intensities that closely match that of the training light and will decrease as the intensities are progressively different. In other words, *generalization* occurs. This phenomenon, which allows the animal to apply a learned response to somewhat different situations, is found across many species, including human beings.

Discrimination and Stimulus Control. Operant conditioning is unlike classical conditioning in that particular stimuli do not directly elicit a response; they do, however, come to "set the occasion" for a response. Consider the behavior typically exhibited by the rat in a Skinner box, a specialized experimental chamber. The animal has little difficulty learning that pressing a bar will result in the delivery of a pellet of food. If reinforcement is then provided only when the bar is pressed in the presence of a light, the animal will soon limit its responding to the time during which the light is on. The light has become a *discriminative stimulus* for the behavior; it enables the rat to discriminate the condition under which reinforcement will occur.

Such stimulus control is at the heart of adaptive functioning, for even behaviors we wish to strengthen in a variety of situations would not be desirable in all situations. Eating, for example, is a vital behavior that must be brought under stimulus control; although we want to encourage children to eat meat and vegetables, we do not wish them to attempt to eat string, sticks, or the contents of the bottles in the medicine cabinet. Effective and appropriate stimulus control involves the ability to discriminate between the presence of the informative stimulus and its absence, and thus requires a variety of perceptual skills. It also requires that differential responsiveness to the presence and the absence of the stimulus have some functional significance for the consequences that are received. Most people can differentiate a blue police car from a white police car; nonetheless, they do not differentially respond to these two stimuli when being pursued for speeding.

Stimulus control is easiest, of course, when there is an obvious difference between the presence and the absence of the discriminative stimulus. On the other hand, naturally occurring situations often require that we make subtle and difficult discriminations. How are these increasingly difficult discriminations learned? One potent technique is closely related to the shaping method discussed earlier. We are speaking of *fading*, which is the method of teaching difficult discriminations by gradually eliminating the more obvious distinctive features of a discriminative stimulus. The process is analogous to the situation in which a young child can detect that his or her parents are angry only from a full-blown display of annoyance (stern voice, severe scowl, and deliberate manner), whereas an older child may need fewer and fewer of these cues to know that his or her father is really angry, so that eventually a slightly raised eyebrow will do.

Schedules of Reinforcement

The previous discussions suggest that the effects of reinforcement are either continuously present or absent. While it is certainly true that reinforcement is often given for every desired or appropriate response (a so-called *continuous reinforcement* or CRF schedule), in both laboratory and life situations it is at least as common to find that reinforcement is given only intermittently. Moreover, research has shown quite clearly that the effect of reinforcement varies dramatically according to the schedules, patterns, and context of its administration.

Intermittent (Partial) Schedules. One well-established fact is that it is easier to establish a new response (i.e., acquisition) using a schedule of continuous reinforcement, but that it is easier to maintain a response using intermittent reinforcement. Moreover, the most effective instructional strategy appears to be one in which the individual begins on a continuous reinforcement schedule and then gradually experiences a reduction in reinforcers: both acquisition and maintenance are facilitated.

Schedules of reinforcement that provide intermittent reinforcement are called *partial schedules*. Research by B. F. Skinner and his associates has demonstrated the differential effects of four broad partial schedules.

Partial reinforcement may be set up according to a *fixed interval* of time (FI schedule). With this kind of schedule, the subject is reinforced only for the first correct response emitted after a prescribed lapse of time. *Fixed ratio* (FR) schedules, in contrast, are those in which a response is reinforced only after it has occurred for a fixed number of times without consequences—e.g., a reinforcer after every fourth response. Studies with both animals and humans suggest that FR schedules can be made to produce considerably higher rates of responding than either CRF or FI schedules. Moreover, an experimenter may begin an organism on a particular FR schedule and slowly decrease the ratio of unreinforced to reinforced responses until the organism is rewarded as infrequently as one response in every thousand.

Reinforcement also may be provided on variable schedules—that is, after a variable time lapse (*variable interval,* or VI) or a variable number of unreinforced responses (*variable ratio,* or VR). The subject therefore never learns exactly when reinforcement will occur. Responding usually becomes very steady with variable schedules, with the rate depending upon the length of the time interval or the ratio first employed. The VR schedule is particularly potent for evoking high rates of responding. It is as if the subject knows that the more frequent the responding, the more frequent the payoff, even though it is not possible to predict when the payoff will come. Variable schedules are probably extremely common in human experience.

Bijou (1957) provided the classic example of the differential effects of CRF and VR schedules in resistance to extinction among preschool children. The correct response in Bijou's study consisted simply of picking up a ball and moving it to a different location. In one group, each child was given a trinket for completing five consecutive responses (a CRF schedule); the second group was given the same number of reinforcers for five randomly selected responses out of a series of twenty-five trials (a VR schedule). During the extinction phase, when no trinkets were provided, the children trained on the CRF schedule responded far less frequently than those exposed to the partial schedule (see Figure 6–3).

Interestingly, such findings suggest that continuous reinforcement during childhood may have potentially dangerous implications for behavior during adulthood. According to Lundin (1961), for example:

> ... we find that those who break down easily or are readily set to aggression were as children too often *regularly* reinforced. Every demand was granted by their acquiescent parents. In youth they may have been so sheltered that failure was unknown to them. As a result these children have never built up a stability of response which would enable them to undergo periods of extinction and still maintain stable activity. The poor resistance to extinction is exemplified in their low frustration tolerance. As adults they are still operating like the rat who was reinforced on a regular schedule. [P. 82]

FIGURE 6–3
Mean number of responses (cumulative) during the extinction period in Bijou's experiment. Adapted from S. W. Bijou, Patterns of reinforcement and resistance to extinction in young children. **Child Development,** 1957, 28, 47–54. Copyright 1957 by the Society for Research in Child Development, Inc. Reproduced by permission.

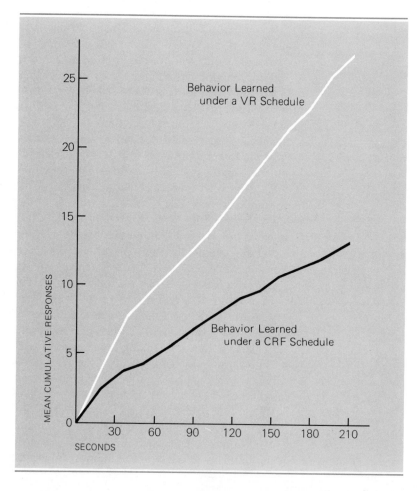

But there is also the other side of the coin. Variable schedules, by virtue of their ability to produce both high rates of responding and considerable resistance to extinction, are probably responsible for many inappropriate but persistent behavior patterns. A child may begin by requesting a cookie from his or her mother, a request that she turns down the first time. But the youngster has been reinforced for such behavior in the past and persists, perhaps speaking more loudly and generally annoying the mother. If the weary parent now gives in, and continues to do so from time to time on future occasions when nagging becomes intolerable, she has begun to build a durable behavior pattern that may survive even staunch efforts to become more firm. At best it will take a long time to extinguish such harassment; at worst, quite tyrannical behavior may become permanently established.

Contrast Effects.   Schedule differences are not the only patterning effects that influence reinforcement effectiveness. Another type of patterning has to do with the contrast between the consequence administered for correct responses and the consequence (or lack of consequences) that other responses produce. For example, in naturalistic situations one response will often be either rewarded or punished, while an alternative will produce no overt consequence. In these situations children do not respond to nonreaction as if it were neutral, but rather respond as if the nonreaction were the "opposite" of the consequence that they received. Thus children who experience reinforcement paired with nonreaction respond as if the nonreaction were a punishment, whereas children who experience punishment combined with nonreaction respond as if the nonreaction were a reinforcement (Spence, 1970). A parent who always praises good performance can punish with silence.

Even broader contrast effects have been noted. In one study (Waite and Osborne, 1972) elementary school children were reinforced on two schedules and then one of the schedules was put on extinction. In addition to the predictable decrease in responding to the extinguished schedule, the subjects were observed to be responding more under the unchanged remaining schedule. Such a result is consistent with an earlier study in which children who failed on one task returned to another task on which they had been previously successful more frequently than those children who had not recently failed (Liebert, 1966).

Another kind of contrast underlies the so-called *deprivation effect*, in which a reinforcer is more effective when the individual has been deprived of it for some time in the past. Most material reinforcers, such as food and money, are more effective if we have not been exposed to them for a while and less effective if we have recently been satisfied (Reynolds, 1968). But what about nontangible, social reinforcers? Are they, too, subject to deprivation and satiation effects? This question has provoked a continuing debate in developmental psychology (Eisenberger, 1970). The general result of research to date seems to be that social reinforcement shows deprivation and satiation effects only when social approval is irrelevant to the task at hand. When praise and other social reinforcement have a clear informative function, they will often not show a satiation effect (Perry and Garrow, 1975). When a child is learning to ride a bicycle, for instance, general verbal

encouragement (saying, "You're doing fine") fades in its effectiveness. But specific information feedback ("Good, your peddling is getting smoother") will often maintain effect even with repeated use.

The Premack Principle. David Premack (1965) added a new dimension to our thinking about operant conditioning by hypothesizing and then demonstrating that access to activities can serve as a powerful consequence for changing the likelihood that other activities will be performed. Formally the Premack principle states that given any two activities of differing values for an individual, performance of the less valued activity can be reinforced if access to the more valued activity is provided. In a well-known application of the Premack principle, Homme and his associates (Homme, C' de Baca, Devine, Steinhorst and Rickert, 1963) modified the behavior of a class of preschool children who appeared to prefer running and screaming to the classroom activities that their teachers had designed for them. The children were permitted to "earn" periods in which they could run and scream as much as they pleased by first working quietly for a period of time. These investigators succeeded in teaching the youngsters to work quietly.

In addition to reinforcing valued behavior, the Premack principle also provides a hint as to how to use activity contingencies to discourage undesirable behavior. Many forms of misbehavior can be eliminated by applying the contingency of a relevant low-value activity. For example, a child who makes a mess can be obliged to straighten it up; often this contingency alone will encourage a greater degree of neatness.

So far we have emphasized positive reinforcement, or the presentation of desired stimuli (i.e., rewards). This can be contrasted with negative reinforcement, which, it will be recalled, involves the termination of an unpleasant stimulus as the reinforcement for a particular response. *Escape* learning and *avoidance* learning reflect the two broad types of negative reinforcement.

In escape learning the individual first experiences a noxious stimulation and then terminates it by making an appropriate response. Avoidance learning involves emitting a response that completely forestalls the negative stimulation so that it is not experienced at all. There are several important functional differences between escape and avoidance learning, which have considerable significance for understanding the effects of negative reinforcement in childhood and throughout the life span.

Escape responses are highly sensitive to changes in environmental contingencies. Children whose experience suggests that they can terminate physical punishment by starting to cry (perhaps signaling parents that they have been hurt enough) will quickly shift to other escape efforts if the crying is unsuccessful in terminating the ongoing disciplinary action. Avoidance responses, on the other hand, can be remarkably impervious to changes in environmental contingencies because often the individual will not learn that he or she is no longer threatened by noxious stimulation. For example, a person who drives to work daily learns through experience that a particular street is studded with large potholes. The person then chooses an alternate path, but may persist in avoiding the damaged roads long after they have been repaired. Simply put, in the avoidance situation the individual avoids not only noxious stimulation, but also avoids any information that might reveal that the noxious stimulation has been removed from the situation entirely. As we shall see later, much of the child's training in the moral sphere involves avoidance learning.

Punishment obviously plays an important role in the practices of many parents. According to one survey, virtually all parents (98 percent) used it at least occasionally (Sears, Maccoby, and Levin, 1957). Whereas reinforcement is most effective in building new patterns of behavior, the effects of punishment are primarily *suppressive;* when punishment "works," it reduces the likelihood of certain noxious or potentially dangerous responses. In this section we shall focus upon what is known concerning the circumstances under which punishment is most and least likely to be an effective means of inhibiting unacceptable behavior by children.

The Timing of Punishment. Perhaps no factor is more important in the naturalistic use of punishment, particularly with the young child, than its timing, relative to an act of transgression. If a child acts in an extremely antisocial way, whether by hitting a younger sibling, stealing, lying, or committing an act of vandalism, some time inevitably will pass before the transgression is detected. Even after detection, an extended waiting period may be present before potential punishment, as in the familiar "Wait till your father comes home!" situation. It is therefore important to determine the relationship between the timing of punishment and its effectiveness.

As a general rule, mild punishment will be maximally effective if it occurs at the outset of a deviant act, or while the act is occurring, and will be much less effective if periods of considerable delay are introduced. There are many theoretical reasons that can explain why this is so, but most involve the following two points.

First, a transgression usually is an instrumental response, producing some positive outcome for the child. Taking forbidden candies or cookies provides the pleasure of eating these treats, and a temper tantrum in a department store may effectively intimidate one's mother into buying a five-dollar notebook. These outcomes are reinforcers for the child, and the longer they are held or savored, the more likely they are to "balance out" the unpleasant experience of punishment.

Second, very late punishment may be confusing in its purpose, at least for very young children. A young boy who seriously breaks some rule subsequently may try to "be good all day" (perhaps to forestall punishment). If he is then punished in the evening for the morning's transgression, the parents have created a situation in which aversive consequences follow some very desirable behavior which they would ordinarily wish to encourage and reinforce.

Effects of Punishment as a Function of its Intensity.   Another factor that plays an important role in the effectiveness of punishment is its intensity. Research with laboratory animals has shown consistently that very mild levels of punishment usually do *not* permanently eliminate responses; however, moderate punishments often tend to suppress the behaviors that they follow and quite intense punishments are very effective in completely eliminating certain kinds of well-practiced responses (Solomon, 1964).

Although ethical considerations obviously preclude using very intense punishments with human subjects, a few carefully designed studies with children have varied the intensity of a punishing noise (e.g., Parke, 1969, 1970). These investigations clearly mesh both with other laboratory studies and with certain naturalistic investigations: ". . . the overall findings from field and laboratory studies generally support the expectation that high-intensity physical punishment in most circumstances more effectively inhibits the punished behavior than does punishment that is less intense" (Parke, 1970, p. 86).

One particularly striking finding is the manner in which the intensity and timing of punishment interact. Parke (1970) has presented evidence to show that late punishment is less effective than early punishment *only* when the punishment is relatively mild, but that children are quite responsive to late punishments of high intensity. This relationship is shown in Figure 6–5.

The Adult-Child Relationship.   The effectiveness of a particular punishment will depend on many other factors. For example, research (Aronfreed,

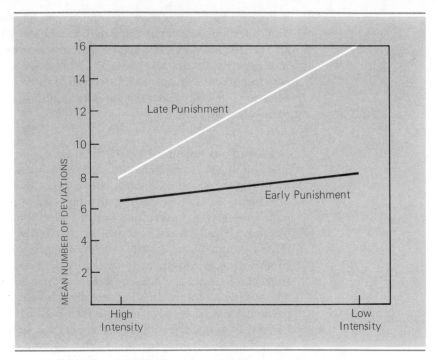

FIGURE 6-5
The relationship of intensity and timing of punishment.
Adapted from R. D. Parke, The role of punishment on the socialization process. In R. A. Hoppe, G. A. Milton, and E. C. Simmel, eds., **Early Experiences and the Process of Socialization** (New York: Academic Press, 1970). By permission of the author and Academic Press.

1968; Parke, 1967; Whiting, 1954) suggests that punishment from an adult who is usually rewarding and nurturing to the child is likely to be more effective than the same punishment from one who is usually cold and distant. What is more, explaining the reason for punishment increases its effectiveness (Parke, 1969). Certain types of consistency also are critical; adults who practice what they preach are likely to be more effective in their reprimands than those who do not (Mischel and Liebert, 1966). On the other hand, the parent who follows punishment with a display of affection toward the errant child may counteract the impact of the punishment and will probably strengthen the undesirable response (Parke, 1970).

All of these findings, along with those mentioned above, provide clues as to how caretakers can maximize the effects of punishment. An additional point is worth mentioning here. In most instances when punishment is used, it is desirable that the child learn another response to substitute for the punished one. For example, if a child is consistently fighting with peers, it might be desirable if the fighting were reduced and cooperation were substituted. The optimal way of achieving this would be to punish aggression and simultaneously reinforce cooperation.

Side Effects of Positive Punishment.   Positive punishment, the presentation of an unpleasant or noxious stimulus or experience, can have four possible side effects: pain-elicited aggression by the subject, avoidance of punishing agent, emotional behavior, and application of the punishment to others by the subject (Whitehurst and Vasta, 1977). For example, aggressive delinquent adolescents tend to be individuals who were themselves subject to physical punishment as children (Bandura and Walters, 1959). Such side effects need not occur, however, if punishment is employed judiciously and in combination with positive reinforcement for alternative activities. Parents and other socializing agents who administer a generous reward for one behavior but express a willingness to punish another behavior are often seen as fair rather than cruel.

Negative Punishment.   Negative punishment, the removal of some desirable stimulus or experience, is of particular interest because it appears to avoid various ethical and moral issues that positive punishment often raises.

There are two types of negative punishment: time-out and response-cost. *Time-out* is an abbreviated way of saying "time-out from positive reinforcement," and has been shown to be effective in a variety of settings (Sherman and Bushell, 1975). For example, in one study (Wahler, 1969) parents were able to dramatically reduce the oppositional behavior of their elementary school-age boys by isolating them in their bedrooms for five minutes (time-out) for each instance of such behavior they displayed. (Oppositional responses might include such behaviors as refusing to do one's homework or fighting with parents about their selection of a television program chosen for family viewing.) Whereas time-out removes the opportunity to continue the oppositional behavior, *response-cost* removes some tangible reinforcer already in the subject's possession or one that would otherwise be due to the subject. Fines are one of the most obvious examples of response-cost applications.

Response-cost and time-out techniques have been shown to be clearly effective when the loss to the individual being punished is substantial enough to outweigh the reinforcers associated with the response to be eliminated. Plainly, however, imposing a small fine on those who are caught engaging in some intrinsically rewarding activity (or, of course, in an activity that produces much extrinsic reinforcement) is hardly likely to be effective. As with positive punishment, the effectiveness of negative punishment increases as the punishment becomes more severe (Burchard and Barrera, 1972).

OBSERVATIONAL LEARNING

Observational learning, as the name implies, refers to learning that occurs through exposure to the behavior of others, the others being presented either live or symbolically in literature, films, television, and the like. Its importance in human affairs was recognized even in ancient times; more than two thousand years ago Aristotle wrote that "man is the most imitative of living creatures, and through imitation learns his earliest lessons."

Developmental Trends

Early roots of observational learning can be detected in the vocal and gestural imitations displayed by human infants, a phenomenon so pervasive as to suggest that certain types of copying may indeed be considered a form of prepared learning in humans.

The extent of early imitation, of course, is limited by various biological developments and acquired skills. Thus almost all infants will imitate an adult's cooing sound by age three months, but it is not until the child is twenty-four months old that he or she can be relied upon to be able to imitate new words. The reason is clear enough: The perceptual, cognitive, and motor development of the three-month-old simply does not permit the more complicated form to be imitated (Uzgiris, 1972).

The Many Faces of Observational Learning

Observational learning encompasses a surprisingly large range of phenomena. Most simply, even certain kinds of stimulus control seem to be acquired without the occurrence of any visible response and thus can be thought of as a rudimentary form of observational learning rather than as operant conditioning in the sense of response followed by reinforcement or punishment. An early study provides a good illustration of the process. Longstreth (1962) had preschool children stand in front of an apparatus that alternately flashed red and blue lights and also dispensed candy. Each child observed that candy was dispensed when one of the lights came on, but not when the other came on. The children did not have to do anything to get the candy and thus the only reinforcement that they received during the acquisition phase was not contingent on any response. Then, during a testing phase, Longstreth instructed the subjects to stand a few feet from the device and to go to it whenever one of the lights came on. The children ran much more quickly to the machine when the light that had been paired with reward came on than when the other light came on.

FIGURE 6–6
Children learn both specific skills and more general role behaviors through observing adults.
Nancy Hays,
Monkmeyer Press
Photo Service.

Miller and Dollard's Analysis.   Neal Miller and John Dollard were among the first to seriously discuss the developmental implications of observational learning in their book *Social Learning and Imitation* (1941).

These writers emphasized the importance of imitation in everyday life, saying that "the young, the stupid, the subordinate, and the unskilled must depend on the older, the brighter, the superordinate, and the skilled . . ." (1941, p. 97). Furthermore, they assumed that imitativeness, like the desire for money, prestige, and the companionship of others, must be acquired as a joint function of the operation of instrumental learning and the presence of social conditions that foster its development and maintenance. They noted that "if matching or doing the same as others do, is regularly rewarded, a secondary tendency to match may be developed . . ." (1941, p. 10). Many years later Donald Baer, James Sherman, and their associates continued to investigate how imitativeness is learned, focusing on the generalized tendency to imitate others (e.g., Baer & Sherman, 1964).

Social Learning and Modeling

So far in this discussion the emphasis has been placed on the manner in which imitation as a *mode of responding* is acquired and maintained. In the remainder of this section we will consider observational learning within the framework of social learning, including the kinds of behaviors that can be learned and the complex subprocesses that are involved. The investigator most widely recognized in this area is Albert Bandura, who, along with a host of associates, has given us innumerable studies showing that children learn about many behaviors—aggression, sharing, social interaction, delay of gratification, cooperation—by watching others perform them. Bandura also has provided valuable analyses of observational learning as a basic process.

In one well-known experiment dealing with aggression, Bandura (1965) presented a view of observational learning in which the learning or *acquisition* of the modeled acts is distinguished from the *performance* of the modeled acts. The study also demonstrated the importance of *vicarious consequences*—i.e., outcomes that the observer sees accrue to the model for the behavior. When these outcomes are positive, they are called *vicarious reward*; negative outcomes are called *vicarious punishment*. In Bandura's experiment, modeling and vicarious consequences were provided by showing nursery school children a remarkable five-minute film on the screen of a television console:

> The film began with a scene in which a model walked up to an adult-size plastic Bobo doll and ordered him to clear the way. After glaring for a moment at the noncompliant antagonist the model exhibited four novel aggressive responses each accompanied by a distinctive verbalization.
>
> First, the model laid the Bobo doll on its side, sat on it, and punched it in the nose while remarking, "Pow, right in the nose, boom, boom." The model then raised the doll and pommeled it on the head with a mallet. Each response was accompanied by the verbalization, "Sockeroo . . . stay down." Following the mallet aggression, the model kicked the doll about the room, and these responses were interspersed with the comment, "Fly away." Finally, the model threw rubber balls at the Bobo doll, each strike punctuated with "Bang." This

sequence of physically and verbally aggressive behavior was repeated twice. [Bandura, 1965, pp. 590–591]

The independent variable manipulated in this study involved the consequences the model received. One group of children saw, in addition to the film segment described above, a final scene in which the model was rewarded generously for assaults upon the clown. Specifically:

> For children in the *model-rewarded* condition, a second adult appeared with an abundant supply of candies and soft drinks. He informed the model that he was a "strong champion" and that his superb aggressive performance clearly deserved a generous treat. He then poured him a large glass of 7-Up, and readily supplied additional energy-building nourishment including chocolate bars, Cracker Jack popcorn, and an assortment of candies. While the model was rapidly consuming the delectable treats, his admirer symbolically reinstated the modeled aggressive responses and engaged in considerable positive social reinforcement. [P. 591, italics added]

A second group of children watched the film end with a final scene in which the model received punishment for his aggressive behavior. For children in this group

> ... the reinforcing agent appeared on the scene shaking his finger menacingly and commenting reprovingly, "Hey there, you big bully. You quit picking on that clown. I won't tolerate it." As the model drew back he tripped and fell, the other adult sat on the model and spanked him with a rolled-up magazine while reminding him of his aggressive behavior. As the model ran off cowering, the agent forewarned him, "If I catch you doing that again, you big bully, I'll give you a hard spanking. You quit acting that way." [P. 591]

A final group that served as a control group also saw the film, but without any final scene.

Thereafter, all children were brought individually into an experimental room that contained a plastic Bobo doll, three balls, a mallet, a pegboard, plastic farm animals, and a dollhouse equipped with furniture and a miniature doll family. This wide array of toys was provided so that the child would be able to engage either in imitative aggressive responses—i.e., the model's responses—or in alternative nonaggressive and nonimitative forms of behavior. Each child was left alone with this assortment of toys for ten minutes while his or her behavior was periodically recorded by judges who watched from behind a one-way vision screen. The frequency of imitative aggressive behavior in this situation constituted the *performance* measure of the study. Not surprisingly, it was found that children who saw the model punished exhibited far fewer imitative aggressive responses than did those in either of the other two groups. But—and this is the major point of Bandura's analysis—it would be inappropriate to conclude that because the children in this group did not spontaneously imitate, they had learned nothing.

To demonstrate that learning had occurred in all groups, irrespective of whether it was spontaneously revealed in performance, the experimenter reentered the room well-supplied with incentives (colored sticker pictures, sweet fruit juices in an attractive dispenser, and so on) and told the child that, for each act of imitative aggression that he or she could reproduce, an additional juice treat and sticker would be given. The youngster's ability to reproduce the model's behavior in this situation (i.e., when asked to display what he or she had learned) constituted the *acquisition* measure. The results provided direct support for distinguishing between two separate aspects of imitative learning, acquisition and performance. As expected, when incentives were specifically offered for demonstrating acquisition of the models' acts, the effects of punishment were wiped out, with all groups showing the same very high level of learning.

This work, as well as a number of successful replications that have followed (e.g., Liebert and Fernandez, 1970; Liebert, Sobol, and Copemann, 1972), has practical implications. Consider, for example, popular television shows or motion pictures that display to children the intricate details and planning required for the execution of remarkable acts of larceny or homicide. Widespread showing of such "adventure" is often justified by the fact that the performers of such felonious acts are inevitably punished. However, even though witnessing punished crimes may be unlikely to lead to spontaneous imitation, Bandura's work shows that punishment does not impede the learning of them; later they may be reproduced in "real life," should the environmental contingencies favor their occurrence.

The Forms and Sequence of Observational Learning

Just as respondent and operant conditioning show generalization (i.e., they extend beyond the situation in which learning originally occurred), observational learning involves more than the recall and exact reproduction of a model's responses. To understand these additional processes, we must distinguish between direct imitative effects and inhibition-disinhibition.

Direct Imitative Effects. We have seen that exposure to a model can lead to relatively exact duplication of the exemplary behavior, either immediately or when the environmental conditions are made conducive; this is *direct imitation*. Observing another's behavior also can *reduce* the probability of matching. The child who sees a peer burned by a hot stove, for example, typically will become *less* likely to touch the dangerous appliance than previously: The exemplar's actions and its consequences are accepted as a guide for what should not be done. Such an outcome may be thought of as *direct counterimitation*.

Inhibitory and Disinhibitory Effects. Observational learning may also apply to actions that fall into the same general class as those observed, but which are different in virtually all particulars. Youngsters who watch a movie filled with shooting and brawling, for example, may become more likely to yell at or push a younger sibling than if they had not seen exemplary hostilities. In such a case we note that aggressive responses in general have increased or been *disinhibited.* Similarly, a child who, on the first day of class, sees that the new teacher punishes a classmate for disrupting the lesson may subsequently be less likely to turn in homework assignments late. Failing to turn in homework and speaking out inappropriately in class, though far from identical, fall into a common category of behavior—disobedience to the dictates of the teacher—and thus the second child's general *inhibition* regarding breaking the rules may be traced to the first child's disruption of the class and the vicarious punishment that followed.

As outlined above, observational learning is a complex process that involves three steps: *exposure* to the responses of others, *acquisition* of what one has seen, and subsequent *acceptance* of the modeled acts as a guide for one's own behavior (Liebert, 1972; Liebert and Poulos, 1975). This sequence is presented in Figure 6–7.

This conceptualization of observational learning is actually very different from that posited by traditional learning theorists, who sought to explain learning (both classical and instrumental) in terms of the association of stimuli and responses. Strict S–R theorists view the child as a more or less passive responder, whereas the foregoing social learning formulation emphasizes cognitive processes—attention, memory, and problem solving—

FIGURE 6–7
The three stages of observational learning.

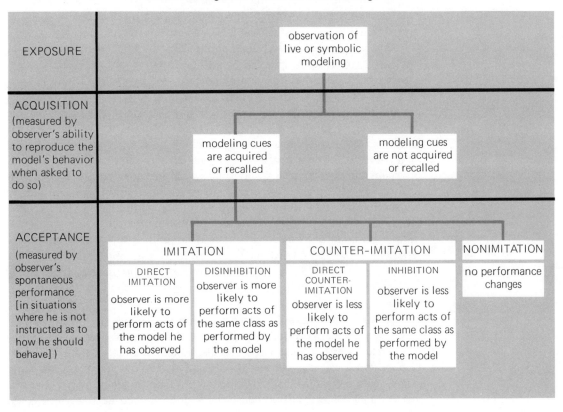

all of which are at least partially instigated by the observer. The remaining portion of his chapter discusses complex processes in learning and sets the stage for chapter 7, where these cognitive processes are explained more fully.

COMPLEX PROCESSES IN LEARNING

Learning to Learn

Finding the solution required by a new problem situation is one important kind of complex learning. Historically, two types of approaches to problem solving have been recognized: trial and error, and insight. Trial and error, as we have already seen, was first experimentally studied by Thorndike, who placed his subjects (chicks, dogs, and cats) into a box from which they could escape to obtain food only by performing a specific response. According to his observations, reasoning was not involved. But the trying out of behaviors, more or less randomly, or accidentally stumbling on correct solutions is not typical for humans, although it may be found in the very inexperienced. Most instances of trial and error involve some selection of particular acts that have been successful in the past (Berlyne, 1970).

Long ago, Wolfgang Köhler suggested that organisms come to solve problems by discovering relations or principles inherent in the situation. Such apparently insightful behavior was demonstrated in Köhler's studies of apes who were given food placed just beyond their reach. At some point the animals suddenly appeared to realize the solution—using a stick to pull the food toward them. Insight involved, then, an internal restructuring of the situation in terms of the relations of its aspects to each other.

As it turns out, trial and error and insight are not as distinguishable as they once appeared. Insight can be interpreted as the result of previous experiences in somewhat different situations. One psychologist who has applied this perspective is Harry F. Harlow.

Harlow's work began with simple discrimination problems, employing both young children and monkeys (Harlow and Harlow, 1949). For example, in the simplest experiment, monkeys were shown two objects that had been placed on a board. The objects always had some distinctive dimension, such as color (e.g., one black and the other white). The experimenter predetermined the "correct" attribute, and if the animal touched the object that possessed it, a reward—a peanut or a raisin—was found underneath. The test apparatus (Figure 6–8) allowed for the consecutive presentation of different pairs of black versus white objects that varied unsystematically on other dimensions (such as form and object position). The number of pairs that had to be presented before the monkey consistently chose the object of each pair that had the correct attribute was the measure of learning.

Initially, the monkeys learned the correct response by a "fumble and find" process that required them to view many pairs of objects. The problem could always be solved in two trials, though. If black was the correct attribute and black was chosen and rewarded on Trial 1, the animal could "stay" with the choice black from then on. If, on the other hand, white was correct and the animal first chose black and received no reward, it could

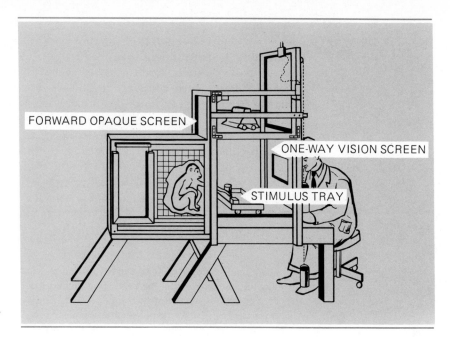

FIGURE 6–8
The Wisconsin General Test Apparatus used by Harlow for· discrimination-learning tasks.
Adapted from Harlow, 1949.

shift to white on Trial 2, receive a reward, and then "stay" with white on all subsequent trials. However, this rapid solving by a "win-stay, lose-shift" strategy is possible only if the animal has "insight" into the solution. Harlow found that with experience the monkeys did indeed gain such insight (Harlow, 1949). As indicated in Figure 6–9, the greater the number of problems presented, the more rapidly the monkeys solved them.

Research with children showed essentially the same phenomenon, although learning occurred more rapidly. The youngsters made many errors at the beginning, usually of the same type as those made by the monkeys, but they gradually came to solve the class of problems—for example, by al-

FIGURE 6–9
Percentage of correct responses occurring rapidly (on Trials 1–6) according to the number of discrimination problems presented to monkeys. The more experience the animals had in solving the problems, the more rapidly they solved them.
Adapted from Harlow, 1949.

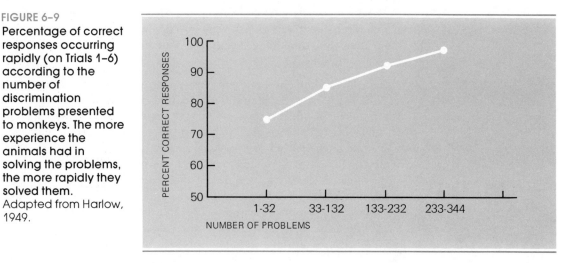

ways picking the white object—in a single trial. This progressive learning about common features of problems has been called "learning to learn."

Further evidence that a true organizational habit has been established comes from research in which the relevant attribute is suddenly reversed; that is, the previously incorrect attribute is now rewarded, while the one that had been correct no longer leads to reward. Such switchovers, called *reversal shifts*, lead to many errors initially, but after extensive experience, learning occurs. We see, after training, perfect performance immediately following the first reversal trial, which is retained for long periods of time. When problems that took weeks to master are reintroduced after a whole year without practice, monkeys will return to top efficiency after a few hours of practice—and sometimes after only a few minutes.

What are the implications of these findings? In a classic description, Harlow and Harlow (1949) first put it this way:

> Suppose we picture mental activity as a continuous structure built up, step by step, by the solution of increasingly difficult problems, from the simplest problem in learning to the most complex one in thinking. At each level the individual tries out various responses to solve each given task. At the lowest level he selects from unlearned responses or previously learned habits. As his experience increases, habits that do not help in the solution drop out and useful habits become established. After solving many problems of a certain kind, he develops organized patterns of responses that meet the demands of this type of situation. These patterns, or learning sets, can also be applied to the solution of still more complex problems. Eventually the individual may organize simple sets into more complex patterns or learning sets, which in turn are available for transfer as units to new situations. . . . At the highest level in this progression, the intelligent human adult selects from innumerable, previously acquired learning sets the raw material for thinking. His many years of education in school and outside have been devoted to building up these complex learning sets, and he comes to manipulate them with such ease that he and his observers may lose sight of their origin and development. [P. 5]

Although it is apparent that learning sets are acquired and used, even by young children, we must still ask what psychological processes underlie or facilitate their formation. One answer lies in mediation.

Mediation and Discrimination

A *mediator* is some internal event intervening between a stimulus and an overt response. The initial stimulus results in a mediator that, in turn, acts as a stimulus for the final response. Thus the sequence $S-M_s-R$ replaces the strict behaviorist sequence $S-R$. It is possible, too, that several mediators may be linked together before the final response is made.

Tracy and Howard Kendler were among the first to focus on the role of *verbal mediation* in learning, postulating that the intervening response involves the use of covert language (Kendler and Kendler, 1962; Kendler, 1963, 1974). To demonstrate the utility of this approach, the Kendlers tested children in a discrimination-learning task. First, pairs of stimuli that differed on two dimensions were presented. Rewarded each time that they

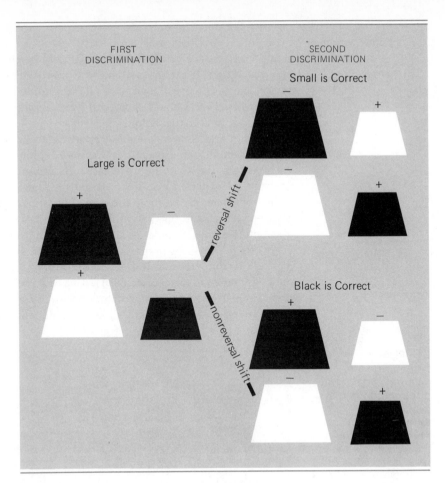

FIRST DISCRIMINATION

SECOND DISCRIMINATION

Small is Correct

Large is Correct

reversal shift

Black is Correct

nonreversal shift

FIGURE 6-10
Examples of a reversal and a nonreversal shift, where (+) indicates the rewarded and (–) the nonrewarded stimuli. Adapted from H. H. Kendler and T. S. Kendler, Vertical and horizontal processes in problem-solving. **Psychological Review**, 1962, 69 1–16. Copyright 1962 by the American Psychological Association. Reproduced by permission.

responded to one attribute of one of the dimensions, children learned the solution to the problem. For example, a child was shown two cups. One was black and the other white (color dimension); one—sometimes the black cup, sometimes the white—was large and the other small (size dimension). Each time the large cup was selected, regardless of whether it was black or white, a reward was received; selecting the small cup never led to reward during training. Thus the child learned that size was the relevant dimension, with large the correct attribute.

Nonreversals should be learned more easily than reversals because it should be easier to strengthen a response that has already been rewarded. An example of a nonreversal shift would be if we changed the correct choice from the large cup to the *black* cup; the subject will have been re-warded already for picking the black stimulus on half of his or her previous trials (when the correct choice was large and black). On the other hand, if the large cup has been the correct choice and we then shift it to the *small* cup, we have made a reversal shift. The subject will *never* have been re-warded before for picking the small cup. From this we can theorize that a nonreversal shift is more easily learned. But the mediational hypothesis predicts the opposite outcome—that reversals are more easily learned. The mediator in reversals must shift only within a dimension (from large to small), not across a dimension (from large to black) as in nonreversals (see Figure 6–10, p. 179). Thus learners who approach the problem by implicitly saying "large is correct" will have an easier time realizing that things have been reversed (now small is correct) than learners who never thought that large was correct in the first place.

Kendler and Kendler found support for this conceptualization: Human adults accomplished a reversal shift more rapidly than a nonreversal shift, whereas rats dealt with nonreversal shifts more easily than with reversals, as would be expected by strict S–R theory. These findings posed the interesting problem of locating the transition point from simple stimulus-response learning to mediation. In an experiment designed to explore this question (Kendler, Kendler, and Learnard, 1962), children from three to ten years of age showed a progressive change in their problem solving that indicated that 50 percent of those between four and six years of age were employing mediation (see Figure 6–11). It has also been shown that when children are instructed to use mediators during discrimination shift problems, the younger ones perform more like the older children. Being instructed to

FIGURE 6-11
Percentage of children of different ages responding in a mediational manner. Adapted from H. H. Kendler and T. S. Kendler, Vertical and horizontal processes in problem-solving. **Psychological Review,** 1962, 69, 1–16. Copyright 1962 by the American Psychological Association. Reproduced by permission.

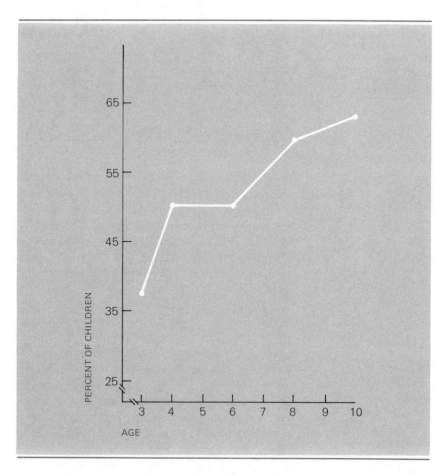

label apparently helps nonmediators adopt a mediational mode. Similar results have been demonstrated in a very different process—that of memory. Memory will be explored in chapter 7.

Hypothesis Testing

According to investigator Marvin Levine (1974; Phillips and Levine, 1975), when individuals are presented with a discrimination task, they begin with a hypothesis about what attribute is correct and they choose the object that displays the attribute that their initial hypothesis calls for. If they subsequently find out that they have chosen an incorrect attribute, they switch to another hypothesis. In this manner, by eliminating incorrect selections, people attempt to solve the problem in some systematic way.

Levine and his associates examined hypothesis testing by presenting stimuli in pairs, shown in Figure 6–12, that involved four dimensions, each with two attributes: letter (T or X), size (large or small), color (black or white), and bar (bar up or bar down). Within the procedure, the person views the paired stimuli presented on Trial 1, selects one or the other of the pair based on the hypothesis held, and is told "right" or "wrong" by the experimenter. Then Trial 2 is presented, one of the pair is chosen, and so on.

It is obvious that being told "right" or "wrong" applies to more than one dimension. If the individual holds the hypothesis *bar up* on Trial 1, he or she will choose the left-hand stimulus. But the feedback "right" means that *T* or *large* or *black* or *bar up* could be the solution. (If the right-hand stimulus was selected, the feedback "wrong" would provide the same information indirectly.) How does the person eliminate all the wrong choices to come up with the one correct answer? Table 6–2 explains four problem-solving strategies that are used. Focusing is the most efficient method because it re-

FIGURE 6–12
An example of the stimulus pairs presented in Levine's hypothesis-testing procedure. If the most efficient strategy, focusing, is used, the problem can be solved in four trials. For example, assume T is the correct answer. Ask someone (or try yourself) to choose one of the pairs on Trial 1. Give them appropriate feedback—"right" whenever the pair with T is selected, "wrong" when the T is not selected. After the first trial, the person should logically know that the answer must be either large, black, T, or bar-up because these were the four features of the right response (small, white, X, and bar-down can be eliminated because they were features of the wrong response). On Trial 2, large and black will be incorrect, leaving only T and bar-up as possible, correct answers. On Trial 3, bar-up will be wrong, leaving T as the correct solution. Want to try again? Choose any of the eight dimensions as the correct solution and start over.

STIMULI PRESENTED

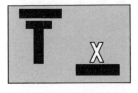   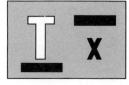

| TRIAL 1 | TRIAL 2 | TRIAL 3 | TRIAL 4 |

TABLE 6-2
Some Possible Ways of Trying to Solve Complex Discrimination Tasks, in Decreasing Order of Efficiency

Focusing	Individual logically eliminates all disconfirmed attributes.
Dimension Checking	Individual systematically checks all four dimensions, one dimension at a time.
Hypothesis Checking	Individual systematically checks all eight attributes, one at a time.
Stimulus Preference	Individual repeatedly selects one attribute even after being told it is incorrect.

Source: Adapted from Levine, 1974.

quires only four responses (see caption for Figure 6–12 for an example of focusing). The other strategies are less efficient. For example, in dimension checking a person investigates only one dimension at a time, such as size.

In order to learn more about this area, Levine devised a method to compare the hypothesis testing behavior of individuals of different ages. In initial experiments, second-, fourth-, and sixth-graders and college students participated (Gholson, Levine, and Phillips, 1972). Figure 6–13 shows the frequency with which different age groups used the four problem-solving strategies: focusing, dimension checking, hypothesis checking, and stimulus preference, in order of efficiency (see Table 6–2). The first three strategies can lead to the solution whereas stimulus preference does not (unless the one choice just happens to be correct). In fact, stimulus preference—choos-

FIGURE 6–13
The frequency with which different age groups used four methods to solve the problems. The methods are ordered from the most to the least efficient, with the latter being a stereotyped behavior. From Levine, 1974.

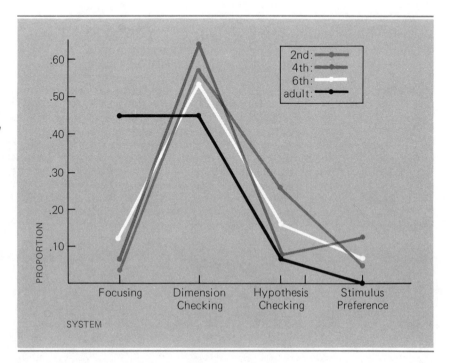

ing the same attribute repeatedly even after it has been identified as in-correct—is considered a primitive stereotypical behavior. Note, however, that all the children most frequently used the second most efficient strategy, whereas adults used their focusing and dimension checking equally as often.

A later experiment, involving second-graders and kindergartners, dem-onstrated an even more interesting developmental difference. Here the re-sults for second-graders were essentially the same, except that there was slightly more stimulus preference and a small amount of position alterna-tion and position preference. The latter two strategies, like stimulus pref-erence, are stereotypical behaviors. In position alternation the individual al-ternately selects the stimulus on the right, then the left; in position preference, either right or left is the consistent basis for selection. These stereotyped choices are striking in their failure to solve the problems and in their insensitivity to feedback. Nevertheless, kindergartners over-whelmingly employed them in this situation (see Figure 6–14).

The difference found between kindergartners and second-graders in these and other studies (Gholson and Danziger, 1975; Weir, 1964) is fasci-nating because it is consistent with a general finding of dramatic change that occurs somewhere between the ages of five and seven years. We have already noted that, according to the Kendlers, children switch, for the most part, to a mediational framework by this time. The same has been found for a variety of other tasks.

Many researchers have attempted to explain this pattern, often pointing to the development of language and the commencing of formal education as of possible importance. According to an analysis by Sheldon White (1965),

FIGURE 6–14
The frequency with which second-graders and kindergartners used different methods in attempting to solve the problems. The methods are ordered from the most to the least efficient, with the latter three methods being stereotyped behaviors.   From Levine, 1974.

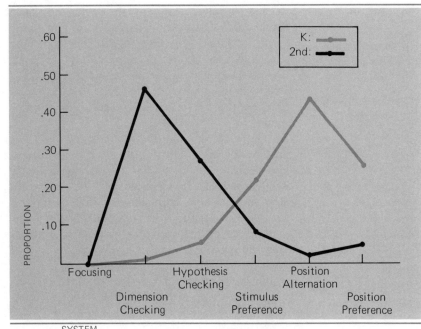

early learning, that which occurs before five years of age or so, is funda-mentally associative. Responses are connected to stimuli more or less directly, and learning is rapid. Between the ages of five and seven, White contends, a new mode emerges that involves coding stimuli and linking them together, even though they may have been separated by time and sit-uation. This "cognitive" mode, made possible primarily by verbal media-tion, can act to inhibit associative action and is itself reflective. In short, it is complex information processing.

SUMMARY

Learning refers to all processes by which an activity originates or is changed through reacting to an encountered situation. Learning always de-pends upon a degree of *readiness* in the individual as well as on a suitable environment and the degree to which we are biologically *prepared* as a spe-cies to learn certain things. Behaviorists view learning in stimulus-response terms, while cognitivists view it in terms of creating and manipulating in-ternal representations of experience. Four basic processes of learning are widely recognized: habituation, classical (or respondent) conditioning, oper-ant conditioning (or instrumental learning), and observational learning. All four processes of learning are displayed by infants, but changes occur with further development.

Habituation is a primitive learning response that is present at birth. It in-volves a simple discrimination between familiar and unfamiliar stimuli, with familiar stimuli no longer eliciting orienting or startle responses after repeated exposure. In *classical conditioning* the individual begins to make a response to situations that have *not* previously elicited the response. Pavlov first systematically investigated classical conditioning, showing how a response (CR) comes to be elicited by a previously neutral stimulus (CS) af-ter the stimulus has been paired with the unconditioned stimulus (UCS). Pavlov also discovered that generalization, discrimination, and extinction occur in classical conditioning. In generalization, stimuli similar to the CS elicit the conditioned response without any additional conditioning trials. Discrimination involves the response of individuals to stimuli that have been paired with a UCS, but not to stimuli that have not been so paired. Ex-tinction of a CR occurs when the CS is presented without the UCS many times.

Operant conditioning (instrumental learning) is based on Thorndike's orig-inal law of effect, which states that the consequences of an act determine the probability of its future occurrence. Four different types of con-sequences control our actions: positive and negative reinforcement and pos-itive and negative punishment. Reinforcement, positive or negative, in-creases the probability of an act, whereas punishment decreases it. Positive reinforcement involves the presentation of a desired stimulus, while nega-tive reinforcement involves the removal of an aversive or unpleasant stimu-lus. As in classical conditioning, extinction, generalization, and dis-crimination occur in operant conditioning. Extinction occurs when a response that once led to reinforcement no longer does so. Generalization of a learned instrumental response occurs when individuals exhibit a response in situations that are similar but not identical to the setting in which reinforcement occurred in the past. Discrimination means that individuals distinguish settings in which reinforcement was previously given. Reinforcement can be provided on a continuous or intermittent schedule; the former leads to rapid acquisition, but the latter results in learning that is more resistant to extinction and thus more easily maintained. Chaining and successive approximation are effective reinforcement procedures for building desirable behavior. Contrast effects, such as the deprivation effect, and Premack's principle, may influence the effectiveness of reinforcement by manipulating the context of its occurrence. The two types of negative reinforcement are escape and avoidance. They differ on whether or not the individual experiences some noxious stimulation that is then terminated or avoids the noxious stimulation altogether.

The effectiveness of punishment is influenced by its timing and intensity, as well as by the relationship between the learner and the punishing agent. The two major types of negative punishment are time-out and response-cost. Both can be quite effective in modifying behavior.

Observational learning is a function of viewing the behavior of others. Its possible effects consist of direct imitation and counter-imitation, as well as inhibition and disinhibition, both of which involve generalization. Observational learning occurs in three steps: exposure, acquisition, and acceptance. Any complete account of observational learning must involve the variables that influence these steps. Thus we must consider characteristics of the stimulus, observer, and model, including vicarious consequences—the consequences that accrue to the model as a result of his or her action. Inasmuch as this analysis also focuses on internal events, such as memory and coding, it moves away from the traditional S–R account into the realm of complex thinking processes.

In demonstrating the "learning to learn" phenomenon, Harlow provided a model for the way in which complex learning processes can be built on relatively simple learning experiences. Learning theorists such as the Kendlers have turned to the concept of mediation to explain discrimination learning. The original stimulus results in an internal label that, in turn, leads to the response.

Children use mediators early but their efficiency grows progressively. The ability to actually produce the mediators is critical. Research into hypothesis testing demonstrates growing sophistication in children's ability to process information to solve discrimination problems.

7 Cognitive Development

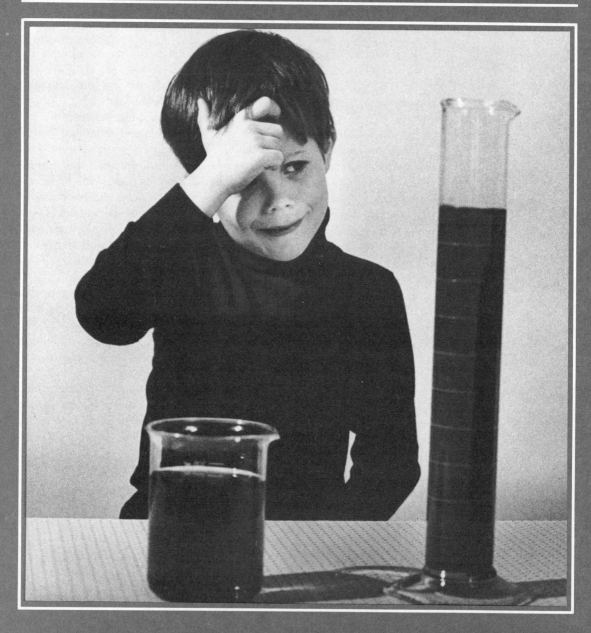

During the decades when most psychologists in the United States were following the strict behavioristic approach, relatively little was learned about the development of human thought, language, and intellectual functioning. Such processes, with the exception of speech per se, cannot be observed directly; accordingly, they were often rejected as inappropriate topics for research. In recent years, however, this has changed as psychologists have become more interested in cognitive processes. Spurred on by promising findings, developmental psychologists have made enormous progress over the past decade in understanding these processes. The focus of this chapter is on the fundamental questions that are now being asked—and answered—about the unfolding of the uniquely human ability to build complex representations of the world and to manipulate these representations so as to explain the past and draw conclusions about the future. This ability "to know" is the essence of cognition (Carroll, 1964). Thus the study of cognitive development covers quite a broad area.

There are two contemporary approaches to cognitive development. One is the information-processing approach, which has been greatly influenced by those cognitive psychologists who have tried to understand human thinking and reasoning by comparing the human mind to a sophisticated computer system that must acquire, process, store, and utilize information according to various programs. The other approach rests heavily on the work of Jean Piaget and emphasizes the biological and structural underpinnings of the development of thought and reasoning. In comparison to information-processing theorists, Piaget concentrates more heavily on the development of cognition, and is regarded as the foremost writer in this area. Therefore, we will begin with an indepth discussion of his theory.

PIAGET'S THEORY

The nature-nurture controversy is expressed in the study of cognitive development by the question: How much of developmental change stems from experience with the environment and how much stems from maturation guided by the blueprint of genetic inheritance? Piaget takes the position that both forces profoundly influence development, and this emphasis on the biological as well as the environmental origins of change is harmonious with his lifelong interest in the biological sciences. Piaget's first intellectual inquiries were in zoology, a branch of biology dealing with the animal kingdom, and his current psychological theory reflects sensitivity to the human species' position in that kingdom.

Adaptation

Adaptation is a central concept in the field of biology. To maintain a favorable interchange with their environments all animals must adjust to ecological change. Herds instinctively seek new grazing in a drought, while chameleons change color to conceal themselves from predators. Humans too have unique methods of adaptation. More than any other animal, we rely on the acquisition and use of higher mental processes as a means of adaptation. For Piaget, then, cognitive development is an extremely active

process. Knowledge and understanding are "built" by organizing and interpreting one's experiences according to the best of one's ability.

Assimilation and Accommodation.   Piaget sees the child's cognitive adaptation in terms of two basic processes, assimilation and accommodation. *Assimilation* is a process whereby the child interprets reality in terms of his or her internal model of the world constructed from previous knowledge. *Accommodation* is the complementary process of improving one's model of the world by adjusting it to external reality. Thus, as Flavell (1977) has noted, assimilation and accommodation are "two sides of the same cognitive coin" (p. 7). Here is an illustration of the role these two processes play in cognitive adaptation:*

> Suppose an infant of 4 months is presented with a rattle. He has never before had the opportunity to play with rattles or similar toys. The rattle, then, is a feature of the environment to which he needs to adapt. His subsequent behavior reveals the tendencies of assimilation and accommodation. The infant tries to grasp the rattle. In order to do this successfully he must accommodate in more ways than are immediately apparent. First, he must accommodate his visual activities to perceive the rattle correctly; then he must reach out and accommodate his movements to the distance between himself and the rattle; in grasping the rattle he must adjust his fingers to its shape; in lifting the rattle he must accommodate his muscular exertion to its weight. In sum, the grasping of the rattle involves a series of acts of accommodation, or modifications of the infant's behavioral structures to suit the demands of the environment.

*Ginsburg & Opper, *Piaget's Theory of Intellectual Development: An Introduction,* © 1969, p. 19. Reprinted by permission of Prentice-Hall, Inc., Englewood Cliffs, New Jersey.

Grasping the rattle also involves assimilation. In the past the infant has already grasped things; for him, grasping is a well-formed structure of behavior. When he sees the rattle for the first time he tries to deal with the novel object by incorporating it into a habitual pattern of behavior. In a sense he tries to transform the novel object into something that he is familiar with; namely, a thing to be grasped. We can say, therefore, that he assimilates the object into his framework.

Adaptation, then, is a basic tendency of the organism and consists of the two processes of assimilation and accommodation. How do the two relate to one another? First, it is clear that they are complementary processes. Assimilation involves the person's dealing with the environment in terms of his structures, while accommodation involves the transformation of his structures in response to the environment. Moreover, the processes are simultaneously present in every act. When the infant grasps the rattle his fingers accommodate to its shape; at the same time he is assimilating the rattle into his framework, the grasping structure. [Ginsburg and Opper, 1969, p. 19]

This example illustrates an infant's ability to adapt, but it should not be assumed that assimilation and accommodation are the devices only of the young. These processes continue throughout the life span of the individual. Piaget has offered in his notion of accommodation and assimilation "a description that holds true of any mind interacting with any environment in any given moment of time" (Flavell, 1977, p. 8).

Schemes.* Piaget has assigned the unique term, *schemes,* to describe the miniature models of the world that we build from birth. A scheme is the structure underlying a sequence of behaviors, such as grasping. Schemes differ in complexity, but even simple grasping organizes the actions of reaching, finger-curling, and drawing in. As the infant gains experience, it will learn to grasp in different ways—e.g., "for something far away," "for something nearby," "for something small," "for something large," and so on. The grasping scheme then becomes a kind of category or underlying strategy that subsumes a collection of distinct but similar action sequences.

The first schemes exhibited by the newborn infant are almost entirely reflexive and inborn. Thus the neonate exhibits a sucking scheme when almost anything comes into its mouth. All schemes give rise to organized behavior patterns and all schemes (even those that are innate) are subject to modification (i.e., adaptation) through the interplay of the individual with its environment.

The most important property of schemes in relation to cognitive development is that they can be combined to form larger units. As we shall see, the initial schemes of looking, listening, and grasping become woven together over the course of early cognitive development until the infant is able to execute an intelligent search procedure for a missing person or object. Schemes formed during early infancy either change or give way to increasingly sophisticated models of the world, which emerge in later life and

---

*In earlier editions we referred to a scheme as a *schema* and to schemes as *schemata.* Flavell (1977) has pointed out that these latter terms result from a mistranslation of the original French, in which Piaget used the word *schème.*

define the most advanced forms of human thought. But according to Piaget the child's changing way of viewing the world, his or her level of cognitive development, does not change in an entirely smooth or continuous fashion. Rather, Piaget feels that the emergence of intellectual sophistication and an adult view of the world involves four distinct periods of cognitive development:

1. Sensorimotor period (0 to 2 years)
2. Preoperational period (2 to 7 years)
3. Period of concrete operations (7 to 11 years)
4. Period of formal operations (11 through adulthood)

It is important to note, though, that the ages shown are only approximate averages and will vary considerably with the environment and background of the child. Despite these qualifications, the major periods identified in Piaget's theory serve as useful guidelines for describing the overall course of cognitive development.

The Sensorimotor Period (0 to 2 Years)

Though untutored by experience, the newborn infant is not completely helpless because he or she is born with inherited reflexes and a number of innate perceptual abilities (see chapter 4). During the first two years of life these inborn abilities will evolve so that the child is able to engage in increasingly flexible and planful actions.

Piaget casts the sensorimotor period into six substages. Like the larger periods described in Piagetian theory, the chronological ages associated with each substage are approximations. Nonetheless they aid in clarifying the stages.

The First Month of Life (Stage 1). During this stage the infant displays increasingly smooth and systematic use of its natural reflexes, engaging in what Piaget calls "reflex exercise." Developmental emphasis is thus on refinement of already existing ability and structure. For example, it appears that subtle but noticeable advances in the coordination of the sucking scheme occur during the first month of life (Flavell, 1963). Similar refinements can be observed in the infant's perceptual abilities. Within a few days after birth the neonate is able to visually track some moving objects, but the ability to track is uneven and objects are easily "lost." By the end of the first month visual tracking has improved noticeably (cf. Bronson, 1974).

The Second to the Fourth Month (Stage 2). The infant's response to external stimulation changes rapidly during this time, as a result of both physiological development and growing experience. For example, when a newborn is presented with a novel visual stimulus it will typically turn and fixate on the first edge that it sees; two-month-old infants, in contrast, will scan the stimulus in a more active effort to secure information (Salapatek, 1975).

Equally impressive perceptual development occurs in the infant's hearing. One-month-olds have difficulty localizing sound, but by the age of four months infants appear able to localize sounds quite well (McGurk and Lewis, 1974). Infants as young as two months are able to discriminate the difference between their mother's voice and that of a strange female and can also hear the difference between a soft and a harsh intonation when the same passage is being read (Horowitz, 1974). These and other perceptual developments make further development of the infant's cognitive schemes possible. Basic reflexive schemes can now be coordinated and integrated with one another, as seen in the appearance of the first *circular reactions*.

A circular reaction is a sequence of events consisting "first, of stumbling upon some experience as a consequence of some act, and second, of trying to recapture the experience by re-enacting the original movements again and again in a kind of rhythmic cycle. The importance of circular reactions lies in the fact that it is the sensorimotor device par excellence for making new adaptations, and of course new adaptations are the heart and soul of intellectual development at any stage" (Flavell, 1963, p. 93). *Primary circular reactions* are typical of Stage 2. They are repetitive acts that center on the infant's own body; thumb-sucking, frequently seen in three- and four-month-old infants, is a good example.

The Fourth to the Eighth Month (Stage 3).   Between the fourth and eighth months of life *secondary circular reactions* appear. Circular reactions at this stage are aimed at maintaining environmental events originally brought about by chance. For example, suppose the infant accidentally shakes a rattle and hears a noise. The infant will repeatedly shake the rattle trying to produce the noise again—perhaps unsuccessfully at first. This action pattern requires the coordination of two action patterns heretofore used separately, that is, grasping and hearing. Typically, coordination between previously isolated behaviors occurs during this stage. Thus, for example, the first coordinations between vision and movement take place at this time:

> The baby starts grasping and manipulating everything he sees in his immediate vicinity. For example, a subject of this age catches hold of a cord hanging from the top of his cradle, which has the effect of shaking all the rattles suspended above him. He immediately repeats the gesture a number of times. Each time the interesting result motivates the repetition. . . . Later you need only hang a new toy from the top of the cradle for the child to look for the cord, which constitutes the beginning of a differentiation between means and ends. [Piaget and Inhelder, 1969, p. 10]

The Eighth to the Twelfth Month (Stage 4).   Examples such as the foregoing suggest at least the threshold of intelligent behavior. However, Piaget theorizes that it is not until Stage 4 that truly planful behavior appears. Piaget finds evidence for this process by setting up problems derived from natural situations and observing the reactions of children. Here is an example in which his son Laurent had to move an obstacle in order to reach a toy:

Until now [he was seven months and thirteen days old] Laurent has never really succeeded in setting aside the obstacle; he has simply attempted to take no notice of it. . . . For instance . . . [at six months] I present Laurent with a matchbox, extending my hand laterally to make an obstacle to his prehension. Laurent tries to pass over my hand, or to the side, but he does not attempt to displace it. . . . [At seven months, ten days,] Laurent tries to grasp a new box in front of which I place my hand. . . . He sets the obstacle aside, but not intentionally; he simply tries to reach the box by sliding next to my hand and when he touches it, tries to take no notice of it. . . . Finally [at age seven months, thirteen days,] Laurent reacts quite differently almost from the beginning of the experiment. I present a box of matches above my hand, but behind it, so that he cannot reach it without setting the obstacle aside. But Laurent, after trying to take no notice of it, suddenly tries to hit my hand as though to remove or lower it; I let him do it to me and he grasps the box. . . . I recommence to bar his passage. . . . Laurent tries to reach the box, and bothered by the obstacle, he at once strikes it, definitely lowering it until the way is clear. [Piaget, 1952b, p. 217]

Pushing the obstacle aside is now not an "accident"; rather, it is an act recognized as necessary for reaching the object. It seems that secondary circular reactions (which conserve knowledge originally hit upon by accident) combine to launch new behavior that is intentionally goal-directed, as the first glimmer of real intelligence appears.

The Twelfth to the Eighteenth Month (Stage 5).   The fifth stage, twelve to eighteen months, gives rise to *tertiary circular reactions.* In the secondary circular reaction the child tries to recapture an external event by activating the behavior that led to it in an almost stereotyped and mechanical way. In the tertiary circular reaction the infant seems to be exploring the relationship between action and object. The child experiments with objects in order to see, understand, and pursue the novel. Consider the following example of the tertiary circular reaction:

Jacqueline holds in her hands an object which is new to her; a round, flat box, which she turns all over, shakes, rubs against the bassinet, etc. She lets it go and tries to pick it up. But she only succeeds in touching it with her index finger, without grasping it. She nevertheless makes an attempt and presses on the edge. The box then tilts up and falls again. Jacqueline, very much interested in this fortuitous result, immediately applies herself to studying it. Hitherto it is only a question of an attempt at assimilation . . . and of the fortuitous discovery of a new result, but this discovery, instead of giving rise to a simple circular reaction, is at once extended to "experiments in order to see."

In effect, Jacqueline immediately rests the box on the ground and pushes it. . . . Afterward Jacqueline puts her finger on the box and presses it. But as she places her finger on the center of the box she simply displaces it and makes it slide instead of tilting it up. She amuses herself with this game and keeps it up (resumes it after intervals, etc.) for several minutes. Then, changing the point of contact, she finally again places her finger on the edge of the box, which tilts it up. She repeats this many times, varying the conditions, but keeping track of her discovery. . . . [Piaget, 1952b, pp. 268–272]

FIGURE 7–2
During the sensorimotor period infants begin to construct reality by integrating sensory and motor experience.
Censer, Monkmeyer.

Stage 4 children can only construct means to goals by coordinating actions that by chance exist in their repertoires. In contrast, Stage 5 children, through trial-and-error experimentation, actively search for new means. Suppose a Stage 5 infant in a playpen wants a long stick lying outside the playpen bars. The situation is new, and no familiar method of solution is at hand. A Stage 4 child would probably not find a successful approach; on the other hand, the Stage 5 child will use trial and error, performing "experiments in order to see," just as Jacqueline did in Piaget's example. And, eventually, this method will work. Sooner or later the Stage 5 child will tilt the stick parallel to the opening between the bars of the playpen and draw it through.

The Eighteenth to the Twenty-fourth Month (Stage 6).   During the sixth and final stage of the sensorimotor period the ability to covertly plan without trial-and-error experimentation emerges. This new process is "insight."

> ... Jacqueline (at 1 year, 8 months, 9 days) arrives at a closed door—with a blade of grass in each hand. She stretches out her right hand toward the knob but sees that she cannot turn it without letting go of the grass. She puts the grass on the floor, opens the door, picks up the grass again and enters. But when she wants to leave the room things become complicated. She puts the grass on the floor and grasps the doorknob. But then she perceives that in pulling the door toward her she will simultaneously chase away the grass which she placed between the door and the threshold. She therefore picks it up in order to put it outside the door's zone of movement. [Cited in Flavell, 1963, p. 119]

The exceedingly important, newly developed process that underlies the emergence of insightful behavior is called *representation*. The process of representation allows the child to search for an appropriate solution through the manipulation of internal symbols instead of physical objects. An interesting development of this stage is the ability to recognize representations of oneself. Amsterdam (1972) placed children under the age of two in front of a mirror so that they could see an image of themselves. The aim of the study was to see whether they would recognize that what they saw was indeed an image of themselves (for example, by touching their own faces rather than the mirror). Amsterdam reported:

> The first prolonged and repeated reaction of an infant to his mirror image is that of a sociable "playmate" at about 6 through 12 months of age. In the second year of life wariness and withdrawal appeared; self-admiring and embarrassed behavior accompanied those avoidance behavior starting at 14 months, and were shown by 75% of the subjects after 20 months of age. During the last part of the second year of life, from 20–24 months of age, 65% of the subjects demonstrated recognition of their mirror images (1972, p. 297).

In summary, the six substages of the sensorimotor period describe in orderly sequence the different stretches of terrain through which the infant passes on a journey from automatic, reflexive reactions to planful behavior efficiently coordinated with the infant's own goals and desires. The most important cognitive accomplishment during the sensorimotor period is that by its end the child is able to use and comprehend symbols.

The Preoperational Period (2 to 7 Years)

The end of the sensorimotor period coincides with the beginning of the preoperational period. Henceforth the child will begin to deal with increasingly complex problems and will gradually come to rely on mental representations in solving them. During the preoperational period, then, the child begins to develop a perspective of the world and displays an increased ability to accommodate to new information and experience. At first, however, the emerging perspective is *egocentric*, meaning that children have trouble understanding that others will often view the physical and social environment differently than they do. Frequently unaware of the possibility of varying perspectives, the preoperational child is an unknowing prisoner of his or her own point of view.

Egocentrism in Preoperational Thought. In the classic demonstration of egocentrism (Piaget and Inhelder, 1956, chapter 8), children were seated on one side of a display consisting of three toy mountains of unequal heights and were asked to show how the display looked to a doll seated elsewhere in relation to the display. Piaget and Inhelder found that children under the age of seven or eight generally indicated that the doll saw what they themselves saw. Egocentrism diminishes during the preoperational period by the thrust of contact with friends, siblings, and classmates who convey the fact of their own differing perspectives (Piaget and Inhelder, 1969; Flavell, 1974).

Much recent research has explored the extent of egocentrism in children's thought (Hoy, 1974; Shantz and Wason, 1970; Brodzinsky, Jackson, and Overton, 1972; Masangkay, McClusky, McIntyre, Sims-Knight, Vaughn, and Flavell, 1974). In one study Liben (1975) asked children to describe what a white card looked like both to themselves and to an experimenter (a) when the children wore yellow-tinted sunglasses and the experimenter wore none, (b) when the experimenter wore green-tinted sunglasses and the children wore none, and (c) when the children wore yellow-tinted sunglasses and the experimenter wore green-tinted sunglasses. Almost half of the three-year-olds tested answered correctly, and the four-, five-, six-, and seven-year-olds tested were extremely successful. These results indicate that when the problem is simple enough even three-year-olds show some ability to take another's perspective, though with more difficulty than older children.

According to Piaget, the preoperational child's generally limited perspective on the world is not only evident when he or she is asked to take another's point of view. It is a general characteristic of thought processes at this age, reflected in all the child's efforts to solve problems. To better understand just how the preoperational child thinks, let us examine the so-called conservation problems.

The Conservation Problems. In classical physics there is a law that states that the amount of matter in the universe remains the same through all time, regardless of the form it takes. A similar idea, if on a less grand scale, is held by most adults. If we start with a sack containing exactly ten pounds of sand, and the sack accidentally falls to the floor and breaks, the amount of sand will remain the same—will be conserved—regardless of the change in its location and form. If there were ten pounds of sand in the sack before, there must be ten pounds of sand on the floor now. Piaget's work on the development of the conservation concept has attracted more attention than perhaps any other aspect of his work because he has demonstrated that young children do not reason this way. They fail to appreciate that some features of objects (such as number and length) will remain invariant despite changes in other features (such as shape and position).

In tests of conservation of *liquid quantity*, for example, children are presented with two identically shaped beakers of milk and adjustments are made until they agree that each contains the same amount to drink. Then the contents of one of the beakers is poured into a third beaker, which differs in shape from the other two. The transition, which occurs entirely in the child's presence, is depicted in Figure 7–3. The preoperational child (in contrast to older children) is likely to say that beakers A and C do not have the same amount of milk.

What distinguishes the two age groups in this situation? According to Piaget's terminology, older children are able to show *conservation*. They understand, at least in this situation, that no change necessarily occurs in one or more aspects of an object or relationship simply because of changes in other, independent features or aspects.

Conservation of liquid quantity is only one of a number of types of

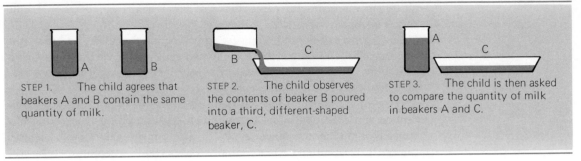

STEP 1.   The child agrees that beakers A and B contain the same quantity of milk.

STEP 2.   The child observes the contents of beaker B poured into a third, different-shaped beaker, C.

STEP 3.   The child is then asked to compare the quantity of milk in beakers A and C.

FIGURE 7–3
A typical sequence for studying conservation of liquid quantity.

transformations in the physical universe that reveal cognitive differences in children's understanding. Studies of conservation of *amount*, for example, begin by showing the child two equal-sized balls of plasticene clay. Then, while the subject watches, one of the balls is transformed in shape (e.g., rolled up like a sausage, made into a flat pancake, or divided into several pieces). Children up to about five years of age usually are unable to "see" that the quantity of plasticene has remained constant despite these changes and will identify one of the shapes as now having more clay than the other. By the age of seven or eight they understand that no change in amount has occurred (Piaget and Inhelder, 1941).

Why Does the Preoperational Child Fail to Conserve?   Piaget and his associates have suggested that the preoperational child fails to conserve because he or she is unable to recognize the operation of certain processes in the physical world. We shall consider three of these processes. First, the preoperational child apparently fails to see the *reversibility* of certain physical operations. If adults were asked how they know that the amount of fluid remains the same in the example provided in Figure 7–3, they might say that if the operation were reversed (if the fluid in beaker C were poured back into beaker B), then the equality would be obvious. The preoperational child, on the other hand, does not appear to recognize this.

A second characteristic of preoperational children that appears to prevent their conserving is *centration*. This notion refers to the tendency to center or focus on a single detail of a question or problem and subsequently to be unable to shift to another detail or dimension. In the conservation of liquid, for example, the child may attend either to the height of the beaker (and thus say that the taller beaker has the greater volume) or to the width (and thus say that the wider and squatter beaker has the larger quantity of fluid). To solve the problem correctly, the child must *decenter*—that is, attend simultaneously to both the height and the width of the beakers—in order to see the relationship between the changes in one of these dimensions and the compensatory changes in the other. Despite the fact that the column of fluid becomes wider as it gets lower (or taller as its gets narrower), the overall quantity remains the same. It is this fact that the preoperational child seems unable to appreciate.

Centering and decentering refer to perceptual processes, and thus it is important to ask whether there is any perceptual evidence that young children differ from older children in the way they perceive (that is, visually take in) the conservation displays. There is.

One of the most fascinating demonstrations of the link between perception and cognition in dealing with conservation problems is found in a study by O'Bryan and Boersma (1971). These investigators built a special camera that permitted them to actually track a child's eye movements as the child attempted to deal with several conservation tasks. The findings clearly verify that the type of relationship between perception and cognition suggested by Piaget was an excellent characterization of what children actually do:

> There seems little doubt that the nonconserver centrates on the dominant part of the visual display, and that the transitional [child] displays a type of dual centration on both parts, shifting infrequently between the two. By contrast, the conserver appears to have overcome the perceptual distortion presented by the transformed element in that she displays many shifts of fixation and seems completely decentered (O'Bryan and Boersma, 1971, pp. 167–168).

Although it seems clear that the preoperational child tends to center upon one of the stimulus dimensions in a conservation problem, there is more than one possible interpretation of why this should occur. Inasmuch as the problems typically involve the use of relational terms (i.e., the experimenter asks: "Which one is *bigger*?"), it is possible that the child's responses result from a misunderstanding of the words rather than from deficiencies in logic or perception. The child may, for example, interpret the word "bigger" or "more" to mean "taller" (Braine and Shanks, 1965).

Do younger children fail to conserve simply because they do not understand the meaning of relational terms, or is there a real difference between their mental processes and those of older children and adults? To find out, Kempler (1971) designed a test of conservation in which potentially confusing relational terms were not used at all. He constructed a set of one hundred rectangles of varying shapes and areas, so that almost all the possible combinations of height and width were represented in the set. For example, there were tall, narrow rectangles; short, wide ones; and even rectangles that were in effect perfectly square. The subjects of the study, six-through thirteen-year-old children, were shown the rectangles one at a time and were simply asked to indicate whether each was large or small. Using an ingenious mathematical technique, Kempler was able to take these data and calculate the relative importance children of each age group gave to height and to width in making their judgments of large or small. He found that all the younger children overestimated the importance of height, and equal reliance on height and width appeared only in the twelve- and thirteen-year-old group. In a related study, Holland and Palermo (1975) successfully taught four- and five-year-old children how to use the terms "more" and "less," but this training did not appear to assist them at all in solving the conservation tasks. These findings suggest strongly that the general problem that Piaget identified in his conservation tests is not reducible to a confusion in word usage on the part of younger children.

A third characteristic of preoperational children that prevents the solving of conservation problems appears to be that they perceive *states* rather than *transformations*. That is, they attend to the series of successive conditions that are displayed in the experiment rather than the process by which the researcher changes or transforms one display into another. It is as if the nonconserving child sees a series of still pictures, whereas a more advanced observer sees a moving picture. The difference is critical, for only by appreciating the transformation or continuous character of conservation problems can we be confident that quantity has remained the same.

Can Children Learn to Conserve?   Piaget considers an understanding of conservation to be "a necessary condition for all rational activity." To the extent that such an assertion is even partially accurate, there would be important educational advantages in speeding the acquisition of conservation. Moreover, the paradox of children contending that the amount of milk changes when an experimenter merely pours it from one glass to another has proved an irresistible challenge, especially for those interested in the development of intelligence.

According to Piaget, children below the age of six cannot learn conservation because of a cognitive immaturity that renders all relevant experience useless. The failure of early experimenters to induce conservation in young children was interpreted by some as confirmation of this position (Flavell, 1963). More recent experiments, however, have met with greater success, yielding important information about the various means by which children learn about and come to understand the world around them.

Teaching Logical Operations.   Certain logical operations are assumed by Piaget to be prerequisites for conservation mastery, and an inability to grasp them is said to doom the young child to failure on all conservation problems. Efforts to teach these logical operations and thereby stimulate mastery of conservation have been made in several investigations (Shantz and Sigel, 1967; Sigel, Roeper, and Hooper, 1968). For example, Sigel and his associates (1968) assumed that in order to understand the notion of conservation, children must be able to respond to two dimensions simultaneously. Therefore they gave young children who had failed various tests of conservation practice in utilizing several dimensions at once. Children were asked to list single attributes (color, shape, and function) of common objects. Eventually they were asked to think in terms of two dimensions at once—e.g., "Can you think of two things that you are at the same time?" Training of this sort was supplemented by practice in thinking with reversibility. The majority of four- and five-year-olds who received training showed some increase in comprehension of conservation on a posttraining test, but it also became apparent that logical training alone was insufficient to produce dramatic results.

Teaching Relevant Skills. Kingsley and Hall (1967) argued that unsuccessful attempts to train conservation almost invariably "ignored the large amount of specific background knowledge necessary and the time needed to train children for conservation mastery." Rather than teaching *logical* prerequisites as Sigel had, Kingsley and Hall concentrated on teaching *skills* directly involved in the task. In training children in the conservation of length (the notion that relative length does not change when two aligned sticks are moved out of alignment), their goal was that the child (1) know the meaning of specific terms (*longer, shorter*) used in test questions, (2) know how to measure length with an independent third measuring instrument, (3) know that use of a measuring stick is more accurate than visual cues, (4) know the effects of adding and subtracting length at the ends, and (5) know the effects (or lack of effects) of moving the objects. Each of the five components was taught separately, as were similar skills in a conservation-of-weight task. The techniques were quite successful. Later, using similar procedures, Rothenberg and Orost (1969) were able to teach conservation of number (the notion that the number of pennies in a row does not change when the pennies are squeezed closer together or spaced more widely apart).

A training procedure like that of Kingsley and Hall raises the question, Is an understanding of conservation derived from direct training good enough to aid children in situations for which they have not been specifically trained? This is the question of *transfer of training*. Kingsley and Hall, who trained children on conservation of length and weight, found improved understanding of conservation of amount, a conservation problem for which no training had been given.

Teaching Rules. Beilin (1965) was the first to try the most direct approach of all, teaching the child the conservation rule itself. In teaching conservation of length, for example, his experimenters would respond to an error by the child with a clear statement of the rule: "Whenever we start with a length like this one (pointing) and we don't add any sticks to it or take away any sticks . . . it stays the same length even though it looks different. See, I can put them back the way they were, so they haven't really changed." While reciting the rule, the experimenter made the appropriate changes in the object so that the child would have a physical as well as a verbal representation of it. Beilin was quite successful in inducing specific conservation on the training task, but his simple procedures failed to produce significant generalization to related tasks. Later investigators have been much more successful with generalization (Gelman, 1969; Siegler and Liebert, 1972a, 1972b) because they have taken additional steps to bolster the rule training.

Gelman (1969) succeeded in obtaining high levels of both specific and general conservation mastery by teaching conservation rules through a discrimination-learning procedure similar to the one used by Harlow and by Kendler and Kendler (see chapter 6, pp. 176–180). A related strategy was later used by Siegler and Liebert (1972a, 1972b) to determine the relative contribution of verbal rules and of feedback to conservation learning. Their

Challenges to Piaget's View of Cognitive Abilities in the Preoperational Child

In recent years there has been growing criticism of Piaget's conclusions regarding the limited mental capacities of the pre-operational child. Although many specific issues have been raised, the general point made by critics is that Piaget has often underestimated the abilities and capacities of children because of his insensitivity to certain methodological problems that have just recently come to be understood or appreciated. Perhaps the most outspoken of Piaget's critics is Rochel Gelman, whose doctoral dissertation on teaching young children conservation skills (Gelman, 1969) was discussed previously.

Gelman (1978) has now taken the general position that children of preoperational age (two to seven) have a considerably greater range of cognitive capacities than Piagetians have supposed. Gelman feels that one problem with Piaget's work is that it has led many investigators into believing that Piaget's tests are the tests of various cognitive capacities. She believes that the young child has many more capacities than has been commonly supposed but that the capacities are "fragile" and thus are typically not manifested except in the simplest situations. Successful training studies, such as those we reviewed on the conservation tasks, are in Gelman's view evidence that preschool children have an existing capacity that can be built on, and that none of the training studies to date could be considered as "establishing a capacity from scratch."

Another point that Gelman stresses is that the young child often does not understand the rules of the experimenter's game. She points out that it is a basic rule of conversation not to state the obvious, and that young children are less likely than older children or adults to break this rule in order to show the experimenter that they know something that is "obvious."

A good example of the empirical basis for these criticisms can be found in Gelman's challenge to the Piagetian conclusion that children below ages six or seven are egocentric (see p. 195) in a way that older children are not. In one study cited by Gelman, four- and five-year-old children were asked to help decide about toys that were to be given either to a two-year-old or another child their own age.*

Depending on which condition they were in, they were shown a picture of either a 2-year-old or a 4-year-old boy in order to test whether they could make appropriate choices for others when they had no direct feedback from the recipient. The stimuli consisted of four toys: two that were deemed appropriate for 2-year-olds and two deemed appropriate for 4-year-olds. Subjects who chose presents for 2-year-olds picked significantly more 2-year-old toys than expected by chance. Likewise, "peer condition" subjects chose 4-year-old toys. An analysis of the toy-choice justifications showed that the children rarely gave inappropriate or egocentric ones such as "I like it." Instead children tended to refer to the cognitive and/or affective predispositions of the receiver as illustrated by the following explanation: "I didn't pick this (the number-letter board) because he (the 2-year-old) can't read." (Shatz, 1973, cited in Gelman, 1978, p. 316)

Certainly this situation is a simple and relatively undemanding one, but it nonetheless demonstrates that even very young children are not egocentric under some circumstances. Similarly, Menig-Peterson (1975) found that preschoolers modified their recounting to an adult of an event that occurred the previous week as a function of whether or not the adult had participated in the event. Marvin, Greenberg, and Mossler (1976) have shown that children as young as four are aware that a secret is known only to people who have actually seen the event in question. There is also some recent evidence to suggest that spatial perspective-taking skills can be taught to preschoolers (Priddle and Rubin, 1977). With this evidence in hand, Gelman (1978) concludes:

> If the task is simple enough—where simple refers variously to the use of responses that are well developed, stimuli that are suited to the child's interest, stimuli the child can process, instructions the child can understand—then the young child's nonegocentric abilities will show through. If, on the other hand, the child has to deal with just-learned materials, just-acquired responses, emerging concepts or not-yet-developed concepts, or unavailable strategies, the coordinated demands of the task will surely overload his processing capacities, and, likely as not, lead him to fail. By such a view, perspective-taking abilities become better and better with experience, the acquisition of knowledge in a variety of domains, and sheer practice. It is not an ability that is first absent and then present. It is an ability that continues to develop into adulthood. (p. 319)

What conclusions can be drawn about cognitive development in relation to Gelman's and others' criticisms of Piaget? Certainly it can be said that Piaget underestimated many of the young child's cognitive abilities. Young children can recognize the perspective of others in very simple and obvious situations (such as recognizing that if someone is blindfolded he can't be expected to see what is going on and the incident will have to be explained to him). Nonetheless it is equally clear that the rudimentary capacity of young children to grasp another's perspective will rarely be sufficient to lead to an understanding of the perspective of others in real-life situations. Thus, there is a difference between the cognitive-developmental level of preschoolers and older children. Gelman supports this. She writes that "preschoolers as compared to older children differ in their ability to negotiate a particular cognitive domain. This cannot be denied" (1978, p. 299). The problem, of course, is to describe and explain the differences and it is here that there are increasing challenges to Piaget.

experiments indicated that either providing the relevant rules or providing feedback helped children master conservation problems and also demonstrated that providing both rules and feedback was more effective than providing either alone. Gelman's and Siegler and Liebert's experiments conclusively answer the original question of whether four- and five-year-olds can be taught conservation skills. The numerous unsuccessful and partially successful earlier studies, however, attest to the difficulty of inducing conservation in these children.

The Period of Concrete Operations (7 to 11 Years)

According to Piaget, the period of concrete operations is characterized by an orderliness of thinking that gives rise to the ability to decenter and recognize transformations, an awareness that some transformations are reversible, and of course a grasp of the concept of conservation. Flavell contrasts it with the preceding periods as follows:

... the preoperational child differs profoundly from the sensory-motor infant by virtue of the fact that he operates on a wholly new plane of reality, the plane of representation as opposed to direct action. Since the concrete-operational child also operates on the same plane [as the preoperational child], the question arises: what are the differences between the two? ... It is simply that the older child seems to have at his command a coherent and integrated cognitive system with which he organizes and manipulates the world around him. [Flavell, 1963, p. 165]

The integrated cognitive system of which Flavell writes is an organized network of operations. What kind of mental event is an *operation*? It is an act of representation, such as adding, subtracting, multiplying, or dividing. Piaget has elaborately detailed nine different groupings of logical operations that define the system of concrete operations. However, a consideration of them is beyond the intended scope of this book.*

The accomplishments of the concrete operational stage are many. Besides the ability to conserve, the child has lost much egocentrism and has gained in sensitivity to contradictions inherent in his or her own thought. The child's ability to represent the world symbolically is greatly advanced.

One way to summarize many of these differences is to note that the preoperational child tends to respond to *perceived appearances* rather than to *inferred reality* as the older child does (Flavell, 1977). It is, indeed, the younger child's failure to appreciate the fact that there is an underlying reality behind every phenomenon (rarely identical to its appearance), which is most significant here. The shift that occurs between preoperational and concrete operational thought is a shift in which the child turns from making judgments on the basis of perception alone to making judgments on the basis of his or her conception of the meaning behind various perceptions. (A good test, which anyone can try on children of various ages, is to see whether they understand such differences as "looks bigger" versus "really is bigger.")

Given the accomplishments of children at this age, one may reasonably ask, What sorts of operations can concrete operational children *not* perform? The answer is intriguing.

Although concrete operational children understand relationships among specific events in the environment, they are unable to produce formal, abstract hypotheses. They cannot imagine possible events that are not also real events, and thus they cannot solve problems that involve formal abstractions. As an example, consider Archimedes' law of floating bodies. This principle, which is a formal abstraction, states that an object will float in water if its density (weight per unit) is less than that of water. This law means that if two objects are of equal weight, the smaller object is more likely to sink than the larger. This fact can give rise to an experimental test. Specifically, a child is given a bucket of water and several different small objects, some of which will float in water and some of which will sink. The child's job is to classify the objects in terms of whether they will float or sink, and to look for a rule that will tie the findings together.

*An excellent discussion of these phenomena can be found in Flavell's *Developmental Psychology of Jean Piaget* (1963).

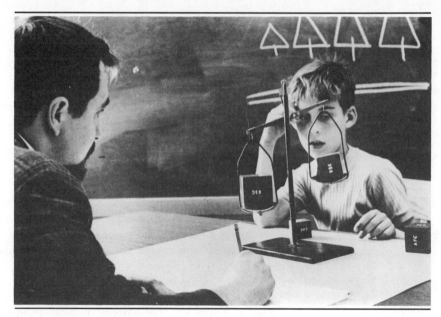

Concrete operational children will say such things as "an object sinks because it is iron," "because it is heavy," and so on. They will be troubled and confused, though, by the dilemmas created by such rules (i.e., a piece of wood may be heavier than a bit of rock, but may float while the rock sinks). In contrast, children who have reached the stage of formal operations appear able to abstract the appropriate statement. The phenomenon is illustrated by Piaget's description of one child who, at age twelve years, six months, comes close to a solution, saying in reference to a penny that "it sinks because it is small, it isn't stretched enough. . . . You would have to have something larger to stay at the surface, something of the same weight and which would have a greater extension" (Inhelder and Piaget, 1958, p. 38).

Concrete operational children are bound up with the world as it is, and they cannot get any further until they begin to delineate all possible explanations at the outset of considering a problem. This ability to appreciate the possible as well as the real characterizes the transition to formal operational thought. It is not that the concrete operational child is unintelligent; by middle childhood youngsters have at their command an impressive array of cognitive tools. Nonetheless, in Flavell's colorful words, the concrete operational child takes "an earthbound, concrete, practical-minded sort of problem-solving approach, one that persistently fixates on the perceptible and inferable reality right there in front of him . . . A theorist the elementary-school child is not." (Flavell, 1977, p. 103).

The Period of Formal Operations (11 Through Adulthood)

Beginning with preadolescence, people begin to display the ability to engage in formal reasoning on an abstract level. They can draw hypotheses from their observations, imagine hypothetical as well as real events, and deduce or induce principles regarding the world around them. They begin to consider all possible explanations to a problem, and only then do they try to discover, systematically, which of the explanations really applies. This advanced way of thinking, in which what occurs in reality is seen as just one among many *possible* alternatives, is part of what makes the thinking of the formal operational child more powerful than it has been at any earlier period.

The Pendulum Problem.   Inhelder and Piaget (1958) have used the following setup to explore formal operational thought. The subject is presented with a pendulum consisting of an object hanging from a string. He or she is permitted to vary the length of the string, change the weight of the suspended object, alter the height from which the pendulum is released, and push the pendulum with varying degrees of force. The problem that must be solved is a classical one in physics: to discover and state which of these factors alone or in combination will influence how quickly the pendulum swings back. (In fact, length of the string is the critical variable. The shorter it is, the faster the pendulum swings.) Because the experimenter plays a nondirective role, the way in which the problem is solved tells us much about the cognitive operations of the performer.

Concrete operational children approach the problem unsystematically and soon fail to give up because their chaotic approach leaves them without any real clue to the answer. Formal operational children, in contrast, handle the problem quite systematically. First, the adolescent envisages all the possible factors and combinations of factors that could influence the speed of the pendulum: string length, weight, height of release, force, length and height, length and weight and height, and so on. This analysis of possibilities can be exhaustive, and the formal operational child can cast the pos-

FIGURE 7-5
Youngsters enter into the period of formal operations about the time when adolescence begins. The ability to conduct scientific experiments depends upon formal operations, according to Piaget.   De Wys, Inc.

sibilities into the form of propositions, which function as hypotheses. Finally, these hypotheses are empirically tested. To construct a valid test of each hypothesis the child varies one dimension, such as length of string, while holding all other dimensions constant. For example, a 100-gram weight with a long string will be compared with a 100-gram weight with a short string. Formal operational thinkers realize that an experiment would yield inconclusive results if both weight and string length were varied together because they would be unable to deduce which factor produced the difference in speed. Inhelder and Piaget give an exemplary case of a fifteen-year-old who

> ... after having selected 100 grams with a long string and a medium length string, then 20 grams with a long and short string, and finally 200 grams with a long and short, concludes: *"It's the length of the string that makes it go faster or slower; the weight doesn't play any role."* She discounts likewise the height of the drop and the force of her push. [1958, p. 75]

Accelerating the Development of Formal Operational Thought. As with the conservation problems, a major question is, Can children below the age of formal operations learn to master formal operational problems? A series of studies by Siegler and his colleagues (Siegler, 1975; Siegler and Atlas, 1975; Siegler and Liebert, 1975; Siegler, Liebert, and Liebert, 1973) indicates that they can. In one of these studies, Siegler, Liebert, and Liebert attempted to teach the pendulum problem to ten- and eleven-year-olds. The instructional procedure included definitions of key scientific concepts, application of these concepts to particular problems, and demonstration of the use of precise measuring instruments. Roughly 70 percent of the children who were provided such instruction mastered the pendulum problem, compared with less than 10 percent of the uninstructed children. The other studies in the series also testify to the ability of concrete-operations-aged children to learn formal operations concepts, although, in accord with Inhelder and Piaget's findings, these children rarely solve the problems without instruction.

As suggested by Inhelder and Piaget's descriptions and by the type of skills Siegler and his colleagues taught to the ten- and eleven-year-olds, the characteristics of the formal operational child are related to those of good scientists. In fact, the intellectual sophistication acquired during the formal operations period seems to be a prerequisite for all scientific thinking. It is with this understanding of the scientific method, according to Piaget, that the basic development of intellectual processes arrives at its most advanced state. It is important to keep in mind, though, that formal operational reasoning is something that most older adolescents and adults are capable of, but not necessarily something that they will typically do all, or even most, of the time. Just as young children may show production deficiencies and thus deprive themselves of the benefits of tactics that they already know so, too, adolescents and adults may often fail to think logically, even when they are capable of doing so and when such thinking would be highly beneficial.

Throughout our discussion of Piaget's theory we saw that mental representation must play an important role in cognitive development, but we have not yet examined the process in any detail. It is time to do so. We begin with Piaget's viewpoint on the nature of mental representation and then contrast it with the theory of Jerome Bruner, who views Piaget's analysis as pioneering but quite incomplete.

Piaget's View of Mental Representation.   Recall that according to Piaget, a major advance in the child's ability to represent events mentally occurs at about two years of age, corresponding closely with the onset of the preoperational period. At this time the child begins to distinguish what Piaget calls *signifiers* (internal symbols and signs) from *significates* (the actual objects, events, and actions to which signifiers refer). In the following passage, famous among Piagetians, Piaget describes an incident in which his daughter Lucienne, two years old, symbolizes an act not yet performed:

> . . . I put the chain inside an empty matchbox (where the matches belong), then closed the box leaving an opening of 10mm. Lucienne begins by turning the whole thing over, then tries to grasp the chain through the opening. Not succeeding, she simply puts her index finger into the slit and so succeeds in getting out a small fragment of the chain; she then pulls it until she has completely solved the problem.
>
> Here begins the experiment which we want to emphasize. I put the chain back into the box and reduced the opening to 3mm. It is understood that Lucienne is not aware of the functioning of the opening and closing of the matchbox and has not seen me prepare the experiment. She only possesses the two preceding schemata: turning the box over in order to empty it of its contents, and sliding her finger into the slit to make the chain come out. It is of course this last procedure that she tries first; she puts her finger inside and gropes to reach the chain, but fails completely. A pause follows during which Lucienne manifests a very curious reaction bearing witness not only to the fact that she tries to think out the situation and to represent to herself through mental combination the operations to be performed, but also to the role played by imitation in the genesis of representations. Lucienne mimics the widening of the slit.
>
> She looks at the slit with great attention; then, several times in succession, *she opens and shuts her mouth*, at first slightly, then wider and wider! Apparently Lucienne understands the existence of a cavity adjacent to the slit and wishes to enlarge the cavity. The attempt at representation which she thus furnishes is expressed physically, that is to say, due to inability to think out the situation in words or clear visual images she uses a simple motor indication as "signifier" or symbol. Lucienne, by opening her mouth thus expresses, or even reflects her desire to enlarge the opening of the box. This schema [scheme] of imitation, with which she is familiar, constitutes for her the means of thinking out the situation. There is doubtless added to it an element of magic-phenomenalistic causality or efficacy. Just as she often uses imitation to act upon persons and make them reproduce their interesting movements, so also it is probable that the act of opening her mouth in front of the slit to be enlarged implies some underlying idea of efficacy.
>
> Soon after . . . Lucienne unhesitatingly puts her finger in the slit and, instead of trying as before to reach the chain, she pulls so as to enlarge the opening. She

succeeds and grasps the chain. [Cited in Flavell, 1963, pp. 119–120, italics added]

Of considerable importance for our understanding of the development of mental representation is Piaget's distinction between two kinds of signifiers: symbols and signs. *Symbols* correspond in a relatively private way to the events that they represent and somewhat resemble them physically (e.g., Lucienne's opening and closing her mouth). *Signs,* on the other hand, bear no obvious resemblance to the events they represent; their meanings are arbitrary, but they are shared by other members of the environment (e.g., formal language).

Piaget argues that representational thought does not have its beginnings in social language, but rather in private symbols that form the basis for later acquisition of language. Language development (which we will discuss in detail in chapter 8) is in Piaget's view dependent upon the usage of certain prelinguistic symbols; later, in turn, language fosters further development of private symbols. This basic view, that early mental representation does not rely heavily on language, lies at the heart of the theory of Jerome S. Bruner, to which we now turn.

Modes of Representation and Cognitive Growth: Bruner's View. How, exactly, do human beings represent their experiences mentally? How does mental representation develop over the course of infancy and childhood? These are the fundamental questions that Bruner and his associates have tried to answer.

Bruner (1964, 1966) suggests that human beings represent the world in three modes: the *enactive*, the *iconic*, and the *symbolic*. The enactive mode involves representation through action. When Lucienne opened and closed her mouth to signify her desire to widen the opening in the box, she used the enactive mode of representation. The iconic mode is representation using visual images, seeing in your mind's eye something that in reality is not in view. The symbolic mode is representation using language. (Note, then,

FIGURE 7–6
The matrix presented to children by Bruner and Kenney (1966). Seven-year-olds can usually reproduce the matrix around one glass that has been transposed by the experimenter (as if the board had been turned), but five-year-olds cannot because they are unable to use the symbolic mode of representation.

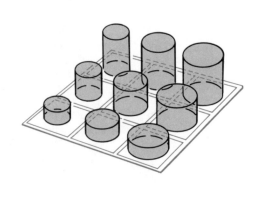

FIGURE 7-7

Percent of children of various ages who succeeded in reproducing and in transposing the matrix presented in Bruner and Kenney's (1966) experiment. On multiple ordering, in J. S. Bruner, R. R. Olver, and P. M. Greenfield, eds., Studies in Cognitive Growth, Copyright 1966. Reproduced by permission of John Wiley & Sons, Inc.

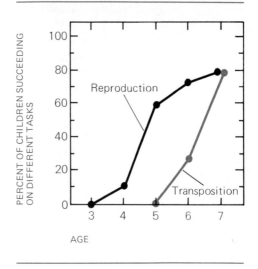

that Bruner's use of the term "symbol" coincides with Piaget's use of the term "sign.") According to Bruner there is a clear developmental sequence for the process of representation. The earliest mode used by the infant is the enactive mode. At about 1½ or 2 years of age the iconic mode emerges, and the symbolic mode appears at about age 7.

A provocative experiment by Bruner and Kenney (1966) illustrates the difference between iconic and symbolic representation, and also directly supports the claim that the iconic mode emerges before the symbolic one. Bruner and Kenney arranged a set of nine plastic glasses in a three-by-three matrix, displayed in Figure 7-6. Along the vertical edge the glasses increased in height, while along the horizontal edge they increased in width. After acquainting children with the display, the experimenters scrambled the glasses and asked the children to reconstruct or *reproduce* the array exactly as it had been originally. Then the glasses were scrambled once more, but this time the glass that was formerly in the southwest corner of the grid (the shortest and thinnest glass) was placed in the southeast corner. Children were then asked to build an array like the original around the newly relocated glass. In short, they were asked to *transpose* the matrix. Although children ranging in age from three to seven years were tested, it is most interesting to focus on the performance of the five-, six-, and seven-year-olds. On the reproduction task a majority of the five-, six-, and seven-year-olds responded correctly. On the transposition task, however, none of the five-year-olds and only a small fraction of the six-year-olds succeeded. Not until the seventh year did the task become performable (see Figure 7-7).

Bruner and Kenney suggested that five-year-olds, not old enough to have mastered the symbolic representation required for this task, had to rely on the iconic mode. These children had a visual image of the original array in memory, a sort of picture taken at the time the array was seen and then stored away. They responded to the problem by "reading" this image and making a copy of it for the experimenter. However, children cannot copy an image of the original as a means of solving the transposition task because they cannot get any match between the transposed glass the experimenter has placed on the board and the picture they have in their heads. Thus, five-year-olds fail at the transposition task because they are being asked to reproduce something they have never seen before. But many of the seven-year-olds succeeded, and we must ask why.

The older children, according to Bruner, had translated their information about the array into the symbolic mode. In short, they used a set of verbal rules to guide them, such as "It gets fatter going one way and taller going the other." Being able to render the matrix into a verbal or symbolic formula allowed the children to preserve and recognize the basic structure of the matrix despite rotation.

Concept Formation: The Example of Object Permanence

Even in early childhood a major portion of human development involves learning to identify and discriminate similarities that exist among otherwise diverse situations. The ability to identify classes of events on the basis of their shared, often abstract properties is referred to as *concept formation*. Rudimentary concept formation has been demonstrated in children as young as two years of age (Denney and Acito, 1974) and the evidence is quite convincing that verbal mediation is not necessary in order for the child to respond to abstract dimensions (Esposito, 1975).

What is a *concept?* It is an abstract grouping of experiences that helps to reduce their complexity. Some concepts are truly abstract, such as the concept of happiness, while other concepts define categories of objects or events that are themselves quite concrete. The concept "ball" encompasses a set of concrete instances that are likely to be seen in similar situations; consequently, this concept appears quite early in the young child's repertoire of abstractions. Developmental psychologists have asked two broad questions about children's concepts: How are they formed during the course of development? How are they used by children in various situations?

As in other cognitive areas, Piaget has contributed a great deal to our understanding of the development of concepts, especially in his investigations of the concept of object permanence. According to Piaget, during the sensorimotor period children gradually make a discovery that will mark their interactions with the world for the rest of their lives. They learn that objects encountered in the world have a permanent existence independent of their own perceptions. The heart of the progression can be seen by following the concept of object permanence through the six substages of development that occur during the sensorimotor period (Flavell, 1970a).

0 to 4 Months. Most researchers seem to agree with Piaget that the infant does not have the concept of object permanence at this early age. In a technique used by Bower (1970), among others, objects are made to "vanish" by sliding a screen between them and the baby. The infant acts as if the object no longer exists, a sort of "out of sight, out of mind" reaction. Even more

FIGURE 7–8
Young infants do not yet have the concept of object permanence. When a toy is taken out of sight, here by interposing a simple screen, it is also out of mind for the infant.   Zimbel, Monkmeyer.

interesting is the fact that most infants will seem *more* surprised if the object is still there when the screen is moved away than if it is missing.

4 to 8 Months.   Infants at this stage seem to have the first glimmerings of object permanence and will try to regain visual contact with an object that has disappeared from view. We would only expect this reaction, of course, if the infant believed that the object did still exist somewhere. But the concept is far from completely formed, as the following description shows:

> First, the child makes a primitive beginning at regaining contact with absent objects by extrapolating the accommodatory movements made to them during their presence; thus he may lean over to look for an object that fell to the floor rather than simply stare at the point where it disappeared from view. . . . Second, he acquires the ability to anticipate a whole object on the basis of seeing only a part of it. However, his behavior in this situation also testifies to the immaturity of his object concept: if a sufficient fraction of the object shows from behind the screen, he reaches for it; if this fraction is then made to decrease, the reaching hand abruptly drops. More generally, it is characteristic of this stage that the child makes no attempt to retrieve an object manually once it has disappeared from view (e.g., by being covered with a cloth), in spite of the fact that such activity would by this age be well within his physical capabilities. [Flavell, 1970a, p. 1010]

8 to 12 Months.   Children will begin to search regularly for objects they have seen disappear, first only if the object has just been seen a moment ago and then even after periods of considerable delay. But there is a wrinkle, for the search process itself reveals that the child is not yet integrating what has been seen with what has been done. Baldwin (1967) provides this example, which can be repeated by anyone who has two pillows of different colors and a small object that can initially capture the infant's interest:

> The object is put under the red pillow and the child is allowed to retrieve it. Then, while the child watches, it is placed under the red pillow, taken out, shown to the child, and placed under the blue pillow. The question is, where will the child look for it? *At Stage 4, [8–12 months] he looks under the red pillow.**
>
> What does this mean? It actually represents an important failure in the child's understanding. The belief that objects continue to exist when they are invisible also requires some belief that objects are located at some point in space. When objects move they go to the point at the end of the path of movement. Therefore, we look for objects where they were last seen or at the end point of the pathway we think they followed. This strategy for recovering vanished objects is in some ways the exact opposite of what the child discovered in Stage 3, namely, to repeat the action that produced the interesting event. When the child obtains the object from under the red pillow and now looks for it there even though he has seen it put under the blue one, he is repeating the action that found him the object last time rather than looking for it where he saw it. [Baldwin, 1967, p. 213, italics added]

12 to 18 Months. Children of this age are usually able to recognize that they must search for missing objects where they were last seen and that this factor is more important than where the object was found before on previous trials. Even so, the concept is not yet complete because the child cannot yet infer invisible displacements. Flavell, for example, describes a child at this age who watches an experimenter carry a small object across a room in his closed hand and then deposit it in a hiding place. The child is only partly able to see this happening; that is, she sees the hand movements of the experimenter but does not catch a glimpse of the object itself during the transfer. Rather than going to the hiding place, the child first goes to the experimenter's now empty hand—for that is where the object was actually seen last.

18 to 24 Months. The development of the concept of object permanence is completed during this stage and has been well described by Flavell:

> At the end of the sensorimotor period the child becomes capable of representing whole sequences of invisible but inferable displacements, for example, if object-in-closed-hand is transported in succession to hiding places *A, B, C,* and *D,* the child will systematically search in all of them (and in the hand), as if he knew exactly what the possibilities were. At this point in development, Piaget is ready to credit him with a full-fledged concept of the independent and enduring object. [Flavell, 1970a, p. 1010]

The Role of Language in Later Concept Development. According to Piaget, the concept of object permanence and other basic, rudimentary con-

---

*The stages that Baldwin refers to are the Piagetian substages of the sensorimotor period (see pp. 191–195).

cepts spring from assimilation and accommodation by the child in the world of objects and do not depend on language. However, there are other concepts, like "brother," "red," and "on time." How are these concepts acquired? According to Benjamin Whorf (1956), the development of at least some concepts *is* influenced by the language that the child learns to speak:*

> We dissect nature along lines laid down by our native languages. The categories and types that we isolate from the world of phenomena we do not find there because they stare every observer in the face; on the contrary, the world is presented in a kaleidoscopic flux of impressions which has to be organized by our minds—and this means largely by the linguistic systems in our minds. We cut nature up, organize it into concepts, and ascribe significances as we do, largely because we are parties to an agreement to organize it in this way—an agreement that holds through our speech community and is codified in the patterns of our language. The agreement is, of course, an implicit and unstated one. But its terms are absolutely obligatory; we cannot talk at all [unless we subscribe] to the organization and classification of data which the agreement decrees. [Whorf, 1956, p. 214]

Carroll and Casagrande (1958) collected data that lend some support to Whorf's suggestion. Two groups of Navaho children were studied, one group came from families where Navaho was spoken and the other came from families where English was spoken. The Navaho language has an interesting feature that English does not have, namely, certain verbs—such as the verbs "to pick up," "to drop," or "to hold in the hand"—require special forms, depending on the shape of the object handled. There is a special verb form for round spherical objects, for round thin objects, for long flexible objects, and so on. Given this distinctive feature of the Navaho language, the experimenters expected that Navaho-speaking children would show awareness of shape before English-speaking Navaho children. The two groups were compared with respect to how often they used shape rather than color as a basis for sorting some objects. Carroll and Casagrande's results showed that Navaho-speaking children did indeed tend to sort according to shape before English-speaking children did, and these findings suggest that in some instances language may play a role in concept development.

INFORMATION PROCESSING AND COGNITIVE DEVELOPMENT

The course of cognitive development as charted by Piaget is only a partial representation of cognitive developmental theory and research. In addition to challenging some of Piaget's methods and conclusions, many psychologists have approached cognitive development using a different model, asking questions about the emergence of information-processing skills as a result of maturation and experience.

The information-processing approach to cognitive development is quite similar to Levine's conceptions of the development of hypothesis testing in discrimination learning discussed in chapter 6. The prototype task for re-

*Reprinted by permission of the MIT Press from Benjamin Lee Whorf, *Language, Thought and Reality*, Copyright © 1956 by the Massachusetts Institute of Technology.

search within this framework is the game "Twenty Questions"; subjects must identify a person, place, or thing by asking yes/no questions, such as "Is it alive?" or "Is it bigger than a shoe box?" Marked changes occur with increasing age in this game, with older questioners being more likely to "narrow down" from the more general to the more concrete (Neimark, 1970; 1975). This is the core aim of computer information-processing as well: to become more efficient by probing for information in the fewest steps and/or in the least time possible.

The cognitive processes we talked about earlier, such as the ability to perform logical operations or symbolize events, all involve manipulating already processed sensory experiences (bits of information) in order to perform a cognitive task or solve a demanding problem. But none of the processes would be of much value unless the raw material for thought, information itself, was available. Two aspects of information processing have been explored sufficiently to enable a developmental picture to emerge: selective attention and memory.

Selective Attention

Some of the earliest research in psychology asked: How much information can the mind simultaneously survey? Early answers to this question (Hamilton, 1859, as cited by Posner, 1973) as well as later ones (Miller, 1956) have suggested that the adult mind can encompass only about seven discrete pieces of information at one time. In short, our capacity for simultaneous processing of information is very limited. In order to cope with limited capacity, humans must be selective in the information they choose to process.

Selective attention involves noticing and attending to (i.e., perceiving) certain features and aspects of the environment while at the same time ignoring or somehow filtering out other aspects (Pick, Frankel, and Hess, 1975).

One way to study selective attention is to construct a task for children in which some information is relevant for successful solution and other information is incidental. Performance of the central task can be compared with recall of incidental information. Low incidental learning in combination with successful performance of the central task would indicate selectivity in attention—that is, attention directed primarily to task-relevant rather than task-irrelevant stimuli (Hagen and Hale, 1973; Maccoby and Hagen, 1965).

A major shift in the degree to which children attend selectively occurs during middle childhood. Generally, incidental learning seems to increase until children are about ten or eleven years old, probably because through this period there is a gradual increase in the child's attention to and retention of all the features in the learning situation. However, after about age eleven there is a *decrease* in incidental learning, suggesting that by age eleven children have learned to selectively ignore certain features of a situation as a complement to selectively attending to other features (Mackworth, 1976).

The notion of selective attention has been discussed in other contexts in earlier sections of this book. Piaget's notion of *centration*, for example, involves a kind of selective attention in which the child rigidly focuses on one detail of the problem and is unable to shift attention to other task-relevant stimuli. A process similar to selective attention may also underlie the "learning to learn" phenomenon observed by Harlow (chapter 6), in which youngsters who generally made many errors at the beginning of a series of discrimination learning problems gradually came to solve such problems in a single try. In addition, selective attention is probably involved in gaining facility with "reversal shifts," as studied by Kendler and Kendler (1962, see chapter 6). The work of Maccoby and Hagen (1965) illustrates that attentional processes greatly influence memory. It is to the general topic of memory development that we now turn.

The Development of Memory

There has been an explosion of interest in memory and memory development in the past decade. One reason is that memory has now come to be seen as a much more active cognitive process than had been realized previously. We do not store our experiences as mere mental tape-recordings or exact duplicates of the things that we see, hear, feel, and smell. The act of remembering is in part an act of problem-solving, and the evidence is clear that inference processes play an extremely important role in what human beings recall and remember from their own past experiences (Frijda, 1972).

What Is Memory?   Memory is an elusive concept. When we say someone "has a good memory," we may mean that the person is good at storing indi-

FIGURE 7-9
As children grow older, the ability to "operate" their own memory increases dramatically.   Paul Conklin, Monkmeyer Press Photo Service.

vidual facts, or good at remembering which names go with which faces at a party, or that the person seems to be good at remembering demonstrations of how things work. Psychologists identify two bipolar dimensions of memory, depending on *what is remembered* and *how it is retrieved.* Episodic memory and semantic memory are related to what is remembered, whereas recognition and recall are two types of retrieval.

What we remember includes specific facts and bits of information (ranging from remembering a friend's phone number to remembering the specific details of a recent vacation), but that is not all. What we remember also encompasses the distillation of all we have learned; that is, our general knowledge. Piaget and Inhelder (1973) speak of this distinction as "memory in the strict sense" and "memory in the wider sense." Another distinction made about what we remember is whether the material is *episodic* or *semantic* in character (Tulving, 1972). Episodic memory is memory for specific, usually timebound facts or events (e.g., a dentist appointment today at 3:00 P.M.). Semantic memory is knowledge about recurring facts and relationships; for example, most people would say that they *know* the sun rises in the morning, not that they *remember* the sun rises in the morning.

Retrieval—how we remember—varies in terms of the cues available to us to obtain a piece of information from memory. At one extreme, *simple recognition* occurs when we are presented with a stimulus and remember that we have seen it before. At the other extreme is *free recall*, in which we are asked for information in a way that defines the question but gives little hint as to what the actual information to be remembered is. Recognition is easier than recall because of the intrinsic prompt in the former. For example, fewer people can correctly answer the question, "What is the capital of Nevada?" than can answer the question, "Is Carson City the capital of Nevada?"

Memory can also involve *reconstruction*, a process intermediate between recognition and recall in which the subject recreates an event by drawing inferences from recalled information until the puzzle is solved (Piaget and Inhelder, 1973).

The process of simple recognition is present from birth, at least in the sense that habituating to a stimulus means that the infant "remembers" it

FIGURE 7-10
**Movement of
information within the
memory system.**
From "The Control of
Short-Term Memory"
by Richard C. Atkinson
and Richard M. Shiff-
rin. Copyright © Au-
gust 1971 by Scientific
American, Inc. All
rights reserved.

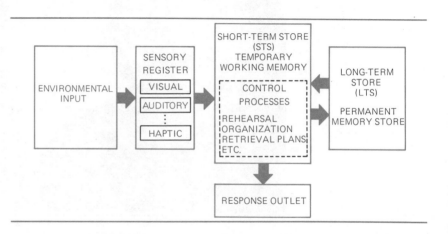

from previous exposure. Using habituation as the response measure, it has been shown that infants as young as four months can remember a photograph seen for only a few minutes, two weeks prior to the second exposure (Olson, 1976). Most memory tasks are more difficult, however, and age-related improvement in memory seems to depend on the development of a number of memory-related skills and strategies.

What kinds of changes are involved in memory development? The question cannot be answered unless we begin with a reasonable model of how memory operates. According to one information-processing view (Atkinson and Shiffrin, 1968, 1971; Ornstein, 1977), memory is like a mental computer system consisting of structural features, the "hardware" of the system, and techniques or programs for using and operating the system, the "software."

Figure 7–10 shows a diagram of the components of memory as envisioned within this model. The hardware consists of three components: (1) a *sensory register* where information arrives from the environment in a raw sensory form (visual, auditory, etc.) and is held for no more than about one second; (2) *short-term store*, a temporary working memory of quite limited capacity; and (3) *long-term store*, a permanent storehouse of information containing our knowledge of the world, assumed to be of very great capacity. When information arrives from the environment it can be held only momentarily in the sensory register. It will either be immediately forgotten or categorized and passed on to the short-term store. (Ornstein [1977] cites the following as an example of using short-term memory: He asked subjects to try to remember an unfamiliar telephone number they had just looked up and he asked them to dial it. If a subject waited a moment too long, the number would be forgotten. Try this experiment yourself.)

Control processes, such as rehearsal techniques, are instrumental in the transfer of information to long-term store. Once information reaches long-term store, very little of it, if any, is lost. Failure to remember at this stage is believed to be due to one's temporary inability to retrieve information rather than an actual loss of memory; people have better recall when given "retrieval cues" that help in remembering previously learned information (Tulving and Pearlstone, 1966). (A good example of the difficulty one can encounter in accessing information from the long-term store is the frustration of trying very hard to remember something like your third-grade teacher's name, only to wake up the next morning thinking of the name "Mrs. McGuillicutty.")

Though recall memory has long been known to improve with age, at least until adulthood is reached, an adequate understanding of the underlying process of development has been unavailable. Guided by the computer model of memory, psychologists have begun to break down the study of memory and look separately at developmental differences in the hardware and the software of the memory system. There appears to be very little change with age in the structural components (hardware) of memory, but that the control processes (software) used to operate the memory system do improve with age (Sheingold, 1973; Ornstein, 1977; Ornstein, Naus, and Liberty, 1975).

In fact, a considerable amount of evidence suggests that what develops

in memory is the ability to operate the memory system by devising and utilizing increasingly more effective strategies for memorization.

Development of the Ability to "Operate" Memory. Rudimentary strategies for remembering appear at a very early age. In an unusually clever
study, Wellman, Ritter, and Flavell (1975) played a game with two- and
three-year-old children to determine whether they were able to act plan-
fully when they had been asked to remember something "important." The
procedure began with the experimenter and child seated at a table with a
toy dog and four cups. The experimenter explained to the child:

> I want to tell you a story about this dog. See, here he is on the playground
> [table top]. He loves to play, he runs, he jumps, . . . but he was playing so hard
> he got very hungry. So he went to look for some food. When he was looking he
> went by this dog house, and this dog house, and this dog house, and this dog
> house [dog is walked by all four cups]. And then he went in this dog house to
> find some food [dog is hidden]. You know what, I have another toy I could get
> to help us tell the story. I'll go get it because we need it for the story. [p. 781]

At this point half the children were told: "You *remember* where the dog
is." The remaining children served as experimental controls and were
merely told: "You *wait* here with the dog." All subjects were surreptitiously
observed during the ensuing delay period, and the amount of time they
spent looking and touching the cup under which the toy dog had been hidden was recorded. The results showed plainly that among the three-year-
olds the *remember* instructions produced more of these planful behaviors
than the *wait* instructions—and they actually remembered better as a result.
Wellman and his associates thus concluded that their study demonstrates
convincingly that "3-year-old children can and do engage in deliberate
memory behavior in at least one task situation." (p. 787)*

Nonetheless the quality of the child's deliberate memory improves
markedly at least into adolescence. Older children generally have greater
access to a variety of things that can help them to remember, including the
use of rehearsal and the application of names, labels, and other easily stored
symbolic representations (Moely, Olson, Halwes, and Flavell, 1969;
Neimark, Slotnick, and Ulrich, 1971).

The ability to *organize* to-be-remembered material also plays an extremely important role in successfully using one's memory. Adult's recall of
categorical material has been shown to depend on the ability to recall in
"clusters" of related items or, when there is no obvious category structure,
to impose a personal organization upon the materials (Mandler, 1972).

To test the extent to which organizational factors account for age
changes in recall performance, Liberty and Ornstein (1973) presented
fourth-graders and college students with a list of twenty-eight items to

---

*Interestingly, the *remember* instructions did not have any effect on two-year-olds, though, as
Wellman and his associates note, this does not mean that two-year-olds might not have succeeded in some other situation.

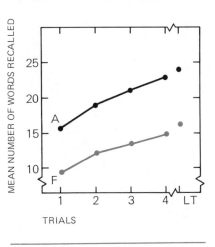

FIGURE 7–11
Mean recall as a function of trials for free-sorting adults (A) and fourth-graders (F). These data are indicated both for Trials 1–4 and for the last sorting trial (LT). From Liberty and Ornstein, 1973.

learn. The items were not completely unrelated, but they did not fall into distinct categories. Subjects were told to sort the words, which were printed on cards, into groups that would help them to remember as many words as possible; they were allowed to use between two and seven groupings. Not surprisingly, the college students' performance was superior to that of the children (see Figure 7–11). College students tended to group the words into four fairly definite content clusters, while the fourth graders structured the items to some extent, but their categories were less content defined. For example, 70 percent of the fourth-graders sorted *flower* and *seed* together, but only 58 percent also agreed upon the inclusion of *tree* with this group. The differences in sorting strategy were significantly correlated with level of recall, with the superior strategy of the college students resulting in better memory.

Liberty and Ornstein (1973) were not content with correlational evidence alone for their hypothesis, and so devised an experimental manipulation to test the hypothesis that organizational differences actually caused (or contributed to) the recall differences. Additional groups of subjects were required to learn sorting patterns that had been used by individual subjects in the first part of the experiment. One-half of the fourth-graders were required to use sorting patterns that the college students had used, while the remainder used the patterns of the other fourth-graders. The same was true for the adult subjects—half used sorting patterns of children and the other half learned adult patterns. If the superior recall of the college students in the first part of the experiment had been due at least in part to their superior organizational clusters, then children's recall should improve when they are trained in adult techniques. Also, adults who were required to use less efficient fourth-grade strategies should do less well than adults using adult strategies. Figure 7–12 shows that this is exactly what happened. Adults using adult strategies performed best of all. The adults using fourth-grade strategies performed less well, but their performance was still superior to the fourth-graders. Fourth-graders who had learned adult strategies

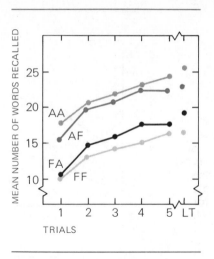

FIGURE 7-12
Mean recall as a function of trials for constrained sorting conditions (adults yoked to adults, AA; adults yoked to fourth-graders, AF; fourth-graders yoked to adults, FA; fourth-graders yoked to fourth-graders, FF). These data are indicated both for Trials 1-5 and for the last sorting trial **(LT).** From Liberty and Ornstein, 1973.

performed better than those who had used fourth-grade patterns, indicating not only that control process strategies are in part responsible for better memory, but also that training can improve recall.

Development of Metamemory. *Metamemory* is a term used to describe a person's knowledge about the memory process. It is thus a cognitive function that demands thinking and reflection. A fascinating interview study by Kreutzer, Leonard, and Flavell (1975) probed the understanding of kindergarten through fifth-grade children as to exactly how memory works. Here is a typical item from their interviews:

> Jim and Bill are in grade _____ [children's grade]. The teacher wanted them to learn the names of all the kinds of birds they might find in their city. Jim had learned them last year and then forgot them. Bill had never learned them before. Do you think one of these boys would find it easier to learn the names of all of the birds? Which one? Why? [p. 8]

Unsurprisingly, metamemory shows a dramatic increase over middle childhood. For example, kindergarten and first-grade children will recognize that the relearner has the advantage of recognition (saying such things as "the names will come back to Jim when he hears them"), but do not yet understand how subtler, psychological factors influence memory. In a notable instance, one psychologically minded third-grader told the experimenters that the advantage was actually with the new learner "because the kid who learned them might think he knew them, and then he would get them wrong, but the kid who didn't learn them last year might study more than the kid who *thought* he knew them" (Kreutzer, *et al.*, 1975, p. 9).

There is also very clear evidence that kindergarten and first-grade children have more difficulty than children in the higher elementary school grades in realistically assessing their own memory abilities (Flavell and

Wellman, 1976). For example, when these two age groups were asked to study a series of items until they were sure they could remember them perfectly, the older subjects usually studied for a period of time, and when they announced that they were prepared, they usually were. Younger children also tended to study for awhile and then announce that they were prepared, but usually they were not!

In conclusion, the evidence is indeed convincing that age differences in memory are due to advances in the software of the memory system; that is, the development of techniques or strategies that aid the memory process.

SUMMARY

One contemporary approach to cognitive development is based on Jean Piaget's biological and structural approach; the other, an information-processing approach, compares the human mind to a computer system, which acquires, processes, stores, and utilizes information.

According to Piaget, cognitive adaptation consists of two basic processes—assimilation and accommodation. Schemes are structures underlying a sequence of behavior. Piaget identified four periods of cognitive development. In the *sensorimotor period*, from birth to about two years of age, the child gradually passes through six stages of development, changing automatic reflexive reactions to planful behavior. Several developmental processes are involved in this period: primary circular reactions, secondary circular reactions, tertiary circular reactions, and representation. The *preoperational period*, from two to seven years of age, is characterized by the child's egocentric perspective, and by limitations in thinking demonstrated by the failure to solve conservation problems. During this period the child fails to see the reversibility of certain physical operations, perceives states rather than transformations, and tends to focus on a single detail of a problem without being able to shift to another dimension. Although Piaget believed that children below the age of six lacked the cognitive maturity to learn conservation problems, several training procedures have been successful in teaching them to younger children.

In the *concrete operational period*, from seven to eleven years of age, the child acquires an orderliness of thinking that involves the ability to decenter, recognize transformations, and understand reversibility and conservation problems. The last stage, the *formal operations period*, begins with preadolescence and is characterized by the ability to engage in formal reasoning on an abstract level, such as being able to solve the pendulum problem.

There have been numerous challenges to Piaget's conclusions about various aspects of cognitive development. Gelman particularly has challenged some of Piaget's claims about egocentrism during the preschool years and has argued that preschoolers can see another's point of view in certain situations.

The periods identified by Piaget are accompanied by the concurrent development of several important mental processes, which are required for adaptive and intelligent behavior. Mental representation, according to Piaget, first occurs at about age two when the child distinguishes signifiers (symbols and signs) from significates (the actual objects). Expanding on the work of Piaget, Bruner has identified three modes of mental representation—enactive, iconic, and symbolic. In one study, Bruner demonstrated that older but not younger children were able to use the symbolic mode of representation and thus were able to solve an otherwise impossible transposition problem.

Concept formation is the ability to identify classes of events on the basis of their shared, often abstract properties. Concept formation develops by the end of the sensorimotor period, with one of the first and most important concepts being that of object permanence.

Two major aspects of information processing have been identified—selective attention and memory. Selective attention to task-relevant information apparently is a developmental process, and it has a strong influence on memory. Four types of memory are "memory in the strict sense," "memory in the wider sense," episodic memory, and semantic memory. Retrieval—how we remember—may involve simple recognition, free recall, or reconstruction.

In studies based on a computer model of memory, developmental improvement in memory of recall tasks involves the acquisition of strategies and techniques for operating the memory system (software). Little or no age differences have been found for tasks involving the structural features of memory (hardware). Metamemory, a term used to describe a person's knowledge about the memory process, also improves dramatically with age.

8 Language and Communication

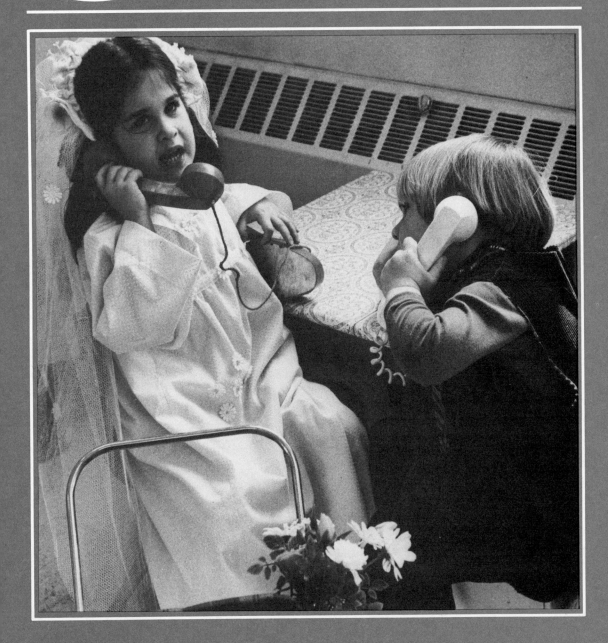

A child's first spoken word is one of the most momentous events in human development. The ability to communicate with others through speech begins at a very early age and opens up many new avenues of learning. We speak to one another at school, at home, and in business. Through written language we are able to preserve our ideas and benefit from the accomplishments and understanding developed by preceding generations as well. Successful and appropriate language use is also linked closely to a mastery of social situations, so the inability to understand and communicate with others can hamper a person's ability to cope with even the simplest of problems.

This chapter begins with a basic description of the course of language development from the individual's earliest babbling in the crib. We then focus on the separate aspects of language, including the issues of how meaning is attached to words and the processes through which words are arranged into grammatical and understandable sentences. And, finally, we examine language as it is actually used by children and adults in social contexts.

BEHAVIORAL AND COGNITIVE APPROACHES TO LANGUAGE AND COMMUNICATION

How is language acquired? Although the question has intrigued philosophers, parents, and scientists for thousands of years, we shall see that answers to it have not come easily and many important theoretical disputes are still unsettled.

The most important dispute revolves around the now familiar behaviorist-cognitivist schism. Behaviorists tend to view language acquisition and use as functional developments in the ability to communicate. The behaviorist looks to the child's environment, experience, and learning history (including responses obtained for various communication efforts) to explain various attainments in language development.

According to behaviorists, adults react differently to random sounds emitted by their infants, thereby increasing the frequency of some sounds and decreasing the frequency of others. Supporting this viewpoint, a series of studies conducted over a period of almost twenty years has suggested that external social reward can increase the rate at which infants vocalize (Bloom and Esposito, 1975; Rheingold, Gewirtz, and Ross, 1959; Weisberg, 1963).

Those holding the cognitive view insist that behaviorists ignore the marvelous structural complexity of human language. The processing of even the simplest sentences, according to the cognitivists, involve a myriad of complex mental operations. Cognitive-oriented theories therefore attempt to describe the maturation of mental capacities and/or the operation of mental processes on which language is presumably based. Despite their shared general orientation, however, cognitivists still differ sharply among themselves about how to best conceptualize language acquisition.

THE ROOTS AND SOUNDS OF LANGUAGE

Developmental psychologists are in substantial agreement when describing the roots and sounds of language itself. The belief that human language is made possible by our species' unique biological endowment is also generally accepted. Many nonprimate animal species are able to communicate with members of their own kind in various ways (the songs of birds, for example, appear to function as signals, as do the unique flying patterns or "dances" displayed by some types of bees), but their methods are almost completely innate and unmodifiable (McNeill, 1970a). Chimpanzees have been taught to communicate in a language-like way, using hand symbols taken from sign language (Gardner and Gardner, 1969), or using distinctively designed plastic chips as "words" (Premack, 1970). But it has proven impossible to teach apes to use speech in even its simplest conversational form, despite elaborate training efforts (Kellogg and Kellogg, 1933; Hayes, 1951). Thus members of the human species remain alone as true speakers, probably because of our unusual control of the vocal tract (the apparatus itself is present in the ape) and an innate capacity to handle complex symbols linguistically.

Preverbal Behavior

Children normally do not begin to speak meaningfully until after the first year of life, but such "real" speech is preceded by various forms of vocalization and reaction to vocalization in others. Sanger (1955) traced the development of prelinguistic behavior in infants at successive ages and found that infants responded to the sound of the human voice before the age of two months. Soon after (between the ages of two and four months), they also stopped vocalizing in order to listen to adults.

Infants have an impressive ability to perceive some very subtle differences in adult speech. For example, if a one-month-old infant is presented with the sound *pa* and then with successive versions of *pa* that sound more like *ba*, the infant will respond as if the sound had suddenly shifted from *pa* to *ba* rather than behaving as if the shift had been gradual. Moreover, the shift seems to occur at the same "boundary" as it does when adult listeners discriminate the two sounds in normal conversation (Eimas, Siqueland, Jusczyk, and Vignito, 1971; Eimas, 1975). Eimas (1975) interprets these results as showing that infants have inborn "feature detectors" that are designed to pick up and discriminate certain properties of speech but not others.

Cries and Cooing. The content of children's vocalization changes rapidly during infancy. For the first two or three months of life cries and grunts predominate; then, at about three months, cooing begins. These early sounds have been studied with a sophisticated device called the sound spectrograph, which provides a visual record of the physical aspects and the acoustic qualities of sound. Spectrograms show crying to be little more than the blowing of air along the vocal tract. With the exception of the opening and closing of the mouth, there is little articulation. Cooing produces a sound spectrogram that is quite different. The coo lasts about one-half second in duration—much shorter than the cry—and the articulatory organs, mainly the tongue, move during cooing. Infant cooing sometimes sounds

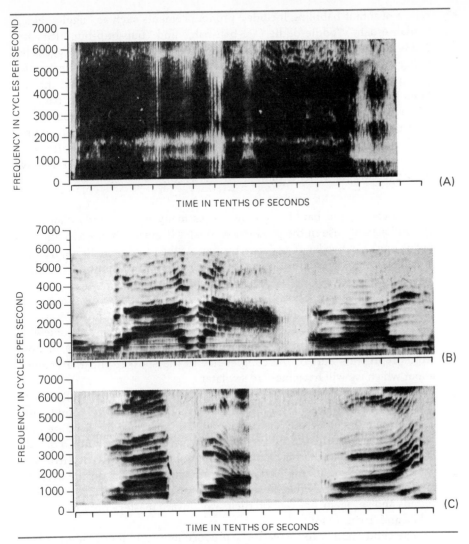

FIGURE 8-1
Some sample spectrograms of infant and mother's speech. (a)
Spectrogram of a 2-week-old boy crying vigorously; (b) a 3-month-old boy
cooing; (c) mother imitating her child after listening to a tape on which the
baby's noises are recorded.   From E. H. Lenneberg, **Biological Foundations
of Language**. Copyright 1967. Reproduced by permission of John Wiley &
Sons, Inc.

"vowel-like" but differs from adult vowel production functionally and
acoustically. The difference between the sound production of an adult
speaker and that of a prelanguage child is illustrated in Figure 8-1. Note
that even when the mother tries to imitate her own child, she makes very
different sounds than does the infant.

Social Babbling.   Social babbling develops after cooing, and often sounds
like an effort to communicate in a foreign language. One early investigator's

report of infant babbling included pronouncements such as "uggle-uggle," "erdah-erdah," "oddle-oddle," "a-bah-bah," and "bup-bup-bup" (Shirley, 1933). Some observers, noting that the vocalizations of infants suggest the rising and falling of the voice associated with questions and declarative statements in adult speech (Miller and Ervin, 1964), have argued that infants imitate the pitch, loudness, and intonation of adults when babbling (Weir, 1962). While babbling probably plays some role in later speech, the course of development between babbling and real language does not appear to be direct. Some children continue to babble for several months after they begin to produce real speech, whereas for others a short period of relative quiet precedes the onset of talking (Menn, 1976).

Phonemes: The Raw Materials of Speech

The cooing and babbling infant makes many more sounds than he or she will actually use in the production of later language. Some sounds drop out as one's "native language" is acquired. At the same time, though, single sounds are transformed into groups called *phonemes*, which are the raw materials from which all later speech will be composed.

In a general way, phonemes correspond to the usual vowel and consonant sounds of a language. But the letters alone are not quite enough to represent the phoneme. The letter *b*, for example, is pronounced somewhat differently in *bat* than in *tab*. That the sound is recognized as *b* in both words represents part of the competence of the speaker and the listener, about which we will have more to say later.

Vowel sounds begin to emerge during the first ten days of life. By one to two months of age the child commands an average of 4.5 vowel sounds, and at thirty months he or she has control of 11.4. Inasmuch as there are only fourteen vowel sounds in the English language, the thirty-month-old child is doing quite well in terms of mastery. Of approximately twenty-five consonants in English, infants of one to two months produce, on the average, 2.7. But by thirty months they are up to an average of 15.8 consonant sounds and so, again, are well on their way toward mastery before age three (Chen and Irwin, 1946).

The child's ability to increasingly produce more and more different language sounds, sometimes called *phonetic expansion*, roughly parallels a quite different occurrence, *phonetic contraction*. Several researchers have suggested that the infant, especially between the ages of six and twelve months, is able to, and in fact does, produce almost all of the sounds heard in human language, including the French vowels and German umlaut, which are extremely difficult for English-speaking adults to master (Jespersen, 1922). As children become more proficient in their native tongue, however, they cease to produce exotic language sounds. This contraction occurs as they apparently learn to limit themselves to the sounds of their own language.

Phonetic development has recently been cast as a type of learning based on hypothesis testing (Clark and Clark, 1977; see also chapter 6, p. 181). This view assumes that children are motivated to produce the "correct" (recognizable) sounds required by their language and that they try out various hypotheses in an effort to produce each required one. There is a certain discontinuity between one hypothesis and another as the child proceeds in the direction of accuracy; for example, a child may first say *dodi* and then shift to *goggie* before finally learning to produce a recognizable version of the adult, *doggie.* According to the hypothesis testing view children "have a clearly defined goal from the very start: they are trying to learn how to say recognizable words. They have to learn not only how to produce a sound close to the adult target, but also just how close they have to be before others can identify the segment they are aiming at" (Clark and Clark, 1977, p. 397).

The Mispronunciations of Young Children. Children are able to produce some phonemes before others and this fact, in turn, helps us to understand why certain mispronunciations are often found in the speech of young children. For example, the sounds called *fricatives* are almost invariably acquired later than the sounds called *stops*. F and S (fricatives) are produced later than P and T (stops). As a result children may pronounce *fish* as *pish* and *suit* as *toot*. The so-called *affricates* (for example, the *ch* in chair) are also acquired later than the stops. For this reason children will often pronounce *chair* as if it were *tair*.

Children seem to be aware of their own mispronunciations and many young children will simply avoid using words containing sounds that they cannot pronounce with ease (Ferguson and Farwell, 1975). Children also practice new words, word segments, and word rhymes in spontaneous monologues throughout much of early childhood (Weir, 1962, 1966). Through practice they learn to master difficult sounds.

Interestingly, children are often able to distinguish correct and incorrect pronunciations in the speech of adults that they are not yet capable of producing themselves. This differential ability leads to some amusing interchanges. Here is a marvelous example provided by Berko and Brown (1960), which has come to be called the "fis phenomenon."

> One of us, for instance, spoke to a child who called his inflated plastic fish a *fis*. In imitation of the child's pronunciation, the observer said: "This is your *fis*?" "No," said the child, "my *fis*." He continued to reject the adult's imitation until he was told, "That is your fish." "Yes," he said, "my *fis*." (p. 531)

LINGUISTIC COMPETENCE

So far our emphasis has been on the development and recognition of speech. But an understanding of these aspects of language provides only a small part of the answer to the central question, "How does language develop?" We must also explain the development of the ability to recognize, produce, and transmit sentences that are meaningful and grammatically correct, for it is this ability that is demonstrated by adult human beings in every culture and society.

Technically, the study of the relationship of language to meaning is called *semantics,* and the study of the rules followed in producing "permissible constructions" is called *grammar.* The study of grammar is divided into two parts—*syntax* concerns itself with how words are combined into phrases and sentences, and *morphology* examines the formation of words themselves. An accomplished speaker's knowledge of the semantics and grammar of a particular language, then, reflects his or her *linguistic competence*, the set of principles and specific information a person must have in order to be a speaker of that language. Viewed in this manner, one major task undertaken by developmental psycholinguists is to chart the emergence of this competence from birth to adulthood and to identify the underlying processes that account for it.

The ability to communicate, however, entails more than linguistic competence. Sophisticated communication entails knowing what to say as well as how and when to say it, and thus demands that the speaker be sensitive to the person(s) to whom he or she is communicating as well as to the context in which the communication occurs. The picture of development that has begun to emerge from recent studies is that linguistic competence is achieved fairly early in development, whereas the broader ability to communicate effectively continues to develop well into adolescence and perhaps throughout most of the life span.

We will now more deeply explore early communication skills and lin-

FIGURE 8–2
Pointing is an early but highly effective form of communicating.
© 1979 Jan Lukas, Photo Researchers, Inc.

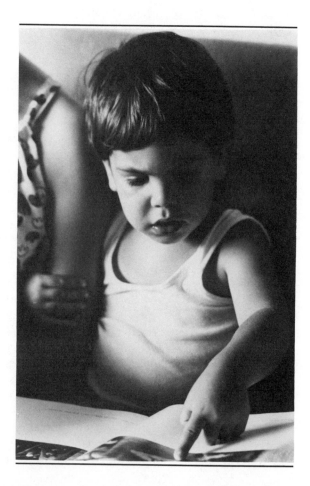

guistic development during the first three years of life. As we shall see, the period is one of remarkable achievement.

Early Communication Skills

The need to communicate exists for every living being. Spoken and written language are the unique means of human communication, but humans also display, recognize, and use a variety of nonverbal signs and signals from a very early age. Effective communication patterns, including verbal and nonverbal modes, develop over time as a result of both direct and vicarious experience and the maturation of underlying motor, perceptual, and cognitive processes.

Gestural Communications in Preverbal Infancy. Escalona (1973) found that adults begin to bring objects to infants while naming the objects by the time the infant is three or four months old. Within a few months thereafter children begin to reciprocate by spontaneously bringing objects to adults. By the time the infant is about eight months old the gesture of pointing will be comprehended by the infant and, again, the child will learn to reciprocate before his or her first birthday, pointing out interesting or attractive objects in the presence of others.

By the age of one year children seem to show a real understanding of the concept "listening." They will point or gesture to show an adult something and then check to make sure that the adult has really been following the communication (Carter, 1975).

The Relationship Between Gestures and Words. A considerable body of evidence suggests that gestures and speech acts have parallel functions as systems of communication. (Think of the one-year-old who says "bye-bye" and waves her hand at the same time.) The gestures of very young children are also readily characterizable according to their function (Bruner, 1975). Some gestures make a request (e.g., reaching for a distant toy as a way of asking an onlooker, "[Please] get me that toy"), while others advance an assertion (e.g., pointing at someone passing on the street to communicate, "Look").

The Child's First Words

The first word that children almost everywhere produce sounds very much like *mama*, and it is believed that *mama* appears in so many diverse languages because it is derived from the natural nasal-like murmur that infants make when sucking ("mmmh-ah"). As a bit of meaningful speech, *mama* is most often used to demand that a need be filled (Jakobson, 1962), but the specific age at which it is first pronounced may precede its meaningful use. Other meaningful words do not usually appear until around the child's first birthday (McCarthy, 1954). The three categories that are most popular in children's first ten words are animals, food, and toys. In one study (Nelson, 1973) *juice, milk,* and *cookie* tended to be the first food words; *dog* and *cat* tended to be the first animal words; and *ball* and *block* were the first toys to be named.

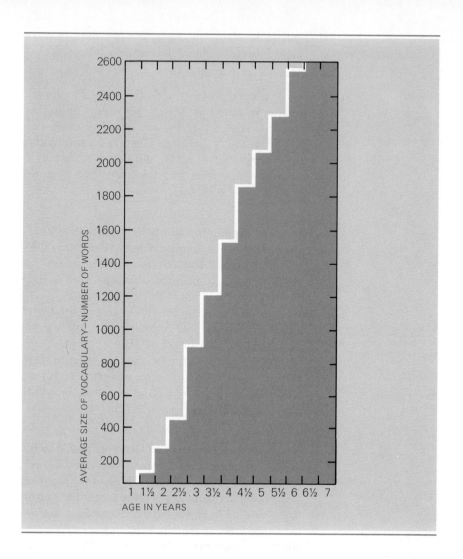

By the age of twenty-four months vocabulary has multiplied two-hundred to three-hundred times. The number of words used continues to increase thereafter at a rapid rate (see Figure 8–3). With such a substantive vocabulary it seems logical that the child's next step would be sentence building.

The Development
of the Sentence

The sentence is considered by most modern linguists to be the basic unit of language because it is the simplest unit that can perform in actual language use. The sentences produced by young children, like those produced by older children and adults, must be constructed from the child's ever-expanding vocabulary. The question is, How does the child know how to construct a sentence?

The One-Word Sentence: A Linguistic Universal. Research has shown that in virtually every language and culture the child's first sentences consist of single words. That is, children everywhere begin by using the individual words in their vocabularies as independent statements expressing assertions, commands, or questions. This fact has led some theorists to suggest that the concept of a sentence is part of the human organism's inborn capacity, a linguistic universal which is not itself learned but on which grammar and speech are built through learning. McNeill (1970a) has put it this way:

> The facts of language acquisition could not be as they are unless the concept of a sentence is available to children at the start of their learning. The concept of a sentence is the main guiding principle in a child's attempt to organize and interpret the linguistic evidence that fluent speakers make available to him. . . .
>
> Children everywhere begin with exactly the same initial hypothesis; sentences consist of single words. The entire structure of a sentence must be squeezed through this tiny space. This simplest hypothesis leads to the most peripheral of differences between children learning different languages. Only the words differ. A child exposed to English might use *hot* as a comment and a Japanese child would use *atusi*, but the difference is merely in sound, not in conceptual or linguistic structure. Not only are words sentences at the beginning, they are the same sentences in different languages. [p. 2]

The child's first single word sentences are likely to appear as accompaniments to gestures (Greenfield and Smith, 1976, see Table 8–1), and the gestures, like the words, typically imply either assertions or requests in themselves.

The Two-Word Sentence.   Within a few months after uttering his or her first meaningful one-word sentence, the child will begin to produce pairs of words that make some type of statement. Careful observation has shown that the transition from two one-word sentences to a functional two-word sentence is a gradual one. After beginning to use a few single words, the child will string them together, pausing between each. Then the location of the pause will gradually change so that, for example, the child will begin by saying "baby" and "chair" together, but will soon combine them to form "baby chair." (Bloom, 1973).

TABLE 8–1
Examples of Assertions and Requests Communicated by the Combination of Gestures and One-Word Sentences

CHILD	FUNCTION	COMMUNICATION	CONTEXT
Nicky	Assertion	Ba + look	Looking at ball
	Request	Mama + whine + reach	Reaches toward any object desired
Matthew	Assertion	Dada + look	Looking at father
	Request	Ma + whine + point	Pointing at microphone

Source: Based on Greenfield and Smith, 1976.

TABLE 8-2
Assertions and Requests at the Two-Word Stage

SPEECH ACT	UTTERANCES
Assertions	
Presence of object	See boy. See sock. That car.
Denial of presence	Allgone shoe. No wet. Byebye hot.
Location of object	Bill here. There doggie. Penny innere.
Possession of object	My milk. Kendall chair. Mama dress.
Quality of object	Pretty boat. Big bus.
Ongoing event	Mommy sleep. Hit ball. Block fall.
Requests	
For action	More taxi. Want gum. Where ball?
For information	Where doggie? Sit water?
Refusal	No more.

Source: Adapted from Clark and Clark (1977); based on data from Slobin (1970), Bowerman (1973a), and R. Brown (1973).

Two-word and longer sentences can more easily stand as communications than one-word utterances can, but they, too, may be accompanied by gestures and are readily classifiable in function as assertions or requests (Clark and Clark, 1977; see Table 8-2).

Once the child begins to produce two-word sentences their use expands at a very rapid rate. It is as if the child suddenly discovers the power to express an almost unlimited set of ideas and cannot resist doing so. One case study has shown that more than one thousand new and distinct two-word utterances per month appear during this phase of development (Braine, 1963).

Emergence of the Full Sentence. If children everywhere begin with one- and then two-word sentences, as appears to be the case, this situation is rapidly modified by environmental experience. Brown (1965) has pointed out that "by the age of thirty-six months some children are so advanced in the construction process as to produce all of the major varieties of English simple sentences up to a length of ten or eleven words" (p. 286).

The Child's First
Conversations

Although children communicate their assertions and requests from a very early age, there is an unmistakable one-sidedness to these communications. It is not until the age of two or so that real interchange—the beginnings of conversation—emerges.

We shall start with an excerpt (taken originally from the records of Brown and Bellugi, 1964) to provide the general feeling of what such a conservation might be like (Table 8-3). Note that certain words are missing from the child's part of the interchange. The glaring absence of most articles, auxiliary verbs, and inflections is noticeable, particularly in phrases such as "put suitcase . . . for?" "Where birdie go?" "What inere?" and "Yep, it fit." But despite the deletion of many elements, including "what," "did," "you," "it," "in," and "the," from the child's sentence "Put suitcase . . . for?" the essential message can be successfully communicated.

| TABLE 8-3 |
| Typical Conversation between an Adult and a Young Child |

Child (28 Months)	Adult
What dat . . . somebody pencil	Whose pencils are they?
Floor	Floor?
Where birdie go?	
Birdie	
Birdie up dere	
Birdie	
Read dat?	
Read dat?	Will you read it to me?
What inere?	Is that a hammer, Adam?
Hammer	
Hit hammer, mommy	
No Cromer _____, mommy?	
Hurt	Poor Adam. Did you hurt yourself?
	What happened, Adam?
Screw (did) happen	Screw happened? You didn't even have
	a screw.
have screw	
_____ no down there . . .	
table . . . get broom	Does that one fit?
Yep, it fit	
Yep, it fit	Does it fit?
No . . . fit	
Put suitcase . . . for?	What did you put it in the suitcase for?
What dat?	That's tape. We'll use that one tomorrow.
All right 'morrow	Shall we use it tomorrow?
Yep	
Use morrow, yep	
Sure, use morrow	

Source: R. Brown and U. Bellugi, "Three Processes in the Child's Acquisition of Syntax," Harvard Educational Review, 1964, 34, 133–151. Copyright 1964 by the President and Fellows of Harvard College.

Telegraphic Communication. Because of the similarity between the well-trimmed telegram and the pared down verbal communications of the young child, many writers have described the young child's speech as *telegraphic*. This is an appealing and graphic term, but we should not overlook its deeper significance. The fact that the child's first communicative speech sounds like telegraph messages is not important—most three-year-olds would not be able to tell you what a telegraph is. Rather, what is important is that adult telegraph messages are remarkably like children's early speech. The basic developmental principle seems to be that the essentials always come first, with refinements and frills appearing later.

Table 8–3 actually shows two levels of telegraphic simplification. One is at the word level, as in the child's reduction of tomorrow to " 'morrow,"; the other is at the sentence level, as in the child's "Where birdie go?"

Smith (1973), in a detailed analysis, describes four distinct ways in which children may simplify the production of individual words:

1. *Omitting unstressed syllables.* The child's *'morrow* in Table 8–3 is an example of this form of simplification.

2. *Omitting final consonants.* Children will often say such things as *cuh* for cookie or *ba* for ball.

3. *Reducing consonant clusters.* Young children will often omit one or more consonants from a consonant cluster; for example, a child may say *kirt* for skirt.

4. *Syllable reduplication.* Children may simplify words while maintaining the "length" of the word by repeating the first syllable rather than supplying the actual second syllable. Thus daddy becomes *dada.*

Imitation with Expansion and Reduction. All communication includes at least two people, so we should not overlook the role of the adult in our sample conversation. The passage in Table 8–3 contains several instances in which the adult rephrases or expands something the child has said, often taking something that is ungrammatical and recasting it properly. For example, the child's question "Read da?" is recast by the adult into "Will you read it to me?" and "Put suitcase . . . for?" is expanded into "What did you put it in the suitcase for?" In imitative expansion, then, the adult adds to the child's telegraphic message, making the utterance clearer as well as more grammatically correct. Children even seem to have a preference for being spoken to in adult terms. In one investigation (Shipley, Smith, and Gleitman, 1969) it was reported that young children are actually more responsive to adult commands given in adult form (*Throw me the ball*) than the same command in a form that approximates the child's own level of syntactic production (*Throw ball*).

McNeill (1970a, 1970b) has suggested that an adult will select an expanded sentence to fit the child's intended meaning, manufactured from both the child's utterance and the situation which exists. Thus, if the child's meaning is correctly guessed, the adult is actually presenting to the child a grammatically appropriate way to express the meaning the child has in mind.

Several excellent examples of the expansion process can be found in an intensive study of the natural language development of three children, "Adam," "Eve," and "Sarah," from the time they were about two years old (Brown, Cazden, and Bellugi-Klima, 1969):

> Every second week we visited each child for at least two hours and made a tape recording of everything said by the child, as well as of everything said to the child. The mother was always present and most of the speech to the child is hers. Both mother and child became very accustomed to our presence and learned to continue their usual routine with us as observers. [Brown, 1965, p. 287]

One of the most striking aspects of these transcripts is that the child learns speech imitatively, through a reciprocal process of interchange with the mother. Specifically, the child tends to show *imitation with reduction* of the mother's speech, whereas the mother imitates some of the child's phrases *but expands upon them.* Both types of imitation are illustrated in Table 8–4.

TABLE 8-4
Examples of Imitation with Reduction (By the Child) and Imitation with Expansion (By the Mother)

IMITATION WITH REDUCTION	
Mother	Child
Daddy's brief case.	Daddy brief case.
Fraser will be unhappy.	Fraser unhappy.
He's going out.	He go out.
No, you can't write on Mr. Cromer's shoe.	Write Cromer shoe.

IMITATION WITH EXPANSION	
Child	Mother
Baby highchair.	Baby is in the highchair.
Mommy sandwich.	Mommy'll have a sandwich.
Pick glove.	Pick the glove up.

Source: Brown, 1965.

Taking Turns in Social Conversation: A First Lesson in Social Cooperation. An important feature of the conversations recorded in both Tables 8–3 and 8–4 is that the adult has structured the conversation so that she and the child are taking turns. Turn-taking is essential not only to communication but also to many other cooperative, social endeavors.

The child's first experience with taking turns typically comes from language interactions with parents. As soon as children begin to talk at all, parents seem to promote the idea of taking conversational turns and alternating the role of speaker and listener. Snow (1977) even found evidence that mothers try to deal this way with their prelinguistic infants, treating the babies' yawns, blinks, and burps as if these were appropriate conversational replies. Clark and Clark (1977, p. 324) provide a simulated dialogue between mother and infant that captures the essence of this form of early conversational training:

Mother: Hello. Give me a smile then [gently pokes infant in the ribs].
Infant: [yawns]
Mother: Sleepy, are you? You woke up too early today.
Infant: [opens fist]
Mother: [touching infant's hand] What are you looking at? Can you see something?
Infant: [grasps mother's finger]
Mother: Oh, that's what you wanted. In a friendly mood, then. Come on, give us a smile.

Parents also use powerful shaping procedures. As soon as the infant is able to produce words he or she is *required* to use words (rather than gestures alone) to keep the conversation going. To assist in this form of training, parents often model both sides of conversation so that their children can learn observationally how the game should be played (Ervin-Tripp, 1970). For example, parents may model the child's role as well as their own in an effort to teach turn-taking, creating such exemplary dialogues as:

Parent: [initiating conversation in role of parent] What's the doggie doing?
Parent: [modeling appropriate reply for child] The doggie is eating!

Talking to Children: Some Adult Ways.   Anyone who has ever tried to talk to a young child conversationally knows very well that one can't speak to a child as one does to an adult. One problem is simply getting the child's attention. Adults use a variety of devices for this purpose, such as using the child's name at the beginning of a sentence ("Bobbie, look at the horse"), using exclamations (such as "Hey!"), repeating portions of what they have said in order to capture and hold the child's attention ("Yes, horsie!"), or looking and pointing at the objects they are talking about (Collis, 1977; Snow, 1972).

Adults also monitor children carefully to be sure that their attention is sustained. Sachs, Brown, and Salerno (1976) found that adults raise the pitch of their voices at the end of sentences when they are telling a story to young children. This is the very device adults generally use when asking questions, and presumably signals to the child that the adult wants some type of feedback (Clark and Clark, 1977).

Adults often simplify their speech in various ways when talking to young children (Snow, 1972). Articles and possessives are frequently omitted so that these words occur least frequently when adults talk to two-year-olds, more frequently when they talk to ten-year-olds, and most frequently when talking to other adults. Adults also avoid pronouns when talking to young children, repeating the relevant noun instead. (For example, an adult would probably not say, "See the boy. He is riding the horse." Instead an adult might say to a young child, "See the boy. The boy is riding the horse.") Presumably these devices make it easier to understand what is being said. An interesting note here is that adults simplify their language in similar ways when talking to foreigners (e.g., Ferguson, 1971).

Adults also vary the modulation in their voices, depending on whether they are talking to adults or to children. In a fascinating dissertation, Garnica (1975) recorded the voices of adults talking to two-year-olds, five-year-olds, and adults in a similar setting and found that the pitch of the adults' voices was highest for the two-year-olds, a bit lower for the five-year-olds, and lowest for other adults. Garnica also found that mothers are considerably more likely to whisper to their two-year-olds than to their five-year-olds, and that they almost never whisper to other adults.

Parental Feedback for Communicative Accuracy.   The detailed observations recorded by Brown and his associates (1969) of parent-child conversations, in addition to the previously mentioned discoveries, also revealed an important fact about the intent of parental training. Parents are considerably less concerned with their children's grammar than with the adequacy and accuracy of the child's communication. Brown and his colleagues report:

> Once in a while an error of pronunciation was noticed and corrected. Most commonly, however, the grounds on which an utterance was approved or disapproved . . . were not strictly linguistic at all. When Eve expressed the opinion that her mother was a girl by saying "He a girl," mother answered "That's right." The child's utterance was ungrammatical but mother did not respond to the fact; instead she responded to the truth value of the proposition the child intended to express. In general the parents fit propositions to the child's utterances, however incomplete or distorted the utterances, and then approved or not, according to the correspondence between proposition and reality. Thus "Her curl my hair" was approved because mother was in fact curling Eve's hair. However, Sarah's grammatically impeccable "There's the animal farmhouse" was disapproved because the building was a lighthouse and Adam's "Walt Disney comes on, on Tuesday" was disapproved because Walt Disney comes on, on some other day. It seems, then, to be truth value rather than syntactic well-formedness that chiefly governs explicit verbal reinforcement by parents. Which renders mildly paradoxical the fact that the usual product of such a training schedule is an adult whose speech is highly grammatical but not notably truthful. [Brown, Cazden, and Bellugi, 1969, pp. 57–58]

HOW DOES THE CHILD ACQUIRE GRAMMAR?

In the detailed conversations recorded by Brown and his associates (1969), we saw that mothers did not tend to correct the child's grammar in the early years. Yet it was also clear that imitation was involved in these conversations. What role does observational learning play in the acquisition of grammar, and what other factors are involved?

The Role of Observational Learning

At one time it was thought that children might learn to speak grammatically by merely listening to and then copying adult sentences in precisely the form they were heard. It has now become apparent, however, that this is not the case. Children produce many more sentences than they have ever heard. More importantly, even when children imitate adult sentences, they do not imitate adult grammar; even in simply trying to repeat *I am drawing a picture*, young children will say *I draw picture*. And, finally, children who cannot speak at all and thus never imitate language may come to comprehend it perfectly (Lenneberg, 1967).

But observational learning, in some form, must be deeply implicated in the acquisition of grammar. Children all over the world come to speak the language and use the grammar of those around them, and this is as true of children adopted from one culture to another as it is of those with "roots" in a particular language. Children must learn a major part of language from exposure to native speakers (an American child who cannot speak will learn to understand English from the language of others, but a child who is

reared in a world where no one else can speak will obviously not understand English at all). The question is, What processes are involved in the
learning? Developmental psychologists interested in observational learning
have increasingly focused on children's ability to abstract the underlying
rules that apparently govern a model's behavior in language and in other
areas as well. Once such rules have been formulated, the observer can generate an endless number of novel responses that are consistent with them
(Zimmerman and Rosenthal, 1974). Both the formation of sentences (syntax) and the formation of words (morphology) appear to be governed by
rules.

Syntax and the Observational Learning of Rules. Applying this type of
reasoning to the study of syntactic development, Leonard (1975) selected
eighteen children between two years, four months of age and three years,
four months of age, all of whom used two- and three-word utterances
("More milk," "That kitty"), but none of whom were producing true
subject-verb sentences ("Man read," "Boy go," "I drink"). Training, though
it varied in minor ways that need not concern us here, consisted of exposure
to an adult model who was rewarded for describing various pictures and
situations in two-word, subject-verb sentences. When he compared children so trained with a group of control children who had received no special training, Leonard found that the modeling groups showed significant
gains in their production of novel, grammatical two-word sentences. The
test he used, which avoided the problem of having to give special verbal
hints or instructions, was to ask children to describe pictures that invited
the subject-verb form of grammatical construction, such as a picture of a
man walking.

Syntax of the Two-
Word Sentence

The appearance of the two-word sentence raises the grammatical question of how such sentences are formed. Observers of all theoretical per-
suasions agree that the child's two-word utterances are rule-governed, at
least to some extent, but theoretical disputes still rage regarding the exact
nature of early syntax.

Autoclitic Frames. In the late 1950s, Skinner (1957) attempted an account
of the emergence and maintenance of language, using as the basis of his
speculation many of the same variables that had shaped and maintained
nonverbal behavior in the laboratory through operant conditioning (see
chapter 6). One important idea in Skinner's theory of language development is the notion of partially conditioned *autoclitic frames.** When a child
has acquired responses such as "the boy's gun," "the boy's shoe," and "the
boy's hat," the partial frame "the boy's——" is presumably available and
may be combined with other responses. Thus when the child notices a boy
who has recently obtained a bicycle, she may compose a new unit "the
boy's bicycle," by inserting the appropriate term in the previously acquired

* Skinner's account of language is quite complex and touches on all aspects of language
structure and function as seen from his thoroughly behaviorist position.

frame. The relational aspects of the situation determine the use of the particular frame, and the specific features of the situation determine the nature of the responses that will fit into it. To illustrate, Whitehurst (1972) trained two-year-old children to use partially conditioned autoclitic frames as defined by Skinner. The procedure involved teaching two subjects to label individual colors or figures with a nonsense vocabulary (eg., "Gol" or "Tib"), and then training them to label the color and figure simultaneously, in a given order. For example, when the color red and a particular figure were presented, the correct answer would be *red car* (except that the subjects' actual responses were in the nonsense vocabulary, e.g., "Gol Tib"). Then a few figure label would be taught and simultaneously presented with the old color, red. The red stimulus, then, was retained as part of each new unit and should become a frame for learning this simple grammar. This is just what happened for both children. They soon learned to produce novel but grammatically correct descriptions of any red object for which they were taught a label, without having to hear or be rewarded for producing the particular description.

Pivot-Open Grammar.   One criticism of the notion of partially conditioned autoclitic frames is that they do not account for the range of two-word sentences that children actually generate. Thus many theorists have pursued a more abstract, cognitively oriented analysis of the rules underlying syntax.

An early suggestion was that children begin with what is called a *pivot-open* grammar (Braine, 1963). Consider the usual two-word sentences of the young child. Sequences such as "my shoe," "a hand," and "see papa" are extremely common, whereas verbalizations such as "shoe my," "hand a," and "papa see" occur infrequently—if at all. According to the pivot-open theory, it is supposed that young children divide their word repertoire into two classes and that one word from each class is selected for certain two-word utterances. The smaller of the classes is called the "pivot" class, and the other is called the "open" class. In the sequences "see papa," "see hand," and "see shoe," *see* is a "pivot" word, and all the other words fall into the "open" category. Any particular pivot word occurs in the same position in every sentence, but some pivot words can appear in the first position only, while others can appear in the second position only. Investigators have found that there are far fewer pivot words than open words, that their number grows quite slowly in our vocabularies, and that pivot words almost never are used as one-word sentences.

Like the notion of autoclitic frames, the pivot-open idea has its limitations. One problem is quite obvious: pivot-open grammar does not seem overtly related to the grammar that develops later. Also, some research has indicated quite contradictory results. Bloom's study (1970) of two young children reports that the overwhelming majority of their sentences were *not* of the pivot-open form.

The "Functional Grammar" of the Two-Word Sentence.   Partly in response to her own observation that children's two-word utterances are of-

TABLE 8–5
Functions of Two-Word Sentences in Child Speech, with Examples from Several Languages

Function of Utterance	English	German	Russian	Finnish	Samoan
Locate, name	there book	buch da (book there)	Tasya tam (Tasya there)	tuossa Rina (there Rina)	Keith lea (Keith there)
Demand, desire	more milk	mehr milch (more milk)	yesche moloko (more milk)	anna Rina (give Rina)	mai pepe (give doll)
Indicate possession	my shoe	mein ball (my ball)	mami chashka (mama's cup)	tati auto (aunt car)	lole a'u (candy my)
Question	where ball	wo ball (where ball)	gdu papa (where papa)	missu palle (where ball)	Fea punafu (where Punafu)

Source: Adapted from Slobin, 1970.

ten not explainable in terms of pivot-open grammar, Bloom (1970) suggested that young children use a grammar in which the function rather than just the position of a word plays a role. The two-word sentence *that book* serves a nominative function (it names something), whereas *mommy lunch* serves a possessive function, and *Eve read* serves to link an agent and its action. Analyzing the speech of many children acquiring languages all over the world, both Brown (1970) and Slobin (1970) reported that a small number of such functional relationships invariably occur in language development (see Table 8–5).

The functional view has been extended to suggest that children develop formulas for generating their two-word sentences, based on past experience and current needs. Not every child invents the same formulas, and so we would expect children to differ in the general form given to their two-word utterances (Braine, 1976). This appears to be just what occurs. Some children combine two "content" words in their two-word utterances such as "Bob car," or "make picture," while other children may regularly combine a content word with a pronoun (I go, I do) or a "location" word (push it) (Bloom, Lightbown, and Hood, 1975).

Morphology and the Application of Rules

Up to now we have spoken primarily of the child's early syntactic development, but *morphology*, the grammar of forming words correctly, is important both in its own right and as a way of better understanding the entire process of language development. As with syntactic development, the bulk of the accumulated evidence now suggests that children develop formulas or rules based on experience and that these rules govern their subsequent language behavior.

Inflection, for example, is an important aspect of morphology that refers to changing the shape (and usually the meaning) of a word by the addition of suffixes (e.g., adding *-ed* to *walk* marks the past tense) or an alteration of the base itself (e.g., converting *swim* to *swam*). In a classic study, Berko (1958) demonstrated quite conclusively that children's inflection of words is rule-regulated rather than merely based on memory of specific forms for

FIGURE 8–4
An example of the pictures used by Berko to show that children know and use morphological rules even by preschool age. Although the child has never heard the word WUG before, he or she will "correctly" pluralize it into WUGS. Adapted from Berko, 1958.

specific words. She accomplished this by presenting children with totally unfamiliar words that required inflection; thus the children had no previous exposure and could not rely on direct past experience. More specifically, Berko showed children some pictures of nonsense objects, such as the one in Figure 8–4, and said "This is a WUG." She then showed the child a picture of two such objects and said, "These are two——," providing the child with an opportunity to supply the plural form of WUG. Her subjects, preschool children, were able to perform remarkably well (i.e., by application of the rule, the plural of WUG ought to be WUGS).

Patterns of rule-regulated language of the type identified by Berko frequently can be observed even in the casual observation of young children's language. For example, children will often "regularize" what are, in fact, irregular English forms by saying "He *doed* it" instead of "He *did* it" or "I see the sheep*s*" rather than "I see the sheep." Inasmuch as it is most unlikely that they have heard adult speakers use these particular phrases, they are presumably operating with rules that they have abstracted, incorrectly in these cases, from the language they have heard. Such overregularization is found not only in English, but in a variety of languages that have quite different rules for the application of the suffix, such as Russian, Latvian, Serbo-Croatian, Hungarian, and German (Clark and Clark, 1977).

If casual observation reveals the child's knowledge of morphological rules by charming but mistaken regularizations, it is less likely to reveal the

TABLE 8-6
Stages in the Acquisition of the Past Tense Suffix in English.

STAGE 1	Little or no use of past tense forms.
STAGE 2	Sporadic use of some irregular forms (examples: went, broke).
STAGE 3	Use of regular suffix -ed for all past tense forms (examples: jumped, goed, breaked).
STAGE 4	Adultlike use of regular and irregular forms (examples: jumped, went).

Source: Based on Cazden, 1968.

surprising sequence of this aspect of language development. Most people would probably guess that a child's first tendency is to regularize irregular words, as in the sentences we have just examined, and that the error is rectified later by overhearing correct adult usage. In fact, this is not the sequence at all. Children usually begin by using the correct form of irregular verbs, such as *came* and *broke,* probably because they are imitating these frequently heard adult forms as particular words. Then, perhaps weeks or even months later, the child will shift from correct to incorrect usage, by regularizing all verbs. The child who begins by saying *I broke it* will "advance" to the stage of saying *I breaked it,* rather than the other way around. By the time they start school, of course, most children will have permanently reinstated commonly used irregular forms as their typical language performance (Ervin, 1964). This entire process involves four relatively discrete stages (Cazden, 1968), summarized in Table 8–6 on p. 243.

Transformational Grammar Theory and Later Syntactical Development

There is much about children's grammar that remains unexplained by merely saying that language is learned through observation and the abstraction of rules. For one thing, youngsters seem able to respond correctly to aspects of language that are not marked in any obvious way in speech, such as the "logical" subject of a sentence. Consider the sentences "John is eager to please" and "John is easy to please." Although *John* may appear at first to be the subject of both sentences, it is actually the subject only in the first. The second, "John is easy to please," actually means that it is easy for someone to please John. The question is not whether people can make the distinction—it is apparent that they can—but *how* the distinction is made. One theorist, Noam Chomsky (1968), has proposed that the answer lies in the theory of transformational grammar.

Transformational grammar theory is primarily designed to provide a cognitive explanation of language processing and its development. One writer (Ehri, 1972) traces the view back to a classic analysis by the eminent neuropsychologist Karl Lashley, who suggested that a three-step sequence of mental events underlies the production of any sentence. First, some event, occurring either in the environment or within the person, arouses a thought. In turn, the thought calls forth learned expressive units—words—which represent components of the thought. Finally, as the last step, the words are arranged into a sequence appropriate to communicate the thought in a particular language. Those who accept this view claim that analysis of the end product, the particular linguistic expression of a thought, can provide only limited information about the process of language generation. It is not the particular form of an expression but its underlying meaning, or *deep structure,* that really matters.

If this view is correct, the same process should also work in reverse. That is, when in the role of listener (and learner), persons would be expected to understand communications of others by processing the grammatical surface structure of sentences they hear to extract the underlying relations and meaning. The superficial structure of the communication would then probably be forgotten, and only the deep structure would be preserved in memory. This expectation has received strong support in research. Children and adults, presented with a number of sentences with varying surface structure but the same deep structure (e.g., "The soldier destroys the bridge" or "The bridge is destroyed by the soldier"), will remember the meaning of the sentences they have heard but have great difficulty in remembering the particular structure on which it was based.

Surface and Deep Structure: a Closer Look. A transformation, for Chomsky, is a relationship between the underlying or *deep* structure of a sentence and its superficial or *surface* structure. The surface structure of a sentence is the apparent relationship among its elements and has been traditionally viewed as the ordered set of phrases or "parts of speech" learned in elementary school. *Visiting relatives can be a nuisance* is readily analyzed into a noun phrase (*Visiting relatives*) and a compound verb phrase (*can be*) (*a nuisance*). But underlying this surface arrangement is a twist: The sentence has two possible underlying meanings. We must transform this sentence in order to detect its message, and here we find that two quite different underlying meanings could be represented by this one string of words, depending on the deep structure we read into it. Transformed in one way the sentence means *Relatives who visit can be a nuisance,* but an equally plausible transformation of the same word string is *It can be a nuisance to visit relatives.* We understand the sentence only when we grasp its underlying structure, which cannot be equated with the initial arrangement of the word string itself.

When the meaning of a sentence is ambiguous from its surface structure, how well can children discern the deep structure that the sentence reflects? To explore this question Carol Chomsky (1969) placed a small, blindfolded doll in front of five-, six-, seven-, eight-, and nine-year-old subjects and asked, "Is the doll easy to see or hard to see?" She found that children answered with considerable self-assurance, but there was a surprising number of errors even up through the age of eight (see Table 8–7). Apparently the deep structures of some sentences are not easily found and children just avoid such constructions in their spontaneous speech.

Chomsky also made the interesting discovery that children confuse *ask* and *tell* during early elementary school years. This is *not* because they don't know the meaning of these words but because in certain sentences the implied underlying structure is confusing to them. The following passage, an actual dialogue between six-year-old Laura and an adult, illustrates the point.

Q. Ask Joanne what color this book is.
A. What color's that book?
Q. Ask Joanne her last name.
A. What's your last name?
Q. Tell Joanne what color this tray is.
A. Tan.
Q. Ask Joanne what's in the box.
A. What's in the box?
Q. Ask Joanne what to feed the doll.
A. The hot dog. [Here Laura has confused *ask* and *tell*.]

TABLE 8-7
Percentage of Children at Various Ages Who Respond Correctly to the Deep
Structure of the Question "Is the Doll Easy to See or Hard to See?"
(The younger children tend to respond as if the question were, "Is it easy
[or hard] for the doll to see?")

AGE OF CHILD	PERCENTAGE RESPONDING APPROPRIATELY TO THE DEEP STRUCTURE
5	22
6	42
7	86
8	75
9	100

Source: Reprinted by permission of the MIT Press from Carol Chomsky, **The Acquisition of Syntax in Children from 5 to 10,** Copyright © 1969 by the Massachusetts Institute of Technology.

Q. Now I want you to *ask* Joanne something. *Ask* her what to feed the doll.
A. The piece of bread. [Laura persists in telling rather than asking Joanne.]
Q. Ask Joanne what *you* should feed the doll.
A. What should I feed the doll?*

[C. Chomsky, 1969, p. 57, italics added]

Transformational Grammar Theory and the Changing Form of Children's Questions. Anyone spending even a few minutes with children will discover that they avidly and often persistently ask questions. There are, however, striking developmental differences in both the structure and the content of these questions as children mature.

Almost invariably, the child's first questions are marked by intonation alone, the simplest way of converting a declarative statement into an inquiry. Soon after a child can declare *My ball* he or she can also ask *My ball?*, and this form of questioning is probably admissible in the deep structure of almost all languages. Only later are transformations to more sophisticated surface structures likely to be seen.

Shortly after a child's first question is asked, advantage is taken of the "wh" words (*who, what, when, where, why*). However, although the use of *wh* words as part of questions appears quite early, they do not at first follow adult form. The young child merely attaches the needed word of inquiry to the beginning of a sentence (*Why him go? What her eat?*), without altering the base sentence at all. Even when the base sentence already has a negative form, the first questions are produced by simply adding *why not* and the questioning intonation while leaving the base sentence intact, as in *Why not Susie can't walk?* (Dale, 1972).

Transformational grammarians assert that all questions derive from a base or kernel string of words, usually a declarative sentence, through a

*Laura gives the correct answer here because the experimenter's question has made it obvious that she and not Joanne must feed the doll.

series of transformations. The child learns the transformations, perhaps by listening to other speakers, but only because he or she is innately capable of noticing and applying them.

Let us begin with the sentence "John will do this." The simplest interrogative form that derives from the same kernel is "John will do what?" However, this sentence is not the usual one produced by English speakers; rather, they say "What will John do?" How does one move from the kernel to the standard interrogative form? The answer offered involves the use of two transformations.

Preposing, a simple transformation that often characterizes the interrogative questions of young children, merely involves bringing the *wh* word to the beginning of the sentence:

1. John will do what?
2. John will do what?
3. What John will do?

Transposing, on the other hand, involves knowing that one must exchange the order of the subject and the auxiliary verb:

1. John will do what?
2. John will do what?
3. What will John do?

Transformational grammar theory, then, proposes a particular sequence in the development of the child's comprehension and production of grammatical sentences based on the emergence of rules of transformation. The theory is historically important because it has paved the way for a deeper understanding of the complex relationship between linguistic development and the overall ability of people to communicate with one another. It has also helped us to understand the close relationship between grammar and meaning.

SEMANTIC DEVELOPMENT: IDENTIFYING THE MEANING OF ⊃RDS AND SENTENCES

We have already defined semantics as the study of the relationship of language to meaning. Developmental psychologists interested in semantics have asked when and how meaning is acquired.

Early Semantic Development: Understanding Words

We noted earlier that during the first few years of life the vocabulary of humans rapidly increases. But how do we come to understand the meanings of these words, and what explanations can be offered regarding the process of semantic development?

The growth of the child's vocabulary proceeds in an orderly way that provides some important hints about the nature of semantic development. First of all, certain words appear very early in the working vocabularies of most children. The outstanding characteristic of these few words is that

FIGURE 8-5
Words that refer to objects that engage children actively, such as articles of clothing they must put on, are among the first to enter their vocabularies.
Christelow/Jeroboam.

they refer to things that move or change by themselves or that can be readily acted on by the child. As Nelson (1974) points out:

> "Dog," "cat," "car," and "ball" are the most common "thing" words produced by young children. . . . Of the clothing items found in early vocabularies, two thirds are shoes and other footwear that the child acts on. It is furthermore noteworthy that early vocabularies do not include items that are just "there," that the child sees but does not interact with and that do not themselves move, for example, furniture. [1974, p. 279]

This finding suggests that semantic development may be based on the child's forming functional concepts out of his or her own experience and then identifying words that seem to fit the concept. Such a view is supported further by the finding that when young children cannot find a word to express a particular meaning, they will often invent one (Werner and Kaplan, 1964).

Obviously, however, an important part of semantic development involves learning to discern the usual or commonly understood meaning of words, and here a theory of the acquisition of meaning is required. It is generally agreed that the process involves some sort of concept formation and that the child's first efforts to tie concepts and words are somewhat imprecise. The clearest example is when the meaning of a word is over- or underextended by a young child (Bowerman, 1976; Nelson, 1973). *Overextension* is evident in the quite common errors among young children of calling all four-legged animals "dogs" or all adult males "Daddy." *Underextension* is illustrated in a report by Bloom (1973) about a nine-month-old girl who used *car* to refer only to cars that she watched through the window, but not to cars she rode in herself. Bloom also noted that some of the words used by infants and young children are not used with their adult meanings. (Recall Werner and Kaplan's finding that children will often invent their own words.) Such idiosyncratic words generally drop out of children's speech rather quickly, though they may survive if parents become responsive to them. One two-year-old, for example, insisted on referring to breakfast cereal as *fafa* and continued to do so until her parents became unresponsive to

FIGURE 8-6
Young children often overgeneralize the meaning of words, for example, by calling all four-legged animals "dogs."
Shumsky, ICON.

fafa (or to pointing to the cereal box), waiting until she verbally requested "cereal."

One theory that explains such overextensions is *semantic feature theory* (Clark, 1973). According to this theory, the child's first attempts at grasping word-thing relationships involves attaching only one or two features of a thing to the word that names it. Then, as a result of exposure to adult correction and usage, new and more discriminating features may be added to the child's meaning of the word until it includes all the features recognized as essential by adults. Thus, a child may at first refer to all four-legged animals as "dogs" because four-leggedness is the only feature associated with the word. Over time, however, many other features will be added (fur, paws, the ability or tendency to bark, and so on) until the child's meaning of "dog" corresponds to the usual adult meaning.

A child's understanding of the meaning of "thing" words almost certainly precedes a grasp of the more abstract connotations that adults may ascribe to words with which the child is already somewhat familiar. *Blue*, for example, is probably known to most four-year-olds as a color word (for example, in *The ball is blue*), but few preschoolers will understand its meaning as an emotional state; *I feel blue* just sounds like an anomalous or "silly" sentence to them.

Understanding Sentences: Combining Semantic and Syntactic Information

In daily language, children beyond the first year or two of life are much more likely to be faced with interpreting the meaning of complete sentences rather than single words, and this may involve more than the ability to understand the individual words themselves. Indeed, we have already discussed some of the problems of determining the meaning of sentences when we considered the problem of relating the surface structure of a sentence to its deep structure (see p. 245). Now we will see even more clearly that semantics and syntax are inextricably woven together in the ongoing process of natural language communication.

Young children find it impossible to understand the meaning of sentences that make no factual sense to them. Strohner and Nelson (1974) found that two- and three-year-old children interpreted both *The cat chased the mouse* and *The mouse chased the cat* as meaning the same thing, that is, that "the cat chased the mouse." Thus, in this instance the children ignored the syntactic information entirely because of the content (semantics) of the message.

The most obvious measure of a child's understanding of the meaning of a sentence is whether he or she will respond to it appropriately. Suppose, for example, a child is presented with red and green toy trucks of the same size and is asked to place them on a table so that "The red truck *is pushing* the green truck." Ten- and eleven-year-old children will respond quite quickly—and they will be correct about 99 percent of the time. But suppose that instead the child is asked to create the situation in which "The green truck *is being pushed by* the red truck." Although the action called for is the same, the likelihood of error is higher and the child takes significantly longer to respond. Why is the second sentence so much more difficult to understand?

Huttenlocher and her associates (e.g., Huttenlocher, Eisenberg, and Strauss, 1968), who have performed a number of experiments in search of an answer to this question, point out that in the first sentence, "The red truck is pushing the green truck," *red truck* is both the logical and the grammatical subject of the sentence. (*Red truck* is the logical subject in the sense that it must be the source of the action and "do the pushing.") But in the second sentence *red truck*, though it continues to be the logical subject responsible for the action, becomes the grammatical *ob*ject of the sentence. In extracting the sentence's meaning, it seems that children must begin with a sort of preliminary grammatical analysis of what they have been told. Only after this analysis can they translate the information contained in the sentence, its meaning, into appropriate action. When the grammatical and logical subject are not the same, as in the second version, the translation task is much more difficult.

Another technique used to trace the course of semantic development simply involves the child's immediate ability to recall word strings that vary

FIGURE 8–7
Percentage of grammatical and meaningful, grammatical and anomalous, and scrambled word strings correctly recalled by children five, seven, and eight years old in McNeill's (1970b) experiment, showing that younger children have difficulty making use of semantic information.
Adapted from McNeill.

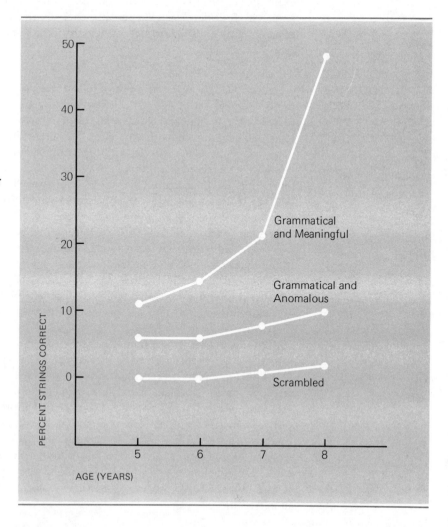

Extralinguistic Sources of Confusion in Young Children's Understanding of Spoken Language

The context of a communication greatly influences the way in which it will be understood, and the ability to correctly interpret communication contexts gradually improves as one's linguistic competency develops. Unfortunately, language development researchers are prone to fall into the trap of confusing the two abilities. An interesting example involves young children's understanding of the words **same** and **different**.

In a widely cited study Donaldson and Wales (1970) asked 3½-year-old children to respond to the following requests as an adult held up a common object (e.g., a toothbrush):

"Give me one that is the **same** in some way."
"Give me one that is **different** in some way."

The children's responses were almost identical regardless of whether they were asked to select an item that was "the same in some way" or "different in some way." In either instance they handed the experimenter the available item that most resembled the adult's example. Thus when the adult held up a blue toothbrush and the children had available to them a blue toothbrush, a red toothbrush, and a variety of nontoothbrush items (e.g., a white egg cup), virtually all the children responded to the two requests by handing the experimenter a blue toothbrush! Does this mean that three-year-olds generally do not know the difference between the words **same** and **different?** Glucksberg, Hay, and Danks (1976) suggested that such a conclusion might not be warranted by Donaldson and Wales's observations:

Should we infer that children cannot differentiate between two words because they do not differentiate between two sentential utterances containing those two words? In normal adult conversation, many utterances containing different and contrasting words are, in fact, responded to in the same way. For example, I might say, "I drank four bottles of gin last night—**do** you believe me?" Or "I drank four bottles of gin last night—**don't** you believe me?" Whether you believe me or not, you would answer both of these utterances in the same way: you would say "yes" to either one if you did believe me, and "no" if you did not. Clearly, it would be inappropriate to infer that an adult does not or cannot discriminate between the words **do** and **don't** simply because he or she responds to utterances containing these words in exactly the same way.

On purely rational grounds, then, the evidence that young children treat pairs of apparently antonymic [opposite] utterances equivalently may say nothing of their ability to differentiate among specific individual words in those utterances. Let us assume as a working hypothesis that children, like adults, respond to utterances by trying to infer what a speaker's intended message might be. In the case of the "same-different" requests, one might argue that children respond in the most appropriate fashion possible, namely, just as adults would. When someone holds up an object, for example, a pencil, and says, "Give me one that is different in some way," one may very well interpret that utterance as a request for another writing implement and not a request for a watermelon, a chair, or any other "different" object in the universe. If this is the case, then the Donaldson and Wale's findings actually demonstrate that children are skilled interpreters of adult speech! (Glucksberg, Hay, and Danks, 1976, p. 738)

FIGURE 8-8

The data show clearly that children do understand the meaning of the words "same" and "different," but that they are misled by the ambiguous nature of the question when the relevant context is not specified. In Test 1 the context was unspecified (the experimenter requested something the "same" or "different" than what he displayed). The context was specified in Test 2, with the experimenter requesting that the three-year-olds choose something that was the "same color" as or a "different color" than the item he displayed. Data from Glucksberg, Hay, and Danks, 1976.

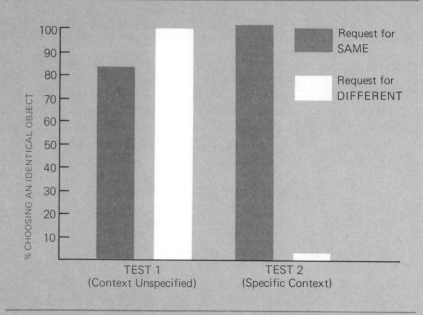

Glucksberg and his associates asked three-year-olds to respond to a **same-different** task that was almost identical to the one used by Donaldson and Wales. The experimenter held up an object and asked the child for something that was either the **same** or **different**. The child had to choose from an assortment containing an identical object, an object of the same class but differing in size and/or color, and two additional objects of a different class. These three-year-olds performed just as those in the Donaldson and Wales's study had, selecting the identical item regardless of whether they had been asked to select something the **same** or something **different**.

Glucksberg and his colleagues, however, also gave each of their subjects a second, contextually clearer test of their ability to understand the words **same** and **different**. In this second test each child was initially shown a solid-color plastic bead (e.g., a red one). He or she was then offered an assort- ment of beads of various colors and asked to give the experimenter "one that's the same color as this [red] bead" or "one that's a different color than this [red] bead." Every child was able to follow these unambiguous instructions, displaying a clear understanding of both communications. Each provided a like-colored bead when asked for one that was the same and a different-colored bead when asked for one that was different (see Figure 8-8).

Misleading contexts may also explain young children's inability to deal with various cognitive tasks that are presented in subtly ambiguous ways. A good example involves the development of logical classification skills, which Piaget concluded were beyond the scope of preoperational children (see chapter 7). In the classical Piagetian test of classification skills (e.g., Piaget, 1952) children were shown a box containing twenty white beads and two brown beads and asked whether there were more white beads or more beads in the box. Up to about age seven most children said that there were more white beads, a result which led Piaget to conclude that certain classification skills required and depended on achieving the concrete operational stage of cognitive development. In a modified replication of the study, Kalil, Youssef and Lerner (1974) presented one group of kindergartners with the bead problem, just as Piaget had constructed it, while another group was given the problem in a modified form. Specifically, the modified method consisted of separating the beads, putting all of the white beads on the left side of the box and all of the brown beads on the right side. The children were then asked whether there were more white beads on the left-hand side of the box or more beads in the whole box. While children presented with the standard version of the problem regularly said that there were more white beads than beads (as reported in Piaget's studies), most of those exposed to the new procedure recognized that there were in fact more beads than white beads. Thus the rudimentary classification skill appears to be present at a much younger age than Piaget supposed, but was masked by a misunderstanding of the relationship between the experimenter's linguistically based question and the context in which it was asked.

In a more recent study challenging Piaget's conclusion that preoperational children cannot classify correctly, Markman and Siebert (1976) presented children who had failed on the standard Piagetian task with a new problem that was posed in one of two different ways. In the standard presentation, the child was shown a pile of red and blue blocks, with blue blocks outnumbering the red ones. The child was then asked whether someone who owned the blue blocks or someone who owned the blocks would have more blocks to play with. The children did poorly on this task: Piagetians would conclude that this was a result of the children's presumed inability to classify objects correctly. However, the remaining children were asked whether the one who owned the blue blocks or the one who owned the pile of blocks would have more. The children performed far better with this type of questioning, suggesting that their lack of verbal understanding rather than their cognitive capacity may have limited them earlier.

in their meaningfulness for adult speakers. In several experiments (Miller and Isard, 1963; McNeill, 1970b) the strings, which always consist of the same number and types of words, have been either *grammatical and meaningful, grammatical and anomolous,* or *scrambled.* Here is an example:

Grammatical and meaningful: *The academic lecture attracted a limited audience.*
Grammatical and anomolous: *The academic liquid became an odorless audience.*
Scrambled: *Liquid the an became audience odorless academic.*

Differences in ability to recall these strings could be based on syntactic information (although the anomalous sentences are meaningless, they are "grammatical") or semantic information (only the first sentence has a comprehensible meaning). As shown in Figure 8–7, both processes operate. Children as young as five years recall and are able to reproduce anomalous sentences better than scrambled ones, and this accords with their already well developed syntactic ability. Semantic cues, on the other hand, though they aid recall at all ages studied, grow steadily in their importance for recall through age eight. As Dale (1972) notes, it is hard to resist the conclusion that semantic development proceeds more slowly than syntactic development.

253

REFERENTIAL
COMMUNI-
CATION: THE
PROBLEM OF
CHOOSING THE
RIGHT WORDS

More than twenty years ago, Roger Brown (1958) pointed out to psychologists interested in language and communication that any particular word can be used to refer to many different things, and any particular thing can be referred to by many different words. Therefore, children must not only learn a vocabulary but must also learn how to select words from that vocabulary in order to communicate most effectively. Brown himself suggested that these choices were typically made by "operating at the level of usual utility," that is, the person chooses a word that makes it maximally easy for the listener to understand the intended meaning in the situation at hand. One implication of Brown's idea is that "the task of selecting the particular words to suit particular social and physical contexts may not be a trivial one and ... learning how to do so may pose formidable developmental problems to be solved as children learn how to use their language effectively" (Glucksberg, Krauss, and Higgins, 1975, p. 308). This learning process leads to the development of *referential communication skills*. The concept itself acknowledges the fact that all communicators must learn how to construct messages that convey their intended meaning as clearly and accurately as possible.

Effective referential communication rests heavily on discrimination learning (see chapter 6) and on a grasp of the discriminative abilities and limitations of the listener. A communicator must know which elements in a situation are discriminating and which are nondiscriminating or redundant, and must also be aware of the ease or difficulty with which a discriminative aspect of the referent can be detected in various situations. For example, most people would include their eye color when providing a brief physical description of themselves, but most would not include eye color in a description provided to a stranger scheduled to meet them at an airport. In the latter instance eye color is omitted simply because it is not discernible at the distances likely to be involved.

Egocentrism in Young Children's Referential Communication

By the time children reach the age of five or so, their literal face-to-face conversations are impressively like those of similar communications among adults. Most major grammatical forms have appeared, and the youngster already possesses an adequate vocabulary. But the child's language is rather self-centered (that is, *egocentric*) and remarkably concrete.

Long ago, for example, Piaget (1926) asked children to teach other youngsters how to use mechanical devices, such as a syringe. Children under six years of age did very poorly at explaining, apparently unable to see the problem from the listener's point of view; they used vague gestures and pronouns such as "this," "something," "here," "there." Even when the child receiving the instruction was blindfolded, the young speakers did not appear to grasp why their communications would be unsuccessful.

Glucksberg, Krauss, and their associates (Glucksberg, Krauss, and Weisberg, 1966; Glucksberg and Krauss, 1967; Krauss and Weinheimer, 1964) also observed communication between children. In their experimental situation children are seated out of sight of each other, as in Figure 8–9, and are asked to play a game called "stack the blocks." One child is the speaker and has the job of encoding a message to relay to another child.

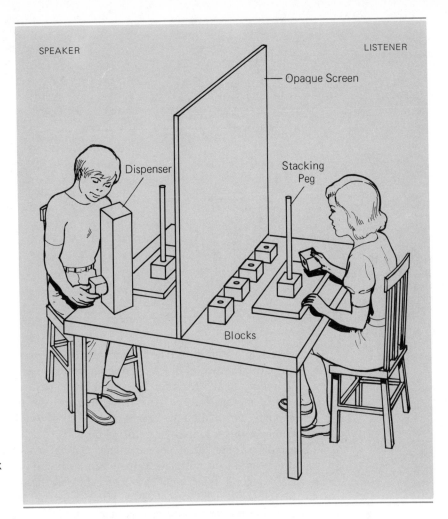

SPEAKER   LISTENER

Opaque Screen

Dispenser

Stacking
Peg

Blocks

FIGURE 8–9
The experimental task
used by Glucksberg,
Krauss, and their
associates.

The second youngster, the listener, must decode the speaker's message and act on the information. In front of each player is an array of six blocks and a peg on which the blocks can be stacked. The speaker receives blocks one by one from a dispenser and must put them on the peg in the order they are received. The listener's blocks, however, appear in a random array on the table. The object of the game is to form two identical stacks of blocks. To accomplish this goal the speaker must verbally instruct the listener in a way that can be understood. Each block carries a design (see Figure 8–10) by which it can be identified. The designs, however, have been carefully chosen and are not ones that have readily available English names.

In the first in a series of such experiments, children of approximately four and five years of age served as subjects. Results showed that the speaker child tended to use reference phrases that were private and idiosyncratic. One youngster, for example, referred to form 5 in Figure 8–9 as "a pipe, a yellow part of a pipe," a phrase that communicates much less well than such labels as a "boot," a "horse's head," or an "ax head"—which represent average adult responses. (Incidentally, the adjective "yellow" con-

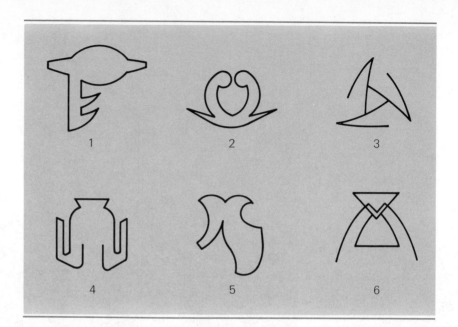

FIGURE 8-10
The six novel forms used in the Glucksberg and Krauss experiments.

veyed no useful information, since the forms were stamped with black ink on natural redwood blocks.) Another young speaker referred to form 6 as "Mommy's hat." Apparently it resembled a particular hat belonging to that child's mother but, for the naive listener, the message did not contain enough information to assist performance. Adults, on the other hand, tended to refer to it as "An upside down cup. It's got two triangles, one on top of the other." It is not surprising that not one of the seven pairs of children was able to complete a single game without error.

A second experiment, however, showed that children of the same age functioned much more effectively in the listener role when they had to respond to reference phrases that had been used by adult subjects rather than by other children. Eight out of twelve met the criterion of two consecutive errorless games. Yet a third experiment was performed to determine whether children would understand their own idiosyncratic labels. Subjects of four and five years of age saw each of the six forms and were asked by the experimenter to "tell me what this looks like." The experimenter then played the role of speaker in the communication game, using the names that had been supplied by the children earlier. The results showed that the children's own names were adequate to guide their actions. One young subject referred to form 4 as "Daddy's shirt" and form 6 as "another Daddy's shirt" but, in each case, selected the correct form.

Research directly extending the Glucksberg and Krauss inquiry has now shown that the frequency of egocentric speech among children depends on the entire speaker-listener relationship and not just on the age of the speaker (e.g., Mueller, 1972; Hoy, 1975). Hoy, for example, found that five- to nine-year-olds could reproduce toy models simply from a peer's verbal description (of either a horse or a random shape) almost perfectly (99 percent correct) if the speaker and listener could see each other in full view and engage in two-way exchanges. When a comparable sample of children had to communicate the same information without the benefit of seeing their listeners at all, accuracy plummeted to 62 percent. These differences occurred despite the fact that in neither group could the listener see the model he or she was to build. Personal contact with one's listener is obviously as important for children's communications as for those of adults.

In addition to experiments based quite directly on the Glucksberg and Krauss paradigm, other investigators have asked more process-oriented questions about what develops in referential communication.

One attractive possibility, suggested by Flavell and his associates (1968), is that the basic referential communication skill is the communicator's ability to take the role of the prospective listener in evaluating a possible message before transmitting it. More specifically, these investigators suggest that the speaker first encodes a referent as if it were a message for her- or himself. The speaker then evaluates the listener vis-à-vis the message, and rephrases the message according to the judged needs of the listener. Such role-taking skill is weak or absent in young children, and must develop with maturation and experience.

Research provides some support for Flavell's role-taking view of referential communication. Saunders (1969) reported that in naming items or events for a listener young children provide the name that they are most accustomed to using (associative frequency) rather than judging the information value of the name selected in the situation. Adults, of course, attend closely to whether the words they select will be useful for listeners. It also appears that children have considerably more trouble than adults do in recognizing poor clues when several are suggested (Pietrinferno, 1973).

Nonetheless, it has been shown (Asher, 1972) that young children can discriminate reasonably well between "good" and "bad" clue words to help a listener understand which of two items in a pair is to be selected, if they are urged to do so. This evidence additionally supports the theory that young children differ from older children and adults in their willingness (rather than their ability) to use the most effective or appropriate strategy in a problem-solving situation.

Glucksberg and his colleagues have defined four different processes that underlie referential communications; each process shows clear change with increasing age. The four processes identified by Glucksberg and his associates are:

1. *Sensitivity to the referent-nonreferent array.* The sensitivity referred to here involves the ability "to provide information to a listener that discriminates between the referent and potentially confusable nonreferents" (p. 328). Early developmental changes regarding this type of sensitivity are quite dramatic. For example, Glucksberg and Kim (1969) asked nursery-school children to tell someone else how to stack a set of colored blocks. The subjects were asked to use one-word communications and the duotone blocks involved differed in one of the colors (a discriminative cue) but shared a second color (a redundant or useless cue). Surprisingly, these young subjects were as likely to name the redundant color as the discriminating one. For example, suppose two blocks, one red and blue and the other red and green, had to be stacked by a listener who could not see

them. The nursery-school-age speaker would be just as likely to tell the listener to stack the "red" block first as to stack the blue or the green one first, even though both of the blocks involved are red.

2. *Sensitivity to characteristics of the listener and the listener's situation.* Even at a very young age children show some sensitivity to the characteristics of the listener and the listener's situation. For example, Gelman and Shatz (1972) asked four-year-olds to communicate to two-year-olds and to adults. The speech of the four-year-olds varied as a function of the age of the listener; when speaking to two-year-olds, the four-year-olds produced sentences that were shorter, simpler, and contained more attention-getting elements (such as saying *look*). Nonetheless, the knowledge displayed by preschool children is rudimentary. Several studies (e.g., Flavell et al., 1968; Higgins, 1973) have shown that the ability to adapt one's messages to one's listener increases at least through the early teen years.

3. *Sensitivity to listener's behavior (sensitivity to feedback).* Glucksberg and Krauss (1967) had kindergarten, first-, third-, and fifth-grade children, as well as adults, play the stack-the-block game under conditions in which the listener provided three different types of feedback to the speaker: "I don't understand which one you mean"; "Tell me more about it"; or "I don't understand which one you mean, tell me more about it." Kindergarten and first-grade children tended to be unresponsive to these communications with the kindergartners being quite likely to respond to the feedback either by repeating exactly what they had already said or by being silent, a reaction displayed by none of the adults. A later study (Peterson, Danner, and Flavell, 1972) found that young children responded reasonably well to explicit feedback such as "Look at it again. What else does it look like? Can you tell me anything else about it?" But the same children were unresponsive to implicit feedback such as facial expressions or statements such as "I don't understand. I don't think I can guess that."

4. *The role of the listener.* The final developmental process involved in referential communication involves improved listener skills in relation to increasing age. Glucksberg and his colleagues (1975) report that adults are considerably better than children at letting the speaker know when his or her message has been inadequate and can also specify the additional information that they need in order to provide a correct response. Here, as elsewhere in the developmental scheme, it is not until the early teen years (the ninth grade in the Glucksberg and Krauss, 1967, study) that youngsters appear to perform as well as adults.

In sum, Glucksberg and his associates suggest that what develops is the ability to impose "editing" upon one's own possible messages to others. Editing skills play an important role in all successful communication.

**MASTERING THE
ART OF
COMMUNICATION**

With increasing age and experience children develop the ability to edit their prospective communications more effectively. In this final section we will consider some of the processes involved in this accomplishment.

Communications specialists in psychology, sociology, political science, and education have increasingly come to view communication as involving an implicit contract between communicator and communicatee. Mastering the art of communication involves refining and complying with this implicit contract, which in turn requires an understanding of its various components.

The "Given-New" Contract. Modern psycholinguists think of sentences as involving both *given* and *new* information. For example, in the sentence, "It was psychology that Bob failed," the given information is that Bob failed a course, while the new information is that the course Bob failed was psychology.

Given information is therefore information that the listener presumably already knows, and it provides the basis or context in which to transmit new information (that is, information not previously known to the listener). Speakers are implicitly responsible for "marking" their communications so that listeners can distinguish which information is new and which information is given. The speaker's obligation to recognize and mark this distinction has been referred to as the *given-new contract* (Clark and Haviland, 1977).

Young children, in their first single-word sentences, typically express information that is *new for the speaker* (Greenfield and Smith, 1976). Thus a child who has recently learned that a particular toy is called a "car" will often delightedly tell every available adult this new word (saying "car" as he or she points to the item in question).

One potential problem: How does a child deal with both given and new information with a repertoire of sentences consisting only of single words? The answer appears to be that the child will begin by announcing the given information repeatedly in a single word and then, after establishing the context for his or her listener, will go on to provide a one word sentence containing new information. Here is a conversation between Brenda (age fifteen months) and her mother, which illustrates how the process works (Scollon, 1974, as cited by Clark and Clark, 1977, p. 318):

Brenda:	Fan. [looking at the electric fan]
	Fan.
Mother:	Hm?
Brenda:	Fan.
Mother:	Bathroom?
Brenda:	Fan.
Mother:	Fan! Yeah.
Brenda:	Cool!
Mother:	Cool, yeah. Fan makes you cool.

The two-word utterance has room for both given and new information in a way that the one-word utterance does not. How, though, do children

mark the distinction between given and new information in their two-word sentences? Wieman (1976) found that young children tend to indicate which information in a two-word sentence is new by giving greater stress to the new information. Thus a child who has recently discovered the color name for her favorite ball is much more likely to say "RED ball" than "Red BALL."

In both one- and two-word utterances children seem to understand the desirability of obtaining an acknowledgment from the listener before proceeding. Note that this was true in Brenda's brief conversation with her mother, described above. The mother repeated Brenda's use of the word *fan* and Brenda interpreted this as a sign that her mother had both listened and understood the context she was establishing. Moreover, even at this young age there is clear evidence of turn-taking.

For two-word utterances it is often possible to indicate to listeners what is given and what is new by using vocal stress, as in our red ball example. As soon as the child's sentences become more complex, however, a further device is needed. The use of the definite article to indicate given information and the indefinite article to indicate new information is used quite frequently by adults and is generally acquired by children during early and middle childhood. Adults will use the indefinite article *a* when first mentioning something and the definite article *the* when mentioning the same piece of information thereafter. For example, an adult may say, "I found *a key* yesterday, and it turned out to be *the key* to my old suitcase." Thus, one way to determine at what age children begin to use the definite and indefinite articles to mark given and new information respectively is to examine their communications in terms of whether a first mentioned piece of information is marked by the indefinite article.

Warden (1976) asked three-, five-, seven-, and nine-year-old children to tell a peer a story based on three cartoon-like pictures. Analysis of the subjects' stories indicated that the three-year-olds used the indefinite article on the first mention of a new piece of information slightly less than half the time, meaning that they used definite and indefinite articles almost indiscriminantly. Five- and seven-year-olds were somewhat more likely to use the indefinite article on first mention of a piece of information, and nine-year-olds used the indefinite article when first mentioning a piece of information most of the time. (The problem is not one of familiarity with the two words, for most children begin to use both *the* and *a* by the time they are three years of age.)

Understanding the Implicit or Subtle Elements in a Communication. A variety of implicit or subtle cues are involved in any communication, and so part of the development of communication skills is found in the ability to understand these nuances.

We have already mentioned intonation as a cue used to mark the difference between given and new information in two-word sentences. Even before they can speak, at the tender age of two months, infants are able to make the perceptual discrimination between a rising and a falling intonation (Morse, 1972). Nonetheless, an understanding of the *use* of intonation comes much later. Cruttenden (1974) exposed seven- and nine-year-old children to BBC radio announcements of football scores in which a team had either won, lost, or tied its opponent. In contrast to adults, who were able to predict the outcome of the game from the tone of the announcer quite well, nine-year-olds had some difficulty and seven-year-olds performed very poorly.

In making requests and in understanding the requests of others there is also a great need to master many subtleties. For example, Grimm (1975) reported a dramatic difference between the way in which five- and seven-year-olds grant permission to a peer. Whereas the permissions issued by five-year-olds sounded much like commands (such as "You can swing"), seven-year-olds were more likely to say something softer such as, "I don't mind your swinging." Likewise, five-year-olds would forbid the action by saying "You mustn't swing!" whereas seven-year-olds were more likely to say something such as, "I'd rather you didn't swing." The older children were also more likely to add *please* when making requests.

Another important subtlety in adult language is the indirect nature of many of our requests. For example, we may say, "Can you open the window?" when in fact we mean, "Will you open the window?" Shatz (1974) found that young children will respond to sentences such as, "Can you open the door?" by actually opening the door, just as adults might. However, the young child is not like an adult because he or she will also respond to communications that are not implicit requests (such as, "Must you open the door?") in the same way (by opening the door). Fully comprehending adult speech in all its aspects takes a good deal of time and experience.

SUMMARY   Language is recognized as central to human social behavior and communication. Behaviorists look to the child's environment, experience, and learning history to explain language development, while cognitivists focus on underlying mental operations. Human language is made possible by our species' unique biological endowment including an unusual control of the vocal tract and an innate capacity to handle complex symbols linguistically.

The infant's impressive ability to perceive subtle differences in adult sounds and preverbal behavior such as cries, cooing, and babbling are the roots of language development. These early, single sounds produced by the infant are eventually transformed into groups of sounds called *phonemes*, the units of raw speech material that correspond roughly to vowel and consonant sounds of a language.

The course of language development is best thought of as an emerging language competence. Growth in this area involves examining both *semantic development* (understanding the meaning of words and sentences) and *grammatical development* (the formation of permissible language constructions). Grammar is in turn broken down into *syntax* (rules governing sentence construction) and *morphology* (rules for forming words themselves). Basic linguistic competence is achieved fairly early in development whereas the broader ability to communicate effectively continues to develop well beyond childhood.

A major discovery made by those studying language development is that there are certain linguistic universals. The first word that children almost everywhere produce sounds very much like *mama*. In all languages the child's first sentences consist of single words, and the usual forms of children's first two-word utterances are also remarkably similar throughout the world. In addition, one- and two-word sentences are accompanied by gestures to express assertions or requests.

Children's first real conversations begin at about age two, typically between mother and child, and they sound much like telegraph messages because they use only the essentials of speech. These early conversations involve turn-taking and imitation (imitation with expansion by the mother and imitation with reduction by the child).

Theories of grammatical development involving reinforcement and observational learning can account for only a portion of language development, and naturalistic observation shows that parents do not use either reinforcement or modeling as perfectly as learning theories of grammatical development would imply. Children learn to speak grammatically by abstracting the underlying rules of language spoken to them. Studies have shown that children's formation of words and sentences depend on rules they have learned from listening. Theories about the syntax of two-word sentences include Skinner's autoclitic frame theory, Bloom's functional grammar, and the pivot-open theory.

Noam Chomsky's transformational grammar theory suggests that linguistic competence involves converting or transforming the surface structure of an utterance into its deep structure or meaning, and research shows that children's use and understanding of grammar may proceed along these lines.

In early semantic development, children will often over- or underextend the meaning of a word until they have developed an exact idea of what the word really means. Young children find it impossible to understand the meaning of sentences that make no factual sense to them.

Studies have shown that both grammatical and semantic features of an utterance influence how well children will remember it, with meaningfulness being more important as the child grows older. Semantic development evidently progresses more slowly than syntactic development, especially when more complex or subtle forms of language are involved.

Referential communication skills include four different processes: sensitivity to the referent-nonreferent array, sensitivity to characteristics of the listener and the listener's situation, sensitivity to the listener's behavior, and learning to play the role of the listener.

Mastering the art of communication involves the recognition and understanding of an implicit contract between speaker and listener. For example, speakers are responsible for "marking" their communications to distinguish between given and new information. An understanding of the implicit and subtle elements in communication such as intonation and making requests of others improves as children grow older.

9 Intelligence

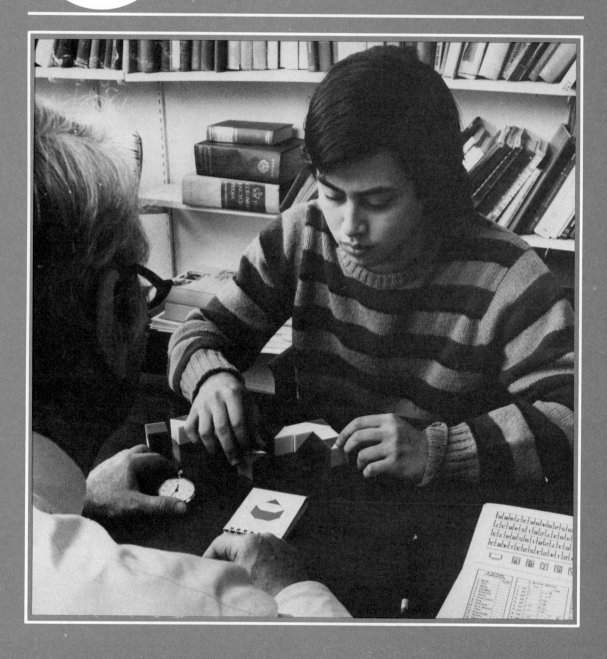

In previous chapters we traced basic processes through which the child comes to know and adapt to the world. Learning, perception, memory, and constructing reality as described by Piaget are fundamental to the intellectual development of children. In this chapter intelligence is examined from a different context, one that is intricately related to its measurement. The many facets of testing will be discussed, as well as the usual course of intellectual development. Also to be considered are the intellectually exceptional—those who either do not achieve the typical standards of intelligence or go far beyond them.

THE CONCEPT OF INTELLIGENCE

What is intelligence? Any discussion of the topic must begin with this question because despite the vast interest by psychologists in intellectual ability and its measurement, there has been difficulty in defining intelligence.

Nature vs. Nurture

As indicated in our discussion of genetics in chapter 5, one focus of concern about intelligent behavior has revolved around the question of whether it is innate or learned. For the most part, the dominant view, at least until the late 1940s, emphasized innate factors. Underlying this view was a belief that intelligence was *fixed* at a particular level and that it was *predetermined* by heredity (Hunt, 1961). Each of these beliefs was deeply embedded and had some empirical support. For example, animal research provided examples of maturation that were relatively uninfluenced by the environment, such as the development of motor ability in the salamander (p. 80). It seemed not unreasonable, then, to consider that intelligence might also be largely independent of experience. Furthermore, in humans, scores on tests of intelligence were known to be more closely correlated as the degree of relationship between the examinees increased—an indication of genetic influence (p. 106). But evidence that intelligence may be changed, sometimes dramatically, by environmental determinants began to accumulate, transforming the concept considerably. This change will be traced later in the chapter.

General vs. Specific Intelligence.

In referring to someone as "bright" or "dull," all of us recognize in a general way that individuals differ in their ability to deal with the world. On the other hand, we also are aware that "'bright" people may not do everything well and that "dull" people are sometimes remarkably adept at certain tasks. Psychologists also have recognized both the generality and the specificity of intelligent behavior.

Theorists who view intelligence as a general attribute refer to it as the ability to learn; the capacity to adjust or adapt to the environment, especially to new situations; or sometimes simply to all of the knowledge a person has acquired (Robinson and Robinson, 1965). From this point of view, intelligence is a single, general attribute possessed to some degree by each individual.

Other theorists, among them L. L. Thurstone (1941) and J. P. Guilford (1966), regard intelligence as consisting of a number of different attributes or capacities. According to multifactor models of intelligence, an individual may be well endowed with one attribute, but deficient in another. Assuming that intelligence is not general, theorists have sought to discover the nature of the specific factors.

The procedure employed is conceptually quite simple. A group of individuals is given a large number of different tests, each of which purports to measure intelligence. It is assumed that success on some of the tests requires skill in one area, while success on other tests requires skill in other areas. For example, some tests might require skill in memory for verbal material while others might require the ability to work effectively with abstract mathematical concepts. The task of the experimenter is to discover the existence of different groups of tests, each of which requires a different skill. To achieve that objective the experimenter employs a statistical technique called "factor analysis." Cattell (1965) has suggested that the logic underlying this technique is similar to the logic a jungle hunter might use in deciding whether a set of dark blobs in a river is three separate rotting logs or a single alligator. To make this decision the hunter watches for movement. If the blobs move together, it is assumed that they are part of the same structure, an alligator. If, on the other hand, they do not move together, they are not part of the same structure but instead represent three different structures, three logs. Similarly, if changes in performance on one test typically are accompanied by changes in performance on a second test—i.e., they move together—one could assume that the tests are measuring the same attribute or *factor*. It remains then for the investigator to give a name to each factor, usually based on a subjective view of the skill involved.

What specific factors have been identified by the use of factor analysis? Thurstone and Thurstone (1941) concluded that there are seven primary ones: perceptual speed, word comprehension, word fluency, space, number, memory, and induction. They also acknowledged a general factor that operated in all tasks but emphasized that analysis of the several factors is more useful in assessing intellectual ability. To make matters more complicated, though, Cattell and Horn conceptualized the primary mental abilities as falling into two dimensions: fluid and crystallized intelligence (Cattell, 1963; Horn, 1970; Horn and Cattell, 1966). Fluid intelligence is the capacity to deal with virtually any problem; that is, to perceive relationships and strategies. It is viewed as the higher cognitive processes that are tied to the biology of the person and are relatively uninfluenced by experience. Crystallized intelligence, in contrast, involves the ability to understand relationships, make judgments, and solve problems based on learning cultural information and skills. A person's crystallized intelligence is a reflection of the individual as a product of her or his culture. The distinction between the two dimensions becomes sharper with age because individuals have time to learn the intelligence of their culture.

Applied
Approach to
Defining
Intelligence

Many psychologists, though, have little interest in theoretical models of intelligence—whether general or specific. Rather, they accept the view that intelligence is not a concrete capacity located somewhere within the individual but a sample of certain behaviors that is useful in describing and predicting other behaviors. This approach is an applied one; it focuses almost exclusively on testing to determine the intellectual tasks individuals can perform or the knowledge they have accumulated. It is expected that test performance will provide helpful information about the present functioning of the individual and, to some extent, about his or her range of future performance on related tasks, such as academic achievement. The implications of this approach can be seen in much of the following discussion.

THE MEASUREMENT OF INTELLIGENCE

From the beginning of the century, when test construction seriously commenced, until the late 1950s, the testing movement was characterized by expansion into many areas: the selection and classification of men in the armed forces, the admission of college students, the evaluation of progress in educational institutions, and the selection of employees (Holtzman, 1971). It is thus appropriate to consider briefly some of the principles of test construction, as well as examples of the more widely used tests.

Principles of Test Construction

Initial Item Selection. The first step in constructing any kind of psychological test is selection of appropriate items, that is, of the test questions. The choice will obviously depend upon the purpose of the test and the theoretical stance of the people constructing it.

Norms and Standardization. Next, the test items must be administered to a representative group of individuals in order to establish *normative* performance. This group, the standardization sample, must be chosen carefully because its scores will be employed as a standard against which later examinees' scores will be compared. For example, if the test is being designed for children of varying ages and socioeconomic backgrounds, the standardization group should include appropriate proportions of individuals reflecting these characteristics.

Still another part of standardization procedures concerns the context within which the test is administered. When classroom tests are given in school, as in spelling or arithmetic, individual teachers may differ widely in their selection of content, the amount of time allowed for taking the test, whether notes may be used, and so forth. Such tests are unstandardized and do not permit direct comparisons from one classroom to another. A child who correctly answered 80 percent of the questions on Mr. Jones's arithmetic test might very well have learned less—or more—than one who earned the same score on Mr. Smith's test. If we are to compare many children from different parts of the country, or even different classrooms, successfully, this problem must be overcome. *Standardization of test procedures* is used for this purpose. Specifically, a standardized test is one in which the apparatus, procedure, and scoring have been fixed so that exactly the same test is given at different times and places (Cronbach, 1960, p. 22).

It is sometimes felt that one of the weaknesses of psychological tests is that such standardization does not allow for optimal conditions under which any one individual may perform. However, if comparison with others is desired, it is necessary that the test be conducted in a standard situation for all individuals.

Reliability. Some time after a test has been standardized, efforts must be made to check its reliability. *Reliability* refers to *the consistency of the test.* If a test is not reliable, it is not useful because measurement could fluctuate haphazardly. One common method of determining reliability is to administer a test to the same individuals on two different occasions. Another consists of administering equivalent forms of the test or items from the same form on separate occasions. In either case the two sets of scores are then correlated—the higher the correlation coefficient, the higher the reliability. Reliability, then, refers to how closely the sets of scores are related or how consistent they are over various time intervals.

Validity. According to many psychologists, questions of validity are the most important that can be asked about any psychological test. Simply, *the validity of a test is the degree to which it actually measures what it purports to measure.*

How does one determine validity? Usually, one or more independent *criterion measures* are obtained and correlated with scores from the test in question. Criterion measures are chosen on the basis of what the test is designed to measure. Anxiety exhibited in a public-speaking situation, for example, might be a criterion measure for a test to evaluate self-consciousness. Thus, if test scores rise and fall as do measures of anxiety, evidence exists that the test enjoys some validity.

The validity of intelligence tests is usually determined by employing, as criterion tasks, measures of academic achievement, such as school grades, teacher ratings, or scores on achievement tests. The reported correlations for the more widely used intelligence tests and these criterion tasks are reasonably high; for example, they fall between .40 and .75 for the Stanford-Binet intelligence test. Furthermore, children who have been accelerated or "skipped" one or more grades do considerably better on the Stanford-Binet than do those who have shown normal progress, whereas youngsters who were held back one or more grades exhibit considerably lower than average scores (McNemar, 1942). So the Stanford-Binet appears to measure intelligence, at least insofar as intelligence is reflected in school performance, and is thus relatively successful in predicting school achievement. Such predictive validity is largely responsible for the wide use of tests of intelligence.

TYPES OF INTELLIGENCE TESTS

In the following sections, examples will be given of a few of the most widely employed intelligence tests. All of the ones discussed are administered individually rather than in groups. Presumably this optimizes the motivation and attention of the examinee and provides an opportunity for the sensitive examiner to assess subjective factors that may influence test performance. The examiner may notice that the examinee is relaxed and therefore is probably functioning at an adequate level or may observe that intense anxiety is interfering with performance. Such clinical judgments are not feasible with group intelligence tests. On the other hand, group tests have the advantage of inexpensively providing information about many individuals quickly and often without the need of highly trained psychologists. For this reason group tests have been used widely for general placement in schools and the like—not, however, without controversy, as we shall see later in the chapter.

The Binet Scales.   In 1905 Alfred Binet and Theophile Simon, commissioned by the minister of public education in Paris, devised the first successful test of intellectual ability, called the "Metrical Scale of Intelligence." Composed of thirty problems in ascending order of difficulty, its goal was to identify children who were likely to fail in school so that they could be transferred to special classes. Systematic comparisons thus were made between normal and mentally retarded children. Later revisions of the test in 1908 and 1911 were based on the classroom observations of characteristics that teachers called "bright" and "dull" as well as on a considerable amount of trial-and-error adjustment. Scores obtained on them agreed strongly with teachers' ratings of intellectual ability.

Beginning with the 1908 revision, the Binet-Simon test was arranged into age levels. For example, the investigators placed all tests that normal three-year-olds could pass in the three-year level, all tests that normal four-year-olds could pass in the four-year level, and so on up to age thirteen. This arrangement gave rise to the concept of *mental age* (MA). A child's mental age is equivalent to the chronological age (CA) of children whose performance he or she equals. A six-year-old child who passed tests that the average seven-year-old passed would be said to have an MA of seven. This procedure, which was simple to grasp as a complement to the youngster's CA, did much to popularize intelligence measurement and the mental testing movement generally.

The Stanford-Binet Tests.   The Binet-Simon tests attracted much interest and translations soon appeared in many languages. Lewis Terman at Stanford University revised the test into the first Stanford-Binet in 1916. The Stanford-Binet was a new test in many ways; items had been changed and it had been standardized on a relatively large American population including about one thousand children and four hundred adults. Furthermore, Terman and his associates employed the notion of the *intelligence quotient* or IQ— the ratio of an individual's mental age to his or her chronological age, muliplied by 100 to avoid decimals. Thus:

$$IQ = \frac{MA}{CA} \times 100$$

This quotient, although no longer used on the Stanford-Binet, was ingenious in its day. If a child's mental age and chronological age were equivalent, the child's IQ, regardless of actual chronological age, would be 100—

reflecting average performance. The procedure also made it possible to more directly compare the intellectual development of children of different chronological ages. If a four-year-old boy has a mental age of three, his IQ will be 75 (¾ × 100), as will that of an equally retarded twelve-year-old with a mental age of nine (9/12 × 100 = 75).

The Stanford-Binet was revised in 1937, 1960, and 1972, with restandardization in 1937 and 1972. Since the 1960 revision an individual's IQ is calculated by comparing his or her test results with the average score earned by those of the same age in the standardization group. The use of statistical procedures allows the average score for each age group to be set at 100, with approximately the same number of scores falling below 100 as falling above it. All possible scores distribute themselves in a normal curve. An IQ score thus reflects how near and how far, and in what direction, one is from the average score of the age group. Moreover, it is possible to calculate the percentage of individuals who perform higher and lower than any particular IQ score. This kind of comparison is now used in many intelligence tests.

Like the earlier versions, the Stanford-Binet consists of many cognitive and motor tasks, ranging from the extremely easy to the extremely difficult. The test itself may be administered to individuals ranging in age from approximately two years to adulthood, but not every individual is given every question. For example, young children (or older retarded children) may be asked to recognize pictures of familiar objects, string beads, answer ques-

FIGURE 9–1
Some of the test materials used in administering the Stanford-Binet to children. From **Introduction to Psychology** by Norman L. Munn, L. Dodge Fernald, Jr., and Peter S. Fernald. Houghton Mifflin, 1972, by permission of the publishers.

tions about everyday relationships, or fold paper into specified shapes. On the other hand, older individuals may be asked to define vocabulary words, reason through to the solution of an abstract problem, or decipher an unfamiliar code. Some of the standardized materials used in the Stanford-Binet children's scales are shown in Figure 9–1. The examiner determines, according to specific guidelines, the appropriate starting place on the test and administers progressively more difficult questions until the child fails all the questions at a particular level. An IQ score is assigned on the basis of how many questions the examinee passed compared with the average number passed by children of the same age.

The Wechsler Scales.   A second set of intelligence scales widely used in

---

TABLE 9–1
The Wechsler Intelligence Scale for Children (WISC)

Verbal Scale	Performance Scale
1. General information A series of questions covering a wide range of information which children presumably have had an opportunity to acquire (e.g., "Who discovered America?"). Specialized knowledge is avoided.	1. Picture completion Picture cards from which some part on each card (e.g., the whiskers of a cat) is missing. Child must identify the missing parts.
2. General comprehension Items in which the child must explain what should be done in given circumstances, why certain practices are followed, and so on. An example: "Why is it better to build a house of brick than of wood?"	2. Picture arrangement Sets of picture cards are shown to the child, who must rearrange them so as to tell a story.
3. Arithmetic Simple, orally presented arithmetic problems, to be solved without paper or pencil.	3. Block design The child is given a set of blocks, with red sides, white sides, and sides that are both red and white and must reproduce a pattern shown by the examiner.
4. Similarities Questions such as "In what way are a piano and a violin alike?"	4. Object assembly Cardboard puzzles which the child is to assemble.
5. Vocabulary Increasingly difficult words are presented orally and visually; the child is asked to tell what each means.	5. Coding A code-substitution test in which symbols are to be paired with digits.
6. Digit span Orally presented lists of digits, which are to be repeated (in order or backwards).	6. Mazes Eight printed mazes are presented; the child must trace in pencil the correct route out.

assessment and research with children is based on the work of David Wechsler. The original Wechsler scale, the Wechsler-Bellevue, was published in 1939 and was geared specifically to the measurement of adult intelligence for clinical use. Subsequent revisions involved instruments for adults (Wechsler Adult Intelligence Scale, or WAIS), for schoolchildren (Wechsler Intelligence Scale for Children, or WISC and WISC-R), and for children four to six years of age (Wechsler Preschool and Primary Scale of Intelligence, or WPPSI). All of these tests follow a similar format, which we can examine by looking at the WISC.

The WISC bears many similarities to the Stanford-Binet, but it does differ in various ways. One major difference is that the subtests are categorized into either verbal or performance subscales, the latter tapping nonverbal symbolic skills. The examinees thus are assessed on verbal IQ, performance IQ, and a combination of the two, the full-scale IQ. A second major difference is that each examinee receives the same subtests, with some adjustments for either age level or competence or both. The subtests themselves are listed and described in Table 9–1.

Infant Tests of Intelligence

Several individual tests of infant behavior have been developed in the United States during the last fifty years; examples are the Gesell Developmental Schedules, the Cattell Intelligence Tests for Infants and Young Children, and the Bayley Scales of Infant Development. Performance on these tests is labeled DQ, for developmental quotient, rather than IQ.

Gesell's test was the first specifically designed to measure mental ability in early infancy and is the most well known (Bayley, 1970). It evaluates behavior in four basic areas: motor, adaptive, language, and personal-social (Figure 9–2). The last scale is scored mainly from a parental interview. The child's performance is compared with norms derived from a relatively small group of middle-class children from New Haven, Connecticut, who were followed longitudinally.

The Bayley Scales of Infant Development are a revision of Bayley's original tests, with the addition of a broader standardization and clarification of scoring and administration (Bayley, 1970). Designed for infants two to thirty months old, they consist of Motor and Mental scales and an Infant Behavior Record. The Motor scale includes such items as holding the head up, walking, and throwing a ball. The Mental scale, designed to assess development of adaptive behavior, includes such behaviors as attending to visual and auditory stimuli, following directions, looking for a fallen toy, and imitating. The Infant Behavior Record is a rating of the child on such responses as fearfulness, happiness, endurance, responsiveness, and goal directedness.

The Relationship between Early Test Performance and Later IQ Scores

Infant Tests. A frequently asked question concerns the degree to which early tests predict scores on tests given at later times (see, for example, Lewis, 1976). From a practical standpoint, a strong positive relationship would indicate that assessment early in life would provide information about the child's later performance. In one study, correlations were calcu-

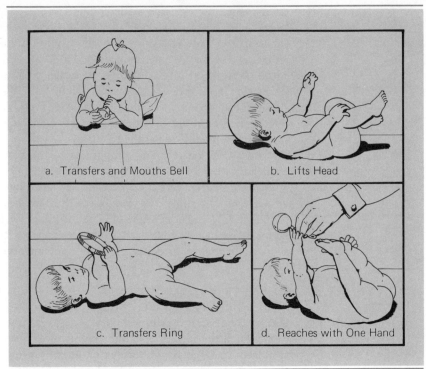

a. Transfers and Mouths Bell

b. Lifts Head

c. Transfers Ring

d. Reaches with One Hand

lated between tests given at three, six, nine, twelve, eighteen, and twenty-four months with Stanford-Binet scores obtained at five years (Anderson, 1939). As seen in Table 9–2 the relationship was low and tended to decrease as the time span between assessments increased. The low correlation between early and later tests has been shown in many subsequent studies (Bayley, 1955; Honzik, MacFarland, and Allen, 1948; Pease, Wolins, and Stockdale, 1973; Rubin and Balow, 1979).

Some investigators note that predictability from early assessment is higher when more global categories, rather than specific IQ scores, are con-

TABLE 9–2
Correlation Coefficients between Infant Intelligence Tests Given at Various Ages and Stanford-Binet IQ at Five Years

Ages	Number of Children	Correlation Coefficients
3 mos.–5 yrs.	91	.008
6 mos.–5 yrs.	91	−.065
9 mos.–5 yrs.	91	−.001
12 mos.–5 yrs.	91	.055
18 mos.–5 yrs.	91	.231
24 mos.–5 yrs.	91	.450

Source: Adapted from Anderson, 1939.

sidered and when clinical judgment is used along with test scores. MacRae (1955) asked examiners to assign infants to one of five categories on the basis of their subjective assessment of test performance; the categories were: superior, above average, average, below average to borderline, mentally defective. Correlations with test scores obtained at nine years, two months were .56, .55, and .82 when the infant tests had been given at zero to eleven months, twelve to twenty-three months, and twenty-four to thirty-five months, respectively. Illingworth (1961) has argued that general mental inferiority can be diagnosed during the first year of life. In one study employing modified Gesell tests, histories, and clinical judgment, he predicted deficiency with 75 percent accuracy as it was measured independently at school age. Such success speaks well for the practical benefits of early diagnosis of problems, primarily because it makes it possible to design treatment plans or appropriately place children into adoptive homes (cf. Knobloch and Pasamanick, 1974). At the same time, a study of four-year-olds with IQs of 140 or higher showed that their superior performance was not predictable from scores on the Bayley Scales obtained at eight months (Willerman and Fiedler, 1974). At this time the evidence is scarce that infant tests alone dependably predict the future performance of those who fall into the middle or high range of intelligence scores.

We might ask why predictive power is not greater. One reason is that there is relatively little room for the display of individual differences during the early months of life (Ames, 1967), and so infants can be differentiated only in a global way. Then, too, early temperamental variations (e.g., activity level or reactivity to stimulation) may influence early performance in a manner different from that in which they affect later performance. Another explanation, perhaps the most important, for low predictability is that infant tests tap abilities other than those evaluated on later tests, placing more emphasis on sensorimotor items and less on tasks involving language and abstract problem solving. At first blush it might be expected that early precociousness or retardation on sensorimotor tasks would foretell later intelligence. Bayley suggests, though, that there is little reason to anticipate a strong relation between early simpler functions and the more complex processes that develop later:

> The neonate who is precocious in the development of the simpler abilities, such as auditory acuity or pupillary reflexes, has an advantage in the slightly more complex behaviors, such as (say) turning toward a sound, or fixating an object held before his eyes. But these more complex acts also involve other functions, such as neuro-muscular coordinations, in which he may not be precocious. The bright one-month-old may be sufficiently slow in developing these later more complex functions so as to lose some or all of his earlier advantages. [Bayley, 1955, pp. 807–808]

Tests Given in Childhood and Beyond.   What happens, then, when test scores obtained by older children are correlated with yet later performance? It generally has been found that the correlations (1) are substantially higher than those for infant tests and (2) progressively decrease as the time interval

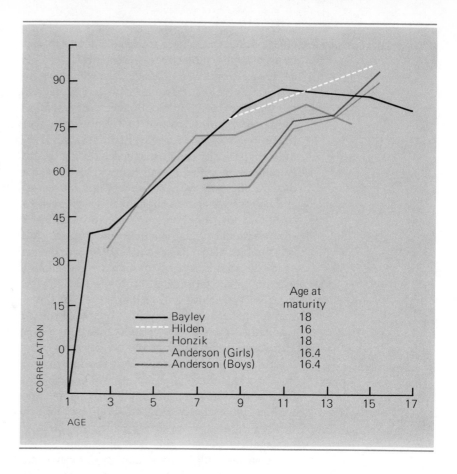

FIGURE 9–3
Correlations between
test scores obtained
at various ages with
those obtained at
maturity. The graph
lines represent data
from different
investigations,
illustrating the
substantial power of
tests obtained during
early childhood to
predict later
performance.
Adapted from B. S.
Bloom, **Stability and
Change in Human
Characteristics.**
Copyright 1964,
reproduced by
permission of John
Wiley & Sons, Inc.

Graph legend:

	Age at maturity
Bayley	18
Hilden	16
Honzik	18
Anderson (Girls)	16.4
Anderson (Boys)	16.4

CORRELATION

AGE

between tests increases. Figure 9–3 represents the correlations, from several studies, of scores obtained at maturity with those obtained at previous ages. These studies clearly show that although the relationship increased progressively as time of testing approximated maturity, even tests obtained during childhood substantially predict later performance when data for groups of people are examined. (Note, though, that any particular child's later IQ score will not necessarily be predicted accurately.)

DEVELOPMENTAL PATTERNS OF MEASURED INTELLIGENCE

Historically, efforts to measure intelligence have been tied to understanding the growth of mental capacity through the life span. The study of age-associated IQ change has become a popular topic, and, indeed, age-associated test performance may tell us much about the functioning of people at various times in the life cycle.

It had been assumed that mental functioning increases with age until adulthood, not an unreasonable view if one adopts the model that development more or less proceeds to "maturity" and then declines, perhaps after reaching a plateau at a certain age. Early data collected from cross-sectional studies confirmed this view for the most part: They showed a performance peak at eighteen to twenty-five years, a gradual decline until approximately fifty years of age, and then more rapid decline after fifty (Botwinick, 1973; Horn, 1970). Recognition of this pattern is built into some intelligence tests. The WAIS, probably the most widely used and researched of the adult scales, assigns IQ on the basis of comparison with others of the same age. But it does consider the fact that performance is not the same at different ages. For example, two people, twenty-five and fifty-six may achieve the same IQ score, but, in fact, the younger person will actually have performed better on the test. Figure 9–4 shows the age decline and the adjustment for age differences on the WAIS.

It is obvious, though, that the curve may show age *differences* as well as age *changes.* The people measured at different ages were different people, and it is thus possible that the decline is due to age-related differences in diet, opportunity for learning, test-taking sophistication, motivation, and the like. Consider, for example, the hypothetical case of a group of sixty-year-olds who obtained an average IQ of 95 while a group of twenty-five-year-olds obtained an average IQ of 105. Can it be concluded that aging itself is responsible for this apparent change over time? No, because the two age groups may have had different experiences relevant to intellectual performance. The twenty-five-year-olds undoubtedly had more formal education and may have experienced greater encouragement to achieve, better nutrition, and more practice in taking standardized tests. Perhaps these cohort differences, rather than age itself, underlie the higher IQ scores obtained by the twenty-five-year-olds. (The reader may recall our more general discussion of the problem of cohort effects in chapter 2).

Green (1969) conducted a cross-sectional study in change in IQ scores among Puerto Rican citizens between ages twenty-five and sixty-four and noted the same kind of pattern that had led other investigators to conclude that from early adulthood there is a steady decrease in intelligence (e.g.,

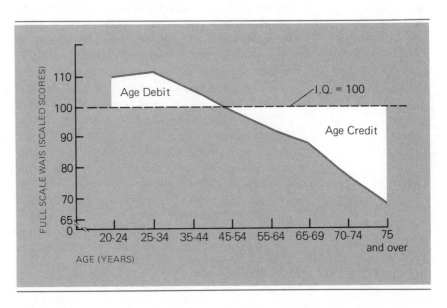

FIGURE 9–4
This graph shows the adjustment in performance (scaled scores) made at various ages so that 100 is the average IQ for all age groups. For younger people points were subtracted; for the older, points were added. Reproduced from Botwinick, 1973, p. 183. Copyright © 1973 by Springer Publishing Company, Inc., New York. Used by permission.

Bromley, 1966). However, Green also observed that the older subjects, on the average, had received fewer years of education, and he hypothesized that reduced educational experience rather than age was responsible for the result. When he adjusted the analysis so that educational level was equated for all age groups, he found that full-scale IQ scores increased until age forty and thereafter remained constant. When verbal and nonverbal sections were examined separately, it was found that verbal intelligence steadily increased from ages twenty-five to sixty-four, while nonverbal intelligence was constant from twenty-five to forty, after which it showed some decline.

Using a longitudinal design, Blum, Jarvik, and Clark (1970) reported trends in IQ change among individuals between ages sixty-five and eighty-five. They found a small decline in intelligence test scores between sixty-five and seventy-three and a much steeper decline between seventy-three and eight-five. Like Green, they also observed that the rate of change for different parts of the intelligence test was not constant. On tests of pure information, such as vocabulary, no decline was observed through age eighty-five, whereas on tests requiring speed or perceptual-spatial reasoning, there was a sharp decline between ages sixty-five and seventy-three. Many other longitudinal studies lead to the conclusion that intelligence test scores obtained from the *same* subjects over time are maintained and may even increase through early and middle adulthood (Horn, 1970). Such results are gladly accepted by those of us who want to believe that adult intellectual ability does not decline rapidly, but we must realize that the picture is far more complicated.

First, the problem of losing subjects (technically called *differential attrition*) inevitably causes trouble. Regardless of the research design employed, with increasing age there is increasing loss of people due to poor motivation, and perhaps more importantly, to illness and death. The tests of the older people thus do not include many who, on the average, would obtain the lower scores (Riegel and Riegel, 1972; Siegler, 1975). Riegel and Riegel (1972), for example, in tracing the subjects who had dropped out of their study, found that as a group these individuals had obtained lower scores on the previous testing. They also noted that many had died since the previous testing.

The Riegels emphasized another implication of their findings. It appears that test performance drops when a person is relatively close to death. As groups of older subjects include a greater number of people close to death, the average performance of the older subjects declines. But, in fact, the average may indicate a greater decline than is actually the case because the performance records of those near death are included.

These considerations make it extremely difficult to interpret the age patterns on tests. Loss of subjects would lead one to believe that the decline in performance has been underestimated while the marked predeath drop in certain individuals would mask the better performance of the majority of the subjects. It is understandable that investigators disagree on the findings, even when the more sophisticated cross-sequential research designs have been used (Baltes and Schaie, 1974, 1976; Horn and Donaldson, 1976). The most widely agreed upon pattern appears to be that performance peaks sometime in the twenties, is at a plateau during the thirties and forties, and declines after that, at first gradually and then more sharply late in life or just prior to death. A finer analysis, though, takes into consideration different patterns for different abilities.

Changes in Different Abilities

We saw in two studies above that verbal abilities, compared to perceptual-spatial abilities (many of which are timed), increase or are maintained well into adulthood, a finding that has often been replicated. What actually is sampled in these types of tasks? To obtain some idea of this, we can review Table 9–1. The verbal abilities being referred to include general information, comprehension, similarities, and vocabulary. The perceptual-spatial tasks are some of the performance tests.

The distinction between abilities that decline more rapidly and those that do not also has been conceptualized along the dimension of fluid and crystallized intelligence (Horn, 1970). Recall that fluid intelligence refers to abilities to solve problems that are relatively uninfluenced by experience, whereas crystallized intelligence involves knowledge of the information and skills of the culture. Figure 9–5 demonstrates the findings of Horn and Cattell that fluid intelligence is high during adolescence but drops throughout the life span, whereas crystallized intelligence follows a reverse pattern. These investigators have also suggested a life span pattern (Figure 9–6). Early in life both abilities would be expected to grow at a rapid and approximately even rate. Fluid intelligence then would begin a downward swing due to biological wear and tear in the central nervous system. Crystallized intelligence would tend to continue to develop with cultural experience, declining only when environmental restriction occurs or when biological wear and tear is overpowering.

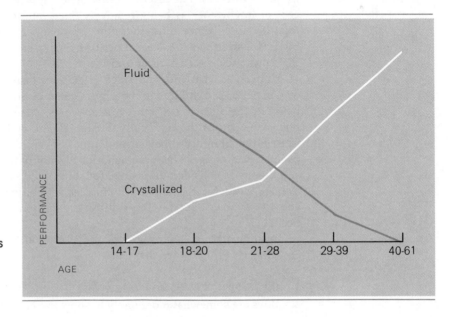

FIGURE 9–5
Performance on tasks utilizing fluid and crystallized intelligence. From Horn, 1970, p. 463.

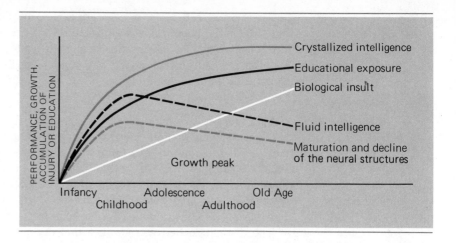

In summary, what can be concluded about the development of intellectual abilities as they are measured on general and specific tests of intelligence? Their peak is evidently not reached as early as once thought, and abilities persevere well into adulthood. But all abilities cannot be lumped together; some follow a different pattern than others. To the extent that individuals biologically age at different rates and accumulate different experiences, their performance will certainly vary.

THE CHANGING VIEW OF INTELLIGENCE

Constancy in Individual IQ Scores

In an earlier section of this chapter it was noted that IQ scores are relatively constant from childhood for many individuals. The studies from which this conclusion is drawn consist of retesting *groups* of people at specific time intervals and then observing whether a correlation exists among the several scores. The results, at first blush, appear to support the old concept of intelligence as being relatively fixed (and some may assume from this that intelligence must therefore be predetermined by biological factors). However, when *individual* performance over time is examined we see that constancy is *not* a hard-and-fast rule.

Honzik, MacFarland, and Allen (1948), for example, found that almost 60 percent of 252 children in the Child Guidance Study, tested several times between the ages of six and eighteen years, changed by fifteen or more points. As part of the Fels Study, Sontag, Baker, and Nelson (1958) administered the Stanford-Binet several times to children between three and twelve years of age. The large majority did not obtain the same IQ scores, and there was considerable change for some children. Figure 9–7 shows the average gains for the thirty-five children exhibiting the greatest increase and the average loss for the thirty-five children displaying the greatest decline.

In summarizing their own work and that of others, McCall, Appelbaum, and Hogarty (1973) noted that:

1. IQ changes of thirty and forty points are fairly often found.

2. Boys are somewhat more likely to show increases in IQ than are girls,

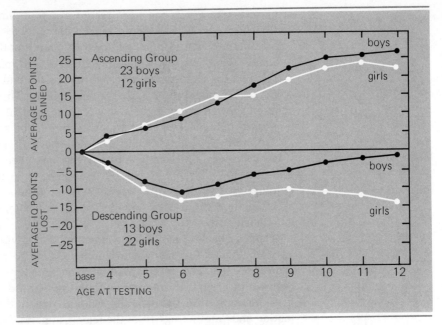

and girls oriented toward masculine roles tend to show more increases than girls not so oriented.

3. Children of low-income families tend to show no change or decrease in IQ scores.

4. Differences in personality have been found between those who show increases and those who show decreases in IQ. Preschool children who gain are independent and competitive; the same is true for elementary school children who gain and they also are self-initiating and problem solving.

Early Studies of Environmental Impact

If IQ scores change with age, it is clear that some form of environmental influence may be operating, a fact that is currently receiving wide recognition. Interestingly, if we glance back into history we see that investigations that pointed to environmental influence on intelligence test scores ignited one of the most intense controversies to ever exist in psychology. It all began when Wellman (1932a, 1932b) reported that children who attended preschool in the Iowa Child Welfare Station showed substantial gains in IQ during their attendance that were not attributable to practice effects. Reactions to the reports were strong. One investigator, in a paper entitled "The Wandering IQ: Is It Time to Settle Down?" suggested that the work reflected statistical incompetence influenced by wishful thinking (Stott and Ball, 1965). Arguments flew back and forth, with claims from other preschool studies that such gains did not occur.

Another series of investigations compared the mental development of youngsters reared in institutions with that of youngsters reared by their own mothers or caring mother-figures. Spitz (1949) compared two groups of infants—one group had been reared in a foundling home and the other had been cared for in an institutional nursery by the infants' own mothers. The foundling home infants at two to four months had developmental quotients averaging 124, while the mother-reared infants had an average of 100. When the children were tested toward the end of one year, their DQ scores had changed to 72 and 105, respectively. Thus, the foundling home children showed an average decline of more than 50 points. Spitz attributed the results to the lack of environmental stimulation and emotional ties.

Goldfarb (1943) examined children who had spent most of their first three years of life in an institution and had then been placed in foster homes, with children who had been assigned to foster homes from the beginning. He reported the same pattern of results as had Spitz: The institutionalized children exhibited a greater percentage of mental retardation and deficient speech.

Harold Skeels (1966) also documented that environmental factors could have an impact on mental development. Due to rather unusual circumstances, he was able to compare orphanage children with a group of children who were transferred before their third birthdays from the orphanage to an institution for the mentally retarded, where they received a lot of attention and "mothering" from the female inmates. Skeels described the two environments in this way:

The orphanage

Overcrowding of living facilities was characteristic. Too many children had to be accommodated in the available space and there were too few adults to guide them . . . Thirty to thirty-five children of the same sex under six years of age lived in a "cottage" in the charge of one matron and three or four entirely untrained and often reluctant girls of thirteen to fifteen years of age. The waking and sleeping hours of these children were spent (except during meal times and a little time on a grass plot) in an average-sized room (approximately fifteen feet square), a sunporch of similar size, a cloakroom. . . . and a single dormitory. The latter was occupied only during sleeping hours. The meals for all children in the orphanage were served in a central building in a single large dining room. . . .

The duties falling to the lot of the matron were not only those involved in the care of the children but those related to clothing and cottage maintenance, in other words, cleaning, mending, and so forth. . . . With so much responsibility centered in one adult the result was a necessary regimentation. The children sat down, stood up, and did many things in rows and in unison. They spent considerable time sitting on chairs, for in addition to the number of children and the matron's limited time there was the misfortune of inadequate equipment. . . .

No child had any property which belonged exclusively to him except, perhaps, his tooth brush. Even his clothing, including shoes, was selected and put on him according to size.

The institution for the mentally retarded

[The children] were placed on wards with older, brighter inmate girls. The wards were in a large cottage that contained eight wards with a matron and an assistant matron in charge and with one attendant for each ward. Approximately 30 patients, girls ranging in age from 18 to 50 years, were on each ward. On two wards (2 and 3), the residents had mental ages of from 9 to 12 years. On two other wards (4 and 5), the mental levels were from 7 to 10 years, and on another (ward 7), the mental ages were from 5 to 8 years. With the exception of ward 7, the wards housed few or no younger children other than the experimental "house guests." It was planned to place one, or at the most two, children from the experimental group on a given ward. . . .

The spacious living rooms of the wards furnished ample space for indoor play and activity. Whenever weather permitted, the children spent some time each day on the playground under the supervision of one or more older girls. Here they were able to interact with other children of similar ages. Outdoors play equipment included tricycles, swings, slides, sand boxes, etc. The children also began to attend the school kindergarten as soon as they could walk. Toddlers remained for only half the morning and 4- or 5-year olds, the entire morning. Activities carried on in the kindergarten resembled preschool rather than the more formal type of kindergarten.

As part of the school program, the children attended daily 15-minute exercises in the chapel, which included group singing and music by the orchestra. The children also attended the dances, school programs, moving pictures, and Sunday chapel services.

In considering this enriched environment from a dynamic point of view it must be pointed out that in the case of almost every child, some one adult (older girl or attendant) became particularly attached to him and figuratively "adopted" him. As a consequence, an intense one-to-one adult-child relationship developed, which was supplemented by the less intense but frequent interactions with the other adults in the environment. Each child had some one person with whom he was identified and who was particularly interested in him and his achievements. This highly stimulating emotional impact was observed to be the unique characteristic and one of the main contributions of the experimental setting. . . .

Skeels was able to follow the children into adulthood, ascertaining that those placed in the institution for the mentally retarded fared better in many ways. More were placed in loving adoptive homes and subsequently attained average intellectual levels, a greater amount of formal education, higher earnings, successful marital circumstances, and higher occupational status.

By no means are the Skeels and the other early studies we have examined without methodological weaknesses. Nevertheless, they contributed strongly to the reconceptualization of intelligence as being shaped by an interaction of genetic and environmental factors, with life experiences being powerful forces that can foster or retard mental growth. This thesis was persuasively documented by Hunt in 1961 when he drew together a wealth of evidence from the laboratories. Like Skeels, Hunt emphasized that a central task of society is to manage children's experiences so that intellectual development is optimized. Today research is continuing at a substantial pace to further explore specific kinds of experiences that influence intelligence throughout the life span. Let us turn to an examination of some important variables that operate during childhood.

A broad understanding of intelligence is provided by examining the factors to which it is related. Most of the studies of the correlates of intelligence are indeed correlational, and, as such, they allow only limited causal inferences to be drawn from them. Nevertheless, they have furnished many hypotheses for further exploration.

Family Variables

Although family variables are presumed to be related to intelligence, it is difficult to draw firm conclusions about them.

Family Size, Birth Order, and Sibling Spacing. Family size is often, but not always, inversely associated with test scores; sometimes no relationship is demonstrated (McCall and Johnson, 1972). Similar results apply to IQ and birth order. For example, McCall and Johnson (1972) found no association after testing elementary school children, but Burton (1968) reported a decrease in IQ with birth order in a college population, with the difference between firstborns and lastborns being 3.3 points. When an association is found, it is customary that the largest effect is between firstborns and all laterborns, who differ little from each other (Jensen, 1974a). This is consistent with the fact that firstborns appear to be academic achievers as compared to laterborns.

The results of a well-controlled study conducted in the Netherlands are noteworthy (Belmont and Marolla, 1973). The investigators examined the relationship between intellectual competence and family size and birth order for almost four hundred thousand men. They found that as scores on a nonverbal measure of intelligence decreased, family size and birth order became progressively larger. As Figure 9–8 shows, firstborns scored higher than did secondborns, secondborns scored higher than thirdborns, and so on, regardless of family size. The "only child" performed less well than did the older children of small families. Furthermore, these effects were found for the three social classes examined. The authors suggested that perhaps mothers become "less effective producers" with an increasing number of children, or that parents pay less attention to individual children as family size increases.

Based on these and similar findings, Zajonc and Markus (1975; Zajonc, 1976) proposed a model to explain the effects of family size and birth order on intelligence. According to the model, the intelligence of any one child depends upon the intellectual environment of the family, defined as the average intellectual level. For example, if 30 is arbitrarily assigned to represent the typical adult input, the intellectual level of the family of a firstborn is 30 (parent) + 30 (parent) + 0 (the newborn), or $60 \div 3 = 20$. If a second child is born relatively soon, the intellectual level may be 30 (parent) + 30 (parent) + 8 (older sibling) + 0 (the newborn), or $68 \div 4 = 17$. Family size thus has a direct influence, with largeness working to decrease the intellectual environment because the proportion of individuals with low intellectual level is high. But spacing of the children also plays a role: As a child matures he or she obtains a higher level. In the previous example, if the older sibling is nearing adulthood the average intellectual level might be

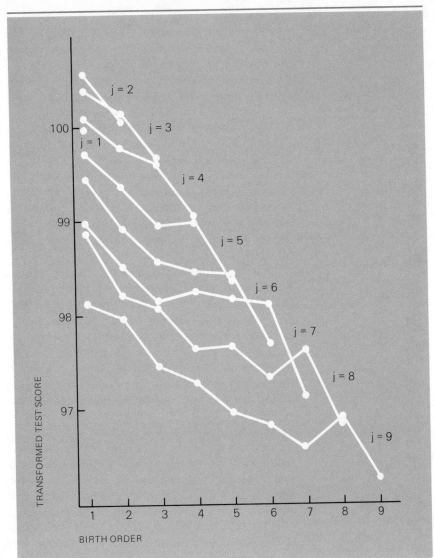

FIGURE 9–8
Scores on nonverbal
measure of
intelligence
according to birth
order in families of
different size (j equals
number of children).
From R. B. Zajonc
and G. B. Markus,
Birth order
and intellectual
development,
Psychological Review,
1975, **82,** 74–88.
Copyright by the
American
Psychological
Association, reprinted
by permission.

30 (parent) + 30 (parent) + 24 (older sibling) + 0 (the newborn), or 84 ÷ 4 = 21. Greater spacing increases the intellectual level and it may even reverse the usual relationship between birth order and intelligence. With regard to the only child performing less well than older children of small families, Zajonc and Markus suggest that the only child is disadvantaged by not having the opportunity to assume the role of teacher for younger children. In attempting to quantitatively relate several social variables to individual differences in intelligence, the model serves as an example of the kind of theory toward which developmental psychology aspires. However, a more recent analysis has challenged the ability of the model to predict intellectual performance and so its ultimate success remains unknown at this time (Velandia, Grandon, and Page, 1978).

Parental Interaction. The relationship between intelligence and the specific ways in which parents deal with their offspring has also been examined. It is not easy to categorize and measure parent-child interaction, and the number of parental behaviors and attitudes affecting children's performance is presumably very large. The following remarks, then, provide only a sample of the kinds of variables being studied and some of what is tentatively known about them.

Using a specially designed inventory to assess the home environment, Caldwell and her associates (Caldwell, Bradley, and Elardo, 1975) found that increases in functioning from six months to thirty-six months were related to maternal involvement with the children and provision of play material. Inadequate organization of the physical and temporal environment was related to decreases. Bayley and Schaefer (1964) reported that hostility in mothers was related to high IQ scores in boys during infancy; for girls, loving, controlling maternal behavior was related to high IQ scores during infancy.

Honzik (1967) related family variables measured when infants were twenty-one months old to test performances obtained between the ages of twenty-one months and thirty years. One of the clearer findings was the positive relation between IQ scores, particularly for boys, and mothers' worrisomeness, tenseness, concern, and energy. The author suggested that such mothers probably are more responsive to the wants and needs of their children and do more for them. The closeness of the relationship also was important. For girls, early closeness to mother was related positively to test scores, but this was superseded during adolescence by the father-daughter relationship. Girls' IQs, unlike those of boys, also appeared related to parental harmony or lack of conflict.

Baldwin, Kalhorn, and Breese (1945) concluded that children of high intelligence came from democratic accepting homes, whereas those exhibiting low performance tended to come from homes categorized as rejecting and autocratic. Kent and Davis (1957) classified parents into demanding, over-anxious, normal, and unconcerned and found that children of demanding families did better than those from normal families, while youngsters of unconcerned parents did less well. This finding appears consistent with the Honzik result in relating concerned, stimulating, and tense parents to high intelligence in their children. Similarly, Sontag, Baker, and Nelson (1958) found that parents of children whose IQ increased over time (see p. 280) tended to apply pressure for optimal performance.

There is some evidence that mothers', compared to fathers', intellectual level is more closely associated with children's functioning (e.g., Willerman and Stafford, 1972). With regard to fathers, they may cast greater influence on their sons' cognitive development than on cognitive development in their daughters. Radin's (1972, 1973) work with boys from lower- and middle-class families showed a positive correlation between paternal nurturance and IQ. Fear of the father did not enhance growth, and a negative correlation was found between restrictiveness of the father and IQ in the lower-class families. It was suggested that nurturant paternal behavior allows the child to identify with the father and internalize the father's ideas and behaviors. Also, in accordance with social learning theory, the father's attitude toward the child may assure the child that his exploratory behavior will be rewarded and increase the incidence of such behavior leading to cognitive growth. The importance of the father's availability on intelligence was demonstrated by Reis and Gold (1977), who studied four-year-old boys with available fathers (average time with child, nineteen hours per week) and less available fathers (spent eleven hours per week with child). They found a positive correlation between availability and three measures of problem solving.

It has been suggested that paternal influence on a daughter operates indirectly through the mother. Honzik (1967) reported an association between paternal friendliness toward the mother and intellectual development in the daughter. Radin (1976) suggested that the father's warmth toward the mother may increase the mother's warmth toward the child. Such positive parental interaction may create the milieu supportive of cognitive growth in girls. However, it is not clear why the effect is not demonstrable in the son's development.

Socioeconomic Status, Race, and Ethnicity

As we have seen earlier (in chapter 5), a clear-cut, positive relationship exists between socioeconomic status (SES) and IQ. The pattern has shown up continuously on standardization of intelligence tests such as the Stanford-Binet and the Wechsler tests. For example, children whose fathers were classified as professionals obtained an average Stanford-Binet score of 115, whereas children whose fathers held slightly skilled occupations obtained an average score of 97 (McNemar, 1942). Table 9–3 indicates a similar relation for the WISC. It has been estimated that, in general, a fifteen-to twenty-five-point difference exists between scores of children of professionals and laborers (Eells, 1953).

TABLE 9–3
Mean IQ Scores for the Normative Sample on the Wechsler Intelligence Scale for Children Categorized on the Basis of Father's Occupation

	Mean IQ		
Occupational Category	Verbal	Performance	Full Scale
Professional and semiprofessional workers	110.9	107.8	110.3
Proprietors, managers, and officials	105.9	105.3	106.2
Clerical, sales, and kindred workers	105.2	104.3	105.2
Craftsmen, foremen, and kindred workers	100.8	101.6	101.3
Operatives and kindred workers	98.9	99.5	99.1
Domestic, protective, and other service workers	97.6	96.9	97.0
Farmers and farm managers	96.8	98.6	97.4
Farm laborers and foremen, laborers	94.6	93.9	94.2

Source: Adapted from Seashore, Wesman, and Doppelt, 1950.

Bayley and Schaefer (1964), among others, found that starting at about two years of age, measures of SES correlated more and more positively with IQ. Before that age, there was either no relationship or a negative one. This is not surprising in light of the apparent qualitative differences of infant tests. But the question remains as to how to interpret the growing correlations with age. It could reflect either the accumulative influence of the environment, the late appearance of genetically based abilities, or a combination of these factors.

Cumulative Deficit Hypothesis.   Recent data support the hypothesis of environmental cumulative deficit, the idea, voiced for several decades, that the effects of a poor environment accumulate over time. Otto Klineberg was the first to use the term "cumulative deficit" in his citing of the early Sherman and Key (1932) test of children from the hollows of the Blue Ridge Mountains, which are approximately 100 miles from Washington, D.C. (Jensen, 1974a). Life in this cultural setting was characterized by an extreme degree of poverty, low literacy, poor educational facilities, and isolation from other communities (Figure 9–9). It was not surprising that the children achieved less than average scores, and performance was related to the cultural level of the individual hollows. Moreover, the average IQ declined from 84 at ages six through eight, to 70 at ages eight through ten, and to 53 at ages ten through twelve.

In reviewing evidence of cumulative deficit, Jensen (1977) harshly criticized the methodological adequacy of the research, concluding that it did not demonstrate the phenomenon. He then proceeded to test the hypothesis in California and Georgia by comparing the performance of both black and white siblings. If older siblings performed less well than younger ones, it could be attributed to cumulative deficit. The California study, which involved kindergarten through grade six students, showed a small cumulative deficit in verbal but not nonverbal IQ for the black population. The Georgia investigation, which included children from kindergarten to twelfth grade, demonstrated a substantial cumulative deficit in both verbal and nonverbal IQ for black children only. Jensen commented:

FIGURE 9-9
A family from one of the isolated hollows studied by Sherman and Key.   From M. Sherman and C. B. Key, The intelligence of isolated mountain children, **Child Development, 3** (1932), 179–290. Copyright 1932 by the Society for Research in Child Development, Inc. Reproduced by permission.

The existing data do not permit a definitive rejection of the genetic or environmental hypotheses. Moreover, the two hypotheses are not mutually exclusive ... However, the present results on Georgia blacks, when viewed in connection with the contrasting results for California blacks, would seem to favor an environmental interpretation of the progressive IQ decrement ... The blacks of rural Georgia, whose environmental disadvantages are markedly greater than in the California sample, show considerable decrements in both verbal and nonverbal IQ ... (1977, p. 190).

It should be noted that our discussion of cumulative deficit began with SES and ended with black/white differences. Because blacks fall disproportionately into the low SES, there is often a confounding of social class and racial variables.

Performance of Blacks on Standard Tests.   It is by now firmly established that blacks do considerably less well on standard IQ tests than whites (Dreger and Miller, 1960; Kennedy, 1969; Shuey, 1966). The difference is in the range of fifteen to twenty points; that is, blacks score about 80 to 85 compared with the white average of 100. For example, one group of investigators (Kennedy, van de Riet, and White, 1963) established norms for eighteen hundred black children of grades one to six in the southeastern United States. The mean IQ on the Stanford-Binet was 80.7. Children from metropolitan schools performed better than those from urban and rural communities. Figure 9–10 shows the distribution of scores of black children, compared with the distribution of the original standardization sample for this test. Note that there is considerable overlap between the two distributions; this means that a large percentage of black and white children score within the same range.

FIGURE 9–10
IQ distribution on the Stanford-Binet for the normative white sample and 1,800 black elementary-school children in the Southeast. Adapted from W. A. Kennedy, V. van de Riet, and J. C. White, Jr., 1963. Copyright 1963 by the Society for Research in Child Development, Inc. Reproduced by permission.

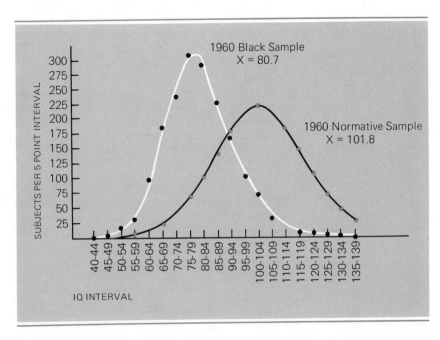

It is also worth noting that differences among blacks and whites generally do not show up until the preschool years; black infants do as well as whites on the kinds of skills required by infant tests. This is particularly interesting because of the well-established higher incidence of prematurity and inadequate medical and dietary care in the black population.

In chapter 5 many of the issues relating to black achievement and test performance were discussed. But one related issue of great importance and controversy remains: cultural bias and testing.

The Cultural Bias of Intelligence Tests. Psychological testing has come under increasing criticism since the 1950s. One of the criticisms is a response to the consistent finding that individuals coming from cultural backgrounds other than the broad middle or upper class perform less well on tests of intelligence than those from the general population. It is asserted that conclusions about the intelligence of various minority groups are based on tests that, by the nature of their construction and administration, are biased against them.

This stance is sometimes referred to as the "Chicago point of view," because much relevant writing and research was carried out at the University of Chicago. Consider the following informal description of cultural bias as it was suggested by one member of the Chicago group, Kenneth Eells:*

> Let us suppose for a moment that you have a friend in Australia and that you have gone to visit him in his home country. He has told you that he is to take an intelligence test that afternoon and suggests that you take it too, just for the fun of it. . . . When you first open the test booklet you say to yourself, "Well, I'm in a foreign country, but since they speak English, I shouldn't have any special difficulty with this." But soon you are in trouble. . . . You realize that because of the mutton and the kangaroo, the strange words, the local information, and the variations in word connotations your friend had an advantage over you. If he thinks this is a good measure of your intelligence you are glad that he cannot compare your score with his. . . . As a measure of your ability to get along in a certain portion of the Australian culture the test might be excellent and you might willingly accept your low score as an accurate reflection of your "current ability." It is the labeling of the test as an "intelligence" test, with its accompanying implication that this is somehow a measure of some basic ability or potentiality of yours, that disturbs you. . . . You wouldn't object to being told you couldn't understand Australian newspapers very well; but to be told you're not very "intelligent" implies something more serious, doesn't it? [1953, pp. 284–285]

Eells goes on to note that children reared on the "wrong side of the tracks" in America are in an analogous situation. They are judged on the basis of test items requiring cultural experiences different from their own. Consider, for example, a test item such as:

A symphony is to a composer as a book is to what?
paper   author   musician   man

*Copyright © 1953 by President and Fellows of Harvard College.

It would surprise no one if children from the upper classes chose the correct answer, simply on the basis of experience, more often than those from the lower classes. And yet, this outcome is frequently interpreted as implying a deficiency in the lower classes in some inherent capability called intelligence.

In one major study, in which eight group intelligence tests were administered in the Midwest, an analysis of test items for higher and lower socioeconomic classes was made (Eells, Davis, Havighurst, et al., 1951). Many items were answered differently by children of different social status; for subjects thirteen or fourteen years old this difference was as high as 85 percent of the items. The largest difference was obtained on verbal items; there was small difference on items communicated in simple vocabulary or those that were common to the social classes.

One investigator, Adrian Dove, has taken a "shoe on the other foot" approach to succinctly demonstrate cultural bias. He composed the "Dove Counterbalance General Intelligence Test, or the "Chitling Test," utilizing general knowledge of black culture. Table 9-4 shows a few of the items, most of which cannot be successfully completed by people other than blacks.

There also have been serious attempts to construct tests that eliminate aspects along which subcultures might vary, such as content, language, and the influence of speed (Anastasi, 1968). Today several culture-fair tests exist that are relatively good predictors of academic success. Raven's Progressive Matrices, for example, consist of designs, each having a missing section (Figure 9–11). Examinees are required to select the missing part from several alternatives; they must abstract relationships, which become increasingly more difficult. There is no time limit and instructions are simple. The Goodenough-Harris Drawing Test requires subjects merely to draw a picture of a man, woman, and themselves. It is reasonably reliable and correlates with other intelligence tests. It should be noted, however, that both of these tests are more culture-laden than originally expected. Raven's Progressive Matrices reflects amount of education (Anastasi, 1968), while the Goodenough-Harris Drawing Test is related to the degree to which repre-

---

TABLE 9-4
A Few of the Items That Appear on the "Chitling Test"

Cheap chitlings (not the kind you purchase at a frozen-food counter) will taste rubbery unless they are cooked long enough. How soon can you quit cooking them to eat and enjoy them? (A) 45 minutes, (B) 2 hours, (C) 24 hours, (D) 1 week (on a low flame), (E) 1 hour.

"Down-home" (the South) today, for the average "soul brother" who is picking cotton from sunup to sundown, what is the average earning (take-home) for one full day? (A) 75¢, (B) $1.65, (C) $3.50, (D) $5.00, (E) $12.00.

If you throw the dice and seven is showing on the top, what is facing down? (A) seven, (B) snake eyes, (C) boxcars, (D) little Joes, (E) eleven.

"Hully Gully" came from: (A) East Oakland, (B) Fillmore, (C) Watts, (D) Harlem, (E) Motor City.

Correct answers: c, d, a, c.

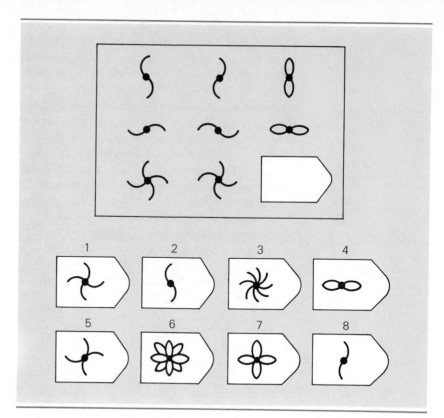

FIGURE 9–11
Materials similar to
those used in Raven's
Progressive Matrices
Test.

sentational art exists in cultures (Dennis, 1966). A study of the Drawing Test, for example, showed that aboriginal Australian boys, but not girls, out-perform the average U.S. child (Money and Nurcombe, 1974). The aborigines have a strong cultural heritage focusing on the painting of totemic designs, with which boys, much more than girls, are involved. It does not seem possible, at this point in time, to construct tests that are *completely* free of cultural content.

With regard to standard tests there is no doubt that injustice has resulted from poor judgment about test use and interpretation. For example, in California pupils with Spanish surnames constituted 28.34 percent of the educable mentally retarded enrollment but only 15.22 percent of the general school-population. Black children constituted 25.5 percent of these special classes but only 8.85 percent of the general population (Leary, 1970). Partially as a result of court order, the state is now using nonverbal tests employing the primary language used in the home and a study of the home environment—procedures that were not originally employed—to reevaluate pupils labeled retarded. Other states and cities have also adopted various procedures to eliminate the abuse of culturally biased testing.

Other Performance Patterns. It has been suggested that useful information can be gathered about the achievement of racial, ethnic, or social groups by an analysis of performance on different kinds of tasks (Dreger and Miller, 1960; Lesser, 1973; Lesser, Fifer, and Clark, 1965). In one such analysis, first-grade children from middle- and lower-class families with Chinese, Jewish, black, and Puerto Rican cultural backgrounds were studied (Lesser, Fifer, and Clark, 1965). Tests were administered that measured verbal ability, reasoning, number facility, and space conceptualization. Although middle-class children obtained higher scores on all the scales, the pattern of performance within ethnic groups differed. For example, Jewish children performed best on the verbal tasks; then, in order of decreasing strength, on number, with space and reasoning almost equal. Puerto Rican children performed best on space tasks and least well on verbal ones.

Jensen has proposed that the relationship between test performance and social class and race can best be understood if intelligence is conceptualized into Level I and Level II abilities (Jensen, 1969, 1973, 1974b; Jensen and Figueroa, 1975). *Level I* involves simple registration, storage, and recall of sensory inputs and is most prominent in rote learning and short-term memory. *Level II* involves mental manipulation of inputs, abstraction, transfer, reasoning, conceptualization, and problem solving. It is dependent somewhat on Level I, but the reverse is not true. Jensen maintains that Level I tasks are performed equally as well by lower- and middle-class children and by whites and blacks, but that middle-class children and whites are superior on Level II tasks. Furthermore, he has produced some evidence supporting his ideas. This work has created a storm of controversy because Jensen favors a genetic explanation for the differential performance between blacks and whites. The controversy between genetic and environmental explanations for the different patterns on IQ tests obtained by various racial/ethnic groups will be long-lived because there are supporters on both sides (see pp. 128–129 also).

MENTAL RETARDATION

Mental retardation has been mentioned a number of times in this chapter as it is related to various aspects of intelligence. Intelligence as it is defined by standard tests has been crucial to the definition of mental retardation. According to the American Association on Mental Deficiency (AAMD), *mental retardation* "refers to significantly subaverage general intellectual functioning existing concurrently with deficits in adaptive behavior, and manifested during the developmental period" (Grossman, 1973, p. 11). It is often estimated that about 3 percent of the total population is classified as retarded (Scheerenberger, 1964; Robinson and Robinson, 1970), but from 1894 this figure has varied from .05 to 13 percent, depending on the current definition (Windle, 1958).

The prevalence of retardation is related to age in an interesting way. Preschool children are rarely termed retarded; the same is true for adults who are out of school and who manage to avoid encounters with police and other societal agents. However, the abstract conceptual and verbal proficiency required for school-age children, together with the fact that most wide-scale IQ testing is done during this period, results in a larger percentage of the population being termed retarded during the school years than at any other time (Granat and Granat, 1973). Figure 9–12 shows the usual pattern.

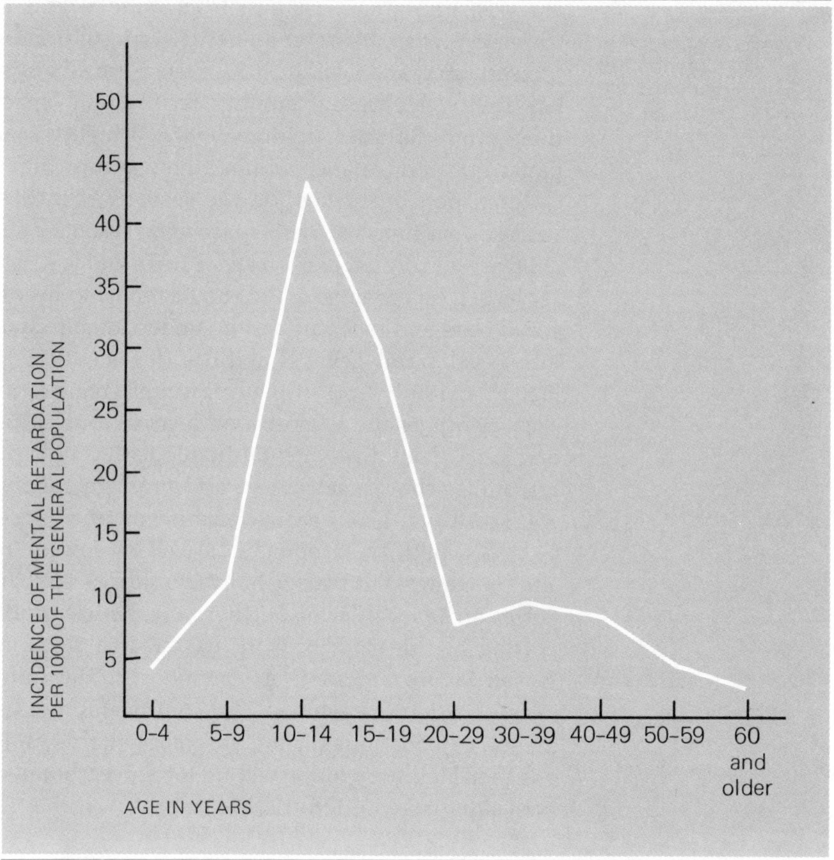

FIGURE 9–12
Relative frequency of being labeled mentally retarded as a function of age. Note that school-age children are particularly likely to be termed retarded. Adapted and reprinted with permission from N. O'Connor and J. Tizard, **The Social Problems of Mental Deficiency**, copyright 1956, Pergamon Press Ltd.

Levels and
Measurement of
Retardation

Historically retardation has been classified according to severity. Over the years three or four categories have generally been recognized, although the labels associated with them have varied with the time and the setting. The terms moron, imbecile, and idiot, for example, were once standard designations for retarded individuals. Today the AAMD uses the terms *mild, moderate, severe,* and *profound.* Current labels used by educators in the United States reflect the school capabilities of each group; here we find that *educable* (EMR), *trainable* (TMR), and *custodial* levels are distinguished. Table 9–5 shows the parallel between these classification schemes, as well as the accepted IQ range for each category. It should be noted that the variations in the labels themselves are not due simply to linguistic fashion or whimsy. Rather, they reflect a specific orientation toward retardation. Changes in labels have also served the beneficial purpose of helping to overcome prejudices and stereotypes that have accumulated over the years. Today most of us would be aghast to hear a mentally retarded person referred to as an imbecile or idiot, as these terms have taken on an extremely unpleasant connotation. Also, it has been shown that children labeled as slow learners are judged more favorably than those termed mentally retarded (Hollinger and Jones, 1970).

TABLE 9–5
Categories of Mental Retardation and the Associated IQ Ranges

System	IQ 100 95 90 85 80 75 70 65 60 55 50 45 40 35 30 25 20 15 10 5 0
American Association on Mental Deficiency	Mild | Moderate | Severe | Profound
American Educators	Educable | Trainable | Custodial

Source: From D. P. Hallahan and J. M. Kauffman, Exceptional Children, © 1978, p. 68. Reprinted by permission of Prentice-Hall, Inc., Englewood Cliffs, New Jersey.

Identifying levels of retardation on the basis of adaptive functioning is nowhere near as precise as is using intelligence test scores. Ideally it would involve numerous observations of the individual in various settings. In practice it is based on interviews and rating scales. The Vineland Social Maturity Scale, developed by Edgar Doll in 1935, consists of 117 items arranged hierarchically into several categories: self-help general, self-help eating, self-help dressing, self-help direction, occupation, communication, locomotion, and socialization. The AAMD Adaptive Behavior Scale, 1974 Revision, is composed of two major sections and subdivisions, listed in Table 9–6. These two scales are among the most frequently used to evaluate adaptive behavior, but they have not been constructed as meticulously as the IQ tests. Partly for this reason they are used as general measures of functioning.

TABLE 9–6
Behavioral and Personality Domains Evaluated by the AAMD Adaptive Behavior Scale

Part I	Part II
independent functioning	violent and destructive behavior
physical development	antisocial behavior
economic activity	rebellious behavior
language development	untrustworthy behavior
numbers and terms	withdrawal
domestic activity	stereotype behavior and odd mannerisms
vocational activities	inappropriate interpersonal manners
self-direction	unacceptable vocal habits
responsibility	unacceptable or eccentric habits
socialization	self-abusive behavior
	hyperactive tendencies
	sexually aberrant behavior
	psychological disturbances
	use of medications

Source: Adapted from J. M. Kauffman and J. S. Payne, eds, Mental retardation: Introduction and personal perspectives (Columbus, Ohio: Charles E. Merrill, 1975), pp. 99–101.

As a group, mentally retarded children are slow to walk, talk, and feed themselves. They also take unusually long periods of time before they are toilet-trained. In the more severe cases, retardation extends to almost all areas of anatomical, motor, and verbal development. Because intellectually normal children also may display one or more of these indicators, it usually is not assumed that a young child is retarded unless an extensive pattern of deficits is present.

By far the largest group of retarded individuals are classified as mildly or educably mentally retarded; they are rarely institutionalized. Of course even with this mild level of retardation a child will have a difficult time in school and is likely to lag behind intellectually average children of the same age. An educably retarded youngster can acquire many of the academic skills mastered by elementary school children, but reaches this level of achievement at a later age. There are many jobs that the mildly retarded are quite capable of filling; they have become welders, miners, painters, tailors, and the like. It has been found that their out-of-school success usually depends more on social skills than on occupational ones (Telford and Sawrey, 1972). Thus, parents of these children must avoid the temptation to foster dependency, sloppiness, and other socially undesirable characteristics, "excusing" them because of intellectual deficit.

The moderately or trainably retarded are usually unable to hold jobs except within sheltered workshops; they rarely marry and often are institutionalized. For the profoundly retarded—with IQs below 25—institutionalization is virtually inevitable. Among these individuals, interpersonal communication is minimal or entirely lacking, and learning even the simplest kind of self-care often proves extremely difficult or downright impossible.

Etiology

Although the causes of mental retardation vary considerably, two distinct etiological categories have been identified and can help us understand the range of characteristics and abilities displayed by retarded individuals.

Familial mental retardation is said to account for roughly 80 percent of all mental deficiency. A familially retarded child may be viewed as having an IQ within the lower range of the normal IQ distribution. As we would expect from this distribution, most children in this category are only mildly retarded. They are physically normal and have no history of brain damage or neurological defect.

Biologically caused mental retardation, as the name implies, is caused by some particular biological damage or defect. These include chromosomal anomalies such as Down's syndrome (mongolism) and gene defects such as phenylketonuria, both of which were discussed in chapter 5, as well as brain damage caused by infectious disease, oxygen deprivation, or physical trauma. Most, though not all, individuals with IQs below 50 appear to be in this category.

Cognitive Deficits of the Retarded

It is generally agreed that cognitive deficits are at the heart of the varied problems of mental retardation, whether they are viewed from the learning theory or Piagetian point of view.

Learning Processes. Research growing from the learning standpoint has revealed clear differences between the retarded and nonretarded on many learning tasks. Here we will briefly describe a few, drawing on Robinson and Robinson's (1976) extensive summary.

1. *Memory.* Short-term more than long-term memory is affected. We have seen that rehearsal is crucial for memorization and that children customarily use spontaneous rehearsal by the third grade. Retarded individuals do not tend to rehearse, thereby losing information. They also do not organize material by clustering, and so have difficulties in retrieval. To some extent training in rehearsal and clustering can increase memory, but success is limited with complex information and when generalization to a new problem is required.

2. *Paired Associate Learning.* In this learning task a pair of stimuli is initially presented and then subjects are given one stimulus of the pair and requested to recall or reproduce the other. By age five or six children usually employ a variety of strategies to help them relate the two stimuli of the pair, including visual imagery and verbal elaborations. Retarded children are able to use such mediators but do not readily produce them. Moreover, although they respond to training in the production of mediators, they tend to abandon the techniques unless training has been extensive.

3. *Discrimination Learning.* A good deal of research has been directed to discrimination learning; that is, to situations in which the individual is required to select one correct stimulus from two or more on the basis of feedback from previous trials. Nonretarded individuals appear to suddenly learn the solution after a number of trials, during which they first attend to the dimensions and then learn the correct one. When the retarded solve discrimination problems they too follow this pattern; however, they appear to have difficulty in attending to the relevant dimensions, thereby delaying learning.

4. *Learning to Learn.* Recall from chapter 6 that learning to learn involves subjects being given a series of problems, each series consisting of, for example, a simple discrimination or reversal problem. Learning becomes progressively rapid over the sets of problems until the solution occurs after one feedback trial, when the subjects form a learning set. Retarded children do not learn as rapidly as normal children, apparently due to unresponsiveness to feedback. Instead of using the information they are provided with by feedback they continue with initial preferences, such as a position preference.

In summary, research into the learning processes of the retarded demonstrates that learning occurs slowly, if at all, due to deficits in attention and the employment of mediators and problem-solving strategies. The retarded do not seem to plan ahead or to manipulate and transfer information as various tasks require.

The Piagetian View. In spite of the fact that Piaget himself has written little about retardation, his long-time associate, Bärbel Inhelder (1968), has described levels of retardation in terms of Piaget's stages. The mildly retarded are viewed as functioning no higher than at concrete operations; the moderately retarded as not surpassing the preoperational stage; and the severely and profoundly retarded as functioning at the sensorimotor stage. There is evidence for the accuracy of this description (Robinson and Robinson, 1976). Retardation thus can be considered a failure to progress beyond certain stages—an intellectual fixation that involves fluctuation between different modes of function. The child passes through the usual stages of cognitive development more slowly than the nonretarded child and reaches a lower limit. This view is referred to as the *developmental* view in contrast to the *difference* view, which maintains that retardation involves qualitatively different processes than normal development, not merely a slower rate and lower ceiling.

The distinction between the developmental and difference viewpoints of retardation applies not only to the Piagetian framework, but Piaget's theory lends itself to the testing of the two ideas. In a recent review of studies on this issue, Weisz and Zigler (1979) concluded that the preponderance of the evidence supports the developmental view, with the possible exception being the subgroup of retarded who suffer EEG abnormalities.

Social and Emotional Factors in Retardation

If mental retardation is thought of as simply an intellectual disadvantage, then little attention is given to the way in which it may be intertwined with social and emotional factors. Yet it is clear that these other factors are important, for biological as well as familial retardation. Regardless of the depth or cause of a child's intellectual disability, the home environment and the incentives provided to learn important skills can do much to relieve the problem—or make it worse.

Home Environment. In previous chapters we have seen repeatedly that a child's home environment plays a primary role in all aspects of social and emotional development. It is not surprising, therefore, to discover that some distinct patterns of home and family environment accompany retardation. The President's Task Force on Manpower Conservation (1964) found that the families of draftees rejected for intellectual deficits were characterized by poverty and poor education. Benda, Squires, Ogonik, and Wise (1963) indicated that among 205 retardates with IQs greater than 50, the majority had another retardate in the immediate family and three-quarters of the families either were separated or were not able to provide even bare necessities. Other family factors related to retardation include low achievement motivation of the parents, father's absence, lack of appropriate sex-role models, impoverished financial status, and low emphasis on education (Chilman, 1965; Robinson, 1967; Robinson and Robinson, 1970).

A rather specific effect of early home experiences on retardation has to do with the child's motivation. Retarded children, it has been suggested, may have more frequently been neglected by adults in their early lives and therefore crave attention and praise to a greater degree than their mental age alone would predict. To test this formulation, Zigler and Balla (1972) compared the influence of social praise on the behavior of normal and retarded children of mental ages seven, nine, and twelve, predicting that younger and retarded children, if given praise, would continue to perform a boring task for a longer time than older and normal individuals. The results confirmed their expectation; younger children performed the boring task longer than older ones and retarded children persisted more than normals. Especially striking was the finding that even the oldest retardates performed the boring task for a greater period of time than the youngest normal children.

And, finally, the home environment may influence the most important decision of all: whether the child is institutionalized. Studies have shown that, for brighter retardates, institutionalization is much more likely when the home environment has been inadequate than when parents have been able to provide the attention and care needed by these children (Zigler, 1968).

Educational Environment. All education is based on incentives of one sort or another, but it has been suggested that retarded children may be motivated by different incentives than are the typical middle-class youngsters, whose needs and tastes determine so many of our educational practices. Zigler and de Labry (1962) found clear support for this possibility, in an experiment that was later recapped this way:

> These investigators tested middle-class, lower-class, and retarded children *equated on MA* on a concept-switching task . . . under two conditions of reinforcement. In the first condition . . . the only reinforcement dispensed was the information that the child was correct. In the second condition, the child was rewarded with a toy of his choice if he switched from one concept to another. In the "correct" condition . . . retardates were poorer in the concept-switching than were middle-class children. . . . [But] in the toy condition this inferiority disappeared, and retarded and lower-class children performed as well as the middle-class children. [Zigler, 1968, p. 590]

FIGURE 9-13
With well-planned instruction, some severely retarded children can learn important academic skills. Sybil Shelton, Monkmeyer.

If material incentives are particularly important for retarded children, as Zigler and de Labry's findings suggest, then it becomes essential to determine what type of incentive conditions are most effective. Addressing this question, Talkington (1971) trained educable mentally retarded adolescents to perform a rather complex motor task under four incentive conditions. In the *reward only* condition, students simply received a token reward (later exchangeable for money) for each correct response; in the *response cost* condition, participants received twenty tokens as a sort of legacy at the beginning of each training session but lost one token for each error; youngsters in the *reward and cost* condition received ten tokens at the beginning of each session and subsequently received a token for each correct response but lost one for each error; finally, subjects in the *no reward, no cost* condition served as a control group and received no incentives.

Talkington's results were very clear. The *response cost* condition was by far the most effective way to teach these youngsters, and it resulted in fewer errors than reward alone regardless of whether it was used by itself or combined with reward. What is more, performance was at essentially the same level for the *response cost* and *reward and cost* groups, indicating that the reward element provided no additional motivation beyond that obtained by response cost alone. Talkington interprets the token removal procedure as a failure experience and suggests that the *response cost* technique was so highly effective for these retarded youngsters precisely because it elicited their strong motivation to avoid failure.

The theoretical significance of Talkington's study is that it meshes with a considerable body of earlier evidence showing that retarded persons are generally more motivated to avoid failure than to achieve success (Cromwell, 1963; Zigler, 1968). The underlying process appears to arise from the fact that retarded individuals have a background of many failures. As a result, the desire to avoid failure is particularly important for them when faced with a new problem. Retarded children are therefore more likely than normal children of the same *mental* age, that is, their intellectual peers, to "settle for" poor performance even when they can do better (Stevenson and Zigler, 1958). Building positive self-concepts and reducing the overwhelming motive to avoid failure is, or at least should be, a high priority goal for anyone teaching retarded children.

Social Skills and Intellectual Functioning

A question that frequently arises regarding intellectual retardation is whether it constrains the development of appropriate social skills. There is a clear correlation between mental age and social competence (Copobianco and Cole, 1960; Goulet and Barclay, 1963). It has been argued, though, that the relationship may not be a direct result of mental retardation. Perhaps, for example, it is not mental retardation itself but the failure to train retarded children in more advanced social skills that gives rise to the correlation (Gunzburg, 1965).

Severy and Davis (1971) have provided evidence that supports this view. They studied helping behavior of normal and retarded children under conditions in which the retarded children were "in a milieu containing models of and rewards for helping behavior" (p. 1019). There was no evidence of a deficit in helping behavior among retarded children in this situation; in fact, the older retardates actually attempted to give help more often—and succeeded in helping as often—as any of the groups of intellectually normal children.

Even among severely retarded children, careful and systematic use of modeling and reinforcement can be used to cultivate positive social skills and interactions. In one study (Paloutzian, Hasazi, Streifel, and Edgar, 1971) severely retarded children were trained in such tasks as passing a beanbag to another child or pulling another child cooperatively on a wagon. Before these experiences the children had made no attempt to interact with others and simply played aimlessly by themselves; after training, the children began to observe the play of more advanced peers and in some cases initiated appropriate interactions themselves.

Unfortunately, behaviors developed in severely retarded children through such special training will often disappear if reinforcement is not continued. Following up a one-year training program in social competence skills, Lawrence and Kartye (1971) found that the severely and profoundly retarded girls who participated had lost most of their earlier gains in communication and social skills within four months, although most of the self-help skills learned during the program were retained. The results suggest, then, that either long-term training or continued external reinforcement, or perhaps both, are needed in training severely retarded children to adapt socially. On the other hand, the findings also suggest that the task *can* be accomplished.

THE INTELLECTUALLY GIFTED AND CREATIVE

We now turn to the opposite end of the IQ spectrum, to the exceptionally gifted. Because we are virtually always fascinated by the unusual, it is not surprising that many presumptions have been made about the exceptionally gifted and talented. Historically the gifted have been associated with either the gods or madness (Albert, 1975). Their unusual talents or genius were attributed to supernatural powers; Goethe spoke of poets as "plain children of God," and it is not uncommon to find the word "divine" applied to artists. For Aristotle, "there is no genius without madness."

These attitudes still exist today in stereotypes of the gifted as being strange, odd, socially inept, maladapted, and downright mad. But their force has been lessened by studies of the gifted that paint a strikingly different picture. The 1920s and 1930s witnessed the beginning of several studies of the intellectually gifted. Among the most influential of the investigations is the Stanford study of the gifted begun in 1922 by Lewis Terman, which is still active. In the following excerpt, written in 1954, Terman describes his motivation for the project as well as some of his findings.

Terman's report also describes the attempt to identify factors that influenced life success among gifted men. The subjects first were rated on life success—the extent to which they made use of their abilities—and then the 150 who rated highest (the *A*s) and the 150 who rated lowest (the *C*s) were

The Discovery and Encouragement of Exceptional Talent   Lewis M. Terman

I have often been asked how I happened to become interested in mental tests and gifted children. My first introduction to the scientific problems posed by intellectual differences occurred well over a half-century ago when I was a senior in psychology at Indiana University and was asked to prepare two reports for a seminar, one on mental deficiency and one on genius. Up to that time, despite the fact that I had graduated from a normal college as a Bachelor of Pedagogy and had taught school for five years, I had never so much as heard of a mental test. The reading for those two reports opened up a new world to me, the world of Galton, Binet, and their contemporaries. The following year my MA thesis on leadership among children (Terman, 1904) was based in part on tests used by Binet in his studies of suggestibility.

Then I entered Clark University where I spent considerable time during the first year in reading on mental tests and precocious children. Child prodigies, I soon learned, were at that time in bad repute because of the prevailing belief that they were usually psychotic or otherwise abnormal and almost sure to burn themselves out quickly or to develop postadolescent stupidity. "Early ripe, early rot" was a slogan frequently encountered. By the time I reached my last graduate year, I decided to find out for myself how precocious children differ from the mentally backward, and accordingly chose as my doctoral dissertation an experimental study of the intellectual processes of fourteen boys, seven of them picked as the brightest and seven as the dullest in a large city school (Terman, 1906). These subjects I put through a

great variety of intelligence tests, some of them borrowed from Binet and others, many of them new. The tests were given individually and required a total of 40 or 50 hours for each subject. The experiment contributed little or nothing to science, but it contributed a lot to my future thinking. Besides "selling" me completely on the value of mental tests as a research method, it offered an ideal escape from the kinds of laboratory work which I disliked and in which I was more than ordinarily inept. (Edward Thorndike confessed to me once that **his** lack of mechanical skill was partly responsible for turning **him** to mental tests and to the kinds of experiments on learning that required no apparatus.)

However, it was not until I got to Stanford in 1910 that I was able to pick up with mental tests where I had left off at Clark University. By that time Binet's 1905 and 1908 scales had been published, and the first thing I undertook at Stanford was a tentative revision of his 1908 scale. This, after further revisions, was published in 1916. The standardization of the scale was based on tests of a thousand children whose IQ's ranged from 60 to 145. The contrast in intellectual performance between the dullest and the brightest of a given age so intensified my earlier interest in the gifted that I decided to launch an ambitious study of such children at the earliest opportunity.

My dream was realized in the spring of 1921 when I obtained a generous grant from the Commonwealth Fund of New York City for the purpose of locating a thousand subjects of IQ 140 or higher. More than that number were selected by Stanford-Binet tests from the kindergarten through the eighth grade, and a group mental test given in 95 high schools provided nearly 400 additional subjects. The latter, plus those I had located before 1921, brought the number close to

Adapted and reprinted from L. M. Terman, The discovery and encouragement of exceptional talent. *American Psychologist*, 1954, 9, 221–230. Copyright 1954 by the American Psychological Association. Reproduced by permission.

1,500. The average IQ was approximately 150, and 80 were 170 or higher (Terman, 1925).

The twofold purpose of the project was, first of all, to find what traits characterize children of high IQ, and secondly, to follow them for as many years as possible to see what kind of adults they might become. . . .

The more important results can be stated briefly: children of IQ 140 or higher are, in general, appreciably superior to unselected children in physique, health, and social adjustment; markedly superior in moral attitudes as measured either by character tests or by trait ratings; and vastly superior in their mastery of school subjects as shown by a three-hour battery of achievement tests. In fact, the typical child of the group had mastered the school subjects to a point about two grades beyond the one in which he was enrolled, some of them three or four grades beyond. Moreover, his ability as evidenced by achievement in the different school subjects is so general as to refute completely the traditional belief that gifted children are usually one-sided. I take some pride in the fact that not one of the major conclusions we drew in the early 1920's regarding the traits that are typical of gifted children has been overthrown in the three decades since then.

Results of thirty years' follow-up of these subjects by field studies in 1927–28, 1939–40, and 1951–52, and by mail follow-up at other dates, show that the incidence of mortality, ill health, insanity, and alcoholism is in each case below that for the generality of corresponding age, that the great majority are still well adjusted socially, and that the delinquency rate is but a fraction of what it is in the general population. Two forms of our difficult Concept Mastery Test, devised especially to reach into the stratosphere of adult intelligence, have been administered to all members of the group who could be visited by the field assistants, including some 950 tested in 1939–40 and more than 1,000 in 1951–52. On both tests they scored on the average about as far above the generality of adults as they had scored above the gen-

erality of children when we selected them. Moreover, as Dr. Bayley and Mrs. Oden have shown, in the twelve-year interval between the two tests, 90 percent increased their intellectual stature as measured by this test. ''Early ripe, early rot'' simply does not hold for these subjects. So far, no one has developed postadolescent stupidity!

As for schooling, close to 90 percent entered college and 70 percent graduated. Of those graduating, 30 percent were awarded honors and about two-thirds remained for graduate work. The educational record would have been still better but for the fact that a majority reached college age during the great depression. . . .

The achievement of the group to midlife is best illustrated by the case histories of the 800 men, since only a minority of the women have gone out for professional careers (Terman, 1954). By 1950, when the men had an average age of 40 years, they had published 67 books (including 46 in the fields of science, arts, and the humanities, and 21 books of fiction). They had published more than 1,400 scientific, technical, and professional articles; over 200 short stories, novelettes, and plays; and 236 miscellaneous articles on a great variety of subjects. They had also authored more than 150 patents. The figures on publications do not include the hundreds of publications by journalists that classify as news stories, editorials, or newspaper columns; nor do they include the hundreds if not thousands of radio and TV scripts.

The 800 men include 78 who have taken a Ph.D. degree or its equivalent, 48 with a medical degree, 85 with a law degree, 74 who are teaching or have taught in a four-year college or university, 51 who have done basic research in the physical sciences or engineering, and 104 who are engineers but have done only applied research or none. Of the scientists, 47 are listed in the 1949 edition of **American Men of Science.** Nearly all of these numbers are from 10 to 20 or 30 times as large as would be found for 800 men of corresponding age picked at random in the general population, and are sufficient answer to those who belittle the significance of IQ differences.

The follow-up of these gifted subjects has proven beyond question that tests of "general intelligence," given as early as six, eight, or ten years, tell a great deal about the ability to achieve either presently or 30 years hence. Such tests do not, however, enable us to predict what direction the achievement will take, and least of all do they tell us what personality factors or what accidents of fortune will affect the fruition of exceptional ability. Granting that both interest patterns and special aptitudes play important roles in the making of a gifted scientist, mathematician, mechanic, artist, poet, or musical composer, I am convinced that to achieve greatly in almost any field, the special talents have to be backed up by a lot of Spearman's **g**, by which is meant the kind of general intelligence that requires ability to form many sharply defined concepts, to manipulate them, and to perceive subtle relationships between them; in other words, the ability to engage in abstract thinking.

examined. Table 9–7 summarizes these findings. The most spectacular difference, according to Terman, was the greater drive to achieve and the greater mental and social adjustment of the *A* group. With regard to the preconceived notion that the gifted are strange, Terman said:

> Our data do not support the theory of Lange-Eichbaum (1932) that great achievement usually stems from emotional tensions that border on the abnormal. In our gifted group, success is associated with stability rather than instability, with absence rather than with presence of disturbing conflicts—in short with well-balanced temperament and with freedom from excessive frustrations. The Lange-Eichbaum theory may explain a Hitler, but hardly a Churchill . . . a Jefferson or a Washington.

TABLE 9–7

Ways In Which the Most Successful (the As) and the Least Successful (the Cs) Gifted Men In Terman's Study Differed

---

During high school the Cs began to slump academically.

Fifty-two percent of the As and only 14 percent of the Cs graduated from high school with honors.

As were more accelerated in school; they were 15 months younger at college graduation.

Half the As but only 15 percent of the Cs had fathers who were college graduates.

Twice as many of the As had siblings who had graduated from college.

The number of books in the homes of the As was double that in the homes of the Cs.

By age sixteen, half as many of the As' parents had divorced compared to the Cs' parents.

As children As rated markedly higher in prudence, self-confidence, perseverance, desire to excel. They also rated higher in leadership, popularity, sensitivity to approval and disapproval.

By middle adulthood four-fifths of the As and two-thirds of the Cs had married. The divorce rate of the As was half that of the Cs.

By middle adulthood, As rated higher in persistence in the accomplishment of ends, integration toward goals, self-confidence, and freedom from inferiority feelings.

Source: From Terman, 1954. Copyright 1954 by the American Psychological Association. Reprinted by permission.

Terman also expressed concern that the gifted be provided with proper educational experiences. But despite the passage of many years several unresolved issues still exist regarding the way in which the intellectually superior child should be treated.

What is Creativity?

Most people recognize in others and themselves something that seems to go beyond intelligence as it is usually conceived, something that might be labeled creativity. An exact definition, though, is hard to come by. Researchers have begun by asking whether creativity can, in fact, be distinguished from intelligence.

One strategy employed to test the validity of this distinction has been to compare "average" people with very successful people in various occupations, such as art, scientific research, mathematics, and writing. Are those who have made the most significant adult contributions the ones with higher intelligence? Did they have the better grades in school? In one study (Helson and Crutchfield, 1970) involving mathematicians, the index of creativity was nominations by other mathematicians for significant accomplishment in mathematics research. The highly creative scholars were compared with others, matched for age (they were all in their late thirties), who had doctorates from universities of equally high standing. The men in the two groups were approximately equivalent in terms of the amount of time they spent on their work, yet, by agreement of their peers, they differed markedly in terms of the quality of their products. It came as a surprise, then, that the two groups were entirely comparable in terms of IQ as usually measured; at this range of ability, intelligence was unrelated to creativity.

In fact, those who are creatively accomplished as adults are often unidentifiable by school grades. "As students," writes researcher D. W. MacKinnon of one sample of creative individuals, "they were, in general, not distinguished for the grades they received, and in none of the samples did their high school grade-point average show any significant correlation with their subsequently achieved and recognized creativeness" (1968, p. 103).

Similar findings emerge from many other reports. Scientists' later professional standing is not related to their undergraduate grades, even in science itself (Harmon, 1963). Nor are grades as a graduate student relevant. Mednick (1963), for example, asked psychology professors to rate their graduate students in terms of creativity—the level of imaginativeness and potential for their research efforts—and found that this index of creativity was unrelated to intelligence. More striking, creativity was not even related to the grades the subjects were receiving—from the same professors—for their graduate course work in psychology.

Employing a different strategy, Getzels and Jackson (1975) were able to distinguish, on the basis of tests, two groups of adolescents attending a private school whom they labeled "highly intelligent" and "highly creative." The groups were equally superior in academic achievement, but the former was in the top 20 percent on standard IQ measures but not in the top 20 percent on measures of creativity, whereas the highly creative showed the reverse pattern. Several differences were apparent between the groups.

Teachers expressed a clear preference to have the high IQ students in class compared to the highly creative; preference for the creative did not differ from preference for the total student body. The high IQ students displayed a desire to possess immediately qualities that would lead to later success, but the creative students did not appear to select present goals on the basis of future success. They also rated high marks, IQ, pep and energy, character, and goal directedness lower than did the highly intelligent group, valuing instead a wide range of interests, emotional stability, and a sense of humor. And finally, the relationship between students' personal aspirations and the qualities that they believed teachers preferred differed for the two groups. The high IQ students held a self-ideal that was harmonious with the attributes they believed teachers approved of; the self-ideal of the highly creative was not only *not* harmonious but also was negatively correlated with what they believed to be the teachers' ideal qualities.

Wallach and Kogan (1965) similarly identified school children who fell into four categories: high intelligence-high creativity, high intelligence-low creativity, low intelligence-high creativity, low intelligence-low creativity. As can be seen in Table 9–8, the high intelligence-high creativity child appears to possess extremely positive characteristics, while children in the other categories seem to have difficulties of some sort. However, we must be cautious in applying stringent values to these descriptions. The relationship between these childhood behaviors and later adult behaviors is not well understood: Who is to say that extreme aspirations for academic success or conflict with school or oneself cannot lead eventually to a satisfactory life in terms of both individual and societal goals?

From the several studies described above it can be seen that *at least within a certain range,* creative accomplishment seems to involve something other than, or in addition to, high intelligence. It is important to note,

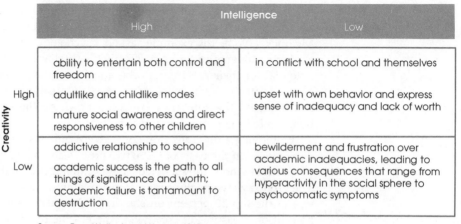

TABLE 9–8

Characteristics of Thirty-two Children Identified by Degree of Intelligence and Degree of Creativity

		Intelligence	
		High	Low
Creativity	High	ability to entertain both control and freedom adultlike and childlike modes mature social awareness and direct responsiveness to other children	in conflict with school and themselves upset with own behavior and express sense of inadequacy and lack of worth
	Low	addictive relationship to school academic success is the path to all things of significance and worth; academic failure is tantamount to destruction	bewilderment and frustration over academic inadequacies, leading to various consequences that range from hyperactivity in the social sphere to psychosomatic symptoms

Source: From Wallach and Kogan, 1965.

though, that creativity and IQ are unrelated only among individuals with a relatively high level of intellectual ability. We do not usually find exceptionally creative individuals below the average IQ range.

Still we have not determined what are the attributes of creativity. Psychologists have devised many ways by which they attempt to measure creativity; usually pictures, words, or stories are presented to the individual, who is then asked to generate a product of some kind that is then judged for creativity (see Figure 9–14 on the following page). These tests are constructed around various characteristics viewed as essential to creativity. Let us look at some of the most widely accepted ones.

One way to define creativity, proposed by Jackson and Messick (1968), involves judging a person's products in terms of four criteria: novelty, appropriateness, transcendence of constraints, and coalescence of meaning. It is perhaps obvious that a creative product must be *novel* in the sense of being unusual, but more is also required. If we asked a nine-year-old boy: "How much is 2 + 2?" and he replied "17," we would be obliged to call the response unusual, but hardly creative. Thus, we add the criterion of *appropriateness.* In practice, though, appropriateness is not always easy to agree on. An artist dismissed as merely unusual and vulgar by one generation may be hailed for true creativity by the next.

The third criterion, *transcendence of constraints,* refers to combining elements in a way that at once defies tradition and yields a new perspective. The final criterion, *coalescence of meaning,* suggests that creative products do not divulge themselves fully at first glance. The implications of a scientific innovation and the subtleties of great art both require careful and repeated inspection.

J. P. Guilford (1957, 1966) and his associates have proposed that the distinction between *convergent* and *divergent* modes of thinking is directly relevant for understanding creativity. Convergent thinking involves integration of established information so as to arrive at the standard, correct answer. Divergent thinking goes off in many directions to arrive at an answer in instances where no one answer is necessarily correct. It is this divergent mode that indicates creativity, according to Guilford.

Related to divergent thinking is the ability to generate a plentiful number of ideas that are appropriate to a task, or *ideational fluency.* Wallach and Kogan (1965) have established that children differ in ideational fluency and that the differences are related to later creative accomplishments. They devised a number of tasks to measure ideational fluency in children. One, an "alternative uses" test, involved asking youngsters to name as many uses as they could for a number of common objects, such as a shoe or a cork. Another required the subjects to point out all of the similarities they could think of between a pair of objects—for example, a train and a tractor or a potato and a carrot. A third involved naming as many concrete instances as possible of an abstract category such as round things or things that make noise. The fourth test required children to generate ideas when presented with visual arrays; for example, they were asked to identify all the meanings they could think of for abstract patterns or abstract line drawings. Using these measures, Wallach and Kogan then studied 151 fifth-grade chil-

Children are asked what these lines mean to them. Adapted from M. A. Wallach and N. Kogan, Modes of Thinking in Young Children, *page 36, figure 3. New York: Holt, Rinehart & Winston, 1965. By permission of author and publisher.*

A Usual Answer:
Mountains

An Unusual Answer:
Squashed piece of paper.

Children were given colored materials and asked to make mosaics (similar to Hall, 1958).

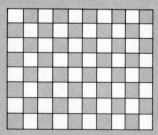 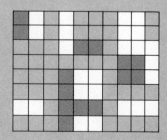

Children were asked to tell a story about a picture of a man working late or early in an office. Adapted from Getzels and Jackson, 1962.

There's ambitious Bob, down at the office at 6:30 in the morning. Every morning it's the same. He's trying to show his boss how energetic he is. Now, thinks Bob, maybe the boss will give me a raise for all my extra work. The trouble is that Bob has been doing this for the last three years, and the boss still hasn't given him a raise. He'll come in at 9:00, not even noticing that Bob has been there so long, and poor Bob won't get his raise.

Judged Less Creative

This man has just broken into this office of a new cereal company. He is a private eye employed by a competitor firm to find out the formula that makes the cereal bend, sag, and sway. After a thorough search of the office he comes upon what he thinks is the current formula. He is now copying it. It turns out that it is the wrong formula and the competitor's factory blows up. Poetic justice!

Judged Creative

FIGURE 9–14
Examples of the tasks given to individuals to test creativity, and judgments of the projects.

Children were asked to draw a picture around the theme "playing tag in the school yard." Adapted from J. W. Getzels and P. W. Jackson, Creativity and Intelligence. *Copyright 1962, reproduced by permission of John Wiley & Sons, Inc.*

Judged Less Creative   Judged Creative

dren, both boys and girls. The investigators noted that at least two types of measures could be derived from their results, the actual number of responses produced by a child and the number that are original. Interestingly, the two measures were highly correlated. Also children who tended to generate a larger number of ideas—or larger numbers of original ideas—in response to one of the tasks tended to do so for the others as well. Finally, ideational fluency was not related to IQ scores. Wallach and Wing (1969) then found a clear association between measures of ideational fluency and creative products among a sample of about five hundred college students. Looking at attainments such as prizes in art and science contests, political leadership, roles in major dramatic productions, and awards in the fine arts, they found that while differences in intelligence test scores failed to predict any kind of *nonacademic* attainment, ideational fluency did predict accomplishments in many of these areas (Figure 9–16). Finally, in one of the first longitudinal studies of creativity, Kogan and Pankove (1972) tested a group of tenth-grade boys and girls who had been tested five years earlier as fifth-graders. Although the results were in many ways complex, they did suggest considerable stability in ideational productivity over the five-year span and also showed that some early measures of creativity were predictive of extra-curricular accomplishments in the tenth grade. While the investigators are careful to avoid premature claims about the predictive power of any one measure, their findings do provide evidence that a person's creative ability is an important and more or less stable characteristic that can be discriminated from IQ.

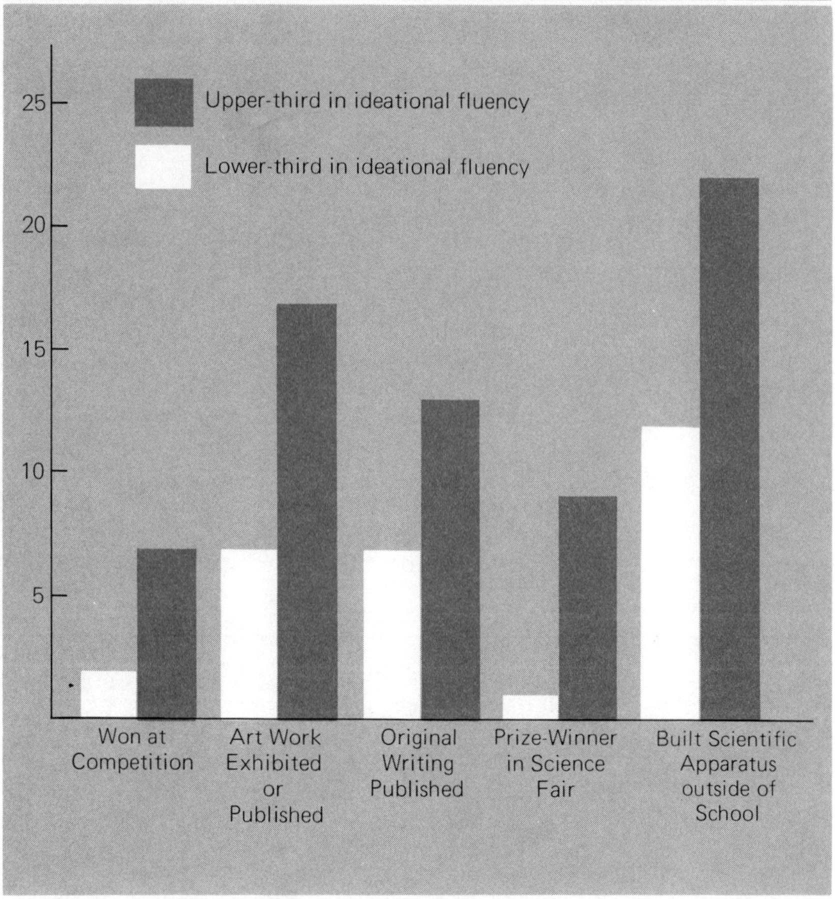

FIGURE 9–16
Differences in
productivity of
college students high
and low in ideational
fluency (a measure of
creativity) in Wallach
and Wing's research.
Adapted from M. A.
Wallach and C. W.
Wing, **The Talented
Student: A Validation
of the Creativity-
Intelligence
Distinction.** New York:
Holt, Rinehart, &
Winston, 1969, by
permission.

Fostering
Creativity

The possibility that creativity can be identified as a characteristic that predicts accomplishment leads us to the practical question of whether it is possible to train for creativity. Evidence in this area is limited, but there are two sources to which we can turn for some preliminary information.

Family Variables.   One of the places where we can look for answers is in the retrospective accounts of creative persons; from these we can determine something of the background, home life, and pressures (or lack of them) that are associated with later accomplishment. Using this strategy, MacKinnon (1962) has reported that his sample of creative architects often received extraordinary respect from their parents, who expressed confidence in their ability to do what was appropriate. These same parents granted much freedom of exploration and decision, believing that their children would act independently, reasonably, and responsibly. At the same time, strong emotional parental ties were frequently absent. It was not only that closeness was lacking but that the overdependency and fear of rejection which often characterize parent-child relationships were not experienced. Fathers were models of effective behavior in their careers while mothers were active women with autonomous careers and interests. Furthermore, one or both parents frequently were of artistic skill and temperament.

As children, many of the architects showed early interest in painting and drawing; this was rewarded and encouraged primarily by the mother but was allowed to develop without undue pressures. There also was little parental pressure in regard to a particular career, even when parents were themselves architects. Nonetheless, within the family explicit rules and standards existed. Discipline was predictable and consistent and there was relatively little corporal punishment. Religious practices varied considerably, with two-thirds of the families practicing only perfunctory or no formal religion. Emphasis was placed instead on the development of one's own code of ethics, with integrity, pride, joy in work, intellectual and cultural endeavors, success, ambition, and doing the right thing being highly valued.

Reports of shyness, isolation, aloneness, and little adolescent dating were frequent. MacKinnon suggests that this may have been related to the high incidence of moving or perhaps to unusual introversion or sensitivity. In either case, the apparent isolation may have fostered an awareness of inner life and interests in imaginal, symbolic processes.

Another investigator (Siegelman, 1973) has since looked at the relationship between parent behavior and the presence of creative potential in male and female college students. Those with traits suggesting they had creative potential tended to describe their parents as more rejecting than loving. In contrast, students with less creative potential often described their parents as more accepting and affectionate. Siegelman's findings are consistent with those of other studies (Arasteh, 1968; Domino, 1969) showing that usually there is little warmth between creative individuals and their parents. One possible reason for this consistent finding is that children with loving parents tend to accept parental attitudes and thus become somewhat conformist. Cooler and less-accepting parents, on the other hand, may encourage a rebellious attitude in their children that leads to independent thinking and action.

Training for Creativity. Attempts to train creativity basically involve encouraging students to think divergently—to envision novel, unusual, or a greater number of procedures, uses, or ideas. In a relatively early study, for example, Anderson and Anderson (1963) trained groups of sixth-grade boys to think of unusual uses for familiar objects by pointing out the unique properties of each object and then rewarding them for offering interesting possibilities. As hoped for, some generalization effects were observed. The boys were now able to generate more novel uses for other familiar objects that had not been included in the training series.

Ward, Kogan, and Pankove (1972) administered several standard tests of creativity to fifth-grade boys and girls from a predominantly black, urban, lower-class community. Each child was then given another test of creative performance after being randomly assigned to one of three treatments: a control group that received no rewards, an immediate reward group that received a penny for each creative idea after verbalizing it, and a delayed re-

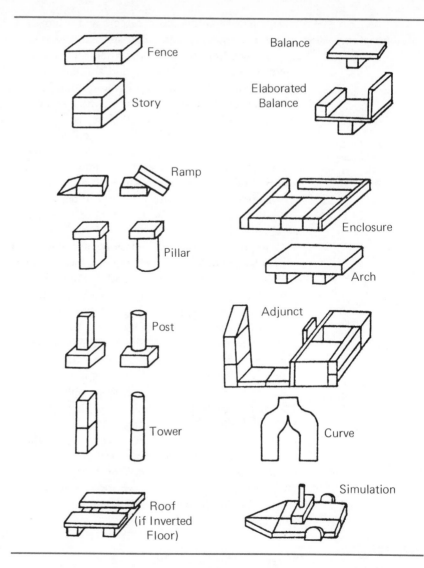

FIGURE 9–17
Examples of
frequently seen forms
in preschoolers' block
building. From Baer,
Rowbury, and Goetz,
1976, p. 12.

ward group that was told that its members would receive a penny for each idea after they completed the task. Both reward groups did offer more creative ideas during this second test than did youngsters in the control group. Nonetheless, the relative order of the students did not change. Those who had few ideas without reward did not catch up with those who had many, and reward seemed only a minor facilitator of performance. Ward and his associates concluded that performance on measures of creativity reflect real individual differences in the capacity for creative thinking, and that this capacity is more important than motivational variables in accounting for the wide differences that exist among people.

Although all of the above studies were conducted with elementary school children, Goetz and Baer have demonstrated the possibility of fostering creativity as early as the preschool years (Baer, Rowbury, and Goetz, 1976; Goetz and Baer, 1973). They chose block building for their research because blocks are commonly available and are customarily considered valuable in lessons involving space, mass, gravity, measurement, aesthetics, and fantasy. Goetz and Baer set out to determine whether they could reinforce diversity in block forms, defined as the creation of different shapes with two or more blocks. After identifying twenty frequently seen forms (Figure 9–17), baselines were taken during individual sessions with three girls. During subsequent phases the teacher reinforced only different forms ("Oh, that's very nice—that's different!") or only same forms ("How nice—another arch!"). Figure 9–18 shows that form diversity in all three preschoolers seemed to be influenced by social reinforcement. An example of one child's work during baseline and reinforcement for diversity appears in Figure 9–19.

Some researchers have begun to develop curricula for creativity training. Reese and Parnes (1970), for example, have developed programmed materials—a sequence of twenty-eight booklets designed to teach the principles of creative problem solving—for stimulating creativity in junior high school students. Their experimental evaluation of the program in six schools showed it to be highly effective (e.g., in producing greater flexibility and originality as measured by standard tests). Most interestingly, significant increments in creativity occurred relative to a control group even when the program was delivered in "do-it-yourself" form without a classroom instructor.

FIGURE 9–18
The form diversity of three preschoolers' block building during baseline, reinforcement for different forms, and reinforcement for same forms.   From Baer, Rowbury, and Goetz, 1976, p. 21.

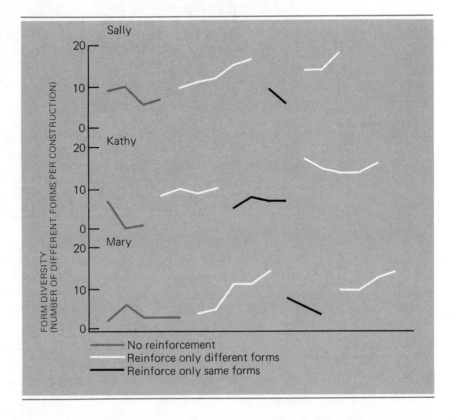

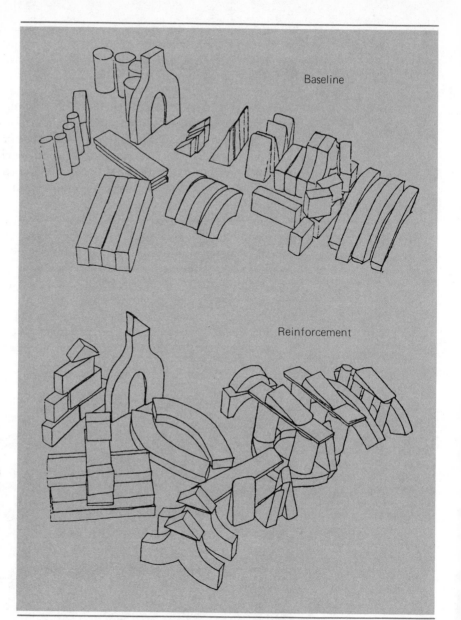

Baseline

Reinforcement

FIGURE 9-19
An example of Mary's block building during the baseline condition and after the third session of reinforcement for form diversity. From Baer, Rowbury, and Goetz, 1976, p. 23.

Overall, then, several demonstrations have shown that under certain conditions one can train for creativity, although there may be limits to the extent that training is effective. Certainly the prospects are encouraging and exciting.

SUMMARY   The nature of intelligence has long been debated. Two major issues are involved: (1) whether intelligence is learned or innate and (2) whether it

314

consists of one general ability or several different abilities. Some psychologists, however, view intelligence less as a capacity of the individual than as a sample of behavior that is related to other intellectual tasks, such as school performance. Within this framework, IQ scores can be useful in predicting academic success.

The construction of an IQ test involves the choosing of appropriate items, standardizing of test performance and procedures, and checking for reliability and validity. *Reliability* refers to the consistency of the test. *Validity* refers to whether the test is actually measuring what it was designed to measure.

Intelligence tests vary in many ways. Group tests are efficient to give but preclude the sensitive evaluation of the child that is possible in individual tests. The first individual test, the Binet, was constructed by Binet and Simon at the beginning of this century to identify French schoolchildren who were likely to need special education. The three Wechsler tests, like the Binet tests, are widely used to evaluate children and adults. All of these tests present a variety of tasks and evaluate performance by comparing it in some way with the performance of age-mates. The Wechsler tests, unlike the Binet, produce a verbal, performance, and full-scale IQ.

Infant tests differ from others most dramatically in their lack of verbal tasks. Performance on infant tests does not correlate highly with that of tests given at a later time; that is, they do not predict how the child will perform intellectually in later years. They are useful, however, in helping to diagnose infants for placement into adoptive homes and the like. In general, the correlation between tests scores increases as the time interval between the tests decreases.

There is ongoing disagreement about age changes in performance on IQ tests and their interpretation. Cross-sectional studies show decline with age, but longitudinal studies indicate that IQ may remain fairly stable until late in life. It also appears that verbal ability and crystallized intelligence are maintained more easily than perceptual-spatial ability and fluid intelligence. The role of life history, motivation, and illness must all be considered in interpreting age changes.

Intelligence has frequently been viewed as being innate and fixed over time. We now know that although there is a degree of stability in test scores, there also is much individual change over time. People may fluctuate 30–40 points during their childhood. Some of this fluctuation is undoubtedly due to the influence of the environment, as earlier studies, such as the Skeels study, suggested. Thus, intelligence is now viewed as resulting from an interaction of innate and environmental influences.

In an attempt to better understand intelligence, many correlational investigations have been conducted. There is some evidence that family size is negatively related to IQ performance and that firstborns perform better than later-borns. The relationship between IQ and parental practice is difficult to ascertain. Mothers may have greater influence on offspring performance than fathers, and perhaps fathers' influence is greater on their sons than on their daughters. Socioeconomic status and IQ are correlated positively, partly because intelligence tests are culture bound and are therefore biased against children who are reared in an environment other than that of the middle or upper class. The effect of such an environment appears to accumulate throughout childhood.

The term *intellectually exceptional* includes not only the mentally retarded but also the highly gifted and creative. Mental retardation refers to subaverage functioning associated with impairment in adaptive behavior. It can be subdivided into four categories: mild, moderate, severe, and profound. The mildly retarded can hold many types of jobs, depending on their social skills; institutionalization is more likely for the other categories. Two distinct etiologies have been identified for retardation: (1) familial mental retardation, involving no apparent physical damage or impairment and may be viewed as the lower range of the normal IQ distribution, and (2) biologically caused mental retardation, which does involve some kind of chromosomal anomaly or brain damage.

Several intellectual deficiencies have been demonstrated in the retarded: deficiencies in memory, paired-associate learning, discrimination learning, and learning to learn. Retardation has been conceptualized with the Piagetian framework as a slower rate of growth and as acquisition of lower stages of cognitive development.

Due to a background of failure, retarded children are more motivated to avoid failure than to achieve success; they are also more motivated by material incentives, possibly due to neglect in the home environment. Modeling and reinforcement have been used successfully to teach the retarded academic lessons and social skills, but studies suggest that long-term training or continued reinforcement are required to maintain these skills in the more severely retarded.

Terman's studies found that intellectually gifted children were superior to others in physique, health, and social adjustment as well as in their academic subjects. A follow-up of these children thirty years later found them still well adjusted socially and well advanced academically and professionally, with many publications and other achievements to their credit.

Creativity seems to involve something distinct from, or in addition to, high intelligence. One definition of creativity involves judging a person's products in terms of four criteria: novelty, appropriateness, transcendence of constraints, and coalescence of meaning. Studies indicate that one successful measure of creativity is ideational fluency, which predicted creative accomplishments in many areas. Divergent, rather than convergent, thinking also has been associated with creativity.

In any event, creative children can be distinguished from highly creative children, although these attributes surely can overlap. Creative children often have been viewed by society somewhat negatively, perhaps partly because their views are less harmonious with society's than the views of the less creative. Many family variables have been associated with creativity, but the one identified in several studies is the lack of strong emotional pa-

rental ties—creative students tend to describe their parents as more rejecting than loving. Several demonstrations indicate that training can increase
creativity, although the limits of effective training are yet to be explored.

IV Social Development

The more basic developmental processes culminate in the functioning, socialized person that each of us becomes. Social development is greatly influenced by our cultural and economic environment and by the people in our families, as explained in chapter 10. Chapter 11 goes on to discuss the child's early social experiences in some detail, and explains the development of social attachments from the ethological, psychoanalytic, and social learning viewpoints.

The remaining chapters in the section deal with important aspects of social development that have been studied extensively. Chapter 12 explains the concept of sex roles and considers fascinating questions about whether various sex differences are culturally or biologically determined. Chapter 13 outlines various aspects of self-control, including resisting temptation and setting standards for oneself, concluding with a discussion of achievement and its correlates. Chapter 14 is devoted to interpersonal values, expressed in behaviors that help (or hurt) others and in the moral reasoning we offer when questioned about various situations.

Chapter 15, the last in the section, overviews the various behavior problems that can arise in childhood and describes many of the currently practiced treatment approaches.

10 Effects of the Social and Economic Environment

In this chapter development is discussed in light of social and economic factors. For the most part, influences will appear to operate in one direction: from the environment to the child. Actually, of course, mutual effects occur, but this one-sided approach is a reflection of the emphasis that has existed in research over the years. For organizational purposes, the child will be viewed as a member of three fundamental and overlapping units: a culture, a family, and a socioeconomic group.

Before we begin, a few definitions are in order. We shall use the term *society* to refer to a group of people who live together and share common institutions, traditions, activities, behaviors, interests, beliefs, and values. The content of their sharing is their culture. *Socialization* refers to the processes by which individuals acquire the knowledge, skills, attitudes, and values of the society or subgroups of the society to which they belong. Although socialization occurs throughout the life span, in this chapter we shall focus on the socialization of the child as, indeed, have most psychologists. Moreover, of the several recognized agents of socialization—family, schools, religions, peer groups, the workplace, and the mass media—emphasis will be placed on the family as the primary agent of socialization.

THE CULTURAL CONTEXT

People have probably always been fascinated by the ways in which others live, but anthropologists can be credited with understanding the advantages of systematically studying different societies. By the 1920s anthropologists were going into the field and bringing back detailed descriptions of cultures around the world. From Freud they borrowed a theoretical framework and they began to direct their energies to the issues of child development and personality (Sears, 1975). Two classic studies are Bronislaw Malinowski's test of Freudian theory conducted in the Trobriand Islands and Margaret Mead's examination of adolescence in Samoa. Malinowski (1927), for example, observed that in a culture in which uncles played a dominant role in family life, boys did not come into conflict with their fathers in the way Freud predicted. Mead (1928) reported that the Samoan adolescent years were more serene than those in the United States. Both anthropologists tested the universality of theory, suggested causes of development, and provided a picture of the possible range of human behavior. These benefits of cross-cultural research, widely valued by psychologists today, were recognized by two colleagues at the Institute of Human Relations at Yale University, John W. M. Whiting and Irvin L. Child.

The Whiting and Child Study

Whiting and Child (1953) were interested in the relationship between culture and personality. Their conceptual system took into account the effects of child-rearing practices on the development of personality, which, in turn, affected cultural characteristics. They drew from both Freudian theory and general behavior theory to construct hypotheses about these relationships. We shall not delve into their specific hypotheses here, but instead examine their research method and their two general conclusions.

The data were descriptions of seventy-five cultures that had been provided by different investigators and collected at Yale University. Judges independently rated these so-called ethnographies with regard to certain cultural characteristics and child-rearing practices related to five systems of behavior. All five systems were considered prevalent around the world. Three of them (oral, anal, and sexual behaviors) were viewed as innate and were obviously tied to Freudian theory; the other two (dependence and aggression) were considered to be learned. For all systems, the judges assessed the degree to which particular socialization practices were indulgent or severe.

One of the main conclusions drawn from the study was that child training is identical the world over in that all societies are concerned about the same issues. They must all deal with eating behavior, evacuation of waste products, and the development of sexuality. Aggressive impulses and the growth of independent and responsible actions also must be shaped. In the words of Whiting and Child:

> . . . there is no clear evidence in any case that any of these basic problems are in fact absent from the life of any people. Child training everywhere seems to be in considerable part concerned with problems which arise from universal characteristics of the human infant and from universal characteristics of adult culture which are incompatible with the continuation of infantile behavior. (1953, pp. 63–64)

The second conclusion, however, pointed to the great variability in the specific goals of socialization and the ways in which they are attained. This can be seen dramatically in the accounts given below of the toilet-training practices found in two cultures. The Dahomeans were rated as being severe in their practices:

> A child is trained by the mother who, as she carries it about, senses when it is restless, so that every time it must perform its excretory functions, the mother puts it on the ground. Thus, in time, usually two years, the training process is completed. If a child does not respond to this training, and manifests enuresis [bedwetting] at the age of four or five, soiling the mat on which it sleeps, then, at first, it is beaten. If this does not correct the habit, ashes are put in water and the mixture is poured over the head of the offending boy or girl, who is driven into the street, where all the other children clap their hands and run after the child singing.
>
> > Adida go ya ya ya
> >
> > "Urine everywhere."
> >
> > > [Herskovitz, as cited by Whiting and Child, 1953, p. 75]

In the practices of the Siriono, on the other hand, considerable overindulgence can be seen:

> Almost no effort is made by the mother to train an infant in the habits of cleanliness until he can walk, and then they are instilled very gradually. Children who are able to walk, however, soon learn by imitation, and with the assistance of their parents, not to defecate near the hammock.

When they are old enough to indicate their needs, the mother gradually leads them further and further away from the hammock to urinate and defecate, so that by the time they have reached the age of 3 they have learned not to pollute the house. Until the age of 4 or 5, however, children are still wiped by the mother, who also cleans up the excreta and throws them away. Not until a child has reached the age of 6 does he take care of his defecation needs alone. [Holmberg, as cited by Whiting and Child, 1953, pp. 75–76]

Similar differences are found for feeding and weaning practices. The Kwoma tribe, for example, is extremely indulgent:

Kwoma infants up to the time they are weaned are never far from their mothers. . . . Crying . . . constitutes an injunction to the mother to discover the source of trouble. Her first response is to present the breast. If this fails to quiet him, she tries something else. . . . Thus during infancy the response to discomfort which is most strongly established is that of seeking help by crying or asking for it. [Whiting, as cited by Whiting and Child, 1953, pp. 91–92]

In contrast, Ainu children have considerably different experiences:

Put into the hanging cradle . . . the poor little helpless creatures could not get out, and for the rest they were free to do whatever they were able. This usually meant a good deal of kicking and screaming until tired of it, followed by exhaustion, repose, and resignation. [Howard, as cited by Whiting and Child, 1953, p. 93]

Child-Rearing Variability in Industrially Developed Societies

Whiting and Child's examples of variability in child rearing are taken from descriptions of "primitive" societies, but differences along many dimensions are also found in modern ones. Consider, for example, that in the Israeli kibbutz the child is tended to by many adults and actually lives with peers in a building that is separate from the residence of his or her biological parents (Bettleheim, 1969). On the other hand, infants in isolated communities in Guatemala spend their first year or so in small family huts with no windows. Seldom spoken to or played with, they are given simple toys of corn ears, wood, and clothing (Kagan and Klein, 1973). In contrast, children in middle-class New England, viewed as unshaped newcomers to society, are stimulated by parents and provided with pets and a large number of toys, including blocks, stuffed animals, dolls, and trucks (Fischer and Fischer, 1963). It is obvious from these brief comparisons that child-rearing practices greatly vary among different cultures. Let us look at two examples in more detail.

Child Rearing in the USSR.   From 1960 to 1967 Urie Bronfenbrenner, an American psychologist, visited the Soviet Union seven times as part of a research project on cross-cultural studies of child rearing. The insights he gained from his own observations and interviews were published in *Two*

Worlds of Childhood: U.S. and U.S.S.R. (1970). According to Bronfenbrenner, Russian infants receive much more physical contact and affection—holding, kissing, hugging, cuddling—than American babies. However, they are given little freedom of movement and initiation, perhaps because there is considerable concern about environmental dangers (e.g., low temperatures in the home) and the possibility that the child might hurt him- or herself. Maternal responsibility is diffused to relatives and even strangers. In this regard, Bronfenbrenner notes that it is not unusual when riding public transportation to have a child placed in your lap by a parent or guardian. Strangers easily interact with children and are quickly called "tyotya" or "dyadya" (aunt or uncle).

Despite much affection and care, however, emphasis is placed on the development of obedience and self-discipline. In the preschools children learn early to care for themselves. By eighteen months of age they are expected to have bladder and bowel control and are learning to dress themselves. They are exposed to programs designed to facilitate sensorimotor and language development. Socially their experiences are communal. Babies nap in dormitory-like rows and play in pens that provide close contact with the staff (see Figure 10–1). Even very young children are given communal chores, such as shoveling snow and caring for animals, and they are taught to be altruistic and cooperative. Emphasis on competence and comraderie continues into elementary school, where character building is an explicit goal (Table 10–1). The outcome of these practices, Bronfenbrenner suggests, is that Russian children display "good" behavior; they are well mannered and industrious and possess strong motivation to learn and serve their society.

Child Rearing in Japan and the United States: A Comparison. Caudill and Weinstein (1969) analyzed the way in which thirty Japanese and thirty American mothers interacted with their three- to four-month-olds. The Japanese babies were held, carried, rocked, and verbally lulled a good deal. Their crying or fretting brought quick maternal responses, often with offers of food. They slept in the same room as their parents. The American infants were treated in subtly different ways. Mothers chatted in a lively manner and stimulated their babies to smile and vocalize. Crying aroused a slower response from mothers, and at this early age many of the infants already slept in rooms separate from their parents. The authors suggest that these cultural variations are embedded in the way in which parents view their children with regard to the goals of socialization. The Japanese child is seen as an independent organism who must be drawn into interdependence with others. In the United States, it is important to shape independence and assertiveness. Although it is difficult to relate early child-rearing practices to specific behaviors later in life, the babies in this study demonstrated some immediate behavioral differences: Japanese infants were more passive than the American infants, whereas American infants responded with more activity and happy vocalizations and motor activity.

In a later study Caudill and Frost (1975) examined Japanese-American families who were genetically Japanese but who had migrated to the United

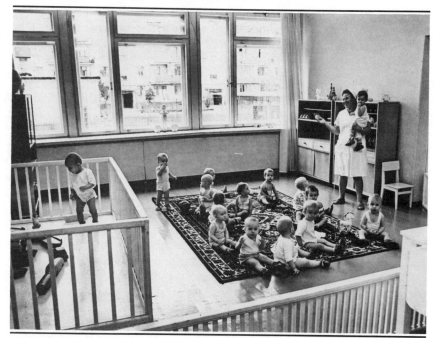

States. Although the mothers had retained some of the style of Japanese mothers (e.g., they lulled and carried their infants), they tended to resemble the American mothers more. In particular they chatted a great deal with their babies who, in return, displayed the happy vocalizations and physical activity characteristics of American infants. Thus it appears that even

TABLE 10-1

A Summary of Stated Objectives for Two Age Groups, Indicating the Explicit Goal of Character Training in the Soviet Union

Ages 7-11	Ages 16-18
Communist morality	
Sense of good and bad behavior Truthfulness, honesty, kindness Atheism: science vs. superstition Self-discipline Diligence in work and care of possessions Friendship with classmates Love of one's own locality and the Motherland	Collectivism, duty, honor, and conscience Development of will, patience, perseverance A Communist attitude toward work and public property Socialist humanism Soviet patriotism and proletarian internationalism
Responsible attitude toward learning	
Interest and striving for knowledge and skill Industry in study Organizing intellectual and physical work Striving to apply one's knowledge and ability in life and work	Understanding of the social significance of education Perseverance and initative in learning Increasing one's power of intellectual work (learning to plan one's work better, development of good work habits, self-criticism, etc.)
Cultured conduct	
Care, accuracy, and neatness Courtesy and cordiality Proper behavior on the street and in public places Cultured speech	Assimilation of norms of socialist community life Good manners and standards of behavior
Bases of esthetic culture	
Understanding of the beautiful in nature, in the conduct of people, and in creative art Artistic creativity	Esthetic appreciation of nature, social life, and works of art Artistic creativity
Physical culture and sport	
Concern for strengthening and conditioning one's body Sanitary-hygienic habits Preparation for sport and athletics	Maximizing the development of physical skills Mastering the rules of personal and social hygiene and sanitation Training and participation in sports Mastering hiking and camping skills

Source: From U. Bronfenbrenner. Two Worlds of Childhood: U.S. and U.S.S.R., © Russell Sage Foundation, Basic Books, Inc., Publishers, New York, 1970.

though differences in social disposition may have a genetic basis (pp. 133–141), social behavior may shift as cultural practices shift. Such interaction of biological and cultural factors and malleability of behavior is not, of course, surprising.

The Relationship between Cultural Experiences and Later Behavior

The diversity of cultural experience is fascinating in itself, but researchers have also been interested in relating these experiences to behavior. As we saw above, some studies provide evidence that the manner in which a child is treated affects his or her behavior. At the same time, the evidence is not as clear as one would hope. For example, in the Whiting and Child (1953) investigation severe socialization within a behavior system tended to be related to anxious beliefs about that system, but indulgent practices were not related in any way. Turning to the previously mentioned Guatamalan study of children confined to their huts early in life, it was found that the infants were exceptionally quiet, fearful, and passive, as well as behind in intellectual development as compared to American infants. However, when they were tested at eleven years of age, they performed as well as American middle-class children on several intellectual tasks (Kagan and Klein, 1973). It is quite possible, then, that their early restriction did not have long-range impact. Because it is difficult to apply and interpret tests given to children from different cultures, there is an obvious need for continued research into this matter. Furthermore, perhaps it is not surprising that a clear link between child-rearing practices and behavior, and particularly later behavior, is difficult to establish. Child rearing is associated with many other customs in a society and any behavior is determined by many factors. Ferreting out these complexities is a difficult task.

Conceptualizing Cultural Influences

Figure 10–2 presents a scheme for drawing together various cultural influences on behavior. Like all schemes, it is a simplified version, but it allows us to begin to conceptualize the issues.

Every society exists in a particular *ecology,* which can be defined as a broad setting that includes geography, topography, and the like. It is useful to recognize that the ecology has both relatively direct and indirect effects on development. As an example of a relatively direct effect, consider that cross-cultural differences in perception have been recognized for many years and that they are not easily attributed to genetic factors (LeVine,

FIGURE 10–2
A scheme for conceptualizing interacting cultural influences on behavior.

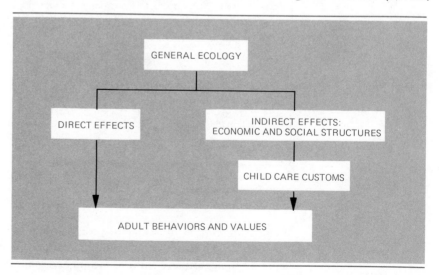

1970). Is it plausible that visual skills, for example, are at least partially determined by the visual environment? Some researchers think so. Turnbull's (1961) description of the Pygmy people living in the Congo in Africa captures the essence of this position. In the following section Turnbull depicts the experience of his Pygmy friend, Kenge, when Kenge ventured out of his deep, lush, forest home for the first time.*

. . . I asked him if he would like to have a holiday and go over there, to see the outside world for himself. He hesitated a long time, and then asked how far the mountains were beyond the forest. I said that they were not more than a day's drive from the last of the trees, to which he responded with disbelief, "*No* trees? *No* trees at all?" He was very dubious about this, and asked me if it was a good country, and what the villagers were like there. I told him that it was very much like my own country in some ways, that it was very good, and that there were few villages.

This decided him and he agreed to go, providing that we brought enough food to last us all the time we were to be out of the forest. He was going to have nothing to do with savages who lived in a land without trees.

. . . As we got to the top of the first incline, there was a flat stretch and then a steep rise. Halfway up this the car sank down into the mud and would not move. Henri and Kenge got out and started pushing, and after half an hour of hard work we reached the top. Once the wheels began gripping I did not stop but kept going until I was at the very crest. There I stopped the engine and waited for the other two, who came running up the hill after me, joking and shouting, covered from head to foot with smelly black slime.

When Kenge topped the rise, he stopped dead. Every smallest sign of mirth suddenly left his face. He opened his mouth but could say nothing. He moved his head and eyes slowly and unbelievingly. Down below us, on the far side of the hill, stretched mile after mile of rolling grasslands, a lush, fresh green, with an occasional shrub or tree standing out like a sentinel into a sky that had suddenly become brilliantly clear. And beyond the grasslands was Lake Edward—a huge expanse of water disappearing into the distance, a river without banks, without end. It was like nothing Kenge had ever seen before. The largest stretch of water in his experience was what he had seen when we had stood, like Stanley, at the confluence of the Lenda and the Ituri. On the plains, animals were grazing everywhere—a small herd of elephant to the left, about twenty antelopes staring curiously at us from straight ahead, and down to the right a gigantic herd of about a hundred and fifty buffalo. But Kenge did not seem to see them.

. . . The lower slopes shone green with the dense forest, the upper slopes rose in steep, jagged cliffs, and above them the great snow-capped peaks rose proudly into the clearest possible sky. There was not a cloud to match the pure whiteness of the snow.

Kenge could not believe they were the same mountains that we had seen from the forest; there they had seemed just like large hills to him. I tried to explain what the snow was—he thought it was some kind of white rock. Henri said that it was water that turned color when it was high up, but Kenge wanted to know why it didn't run down the mountainside like any other water. When Henri told him it also turned solid at that height, Kenge gave him a long steady look and said, "*Bongo yako!*" ("You liar!")

... Then he saw the buffalo, still grazing lazily several miles away, far down below. He turned to me and said, "What insects are those?"

At first I hardly understood; then I realized that in the forest the range of vision is so limited that there is no great need to make an automatic allowance for distance when judging size. Out here in the plains, however, Kenge was looking for the first time over apparently unending miles of unfamiliar grasslands, with not a tree worth the name to give him any basis for comparison. The same thing happened later on when I pointed out a boat in the middle of the lake. It was a large fishing boat with a number of people in it but Kenge at first refused to believe this. He thought it was a floating piece of wood.

When I told Kenge that the insects were buffalo, he roared with laughter and told me not to tell such stupid lies. When Henri, who was thoroughly puzzled, told him the same thing and explained that visitors to the park had to have a guide with them at all times because there were so many dangerous animals, Kenge still did not believe, but he strained his eyes to see more clearly and asked what kind of buffalo were so small. I told him they were sometimes nearly twice the size of a forest buffalo, and he shrugged his shoulders and said we would not be standing out there in the open if they were. I tried telling him they were possibly as far away as from Epulu to the village of Kopu, beyond Eboyo. He began scraping the mud off his arms and legs, no longer interested in such fantasies.

The road led on down to within about half a mile of where the herd was grazing, and as we got closer, the "insects" must have seemed to get bigger and bigger. Kenge, who was now sitting on the outside, kept his face glued to the window, which nothing would make him lower. I even had to raise mine to keep him happy. I was never able to discover just what he thought was happening—whether he thought that the insects were changing into buffalo, or that they were miniature buffalo growing rapidly as we approached. His only comment was that they were not real buffalo, and he was not going to get out of the car again until we left the park. (Turnbull, 1961, pp. 248–253)

In this remarkable account Turnbull forcefully presents the possibility that due to the forest environment Kenge had developed only limited distance perception. Thus he illustrates a direct relationship between the ecology and development.

Other influences of the ecology appear indirect, by comparison, in that they are more clearly mediated by economic and social systems. In order to maintain itself in its ecological niche, each society evolves particular economic and social structures, and the value systems to support them. They account for the innumerable workings of the society: its institutions, family patterns, work habits, sex relationships and roles, and leisure customs, to name a few.

The influence of the size and composition of the primary group in which the child is reared is an example of an indirect effect. In some societies children are reared in *monogamous nuclear* families consisting of parents and siblings. In others, the family is both *monogamous and extended*, including grandparents, aunts, and other relatives. Children of *polygynous* communities, in which males may have several wives simultaneously, live with their mothers, but the working domestic unit may be comprised of the other families of their fathers as well. Depending upon the characteristics of the primary group, children are bound to have different experiences and as a result, they may ultimately display quite varied behaviors as adults.

Universal Goals of Parenting

From a cultural analysis of child-care customs, Robert LeVine (1974) has proposed a useful framework for relating child care to the overall setting and development of cultures. LeVine came to his formulation after he noted that a common hazard for African infants of the Gusii (Kenya) and Hausa (Nigeria) people is the cooking fire, especially when the fire is kept burning through the night for warmth. Perhaps, he speculated, recognition of this hazard had led to children being carried on the backs of adults or otherwise restricted in mobility. Although such limitation might adversely affect the development of certain skills, it would at least facilitate survival, which must be of first priority.

LeVine proposed that many child-rearing customs might have been established in order to promote survival, although this initial reason might have been masked over time with religious or social explanations. This is not to say that considerations other than survival do not figure heavily into

FIGURE 10–3
Nigerian girls pounding millet with their baby sisters on their backs. Photo Researchers, Inc.

determining child-care practices. LeVine, in fact, suggests the following hierarchy of determinants, which he casts in terms of universal parental goals.

1. The physical survival and health of the child including (implicitly) the normal development of his or her reproductive capacity during puberty.
2. The development of the child's behavioral capacity for economic self-maintenance during maturity.
3. The development of the child's behavioral capacities for maximizing other cultural values—e.g., morality, prestige, wealth, religious piety, intellectual achievement, personal satisfaction, self-realization—as formulated and symbolically elaborated in culturally distinctive beliefs, norms, and ideologies. (1974, p. 230)

These universal goals are arranged in an order that is by no means haphazard. Sheer physical survival during childhood is the requirement for the development of any later capacities and so assumes paramount importance in environments that pose great danger to the young. In much the same way, it is reasoned that economic self-maintenance must be considered before the relative luxury of maximizing one's status and prestige can be pursued. Do things really work this way? The evidence suggests that they do.

LeVine's review of studies done in African, Latin American, and Indonesian communities with very high infant mortality rates shows that practices in these societies are highly responsive to environmental threats. The general pattern in these cultures is to keep the infant on or near the caretaker's body at all times, day or night, and to respond quickly to crying, usually by feeding. On the other hand, development of self-maintenance skills receives little attention during this period. By Western standards these mothers rarely smile at their infants or even make eye contact with them.

In societies in which food and related materials for subsistence are scarce, we would expect that child-rearing customs would emphasize the development of behaviors that would ensure economic self-maintenance. The pattern that is found is an emphasis on obedience, presumably because an obedient child can contribute to food and craft production or at least baby-sit competently, thereby freeing parents to do the productive labor. In the long run these children would benefit from obedience training as much as or more than their parents. "The African parents with whom I have worked," writes LeVine, "want their children to become obedient in part because they believe it is the single most important quality involved in adult economic adaptation, and they are concerned that their children have the capacity to survive in a world of scarce and unstable resources" (1974, p. 237).

Following LeVine's hierarchy it would not be surprising to find, then, that societies like the United States would probably list as their first priorities maximizing children's achievement, self-realization, and the like. As we shall see later in the chapter, this appears to be true at least for middle-class Americans.

THE FAMILY

The family has many functions in societies: It serves as an economic unit, it helps satisfy adult sexual drives, and it assumes central responsibility for a small number of people as they move through life. But perhaps its most widely recognized function is the care and socialization of new generations.

The family is recognized as a unit of interacting personalities and roles, but it is difficult to conceptualize these interactions. Psychologists focus most heavily on parental handling of their children, and on the effects of the family structure. As we have seen, the exact form of the family may vary from society to society, and, indeed, different structures may exist within one society. In no society, however, is there a complete lack of family influence on the developing child, even when the responsibility for child rearing is more diffuse than in the United States. Parents are, in fact, usually considered the primary agents of socialization because their influence begins so early in life.

The Differential Roles of Mother and Father

Among the many descriptions of the roles of mother and father in the family, those offered by Freud, Parsons, and social learning theorists are perhaps the most influential (Lynn, 1974).

The Psychoanalytic View. The parent-child relationship is central to Freudian conceptualizations of development. It is the mother, however, who is viewed as important during the first few years of life, due to her role in satisfying the infant's physical needs. Freud described the mother-child relationship as *anaclitic* (literally, "leaning on") to denote the child's dependence on his or her mother for sustenance (Ainsworth and Bell, 1969). In her capacity to arouse both pleasurable and unpleasurable sensations in the infant the mother becomes, ".... unique, without parallel, established unalterably, for a whole lifetime as the first and strongest love-object and as the prototype of all later love-relations for both sexes" (Freud, 1949, p. 45). The father takes on particular importance when the child reaches the *phallic stage*. The child is generally between 3 and 5½ years old at this stage. The male child, desirous of his mother as a love-sex object, fears castration at the hands of his father. He solves this *Oedipal conflict* by identifying with his father, thereby vicariously possessing his mother. Identification involves the young boy "introjecting" the attitudes, ideals, and behaviors of his father—that is, becoming like his father. The female child experiences a parallel situation, the *Electra conflict*, brought about when she notes her lack of a penis and blames her mother for the deficiency. At the same time she becomes desirous of her father because he possesses a penis. Although the girl cannot fear castration, she does fear the loss of her mother's love. To allay her anxiety and prevent such a loss, the daughter identifies with her mother in a manner similar to the identification of a son with his father. The identificatory process in both boys and girls is central to psychoanalytic explanations of sex-role and moral development. Freud also proposed that because early intrapsychic conflicts are not completely resolved, their influence carries into adulthood. And as much as he regarded the mother as the prototype for love relationships, Freud identified the father as the par-

ent who motivates children, especially boys, to incorporate the rules, prohibitions, and values of society into their behavior (Lynn, 1974). Freud's psychoanalytic view will be more fully discussed in chapter 11.

Parsons's Sociological Analysis. Sociologist Talcott Parsons's descriptions of parental figures focuses on the claim that all societies must work
out roles for expressive and instrumental behaviors (Parsons and Bales,
1955). Expressive behaviors include nurturance, empathy, emotional support, and mediation of personal relationships; instrumental behaviors include achievement, competence, and the pursuit of society's goals. According to Parsons, sex roles are differentiated along these dimensions, with
females largely responsible for expressive functions and males primarily responsible for instrumental functions. Mothers thus help maintain smooth
family interaction, guard family solidarity and provide emotional support.
Love for their children is complete, unconditional, and needs no confirmation: The child is loved for itself. Fathers, more in tune to society as a
whole, relate the family to societal concerns. They are expected to be dis-
ciplinarians, to introduce role prescriptions, and to otherwise prepare the
child for independence. Paternal love is viewed by some as depending upon
how the child performs (Lynn, 1974). The instrumental functions of the father come into play when the child is perhaps four or five years of age; before that time the mother controls both expressive and instrumental functions (Lamb, 1976e).

Social Learning Theory. Social learning theorists rely heavily on learning
principles in describing the family. According to this view both mothers
and fathers shape their children's behaviors by dispensing reinforcement
and punishment and serving as models for behavior. Because parents satisfy the infant's physical needs and because they are in relatively frequent
contact with their children, they rapidly become influential in the lives of
their children. Research shows that in general parents who are nurturant
and competent are in the best position to shape their children in the manner
that they prefer. However, there are many complex issues surrounding the
learning that goes on between parents and children, as we shall see in further discussions.

But is the Father Really Important? Despite the fact that all theorists have
recognized the importance of both parents, mothers, more than fathers,
have been inextricably linked with children. There can be no refutation that
a mother's child belongs to her, but a father's biological role is questionable. With little exception, mothers assume most of the early care of the infant. Moreover, fathers do not spend as much time with children as do
mothers, partly because of their responsibility to support the family economically. In the United States, for instance, economic survival once depended upon agriculture or small trade, both of which encouraged the family to interact as a unit, generally with the father as head (Nash, 1976). With
the coming of the Industrial Revolution the life style of the family changed.

It was at first disrupted because all members worked long hours at a distance from the home. Labor laws limiting the work of women and children eventually returned them to the home; the employment of men, however, was not curtailed. One result of the Industrial Revolution thus was that men were not as intimately involved with their families. For this reason the father's role in child development was viewed as weaker than the maternal role.

The situation has recently begun to change, however. Lamb (1976e) suggests three factors that have led to the new trend. The first is a reaction to the previous overemphasis on the role of the mother in socialization; this focus was so skewed that many researchers began to question the implied irrelevance of the father and to reexamine the paternal role. Second, the family, particularly in contemporary America, is rapidly changing, calling for a reevaluation of all family roles. Finally, infants have become recognized as active participants in the family, and their social world has been viewed as more complex and as extending beyond their mothers, thereby demanding further investigation.

One of the ways in which the broadened picture of the family has been exhibiting itself is by comparison of father-infant interaction with mother-infant interaction. In general it had previously been assumed that infants form strong bonds with their mothers but not with their fathers. Nevertheless, the assumption is being challenged by the findings that infants, in the home and in laboratory settings, protest being separated from their fathers as well as their mothers. Furthermore, they may show a preference for mother, father, or no preference at all, depending upon their age and the situation (Lamb, 1976e). It seems clear that both parents are important quite early in life.

Turning to the quality of interactions, evidence is growing that mothers and fathers relate differently to their infants. Weinraub and Frankel (1977) found that mothers displayed more nurturance and vocalized more to their infants, whereas fathers were more active in roughhouse play with their children. Also, parents tended to play more with the same sex child. Clarke-Stewart (1978) observed fourteen infants from various economic levels at fifteen, twenty, and thirty months of age with their mothers and fa-

FIGURE 10-4
Developmental psychologists have come to appreciate the important role that fathers play in caring for their infants. Sybil Shelton, Monkmeyer Press Photo Service.

thers together, as well as with their mothers alone. Fathers engaged in more physical-social play; the mothers' play concentrated on intellectual activities and interactions with objects. It appeared that the infants responded and cooperated more with the fathers; however, this may be more a reflection of the style of play rather than a parental preference on the part of the children. In the presence of the father the mother tended to take a low keyed role, verbalizing less with the infant, and generally not interfering in the father-infant interactions. It is apparent that the interaction between parents and child is not a simple situation to analyze. All members of the family affect and are affected by each other. Clarke-Stewart tentatively hypothesized that the mother influences the behavior of the child, who in turn influences the father, who affects the behavior of the mother.

Although only limited conclusions can presently be drawn, it seems that fathers play more than mothers with infants, or at least in a more rough-and-tumble way (Field, 1978; Lamb, 1976e). The characteristics of the father that are most clearly correlated to the child's development are paternal warmth, acceptance, and involvement (Weinraub, 1978). Further studies are needed to delineate the similarities and differences in mother-infant and father-infant interactions. In addition, we might question whether the primary caretaker role itself largely determines interactions. If fathers are primary caretakers, are they similar to mothers who maintain this role? There is some evidence that this is so. In one study with four-month-old infants, primary caretakers—both mothers and fathers—smiled and imitated the grimaces and vocalizations of their infants more than fathers who were secondary caretakers (Field, 1978).

Although there are difficulties in adequately controlling for socioeconomic and other influencing variables, studies of father-present families leave little doubt that fathers make a significant contribution to the development of sex roles (Biller, 1969; Hetherington, 1967; Sears, Maccoby, and Levin, 1957), cognitive abilities (Busse, 1969; Blanchard and Biller, 1971; Epstein and Radin, 1975), and achievement motivation for sons (Lynn, 1974) and daughters (Aldous, 1975; Crandall, Dewey, Katkovsky, and Preston, 1964). Paternal influence is also reported in several studies of the relation of father absence and measures of their children's IQ. Children reared in families without fathers do less well on standardized measures of IQ than children raised in two-parent families (Biller, 1974; Carlsmith, 1964; Lynn, 1974).

Parental Styles during the School Years

If we were to observe parents as socializers, could we identify pervasive patterns in the handling of children that relate to child behavior? Investigators have attempted to answer this question through studies involving interviews, questionnaires, and ratings of parents and children. The overall results repeatedly suggest the importance of two dimensions of parental behavior: acceptance-rejection and permissiveness-restrictiveness (Becker, 1964; Martin, 1975; Sears, Maccoby and Levin, 1957; Symonds, 1939).

Acceptance-rejection refers to the respect and love—or lack of both—that parents feel for their children. At the extremes, accepting parents show warmth, affection, approval, and understanding. When discipline is used, it tends to include praise and encouragement and little physical punishment. Rejecting parents, on the other hand, are cold, disapproving, and punitive. They do not enjoy their children, nor are they sensitive to their needs.

Permissiveness-restrictiveness refers to the degree to which parents permit their offspring autonomy and freedom in their actions. Permissive parents allow relative freedom in decision making and in carrying out the decisions. They tend not to set forth rules and/or to enforce rules consistently. In contrast, restrictive parents maintain control, exhibiting behaviors that are opposite to those of permissive parents.

Schaefer (1959) has proposed an integration of these dimensions, based on several observations of mothers' interactions with their children from one month to three years of age. As Figure 10–5 shows, Schaefer has arranged maternal behaviors in a circular order around the two dimensions of love-hostility (acceptance-rejection) and autonomy-control (permissiveness-restrictiveness). This model indicates a range of parental behaviors, and also shows that both permissive and restrictive parents can be either accepting or rejecting. Very different environments are thus provided for the child, depending on the parents' position on these dimensions. For example, permissiveness coupled with rejection allows the child considerable freedom combined with parental detachment, indifference, neglect, or outright rejection. Permissiveness paired with acceptance, on the other hand, provides freedom with democratic, cooperative, or accepting parental treatment. The pairing of restrictiveness and rejection leads to a

FIGURE 10–5
Schaefer's conceptualization of two important dimensions of maternal behavior.
From E. S. Schaefer, A circumlex model for maternal behavior. **Journal of Abnormal and Social Psychology**, 1958, **59,** 226–235. Copyright 1959 by the American Association. Reprinted by permission.

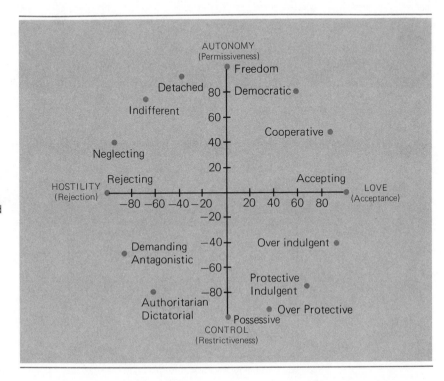

demanding, authoritarian environment, whereas restrictiveness and acceptance can combine to produce overprotection and overindulgence.

Several investigators have examined the consequences of parental
acceptance-rejection and permissiveness-restrictiveness. Becker's (1964)
summary, shown in Table 10–2, takes into account the interactions of such
dimensions. As can be seen, permissive-accepting treatment is related to
children being independent, outgoing, creative, active, and nonhostile. Permissiveness coupled with rejection is related to aggression, noncompliance,
and delinquency. It is as if children learn punitiveness from their parents
and, not having experienced any restriction of their behavior in the home,
use their lessons about punitiveness to deal with the world. Children who
are reared in restrictive but accepting homes tend to be dependent, polite,
obedient, and compliant. And finally, those who experience restrictiveness
and rejection tend to be socially withdrawn, quarrelsome, and inhibited;
they may also have suicidal tendencies.

The outcomes are what we might expect, and yet they should be viewed
with a certain amount of caution (Martin, 1975). Interview data is filtered
through memory, verbal ability, and perhaps defensive distortions. Because
the studies are correlational, care must be taken not to draw firm causal
conclusions. Also, the domain of behaviors studied so far has not been very
large so the picture is a limited one at best. This is particularly troublesome
if we allow ourselves to rely on stereotypes of what is "good" and "bad." It
is easy to believe that acceptance invariably leads to positive outcomes, but,
in fact, it could lead to self-centeredness or self-indulgence. Extreme permissiveness may not always be optimal either; children frequently need
guidelines for their behavior as they meet new developmental challenges.

With the latter point in mind, it should be noted that the
permissiveness-restrictiveness dimension has been further analyzed in light
of two factors (Schaefer, 1965). One of them, *psychological autonomy versus psychological control*, involves covert methods (such as guilt or anxiety induction)
of controlling the child that prevent independent development. The other,
firm control versus lax control, refers to the extent to which rules, regulations,
and limits are set and enforced by parents.

TABLE 10-2
Relationship of Parental Child-Rearing Behaviors and Children's Behaviors

	Permissiveness	Restrictiveness
Acceptance	independent outgoing; friendly creative low hostility active	dependent polite obedient compliant
Rejection	noncompliance delinquency hostility criminality	social withdrawal quarrelsome self-hostility inhibition

Source: From Becker, 1964. © Russell Sage Foundation, Basic Books, Inc. Publishers, New York.

Child Abuse

Although the family functions to care for, socialize, and optimize the potential of children, it sometimes falls short of these goals. Children may be neglected, both physically and psychologically, and they may be abused—that is, physically or sexually harmed. Such untoward treatment has existed for centuries. This grave problem has not been solved, but we are learning more about it and so hopefully we will be better able to deal with it.

In the United States concern for children led to the organization of the Society For the Prevention of Cruelty to Children in 1874. More recently, in the 1940s, social concern about physical abuse was precipitated by physicians' reports of unexplainable multiple-bone fractures and swelling and bleeding in the skulls of children (Gil, 1970). In 1962 Kempe and his coworkers, in describing 749 cases of child abuse, coined the term "battered child" to refer to children who had received nonaccidental physical injury from acts of caretakers (Kempe, Silverman, Steele, Droegemueller, and Silver, 1962). Child abuse became sufficiently pervasive to motivate professionals and the government to act. During the 1960s every state in the nation enacted laws requiring or recommending that health professionals report cases of suspected child abuse to state or local authorities.

One of the startling aspects of such physical abuse is the very act itself. That adults would physically harm children who are defenseless against them and who are entrusted to their care is nothing short of repugnant to most people. And although some of the injuries are relatively mild, the range includes serious damage leading to death—children "have been beaten, burned with cigarettes, thrown downstairs, had their heads banged against walls and

radiators, plunged into boiling water, suffocated, and otherwise tortured. . . ." (Earl, 1974, p. xi).

Children of all ages are abused, although many investigators propose that children in their first three years of life are the most vulnerable (Fontana, 1973; Kempe et al., 1962). Sons are somewhat more likely to be abused than daughters; moreover, a particular child in a family may be the only one to be abused. It appears that children who are born prematurely are at high risk for abuse, as are the physically and mentally handicapped, and perhaps those of particular dispositions (Friedrich and Boriskin, 1976).

The extent of physical abuse is difficult to estimate. One reason is that confrontations usually occur in the home. Also, some victims are afraid to mention the situation or are not in a position to do so; for example, preschoolers often are unable to report their troubles, or perhaps adults question the credibility of their stories. Abusers, too, are afraid or ashamed to tell the truth about their behavior. And physicians, at least until recently, have seemed amazingly unaware of the problem; of three thousand reported cases of child abuse collected from New York City's Central Registry, only eight had been reported by physicians (Light, 1973). Perhaps physicians have not wanted to become involved because some cases are difficult to identify; injuries limited to bruises and the like can occur in any number of accidental ways. But even severe damage is sometimes difficult to identify as child abuse; parents may bring the child to the hospital with elaborate explanations of accidents that cannot be easily refuted by authorities. It is the watchful medical or social worker who notes that the story is suspect or that the child's x-rays indicate more than one broken bone in various stages of healing.

Given all these considerations, it is understandable that estimates of abuse widely vary. In a particularly interesting study Gelles (1979) interviewed 1,146 parents from a national cross section of homes in which a couple and at least one child between the ages of three and seventeen were living. One adult in each home was interviewed about his or her behavior with one particular child. Table 10–3 shows the percentage of parents who reported violently harming their children in various ways. Extrapolating these data to the child population at large, Gelles concluded that between 3.1 and 4.0 million children have been kicked, bitten, or punched at some time in their lives; that between 1.4 and 2.3 million have been beaten up; and that between 900,000 and 1.8 million have been attacked by their parents with a gun or knife. He also suggested that these estimates are low because of the many unreported cases.

In attempting to understand why children are abused, investigators have frequently asked, "What kind of adults are involved?" Simple data indicate that females are more likely to be abusers (Blumberg, 1974; Gelles, 1979), perhaps because they spend more time with children and bear primary responsibility for child care. Gladston (1965), after his study of child-abusing parents of victims admitted to Children's Hospital Medical Center in Boston over a five-year period, concluded that a major role reversal occurs between caretaker and child. This role reversal, which Gladston termed "transference psychosis," involves a gross distortion in the perception of the victim by the parent. Gladston reported the child being referred to as if he or she were an adult, and often a hostile, persecutory adult. One mother, for example, made the following statement about her three-year-old daughter: "Look at her give you the eye! That's how she picks up men—she's a regular sex-pot." The father of a nine-month-old boy, a military police sergeant who had split his son's head, said, "He thinks he's boss—all the time trying to run things—but I showed him who is in charge around here!" (p. 442).

As compelling as these descriptions are, researchers have not been able to draw a concise personality profile of abusing parents. There is agreement, though, that at least a small percentage of abusing parents were themselves abused and neglected as youngsters (Blumberg, 1974; Kempe, et al., 1962; Parke and Collmer, 1975). It is reasonable to assume that they had been exposed to a model of aggressive child-rearing practices and had learned to be aggressive. Furthermore, perhaps a fundamental lack of mothering—not being cared for and cared about—somehow is the root of abusive behavior in adults (Steele and Pollock, 1968).

The more comprehensive explanations of

TABLE 10-3
Percentage of Parents Who Reported Acting Violently Toward Their Children

Incident	Occurrence Once in Past Year	Occurrence More Than Twice in Past Year	Occurrence Ever
Slapped or spanked	5.2	43.6	71.0
Pushed/grabbed/shoved	4.3	27.2	46.4
Hit with something	1.0	9.8	20.0
Threw something	1.3	2.3	9.6
Kicked/bit/hit with fist	0.7	1.7	7.7
Beat up	0.4	0.6	4.2
Threatened with knife/gun	0.1	0.0	2.8
Used knife or gun	0.1	0.0	2.9

Source: Reprinted by permission of the publisher, from **Critical Perspectives on Child Abuse** edited by Richard Bourne and Eli Newberger (Lexington, Mass.: Lexington Books, D.C. Heath and Company, Copyright 1979, D.C. Heath and Company).

child abuse take into account not only characteristics of the abusers and victims but also broad social factors. This approach is exemplified by David Gil (1970; 1979), who conducted one of the first large studies in this area and Richard Gelles (1973), whose schema is presented in Figure 10–6. Considerable research shows the relationship between abuse and the stress of poverty: large family size, low educational level, unemployment, and poor housing are all contributory circumstances. Abuse and stress occur also in the middle and upper classes, and, as Parke and Collmer (1975) have noted, it would be profitable to study stress and its relationship to abuse across all classes. An-

other factor concerns the permissive attitudes held in the United States with regard to violence being used in the child-caretaker relationship. There is evidence that the level of general violence in the United States is high compared to several other nations and that this is reflected in the levels of violence in the family. As a culture we seem to sanction physical force as a way of resolving interpersonal conflict, and this attitude makes its way into child-rearing practices as well. Moreover, different social classes and ethnic groups appear to differ in their use of physical force in rearing children (e.g., Bronfenbrenner, 1958).

Attempts to reduce child abuse fall into

FIGURE 10–6
A social-psychological model of the causes of child abuse. From R. J. Gelles, Child abuse as psychopathology: A sociological critique and reformulation. **American Journal of Orthopsychiatry**, copyright 1973 by the American Orthopsychiatric Association, Inc.

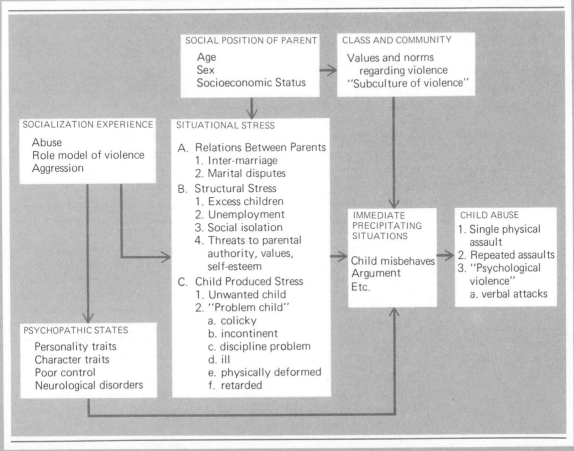

two broad categories: (1) immediate rehabilitation for the family and child, and (2) recommendations for long-range efforts to change societal attitudes and structures. Immediate treatment may include decisions about removing the child from the abusive environment, therapy for parents to help them understand and manage their behavior and to manage their children, and obtaining community support for the family. Recommendations for societal changes include the alleviation of poverty, comprehensive health care and family planning, adequate housing, appropriate education, instruction for proper family functioning, and increased community support (Gil, 1970).

Not surprisingly, children perceive changes over time in the way parents treat them. When second, third, and fourth graders from a middle-class surburban area completed a questionnaire concerning their parents, they reported a decline over time in acceptance, with paternal acceptance declining earlier than maternal acceptance. These youngsters also indicated that while psychological control decreased from year to year, firm control increased (Burger, Lamp, and Rogers, 1975). The same pattern of control was reported, too, by fourth to sixth graders in middle-class Catholic schools (Armentrout and Burger, 1972). Seventh and eighth graders, in contrast, reported a lessening of both psychological and firm control. Thus, children seem to perceive progressive freedom to act independently, while instead pressure to obey parental rules and regulations at first increases and then declines with the advent of adolescence.

The Family
Configuration

Siblings and Birth Order.   Growing up in a family as an only child must be a markedly different experience than being the fifth of five daughters, or having two older brothers and a younger sister. Not only do the number, configuration, and spacing of siblings have effects, but the different reactions of parents to these variables will also be influential. The following account provides a personal description of one daughter's experience.

I had the distinction of having one brother 6 years older than I—who reportedly greeted me with considerable pride and love. I was followed in 3 and ½ years by two more brothers. This was our family until my sister arrived when I was almost 10 years old. My older brother was a model for me. Perhaps he was presented that way; my mother once said, when I was quite young, that the first child is always special. In any event, I was able to follow my brother in important ways, primarily by doing well in school and being active and agile physically. The entire family worked in the family business, which required fairly heavy outdoor physical activities. But as the only female besides my mother for many years, I also participated in household tasks and in caring for my younger brothers. In this respect I became a little mother, caring and bossy. This role was so strong that when I had two sons close in age many years later, I occassionally called them by the names of these brothers—in the correct age order. Despite the fact that I consider my childhood happy, I was lonely for a sister. Not another sibling, but a *sister*. One of the greatest joys of my life occurred early one Monday morning when my older brother returning on his bicycle from a telephone (as we had no home phone) announced, "it's a girl." Because my older brother was already 16 years of age he was able to visit our sister in the hospital; I had to wait several days. On the day she came home I pretended a stomach ache so that my father allowed me to skip school. I rushed to clean furiously so that all would be ready. For years I believed that my father thought that I had a stomach ache. My sister has always been special to me. We talk sometimes of how different her family experiences were, as the last child with siblings so much older than she. In a real way, she grew up in a different family than I did.

It has not proven easy to decipher the possible influences of the many patterns of siblings (Sutton-Smith and Rosenberg, 1970; Hetherington and McIntyre, 1975), and extreme caution must be exercised in generalization.

One of the clearest pictures emerges for firstborns. In a variety of ways they are more successful than later-born children. They speak at an earlier age, tend to perform better on tests of intellectual ability, are more likely to attend college, and are more likely to be recognized as scholars (Altus, 1965; Clausen, 1966; Koch, 1956). There is also evidence that they are achievement oriented, somewhat conformist, and adopt the standards and values of their parents (Altus, 1965; Schachter, 1959). What accounts for these behaviors? Parents place great importance on their first child; they are tense about handling them; they hold high expectations for them; they give them attention and affection (Clausen, 1966; Jacobs and Moss, 1976; Sutton-Smith and Rosenberg, 1970). Firstborns become the "little adult" in the family, garnering knowledge, power, authority, and responsibility (Sears, Maccoby, and Levin, 1957). The apparent result is a child who is highly socialized by parents, according to their standards.

Another consistent pattern for which there is substantial data involves the influence of older siblings (Brim, 1958; Koch, 1954; Sutton-Smith and Rosenberg, 1970). Boys of preschool age exhibit more feminine behavior when they have older sisters and more masculine behavior when they have older brothers. Girls who have older brothers, compared to those with older sisters, tend to be "tomboyish," and having brothers rather than sisters is related to girls being more aggressive and ambitious and performing better on tests of intellectual capacity. There is an interesting twist, however. Research indicates that boys with two sisters have been found to be more masculine than boys with one sister, and fathers have been found to be less feminine in girl-girl families than in girl-boy families (Rosenberg and Sutton-Smith, 1964).

Families with Employed Mothers. Of growing interest to developmentalists, as well as to our entire society, is the question of how children are affected by maternal employment outside of the home. Almost 50 percent of all women are now in the labor force, and, most significantly, work-force participation of women with children increased fivefold from 1940 to 1974 (1975 Handbook On Women Workers). As Figure 10–7 shows, more than one-half of all mothers with school age children, and approximately 37 percent of those with children under six years of age, were working outside of the home in 1974.

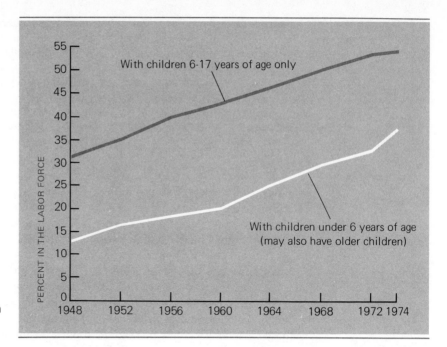

FIGURE 10-7
Percent of mothers in the labor force, according to age of children. From 1975 Handbook on Women Workers, U.S. Department of Labor.

Lois Hoffmann extensively reviewed the literature on the influence of maternal employment (1963a, 1963b, 1974a, 1974b). In order to organize the complex findings, she summarized them in relation to these five hypotheses (1974a):

1. Working mothers, and possibly their husbands, provide particular models of behavior for their children, especially with regard to sex-role behavior.

2. The mother's emotional state is influenced by employment and this affects her interaction with her children.

3. Employed and unemployed mothers use different child-rearing practices because of different emotional states and because the situational demands warrant them.

4. The working mother provides less personal supervision than the nonworking mother, and it may be less adequate.

5. The child is deprived, emotionally or cognitively, or perceives the mother's absence as rejection.

As can be seen from Table 10-4, the findings are quite complex, but they provide at least sketchy support for the first four of Hoffmann's hypotheses. Furthermore, the effects of maternal employment clearly depend on many variables, most notably the mother's attitude and satisfaction toward work, amount of maternal strain, age of the child, and socioeconomic class of the family. Research is required to further test the hypotheses and to understand better the interactions of the many variables. At this point in time, one of the most secure conclusions appears to be that employed

TABLE 10-4
Summary of the Research Findings on the Effects of Maternal Employment on Children

Hypotheses	Findings
1. Working mothers (and fathers) provide particular models of behavior, especially with regard to sex-role behavior.	a. Children tend to be less sex-role stereotyped. b. Daughters are more likely to note a wide range of activities for both men and women; want to work when they become mothers; have higher educational and occupational aspirations. c. Division of household tasks is more egalitarian although women do most household tasks. The greater the father's participation, the more accepting are adolescents of maternal employment. d. Findings about daughters' self esteem are mixed. e. Sons in the lower-socioeconomic class tend to hold their fathers in low esteem; middle-class sons tend to view their fathers as more nurturant.
2. Women's emotional states are influenced by whether they work or not, and this affects their interactions with their children.	a. A woman's motivation for work affects her role as mother. When work is self-oriented and satisfying, it enhances the mother role. b. Nonworking women who prefer not to work obtain higher scores on mother adequacy tests than working mothers who prefer to work. The dissatisfied homemaker obtains the lowest scores on adequacy. c. Children of satisfied workers are adjusted when maternal strain is minimal. d. Many working mothers are concerned about their employment being "bad" for their children. Many feel guilty. Those who feel guilty may overcompensate by being sympathetic, less harsh in discipline, less demanding; they may overprotect. e. Children of working mothers have more positive attitudes toward maternal employment when conflict and strain on the mother are minimal.
3. Working mothers use different child-rearing practices.	a. Children appear to be more involved with their fathers and other people as caretakers. b. Working mothers often compensate by spending more actual time with their children. c. Working mothers emphasize independence training except mothers of younger children who are educated and enjoy work. d. Children have more household tasks except for young children of educated mothers who enjoy work. e. Among the less educated, there is more conformity to rules.
4. Working mothers provide less personal supervision.	a. In lower-socioeconomic classes, working mothers may provide less adequate supervision, but there is no evidence that their children are more likely to be delinquent. b. In the middle-socioeconomic class, adequacy of supervision has not been well studied, but there is weak evidence for a higher delinquency rate among children.
5. Maternal deprivation.	a. Infants: It is generally believed that one-to-one personal stimulation is important, but the effects of employment are still not understood. b. School-age child: There is little evidence of deprivation or perception of rejection.

Source: From "Effects of Maternal Employment on the Child—A Review of The Research" by L. W. Hoffman, Developmental Psychology, 1974, 10, 204–228. Copyright 1974 by the American Psychological Association. Reprinted by permission.

mothers provide a particular model for their children that leads to less traditional sex-role stereotyping, higher approval of maternal employment, and higher evaluation of female competence.

Single-parent Families. When we think of the family in the United States, we tend to consider the intact nuclear family that predominates. Nevertheless, it is estimated that 16 percent of all households are headed by a single parent (Sussman, 1978), and that about one in every six children under the age of eighteen is living in a single-parent family (Bronfenbrenner, 1978). Although death obviously contributes to these statistics, divorce and separation are heavily responsible. And despite the recent trend of fathers retaining custody of their children, most single-parent families are headed by women. There is thus considerable interest today in understanding the effects of father absence on children. Most investigations have examined children's intellectual ability, social adjustment, and sex-role identity (Herzog and Sudia, 1973; Lynn, 1974; Shinn, 1978).

With regard to intellectual development, Shinn (1978), in her review of fifty-four studies, considered twenty-eight of them methodologically sound; of those twenty-eight, sixteen reported detrimental effects of father absence, nine found no significant effects, and three found positive or mixed effects. The measures used were performance in school and on achievement and IQ tests. There was some evidence that both absence caused by divorce and absence occurring during the preschool years are more strongly related to deficits. The data were inconclusive with respect to the length of absence. Children of all ages and both sexes in homes where the father is absent showed poor intellectual performance.

Turning to effects on social adjustment, numerous studies have demonstrated that parental loss is related to depression, anxiety, aggression, and delinquency. Two general themes have emerged: (1) children from divorced families display more aggressive, assertive behaviors, whereas those from widowed families show more evidence of withdrawal and depression; and (2) the earlier the separation the more strongly it is associated with detrimental adjustment (Young and Parish, 1977). Many investigations have established a relationship between length of absence and maladjustment, and also have shown that divorce is a stronger correlate of maladjustment than is parental death (Lynn, 1974). Still, maladjustment has not been demonstrated in all studies involving divorce, and divorce and death may well have different effects.

The possibility of such differential influence is suggested by Hetherington's (1972) study designed to determine if father absence might be related to girls' behavior in adolescence. The participants were thirteen- to seventeen-year-olds from lower- and lower-middle class white families in which there were no male siblings. The first group came from intact homes; the second from homes in which father absence was due to divorce; and the third group in which absence was due to death. The five measures taken were based on direct observations of the girls, interviews with the participants and their mothers, and personality tests. The results showed that girls in both father-absent groups displayed more dependency on female adults than did those in the father-present group. Girls who were being reared without a father also demonstrated differences in interactions with males. Daughters of divorced parents sought male attention and proximity, were verbally responsive to males, and reported earlier and more heterosexual activity. In contrast, daughters of widows held themselves rigidly when they were with males, and avoided eye contact, verbal interaction, and proximity. They also reported less heterosexual activity.

There is some evidence that fathers are more concerned than mothers about sex-role development, and in any event we might expect that the loss of either parent would have implications for daughters and sons adopting masculine and feminine behaviors. Most investigations, however, have focused on the hypothesis that the lack of a masculine model leads to problems in sex-role identity for sons. The results of numerous studies indicate that this may be the case as measured on standardized masculinity scales, questionnaires, and projective tests. Nevertheless, the evidence is not considered strong by all researchers (e.g., Herzog and Sudia, 1973). The exact function of parents in sex-role development is presently one of the most intriguing problems in psychology and we shall return to it in detail in a later chapter.

Despite the high interest in, concern about, and investigation into the effects of father absence, our understanding is far from complete. Early research frequently lacked adequate controls and dependent measures of the projective type are suspect; moderating variables, such as socioeconomic status, age and sex of the child, and length and kind of absence have not been sufficiently studied. And once again it must be pointed out that the research is correlational in nature, leaving open this question: Even if father absence is associated with certain developmental outcomes, is it the direct cause of the outcomes? It is evident that families in which the father is absent may differ in many ways from two-parent families. On the whole, financial stress is higher and mothers may feel burdened by the sole responsibility for the supervision and care of the family, as well as feeling lonely and depressed (Burgess, 1970). On the other hand, the coping capacity of mothers varies, and some, particularly with the support of the women's movement, may enjoy the independence and challenges inherent in being alone. The attitudes of mothers toward their dead or divorced husbands, or toward men in general, might influence children's development in certain areas. Finally, the loss of a father is inextricably bound with the previous dynamics of the family and the specific contributions heretofore made by the father. As one researcher has put it:

> . . . we should not assume that all fathers, when present, give their children love, guidance, and security and their wives companionship and sexual satisfaction. If these attributes are absent in the first place, separation from such a father would naturally not represent much loss. In fact, the father is commonly absent precisely because he could not give these qualities to his family. Moreover, the idea that two parents are better than one is true only when the marriage and the parent-child relationships meet certain minimum standards. (Lynn, 1974, p. 255).

Only casual observation is necessary for the realization that the family structure in the United States has markedly changed in recent years. On the whole, this transition has been greeted with considerable apprehension. It can be argued that the nuclear family as we know it is failing because it no longer meets the needs of many individuals in our society—and is not supported by society. Thus, new structures are emerging. There is no assurance that these new structures will succeed, and at least during this time of transition some negative consequences are apparent. For example, remarriage of persons both of whom have children produces an entirely new family unit with unique relationship patterns that are just beginning to be studied (Sussman, 1978).

SOCIO-ECONOMIC FACTORS

Although the United States prides itself on being a "melting pot," it is, like most nations, stratified on the basis of social and economic variables. *Socioeconomic status (SES)* is commonly indicated by occupation, income, and education, which correlate with each other. This system of stratification brings with it broad variations of environmental conditions, attitudes, values, life styles, and expectations that have implications for development. These variations help set the social context for the manner in which children are socialized. Furthermore, although SES characteristics overlap and may decrease in importance throughout the life span, social-class origins probably remain a strong reference point for most people. Thus, for some time developmental psychologists have been interested in possible differences among individuals of varied economic and social background.

Logically, we might expect that the study of socioeconomic influences would cover the range from the very wealthy and highly placed through the upper-middle and broad-middle class to the very poor and socially disadvantaged. In fact, however, research efforts have not been evenly divided among these groups. Studies have overwhelmingly focused on comparisons or contrasts between the middle class and the disadvantaged. There are several reasons for this bias in emphasis. One is simply that the very well-to-do and socially elite are often unavailable to participate in voluntary research. Then, too, it seems that the problems of the disadvantaged are more urgent than those of the wealthy. Evidence regarding the psychological consequences of being disadvantaged has been in demand, both by those who wish to provide compensatory experiences for the disadvantaged (especially children) and those who do not favor the idea. It is for these reasons that the following discussion focuses heavily (though not exclusively) on the disadvantaged and on comparisons between the disadvantaged and the broad middle class.

Who are the Disadvantaged?

How can the socially disadvantaged be characterized? First, they are economically poor. The disadvantaged child is a product of poverty—or more accurately, is caught up in the self-perpetuating cycle of poverty and failure. Also, the poor are more likely to belong to certain ethnic groups than to others. Havighurst (1970) found that among the approximately 32 million individuals whose family incomes were below the poverty line, approximately 20 million were English-speaking caucasians, 8 million were blacks, 3 million were of Hispanic descent, and 500,000 were American Indians. Thus, most of the poor are whites; however, minority groups are more frequently represented than their percentage in the total population would indicate. Blacks, for example, comprised about 11 percent of the population in 1975, but 27 percent fell into the officially defined poverty class. Although the average income of nonwhite families has been increasing in relationship to that of whites since World War II, blacks still earn less than two-thirds of what whites earn. Black unemployment rates are two times that of whites, and the rates are even higher among adolescents (Beeghley, 1978; Duberman, 1976).

Related to poverty is occupational status, an area that has been well researched over the years by asking individuals to rate the standings of occupations. Professional and managerial occupations clearly are considered more desirable than service or labor occupations. By definition members of the low socioeconomic class overwhelmingly hold the less desirable jobs. Monetary rewards are linked with the status of occupations, of course, but so are working conditions, values, and attitudes of what is "good."

Finally, the disadvantaged are as a group less successful in school. Havighurst (1964) contrasted achievement test performance of middle- and lower-class children in twenty-one Chicago school districts. He found that the scores of sixth-grade students in the seven districts with the highest average socioeconomic status ranged from grade level to one year above grade level on reading and mathematics tests; in the seven lowest SES districts, the test scores clustered around one year below grade level. The Coleman Report, an extensive survey made by the U.S. Office of Education, shows that black first-graders are already behind their white peers one full grade level, with the difference being most pronounced in the South (Coleman et al., 1966). Moreover, an increasing gap between blacks and whites as they advance to higher grades has frequently been noted (Coleman et al., 1966; Hess, 1970).

Level of education, another index of school success, is directly related to SES. Table 10-5 is of particular interest not only because it shows this asso-

---

TABLE 10-5
Percentage of 1957 High School Seniors Who Had Graduated from College within Seven Years, According To Socioeconomic Status and Intelligence, Males Only

Socioeconomic Status Levels	Low	Lower Middle	Upper Middle	High	Total
		Intelligence Levels			
Low	.3	7.9	10.9	20.1	7.5
Lower Middle	2.3	7.4	16.7	34.4	14.2
Upper Middle	4.4	9.8	24.4	46.7	21.7
High	10.5	23.3	38.5	64.0	42.1
Total	3.2	11.5	23.9	47.2	21.8

Source: From Duberman, 1976, p. 208. Adapted from Sewell and Shah, 1967.

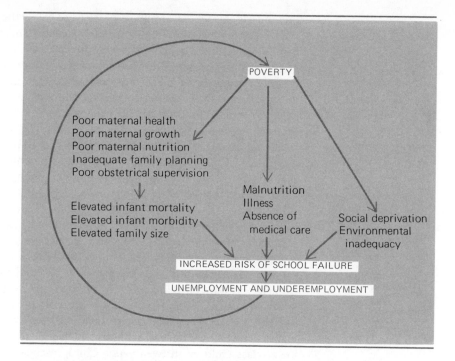

ciation but also because it indicates that the lower the SES, the smaller the percentage of college graduates, *regardless* of intelligence level. Thus, while about 20 percent of low SES students with high intelligence had graduated from college, 64 percent of high SES-high intelligence students had done so.

The picture that emerges, then, is that the disadvantaged individual is poor, undereducated, under- or unemployed, and suffering from a multitude of related conditions that works against mobility from a low status. Figure 10–8 depicts some of the factors involved in the cycle of poverty. Let us further examine them and other correlates of social class.

The Chance for a Long and Healthy Life

From the first moment of conception social and economic factors are related to one's chance of being born alive and healthy and of remaining healthy to an old age. Figure 10–9 depicts death of infants under one year of age for the total population and for black and white people. Although progress has been made overall, blacks are clearly disadvantaged. When infant deaths are analyzed strictly according to SES (income and education of parents), the expected pattern is found. Low infant birthweight is also more strongly associated with low SES and with the black population, and so we would expect a disproportionate amount of developmental deviations among these groups.

A National Health Center survey conducted in the 1960s showed what other studies, too, have indicated: The rates of heart disease, arthritis, hypertension, rheumatism, eye and ear disease, and other chronic illnesses are higher among the poor, as are rates of hospitalization, time lost from work, and restricted activity (Duberman, 1976). Similarly mental illness occurs more frequently among the poor (e.g., King, 1978). And over thirty studies

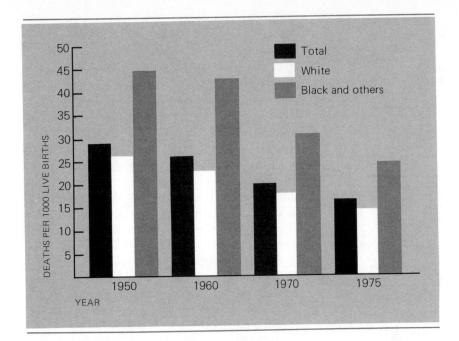

FIGURE 10-9
Deaths of infants
under one year of
age.   Adapted from
U.S. Bureau of the
Census, Statistical
Abstract of the U.S.
1977 (98 ed.),
Washington, D.C.,
1977.

of life expectancy from the nineteenth century to the 1950s show that socioeconomic class is positively related to length of life (Antonovsky, 1974).

Rainwater (1974) has analyzed the attitudes and behaviors of lower-class people that he feels prevents them for taking advantage of medical and other professional services. Because the lives of the poor are so frequently crisis oriented, slight health needs that do not interfere with functioning and health maintenance get pushed aside when more pressing concerns arise. Rainwater suggests, too, that poor people more readily accept poor health because they are so accustomed to making do and to low evaluations of themselves. Then, also, there tends to be a greater reliance on luck, brought about perhaps by the pervasive lack of control the poor have over their lives. Finally, practical conditions—such as heavy financial responsibilities—and discomfort with medical institutions contribute to this situation. All of these considerations, according to Rainwater, unfortunately extend to the children of the poor.

The tragedy of health and medical conditions of the poor is exemplified in this statement from one U.S. government report:

> The infant deaths in the lowest socioeconomic group that are in excess of the number expected on the basis of rates in the highest socioeconomic group may be considered, in a broad sense, preventable. On this assumption it can be estimated that almost 50 percent of infant deaths in the lowest socioeconomic group are preventable (Vital and Health Statistics 1972, p. 1).

Expectancy and
Self-esteem

A substantial body of literature indicates that behavior frequently conforms to the expectations that are set for it. The relationship between expectancy and SES, and the fact that expectancy exerts its influence early in life, can be gleaned from observations of the classroom.

Brophy and Good (1970) provided information on the different ways that teachers interact with children for whom high and low success is expected. After asking teachers to rank their first-graders' level of achievement, the investigators selected the six highest and six lowest in each class for observation. Pupil-teacher interactions were carefully observed and records were kept of the frequency of various teacher and student behaviors, such as hand raising, providing correct answers, giving praise, and giving criticism. With those pupils for whom they held high expectations, teachers were more likely to praise correct answers, less likely to criticize wrong answers, more likely to follow wrong answers with a restatement of the problem (giving the child a second chance), and more likely to provide some kind of feedback after each answer. It seems reasonable to expect that the effect of such teacher behavior would be to improve future performance of those thought to be higher achievers and, conversely, to depress the relative standing of those from whom little was expected.

A telling example of how expectancy is set up on the basis of social class was provided by Rist (1970), who observed a group of black children as they moved from kindergarten through to second grade in an all black urban public school. By the eighth day of kindergarten the youngsters had been placed at Tables 1, 2, or 3 according to the teacher's estimate of their ability to learn. Table 1 was occupied by, in the teacher's own words, "fast learners," whereas the other two tables were occupied by students who "had no idea of what was going on in the classroom." Rist reviewed the information available to the teacher for her decision about ability grouping. For eight days she had been able to observe the children's academic performance, as well as social behavior, appearance, dress, and the like. Even before this she had had information about the medical condition of the children, previous school experience, problems reported by the mothers, place of residence of the family, the number of siblings and parents in the home, and whether or not the family was on welfare. In short, much was known about social and family conditions. In observing the compositions of the tables, Rist noticed that they differed in the following ways:

1. Table 1 children were dressed in neat and clean clothes that suited the weather. The other youngsters were poorly dressed. Their hair was also not cared for and the odor of urine increased from Table 2 to 3.
2. Those at Table 1 became the leaders and interacted easily with the teacher.
3. Table 1 children were quite verbal and used more standard English than the other youngsters, who used black dialect and frequently did not respond to the teacher's questions.
4. With regard to income, education, and family structure and size, Table 1 children came from intact, smaller, more educated, and wealthier families. These middle-class characteristics dropped off progressively from Table 2 to 3.

The Table organization of the classroom became the basis for differential treatment of the children for the rest of the year. The "fast learners" received much attention, whereas the other youngsters were ridiculed, gradually withdrew, and became verbally and physically hostile among themselves. Furthermore, the children tended to be organized in the same pattern in the first and second grades. As Rist pointed out, by this time the other teachers had additional information about them—how they had performed in the previous grades.

The Rist study is important in that all the teachers, administrators, and staff, as well as the pupils, were black, so that racial background was not likely to account for the happenings. Instead, the teachers themselves appeared to hold middle-class values and low expectations for children who fit into the lower class. One wonders how the poorer children would have fared in school had low expectancy not been operating.

Aside from being shaped by expectations of others, behavior is shaped by self-expectancy and self-esteem, which, in turn, arise from a host of environmental experiences. Children who expect to succeed in school tend to do so and it is likely that the ability to maintain academic achievement depends partially upon self-esteem (Crandall, 1967). Considering the experiences of poor children, it would not be surprising that their self expectancy and esteem would be low. Many do not do well in school and Rosenberg (1965), for example, has demonstrated that students who did not achieve high grades typically had relatively low self-images and low occupational expectations. Additionally, they frequently described themselves as withdrawn, overly sensitive, and suspicious—qualities not likely to lead to experiences that might improve their self-esteem.

It has often been hypothesized that individuals recognize early in life their membership in ethnic/racial groups, and that members of groups not highly valued by society have low self-esteem. In fact, the evidence indicates that the ability to make racial distinctions, that is, to be aware of and recognize differences between oneself and others, appears at approximately age three and increases gradually. By age six or seven all children can make such racial distinction. Ethnic awareness is not as easily cued as racial awareness, perhaps arising somewhat later in development (Proshansky and Newton, 1968).

The question of whether children of disfavored groups have low self-esteem has no simple answer. A good deal of research with black children had at one time been interpreted as showing that they do not like being black and devalue blackness (Deutsch, Katz, and Jensen, 1968; Proshansky, 1966; 1968). This was interpreted as an indication of low self-esteem and was presented as an argument against school segregation in *Brown v. Board of Education,* the Supreme Court case that outlawed school segregation (Kluger, 1976). More recently this conclusion has met with some suspicion due to criticism of the early work as well as later findings on the subject (e.g., Taylor, 1976; Teplin, 1976). Moreover, Taylor (1976) argues that poverty, low racial stereotypes, poor school performance, broken homes, and the like are not crucial in the development of self-esteem in black children. Rather, it is shaped by the attitudes of significant others in day-to-day contacts: parents, siblings, friends, and teachers. Black families certainly vary in socioeconomic status and attitudes (Willie, 1974), and this too must be taken into consideration in any analysis of self-esteem.

In the Rist study of teacher expectancy one of the variables that distinguished the children at Tables 1, 2, and 3 was their use of certain modes of language. In fact, language differences among socioeconomic groups have often been noted. The lower-class child, it is frequently concluded, is deficient in many aspects of language development, such as sentence length, vocabulary, grammar, and syntax. Because language not only serves a communicative function but also is intricately involved in thinking, there is much interest in this finding.

One investigator, Basil Bernstein, recorded group conversations among lower- and middle-class British adolescents. He reported that lower-class individuals used longer phrases and hesitated less between phrases, almost as if they were stringing together a set of prefabricated ideas. Middle-class youngsters employed a great number of uncommon adjectives and adverbs, more unusual sentence constructions, and fewer diffuse pronouns such as *they* and *we* (Bernstein, 1962a, 1962b). Bernstein thus distinguished between *restricted* and *elaborated* language codes and argued that reliance upon the former by lower-class children limits their learning of conceptual skills. In restricted language there is a dependence upon a relatively small number of words and phrases, so that another individual will be able to predict fairly accurately what will be said and how it will be phrased on the basis of the situation. There is also little attempt to communicate fine nuances of ideas or feelings. Middle-class speakers are capable of using a restricted code, but additionally possess an elaborated structure with which they can express themselves more precisely. Relying implicitly on the theory that the way people talk influences the way they think, Bernstein contends that, lacking an elaborated code, lower-class youngsters have difficulty developing and applying abstract ideas. He also predicts that their power of analysis will be handicapped by their language.

Bernstein's position has not gone uncriticized. Higgins (1976) has reported that of the many language differences suggested by Bernstein, only a few have consistently been confirmed. Robinson (1965) has argued that lower-class individuals are able to speak either in elaborated or restricted codes, but that they do not feel compelled to use more formal language in experimental situations. To test this hypothesis, he instructed twelve- and thirteen-year-old English children to write two letters, one to a friend and the other to a school administrator. There were few differences between the middle- and lower-class letters written to the administrator; however, letters written by lower-class children to friends contained more restricted language. Robinson concluded that the difference resided in the type of speech used in everyday life rather than in any inability to use elaborated language.

Beginning in the mid-1960s counterarguments to the *deficit* model, exemplified by Bernstein, began to be heard. In essence the *difference model* assumes that the dialect used by lower-class people is different but not lacking in complexity, sophistication, or development (Cazden, 1966; Labov, 1970; Williams, 1970). For example, Labov, Cohen, Robins, and Lewis (1968) studied the language of lower-class blacks in the United States. Observing adolescent residents of Harlem, they noted discrepancies between Standard English and black English. Among these are differences in use of the verb "to be," nonstandard use of verb forms, double negatives, and unusual use of pronouns. Labov and his colleagues argue that these features do not indicate inferiority of the black language but merely *differences*. Such language follows consistent rules, and someone competent in the language can clearly discern what is meant by each statement. Labov and his associates also note a richness in lower-class black language that does not manifest itself in the school setting, but rather in out-of-class verbal activity. Motivational and attitudinal factors and not language, they argue, are responsible for discrepancies in academic performance between lower-class blacks and middle-class whites.

Thus it is increasingly apparent that lower socioeconomic status blacks have developed a language that differs in several aspects from Standard English but is rich in its own right. However, it is unclear how this language is related to the type of conceptual precision required in school situations. It is also difficult to assess the extent to which lower-class language aids or hinders cognitive development. That lower-class members use uncommon adjectives and adverbs less often than middle-class individuals may be more directly related to their vocabulary and usage than to thought processes.

Family Structure, Values, and Child-rearing Practices

There are many well-established social class differences with regard to marriage and family life. In general, those of lower status marry at younger ages; they marry more often as a consequence of pregnancy; they have more children and at a faster rate; and their marriages more frequently end in divorce, separation, and desertion. Because illegitimacy also occurs more often, female-headed households are very common. This profile leads to the description of low SES families as being disorganized, a label that has especially been applied to black families (e.g., Moynihan, 1965). There is some evidence for greater disorganization among blacks, if disorganization is defined by the above statistics, but some investigators argue that the fundamental distinction is class, not race. Duberman (1976), for example, notes that although in 1970 the number of divorces per 1,000 marriages was 33 for white men and 60 for black men, social-class differences account for the seemingly different rates. Schneider and Smith (1973) present the alternate perspective that lower-class families are organized, but not around the nuclear unit, as are middle-class families. Thus, their organization goes unrecognized by the middle-class researchers. A number of factors surely work against the stability of lower-class families, as defined by middle-class standards. Poverty itself is an important factor. Individuals with inadequate incomes are harassed constantly by financial worries and tensions that strain marital bonds. In addition, the disadvantaged are frequently powerless to change the factors that affect their livelihood, or to save an adequate sum of money for emergencies or improvements. It is also unfortunate that under certain welfare systems it is easier for a mother to obtain financial aid when no man is present in the home.

It is difficult to imagine that such conditions would not adversely affect children, and, in fact, child neglect is associated with low SES. At the same time, many lower-class women are adequate mothers. In an attempt to examine factors that might distinguish adequate mothers from neglectful ones, Giovannoni and Billingsley (1971) related interview data from 186 low-income black, Caucasian, and Hispanic mothers to judgments of their adequacy as parents. It was concluded that current situational stress distinguished the neglectful mothers: they were likely to have more children, to be without a husband, to have experienced recent marital disruption, and to be poorer. Impoverishment of relationships with extended kin also existed among neglectful parents, while adequate mothers enjoyed frequent and rewarding contacts with relatives. In interpreting their results, the investigators suggested that poverty is not an "invariant concomitant of neglect. Rather, the implication is that poverty exposes parents to the increased likelihood of additional stress that may have deleterious effects upon their capacities to care adequately for their children" (pp. 332–333).

To the extent that families of different social class vary in their values, goals, and interactions, their children might be expected to develop in somewhat different directions and perhaps at different rates as well. So far we have said little about the range of values and goals that differentiate social classes. Table 10–6, which focuses on some characteristics of family life and marriage, serves to stimulate consideration of the many subtleties to which children of different SES are exposed.

The most notable class difference in child rearing itself concerns the degree to which lower-status parents, compared to middle-status parents, permit children self-direction and freedom. It is generally agreed upon that

---

TABLE 10-6
Social Class Differences in Marriage and Family Life

lower	spouses emotionally and socially isolated strong female bonds men cannot fulfill masculine role in job market strict sex division of labor world uncontrollable

working
(blue collar
workers)
	traditional:
	  strong sex segregation
	  women isolated, passive, submissive, constricted to
	    home
	modern:
	  more equalitarian than traditional working class
	  sharing of duties, decisions, sexual pleasures

lower middle (white collar workers)	emphasis on respectability, which may lead to rigidity strong family ties wives are junior partners to husbands
upper middle (business and professional)	career oriented, especially husbands' financial security and ease social prestige wife often modifies self for husband's career
upper	graceful living, financial security, prestige emphasis on tradition emphasis on family lineage men must follow in family footsteps women must merge identities with husband

Source: Adapted from Duberman, 1976.

FIGURE 10-10
There are enormous social differences in the activities and experiences to which we are exposed.   UPI Photo.

lower-class parents are more restrictive. Bronfenbrenner (1958), for example, found that lower-class mothers more frequently punish failures of self-control such as toilet mishaps, are more likely than middle-class mothers to rely on physical punishment, are more concerned with appearances, and expect less independent activity from their children. This description is reminiscent of LeVine's portrayal of parental goals in societies where economic self-maintenance is paramount; in such societies obedience is considered necessary for survival in adulthood. Perhaps a parallel can be drawn between those societies and the life of lower classes in the more developed nations of the world.

Child-rearing practices have been associated with economic survival in another way as well. Kohn (1963) has proposed that one of the chief differences between the occupations of the lower and middle classes is the way they foster either self-direction or compliance. The lower-class occupations place more emphasis on manipulation of concrete things than on abstraction, ideas, and interpersonal relations; they are also more likely to be supervised and routinized, and to depend upon group efforts rather than individual initiative. As parents, lower-class adults may carry these experiences over to the way in which they control their youngsters.

Robert Hess and Virginia Shipman (1965; 1968) have examined parent-child interaction with the specific intent of determining if and how it might be related to cognitive growth. They argue that patterns of socialization are rooted in the larger social and cultural matrix of which the family is a part, that as part of socialization practices children of poor families acquire a pattern of learning that is unadaptive in the classroom, and that these patterns are learned very early, primarily through maternal contact.

What is the pattern of learning that is hypothesized to characterize the lower class? It is a certain restrictiveness that precludes reflection, consideration, and choice among alternatives of speech, thought, and action. The child develops modes for dealing with stimuli and with problems that are impulsive rather than reflective, that deal with the immediate rather than the future, and that are disconnected rather than sequential. These modes, in turn, reduce the likelihood of achievement and success within the middle-class system.

According to Hess and Shipman, lower-class families are status oriented; that is, they accept the status quo and exhibit passive compliance to rules as unquestionable and appropriate. Status orientation underlies the restrictive mode of dealing with the world that is taught through mother-child interaction. Middle-class families, in contrast, are hypothesized to be person oriented. Because this approach emphasizes attention to individual feelings and roles, it leads to consideration of alternatives and variations rather than simple rule obedience.

To test these hypotheses, 163 black mothers and their four-year-old children were selected from four different social status levels: Group A came from college-educated professional, executive, and managerial occupational levels; Group B came from skilled blue-collar occupational levels, with not more than high school education; Group C came from unskilled or semiskilled occupational levels, with predominantly elementary school education; and Group D came from unskilled or semiskilled occupational levels, with fathers absent and families supported by public assistance.

The mothers were interviewed twice in their homes and were brought to the university for testing and for an interaction session with their respective children. During the latter, each mother was taught three simple tasks by a staff member and was then asked to teach these tasks to her child. The tasks involved grouping plastic toys by color and function, grouping blocks by two characteristics simultaneously, and working together to copy patterns on an Etch-a-Sketch.

One of the more striking results was that person orientation increased with social class and status orientation decreased. The significance of the

---

TABLE 10-7
Examples of Contrasting Replies of Mothers When Asked What They Would Tell Their Children Prior to the First Day at School

A	B
"First of all, I would take him to see his new school, we would talk about the building, and after seeing the school I would tell him that he should meet new children who would be his friends; he would work and play with them. I would explain to him that the teacher would be his friend, and would help him and guide him in school, and that he should do as she tells him to." [P. 96]	"Well, I would tell him he going to school and he have to sit down and mind the teacher and be a good boy, and I show him how when they give him milk, you know, how he's supposed to take his straw and do, and not put nothing on the floor when he get through." [P. 96]

Source: Reprinted with permission of the publisher from Hess and Shipman, 1968. Copyright © 1968 by Teachers College, Columbia University. All rights reserved.

difference is captured in mothers' replies to the question, "Suppose your child was starting to school tomorrow for the first time. What would you tell him [her]? How would you prepare him [her] for school?" Table 10-7 contains the contrasting answers provided by two mothers, one person oriented and the other status oriented. Mother A has provided numerous reasons that the child could use in deciding that school will probably be a pleasant and rewarding experience. While telling the child to obey the teacher, the mother has also given several reasons why this is a good idea. Mother B not only concentrates on a relatively minor aspect of the school experience but also gives the child little reason to look forward to school. There is no basis to form any expectation, and the child can only carry out a set of instructions for which he or she has not been given a rationale. Thus, this finding serves as an example of the ways in which broad social context may be related to parent-child interaction and children's development.

SUMMARY

Socialization, the process by which individuals acquire the knowledge, skills, attitudes, and values of their society, occurs throughout the life span, but socialization during childhood has always been emphasized. The *society* in which these processes occur can be defined as a group of people who live in near proximity, sharing institutions, traditions, activities, behaviors, interests, beliefs, and values. It is helpful to study the socialization of youth in the context of three units: a culture, a family, and a socioeconomic group.

The Whiting and Child study (1953) was a probe into the relationship between culture and personality. They concluded that all societies are concerned about the same general areas in which they must shape their children. At the same time, there is great variability in the specific goals of socialization among societies.

It is important to realize that variations in child rearing and social development are evident in modern societies, as well as in the primitive societies investigated by Whiting and Child. The child-rearing methods and goals of Russia and Japan, for example, are both quite different as compared to those of the United States.

Regarding cultural experiences and later behavior, researchers observe that early restriction does not always result in long-range effects. In general, a relationship in this area is difficult to establish because so many variables are involved.

The *ecology* of a society is its general setting, which includes a particular geography and topography. The ecology of a society is influential both directly and indirectly. Cross-cultural differences in perception, for instance, may be directly affected by topography, while child-care customs may be indirectly influenced by economic and social structures. In relating child care to cultural influence, LeVine suggested a universal hierarchy of parental goals for their children: survival, economic self-maintenance, and maximizing cultural values.

The family is the primary agent of socialization. Its many functions include serving as an economic unit, satisfying adult sexual drives, assuming central responsibility for a small number of people throughout their life spans, and perhaps most importantly, assuming the responsibility for the care and socialization of upcoming generations. The unit "family" varies from society to society. Parents, however, can generally be considered the most important agents in the early socialization of children because of their primary influence in early development. The roles of mothers and fathers as presented by Freud, Parsons, and social learning theorists are among the most influential in the study of developmental psychology.

The parent-child relationship is vital to the psychoanalytic theory presented by Freud. When children reach the phallic stage they sexually desire the parent of the opposite sex, but because of various fears, they come to identify with the same-sex parent. The male child experiences the Oedipal conflict, while the female child's parallel experience is called the Electra conflict. Parson's sociological analysis concentrates on the expressive (nurturance, empathy, emotional support, and mediation of personal relationships) and instrumental (achievement, competence, pursuit of society's goals) roles developed by societies. Parsons suggests that these behaviors are differentiated according to sex roles, with females responsible for expressive functions and males for instrumental ones. Social learning theorists suggest that both parents shape the behavior of their children by dispensing reinforcement and punishment and by serving as models.

Two important dimensions of parental behavior in relation to children beyond the infancy and preschool stages are acceptance-rejection and permissiveness-restrictiveness. *Acceptance-rejection* refers to the respect and love that parents feel for their children and how they express it. *Permissiveness-restrictiveness* defines the range of autonomy and freedom that parents allow their children. The consequences are many, and are influenced by the interaction of both dimensions. For example, a child raised in a permissive-accepting environment will generally be independent, outgoing, creative, active, and nonhostile, wheras parents who have been both permissive and rejecting will often have offspring who are aggressive, noncompliant, and delinquent.

Child abuse and neglect in the family is of much concern today. A full analysis of its cause requires examination of society's values, the characteristics and experiences of care-takers and victims, situational stress, and precipitating events.

In addition to parental influence, the number of siblings, their birth order, the number of parents in the home, and the employment status of mothers are important to human development. In recent years the family structure in the United States has greatly changed, primarily in response to the new demands made by society.

The United States is stratified on the basis of socioeconomic factors; namely, occupation, education, and income of its inhabitants. Because socioeconomic (SES) characteristics vary greatly across the nation, Americans experience very varied life styles. These social class origins play a significant role in most people's lives. Studies have generally concentrated on the middle class and the disadvantaged.

The disadvantaged are caught in a cycle of poverty, poor medical care, inadequate education, and unemployment. They also suffer from low expectations of others. For example, Rist (1970) observed a classroom situation in which teachers who held middle-class values appear to immediately set low expectations for children who belonged to a low socioeconomic class. Self-expectancy and self-esteem are also important. People learn early in life which groups are preferred by society and which ones are not, and they may judge themselves accordingly. Low self-esteem and low expectancy are associated with school failure. Finally, SES is related to language differences, child-rearing practices, and a broad range of values, all of which may interact to create particular environments for children.

II Perspectives on Early Experience

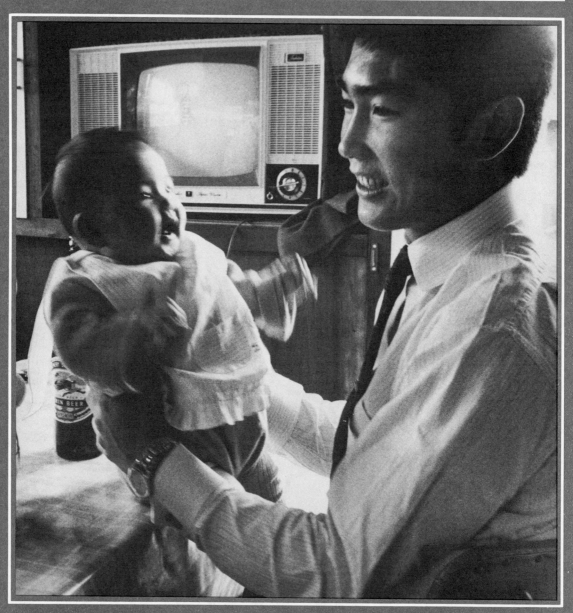

There are many reasons why developmental psychologists have been especially interested in the infant's first social and emotional responses. One is that each child appears to take on a unique "self" during the early years. An individual's personality—patterns of dealing with others and reacting to them—would probably be utterly confusing without an examination of its possible psychological roots in infancy.

A second and equally important issue is the now very familiar nature-nurture question. We would like to know which aspects of personality, if any, have an inherent component that is present at birth and which aspects are shaped largely or entirely by social experiences and the environment. A careful examination of the child's first social responses might provide some answers.

And, finally, woven into the fabric of all our discussions in this chapter is the question of early deprivation and trauma: Are certain early experiences necessary in order that the young child may develop into a psychologically well adjusted adult? Are other early experiences to be avoided because they may permanently scar an individual psychologically?

Interestingly the idea that early experience is of special importance for later development was not taken very seriously until after World War II. As we will see, research on the effects of early experience has produced so many specificities that it is often difficult to generalize, but the evidence has regularly lent support to the conclusion that early experience lays the groundwork for many facets of later social development.

Early experience has been examined from many vantage points: There have been simple case study observations, complex longitudinal studies spanning many years, and innovative and sometimes daring experimental studies with animals. Most studies of early experience have been influenced by one (or more) of the major theories of early social development. Three broad theoretical views have had an impact on studies of early experience: psychoanalytic theory, social learning theory, and ethological theory. All three views stress the importance of early experience for later social development, but each envisions its role differently.

Chapter 6 introduced us to the learning view of social development. We begin this chapter with an extensive review of the psychoanalytic and ethological viewpoints. Attachment, a very important aspect of early social development, is then considered, often in reference to theoretical accounts of the process (e.g., how attachment develops and how attachments, once formed, influence later development). Until recently researchers have emphasized the attachment between mother and infant, but many have now begun to acknowledge and to examine father-infant attachments. In addition to recognizing the paternal role in early development, researchers have also come to appreciate the importance of the parent-child interaction. Both of these new areas of research are given special attention in our discussion of early experience. Finally, the chapter concludes with an examination of the questions surrounding early deprivation, including questions about parental absence and the effects of day care, which are of great practical concern.

The major influence in alerting both lay people and professionals to the importance of early experience was the writings and work of Sigmund Freud. His psychoanalytic theory was the first to stress that certain experiences in infancy establish personality patterns that will endure throughout the entire life span. Freud's theory, highly controversial since it was introduced in the early part of the century, is a comprehensive description of psychological development that emphasizes internal, or *intrapsychic*, events. Although few developmental psychologists today would subscribe to all of Freud's views—and many would shun most of his sweeping generalizations—psychoanalytic thinking has had an enormous impact on the development of contemporary research and has stimulated valuable theoretical debate. (Even the many developmental psychologists who consider themselves completely non-Freudian share Freud's belief that early experience is of great importance for later social development.)

Structures of Personality

Perhaps the best-known aspect of Freud's theory is the idea that personality consists of three components or structures: *id, ego,* and *superego*. The id, characterized as a reservoir of primitive instincts and drives, is present at birth; it is the force that presses for immediate gratification of bodily needs and wants. The ego is the practical, rational component of personality. Freud posited that the ego begins to emerge during the first year of life, in response to the fact that the infant cannot always have what is wanted. An example of the work of the emerging ego is the child's learning other strategies for coaxing adults into action when crying does not produce immediate results. Finally, between the third and fourth years of life the superego or "moral agent" of personality develops as the child identifies with its same-sexed parent and begins to incorporate adult standards of right and wrong.

Psychosexual Stages of Development

Freud believed that human development proceeds as a series of universal stages that all individuals pass through from infancy to adulthood. These stages are largely determined by an innate tendency to reduce tension and achieve a pleasurable experience. Each stage is given its unique character by the development of sensitivity in a particular part of the body or *erogenous zone*—that is, an area that is particularly sensitive to erotic stimulation—at a particular time in the developmental sequence. Freud described these stages as "psychosexual" to indicate that development is the outcome of the successive focusing on and reduction of tension in various erogenous zones that predominate at different times in life. Each stage is associated with a particular conflict that must be resolved before the child can move psychologically to the next stage.

Fixation. There are two reasons why difficulty may be experienced in leaving one stage and going on to the next. One is that the child may not be able to satisfy the demands others make at a particular stage; in this case the child's own needs will also not be satisfied and the resulting conflict, according to Freud, can leave a permanent residue of frustration in the individual's psychological makeup. Alternatively, needs may be so well satisfied that the child is unwilling to leave the stage and, as a result, the behaviors that characterize that stage may continue. Thus, either frustration or overindulgence or a combination of the two is presumed to result in some *fixation* at a particular stage of development, although chronologically the individual has already passed through it.

Freud drew an analogy between this situation and military troops on the march. As they advance, they are met by opposition or conflict. If they are successful in winning the first battle (resolving the conflict), then most of the troops (psychological energy or libido*) will be available to move on to the next battle (stage). However, the greater the difficulty in winning the battle, the more troops will be left behind on the battlefield (fixation) and the fewer will be available to go on to the next confrontation. Presumably all individuals have some psychological investment remaining at each of the stages through which they pass; when the amount is relatively small, only vestiges of earlier patterns of behavior will remain to recur as the individual matures. On the other hand, when a substantial investment of energy has been made at an earlier stage, the individual's personality may become dominated by those techniques of obtaining satisfaction or reducing tension that were used at the earlier period.

Oral Stage. From birth through approximately the first year of life the infant's mouth is presumed to be the prevailing source of pleasurable sensations—for example, the pleasurable sensations associated with sucking.

At the same time, children of this age are quite physically and psychologically immature, so that they must be cared for by others. They may, therefore, be characterized psychologically in terms of relations of *dependence* (upon the mother or other caretakers) and behavior involving chiefly acts of *incorporation* (taking things in). But, according to psychoanalytic theory, these behaviors are more than specific events; the represent durable or potentially durable styles of interaction with the world. Thus, Strupp (1967) points out that "the focal point of the child's personality organization at this period is not necessarily the mouth per se but the total constellation of immaturity, dependency, the wish to be mothered, the pleasure of being held, the enjoyment of human closeness and warmth" (p. 23).

Freud believed that individuals who become fixated at the oral stage are likely to develop an optimistic view of the world, to have relationships in adulthood that are primarily dependent in character, to be friendly and generous, but to expect, in turn, that the world will "mother them." We can readily see how this type of theorizing, which is central to psychoanalytic theory, attempts to explain patterns of later behavior in terms of earlier experiences.

The oral stage is said to end when the child is weaned, and with weaning comes the conflict that is presumed to be crucial during this period. That is, the more difficult it is for the child to leave the mother's breast or

Libido is often described as the energy of the "sexual instincts." But in this context "sex" refers to all pleasurable actions and thoughts, not only those that are principally erotic (cf. Liebert and Spiegler, 1978).

the bottle and its accompanying pleasures, the greater will be the proportion of libido left at this stage.

Anal Stage.   From about one to three years of age, the focus shifts to the
anal zone, with its functions of elimination and retention. Until this time,
the infant presumably has experienced few demands from others, but now
there appear to be direct attempts by parents to interfere with the pleasure
obtained from the excretory functions. Thus, the conflict of this stage is between these demands from society and the sensations of pleasure associated
with the anus.

Various aspects of the anal period may be related to later behavior. If
children view their feces as a possession, toilet-training experiences may be
the foundation for a host of attitudes about possessions and valuables
(Baldwin, 1967). If the bowel movement is viewed as a gift to parents, love
may become associated with material possessions or bestowing gifts. Excessive cleanliness or being pedantic also are viewed as stemming from the demands of toilet training. Still other psychological features of this stage involve the development of shame, shyness (a reaction to being looked at),
and impulsivity.

Toilet training is therefore the major focus of resolving the conflicts of
the anal stage. According to psychoanalytic theory if parental demands are
met with relative ease, then the basis for self-control is established. If there
is difficulty, children may "fight back" by, for instance, deliberately defecat-
ing when and where they please—or, more precisely, when and where it dis-
pleases parents. Such aggressiveness and hostility, it is reasoned, may be
carried into adulthood, where they take the form of excess stubbornness,
willfulness, and related behavior. On the other hand, the child may react by
retaining feces, thus setting the stage for the later characteristics of stinginess and stubbornness.

Phallic Stage.   At about four years of age, the genital region becomes the
focus of libidinal pleasure, as reflected in the young child's masturbation,
curiosity, and inspection of the sexual organs. The conflict of this stage, according to Freud's theory, is the desire of the child to possess the opposite-
sexed parent and fear of retaliation from the same-sexed parent. The reader
is referred back to chapter 10 for a complete discussion of the Oedipal and
Electra conflicts.

Latency and the Genital Stage.   The final two stages postulated by Freud,
latency and the genital stage, are of less importance to understanding the
early foundations of social and emotional behavior. Not only do they occur
after the age of five or six years, but Freud himself considered them insignificant to the development of the basic structure of personality (Baldwin, 1967). Latency includes the years from the resolution of phallic conflicts to puberty and, by definition, is a time during which the libido lies
dormant. The latency years are described as a relatively stable and serene
period during which the child acquires many cultural skills. During the last

FIGURE 11-1
Erik Erikson. Photo
by Jill Krementz.

psychosexual stage, the genital stage, the libido is seen as being reactivated and directed toward heterosexual involvements. Providing that strong fixations at earlier stages have not taken place, the individual is well on the way to establishing fruitful relationships with others and otherwise leading a "normal," satisfying life.

Erikson's Views

One weakness of Freudian theory is its lack of attention to the latency period, which coincides with the child's first major contact with the larger society, school. The importance of this time was ignored by Freud and had to await the attention of other investigators. One such theorist is Erik Erikson, who is regarded as a "neo-Freudian" because he employs the framework of psychoanalytic theory but fashions it in his own direction.

Erikson accepts the notion that libidinal or emotional energy exists at birth and is at the core of human functioning. He also assumes that there are stages of development, several of which coincide with Freudian ones (Table 11-1). Nevertheless, he has made some distinct deviations from Freudian theory; Maier (1969) has noted three major areas in which these differences exist.

First, Erikson places much greater emphasis on the role of the *ego,* or rational part of the personality, whereas Freud concentrated largely on the nonrational, instinctual components of the personality, the *id*. Because society and the changes that occur in it are important to the developing child, the psychosexual stages postulated by Freud are transformed by Erikson into psycho*social* stages. Second, the growing individual is placed within the larger social setting of the family and its cultural heritage rather than in the more restricted triangle of mother-child-father. Third, Erikson stresses the opportunity each individual has for resolving developmental crises,

TABLE 11-1
Comparison of Erikson's Psychosocial and Freud's Psychosexual Stages
of Development

Chronological Stages	Erikson's Stages	Freudian Stages
infancy	basic trust vs. mistrust	oral
1½–3 years (approximately)	autonomy vs. shame, doubt	anal
3–5½ years (approximately)	initiative vs. guilt	phallic
5½–12 years (approximately)	industry vs. inferiority	latency
adolescence	identity vs. role confusion	genital
young adulthood	intimacy vs. isolation	
adulthood	generativity vs. stagnation	
maturity	ego integrity vs. despair	

whereas Freud focused on the pathological outcomes of failure to resolve them adequately. "There is little," Erikson writes, "that cannot be remedied later, there is much that can be prevented from happening at all" (Erikson, 1963, p. 104).

Because of Erikson's emphasis on social context, his theory frequently appears more relevant than Freud's to the kinds of encounters that children have with their everyday world. Additionally, despite his agreement with Freud on the importance of the early years, Erikson's recognition that humans continue to develop throughout the entire life span resulted in a developmental scheme involving eight stages extending from infancy to old

FIGURE 11-2
From birth many socializing agents play a role in the child's social and emotional development. David Strickler, Monkmeyer.

age. Thus he provided both a valuable extension to psychological theory and a personal boon to those unalterably beyond adolescence. For our present purposes, however, discussion will focus on Erikson's interpretation of the four earlier stages of life; we will return to the later ones in chapters 16 and 17.

Basic Trust vs. Mistrust. The foundation of development, according to Erikson, is woven around the theme of trust and hope. Newborns are seen as coming into the world experiencing a change from the warmth and regularity of the uterus. Yet they are not defenseless. Parents, particularly the mother, generally respond to their bodily needs, and the handling of the child largely determines the establishment of attitudes of trust or mistrust. During the early months contact with the world is not only through the mouth but also through the manner in which parents embrace, talk to, or smile at the infant. If a consistent and regular satisfaction of needs is received, certain expectancies about the world are established. The child comes to trust the environment and, in doing so, becomes open to new experiences.

Autonomy vs. Shame and Doubt. The major theme that next evolves, from about 1½ to 3 years of age, is the conflict of whether to assert or not assert one's will. During this time, children rapidly acquire the physical skill to explore the world and begin to see themselves as capable of manipulating some parts of it. The young child attempts to establish autonomy, which sometimes requires disruption of the previously established dependency upon others. But shame and doubt exist alternatively with the thrust for autonomy. They are based on the child's remaining dependency and on fear of going beyond one's capabilities. Toilet training reflects the essence of the conflicts of this stage; shame and doubt result from failure to meet parental expectations and an inability to be assertive, whereas autonomy is the outcome of self-control and assertion.

Initiative vs. Guilt. Coinciding with Freud's phallic stage, Erikson postulates a conflict between initiative and guilt. The environment of three- to five-year-olds now invites—or even demands—that they assume some responsibility and master certain tasks. The child must initiate action in many spheres—action that sometimes conflicts with and intrudes upon the autonomy of others, and thus results in feelings of guilt. Like Freud, Erikson recognizes the increased interest in sex displayed by both girls and boys at this stage. But he sees the child's attraction for the opposite-sexed parent as less incestual and more the result of a reaching out to the one available representative of the opposite sex who has proven herself or himself. The sense of rivalry that naturally occurs with the same-sexed parent leads to a gradual replacement of the desired parent by other love objects. At the same time a more realistic view of the inequality between child and the same-sexed parent results in stronger relations with peers. The rival parent becomes the ideal toward which to strive (Maier, 1969). During this time, then, the child gradually comes to understand the roles and opportunities presented by society and must overcome feelings of failure and guilt with a sense of accomplishment.

Industry vs. Inferiority.   Given the above outcome, the youngster is ready to wrestle with the challenges that arise with entrance into the competitive world of formal schooling. This is the time of latency of sexual striving. With the Oedipal and Electra conflicts settled, peers become increasingly important. The child identifies with peers and regards them as a standard of behavior. The theme of this stage is the mastery of tasks in face of feelings of inferiority. As children achieve such mastery they become capable of facing the turbulent adolescent years that lie directly ahead. Erikson has much to say about this period, as we will see in chapter 16. For now, though, we will move on to the third major theoretical approach to early experience.

THE ETHOLOGICAL APPROACH

The term *ethology* is derived from the Greek word *ethos*, which means habit or convention. The roots of ethology as a scientific discipline are most clearly traceable to zoology (Eibl-Eibesfeldt, 1970). The ethologists have focused their efforts on the study of animals; this strategy permits more detailed examination of social behavior than is usually possible with humans. Like Freud, though, they have taken a strongly biological tack. Ethologists search for universal regularities in the behavior and development of a species.

A basic thesis of the ethological viewpoint is that all animals, including humans, possess species-wide characteristics, which are the foundations for the development of at least some social behaviors. As Freedman (1968) has noted, ". . . [this] emphasis . . . is not meant to deny that familial and cultural institutions do indeed differentially influence behavior and personality. We . . . emphasize that such institutions only support or shape man's behavior and do not create it, as it were, out of the blue" (p. 2). From this point of view, behavioral dispositions are considered to have evolved as the result of a Darwinian process of natural selection. Pressures from the environment exerted over long periods of time ensure that members of a species with the most adaptive behavior are most likely to survive and, thus, pass these characteristics on to their offspring. It is argued, then, that behavioral patterns shared by all members of a species are, or were, necessary for survival. (Recall our discussion of natural selection in chapter 5.)

The manner in which ethologists have employed the evolutionary perspective to account for human behavior can be illustrated by considering the grasp reflex of the human infant. As we saw in chapter 3, the infant will respond to a light touch on the palm by closing the fingers firmly around the object. Figure 11–3 shows a premature infant (gestational age of seven months) hanging by its hands and then by its hands and feet to a clothesline. In an effort to account for this reflex in terms of its presumed evolutionary origins, one prominent ethologist offers the following analysis:

> The grasping reflex undoubtedly served originally the purpose of holding onto the mother's fur. This reflex is often considered a rudiment because man no longer possesses fur and therefore the reflex is thought to be no longer func-

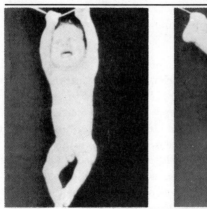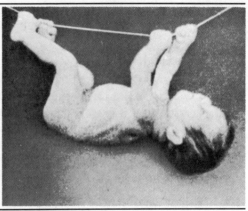

FIGURE 11–3
The grasping reflex in a seven-month-old premature infant. From A. Peiper, Irenaus Eibl-Eibesfeldt, Grundrib der vergleichenden Verhaltensforschung, Ethologie. © Piper & Co. Verlag Munchen 1967.

tional. The behavior does not seem to have completely lost its function, however; one can observe how small infants sleep close to their mothers' body and how they hold onto her clothing. [Eibl-Eibesfeldt, 1970, p. 400]

Grasping and clinging are thus viewed by ethologists as aspects of infant behavior that have been "wired in" to assure that infants become attached to their mothers. This attachment, in turn, greatly increases the infant's chances of survival in an otherwise potentially hostile environment.

ATTACHMENT

Attachment refers to an affectionate, reciprocal relationship that is formed between an infant and another individual. This type of relationship has been observed in almost all infants in all cultures. According to Ainsworth (1977), the disposition to become attached is so strong in human beings that only very gross departures from usual child-rearing practices will prevent it. It seems, then, that entering into close attachments with one or more adults is one of the most universal features of infancy.

The Psychoanalytic View of Attachment

Attachment, according to Freud's psychoanalytic view, is a manifestation of drives and instincts that are present during all stages of psychosexual development. As we discussed in chapter 10, Freud theorized that the mother is the first external object to which psychosexual energy is directed and therefore the first object of attachment. Attachment occurs during the oral stage and is based on the mother's role as nourisher. Freud theorized that the infant's first love object is the mother's breast (Ainsworth, 1969). Experiences with regard to the feeding situation are, not surprisingly, considered crucial in determining later dependency.

The Ethological View of Attachment

Applying the ethological view to human attachment, Bowlby (1969) suggests that pressures on our ancestors, such as the threat of predators, favored individuals who became strongly attached to caretakers. Such attachments, Bowlby reasoned, insured protection from danger and thereby

Feeding vs. Comfort in the Development of Attachment:

An Experimental Study

A classic study of attachment by Harlow and Zimmerman (1959) was aimed at contrasting two maternal roles: her role as food provider, and her role as comforter and a source of warmth.

Newborn monkeys in the Harlow and Zimmerman study were separated from their real mothers and placed individually in a cubicle with both a wire and a terry cloth "surrogate." (See Figure 11–4.) Half of the infants received milk from the wire surrogates, while the cloth mothers "nursed" the remaining newborn monkeys. Observations of total time spent in contact with the surrogates showed that the monkeys preferred the cloth mothers, regardless of the source of nourishment (Figure 11–5). Those who received milk from the wire surrogate went to it for that purpose, but otherwise they remained with the cuddly terry cloth mothers much of the time.

Harlow and Zimmerman went on to demonstrate that the affectional bond between the infants and the cloth mothers is based on far more than the obvious fact that the latter is a comfortable resting place. They observed the monkey's reaction to various fear stimuli, such as a moving toy bear and a bug-like creature (see Figure 11–4, right). Reaching the cloth mothers resulted in a reduction of terror, a highly visible effect that was not achieved by the infants who retreated to the wire mother. When given a choice, the infant monkeys almost invariably

FIGURE 11–4
Left, the wire and cloth "surrogate" mothers used by Harlow and his associates. Right, the infant's typical response was to run to the cloth mother when frightened, even if it had been fed only by the wire one. From H. F. Harlow and R. R. Zimmerman, Affectional responses in the infant monkey, **Science**, 159, **130** (August 21, 1959), 421–432. By permission of the publisher and Harry F. Harlow, University of Wisconsin Primate Laboratory.

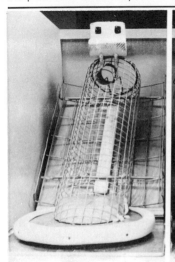

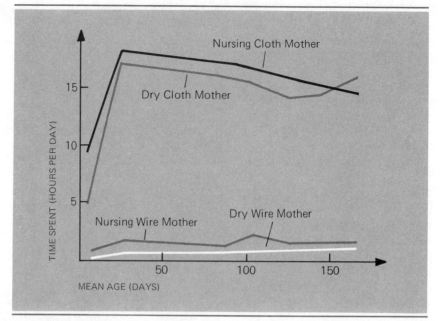

FIGURE 11-5
Amount of time infant monkeys spent with their cloth and wire surrogate mothers. Adapted from H. F. Harlow and R. R. Zimmerman, Affectional responses in the infant monkey, **Science, 130** (1959), 421–432.

sought out the soft mother rather than the nourishing one. Thus Harlow and Zimmerman demonstrated that physical contact, tactile stimulation, and the clinging response (which they labeled contact comfort) was more critical to the attachment bond between mother and baby monkey than was the feeding relationship.

One implication of these findings would come attached to either of their parents, even though fathers are not biologically ca- seem to be that infants can potentially be- pable of breast-feeding. Warmth and phys- ical contact can obviously be provided by either or both parents. It is unfortunate that both ethological and psychoanalytic theo- ries, as well as most learning theories, have so heavily focused their attention on the mother-infant relationship.

increased the infant's chances of survival. Inasmuch as early humans were hunters whose home base shifted with the changing food supply, it was necessary that a young child be carried or be able to follow the mother re- liably during a move or food-gathering expedition. (Even when the infant was carried, the mother had to occasionally put it down.) Thus adaptation favors the child who is inclined to stay reasonably close to his or her mother. However, it is also important (and of considerable survival value as well) for the young child to learn to explore his or her environment. There- fore an interest in exploration also evolved, but it is tempered by a proximity-maintaining mechanism to the mother. The result is a behavior pattern that insures exploration while at the same time providing a reason- able degree of caution.

Research with humans and monkeys has supported, to some degree, the idea that infants use their mothers as a secure base for exploration and that they explore most when their mothers are present. Although most Western

FIGURE 11-6
Patterns of attachment between the infant and its caretaker are quite similar across societies. Victor Englebert © 1979, Photo Researchers, Inc.

homes may provide a relatively safe environment for infants even when left alone, Bowlby believes that the genetically-based species program still disposes infants to behave in ways appropriate to the original environment. Bowlby also claims that infant behaviors such as crying, smiling, clinging, sucking, and following are "wired in" to all human young and form the basis of their attachments.

What is the nature of the evidence that supports this view? In a longitudinal study of fifty-six infants, one team of researchers assessed whether so-called attachment behaviors were related to one another and found significant correlations among visual orientation toward the mother, touching her, crying, and moving in closer proximity to the mother (Coates, Anderson, and Hartup, 1972). They also found that both crying and orientation toward the direction where the mother was last seen occurred more frequently during and following separation than before separation, as would be expected if these responses are viewed as attachment behaviors. Moreover, the process is a reciprocal one: Mothers respond with maternal feelings and attachment to infant smiling and looking (Robson and Moss, 1971). Ainsworth (1967) discovered, from reviewing cross-cultural studies, that patterns of attachment are reasonably similar even in very different societies. Ainsworth considers the cross-cultural data to be evidence for the hypothesis that, as theorized by ethologists, the nature of human infant attachment is universal and inborn.

Imprinting: Support for the Ethologists' View?   The ethological theory of attachment is based in part on a series of studies with birds. One of the earliest findings was reported in 1873 by the English naturalist D. A. Spalding. Spalding observed that newly hatched chicks would approach and follow the first moving object they saw and would become increasingly attached to that object. He theorized that the "following response" was an innate tendency important for survival. Spalding supported his claim that the following response was "wired in" rather than learned very early in life with an ingenious demonstration. Just as a group of new chicks broke out of their shells, Spalding covered their heads with small hoods, thus depriving them of any opportunity for visual learning. Later, when the chicks had reached their presumed *critical period,** the hoods were removed. These chicks then proceeded to follow the first moving object that crossed their field of vision, showing that the following response was indeed prepared or wired in by nature in some way. (Recall our previous discussion of prepared learning in chapter 6.)

Konrad Lorenz continued this line of investigation and demonstrated the following response by making himself the first object that baby ducks saw after birth. Lorenz published a most convincing film showing baby ducklings following him as he walked (Figure 11-7), swimming after him in a lake, and even flying to him as he flapped his arms while standing atop a

---

*With regard to attachment, the term *critical period* is defined as a very short span of time in the early life of an organism, during which a permanent and binding attachment to a particular object (usually the mother) is formed. Spalding's observations played a contributory role in the formation of this concept.

FIGURE 11-7
Konrad Lorenz and ducklings demonstrating the imprinting phenomenon. From "An Adopted Mother Goose," **Life**, August 22, 1955, p. 74. Copyright Thomas McEvoy, **Life** Magazine, © 1955 Time Inc., by permission.

small hill. Lorenz referred to the phenomenon he had uncovered as *imprinting* and described it as an innate, instinctual form of learning that takes place during a critical period in the individual's life.

Critical and Sensitive Periods in Human Attachment. The evidence suggests that something like a critical period for attachment does occur in some species (e.g., Hess, 1959). It is much less clear, however, whether anything analogous to imprinting occurs in human infants. One stumbling block to research (and to the hypothesis itself) is that attachment in humans develops before locomotion skills, so that it cannot possibly be based on a following by ducks and other animals.

Hunt (1979), discussing the possibility of a critical period for the formation of attachment in humans, doubts that there is a strict critical period. Hunt's discussion emphasizes the plasticity of the human species. He points out that "roughly speaking, the higher the species on the evolutionary scale, the longer is the (critical) period and the less resistant and reversible are such attachments. Whether the term *critical* is appropriate for such instances is highly dubious; the term *sensitive* has been suggested and appears to be more appropriate" (p. 128).

The Learning View of Attachment

As noted in chapter 6, learning theorists argue that most of what children become depends on what they have experienced or learned. Thus it should not be surprising that one learning view of attachment casts the phenomenon as a product of reinforcement and analyzes attachment in terms of the principles of operant conditioning (Gewirtz, 1968, 1972; Bijou and Baer, 1965). The operant conditioning view suggests that the interaction between the infant and caretaker is mutually reinforcing so that each comes to exert control over the other's behavior. The mother (or mother substitute) satisfies the basic needs of the child, providing positive reinforcement and removing aversive stimuli. In providing food, a primary reinforcer, the mother and her behavior become secondary reinforcers. The child responds positively by smiling, cooing, or ceasing to cry, which in turn reinforces the parent's behavior. This reciprocal interaction results in mutual attachment. Differences among infants in attachment behavior may result from differences in the kinds of reinforcements they are provided with; for example, a mother who enjoys talking to her infant during feeding may be shaping verbal responses, while another mother who likes to cuddle her infant may be shaping hugging behavior. Also, from a learning viewpoint attachment is a term used to describe behaviors that maintain mother-infant proximity; attachment is *not* seen as an inherent underlying mechanism that can explain behavior.

A number of studies have demonstrated that both smiling and crying can be increased or decreased through operant reinforcement. Brackbill (1958) increased smiling in four-month-old infants by using a reinforcement procedure of picking the baby up, smiling, and talking; she then reduced smiling successfully using extinction procedures. Etzel and Gewirtz (1967) increased smiling and reduced crying in a six-week-old infant and a twenty-week-old infant by reinforcing the infants only for smiling and ignoring their crying and fussing behavior. The investigators thus demonstrated that both crying and smiling can be controlled, at least to some degree, by manipulation of the consequences that immediately follow each act.

Parents may be using contingent responsiveness without being aware of it. As Mowrer (1938) pointed out long ago, failure to respond to infant crying will often lead to louder crying—and few mothers fail to respond to crying that is louder than they are accustomed to hearing from their infants. As a result many parents inadvertently reinforce crying, especially loud crying, on a highly potent intermittent schedule when they are in fact trying to refrain from reinforcing it at all.

So far we have emphasized only the theoretical issues involved in the formation of attachments. It is time to become more concrete by describing the actual developmental course of attachment as it has been observed in humans. Our discussion will reveal a pattern that should by now be somewhat familiar, for social development follows a course that closely parallels other aspects of growth in perceptual, motor, and cognitive processes.

Five Steps in the Development of Human Attachment

Leon Yarrow and his associates (e.g., Yarrow, 1972; Yarrow and Pedersen, 1972) have described the course of social attachment as a series of five ordered steps or accomplishments. These steps occur in the formation of all human attachments; however, with few exceptions, most researchers have emphasized attachment to the mother and the following discussion reflects this fact.

According to Yarrow's model the child must (1) establish boundaries between the self and the external environment, (2) discriminate between people and inanimate objects and animals within the external environment, (3) discriminate between the mother and other people, (4) develop specific expectations toward the mother that distinguish her from other people, and (5) develop trust or confidence in the mother as a source of gratification.

Step 1, Establishing Boundaries between Oneself and the External Environment. This first step in the development of attachment probably is initiated by a strong maturational component, but learning is also involved. Infants learn, for example, that their actions will produce effects (shaking a rattle produces an interesting noise, and crying intensely brings a concerned parent into view), and this certainly helps to discriminate between oneself and the world outside one's skin.

Step 2, Discriminating between People and Inanimate Objects. Newborns look readily at faces because they seem to have an innate tendency to look at things that move and that have light and dark contrast. Infants, as reported earlier, prefer facial representations to other objects and by three weeks of age are more excited by a live human face than by a moving drawing of a face (Stechler and Carpenter, 1967). It appears that most infants will give sustained visual attention to another person by about four weeks of age and will begin to show clearly differential responses to persons and objects shortly thereafter. According to one study of human infants, 65 percent distinguished between people and inanimate objects by one month of age and virtually all seemed able to do so by five months of age (Yarrow, 1967).

Step 3, Discriminating Mother from Other Persons. There are two specific ways in which an infant indicates that it can discriminate familiar from unfamiliar people, and both involve differential responding. Most simply, the infant can be presented with its mother and a stranger; if the child looks at the mother more than at the stranger, then at least passive discrimination must be taking place. We can also look for active discrimination, as when the baby smiles differentially toward its mother or actively reaches out for her. Differential responding appears between thirteen and twenty-four weeks of age in most infants, neatly following the discrimination of familiar and unfamiliar inanimate objects (Bayley, 1970; Yarrow, 1972).

Step 4, Developing Specific Expectations toward the Mother. It is also through changes in response that we detect the infant's special expectations toward its mother. A distressed six-month-old may stop crying as soon as its mother appears, or perhaps actually begin to cry more intensely, either of which would suggest that the baby expects immediate care. And again, the parallels with other aspects of development are important:

Just as the infant must have acquired the capacity for perceptual discrimination to be able to respond differentially to mother and stranger, the acquisition of specific expectations towards the mother is dependent on several cognitive attainments: the development of a rudimentary memory, the acquisition of the concept of the existence of objects outside his immediate perceptual field, some elementary concept of means-ends relationships, and a differentiated schema of the mother. As with other cognitive developments, there are probably differing degrees of object permanence before it is fully established and consolidated. [Yarrow, 1972, p. 89]

As mentioned by Yarrow, smiling is a good example of differential responding. Smiling first occurs when the baby is about five or six weeks old, and initially babies will smile at any human face. By three months of age, infants are more selective and will smile *more* at the mother than at strangers. However, they will still smile at everyone until about six months of age. Cooing and vocalizations that often accompany smiling also become more specifically directed toward mothers. After six months of age, infants smile mostly at familiar people and particularly at those with whom they have formed an attachment.

Step 5, Developing Trust and Confidence in the Mother. The final step in the formation of infant attachment involves establishing trust and con-

FIGURE 11–8
The development of attachment in infants in the Schaffer and Emerson study. Adapted from H. R. Schaffer and P. E. Emerson, The development of social attachments in infancy, **Monographs of the Society for Research in Child Development** (1964), 29, no. 3. Copyright 1964 by the Society for Research in Child Development, Inc., by permission.

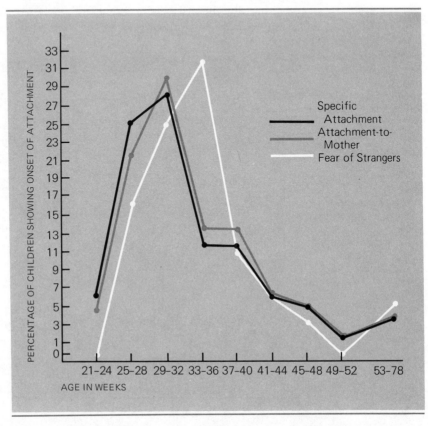

fidence in the mother, which is accompanied by an increasing fear of strangers. Fear of strangers usually occurs about a month after the first clear attachment is formed (see Figure 11–8). This means that fear of strangers is *not* the reason infants keep close to their mothers.

There is controversy about the nature of the infant's emerging fear of strangers (Schaeffer and Emerson, 1964; Spelke, Zelazo, Kagan, and Kotel-chuck, 1973), but it does seem clear that infants show less fear of strangers when the mother is present, and that the presence of the father is as comforting as the presence of the mother in unfamiliar settings, as shown in Figure 11–9 (Lewis and Weintraub, 1974; Lamb, 1976a, 1976b, 1976c, 1976d; Cohen and Campos, 1974; Spelke et al., 1973). Trust and confidence in the attached person is also indicated by greater exploratory behavior in the presence of the mother than in the presence of strangers or when alone.

To Whom are Infants Attached?

Psychoanalytic and ethological theories have strongly implied or stated outright that the first attachment is always between the baby and its mother (or a mother substitute if the mother is absent or deceased). Schaeffer and Emerson (1964) appear to be the first to have examined infant-father attachment. They found that a very high percentage of the infants they studied did indeed form their first attachment with their mothers. But shortly after the first clear attachment was established, or sometimes simultaneously, other attachments were formed with familiar persons such as fathers, grandparents, and siblings (Table 11–2). By six months of age over 50 percent of the infants were attached to their fathers as well as their mothers, and by eighteen months of age over 70 percent were attached to both par-

FIGURE 11–9
Average duration of crying by 36 one-year-old infants when left in a strange room with each of three adults. Although these infants are almost certainly closely attached to their mothers, the presence of their fathers is sufficient to provide comfort to the child in unfamiliar circumstances.
Adapted from Speike et al., 1973. Copyright 1973 by the American Psychological Association. Reprinted by permission.

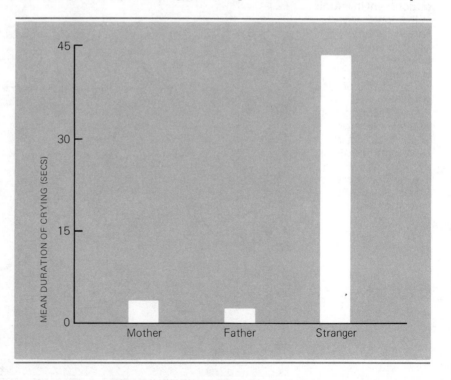

TABLE 11-2
Identity of Attachment Objects: Percentage of Subjects Forming Specific
Attachments According to Identity of Object at Successive Age Period

Identity of Object	Lunar Month Following Age at Onset in First Year						18 Months (CA)
	1st	2nd	3rd	4th	5th	6th	
Mother (sole object)	65	53	32	50	47	17	5
Mother (joint object)	30	35	54	43	50	77	76
Father (sole object)	3	9	7	2	0	5	4
Father (joint object)	27	23	42	29	44	59	71
Grandparent (sole object)	2	0	0	0	0	0	0
Grandparent (joint object)	9	12	14	12	10	29	45
Other relative (sole object)	0	0	0	0	0	0	2
Other relative (joint object)	5	5	5	14	10	18	16
Friend or neighbor (sole object)	0	0	2	0	0	0	0
Friend or neighbor (joint object)	3	7	7	9	3	12	26
Sibling (sole object)	0	0	0	0	0	0	2
Sibling (joint object)	2	5	7	7	7	12	22
Other child (sole object)	0	0	0	0	0	0	0
Other child (joint object)	3	5	14	7	3	12	14

Source: Reprinted by permission from H. R. Schaeffer and P. L. Emerson, "The Development of Social Attachments in Infancy," Monographs of The Society for Research in Child Development, 29:3, Table 8. Copyright © 1964, The Society for Research in Child Development, Inc.

ents. Other results indicated that infants commonly became attached to in-dividuals who played no role in their physical care. (Recall the experimental research of Harlow and Zimmerman, which found that monkeys became attached to cuddly cloth mother surrogates who played no role in their feeding.) Schaeffer and Emerson used as their measure of attachment the reported probability that the baby would cry or protest in response to brief everyday separations from specific individuals. Unfortunately, they relied on mothers as their primary source of information and fathers were neither observed nor interviewed (cf. Lamb, 1978, p. 88).

In a series of observational studies, Kotelchuck and his colleagues (Kotelchuck, 1972; Kotelchuck, Zelazo, Kagan, and Spelke, 1975; Ross, Kagan, Zelazo, and Kotelchuck, 1975) found that infants almost invariably become attached to both parents; twelve- to twenty-one-month-old children showed no preference for one parent over the other, whether observed at home or in laboratory sessions. Cohen and Campos (1974) found that separation protest (a frequently used measure of attachment) did not occur more upon the departure of one parent than the other, but that several measures of proximity-seeking did reveal a preference for mothers over fathers. Using a number of attachment behavior indexes, Lamb (1975, 1976b) found that from the time infants were able to form relationships through thirteen months of age they were attached to both parents and showed no consistent preference for either parent over the other. In a follow-up study during the infants' second year, a significant preference for their fathers was found among the male infants (Lamb, 1977a). All but one of the boys in the sample of twenty male infants showed a consistent preference for their fathers over their mothers. The girls were much less consistent, however.

Some girls preferred their mothers, some preferred their fathers, and some appeared to have no preference. In examining the nature of the father-son relationship, fathers were found to interact much more actively with their sons than with their daughters (and were twice as active in interacting with sons as were mothers), reminding us again that the attachment relationship is a reciprocal one.

The preference of most boys and some girls for fathers appears to be due to differences in the ways that mothers and fathers interact with their children. Close observation has revealed that fathers most often pick up their infants for the purpose of playing with them, while mothers are far more likely to pick up the infants for caretaking purposes or to move them away from undesirable activities (see Figure 11–10).

Determinants of Infant Attachment. The most important factor in the development of attachments is the quality of interaction between parent and child. Quality of interaction may be defined in terms of sensitivity of the parent's response to the child and the emotional intensity of the interaction (Ainsworth and Bell, 1974) or, more simply, as tender loving care (Hunt, 1979). Longitudinal studies suggest that the mutual delight mother and child receive from their interactions may be the most important factor in the infant's relationship with its mother (Ainsworth and Whittig, 1969; Beckwith, 1972; Rheingold, 1961). Ainsworth and Bell (1974) have developed a scale of maternal sensitivity that measures the degree to which the mother perceives and accurately interprets her infant's behavior and the promptness and appropriateness with which she responds. Based on a study of white, middle-class women, Ainsworth and Bell (1974) concluded that nearly half of the women were insensitive to their infant's needs. The

FIGURE 11–10
Reasons why mothers and fathers picked up their infants at seven and eight months of age. Note especially the dramatic differences in caretaking and play. Reprinted with permission from M. E. Lamb, ed., **The Role of the Father in Child Development.** Copyright © John Wiley & Sons, New York, 1976b.

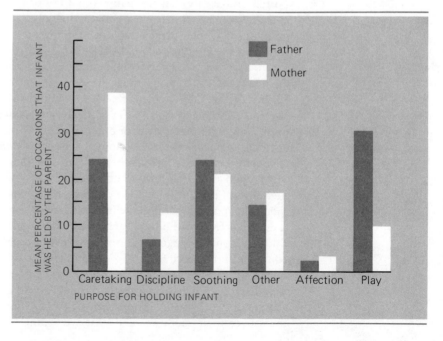

insensitive mothers tended to have disturbed attachment relationships with their children.

On several psychophysiological and observational measures, mothers and fathers have been found to be equally sensitive to infant signals (Frodi, Lamb, Leavitt, and Donovan, 1978; Parke and Sawin, 1976). Studies of infants in their first months of life also indicate that most fathers are eager to interact with their infants and that they are capable of doing so competently and sensitively (Parke and Sawin, 1977; Parke and O'Leary, 1975). The amount of time a parent and child spend together has not been found to predict strength of attachment (Pedersen and Robson, 1969; Schaeffer and Emerson, 1964). Yet, clearly a certain amount of time is required for infant-parent attachment to occur.

How Parents Become Attached.   Remembering that attachment is defined as an affectionate reciprocal relationship, it is surprising that such little attention has been given to how mothers and fathers become attached to their infants.

Pregnancy usually fosters an anticipatory bonding, but if the pregnancy is unwanted the attachment relationship will probably be affected (Hunt, 1979). Acceptance of the mothering role has been shown to be directly related to observed maternal responsiveness to the infant (Moss, 1967; Moss, Robson, and Pedersen, 1969; Robson, Pedersen, and Moss, 1969). Moss (1967) interviewed mothers before the birth of their child and then observed the mother-infant interaction when the infants were three weeks old. Moss found that the attitudes of the mothers were clearly related to the way that they responded to their infants. Ratings of the animation in the mother's voice during pregnancy correlated positively with the amount of stimulation the mother provided the infant at one and three months of age (Moss et al., 1969), and a prenatal measure of interest in affectionate contact correlated positively with the frequency of mother-infant mutual gazing when the infant was one month old (Robson et al., 1969).

Another factor that may influence parental attachment is what happens at and after childbirth. Although there is as yet little or no evidence on the psychological effects of different types of delivery (see chapter 3), there is evidence that the type of hospital care matters. When mothers are separated from their babies during the first hours and days after delivery, they may have difficulty forming an attachment (Klaus and Kennell, 1978). Studies with premature infants as well as those born at full term suggest that the health of the infant and the mother-infant relationship are both improved by early contact following birth (Leifer, Leiderman, Barnett, and Williams, 1972; Klaus and Kennell, 1978). In one study, fathers were also found to markedly increase caregiving after being asked to undress their infants twice and establish eye-to-eye contact with the child for one hour during the first three days of life (Lind, 1973). Most hospital deliveries, however, are followed by several days of separation between parents and child, and this constitutes a deprived interaction according to the definition of deprivation by Barnett, Leiderman, Grobstein, and Klaus (1970). Table 11–3 outlines their definition and levels of interactional deprivation and Table 11–4

TABLE 11-3

Levels of Interactional Deprivation during the First Few Days after Birth. Traditional hospital delivery results in high levels of deprivation, especially in the caretaking interaction.

Levels of Deprivation	Duration of Interaction	Sensory Modalities of Interaction	Caretaking Nature of Interaction
I. No deprivation	Full time	All senses	Complete
II. Partial deprivation	Part time	All senses	Partial
III. Moderate deprivation	Part time	All senses	None
IV. Severe deprivation	Part time	Visual only	None
V. Complete deprivation	None	None	None

Source: From C. R. Barnett, P. H. Leiderman, R. Grobstein, and M. H. Klaus, ''Neonatal Separation: The Maternal Side of Interactional Deprivation,'' Pediatrics, 1970, 45, 197-205. Copyright American Academy of Pediatrics.

shows the deprivation level associated with different birth situations. According to Table 11-4, the best alternative to home delivery (which is still not encouraged by physicians) is the "rooming in" plan, an arrangement where the baby stays in the room with the mother, while the father is allowed to visit and help in the daily care of the infant. A new concept that has been well received is the "birthing center," which attempts to combine the advantages of the home and the hospital; usually birthing centers are independent areas within a conventional hospital that offer a homelike setting. For example, there is a lounge area for the use of family and friends and comfortable beds, chairs, a stereo, and plants may all be part of the furnishings. Fathers are allowed to be present during deliveries at birthing centers, and may even help with the delivery and give the infant his or her first bath.

TABLE 11-4

Deprivation Levels over Time, Related to Birth Situations

Birth Situation	Deprivation Levels, Days and Weeks Postpartum					
	Day 0	Day 1	Day 3	Day 7	Week 8	Week 9
Home, full term	I, no deprivation	I, no deprivation	I, no deprivation	I, no deprivation	I, no deprivation	I, no deprivation
Hospital, full term, rooming-in	III, moderate deprivation	I, no deprivation	I, no deprivation	I, no deprivation	I, no deprivation	I, no deprivation
Hospital, full term, regular care	III, moderate deprivation	II, partial deprivation	II, partial deprivation	I, no deprivation	I, no deprivation	I, no deprivation
Premature, mother allowed into nursery	V, complete deprivation	IV, severe deprivation	III, moderate deprivation	II, partial deprivation	II, partial deprivation (discharge nursery)	I, no deprivation (home)
Premature, regular care (separated)	V, complete deprivation	IV, severe deprivation	IV, severe deprivation	IV, severe deprivation	II, partial deprivation (discharge nursery)	I, no deprivation (home)
Unwed mother, refuses contact	V, complete deprivation	V, complete deprivation	V, complete deprivation	V, complete deprivation	V, complete deprivation	V, complete deprivation

Source: From Barnett et al., 1970. Copyright American Academy of Pediatrics.

There are good reasons for the current rethinking of how to best arrange for the birth and early care of a newborn infant. As Klaus and Kennell compellingly point out:

> Since the newborn baby is utterly dependent upon his parents for his survival and optimal development, it is essential to understand the process of attachment as it develops from the first moments after the child is born. Although we have only a beginning understanding of this complex phenomenon, those responsible for the care of mothers and infants would be wise to re-evaluate hospital procedures that interfere with early, sustained mother-infant contact, to consider measures which promote a mother's contact with her nude infant and to help her appreciate the wide range of sensory and motor responses of her neonate (1978, p. 26).

Just as infants take several months to become attached to their mothers, attachment of a mother for her child is not instantaneous either. Robson and Moss (1971) report that at first mothers perceive their infants as anonymous asocial objects and report only impersonal feelings of affection. When their infants begin to show smiling responses and make eye contact (in the second month), mothers begin to view the infant as a real person with unique characteristics. Thus, it appears that as the infant begins to recognize its mother, the mother responds with an intensification of maternal feelings. Clarke-Stewart (1973) found that the more often the child looked, smiled, and vocalized to the mother, the more affectionate and attached the mother became. Maternal responsiveness to the infant's demands also increased as a result of the infant's social behaviors. On the other hand, if the infant's appearance fails to meet the expectations of the mother or if the child is clumsy at nursing or inactive, the attachment relationship may be retarded or damaged (Blehar, Lieberman, and Ainsworth, 1977). But a considerable amount of early damage can be overcome if mothers who are initially frustrated by the unresponsiveness of their infants begin to interact with them in ways that bring mutual smiles and happiness (Badger, 1977; Hunt, 1979; Hunt, Mohandessi, Ghodssi, and Akiyama, 1976; Levenstein, 1976).

Harlow (1971) reports similar findings from his studies of monkeys who show indiscriminate love for their own or a strange infant during the first week after their infant's birth. When mother monkeys are separated from their infants they are upset by the separation, but they are relieved by the sight of *any infant* until their offspring are a week to ten days old; after this time, however, only the sight of their own infants will help relieve their distress. These observations suggest that the mother monkeys become specifically attached to their own infant only after they have interacted with the infant for a period of time (Jensen, 1965). Studies of mother monkeys also point to the necessity of a reciprocal relationship, particularly in regard to *contact comfort*. Mother monkeys hold their babies close to them during the first month of life, a behavior which seems to be comforting to both mother and infant and also to be an important mechanism in eliciting maternal love. In several experiments, mother monkeys who had been separated from their infants were given substitute infants that would not cling to them (Harlow, 1971). In one such case, the mother monkey was given a kitten. She made every effort to mother the kitten, and even attempted to nurse it! However, when the kitten failed to reciprocate the mother's clinging efforts, the monkey's maternal instincts waned and she totally abandoned the kitten. Similar rejection occurred when a mother monkey was given a one-month-old monkey who had developed an "autistic pattern" of behavior, clutching itself and refusing contact with the mother monkey. Despite this experience, though, the same mother monkey later adopted a second infant that would cling normally.

EFFECTS OF SOCIAL DEPRIVATION AND SEPARATION

Freud and the ethologists agree that the early years are critical for normal social development. Their work has led to increased interest in the effects of early experience, and is particularly concerned with determining the appropriate types and amount of contact with other members of the species that is necessary. But what happens if this contact is not available? Much of our knowledge on this matter comes from early experimental work with animals.

Effects of Social Isolation on Animals

Studies with Dogs. In one series of studies, Scottish terriers were separated from their mothers immediately after weaning and were cut off from the rest of the world by being placed in individual pens with opaque sides (Thompson and Melzack, 1956). The pups, who never saw their human caretakers either, were tested after seven to ten months. Their reactions were compared with those of control Scotties who had spent the same time living with families outside of the laboratory or, in a few cases, living free in the research facilities.

In order to examine fear reactions, the investigators exposed the dogs to strange objects such as an opening umbrella, a human skull, and a swelling balloon. The control animals, who were reared normally, did not show much excitement but simply ran away. The pups reared in isolation, on the other hand, were highly agitated, whirled about, and stalked the objects purposelessly. When retested a year later in the same manner, they had become more like the controls: They were still excitable but exhibited more purposeful avoidance. However, the normal controls had by now developed new reactions—attacking the objects with playful snapping, biting, barking, and growling—not shown by the isolated animals.

Studies with Monkeys. Harlow and Harlow (1970) isolated young rhesus monkeys at birth in a stainless steel chamber in which all light was diffused, the temperature controlled, the air flow regulated, and all environmental sounds filtered. Food and water were provided automatically and the cage was cleaned by remote control. Thus, all physical needs were met, but during the course of early development the animals saw no other living creature. After being raised in this manner for either three, six, or twelve months, each monkey was taken from the specialized chamber and placed in its own individual cage. Thereafter, the Harlows exposed these subjects to a peer (another monkey who had also been reared in isolation) and to two otherwise similar monkeys who had been reared in open cages with others. All four individuals were then put in a special playroom, typically for half an hour a day, five days a week, for six months. The playroom was equipped with a variety of toys designed to elicit activity and play. The Harlows report:

> *Fear is the overwhelming response in all monkeys raised in isolation.* Although the animals are physically healthy, they crouch and appear terror-stricken by their new environment. Young that have been isolated for only three months soon recover. . . . But the young monkeys that had been isolated for six months adapt poorly to each other and to the controls. They cringe when approached and fail at first to join in any of the play. During six months of play sessions, they never progress beyond minimal play behavior, such as playing by themselves with toys. What little social activity they do have is exclusively with the other isolate in the group. When the other animals become aggressive, the isolates accept their abuse without making any effort to defend themselves. For these animals, social opportunities have come too late. . . .
>
> Monkeys that have been isolated for twelve months are very seriously affected. . . . Even primitive and simple play activity is almost nonexistent. With these isolated animals, no social play is observed and aggressive behavior is never demonstrated. Their behavior is a pitiful combination of apathy and terror as they crouch at the sides of the room, meekly accepting the attacks of the more healthy control monkeys. We have been unable to test them in the playroom beyond a ten-week period because they are in danger of being seriously injured or even killed by the others. [1970, p. 95, italics added]

Effects of Parental Separation and Deprivation on Humans

One outgrowth of Freud's theory is the belief that the infant needs a primary love object to develop in a healthy manner, that this should be a single adult figure, and that multiple mothers or dilution of the primary attachment is detrimental (Jersild, 1968). This theoretical position further maintains that such love is an essential element not only for the child's emotional development but also for intellectual growth and physical well-being. Separating a child from his or her mother once an attachment is formed is said to be traumatic and may lead to retarded, impaired development or even death due to "emotional starvation."

Emotional, physical, and intellectual problems are indeed known to occur with some frequency among children in institutions. Spitz (1965) reported that institutionalized children who were adequately cared for in every bodily respect were nevertheless retarded in their physical and emotional development; they frequently withdrew, became depressed, and some even appeared to die as a result of insufficient psychological care. Bowlby (1953) reported similar findings. Both Bowlby and Spitz believed that the negative effects they observed were due to deprivation of maternal love, or lack of love and attention from a mother substitute.

There are many similar accounts, and such deficits in general have been attributed to deprivation of maternal love. But maternal deprivation is a vague term that provides little information about the specific variables that underlie deficiency. A number of years ago, for example, Casler (1961)

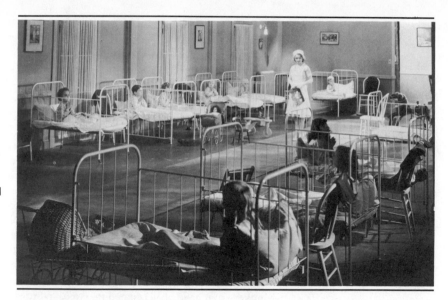

FIGURE 11–11
Foundling home children often have been deprived of intellectual and social stimulation and so fall behind other children in several aspects of their development. The New York Public Library Picture Collection.

made a distinction between children who suffered separation from significant adults before six months of age and those to whom it did not occur until later in life. In regard to children in the former group, he concluded, "evidence is accumulating, both on the human and the animal level, that [the cause] is perceptual deprivation—the absolute or relative absence of tactile, vestibular, and other forms of stimulation" (1961, p. 49). With children over six months old, however, he warned that the problem actually is one of learning about rejection or the severing of an established affectional bond. Later work by Leon Yarrow has offered strong support for Casler's distinction.

Specifically, Yarrow and his associates (Yarrow, Goodwin, Manheimer, and Milowe, 1971) reported longitudinal data on fifty-three adopted children who were followed for a ten-year period. The question asked was, What relationship, if any, exists between the mothering experiences of a child during infancy and the child's personal and social characteristics at ten years of age?

Inasmuch as all children in the study were adopted, it was possible to ask about the impact of early separation upon later personality development.* For this purpose, the investigators compared three groups of children: (1) those who went directly from the hospital to their permanent adoptive homes and therefore experienced *no* separation; (2) those who were assigned temporary foster mothers and then went on to permanent adoptive homes *before they were six months of age;* and (3) those who were separated from their initial foster mothers and placed in permanent homes *after they were six months of age.* The results showed that at age ten there were no differences between the group that was separated early and the group that was not separated at all on any measure of any interpersonal or social adjustment. In sharp contrast, children separated from their initial foster

---

*As we mentioned in chapter 5, but in another context, the advantage of studying adopted children is that parent-child similarities will then certainly be based on social factors, rather than on genetic or hereditary similarities between parent and child.

mothers after the age of six months were markedly lower than the others at age ten on a measure of social discrimination, that is, the child's capacity to establish different levels of relationship with people. The effect, which was clearly present for both sexes, jibes perfectly with findings discussed earlier that attachments are not really formed in humans before the age of six months, but may be quite important thereafter.

Although the children in this study were never institutionalized, the results supported the theory that some of the negative effects experienced by institutionalized children are the result of the separation from attached others and not the absence of maternal love. (Children in all of the above groups had a maternal figure before and after adoption.) Moreover, the results indicated that early separation—before six months of age and before attachments are usually formed—does *not* have the negative effects experienced by those separated after six months when attachments have been formed (Yarrow et al., 1971).

Other data from this study were based on direct observations of the kind of care each infant received in either foster or adoptive homes during the first six months of life. In contrast with the clear long-term effects of separation per se, the kind of care received early in life (provided it was within the normal range) did not seem to influence girls' intellectual or emotional development appreciably. But boys were less resilient. Ten-year-old males whose environment in infancy lacked stimulation and responsiveness fared less well than their peers on measures of intellectual development. These boys were also generally less competent socially, and they experienced greater difficulty than other youngsters in being interpersonally effective or in relating intimately with others (Yarrow et al., 1971).

A similar study with seventy adopted children focused on children who were separated from foster parents between birth and sixteen months of age (Yarrow and Goodwin, 1973). These children were in normal environments both before and after adoption, so it was possible to see the effects of separation (apart from maternal deprivation) at different ages. Only 15 percent of the children were free of all disturbances after the separation, while the remainder had disturbances of varying severity in their sleeping and feeding schedules and in their social reactions, such as decreased social responsiveness, physical rejection of the new mother, or excessive clinging to her (see Table 11–5). Fifty-six percent of the children had lower IQ estimates following adoption. Most interesting is the fact that while *none* of the

TABLE 11-5
Percentage of Children Showing Various Disturbances as an Immediate
Result of Mother-Child Separation

Impact	Percent
No disturbances	15
Mild disturbances	36
Moderate disturbances	23
Severe disturbances	20
Extreme disturbances	6

Source: Based on data provided by Yarrow and Goodwin, 1973. Copyright © 1973 by Basic Books, Inc.

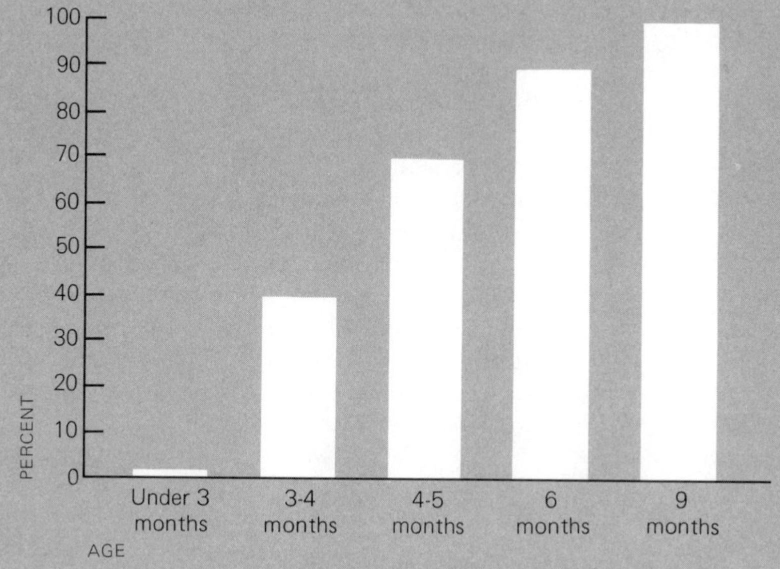

FIGURE 11–12
Percentage of children showing moderate or severe reaction to maternal separation according to the child's age. Adapted from data in Yarrow and Goodwin, 1973.

nine children who were separated before three months of age experienced any serious reaction, *all* of the children who were separated from their foster parents at nine months of age had a moderately severe to severe reaction to the separation. These results are shown in Figure 11–12, which also indicates that between the ages of three and nine months of age, the older the child is at separation, the greater the chance of a severe reaction.

Close-up

Effects of Day Care

Today almost half of all American mothers work away from home, and about 7 million children in the United States under the age of five are enrolled in some kind of day care program (Committee on the Infant and Pre-school Child, 1975). Thus maternal separation in general and day care experiences in particular have become important areas of study.

According to most research day care programs are not necessarily detrimental to children and may even result in positive gains. Kagan, Kearsley, and Zelazo (1975) compared Chinese and Caucasian infants who

attended day care centers from age 3½ months to 30 months with home-reared children of the same age. The groups were matched according to socioeconomic status of their families, ethnicity, and sex. The investigators found no differences in separation protest in the groups and an overwhelming preference for mother over other adults, including the caretaker at the center. The only significant difference found between the groups was that the Chinese infants, both day care and home-reared, exhibited more proximity behaviors and touching of the mother than the Caucasian group; the researchers interpreted these results as showing that the child's attachment to his or her mother is influenced more by the home experience than by whether or not the child has attended day care centers. Kagan and his colleagues concluded that it is the quality of the home experience that is critical to the development of the mother-infant bond, and that day care does not dilute the bond that is formed.

Other studies support the conclusion reached by the Kagan group. Maccoby and Feldman (1972) compared kibbutz-reared Israeli children who are separated from their mothers much of the time and American children of the same age; the investigators found that both groups of children exhibited similar attachment behaviors toward their mothers despite very different rearing conditions. Another study found no differences among day care children and those reared with mothers at home, particularly in relationships with their mothers or in their affiliation, nurturance, hostility, happiness, or emotionality (Caldwell, Wright, Honig, and Tannenbaum, 1970).

However, as in the mother-infant relationship, the quality of day care may make an important difference. The centers studied by Kagan and Caldwell were of unusual quality and it is not at all clear whether their results can be generalized to more typical day care centers (Ashton, 1978). McCrae and Herbert-Jackson (1976) analyzed two contradictory studies on day care and concluded that the term "day care" is meaningless without a description of the characteristics and goals of the particular program in question. Moore (1964, 1969) has identified four factors that influence the effect of day care:

1. The quality of substitute care.
2. Its continuity and stability.
3. The developmental level of the child.
4. The personality of the mother.

Other factors that may play a part in determining the effect of day care are the sex, age, and personality of the child. One investigation reports disturbances in the mother-child relationships of two- and three-year-olds who were enrolled in day care for about five months (Blehar, 1974). These negative findings, which contrast with other studies, may have been due to shorter length of time in the center and, indeed, may have been overcome with time. Alternatively, the results may be due to the later age at which day care began in the Blehar study, or to the poorer quality of the care that was provided. Another study (Brookhart and Hock, 1976) concluded that although in general home-reared versus day care did not predict social behavioral differences in children, there were some indications of social disturbances in males who attended day care programs. Contrary to expectation, some positive outcomes have been noted from difficult encounters in day care situations (Holmes, 1935). Four-year-olds who attended centers in New York slums where encounters were often rough and painful showed far less fear in a variety of fear-inducing situations than did upper-middle-class children who attended nursery school where such treatment was far less common. This research is consistent with similar animal research, which has found that certain early experiences with aversive stimuli decrease the aversiveness of such encounters later (Hunt, 1979).

The importance of individual program characteristics is displayed in yet another study. This study concentrated on an educational day care program that had one trained caretaker for each infant. Twenty children of poor black mothers with IQs of seventy-five or below were involved; the offspring obtained a mean IQ of 124 at age sixty-six months, which was 30 points above that of a control sample! Although the mean IQ of the early educated day care children dropped by the end of the fourth grade in public schools to 109, these children continued to have higher IQ scores than those in the control group (Heber, 1978; Heber, Garber, Harrington, Hoffman, and Falender, 1972).

SUMMARY   This chapter has focused on theory and research concerning early social and emotional behavior, such as the infant's first attachments and social responses, as well as the effects of early deprivation and trauma. No one has been more influential in calling attention to the possible importance of early experience than Sigmund Freud. According to Freud's theory, personality consists of three components; the *id*, the *ego*, and the *superego*. Freud also theorized that all individuals pass through a series of *psychosexual stages* (oral, anal, phallic, and genital). Frustration or overindulgence may result in *fixation* at a particular stage that, according to psychoanalytic theory, is related to personality characteristics in adulthood. Erik Erikson employs Freud's framework in his theory of social development, but has placed greater emphasis on society in his identification of several stages of *psychosocial* development.

The ethological approach also involves the search for universal regularities in the behavior of a species. Behavior patterns are considered to have evolved as the result of a Darwinian process of natural selection. A notable example is the "following response" of some birds called *imprinting*, which occurs during a critical period of the organism's life.

The psychoanalytic, ethological, and learning theories of early development all place much emphasis on the attachment relationship between the infant and its mother. *Attachment*, a universal feature of infancy, refers to a reciprocal affectionate relationship that is formed between an infant and another individual. According to psychoanalytic theory, attachment is a manifestation of sexual drives and instincts; the mother, based on her role as nourisher, is the first object of attachment. Ethological theory views attachment behaviors as "wired in" characteristics of the species that originally served to increase the infant's chances of survival. Learning theorists see attachment as a function of mutual reinforcement.

Research studies have shed some light on the nature and process of attachment, but have not yet fully explained its underlying basis. One very important study did contradict the idea that attachment to the mother was based primarily on her role as nourisher; Harlow and Zimmerman (1959) demonstrated that "contact comfort" was a more critical attachment bond between infant monkeys and a mother substitute than was the feeding relationship. Another study, concerning the infant's willingness to leave the mother, found that infants explore the environment more when the mother is nearby than when left with a stranger; the mother apparently provides the infant with a secure base from which to observe the surroundings. Though attention to infant-father attachments is very recent, the evidence is clear that most infants become attached to both parents. Several studies have found no differential preference for one parent over the other.

The most important factor in the development of infant attachments is the quality of the interaction between parent and child. Involvement in the physical care of the infant is not necessary for infant attachment, but the strength of the attachment may be related to the degree of involvement in caretaking. Quantity of time parent and child spend together also has not been found to predict strength of attachment, although a certain amount of interaction is required for attachment to occur.

393

Summary

Few studies have focused on how parents become attached to their infants; it is clear, however, that the process does not occur instantaneously. Some factors seem to be the prenatal attitude of the mother, the amount of contact (vs. separation) at the hospital, and the responsiveness of the infant. For mother monkeys, contact comfort or clinging has been shown to be a necessary factor for attachment.

Animals have been used to experimentally study the effects of social deprivation. For young monkeys reared completely in isolation, fear is the overwhelming response. Although it is much more difficult to study social deprivation in humans, some studies of children suggest that lack of stimulation and the severing of attachments may result in intellectual and social disturbances.

Of all the ways in which people are categorized, probably none is as influential as classification according to gender. How a person is treated by others, expected to perform, assigned tasks, behaves sexually, deals with social and political power, and perceives the self are all powerfully affected by being male or female. Because gender occupies such a central place in human interaction—and perhaps because it is an inherently interesting topic—it has been the focus of a great deal of speculation and research. Today we are seeing particularly heightened interest due, at least in part, to a renewal of social consciousness that includes a concern for the negative impact of classification according to sex.

SEX STEREOTYPES: HOW WE CATEGORIZE MALES AND FEMALES

If each of us were asked to construct a list of what most females and males are like—or how society classifies them—we would have little difficulty in doing so. The widespread, stable, and consensual images that we hold about the sexes are *sex stereotypes* (Tresemer and Pleck, 1974). Studies confirm that even in this time of enormous change sex stereotypes are pervasive.

Broverman and her associates, for example, have examined the stereotypes held by college students and by mental health professionals (Broverman, Broverman, Clarkson, Rosenkrantz, and Vogel, 1970; Broverman, Vogel, Broverman, Clarkson, and Rosenkrantz, 1972). As can be seen in Table 12–1, college students agreed that many attributes differentiate females and males. In addition, male characteristics were often more valued than female ones. Mental health professionals were in basic agreement with this profile: They generally rated the male attributes as indicative of good mental health! A more recent investigation involving seventh-grade, twelfth-grade, and adult subjects has shown that sex stereotypes are commonly held at all of these ages (Urberg and Labouvie-Vief, 1976).

Even kindergarten children show an appreciable knowledge of stereotypes, although the very young child is limited in both the amount of learning that has occurred and in the mental capacity required to abstract behavioral categories. Nevertheless, Williams, Bennett, and Best (1975) translated the items of a previously used adjective check list into stories such as:

"One of these people is emotional. They cry when something good happens as well as when everything goes wrong. Which is the emotional person?" (p. 127)

Children were asked to select the person from a picture of two adults, one clearly a female and the other a male. The sex-stereotype scores of kindergarteners correlated significantly with their scores on a vocabulary IQ test; that is, the brighter children held stronger stereotypes than the less bright ones. Second graders selected more stereotypic responses than did the younger children, and fourth graders performed at about the same level as the second graders. There was also some indication that male stereotypes are learned earlier than female stereotypes.

How do stereotypes function in society? What implications do they have for development? Although stereotypes are actually ascriptions, (that is, as-

TABLE 12-1

Sterotypes of Masculinity and Feminity. The shaded items are more highly valued than their counterparts.

Masculine	Feminine
Very aggressive	Not at all aggressive
Very independent	Not at all independent
Not at all emotional	Very emotional
Almost always hides emotions	Does not hide emotions at all
Very objective	Very subjective
Not at all easily influenced	Very easily influenced
Very dominant	Very submissive
Likes math and science very much	Dislikes math and sicence very much
Not at all excitable in a minor crisis	Very excitable in a minor crisis
Very active	Very passive
Very competitive	Not at all competitive
Very logical	Very illogical
Very worldly	Very home-oriented
Very skilled in business	Not at all skilled in business
Very direct	Very sneaky
Knows the way of the world	Does not know the way of the world
Feelings not easily hurt	Feelings easily hurt
Very adventurous	Not at all adventurous
Can make decisions easily	Has difficulty making decisions
Never cries	Cries very easily
Almost always acts as a leader	Almost never acts as a leader
Very self-confident	Not at all self-confident
Not at all uncomfortable about being aggressive	Very uncomfortable about being aggressive
Very ambitious	Not at all ambitious
Easily able to separate feelings from ideas	Unable to separate feelings from ideas
Not at all dependent	Very dependent
Never conceited about appearance	Very conceited about appearance
Thinks men are always superior to women	Thinks women are always superior to men
Talks freely about sex, with men	Does not talk freely about sex, with men
Uses very harsh language	Doesn't use harsh language at all
Not at all talkative	Very talkative
Very blunt	Very tactful
Very rough	Very gentle
Not at all aware of feelings of others	Very aware of feelings of others
Not at all religious	Very religious
Not at all interested in own appearance	Very interested in own appearance
Very sloppy in habits	Very neat in habits
Very loud	Very quiet
Very little need for security	Very strong need for security
Does not enjoy art and literature at all	Enjoys art and literature
Does not express tender feelings at all easily	Easily expresses tender feelings

Source: From Broverman, Vogel, Broverman, Clarkson, and Rosenkrantz, 1972.

signed attributes), they act as *prescriptions*, norms, and standards. Socialization efforts thus are aimed at developing all members of society in conformance with the stereotypes: Boys are shaped to be active, competitive, and logical whereas girls are taught to be dependent, emotional, and passive. Moreover, as Tresemer and Pleck (1974) have noted, the boundaries between the sexes are kept relatively clear and rigid so that individuals know when they are stepping out of their prescribed sex roles. For the most part, acceptance and affection are given for conformity to sex stereotypes and punishment is forthcoming for overstepping the boundaries of sex roles.

THE EXTENT OF SEX DIFFERENCES

Historically, there has been a great deal of interest in establishing what differences exist between the sexes. With regard to physical characteristics there is considerable agreement. Males are typically larger and stronger than females throughout the life span. They display a more developed musculature, whereas females have a greater proportion of fat tissue. Females also have a lower mortality rate from the moment of conception and are less susceptible to many diseases and dysfunctions (Hetherington, 1970). Subtle sex differences pertaining to the brain are thought to exist—for example, in the hypothalamus (Money and Ehrhardt, 1972). There is little dispute about these assertions, and about the obvious primary and secondary physical manifestations of the reproductive systems. Many of the physical differences are attributed primarily to biological programming. To be sure, girls would run faster and throw with increased dexterity if encouraged to do so, but their body plan might still set limits on these abilities, just as it serves as the basis for their physical flexibility in gymnastics.

The picture is less clear when psychosocial attributes are examined. In 1974 Maccoby and Jacklin wrote an extremely influential book in which they summarized results from approximately fifteen hundred studies relevant to sex differences, for the most part in the young. They concluded that many presumed differences are actually cultural myths with no basis in reality. Table 12–2 lists the eight myths and also what Maccoby and Jacklin consider to be the accurate facts. They also stated that the research findings in the following areas are simply too ambiguous or inadequate to use in making any firm judgments: activity level, fear and anxiety, competitiveness, dominance, compliance, nurturance and "maternal" behavior, and tactile sensitivity. Finally, they recognized established sex differences in only the four areas that are shown in Table 12–3.

Maccoby and Jacklin's conclusion that so few sex differences have been established has not gone unquestioned. Block (1976) noted that their review included some qualitatively weak studies, gave precedence to behavioral over rating measures, and defined behaviors in ways in which other researchers might not. Block pointed out that it thus led to conclusions that might not have been reached had other procedures been adopted. In addition to these general considerations, several investigators have taken issue with specific areas of the Maccoby and Jacklin study. For example, Maccoby and Jacklin induced that there is no clear tendency for girls to be more sensitive and empathic to social cues than boys. This was based on a review of thirty studies, most of which showed no sex differences and the remainder of which were about equally divided as to which sex was more empathic (Hoffman, 1977). But in his own review Hoffman found that females do appear to be more empathic than males. Hoffman suggested that Maccoby and Jacklin's premature conclusion resulted partly from their including studies that did not clearly pertain to empathy.

TABLE 12-2
Mythical Sex Differences; According to Maccoby and Jacklin

Myth	Facts
Girls are more "social" than boys.	FALSE. Research shows that girls are not more dependent on caretakers than boys, nor are they more responsive to social rewards. At some ages, boys actually spend more time than girls with their playmates.
Girls are more "suggestible" than boys.	FALSE. Most studies show no sex differences here, and a few have shown that boys rather than girls are more likely to give in to peer group pressures which contradict their own values.
Girls lack achievement motivation.	FALSE. Under neutral conditions, girls regularly score higher than boys on measures of achievement motivation. When challenged or put in a competitive situation, the achievement motivation of boys is increased, but only to the level girls have already reached.
Girls are more affected by heredity; boys are more responsive to the environment.	FALSE. Male identical twins are actually more alike than female identical twins. Males are more susceptible to certain types of environmental stress than females but they are not more likely than girls to be influenced by positive environmental factors.
Girls have lower self-esteem.	FALSE. The sexes are highly similar in self-satisfaction and self-confidence in childhood and adolescence. Girls have greatest self-confidence in social competence; boys as dominant, "potent" individuals. The little information about adults shows no differences.
Girls are better at rote learning and repetitive tasks, boys at tasks requiring higher-level cognitive processes.	FALSE. No differences have been found on a variety of tasks such as simple conditioning, paired-associates, discrimination learning, reversal shifts.
Boys are more "analytic."	FALSE. No differences exist in cognitive style. Boys do not excel in disembedding tasks except when visual-spatial ability is needed. Neither sex excels in selecting only those elements needed for the task.
Girls are more auditory, boys more visual.	FALSE. Most studies show no differences at any ages in fixation to and discrimination of visual stimuli, distance perception, and other visual tasks.

Source: Adapted from **The Psychology of Sex Differences**, by Eleanor Emmons Maccoby and Carol Nagy Jacklin, 1974, with permission of the publisher, Stanford University Press.

TABLE 12-3
**Areas in Which Sex Differences Are Fairly Well Established
and the Ages When They Are Exhibited**

Area	Age
Girls have greater verbal ability.	Probably begins early in life, is hardly evident from the preschool years to adolescence, becomes increasingly strong after that into adulthood.
Boys excel in visual-spatial ability.	Is not found until adolescence and remains into adulthood.
Boys excel in mathematical ability.	Begins at early adolescence and is found in adulthood.
Boys are more aggressive.	Begins as early as 2 years old and is consistent through the college years. Little information exists about adults.

Source: From Maccoby and Jacklin, 1974.

Overall, then, the question of sex differences seems to be less resolved than previously was the case. To complicate matters, there is increased awareness that much of the research involves ratings by researchers who know the sex of children being rated. If raters have expectations based on sex, the results may indeed be biased. (It was for just this reason that Maccoby and Jacklin emphasized behavioral observation studies; they reasoned that bias would be smaller). In a fascinating study of rater expectations Condry and Condry (1976) exposed college students to a videotape of a nine-month-old child labeled as either a girl, Dana, or a boy, David. The infant was shown responding to a teddy bear, a jack-in-the-box, a doll, and a buzzer. The students were requested to rate whether and how intensely the infant reacted with pleasure, anger, or fear, and the degree of intensity with which the infant responded. At the end of the videotape presentation they also were asked to describe the infant in terms of several attributes such as quiet-loud, aggressive-passive, and ugly-pretty. The results confirmed the hypotheses that perceptions of the infant varied according to whether the infant had been labeled a girl or a boy. Furthermore, sex of the rater, the amount of previous experience the rater had had with infants, and the actual situation displayed on the videotape were related to the outcome.

These findings serve to remind us of the complexities of conducting and evaluating the research. For the present we would have to conclude that differences between the sexes are less than what they once appeared, but perhaps more substantial than indicated by Maccoby and Jacklin.

DETERMINANTS OF SEX DIFFERENCES

To the degree that sex differences exist, to what can they be attributed? In light of many previous discussions on the determinants of behavior, it is not surprising to find that the most popular stance in American psychology today is that the interaction of biological and social factors accounts for sex differences (Birns, 1976). But as Birns has pointed out, while claiming interactionism, most writers actually emphasize one or the other as the major influence.

Biological
Determinants

Virtually no one claims that there is a direct and rigid path from biology to behaviors and attitudes, except when considering obvious physical differences. This was not always the case, however; in the past the biological position was held much more rigidly.

Hamburg (1974) has drawn attention to two important ways in which the biological model was rigid. First, innate behaviors were perceived as unlearned and independent of environmental factors. Reliance was placed on the fixed-action pattern in which a specific response is released by a specific stimulus. Although this phenomenon occurs frequently in the wider biological world, human behavior is today viewed as considerably more plastic and as adapted through learning. A second way in which the biological model was rigid was in its tendency to focus on general characteristics of populations rather than on the individual. Height, for example, is distributed normally, with males generally being taller than females. But the curves overlap and any one female may be taller than any one male. Investigators espousing the biological stance are now more inclined to recognize that individuals at the ends of the distribution range do not disprove the general pattern for the population. Furthermore, environmental factors are seen as heavily contributing to individual variation. Thus, interaction is inherent in the more moderate approach.

The distinguishing issues of the current biological position have been explicated by Bardwick (1979):

> ... if these [sex] differences exist, do they seem to be inborn or related in some way to physiology? That is, are there any physiological tendencies that would lead cultures toward a sexual division of some roles? Are there gender differences that result in different response preferences or thresholds or tendencies? ... This is not to say that individuals of either sex could not learn the sensitivities and behavior more typical of the other. Rather, it means that in the normal course of events more individuals of one sex would, with greater ease, tend to develop characteristics thought to be typical of that sex. (pp. 162, 165)

That the sexes find it easier to develop in one way rather than in another is at least consistent with the fact that around the world similar sex differences are manifested. In his review of hundreds of anthropological descriptions D'Andrade (1966) pointed to the well-known physical differences and to the common patterns in division of labor. Male activities involve action that is strenuous, cooperative, and may require travel, whereas female activities are physically easier, more solitary, and less mobile. Of special interest to our discussion, D'Andrade reported that males were found to be more sexually active, more deferred to, more dominant and aggressive, less nurturant, less responsible, and less emotionally expressive than females. It is possible, of course, that the data—collected by anthropologists of different people in strange cultures—are biased by stereotypes held by the investigators. Nevertheless, it is sometimes argued that the findings have their foundation in innate tendencies that differ for the sexes.

It is clear that biological variables are implicated in many physical differences and behaviors directly related to sexual function, such as copulation and childbearing (e.g., Ward, 1974). But are they important in aggression, for example? There is some evidence suggesting an association between sex hormones and aggression in animals (Maccoby and Jacklin, 1974; Money and Ehrhardt, 1972). When the male hormone, testosterone, is given to female infant rodents, it appears to increase their tendency to fight in adulthood. On the other hand, administration to males of the female hormone, estradiol, reduces adult fighting (Bronson and Desjardin, 1968, and Edwards, 1969, cited by Maccoby and Jacklin, 1974). Higher levels of male hormones have been reported, too, in the more dominant males of a group of monkeys (Rose, Holaday, and Bernstein, 1971, cited in Maccoby and Jacklin, 1974). The substantial literature in this area, despite its complexities, seems to suggest a relationship between subhuman aggression and biological factors; however, generalization to humans may be hazardous. The part played by biological factors in other human interaction is just as unclear.

Of special interest in this regard is the work of Money and Ehrhardt (1972) with hermaphrodites, children born with sex organs of both genders. The investigation followed twenty-five girls born with some masculinization of the external organs that had been corrected surgically. The malformations had occurred because of a genetic dysfunction of the adrenal glands or because the mothers had been prescribed hormones to prevent miscarriages. In all cases a masculinizing influence had operated during prenatal life. Money and Ehrhardt compared the behavioral characteristics and anticipations of these girls with those of normal matched control groups, using questionnaires and conducting interviews with the girls and their mothers. The results are presented in Table 12–4.

The hermaphroditic girls were generally tomboys of high energy who preferred athletic activities, male playmates, and slacks instead of dresses. While the tomboyishness was considered a long-term style, these girls were not strictly opposed to wearing dresses and feminine adornment for special occasions. Nor did they engage in fighting. With regard to maternalism and marriage, they placed less value on both motherhood and marriage, expressing interest in establishing careers. Typically, masculine toys were preferred; there was also lack of interest in infant caretaking. The findings indicated, though, that manifestations of childhood sexuality and of romantic fantasy and anticipations did not differ from those of the controls. (The hermaphroditic girls nonetheless exhibited delayed dating patterns and they reported having their first love affairs later than the controls.)

Money and Ehrhardt attributed the differences they discovered in the prenatally masculinized girls to influences on the fetal brain. They hypothesized that the specific pathways in the brain involved in dominance (or competitive energy expenditure) and maternal behavior may have been masculinized. Brain pathways related to love and eroticism, it was suggested, were not affected, indicating perhaps that the deciding factors in this area of behavior operate postnatally. The biological hypothesis is indeed intriguing. At the same time, one must wonder whether the girls' his-

TABLE 12-4
Differences between Masculinized Girls and Their Normal Controls; + indicates presence of the characteristic significantly more in masculinized girls than in the controls; 0 indicates no significant differences.

Behavioral Signs	Girls masculinized by maternal hormones versus controls	Girls masculinized by genetic dysfunctions of the adrenal glands versus controls
EVIDENCE OF TOMBOYISM		
Known to self and mother as tomboy	+	+
Lack of satisfaction with female sex role	0	+
EXPENDITURE OF ENERGY IN RECREATION AND AGGRESSION		
Athletic interests and skills	+	+
Preference of male versus female playmates	+	+
Behavior in childhood fights	0	0
PREFERRED CLOTHING AND ADORNMENT		
Clothing preference, slacks versus dresses	+	+
Lacking interest in jewelry, perfume and hair styling	0	0
MATERNALISM		
Toy cars, guns, etc. preferred to dolls	+	+
Lack of juvenile interest in infant care-taking	0	+
No daydreams or fantasies of pregnancy and motherhood	0	+
MARRIAGE		
Wedding and marriage not anticipated in play and daydreams	0	+
Priority of career versus Marriage	+	+
ROMANCE		
Lack of heterosexual romanticism in juvenile play and daydreams	0	0
Lack of adolescent (age 13–16) daydreams of boyfriend and lack of dating relationships	0	0
Lack of homosexual fantasies reported	0	0
EVIDENCE OF CHILDHOOD SEXUALITY		
Attention to genital morphology	0	0
Masturbation 0	0	
Shared genital inspection and play	0	0
Shared copulation play	0	0

Source: From Money and Ehrhardt, 1972, pp. 106–108. © 1972, The Johns Hopkins University Press.

tories influenced the girls themselves or their parents in ways that might account for the results. Perhaps the parents of the hermaphrodites treated them differently in relevant ways. One might guess, however, that such treatment would be in the direction of strengthening the stereotypes of feminine attributes. But expectations and suppositions show up in unexpected ways. Could the interview and questionnaire data have been affected by these factors for either the hermaphrodites or the normal girls? We do not know the answer to these questions, but the study remains a fascinating attempt to discover biological determinants of sex differences.

We know that there is considerable overlap between males and females on all the behaviors and abilities that we have discussed. Many women have become accomplished mathematicians, whereas men have frequently excelled in drama, oratory, and serious fiction—all of which involve high levels of verbal ability. While such overlap may reflect a range of biological capacities, it no doubt also indicates socialization influences, the impact of which is seen in cross-cultural investigations.

Consider, for example, a report of three tribes that differed among themselves on the expression of aggression by the sexes. The study, reported years ago by Margaret Mead (1935), revealed that all combinations of sex-role aggression are possible. The Arapesh, one of the tribes studied by Mead, expect both males and females to behave in ways that would be considered passive and feminine in Western cultures—both sexes are taught to be cooperative and responsive to the needs of others. Among the Mundugumor, in contrast, members of both sexes are expected to act in a way that would be considered almost a stereotype of masculinity by our standards—both men and women are expected to be ruthless and aggressive, and to be unresponsive emotionally in their relationships with others. The third tribe described by Mead, the Tchambuli, shows a pattern of sex-role expectations that is directly opposite to that familiar in Western European and Anglo-Saxon countries—the women are expected to be aggressive and dominant, while their male counterparts are passive and emotionally dependent.

Socialization efforts obviously require time so that we may expect that the very early appearance of specific behaviors lends support to the influence of biological factors. Therefore the time in one's life span when sex differences show up is important in determining biological and environmental influences. Few studies of neonates and infants have demonstrated any sex differences (Birns, 1976). There are exceptions. In a well-controlled investigation, Phillips, King, and DuBois (1978) observed the activity of neonates during the first two days of life, finding higher levels of wakefulness, facial grimacing, and low-intensity motor activity for males. Moss (1967) showed that at three weeks and again at three months, boys cried more and slept less than girls. But according to Birns neither the presence nor the absence of early sex differences is firmly established. She concluded that it is during the years from two to five that the differences emerge. Thus, sufficient time has lapsed for a good deal of socialization to have occurred. Few, if any, doubt that at least to some extent sex differences are learned. But Birns has nicely captured the essence of the environmental position:

> At this time it seems evident that the environment in which all American children mature clearly projects sex-role stereotypes. These stereotypic expectations and the differential responses they elicit are sufficiently clear and unambiguous to account for the cognitive and personality differences in children that ultimately lead to the different roles that they fulfill. (1976, p. 251)

HOW SEX ROLE AND SEX IDENTITY DEVELOPS

So far in our discussion we have primarily emphasized observable behaviors that are basically indicative of sex roles. It is important that we make the distinction between *sex role* and *sex identity*.

Sex (or gender) identity refers to a self-awareness of being of one sex or the other. It is the internal experience, to a greater or lesser extent, that one is a male or female.

Sex (or gender) role is the behaviors and roles that society prescribes for the sexes. The processes of acquiring a sex role is sometimes called *sex typing*.

These concepts cannot always be tidily isolated. Sex typing may depend upon establishing a sex identity, or sex identity may rest partly on adopting sex-role behaviors. Nevertheless, it is helpful to keep the distinction in mind because developmental theories sometimes focus on one or the other.

Developmental views have been offered by virtually all of the life and social sciences and by diverse approaches within each discipline. In psychology three theories presently vie for leadership in explaining how sex identity and sex roles develop. It is not surprising to find that Freud's psychoanalytic view led the way and that his work is still influential. But serious challenges come from social-learning and cognitive-developmental theorists. Each of these three perspectives will be presented in turn. We begin, though, with the work of Money and Ehrhardt (1972), who presented a more comprehensive model, one that integrates biological and social-psychological factors.

Money and Ehrhardt's Model of Gender-identity Development

These investigators liken their model to a relay race in which gender is initiated by the sex chromosomes that are transmitted from the parents and carried along the developmental path by various biological and psychosocial variables. As we can see in Figure 12–1, the XX or XY chromosome pair acts on the indifferentiated fetal gonad (sex organ) so that either ovaries or testes develop. If the gonads are fated to be testes, differentiation begins after the sixth week of gestation; differentiation of the ovaries would commence several weeks later. Direct chromosomal influence ends at that point. Next, the gonads begin to secrete hormones that act in two ways: They differentiate the reproductive systems and institute sexual differences in the nervous system. The latter, although not well understood, include the development of different nerve pathways from the reproductive system to the central nervous system and differential functioning of the hypothalamus of the brain that influence sexual cycles and mating behavior.

According to Money and Ehrhardt, these are the major turning points in prenatal development of gender. At this stage the burden of growth rests with both genital differences (that is, the female or male reproductive systems) and nervous system differences. The factors that come immediately into play are the reactions of other people to the child's sex and the child's own response to its body. Childhood gender identity develops from these variables and the interplay of the nervous system.

At puberty changes in hormonal functioning bring about growth of the reproductive system, development of the secondary sexual characteristics, and increased sexual impulses. Adult gender identity is forged from these, from differential nervous system functioning, and from the juvenile identity that the person already possesses.

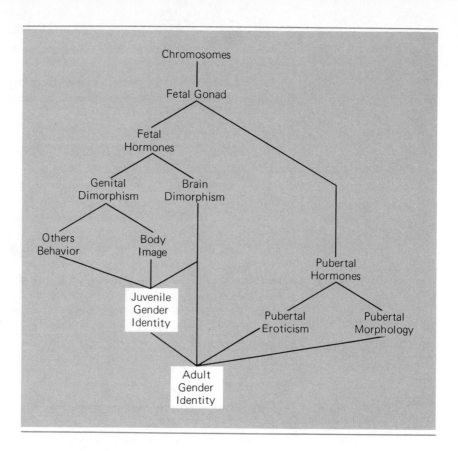

FIGURE 12-1
The major steps in the relay model of gender identity formation by Money and Erhardt.
Adapted from Money and Erhardt, © 1972, The John Hopkins University Press.

Although it seems that the process of gender identity development as described here is long and biologically complex, it should be noted that Money and Ehrhardt believe that basic sex identity is formed during the first two to four years of life and is very much dependent upon psychosocial variables. They have reached this conclusion from their previously mentioned studies of hermaphroditic children. Because these children come into the world with external sex organs that do not match their chromosomes and/or internal sex organs, they are sometimes mislabeled "boy" or "girl" and subsequently reared as such. They develop a healthy gender identity concordant with their *labeling*, providing that they are treated consistently like one sex or the other from early in life. Thus, if a chromosomal girl born with male organs is labeled and reared as a boy, the child will identify as a boy. Even more intriguing, if gender must be reassigned—due, for example, to late decisions about surgical treatment of the sex organs—the child seems to be able to accept the reassignment if it occurs during the first few years of life. As time passes, so does the child's chance of adjusting normally. These cases are dramatic examples of the power of the environment to influence sex identity and sex-role behavior.

Freud first presented his perspective of gender or psychosexual development in the 1905 edition of *Three Essays on the Theory of Sexuality.* In previous sections we have outlined the processes fundamental to this view (see chapters 10 and 11). Briefly, children solve the conflict they experience over their desire for their opposite-sexed parents by identifying with their same-sexed parents, thereby taking for themselves the behaviors, attitudes, and values of the same-sexed parents. Freud initially postulated that the male child was drawn toward his mother, the female child toward her father. However, from the beginning he recognized a problem in this formulation: If *both* sexes develop a libidinal attachment to the mother during the oral and anal stages, what accounts for the transference of the female's attachment to her father? In later years Freud attempted to deal with this theoretical dilemma by postulating penis envy in females; in doing so he ignited controversy and criticism both within and outside of the psychoanalytic circle (Stewart, 1976). Of females he said:

> They notice the penis of a brother or playmate, strikingly visible and of large proportions, at once recognize it as the superior counterpart of their own small and inconspicuous organ [the clitoris], and from that time forward fall a victim to envy for the penis. . . . [The young girl] makes her judgement and her decision in a flash. She has seen it and knows that she is without it and wants to have it. (Freud, 1925, in Stewart, 1976, pp. 49–50.)

According to Freud, penis envy has several far-reaching consequences. If the child does not accept her shortcomings and relinquish hopes of obtaining a penis at some later time she may experience psychological upset and develop masculine traits; at the very least, she may feel a sense of inferiority. Furthermore, the discovery of the inferiority of the clitoris leads the female to give up the clitoris as the organ of pleasure, replacing it eventually with vaginal orgasm. Because the mother is held responsible for the child's lack, maternal attachment weakens. One more step completes the development of the girl into a woman: In some unknown way the wish for a penis is substituted by the wish for a child. This leads to identifying the father as a love object and feelings of jealousy toward the mother. The child now must deal with this Electra conflict, which she does by internalizing her mother's behavior.

One important side effect of Freud's explanations relates to the growth of the superego. (Recall that according to psychoanalytic theory the superego is born out of the resolution of the Oedipal or Electra conflict.) Freud believed this process to be powerful and dramatic in boys because it is motivated by fear of castration. Because the castration complex is lacking in girls, motivation to resolve the conflict is weaker and it may not be well resolved. This, in turn, presumably results in a relatively weaker superego in women.

Social Learning
Theory

Notable among those who have analyzed the development of sex roles from a social learning perspective are Walter Mischel (1966, 1970) and Albert Bandura (1969, 1977). According to both theorists the same learning principles involved in the socialization of other behaviors can be applied to sex-role development. And, typical of this view, the process is seen as accumulative even though the early years may be of greater importance. Bandura has described the early and on-going socialization process in this way:

> Sex-role differentiation usually commences immediately after birth when the baby is named and both the infant and the nursery are given the blue or pink treatment depending upon the sex of the child. Thereafter, indoctrination into masculinity and femininity is diligently promulgated by adorning children with distinctive clothes and hair styles, selecting sex-appropriate play materials and recreational activities, promoting associations with same-sex playmates, and through nonpermissive parental reactions to deviant sex-role behavior (1969, p. 215).

The social learning view emphasizes rewards, punishment, and observational learning for the acquisition of sex roles. It is assumed that parents and others shape appropriate sex-role behaviors in children. In short, girls are taught to be submissive, emotional, and neat, whereas boys are encouraged to be aggressive, independent, and achievement oriented.

The claim that sex roles are heavily influenced by social learning seems beyond question. A growing literature is now beginning to supply researchers with strong evidence that parents treat infants differentially according to sex (Birns, 1976; Lewis and Weinraub, 1974; Moss, 1967; Raskin, 1979).

It is generally believed that observational learning is at least as important as reinforcement contingencies in shaping sex-role behaviors. Children are constantly being exposed to sex-appropriate models—parents and other

FIGURE 12–2
Sex-role learning is reinforced and encouraged both directly and in subtle ways. © Alice Kandell, Photo Researchers, Inc.

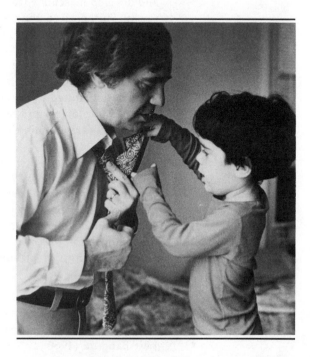

adults, peers, and symbolic models presented in literature, drama, and on television. Cognitive factors are seen as mediating observational learning, with the child absorbing the overall situation (behaviors being exhibited, the consequences that the model experiences, and model characteristics such as nurturance, power, and similarity).

Cognitive-developmental Theory

While the psychoanalytic view rests on emotional confict and the social-learning perspective emphasizes learning experiences provided by agents of socialization, the cognitive-development approach focuses on the child's construction of the concept of sex identity. This analysis, based on Piaget's work, has been most explicitly set forth by Kohlberg (1966; Kohlberg and Ullian, 1974).

Kohlberg outlines the construction of sex identity according to the Piagetian form that is followed for any other concept. It is an especially critical concept, though, because it is one of the few fixed categories into which all people can be placed and is therefore a universal factor of organization. Particular interest has been paid to the formation of one's basic sex identity, which occurs by the age of six. The overall process is thought to occur in three steps (Slaby and Frey, 1975).

1. *Gender identity.* The child recognizes that he or she is either male or female.
2. *Gender stability.* The child recognizes that boys invariably become men and girls become women.
3. *Gender consistency.* The child recognizes that the attribute of being either female or male will not change with changing situations and personal motivations.

By at least age three the child can accurately label itself and can label the gender of others with some correctness (Kohlberg and Ullian, 1974). By four years of age partial awareness exists regarding the fact that gender cannot change. It is not until about age six, however, that a firm concept of sex identity is established, based primarily on physical differences of the sexes. This progression follows the more general pattern of cognitive development, and the constancy of gender may be a special case of object constancy, as discussed in chapter 7. The permanence of gender is not unlike the more general process of recognizing the conservation of properties in the physical universe, and, in fact, children's ability to recognize gender across situations has been shown to be related to their mastery of the concept of conservation (DeVries, 1974). Once basic gender identity has been established, the child actively seeks to shape his or her behavior to match sex identity.

It has been hypothesized by Kohlberg and Ullian (1974) that the structure of the concept of sex identity changes as cognitive development proceeds. At first based on physical differences between the sexes, understanding next rests on social functions. For example, in providing reasons why he thought that men are smarter than women, a fifth-grader implied

FIGURE 12-3
Once basic gender
identity has been
established, the child
actively seeks to
shape his or her
behavior to match sex
identity.   Rita Freed,
Nancy Palmer Photo
Agency.

that it is because men are given the role to work, think a lot, and figure things out. Furthermore, it is thought that although people are not compelled to adhere to specific functions and roles, it is better if they do. Beginning at least in adolescence, sex roles become increasingly freed from prescription; individuals are given more choice of behaviors and are able to break from the stereotypes. By college age the concept includes personal values that provide alternatives to the sex stereotypes.

In examining this formulation it should be noted that stereotypes are always present but that the mode of thinking about them changes. For example, softness and gentleness are always prescribed for women; the reasons change, though. At first it is just because their skin is soft; then it is because of familial and social expectations; and finally these characteristics are assigned to females because they are generally positive attributes. It is these cognitive transformations, viewed as relatively independent of cultural training and reward, that are of interest to cognitive-developmentalists.

Evaluation of Theories and Models

The Money and Ehrhardt model of sex-identity formation is the most comprehensive of the models discussed here. It offers a broad integration of biological and psychosocial variables operating into adulthood. The other perspectives provide finer analyses of psychological factors.

Several aspects of Freud's theory have been criticized. As we have already seen (p. 322), the claimed universality of the Oedipal conflict is doubtful. Concerning female development, the idea of penis envy has been unacceptable to many, and the assumption that the vagina becomes dominant over the clitoris as an organ of sexual pleasure for the female has been refuted. With regard to the weakness of the female superego, there is no empirical evidence to substantiate any sex differences in moral development (Liebert, 1979). Finally, the central concept of identification has been seriously questioned. According to Freud, identification is an emotional tie based on the need to be loved (anaclitic identification) or on the fear of one's parents (aggressive identification). It is this psychological mechanism that brings about introjection of the characteristics and behaviors of the same-sexed parent. Social learning theorists, in particular, have challenged this conceptualization, arguing that identification can be more simply construed as imitation of the same-sexed parent (Bandura, 1969). Overall, the question raised about Freud's formulation certainly cast serious doubt on the validity of many of his claims.

Although social learning and cognitive-developmental theories have very different emphases, each makes a contribution to the understanding of sex-role and sex-identity formation. The social-learning perspective appears to be the more intuitively obvious, but the cognitive-developmental view garners much attention today, regardless of the fact that comparatively little research has been done on it. This is probably due to the generally high interest about cognition that characterizes present-day psychology. Whether Kohlberg's analysis itself will stand the test of time and research remains to be seen.

CHANGES IN SEX ROLES

In spite of the fact that stereotypes are still well recognized, the United States is witnessing important changes in traditional sex roles. One of the most obvious is the continued movement of women into work outside of the home. Along with this transition have come advocacy and pressure for change regarding the social and emotional behavior of both females and males.

As we have seen in Table 12–1, masculinity and femininity have usually been conceived as complete opposites. A person possessing many of the male attributes is considered highly masculine; an individual possessing many of the female attributes is considered highly feminine. Actually, though, people display a mix of characteristics. It is possible to be passive in some situations and aggressive in others; cold in one instance while reacting warmly in another; and dependent one minute and yet independent the next. Furthermore, being able to exhibit a wide variety of behaviors may prove to be beneficial. One ought to profit by being both instrumental and expressive, yielding and assertive, emotional and logical. The term *androgyny* refers to the possession of both masculine and feminine behaviors (Bem, 1974, 1977; Block, 1973; Kaplan and Bean, 1976). In some ways it is an unfortunate term because it implies that characteristics are inherently masculine or feminine. In our opinion, there is little evidence for this. Therefore, we interpret androgyny as referring to the possession of attributes that are stereotypically assigned to one sex or the other. In recent years the hypothesis that androgynous individuals are particularly well adjusted has been supported by research. For example, androgynous college students and adults have been found to have high self-esteem (Spence, Helmreich, and Stapp, 1975; O'Connor, Mann, and Bardwick, 1978).

When we speak of transcending sex roles today, it frequently means that women should be given the opportunity to be more like men, both in occupational roles and in psychosocial behavior. What seems more appropriate, however, is a shift in the value traditionally placed on both masculine and feminine roles. This is exactly what advocates of androgyny seek to do. As one such supporter has explained it:

> It is not just the traditional female role which has disadvantages. Sociologists remind us that, according to statistics, men have a higher criminal record, more stress and illness due to strenuous work, higher suicide rates, and, as a rule, die at an earlier age than women. In school it is the boys who have the greater adaption problems. Men who are divorced and living alone have greater difficulties managing than do divorced women. The interpretation is that the social pressures on the man to assert himself, to fight his way in life, to be aggressive, and not to show any feelings create contact difficulties and adaption difficulties. Sociologists consider that one should not speak of "the problems of woman's role in society" but of "the sex-role problem," in order to emphasize that the problem also concerns traditional male role. (Palme, 1972, p. 241)

Despite the restrictions that rigid sex roles place on individuals, there is strong resistance to disregarding sex boundaries. Social transitions are stressful at best because the social fabric of life comes undone, often with few or no alternative frameworks. And so it is not surprising to see, for example, that although college men are more accepting of the intellectual capabilities and achievement of young women, they have ambiguous feelings about their potential wives relinquishing child and home care (Komarovsky, 1973). Because sex roles are so strongly transmitted culturally, change can be threatening to the concept of the self; that is, it may threaten sex identity. Perhaps the most extreme concern is that a loosening of sex roles will foster changes in sexual behavior itself. Although a time of transition may be stressful, it is highly unlikely that allowing greater overlap between the sexes with regard to occupation and social behavior will bring about such consequences. In this regard, Money and Ehrhardt (1972) have made the distinction between "procreative imperatives"—those tied to impregnation, menstruation, gestation—and the many options for behavior that are peripheral to these functions. They note that children develop a secure sex identity when there are clear cultural signals about procreative imperatives, no matter what the signals are concerning peripheral options.

SUMMARY

Categorization according to gender has a powerful influence on development throughout the life span. Even today stereotypes of sex roles abound and act as prescriptions for socialization. The two questions most frequently asked with regard to sex roles concern (1) the extent of sex differences and (2) the origins of such differences. The sexes show some differences in body size, strength, and susceptibility to disease. Females demonstrate superior verbal ability, whereas males are superior in visual-spatial and mathematical abilities. Aggression is more prevalent in males in many cultures. In their extensive review, Maccoby and Jacklin (1974) claim that no other sex differences have been firmly established. The research issues and findings are complex, though, and some investigators disagree with Maccoby and Jacklin.

Researchers who emphasize biological determinants of sex roles argue that biological influences facilitate one sex developing certain characteristics more easily than the other sex. As support for their position they point to the similarity of sex roles across cultures and the experimental studies of hormonal influence on aggression in animals. Money and Ehrhardt (1972) acknowledge some influence of biological factors on the social development of hermaphroditic girls, although they believe psychosocial influence during the first few years of life is very strong. Researchers who espouse the environmental viewpoint of sex-role development note the variability of sex roles across cultures and the obvious socialization efforts by parents, teachers, and the like.

In examining developmental theories, it is necessary to distinguish between *sex role* (the behaviors and roles assigned the sexes) and *sex identity* (self-awareness of being one sex or the other). Money and Ehrhardt's model of sex identity development is one of the most comprehensive, taking both biological and psychosocial influences into consideration. The psychoanalytic, social learning, and cognitive-developmental views are the dominant psychological theories today. Although each makes a contribution, no one theory completely explains the development of sex role and sex identity.

13

Self-Control and Achievement

Childhood behavior is controlled to a large extent by immediate external constraints: the expectations of others, parental rewards and punishments, and peer pressures, to name a few. Sometimes, however, children behave "appropriately" with seemingly little influence from extrinsic sources. They may, for example, continue to obey rules that have been enforced previously by parents; they may decide, even when alone, to ignore the gratification of immediate rewards in favor of long-range goals; they may impose relatively high achievement standards on themselves; or they may "do the right thing" by others when faced with a moral dilemma.

In this chapter we discuss two closely related aspects of the child's development of a personal value system: self-control and achievement strivings. Each of these areas involves a self-imposed standard of some sort, and each involves and is influenced by the basic processes of learning and cognitive development with which you are by now quite familiar.

SELF-CONTROL

We say that a person is showing *self-control* whenever he or she rises above the immediate pressures of the situation or avoids succumbing to an immediate impulse. Much has been written about self-control, by philosophers and theologians as well as by psychologists. The following discussion investigates the work of research-oriented psychologists who have studied two related aspects of self-control that begin to emerge in childhood: the ability to "resist temptation" and the ability to tolerate "delay of gratification." It will become evident that these behaviors are closely associated with the once popular notion of "will power."

Resistance to Temptation

In its broad definition, *resistance to temptation* refers to refraining from the opportunity to engage in a socially prohibited but otherwise tempting act, such as cheating on a difficult exam or stealing someone else's property. The idea of resistance to temptation differs from other related forms of self-control in that the emphasis is on whether the individual will adhere to or deviate from an established rule. For this reason, the term *resistance to deviation* is preferred by some writers.

In the laboratory, resistance to temptation has been studied mostly in situations that provide the subject with a private opportunity to cheat on a game or to engage in an explicitly forbidden act (i.e., to deviate from the norm of honesty or break a stated rule). Those who deviate are compared in a variety of ways with those who do not deviate.

Discipline and Resistance to Temptation. In a classic study, Burton, Maccoby, and Allinsmith (1961) measured the tendency of four-year-olds, both boys and girls, to resist the temptation to break a rule in light of the child-rearing methods reported by their mothers. To determine the kinds of discipline to which each child had been exposed, the child's mother was interviewed intensively for about two hours. To assess tendencies to violate or adhere to a stated rule, each child was introduced to a beanbag game, told

FIGURE 13-1
An important aspect of self-control is learning to resist temptation. Mimi Forsyth, Monkmeyer.

the rules clearly, and left to play the game alone. The object of the game, as explained to each child, was to hit a wire stretched behind a board on which five lights were displayed in a row. Hitting the wire, it was explained, would turn one of the lights on, and each time this happened a bell would ring, signaling success. Players were to throw each of five bags over the board while standing behind a foot marker approximately five feet from the board; crossing the marker so as to be closer to the target would be a direct violation of the rules of the game in this situation. Before actually playing alone, each child was asked to select from an attractive array the toy he or she would like to win by getting "enough lights to win a prize."

Actually, the game was completely controlled by a hidden experimenter who not only made sure that everyone received the same score but also monitored and recorded each child's behavior. (Controlling the scores in this way was necessary so that the temptation to cheat would not be related to possible differences in the children's throwing ability.) Also built into the situation was a special incentive to cheat; although only one light could be earned honestly, additional ones might be sought by stepping forward, moving the foot marker, retrieving bags incorrectly, and hitting the wire with the hand. After three minutes the experimenter returned to supervise another round of playing for which a prize was awarded. This was done to check whether the children understood the rules, and to soothe feelings of failure among noncheaters and possible guilt among those who did cheat.

Although the interviews disclosed information about many child-rearing variables, we will confine our discussion to those that involve discipline.

Physical vs. psychological punishment during the preschool years. The most interesting finding reported by Burton and his associates was that some mothers generally favored *physical* forms of discipline (slapping, spanking, shaking, and scolding), whereas others favored more *psychological* techniques (reasoning, withdrawal of love, portrayal of suffering by the parent, and so on). The distinction proved to be quite valuable because of its relationship to actual resistance to temptation in the laboratory test situation. Specifically, children of mothers who preferred physical discipline were less likely to deviate from the rules of the beanbag game and therefore showed more self-control than children of mothers who preferred other methods.

The Burton findings suggest that physical modes of training may be more effective than "psychological" discipline when a child is young and unable to comprehend parental reasoning or subtle changes in parental mien. (Recall that these children were only four years old at the time of testing.) With the intellectual sophistication that evolves as the child develops, however, psychological techniques become more effective. In fact, several studies, correlational and experimental, indicate that reasoning and explanation play a very important role in the development of self-control among older children (Aronfreed, 1968; Hoffman, 1975; Leizer and Rogers, 1974). Let us see how these psychological processes operate.

Combining reasoning and punishment. Parents often provide prohibitions for their children that are specific to the situation at hand—for example, "Don't play with your father's sunglasses because if you were to drop them they might break." Such directives, it is thought, help children evaluate their own behavior by explaining exactly *what* activity should be avoided and *why.* To see whether this is in fact the case, Cheyne (1969) conducted an experiment with kindergarten and third-grade boys and girls to explore the effects of a combination of verbal punishment with explicit verbal directives. The children were assigned to one of three conditions:

1. Under the *punishment only* condition, children were told "That's bad" when they selected a certain toy to play with;

2. Under the *punishment plus simple rule* condition, children were told "That's bad. You should not play with that toy" when they selected a certain toy;

3. And under the *punishment plus elaborated rule* condition, children were told "That's bad. You should not play with that toy. That toy belongs to someone else."

Subsequently, when the children were left alone with the forbidden toy, those who had received the most information (those in the *punishment plus elaborated rule* condition) resisted touching and playing with it most often and for the longest periods of time. The amount of time that passed before children touched the toy is shown in Figure 13–2, which also indicates that the elaborated rule was more effective for the older children. This figure additionally suggests that the older children deviated more quickly than the younger ones when behavioral rules were presented without justification, a finding that may indicate that those old enough to benefit from a complete explanation resent not receiving one.

FIGURE 13-2
Amount of time (latency) before first deviation for kindergarten and third-grade boys and girls under various levels of rule structure in Cheyne's experiment. From J. A. Cheyne, "Punishment and Self-Control," paper presented at the R. H. Walters Memorial Symposium at the biennial meeting of the Society for Research in Child Development in 1969.

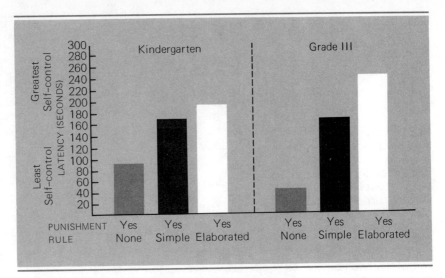

Reasoning vs. verbal reproach. In Cheyne's study various levels of reasoning or explanation were added to the basic punishment experience, and, as expected, these additions increased the punishment's effectiveness. We may still wonder, though, whether resistance to deviation can be taught to older children through reasoning alone, without having to resort to even a small amount of punishment or verbal reproach. One study at least has suggested that this procedure may be effective.

Leizer and Rogers (1974) taught a group of sixty first- and second-grade boys that they were not permitted to play with particular toys, either through verbal punishment ("No! That's wrong. You must not pick that toy") or through moral reasoning (e.g., by explaining that some of the toys were only for older boys). After this training, the experimenter left each child in a room with many toys, and through a one-way mirror observed how quickly the forbidden toy was touched (latency), how often it was touched (frequency), the length of time it was touched (duration), and whether the forbidden or the nonforbidden toy was touched first. On all four measures, resistance to deviation was stronger in the reasoning conditions compared with the verbal reproach condition. Figure 13-3 shows the results for duration of touching the forbidden toy; children in the reasoning conditions spent significantly less time touching the forbidden toy than did those in the verbal reproach condition.* The overall effect was still evident fifteen days later.

Self-instruction and resistance to temptation. We have seen that reasoning and other forms of meaningful verbal instruction can greatly increase children's resistance to temptation. In the past decade many researchers have sought to take the process of verbal instruction a step further by teaching children to provide their own verbal instructions and reminders as they face tempting situations (Hartig and Kanfer, 1973; Meichenbaum and Goodman,

*Leizer and Rogers actually used two moral reasoning conditions, one of which also had a "cognitive" component designed to call particular attention to the forbidden toy. This additional element was apparently not required, and it contributed little to the overall results.

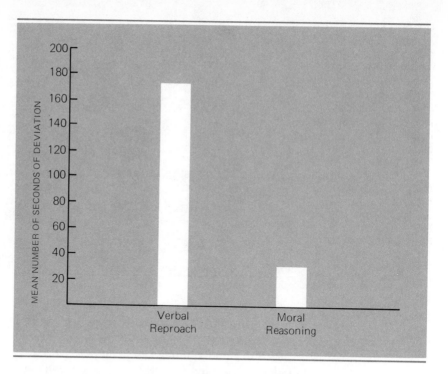

FIGURE 13-3
Mean number of seconds in which first- and second-grade boys in Leizer and Rogers's experiment played with a forbidden toy when alone, as a result of training through either verbal reproach or moral reasoning. Moral reasoning was clearly the superior approach. Data courtesy of Dr. Ronald W. Rogers.

1971). For example, Hartig and Kanfer (1973) asked kindergarten and first-grade boys and girls to participate in a study supposedly dealing with children's evaluations of soon-to-be-marketed toys. Posing as the representative of a toy store, the female experimenter in this study told each child that he or she was to play a surprise game that required entering a room adjacent to the classroom, blindfolded; the blindfold was only to be removed after the child had been seated in the surprise room with his or her back to some enticing new toys. After seating and unblindfolding each child, the experimenter then suddenly announced that she had "forgotten" her paper and pencil in the classroom and that she needed them before she could continue with the game. Before leaving though, she told each child that it "would be bad" and "spoil the surprise" to turn around before she returned. At this point, according to the treatment group to which they had been randomly assigned, the children received one of five further sets of instruction.

In the *verbalization positive* group the children were asked to say to themselves aloud: "I must not turn around and look at the toy. If I do not look at the toy, I will be a *good* [boy, girl]." In the *verbalization negative* group, each child was told to say: "I must not turn around and look at the toy. If I look at the toy I will be a *bad* [boy, girl]." In the third self-instruction condition (*simple verbalization*), children were told to say only the basic self-instruction, i.e., "I must not turn around and look at the toy."

The remaining two groups served as controls. In the *verbalization control* group, the children were asked to recite the nursery rhyme, "Hickory Dickory Dock, the Mouse Ran up The Clock," whereas in the *no verbalization* control condition no instructions to verbalize in the experimenter's absence were given.

The major dependent variable in the Hartig and Kanfer study was the elapsed time (or, more technically, the latency) between the experimenter's departure and the moment the child first turned around to look at the toy. The results were as follows:

1. Children in the three self-instruction groups waited significantly longer than those in the control groups before turning around to look at the toy. This finding shows that the experimenter's request to use relevant self-instruction did effectively increase resistance to temptation.

2. The children in the positive verbalization and negative verbalization groups displayed no more self-control than those in the simple verbalization group, showing that including judgmental labels in self-instruction added nothing to its effectiveness.

3. Although children in the self-instruction condition showed more self-control regardless of whether they verbalized aloud as requested or not, verbalizers in each of the three self-instruction groups showed significantly greater resistance to temptation than those who had been asked to self-instruct themselves but who failed to do so overtly.

4. Overall, younger children (forty to sixty-five months) showed less resistance to temptation than older children (sixty-six to eighty-eight months). Follow-up analysis revealed, however, that the age difference was due to the older children's greater willingness to use the self-instructions that had been provided. Older children made significantly more use of self-instruction than younger children, but the younger children who did verbalize as requested displayed just as much resistance to temptation as the older children in the corresponding treatment conditions.

5. Among those who transgressed by turning to look at the toy before the experimenter returned (174 of the 275 children in the study transgressed sooner or later during the ten minutes the experimenter was gone), over 90 percent flatly denied that they had looked at the toy when questioned later.

6. There were no sex differences on any of the measures.

Situational Factors Influencing Resistance to Temptation. So far we have emphasized aspects of the socializing agent's behavior (such as the use of physical punishment, reasoning, and verbal reproach) as determinants of resistance to temptation. Plainly, however, other factors are also relevant to whether a child will cheat or break a rule in a given situation. For example, it has been shown repeatedly that exposure to rule-breaking peer models can dramatically increase the frequency of rule-breaking by children and adults (Ross, 1971; Liebert, 1979).

Models can also be used to administer vicarious consequences.* In a study conducted by Walters, Leat, and Mezei (1963) four- and five-year-old boys were told not to play with the attractive toys in the room in which they were left alone for fifteen minutes—the boys were told to look at a scholarly

*Recall our discussion of vicarious consequences in chapter 6.

dictionary instead! Then each boy was shown either a movie in which another boy was rewarded for rule-breaking, a movie in which another boy was severely punished for rule-breaking, or no movie at all. In contrast to many breaches of the rule by boys in the other two groups, the boys who saw the punished model exhibited no disobedience at all, even when highly attractive toys were left to tempt them.

There are, however, limitations to controlling rule deviations by modeling vicarious consequences. One is that vicarious consequences seem to have inhibiting and disinhibiting effects only when the model and the observing child are of the same sex; Slaby and Parke (1971) replicated the experiment by Walters and his colleagues with both boys and girls. The results confirmed the earlier results for boys, but girls deviated just as often after seeing a boy punished for such a deviation than after seeing him rewarded for it. Perhaps the girls thought, "Well, he's a boy. They wouldn't punish me."

Resistance to Temptation and the Child's Emotional State. Most studies of resistance to temptation have focused on rewards and punishments and/or on general information relating to the topic. An additional factor has also been shown to influence resistance to temptation: the child's immediate emotional state. In a clear demonstration, Fry (1975) assigned seven- and eight-year-old boys and girls to one of three conditions, which varied in the mood they created. Children in the positive affect (or "think happy") group were induced to think about happy and pleasurable events; children in the negative affect ("think sad") group were induced to think about things that made them sad; and children in the neutral affect group were asked to assemble a very simple jigsaw puzzle, and thus interacted with an adult but presumably experienced little or no mood change as a result of the contact. Subsequently, each child was placed in a resistance to temptation situation similar to the ones we described previously, and measures of the latency, frequency, and duration of deviations were obtained. Induction of a positive mood state increased resistance to temptation on all three measures (see Figure 13–4 for frequency), whereas induction of a negative mood sharply decreased resistance to temptation, i.e., increased the number of rule deviations. As Fry notes, a major implication of this experiment is that children may be taught to control their own mood states in various situations, which, in turn, may help them to maintain self-control in a variety of tempting circumstances. In addition, of course, the results also suggest that children may be less able to follow rules or control themselves when they are sad, depressed, or simply in a bad mood.

Objective Self-awareness and Resistance to Temptation. Psychologists have found that increasing people's awareness of their own behavior, *objective self-awareness,* can substantially increase many forms of self-control in both children and adults (Kanfer, 1970; Wicklund, 1975). Such objective self-awareness may be indirectly fostered by many of the socialization practices we have already discussed; for example, punishing a child for a rule

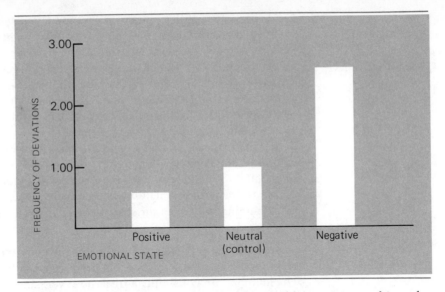

FIGURE 13–4
Frequency of
deviations exhibited
in Fry's (1975)
experiment as a
function of whether a
positive or negative
mood had been
induced. From data
in Fry (1975).

violation may have the effect of calling the child's attention to his or her own behavior. However, the most direct way to increase objective self-awareness is to hold a mirror up to the person's behavior. Investigators have found some intriguing ways to do just that.

A recent field experiment (Beaman, Klentz, Diener, and Svanum, 1980) illustrates how a simple tactic to increase self-awareness can increase resistance to temptation in a naturalistic situation. Beaman and his associates conducted their study on Halloween, 1978. The participants were children who came to trick or treat at thirteen homes that had been specially arranged to accommodate the investigation. Each home had been selected and arranged so that inside a room near the front door there was a large bowl filled with wrapped, bitesized candy bars placed on a long, low table.

Whenever a child or a small group of children arrived at one of these homes they were greeted by a female experimenter who commented favorably on their costumes, told each child that he or she could take only *one* candy, asked each child his or her name and age, and excused herself "to go back to my work in another room." (However, unbeknown to the children, an observer remained hidden in the room and was able to observe how many candies each child actually took after the experimenter left.) In the self-awareness condition of the study a large mirror was placed just behind the table with the candy bowl. The mirror was positioned so that the children would invariably see themselves as they reached for candy. In the control condition, the mirror was simply removed.

As predicted, boys who could not see themselves in the mirror were far more likely to deviate from the standard (by taking more than one candy) than were boys who were made aware of their own actions by self-observation in the mirror. Equally interesting is the fact that introduction of the mirror had virtually no effect on girls, who were quite likely to adhere to the standard even in the no-mirror, control condition.

The effects of inducing objective self-awareness through self-monitoring of one's own behavior is by no means limited to children.

Guided self-observation has also been shown to play a significant role in assisting adolescents and adults to resist temptation in diverse problem areas such as smoking, overeating and failing to complete homework assignments (Caapo, 1979; Rimm and Masters, 1979). In one such study (Adesso, Vargas, and Siddall, 1979) adolescents who had been biting their nails for an average of almost twelve years showed a significant increase in nail length (the "hard" measure of whether nail biting has been reduced) at their four-month follow-up examination, merely as a result of self-awareness training. They were instructed to record every instance of their own nail biting (by keeping a tally on a 3 × 5 card) and chart the frequency of their nail biting, and once a week for four weeks their nails were measured. A comparable group of nail biters who merely had their nails measured at the beginning and end of the study showed little change.

Delay of Gratification

In *Walden Two* (1948), B. F. Skinner's novel describing a utopia built on behavioral principles, preschool children are given lollipops every morning. The lollipops are not simply a treat, however, since they play an important role in teaching self-control. Specifically, the lollipops are all dipped in powdered sugar so that a single touch of the tongue can be detected. The children are allowed to eat the lollipop in the afternoon only if they can refrain from licking it at all in the meantime. In this situation, then, the child who indulges in a small immediate pleasure will have to forfeit a larger but delayed reward, the whole lollipop.

The child's problem is to learn *delay of gratification*, that form of self-control involved whenever children or adults postpone immediate gratification for the sake of more valued outcomes that will only come with patience and effort. A college student who foregoes a weekend movie today in order to study so that next week she can enjoy a movie *and* an "A" on her exam is displaying delay of gratification, as is the teenager who waits for a sale so that he can buy more (or better) clothes with the fixed amount of money he has available. Our interest in this section is to consider how delay of gratification is learned in childhood, and to examine the psychological processes that underlie this learning. Because of its central role in so many aspects of socialization, our discussion begins with a look at the role of modeled examples in acquiring the willingness to delay.

Social Example and Delay of Gratification.   There is a county in Nova Scotia where conflicting subcultural patterns have endured side by side for generations (Bandura and Walters, 1963). In the Acadian community of Lavellée, children are expected to control immediate impulses and to work toward distant goals. Educational and vocational achievement is stressed.

> In terms of time orientation, the main things in life are long-range goals—such as the salvation of the soul, the economic bettering of the area, the preservation and expansion of the Acadian group—even though some of these are unlikely to be achieved by any individual in his lifetime. . . . Work is a moral activity, and a man is enjoined not only to do it but also to take pride and pleasure in it

under almost any circumstance. . . . Life without work would be life without meaning, and people who try only to get as much money as possible while doing as little as they can are disparaged. [Hughes, Tremblay, Rapoport, and Leighton, 1960, pp. 159–60]

In this community parents spend large amounts of time with their children, in the course of which they undoubtedly transmit the adult patterns of their subculture with great efficiency. The children of Lavallée are unlikely to be swayed by the temptation to take an immediate small pleasure when it means forfeiting something worthwhile in the future.

In the same Nova Scotian county lives another group of people whose community is strikingly lacking in cohesion; fighting, drunkenness, theft, and other antisocial acts containing a component of impulse occur frequently. Adults in this subculture believe that "the best thing to do in life is to escape from one's problems as quickly as possible." Children growing up in this subculture are exposed to models exhibiting an overwhelming preference for immediate gratification.

But what would happen, hypothetically, if a child from this settlement subculture were adopted by parents in Lavellée and a child from Lavellée were adopted by settlement parents? Would the behavior of either of these children, who come to their new surroundings with habits, beliefs, and attitudes learned in their original communities, be influenced by the new models with whom they would have contact?

Bandura and Mischel (1965) provided a laboratory experiment that sheds light on this question, and in doing so they demonstrated the importance of modeling in the transmission of delay behavior. In the first part of the study, fourth- and fifth-grade children were given a delay-of-gratification test in which they were to make a series of fourteen choices between a small immediate reward and a larger delayed outcome. For instance, they were asked to choose between a small candy bar that would be given to them immediately or a larger one that would require a week of waiting. Children who displayed either predominant preferences for immediate reward or predominant preferences for delayed reward were thus identified and were subsequently assigned to one of three conditions. In the *live modeling condition* children observed an actual adult model make a series of choices between a less valuable item which could be obtained immediately and a more valuable item which required delay.* The model consistently chose the immediate reward item in the presence of children who demonstrated a preference for the larger delayed reward, whereas the model observed by a child who preferred smaller immediate rewards always selected the delayed reward item. In both cases, the model also briefly summarized a philosophy about the delay-of-reward behavior he was displaying. For example, when the choice was between a plastic chess set to be given immediately and a more expensive wooden set to be given in two

---

*The prizes between which the adult model chose were suitable for adults (chess sets, magazines, and so forth) and were different from the items between which the children subsequently chose. Thus, each child was able to imitate the "principle" underlying the model's behavior but was unable to copy his specific choices.

weeks, the model commented, "Chess figures are chess figures. I can get much use out of the plastic ones right away" (p. 701).

In the *symbolic modeling condition*, children were exposed to the same kind of sequence except that the model's choices and comments were presented in written form. Finally, in the *no model present condition*, children serving as controls for the possible effects of mere exposure to rewards were simply shown the series of paired objects. All children were then given a delay-of-reward test in the model's absence; to assess the stability of any changes in behavior, they also were given a subsequent delay-of-reward test one month later.

The results of the Bandura and Mischel experiment were clear. Children exposed to a model (live or symbolic) who delayed gratification shifted their own preferences so that on posttest about 50 percent of all their choices were for the larger outcomes that required a period of waiting. Even after a month's time these effects were still present. On the other hand, children exposed to models who exhibited little self-control were easily swayed by the impulsive model whom they saw and abandoned their self-control in favor of small immediate gratifications in the majority of cases. We might well expect, then, that our hypothetical child from the settlement culture in Nova Scotia would be influenced by observing the self-restraint in the behavior of the citizens of Lavellée and that, conversely, the behavior of our hypothetical child from Lavellée undoubtedly would be influenced toward less self-restraint through observation of role models in the settlement culture.

Psychological Processes in Delay of Gratification. Although Skinner's utopia would certainly offer children numerous adult models of self-control, more direct efforts to teach delay of gratification are also prescribed. Here is the way Frazier, the storyteller of *Walden Two*, puts it:

> First of all, the children are urged to examine their own behavior while looking at the lollipops. This helps them to recognize the need for self-control. Then the lollipops are concealed and the children are asked to notice any gain in happiness or any reduction in tension. Then a strong distraction is arranged—say, an interesting game. Later the children are reminded of the candy and encouraged to examine their reaction. The value of the distraction is generally obvious. . . . When the experiment is repeated a day or so later, the children all run with the lollipops to their lockers . . . a sufficient indication of the success of our training. [P. 108]

Such training supposes that delaying gratification involves two steps: an initial decision that one wishes to wait and then an effort to maintain one's resolve and bridge the waiting time. Walter Mischel, who has done much of the pioneering experimental work on delay of gratification, has also conceptualized the underlying psychological process as involving these two steps and, what is more, has shown that the steps are influenced by somewhat different factors (Mischel, 1974). Following this lead, our discussion here begins with a closer look at the decision process.

To Wait or Not to Wait. In situations where the child must make a choice between accepting or not accepting the frustration of delay for the sake of earning a superior outcome, he or she probably considers the subjective values of both the immediate and delayed rewards and the probability of obtaining them (Mischel, 1958; Mischel and Metzner, 1962).

In the excerpt from *Walden Two*, for example, the delayed reward (a whole lollipop) probably would be considered superior to the immediate reward (a few licks of a lollipop) by most youngsters. But the course of action also depends on the trustworthiness of the people giving the lollipops, which introduces an element of risk in waiting. And there is another consideration. In most life situations, attaining delayed rewards involves not only simply waiting but also engaging successfully in some required activity. Thus, the child's confidence in being able to perform this activity is undoubtedly related to the decision.

When the difference in value between the immediate and the delayed reward is slight and/or the risk of not being able to obtain the delayed reward despite the delay is great, the rational choice (and the one children presumably make) is to take the immediate reward. On the other hand, when the difference in subjective value is substantial and/or when obtaining the delayed reward is not too risky, the rational choice may be the delayed reward (Mischel and Staub, 1965).

Once the choice has been made to wait for the delayed but superior prize, a question arises as to whether the child will be able to go through with the plan. Although older children tend to exhibit more self-control in this respect than do younger ones (Mischel and Metzner, 1962), delaying reward can be difficult at any age. Experimental work in this area, however, is beginning to provide knowledge of the ways in which a frustrating time span is tolerated.

Maintaining Delay of Gratification. Freud (1959) suggested that delay of gratification could be maintained by creating mental images of the desired object, thereby producing substitute satisfactions that ease the frustration of delay. Others have advanced similar notions—namely, that any process that makes the delayed object-situation salient should facilitate waiting for it.

Using Freud's theorizing as an initial framework, Mischel and his associates have conducted an extensive program of research aimed at a better understanding of delay of gratification. Mischel and Ebbesen (1970), for example, predicted that children would find waiting for a delayed reward easiest when they could see the large reward, whereas waiting would be most difficult when no reward was in sight. It was reasoned that viewing rewards would serve as a vivid reminder that reward was worth waiting for, and would also increase the child's trust in actually receiving the reward. This prediction obviously contradicts the principle of distraction described in the previous excerpt from *Walden Two*.

To test their prediction, Mischel and Ebbesen set up the following situation. Three- to five-year-old children first were asked which of two foods (cookies or pretzels) they preferred, and each youngster then was told that

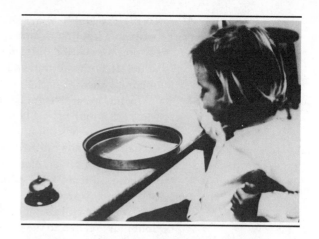

FIGURE 13–5
A preschool child waiting for delayed gratification.
Courtesy of Dr. Walter Mischel.

he or she would wait alone in a room until the experimenter returned, whereupon the preferred food would be provided. The child could also call the experimenter back to the room at any time by a prearranged signal; in this case, however, only the nonpreferred food would be provided. The experimenter then departed, leaving on the table both foods, the preferred food only, the nonpreferred food only, or neither food (see Figure 13–5). He returned in fifteen minutes, or earlier if summoned by the child. The length of time children in the different food conditions waited was the dependent measure of the study. Figure 13–6 shows that the results were opposite

FIGURE 13–6
Average amount of time children were able to wait for the delayed but preferred food in Mischel and Ebbesen's (1970) experiment. Note that children were able to wait longest when no foods were present in the room, and least able to control themselves when both foods were present. Which of the foods (delayed or immediate) was present did not seem to matter.   Adapted from Mischel and Ebbesen (1970). Copyright 1970 by the American Psychological Association. Reprinted by permission.

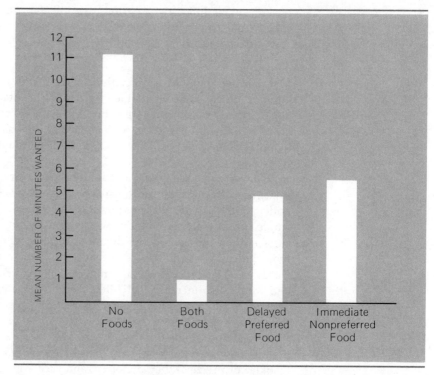

from the investigators' expectations; that is, children who were exposed to neither of the foods delayed significantly more than those exposed to both or one of the foods. It is quite striking that the children in this group were able to sit alone for an average of over eleven minutes—and that 75 percent of them had to be interrupted at the fifteen-minute mark.

Observations of all the children's behavior through a one-way mirror provided a clue as to how time was bridged. Elaborate distraction techniques were designed spontaneously: some children sang, talked to themselves, and invented games. Among those children who successfully waited when food was present, many avoided looking at it by covering their eyes with their hands or resting their heads on their arms. It appeared that any activity that converted the situation into a less frustrating experience could increase delay time, and so Mischel and his associates began to experiment directly with various techniques that might either distract children or help them transform the situation into one in which waiting would become easier.

The focus of these later investigations has been quite cognitive in emphasis, in the sense that what the child *thinks* has been of central interest. One study showed that when children are asked to think about "fun things" their ability to bridge a wait period increases, whereas thinking "sad thoughts" reduces waiting and causes most children to take the immediate reward and terminate the delay (Mischel, Ebbesen, and Raskoff, 1971). But what happens if the child thinks about the rewards themselves? Is that a type of fun thought that increases self-control, or is it a representation of the desired outcome that arouses appetites and decreases the ability to wait just as the presence of the "real thing" did in Mischel and Ebbesen's (1970) original study? The answer to these questions suggests that some subtle and complex mental processes are involved in self-control.

One exciting possibility, suggested by the work of Mischel and Patterson (1976), is that children's ability to delay gratification may be fostered by the availability of clear plans or "blueprints" for action. In the Mischel and Patterson study, preschool children were asked to work on a boring task while an attractive "Clown Box" potentially distracted them. Those given a concrete way to handle the situation, including *what to do* (e.g., say to yourself, "I'm just not going to look at Mr. Clown Box!") and *when to do it* (e.g., "When Mr. Clown Box says to look at him."), were far better able than other children to resist temptation and continue working in this situation. Mischel and Patterson's results also suggest that self-control can be achieved through self-instruction, even among preschool age children. More recent studies, also involving preschoolers, have confirmed that even these very young children are able to wait longer if they have been taught to verbalize about the desirability of waiting, such as the simple statement, "It is good if I wait." (Toner and Smith, 1977; Miller, Weinstein, and Karniol, 1978).

Overall, then, we may say that it is *how* the child thinks about the desired object or outcome that makes all the difference. In one study, children facing real rewards for which they had to wait were able to delay gratification more than twice as long (eighteen minutes vs. eight minutes) if they made believe that the real object in front of them was only a picture.* And thinking about an absent reward in a way that is concrete and arousing (for example, thinking about *eating* the pretzels or marshmallows for which one is waiting) robs the child of self-control almost as thoroughly as looking at the real thing. "It seems likely," Mischel concludes, "that abstract cognitive representations of the rewards [for example, thinking of them only as pictures] permit the subject to remind himself of the contingency, and to engage in self-reinforcement for further delay" (1974, p. 286). His remark raises the question of how children do set standards for themselves and administer self-rewarding consequences. We now turn to these very issues.

ACHIEVEMENT STANDARDS AND STRIVINGS

All people come to set standards for themselves. In general, the higher or more stringent the standard, the more effort must be expended to attain it. People differ, though, in regard to the stringency of their self-imposed standards. Some schoolchildren, for example, will appear pleased and delighted to receive a "B," indicating better than average mastery of academic subject matter, while others will chastise themselves for failing to get an "A," the mark of outstanding achievement. Self-imposed standards of achievement and self-reward are of course largely products of socialization. The question of how they are acquired has long intrigued developmental psychologists.

Self-Reward and Self-Imposed Standards

One experimental situation used to study children's self-imposed standards involves three basic characteristics: (1) the child performs a task that he or she believes to be one of achievement or skill; (2) the child is able to self-administer rewards so that his or her self-imposed criterion determines the amount and frequency of the rewards; and (3) no external socializing agent is present. A report by Liebert and Ora (1968) illustrates such self-imposed standards of children, using the miniature bowling game pictured in Figure 13–7.

At the end of the three-foot runway is a panel of lights; ostensibly they indicate the score earned by rolling the ball down the alley to upset a set of pins. One of the lights—marked "5," "10," "15," or "20"—comes on after each turn. Although the apparatus is preprogrammed to produce a fixed pattern of scores, children actually think the game is one of skill.

Because Liebert and Ora were interested in investigating factors of training and incentive, children in their study were assigned to either the high incentive condition or the low incentive condition. In the *high incentive*

---

*This requires a bit of training, of course. Here is an extract from the actual instructions used, illustrating the point:

. . . Close your eyes. In your head try to see the picture of the _____ (immediate and delayed rewards). Make a color picture of (them); put a frame around them. You can see the picture of them. Now open your eyes and do the same thing. (more practice) . . . From now on you can see a picture that shows _____ (immediate and delayed rewards) here in front of you. The _____ aren't real; they're just a picture. . . . When I'm gone remember to see the picture in front of you. [Mischel, 1974, p. 285]

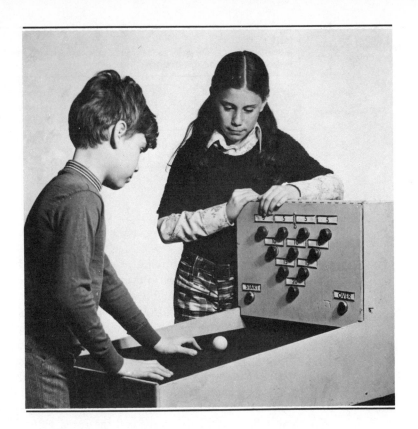

condition each was informed that he or she might win one of a display of prizes ranging in price from ten cents to twelve dollars but that a large number of reward tokens would be required for the most valuable prizes, whereas in the *low incentive condition* the chance to win prizes was not mentioned. Children in the two experimental groups were then either exposed to a model of self-control or given direct instruction to exercise self-control themselves. Those in the *modeling* condition observed an adult male bowl ten trials, rewarding himself with plastic tokens for all scores of 20 but never for lower scores. For each score of twenty he announced, "20, that's a good score. That deserves a chip"; for each score below 20 he announced,—"that's not a very good score. That doesn't deserve a chip." In the *direct instruction condition*, the child bowled ten trials in the training agent's presence and heard the same rules indicating that scores of 20 but not others merited self-reward—e.g., "15, that's not a very good score. I don't think you deserve a chip for that score." Those in the *control* group received no training. Finally, each child was left alone to play the game while his or her behavior was surreptitiously observed.

Children in both training groups—*modeling* and *direct*—adhered to the high achievement standard to a much greater extent than did those in the control group, but the presence of an attractive incentive tended to reduce the stringency of self-imposed standards in all cases (see Table 13–1). Thus it appears that self-imposed standards and patterns of self-reward are set in

TABLE 13-1

Mean Number of Deviations from the Standard Provided by the Training Agent in Liebert and Ora's Experiment

Subgroup	Control	Modeling	Direct Training
Low incentive	7.42	0.92	0.08
High incentive	12.75	3.25	2.92

Source: Liebert and Ora, 1968.

response to the specific demands of a particular situation and, potentially, are modifiable by new training and experiences.

Is self-reward reinforcing? In the Liebert and Ora study children administered consequences to themselves, contingent on their own performance. We may ask, though, whether such self-administered consequences can maintain behavior just as externally administered rewards do. The answer appears to be yes.

Bandura and Perloff (1967) for example, asked seven- to ten-year-old boys and girls to set their own standards on a specially devised crank-turning task and to reward themselves whenever their self-imposed standards had been met. Children in another group had the same standards imposed upon them but were rewarded by an adult for meeting them; that is, these latter children experienced the usual externally imposed reinforcement procedure. Finally there were control groups who received either no reward or a lump sum "inheritance" at the outset. Results, measured in terms of actual effortful behavior, were striking: Those who set their own standards and rewarded themselves were as productive as those rewarded by an adult; both groups substantially outperformed the controls (see Figure 13-8).

Subsequent studies also have shown that highly valuable self-administered rewards are more effective in maintaining one's own productivity than less valuable ones (Liebert, Spiegler, and Hall, 1970), and that self-determined reward standards are as effective in maintaining a more academic task—solving arithmetic problems—as are externally imposed criteria (Felixbrod and O'Leary, 1973). In addition, training in appropriate self-reward can lead to improved school grades among junior high school students (Harris and Trujillo, 1975). All of these findings suggest that the self-administration of consequences might be taught to children for the very practical purpose of influencing their own study habits.

By the end of the 1970s children in experimental classroom situations all over the United States had been taught self-monitoring and self-reward procedures, often with very satisfactory results. While it is too early to evaluate the long-term effects of teaching self-control in the classroom, Rosenbaum and Drabman's (1979) review of studies to date suggests that all of the processes involved can be taught in the classroom setting. Rosenbaum and Drabman write:

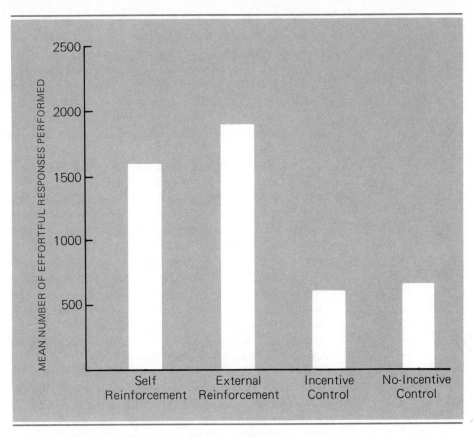

FIGURE 13–8
Number of effortful responses in all groups of Bandura and Perloff's experiment.   From Bandura and Perloff, 1967. Copyright 1967 by the American Psychological Association. Reprinted by permission.

Self-control is a therapeutic goal that is advocated by almost all helping professionals, regardless of their discipline or theoretical orientation. The research reviewed in this article has demonstrated that students can be taught to observe and record their own behavior, determine and administer their own contingencies, and provide instructions to guide their own behavior. (1979, p. 480)

The Achieving Child

The setting of personal standards, discussed above, is integrally related to achievement striving. Achievement-oriented behavior may occur in the arts, academics, sports, or any endeavor where level of performing competence is involved. Competence, however, can be shown only in situations in which there is a "standard of excellence" that may be applied to the performance and that is agreed upon by those concerned. For purposes of the following discussion, then, *achievement behavior* will be defined as any action directed at gaining approval or avoiding disapproval from oneself or from others, for competence in performance where public standards of excellence are applicable (Crandall, Katkovsky, and Preston, 1960a).

Substantial differences in achievement striving among children of five years of age and older have been observed in a number of studies (Crandall,

Preston, and Rabson, 1960; Tyler, Rafferty, and Tyler, 1962; McClelland, 1958). While some children show great persistence with tasks requiring skill and effort at this age, others do not; similarly, while some children tend to seek recognition for achievement, others seem to care little for such reward. And it is not surprising that the emergence of achievement motivation is related to cognitive development, inasmuch as children must recognize intellectually that their own abilities and effort produce success or failure as a precondition for certain kinds of attainment striving (Weiner and Kun, 1976).

How, though, should we conceptualize the differences that exist among children in their striving for success, even from the first school years? Some theorists have viewed these differences as reflecting underlying differences in children's achievement motivation (also called "need achievement"), a concept used in an effort to predict and/or explain achievement behavior. In assessing the relative amount of achievement motivation possessed by a particular child, the examiner listens as the child tells a story about each of several ambiguous pictures. The child's replies are scored according to the frequency of achievement themes in his or her stories; the method, developed by David McClelland, is based on the assumption that, to the degree that achievement motivation is part of the child's personality, achievement imagery will find its way into the youngster's storytelling (McClelland, Atkinson, Clark, and Lowell, 1953).

In a work entitled *The Achieving Society*, McClelland (1961) took an unusual research tack. He attempted to "predict" the economic growth of twenty-three countries between 1929 and 1950 on the basis of the amount of achievement imagery appearing in their children's stories for the period 1920–1929. The achievement motive found in the children's stories correlated +.53 with an index of national economic growth. McClelland concludes from this and other similar studies that children's stories reflect "... the motivational level of the adults at the time they are published, perhaps particularly of the adults responsible for the education of children. ..." (p. 102). These correlational findings dovetail with those of an experimental study in which preschool children's efforts to complete an achievement-related task increased after being read a story relating the achievement-oriented behavior of a child of their own sex (McArthur and Eisen, 1975).

But high achievement motivation as measured by children's storytelling is not always related to real-life achievement strivings (Crandall, 1967), and, more importantly, the focus of achievement efforts varies markedly from one child to another. It is not unusual for a child to spend a great deal of time and effort developing competence in one area, say physical skills, while expending a great deal less time and energy with other kinds of activities, such as artistic or intellectual pursuits (Crandall, 1961).

What Is Achievement • Motivation?

The facts we have reviewed all raise questions about what is meant by concepts such as achievement motivation, intrinsic motivation, personal competence, and a number of others. What all these ideas have in common is that they suggest an underlying motive or need, varying from individual

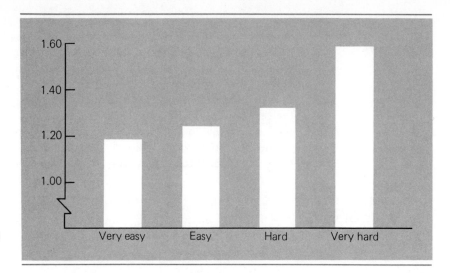

FIGURE 13–9

Mean amount of smiling in Harter's (1977) study as first-grade boys and girls solved problems varying in difficulty. From data reported in Harter (1977).

to individual and, perhaps, situation to situation. Theoretically, the person's level of motivation becomes an explanation for his or her striving behavior. The problem with any such notion is that it is circular and untestable.

As Harter (1979) cogently notes: "There is clearly general support for the operation of a motive that is satisfied by competent performance, and the concept has great appeal [but] little *explanatory* value, given the very breadth of behaviors which are subsumed under such a rubric. . . . Like the weather, it has become something that everyone *talks* about but something about which we have done precious little. That is, there have been few attempts, until recently . . . to view this formulation as one which can be put to an empirical test." (1979, in press).

Harter's own research efforts have been designed to provide the sort of empirical base she deems necessary. For example, one implication of the concept of an intrinsic motivation to perform competently is that accomplishing difficult tasks should be more satisfying than accomplishing easier tasks. To demonstrate the expected relationship empirically, Harter (1977) gave first-grade boys and girls a series of puzzles representing four levels of difficulty. The children were surreptitiously observed by trained recorders, who scored the child's spontaneous smiling upon completion of each puzzle (e.g., no smile = 0; slight or half smile = 1; full smile or grin = 2). As expected, the children were more likely to smile, or to smile more broadly, when they solved difficult puzzles than when they solved easier ones (see Figure 13–9, above).*

The empirical approach often leads to changes in the scientist's initial conceptualizations and, indeed, such self-correction lies at the heart of the scientific enterprise. In the case of Harter's work, she has now found evidence that the relationship between task difficulty and pleasure may change after an "optimally challenging" level of difficulty has been reached. In a

---

*Interestingly, however, this pattern was not present for a group of retarded youngsters who also participated in the study. The reader may recall that differences in the motivational patterns of retarded and nonretarded children were discussed in chapter 9.

study involving sixth-grade boys and girls, Harter (1980) found that problems labeled *very hard* by the youngsters elicited less smiling and were rated as less enjoyable than those rated *hard*. At the same time, *hard* problems were rated as more enjoyable and produced more smiles than *easy* problems, replicating Harter's earlier finding.

When the subjects were questioned after the study, they explained that the very hard problems were simply too time-consuming and frustrating. It seems, then, that the satisfaction of accomplishment comes from things that are neither too easy nor tediously difficult. Rather, Harter concludes, each of us, child and adult, seeks work that is optimally challenging relative to our present abilities.

Factors Related to Achievement Striving

There are many factors influencing achievement striving, including child-rearing practices, self-expectations, and the idea of personal control vs. external control.

Parental child-rearing practices and achievement striving. Among the questions asked by parents and educators, almost none is more frequently heard than, "What factors in child rearing encourage and discourage achievement striving in youngsters?" A complex answer is suggested by a number of different correlational studies. Many parental attitudes and child-rearing practices, including independence training (Winterbottom, 1953; Feld, 1959), reward of achievement efforts (Crandall, Preston, and Rabson, 1960), and encouragement and instigation of intellectual pursuits (Crandall, Katkovsky, and Preston, 1960b), are associated with achievement striving.

Winterbottom (1953), in what is now considered a classic study, gave eight- to ten-year-old boys the rudiments of a story (e.g., "Brothers and sisters are playing. One is a little ahead.") and asked them to elaborate on it. The frequency of achievement themes in the boys' stories was then related to the child-rearing practices to which they had been exposed, as reported by their mothers. Winterbottom's principal finding was that mothers of high achievement-oriented boys differed from other mothers in (1) fostering early independence of thought and action—e.g., encouraging the child to try things for himself, and (2) generously rewarding successful performance with affection and attention.

In another study (Rosen and D'Andrade, 1959), a team of investigators went into private homes to observe youngsters who were either high or low in achievement motivation. Each boy was given a demanding and potentially frustrating task: to build a tower out of irregularly shaped blocks with one hand—while blindfolded. The boys' parents were asked to watch and were permitted to give any sort of rewards they wished so long as they did not touch the blocks or provide direct assistance. Confirming Winterbottom's report, mothers of high-achieving boys were warmer and more encouraging than other mothers. The fathers of low-achieving boys also differed from others in a noticeable way: They tried to make their sons' decisions for them and became quite irritated whenever the boys had any difficulty.

The role of expectancies. In contrast to achievement needs, expectations of success are treated as specific to a particular kind of endeavor—for example, sports, mathematics, or art. But the actual role of expectancies in achievement-related behavior is a question for research. Virginia Crandall and her colleagues at Fels Research Institute have made unique contributions in this area.

One important disclosure from Crandall's work is that the degree to which a child *expects* to succeed has a major bearing on whether he or she actually does or not. In an Ohio junior high school, for example, it was found that students who expected to obtain good grades in mathematics and English actually got the better grades in these courses. In part, we might explain these findings by saying that the more able youngsters simply (and realistically) have higher expectancies. However, when IQ and expectancy diverged (for example, when a student with a low IQ had high expectancies or vice versa), expectation of success rather than IQ was associated with the obtained grade. In other words, to at least some degree, children who expect to succeed actually do better (Crandall, 1967). They will spend more time and effort in studying than the child who expects to fail, for whom such an investment often seems futile.

In light of the importance of expectations, it will be disquieting to many that girls' expectancy estimates are consistently lower than boys'. In a laboratory study performed at Fels Research Institute, for example, elementary school boys and girls were given six kinds of school-like tasks, and each child was asked to estimate how far he or she could go before the task became too difficult. Girls tended to expect to be beaten by the task at much lower levels of difficulty than boys, despite the fact that they actually had *higher* IQs on the average (mean IQ for females 114, mean IQ for males 107).

Although girls often tend to estimate their own intellectual and academic capabilities lower than what an objective observer might expect on the basis of past performance, boys tend to behave in exactly the opposite fashion, estimating their level of competence higher than what past performance would indicate. Why should this be the case? The question has not yet been answered. It is likely that girls get less positive reward for achievement than boys have traditionally received (Horner, 1973), although this is probably not the sole reason for the difference. Crandall and her associates suggest that life experiences can be contradictory in the sense that situations often simultaneously provide reasons to feel competent and reasons to feel incompetent. Thus boys, they suggest, may focus on positive feedback, whereas girls may be unduly sensitive to reproof and thus tend to construct biased pictures of their own capabilities.

Locus of control. Children differ in the extent to which they believe that their own actions can influence the outcome of events. Some tend to assume that they are responsible for their success and failures; others tend to attribute responsibility to outside agents, luck, fate, and other people. The extent to which children believe that the locus of responsibility for achievement is internal rather than external can be measured by the "Intellectual Achievement Responsibility Questionnaire," a thirty-four-item scale that measures responsibility for both pleasant and unpleasant consequences. Each item consists of a description of an achievement-related experience that might have occurred in the child's life, followed by one alternative stating that the event occurred because of the child's own actions and another stating that the event was caused by other forces. Exemplary items from the IAR Scale are presented in Table 13–2.

In answering the questionnaire, the child is asked to pick the answer for each item "that best describes what happens to you or how you feel." It is not surprising to find that children who score high as "internalizers" on this scale tend to get better grades and to do better on achievement tests than do those who score high as "externalizers" (Crandall, Katkovsky, and Crandall, 1965, Gagne, 1975). Internalizers may well show greater initiative and per-

---

TABLE 13–2
Sample Items from the Intellectual Achievement Responsibility Questionnaire (IAR) Used by Crandall and Her Associates

1. If a teacher passes you to the next grade, would it probably be
   _____ a. because she liked you, or
   _____ b. because of the work you did?
2. When you do well on a test at school, is it more likely to be
   _____ a. because you studied for it, or
   _____ b. because the test was especially easy?
3. When you read a story and can't remember much of it, is it usually
   _____ a. because the story wasn't well written, or
   _____ b. because you weren't interested in the story?
4. Suppose your parents say you are doing well in school. Is this likely to happen
   _____ a. because your school work is good, or
   _____ b. because they are in a good mood?

Source: Courtesy Virginia Crandall.

sistence in solving difficult problems and a ready willingness to modify their behavior to achieve the desired goal, whereas externalizers may see little reason to initiate, persist, or modify their behavior inasmuch as they feel the outcome is not under their control. In some situations the IAR scale is a better predictor of achievement than are measures of achievement motivation (Crandall, Katkovsky, and Preston, 1962).

In the past fifteen years much has been learned about locus of control, so that we can now paint a relatively complete picture of this dimension of personality.

The implicit bias of most research in this area is that a belief in internal control is more desirable than a belief in external control. This may be a value judgment, but it has been shown that increasing belief in internal control comes with increasing age (Bachrach, Huesmann, and Peterson, 1977). Moreover, other relationships are consistent with the social relevance of the dimension; for example, delinquent girls are less likely to be internal in their orientation than nondelinquent girls (Duke and Fenhagen, 1975), and, among both black and white children, a higher level of socioeconomic status is associated with greater expectancy of internal control (Rabinowitz, 1978).

What fosters internal control? It has been suggested that the most important factor is fostering the child's self-reliance and independence in a nonauthoritarian environment (Crandall, 1973; Lifshitz and Ramot, 1978; Wichern and Nowicki, 1976). Crandall (1973), for example, found that the earlier in life children were allowed to become independent (e.g., staying at a friend's house overnight) the more internal was their locus of control orientation. This basic finding was later replicated by Wichern and Nowicki (1976), who concluded:

> The finding that earlier independence allowing and independence training were associated with an internal locus of control in a cross-sectional, relatively diffuse low- to middle-class subject population argues for the generality of the relation. It appears that maternal behaviors that include intentional training of skills to make the child self-reliant and also allow him to be "left alone" may be linked with the development of internal perceptions. Mothers of internals seem to allow more room for and provide greater opportunity for cause-and-effect learning to take place. (p. 77)

SUMMARY

Self-control and achievement strivings both involve a self-imposed standard of some sort, and the basic processes of learning and cognition are relevant to the development of all values.

Two aspects of self-control that have been studied are *resistance to temptation* and *delay of gratification*. Young children are more likely to resist temptation if they have been exposed to physical rather than psychological punishment, but reasoning is useful especially with older children and/or in combination with punishment. Self-instruction, exposure to vicarious consequences, and the child's immediate emotional state also influence resistance to temptation.

The tendency to wait for larger rewards, *delay of gratification*, increases with age and is related to such factors as the trust the child places in others. Children can be taught strategies for delaying gratification; one effective strategy is to encourage children to distract themselves from the temptation of the small, immediate reward.

Specific achievement standards are acquired through direct instruction and exposure to social models, which are also the bases through which children learn to reward themselves for various levels of attainment. Such self-reward has been shown to have reinforcing properties and thus has clear potential for classroom application; this potential is now being realized. Achievement motivation has proven difficult to define, but children do seem to most enjoy tasks that are optimally challenging for them. What is optimally (or overly) challenging for a particular child depends very much on the child's expectancies. The belief that one can control one's own outcomes, called *internal locus of control*, has been associated with high levels of achievement striving in a wide variety of comparisons. Internal control, in turn, is related to training in self-reliance during childhood.

14 Moral Standards and Interpersonal Reactions

A major aspect of social development involves coming to deal with others in appropriate and effective ways. Part of what is considered appropriate depends on one's moral values. When broadly defined, the moral sphere encompasses the whole range of interpersonal reactions. Thus, moral development involves attitudes, beliefs, and values on the one hand and actual behavior on the other. Interpersonal behaviors that are perceived as benefiting others, such as sharing, helping, and cooperating, fall into the moral sphere. These are often called "prosocial" behavior. Likewise, actions that threaten or harm others—hurting, killing, cheating, and lying—are considered morally relevant and sometimes are referred to as "antisocial behavior."

This chapter begins with a discussion of theories of moral development and reasoning and then turns to what is known about the development of morally relevant interpersonal reactions.

THE DEVELOPMENT OF MORAL VALUES

There is little doubt that most children develop, during their early years, a set of values or principles regarding correct, appropriate, or good behavior. At one time the study of moral development was considered to be—at best—on the fringes of psychology, but recently it has come to the fore as a worthy topic that has important social implications.

The Psychoanalytic View

The traditional view of morality, favored in nineteenth-century Europe, presumed that values of the kind we call "moral" were provided by God. Then Freud, a revolutionary thinker in his time, suggested that quite the reverse is true. The neonate, he argued, is naturally without concern for the welfare of others. Moral values, if they are present at all, must be cultivated after birth. Psychoanalytic theory offers a view of moral development rooted in the emergence of the *superego*. The superego—a part of each individual's personality—is said to develop as the child "takes in" parental values, at about the fourth or fifth year of life. The formation process itself, intimately linked to the resolution of the Oedipal conflict (see chapter 11), is explained in terms of identification.

The implications of Freud's identification theory, as applied to moral development, are straightforward. The child's moral values either will parallel those of the parents or, if appropriate identification does not occur, the youngster will have an inadequate superego and few moral values or none at all. In either case, though, the critical period is presumed to be the first few years of life.

An extensive review of the available evidence does *not* support this one-process view of moral development (Hoffman, 1975). This does not mean that parents are not important models in the moral sphere, for they certainly are; but it is simply not plausible that a person's early identification with parents is solely responsible for all his or her own moral attitudes and actions in adulthood. Hoffman (1971), for example, points out that young children lack the cognitive skills needed to classify parental examples of moral behavior or infer their motivations and that in any event parents rarely express morally relevant feelings (e.g., guilt or self-criticism) in their children's presence. The importance of Freud's work was that it redirected the public's attention, allowing people to consider the social origins of moral values.

Consistency of Moral Values and Behavior

Parents often expect that the various aspects of a child's moral values and behavior will be quite consistent, as if some youngsters simply have higher standards or a more completely developed conscience than others. One of the most important descriptive studies of moral behavior in children, conducted many years ago, was designed to address this very issue (Hartshorne and May, 1928; Hartshorne, May, and Shuttleworth, 1930).

Hartshorne and May's Research. Hartshorne and May observed thousands of children in many situations—at home, playing party games, in athletic contests—in which the child could commit transgressions such as lying, stealing, and cheating without being aware that they were detected. Contrary to their original expectations, the investigators found little consistency in the actual performance of individual children.

Suppose, for example, that two children, A and B, were placed in a situation where cheating was possible and A cheated while B did not. Could we now safety predict that in another, different situation A would be more likely to cheat than B? Hartshorne and his associates found that the answer to this question was no.

Ironically, though, the investigation revealed a good deal of consistency in the children's responses to queries conducted in their classrooms about their moral values and opinions. But verbally expressed moral values appeared to have little to do with action; often youngsters who cheated expressed as much or more disapproval of cheating as those who did not. And it appeared that even when honesty was not "forced" by concern about detection and punishment, social factors such as approval of one's peers, rather than an inner moral code, were critical.

Burton's Analyses. Hartshorne and May's findings continue to surprise many people, and one may rightly wonder whether their conclusions would have been different if more powerful tools of analysis or experimentation had been used. Roger Burton, who has been a leading contemporary figure in studying the consistency or variability of children's moral behavior, has suggested that the original conclusions were basically sound. Burton (1963) employed highly sophisticated techniques to reanalyze Hartshorne and May's data and found at best a very limited hint that there is some generality to honesty. In a more recent work. Burton (1976) also concludes that "none of the fantasy responses [used to assess conscience development], regardless of their content, can be used in any simple way to predict honesty or cheating." He also reports that children who cheat seem to be the very ones who show strong signs of reparation and guilt, suggesting that these responses may have been learned only to quiet an angry parent and therefore forestall punishment. This is hardly the outcome we would expect if guilt were a measure of a child's underlying conscience. And, finally, Burton reports sex differences that are situation-specific rather than highly general. Girls are more likely to cheat than boys when the adult being cheated is female (Burton, 1976; Hartshorne and May, 1928). But when a male adult is involved, boys are more likely to cheat than girls (Leff, 1969; Stephens, Miller, and McLaughlin, 1969).

Kohlberg's Cognitive Approach to Moral Development

Piaget was the first to suggest the possibility of a sequence of stages of moral growth, roughly paralleling his general theory of cognitive development (see chapter 7). Another cognitive theorist, Lawrence Kohlberg, has explored more completely the development of moral values within a cognitive stage theory framework. He has been concerned primarily with the development of the child's moral judgments rather than moral actions. The child, says Kohlberg, must be viewed as a "moral philosopher."

But what is the child's philosophy? To answer this question, Kohlberg analyzed free responses to hypothetical moral dilemmas such as the following:

> In Europe, a woman was near death from cancer. One drug might save her, a form of radium that a druggist in the same town had recently discovered. The druggist was charging $2,000, ten times what the drug cost him to make. The sick woman's husband, Heinz, went to everyone he knew to borrow the money, but he could only get together about half of what it cost. He told the druggist that his wife was dying and asked him to sell it cheaper or let him pay later. But the druggist said, "No." The husband got desperate and broke into the man's store to steal the drug for his wife. Should the husband have done that? Why? [Kohlberg, 1969, p. 379]

A child's responses to dilemmas such as this one are usually based on one or more general aspects of the problem, such as the motives or intentions of the people involved. After eliciting responses to a large number of dilemmas from many children, Kohlberg feels he has been able to distinguish three levels of moral thinking: *preconventional, conventional,* and *postconventional.*

According to Kohlberg, the preconventional child is often well behaved and sensitive to labels such as good and bad. But the latter are interpreted simply in terms of their physical consequences (punishment, reward, exchange of favors) or in terms of the power of those who make the rules. There is, then, no real standard of morality at the preconventional level. The conventional level is characterized by conformity to the existing social order and an implicit desire to maintain that order. Most American adults, according to Kohlberg, operate at the level of conventional morality. Finally, the postconventional level is said to be governed by moral principles that are universal, and therefore valid independent of the authority of the groups who support them.

Within each of these three levels, Kohlberg (1963, 1967, 1976) suggests, are two discernible stages, producing the full complement of six stages shown in Table 14–1.

TABLE 14-1

Kohlberg's Six Stages of Moral Development

Preconventional Level

Stage 1:
Punishment and obedience orientation. The physical consequences of an action determine whether it is good or bad. Avoiding punishment and bowing to superior power are valued positively.

Stage 2:
Instrumental relativist orientation. Right action consists of behavior that satisfies one's own needs. Human relations are viewed in marketplace terms. Reciprocity occurs, but is seen in a pragmatic way, i.e., "you scratch my back and I'll scratch yours."

Conventional Level

Stage 3:
Interpersonal concordance (good boy—nice girl) orientation. Good behaviors are those that please or are approved by others. There is much emphasis on conformity and being "nice."

Stage 4:
Orientation toward authority ("law and order"). Focus is on authority or rules. It is right to do one's duty, show respect for authority, and maintain the social order.

Postconventional Level

Stage 5:
Social-contract orientation. This stage has a utilitarian, legalistic tone. Correct behavior is defined in terms of standards agreed upon by society. Awareness of the relativism of personal values and the need for consensus is important.

Stage 6:
Universal ethical principle orientation. Morality is defined as a decision of conscience. Ethical principles are self-chosen, based on abstract concepts (e.g., the Golden Rule) rather than concrete rules (e.g., the Ten Commandments).

Concrete examples of the type of moral judgments made in response to the dilemma described in the story of Heinz and his dying wife are shown in Table 14-2. The stages are *not* differentiated by what decision is made, but by the reasoning that underlies the decision.

Kohlberg reports that moral development may be either fast or slow, but that it does not skip stages. Further, this orderly pattern is not related to religious beliefs; no differences are said to exist in the development of moral thinking among Catholics, Protestants, Jews, Buddhists, Moslems, or atheists. Thus moral thought appears to follow a universal pattern typical of all other kinds of thought; progress is characterized by increasing differentiation and integration.

TABLE 14-2

Examples of the Moral Reasoning Employed at Various Stages in Response to Heinz's Dilemma

---

Stage 1
Action is motivated by avoidance of punishment and "conscience" is irrational fear of punishment.

  Pro—If you let your wife die, you will get in trouble. You'll be blamed for not spending the money to save her and there'll be an investigation of you and the druggist for your wife's death.

  Con—You shouldn't steal the drug because you'll be caught and sent to jail if you do. If you do get away, your conscience would bother you thinking how the police would catch up with you at any minute.

Stage 2
Action motivated by desire for reward or benefit. Possible guilt reactions are ignored and punishment viewed in a pragmatic manner. (Differentiates own fear, pleasure, or pain from punishment-consequences.)

Pro—If you do happen to get caught you could give the drug back and you wouldn't get much of a sentence. It wouldn't bother you much to serve a little jail term, if you have your wife when you get out.

Con—He may not get much of a jail term if he steals the drug, but his wife will probably die before he gets out so it won't do him much good. If his wife dies, he shouldn't blame himself; it wasn't his fault she has cancer.

Stage 3
Action motivated by anticipation of disapproval of others, actual or imagined hypothetical (e.g., guilt). (Differentiation of disapproval from punishment, fear, and pain.)

Pro—No one will think you're bad if you steal the drug but your family will think you're an inhuman husband if you don't. If you let your wife die, you'll never be able to look anybody in the face again.

Con—It isn't just the druggist who will think you're a criminal, everyone else will too. After you steal it, you'll feel bad thinking how you've brought dishonor on your family and yourself; you won't be able to face anyone again.

Stage 4
Action motivated by anticipation of dishonor, i.e., institutionalized blame for failure of duty, and by guilt over concrete harm done to others. (Differentiates formal dishonor from informal disapproval. Differentiates guilt for bad consequences from disapproval.)

Pro—If you have any sense of honor, you won't let your wife die because you're afraid to do the only thing that will save her. You'll always feel guilty that you caused her death if you don't do your duty to her.

Con—You're desperate and you may not know you're doing wrong when you steal the drug. But you'll know you did wrong after you're punished and sent to jail. You'll always feel guilt for your dishonesty and lawbreaking.

Stage 5
Concern about maintaining respect of equals and of the community (assuming their respect is based on reason rather than emotions). Concern about own self-respect, i.e., to avoid judging self as irrational, inconsistent, nonpurposive. (Discriminates between institutionalized blame and community disrespect or self-disrespect.)

Pro—You'd lose other people's respect, not gain it, if you don't steal. If you let your wife die, it would be out of fear, not out of reasoning it out. So you'd just lose self-respect and probably the respect of others too.

Con—You would lose your standing and respect in the community and violate the law. You'd lose respect for yourself if you're carried away by emotion and forget the long-range point of view.

Stage 6
Concern about self-condemnation for violating one's own principles. (Differentiates beween self-respect for general achieving rationality and self-respect for maintaining moral principles.)

Pro—If you don't steal the drug and let your wife die, you'd always condemn yourself for it afterward. You wouldn't be blamed and you would have lived up to the outside rule of the law but you wouldn't have lived up to your own standards of conscience.

Con—If you stole the drug, you wouldn't be blamed by other people but you'd condemn yourself because you wouldn't have lived up to your own conscience and standards of honesty.

Source: Rest. 1969. Unpublished doctoral dissertation, University of Chicago, 1969.

Criticisms of Kohlberg's Theory. Kohlberg's conclusions have not gone unchallenged, and in fact his theory and the research on which it is based have been the subject of serious criticism on numerous logical and empirical grounds (Gibbs, 1977; Kurtines and Greif, 1974; Liebert, 1979; Simpson,

1974). We will consider two interrelated examples, dealing with Kohlberg's claims that moral development is universal in its course and invariant in its sequence of development.

Almost certainly, the most distinctive and controversial element in Kohlberg's theory is his claim that there are universal, absolute standards of right and wrong and that he has demonstrated their existence through scientific research. Kohlberg's claim to have discovered universally true moral principles, as the substance of postconventional moral reasoning, is *not* an obvious outgrowth of Piaget's (or his own) cognitive-developmental theory; rather, the whole idea of postconventional morality is a radical departure from Piagetian and related cognitive-developmental theory. For example, at the empirical level there is some support for the sequence of development of moral justifications as proposed by Kohlberg, discovered cross-culturally for Stages 1 through 4 (Edwards, 1975; Kohlberg, 1969; Parikh, 1975; White, 1975). As Gibbs (1977) has pointed out, however, there appears to be almost no evidence to support the claim that Stages 5 and 6 are universal. To the contrary, there seem to be many cultures in which they are simply not found; and in the cultures where they are found, they are found rarely.

The absence of Stages 5 and 6 in most other cultures should not be surprising; postconventional moral reasoning as Kohlberg has defined it requires existential convictions that depend on a specific philosophical commitment. For example, in explaining Stage 6 moral reasoning Kohlberg states: "First of all, recognition of the moral duty to save a human life whenever possible must be assumed" (1971, p. 208). Kohlberg also defines Stage 6 partly in terms of accepting "the assumption that all other actors' claims (in a moral conflict) are also governed by the Golden Rule and accommodated accordingly" (1973, p. 643). Logical considerations alone simply do not give rise to these particular assumptions; rather, they reflect Kohlberg's own preferences and the beliefs of the particular culture of which he is a part.

Kohlberg (1976) has also claimed that his theory is "true" in the sense that "anyone who interviewed children about moral dilemmas and who followed them longitudinally" would come to see the same six stages he did, emerging in an invariant sequence (p. 47). This is quite a remarkable claim because Kohlberg's own report of his only longitudinal data, a follow-up of his initial sample, actually shows relatively little systematic change in moral reasoning over time, and one of the clearest findings seems to be that a number of the subjects displayed a *lower* level of moral reasoning than they had in high school (Kohlberg and Kramer, 1969). An equally significant study was conducted by Holstein (1967), who studied fifty-three families longitudinally to obtain an unusually close look at the course of moral development. During her first assessment, Holstein presented moral dilemmas to a son or daughter in each family who was thirteen at the time. A second assessment was conducted three years later, when the adolescent was now sixteen years old. In direct contradiction to predictions derived from Kohlberg's theory, large percentages of the subjects regressed from higher to lower stages across the three-year period. (Such shifts, by the

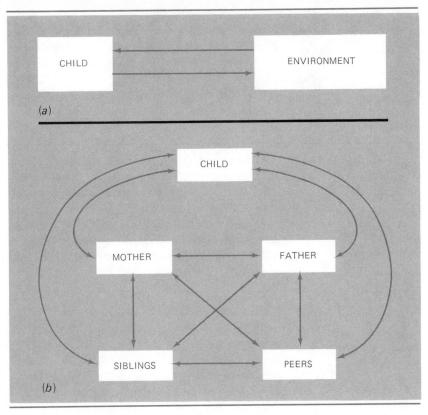

FIGURE 14-1
The child and the environment influence one another in socialization (a), but the interconnections involved are quite complex. Even when simplified by leaving out such factors as the school, church, physical environment, and differences among peers, the environment in which a child develops socially involves the interplay of many forces (b).

way, were equally likely to occur for boys and for girls.) Thus Kohlberg's hypothesis that there is an invariant, universal sequence of moral development was not supported.

If moral development cannot be explained by an innately determined program then how do morally relevant interpersonal reactions develop? One answer, suggested by social learning theory, is that interpersonal reactions such as helping and hurting are shaped or socialized by various forces in the environment.

The shaping process itself, as we saw in chapter 11, is rooted in the child's first relationships with parents and caretakers. But at least by the time the child leaves the crib and high chair, other agents of socialization begin to exert their influence. Siblings and peers play a central role in socialization, and soon relevant training and experiences are provided by such societal institutions as the school, church, and mass media. And socialization is complicated by the fact that children shape their environment, at least to some degree, rather than simply being shaped themselves. The hostilities of the bully, for example, may be a product of past training, but they are also the vehicle through which such a youngster changes siblings, peers, and even parents by eliciting submissive or punitive reactions back from them. The complexity of the process is suggested in Figure 14-1.

The following discussion focuses on two more or less separate aspects of social development: prosocial behavior (sharing, helping, and cooperating with others), and aggression. We cannot hope to fully describe how socializing forces play out for each child, but we can outline some of the basic principles that have been identified in the development of these behaviors. Each aspect is dependent upon basic perceptual, cognitive, and learning processes. It is apparent, though, that socialization always involves some kind of teaching and learning, and so it is not surprising that the various forms of learning have been found to be central.

PROSOCIAL BEHAVIOR

Most parents, most teachers, and most religions try to teach children to act in cooperative, helping, or giving ways—at least some of the time and in some situations. Such behavior is usually thought to be in the greater interest of others and society, and over the past twenty years or so psychologists have come to call all of these behaviors "prosocial." In this section we consider three classes of prosocial behavior that overlap but are not identical, and we describe research that helps us understand how such actions are developed and maintained.

Cooperation

Generally speaking, *cooperation* refers to behavior in which two or more people work together for mutual benefit. Such action is considered prosocial because societies are to a great extent built on the foundation of cooperative enterprises. Nevertheless, most developmental psychologists paid little attention to cooperation among children until Azrin and Lindsley (1956) demonstrated that children become more cooperative when directly reinforced for acting this way.

Developmental Trends and Cultural Influences. In a situation involving valuable resources or desired outcomes that can be obtained only by cooperation, competition is a nonrational as well as a nonprosocial response. When two children of about equal strength pull, tug-of-war fashion, on a single playground swing instead of taking turns on the swing, they will often end up with tired arms and voices, and perhaps with no one having a turn. For this reason, one would guess that cooperation would gradually overcome irrational competitive tendencies as children become more cognitively mature and reasonable, an expectation held by Piaget himself (e.g., Piaget, 1962). But a fascinating series of studies by M. C. Madsen and his associates has revealed that quite the opposite can occur. In some circumstances, practical cooperation *declines* as a child grows older and irrational competition in situations where it cannot possibly pay off comes to be the dominant mode of responding.

Madsen's basic test situation is depicted in Figure 14–2. Pairs of children of the same age are seated at opposite ends of a small table with a curved top that curls down at the sides. A marble is placed directly in the "marble holder" in the center of the table—this holder prevents it from rolling off to the side. A string fastened to each end of the marble holder permits either child to bring the marble nearer by pulling on his or her string and, if there is no interference from the other player, to finally pull the

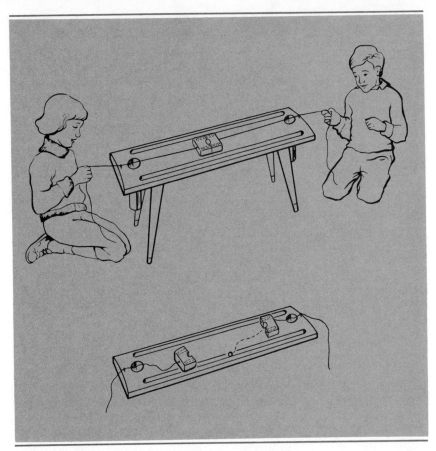

FIGURE 14–2
The marble-pulling game used by Madsen and his associates to measure cooperative behavior in children. A marble is placed in the center, and either child can earn the marble by pulling it to his or her side. But if both children pull at once, the holder will come apart and the marble itself will roll off into the gutter and be lost to both children. Cooperation is therefore required for success.

marble over the mouth of a small cup where it remains as the child's prize. The marble holder is not solid, however; it is held together by magnetic inserts and comes apart quite easily if both players pull at once. When this happens, the marble rolls into the gutter and is lost to both parties. In one major study, Madsen (1971) found that among middle- and lower-class white American children, cooperation during the marble game was quite

FIGURE 14–3
The willingness to cooperate for mutual enjoyment or benefit is evident at an early age. © Peeter Vilms/ Jeroboam, Inc.

likely at ages four and five but was virtually absent among the school-age children. On the first ten trials the four- and five-year-old pairs successfully negotiated to obtain more than half of the marbles on the average; among the seven-, eight-, nine-, and ten-year-old pairs, the great majority did not succeed in obtaining any marbles at all!

Further investigations by Madsen have provided additional support for the pattern, in that retarded children are more cooperative (and therefore more successful) in this situation than are normals; and, among the retarded, the younger children are again more cooperative than the older ones. The key to this paradox, Madsen feels, has been found in his cross-cultural research. Mexican children and children raised on kibbutzim (that is, Israeli collective farms) are far more cooperative than Anglo-Americans and, respectively, more cooperative than Mexican-American and city-dwelling Israeli children as well (Madsen, 1971; Shapira and Madsen, 1974). It seems that urban cultures foster competition to the extent that the bounds of rational cooperation are exceeded. The possibility that competition can become blinding is suggested by the verbal comments of children in situations requiring practical cooperation. In one study it was reported that many children "did not see the cooperative solution. While playing, competitive subjects declared, 'This game is too hard,' or 'No one can win.' When asked after the experiment how they might have gotten some toys subjects most often responded, 'If I could play alone' . . ." (Kagan and Madsen, 1971, p. 38). Perhaps most disquieting of all is the finding that among seven- to nine-year-old American children, situations requiring cooperation often led to participants actively attempting to lower the outcomes of their partners even when there was no direct gain for themselves (Kagan and Madsen, 1972a). Rivalry of this sort increases with age and is greater among boys than among girls (Kagan and Madsen, 1972b).

Except for the sex difference noted above, the generally low level of cooperation found by Madsen seems to be remarkably uniform among American children. No differences have been found between whites and blacks, nor between those coming from the middle and lower classes (Nelson and Madsen, 1969; Madsen and Shapira, 1970). Children in the United States, at least in some situations, are sufficiently imbued with the value of competitiveness so as to preclude consideration of cooperation. Ultimately, of course, a willingness to cooperate in one's own best interests is not incompatible with an entrepreneurial business ethic. Here there is still much that developmental psychologists do not know. Nonetheless, some progress has been made in identifying experiences that might foster a better understanding of the practical use of a cooperative approach in interpersonal behavior.

Stimulating Cooperative Behavior.   What factors will stimulate the development of cooperation? Several have been identified. First, verbally structuring situations in terms of mutual gain by creating a "we" rather than an "I" orientation seems to be important, so that children see themselves as working *with* rather than against each other (Kagan and Madsen, 1971). Second, and not surprisingly, direct experience with the positive consequences of cooperation increases the likelihood that such behavior will occur. Guiding children into a practical cooperative relationship and letting them directly experience its benefits (e.g., actually getting more marbles for themselves than would otherwise be the case) markedly increases cooperation in children of diverse cultural backgrounds (Madsen, 1971).

And, finally, modeled examples of cooperative behavior by other children can have a powerful influence on children. In one study (Liebert, Sprafkin, and Poulos, 1975) children were exposed to a thirty-second television spot designed to teach cooperation through positive example. "The Swing," as this spot was called, opens with a boy and girl running across a field to reach the last remaining swing on a playground; they both reach the swing at the same time and immediately begin to struggle over it, each claiming first rights. After a moment during which battle seems inevitable, one of the youngsters produces the insight that they should take turns and suggests that the other child go first. Each of the children is finally shown taking her or his turn, joyfully swinging through the air with the help of the other while an announcer's voice says, "There are lots of things you can do when two people want the same thing. One is to take turns . . . and that's a good one." Children exposed to this example are considerably more likely than comparable children not so exposed to exhibit cooperative behavior in a test situation similar to the one used by Madsen (see Figure 14–4).

Helping   In the late 1960s experimental social psychologists were profoundly influenced by a dramatic murder in New York, which was later described as follows:

FIGURE 14–4
The effects of exposure to a cooperatively oriented television spot, "The Swing," on children's cooperative behavior. Control group children were shown commercial TV spots that did not have a cooperative message in the test situation; children could cooperate by taking turns or could compete unfruitfully. From Liebert, Spratkin, and Poulos, 1975.

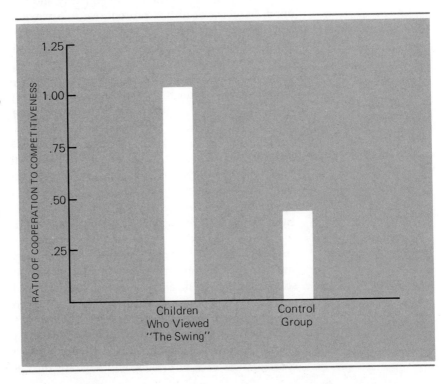

Several years ago, a young woman was stabbed to death in the middle of a street in a residential section of New York City. Although such murders are not entirely routine, the incident received little public attention until several weeks later when the *New York Times* disclosed another side of the case: at least 38 witnesses had observed the attack—and none had even attempted to intervene. Although the attacker took more than half an hour to kill Kitty Genevese, not one of the 38 people who watched from the safety of their own apartments came out to assist her. Not one even lifted the telephone to call the police. [Darley and Latané, 1968, p. 377]

This surprising lack of intervention seemed inconsistent with the humanitarian and cooperative norms that our society tries to foster and raised many questions about the role of prosocial behavior in modern life. Partly as a result, much has since been learned about such behavior in adults (Darley and Latané, 1968; Latané and Rodin, 1969). For example, it has been found that adults are more likely to give assistance in an emergency if they are the only bystanders than if others are present. But an important question remains for developmental psychologists: How is a willingness to help others acquired at all?

Role-playing and Induction. Staub (1971) has hypothesized that at least two factors are critical: the ability to empathize with the needy other and possession of the knowledge or skills to help effectively. To the extent that this reasoning is correct, it should be possible to increase children's willingness to help others by training in empathy and relevant skills. With this in mind, Staub devised two procedures, role playing and "induction," to increase young children's willingness to help other children in distress. Four groups of children were used in the study, one with each of the procedures, one with a combination of both, and a control group.

In the *role-playing* group, pairs of kindergarten youngsters were asked to act out situations in which one of them needed help and the other provided it. The experimenter began by describing a situation in which help was needed. The "helper" child was asked to improvise all of the helping actions he or she could think of; then the experimenter described further ones, each of which was in fact acted out. Finally, the two children changed roles. The five situations that Staub used were: (1) a child had fallen off a chair in an adjoining room; (2) a child was trying to carry a chair that was too heavy; (3) a child was distressed because building blocks were taken away by another youngster; (4) a child was standing in the path of an oncoming bicycle; and (5) a child had fallen and had been hurt. The variety of possible ways of helping, generated spontaneously by the youngsters or suggested by the experimenter, included direct intervention, verbal consolation to the victim, and calling someone else for help.

Staub's *induction* group closely followed the procedures for role playing except that the children were asked merely to describe verbally how they could provide help. Then, as in the role-playing group, the experimenter described other appropriate ways of helping and pointed out the positive consequences each of these would have for the needy child, such as an increase in positive feelings or reduction of pain and suffering. Induction, then, involved pointing out to children the consequences of their behavior for others. (It had been shown [correlationally] in previous research that children whose parents described themselves as using induction techniques tend to show somewhat more frequent prosocial acts in nursery schools than children whose parents use other socialization practices.)

In the *role playing with induction* group children were trained using both procedures. In addition to actually acting out various helping roles, the experimenter explained the positive consequences that would accrue to the needy child.

Finally, there was a control group of children who acted out a variety of scenes that were completely unrelated to helping behavior.

To determine the immediate effects of these treatments, each child in the experiment was taken to a room containing a variety of toys and playthings. After brief interaction with the child, the experimenter went into the adjacent room "to check on a girl who is playing there" and then announced that she (the experimenter) would have to leave for a while. Less than two minutes after the experimenter left, the subject heard a loud crash coming from the adjacent room, quickly followed by about seventy seconds of severe crying and sobbing. Actually the room was empty and the distress sounds were produced by a pretaped recording. From the subject's point of view, though, another child, alone in the next room, desperately needed help and there was no one else to provide it. What could the subject do now?

Staub categorized the children's reactions as: *active help*, if they went into the adjacent room to help; *volunteering information*, if they reported to the experimenter that something had happened in the other room; and *no help*, if they made no effort to provide direct or indirect assistance.*

The test situation described above closely followed portions of the role-playing and induction procedures used during training. It was therefore of interest to determine whether any effects obtained would generalize to situations that were somewhat different from those involved in training. So Staub created a second test in which the subject and an adult experimenter began to play a game, during which time the adult "accidentally" dropped a box of paper clips. She then expressed mild alarm ("Oh, my dear!") and began to pick up the scattered clips. The measure during this circumstance was the number of paper clips the subject picked up, both spontaneously and with prompting (e.g., "Could you help me a little?").

Finally, there was a measure of willingness to share. Later in the sequence each child was given a bag of candy and told that there was a poor child to whom some of the candy could be donated. Thus, in sum, Staub's

*Of course, in such situations it is important to "debrief" the child afterward so as to explain the situation and make sure that he or she does not leave with any negative feelings or misconceptions. Thus, Staub told his subjects ". . . that they had only heard a recording, that no one was really hurt, and that the reason they heard the recording was that [the experimenter] wanted to find out what children thought when they heard another child crying. . . . So that [the children] would have an overall pleasant experience, they engaged in additional activities, for example, making up stories about pictures of pleasant content . . ." (Staub, 1971, p. 809).

experiment involved a total of three measures of prosocial behavior—assisting a child in distress, assisting an adult in distress, and sharing with another child. Some of these tests were given immediately after the induction and/or role-playing treatment and others were given about one week later.

Staub's results suggested generally that role playing could be used effectively to foster prosocial behavior and that its effects were durable over a period of at least one week. The findings were therefore encouraging in that they suggested, as Staub points out in his own conclusion, "that specific training procedures, particularly role playing of specific situations, may enhance the subsequent probability of prosocial behavior" (p. 815).

However, it is of considerable interest that the effects of induction were insignificant. Indeed, inspection of Staub's results reveals that induction may actually have made children somewhat "oppositional"; those exposed to this treatment became somewhat *less* likely to assist the adult in picking up paper clips than were children in the control group. The pressure applied by induction to "be good" apparently created some threat to the child's feeling of freedom, to which he or she responded with resistance.

Effects of Behavioral Example.   As with other forms of prosocial behavior, helping in both children and adults can also be stimulated by social models (Sprafkin, Liebert, and Poulos, 1975; Loye, Gorney, and Steele, 1977; Murray and Ahammer, 1977). Collins and Getz (1976), for example, invited fourth- through tenth-grade children to watch a television action-adventure drama. One version of the program was edited to show the model responding constructively to interpersonal conflict, while the second version showed the actor responding aggressively. The results of this experiment were that children who saw the model respond constructively were more likely to help a fictitious peer complete a task than the children who observed the aggressive model.

Of course, modeling can also be used in combination with other techniques, a general principle that has been known for some time (Mischel and Liebert, 1966). One recent combinational use of modeling and other techniques involves having children watch helpful models on television and then encouraging the children to be helpful through appropriate role-playing situations at home or at school (Singer and Singer, 1974).*

Sharing   Through fate or circumstance, one person is often dependent upon another's charity; indeed, whole institutions in our society are sustained by the voluntary contributions of others. As James Bryan, an expert in the area, has written: "Most children in middle childhood will verbally, if not behaviorally, support the principle that one should aid the needy" (1970, p. 61).

In this section we shall describe some of the research that supports Bryan's statement and ask how a child's willingness to share with others is acquired and maintained. Before doing so, however, it is important to distinguish between *sharing*, the act of giving some or all of one's own goods

---

*The combination of role playing and modeling is also a very potent technique in clinical psychology, both with children and adults.

and resources to another, and *altruism,* which is usually viewed as unselfish action not motivated by self-interest.

Whether or not a child will share can be measured easily—for example, by seeing whether he or she divides a piece of cake with a peer or contributes valuable tokens, money, or toys to others in a controlled situation. But determining whether a child is acting "altruistically" is quite a different matter, inasmuch as altruism implies that the motivation of self-gain is not involved. Certainly it has been observed that children will share even if no adult is around to make them do so, and sharing also occurs even when there is no apparent opportunity for the person helped to reciprocate or even identify the donor. Still, there might be the expectation for delayed or subtle rewards; we do know that children are more likely to share when the arrangement is reciprocal—a sort of "You share with me and I'll share with you"—than when it is not (Floyd, 1964; Staub and Sherk, 1970). Then, too, sharing might occur to avoid possible negative outcomes rather than to produce positive ones. Any of these alternative explanations may plausibly rival the interpretation that children have shared for strictly "altruistic" reasons in any given situation.

Developmental Trends.   In general, a positive relationship between age and children's willingness to share with others has been found; older children are more likely to share or appear to be more generous than younger ones (Ugurel-Semin, 1952; Handlon and Gross, 1959; Rushton and Weiner, 1975). In some areas, though, the relationship between age and generosity is less clear. Liebert, Fernandez, and Gill (1969) found no differences between six- to eight-year-olds and nine- to eleven-year-olds on willingness to share with another child who was described as "not well-liked and has no friends." In this study the younger children actually tended to be more generous than the older ones. With adult subjects the age-sharing relationship similarly may be reversed; thus, for example, young adults are proportionally more likely than older ones to be blood donors (London and Hemphill, 1965).

Mood and Emotional State.   Several studies show that a child's willingness to share is influenced by her or his immediate emotional state. Children who are asked to think happy thoughts share more than those not given this positive set, whereas those asked to think sad thoughts tend to share a bit less than uninstructed control children also invited to share (Moore, Underwood, and Rosenhan, 1973). Related investigations also report that the feeling or experience of being successful seems to produce a "warm glow of success" in children that makes them more generous, whereas failure and its associated feelings decrease generosity in young and old alike (Berkowitz and Connor, 1966; Isen, Horn, and Rosenhan, 1973). And, finally, sharing seems to *produce* positive emotional feelings in donors, apparently because children and adults respond with empathy to the positive experiences of those with whom they share (Aronfreed, 1968).

Effects of Reward and Punishment. Perhaps the most obvious way to elicit sharing from children is to reward them directly for acts of generosity. After doing just this with four-year-old children, Fischer (1963) found that youngsters became more likely to share marbles with unknown peers if such beneficence was, in turn, directly rewarded with bubble gum. The brighter children in this study learned to share at a more rapid rate than the less intelligent ones, a result consistent with correlational data showing a significant relationship between intelligence and the development of a moral code in adolescence (Havighurst and Taba, 1949). However, the length of time these children shared after the experimenter and the promise of external reward were removed is unknown. This is an important question because parents and other adults will not always be present to reward the child for sharing. Other studies showing that bestowing rewards increases sharing are similarly flawed. Until more conclusive studies are done, then, the uncertainty will remain as to whether these incentive-induced increases in sharing persist across time and across situations.

There is also the other side of the coin. One would expect that aversive consequences (punishment) for *not* sharing would also increase a child's sharing in the future. Until very recently developmental psychologists have given little attention to this possibility. But we now know that the threat of punishment for stinginess does increase immediate sharing. Studies have shown that such "help or else" training is extremely effective in transmitting a tendency to share (which often endures even after the threatening conditions are removed). In contrast, merely verbally pointing out the inequity between potential donors and recipients has little effect on children's subsequent sharing (Hartmann, Gelfand, Smith, Paul, Cromer, and Lebenta, 1974; Hartmann, Gelfand, Smith, Paul, Page, and Lebenta, 1976).

There appear to be limits, however, as to the effectiveness of coercion in teaching children to share. In an important experiment, White (1972) simulated a contrast among three training techniques that parents might use to teach sharing. *Guided rehearsal* involved being told during a training session, "What we would like you to do is give one [gift certificate] to the orphans each time you win two," and then being made to follow through on this precept after having in fact won two certificates. Other children were exposed to modeled examples of voluntary sharing, sometimes with an opportunity to rehearse what they would do but always without coercion. A final, control group received no training. At least for these elementary school boys and girls, observation with unguided rehearsal opportunities was the most successful technique overall; exposure to it facilitated sharing and inhibited stealing of the freely available certificates. The pressure of forced rehearsal did have the immediate effect of guiding the children to increase their donations, even when they were alone, but in the long run forcing sharing in this way led to both *decreased* sharing and increased stealing relative to the other groups.

Effects of Behavioral Example. In White's (1972) experiment, discussed above, the combination of a modeled example and voluntary rehearsal was a highly effective long-term training technique for the development of sharing. This should not be surprising, for literally dozens of studies with chil-

FIGURE 14-5
Sharing is often learned by observing others. Photo by Shumsky/ICON.

dren had shown previously that behavioral examples are perhaps the most potent way to elicit and teach sharing (Bryan and London, 1970; Poulos and Liebert, 1972; Rice and Grusec, 1975; Rushton, 1975). In a classic study, for example, Rosenhan and White (1967) asked fourth- and fifth-grade boys and girls to play a bowling game in which gift certificates, exchangeable at a local toy store, could be won. The experimenters varied a number of factors, one of which was whether the children saw an adult model donate to the "Trenton Orphans Fund" by placing some of his gift certificates in a labeled box that displayed children in ragged attire. Of those who saw this example, almost half (47.5 percent) also shared later when they were all alone; in contrast, without the instigation of a generous adult exemplar, none of the children shared. Experimental studies such as these seem to be confirmed by correlational data as well. One study found parents' altruistic values (presumably modeled for their children) to be the single most consistent predicator of altruism in the child (Hoffman, 1973).

That exposure to sharing models can increase children's sharing has been clear for some time, but the model characteristics that can amplify or mute this effect have been studied only more recently. Grusec (1971), for example, found that children were more likely, when alone, to imitate the sharing of a powerful model (an adult who controlled resources of great value to the children) than a nonpowerful one. The same basic effect, that powerful models are more potent as social examples than less powerful ones, has since been confirmed in other studies (Rushton, 1975; Rushton and Owen, 1975). In contrast, Grusec found that a sharing model who was extremely warm, friendly, and rather forgiving was actually imitated somewhat *less* than a sharing adult who had maintained a more neutral demeanor. An overly tolerant and forgiving parent may simply have a more difficult time in transmitting any form of self-denial, including sharing, to his or her child.

Finally, we may wonder whether there is any possible generality in a child's prosocial responses. In other words, is a child who demonstrates co-operation also likely to donate to a charity or help a friend? Investigators have found some evidence for generality among the responses of children (Dlugokinski and Firestone, 1973; Rushton and Weiner, 1975). However, this finding is not consistent across all studies (Yarrow and Waxler, 1976; Rubin and Schneider, 1973). Therefore, it is not clear whether various prosocial responses such as cooperation, helping, and sharing are determined by a common factor or by specific environmental factors.

AGGRESSION

At some time or another virtually everyone aggresses, acting in a way that brings, or might bring, discomfort to someone else. We know, how-ever, that the type of aggression that a person displays and the ability to control such action change in important ways with age and experience. The roots of these patterns and changes have long been of interest to devel-opmental psychologists.

For our purposes the determinants of *aggression* can be divided into two broad classes. Certain kinds of circumstances will draw out aggression more often than others and may therefore be thought of as *elicitors* of ag-gression. When people are attacked, for example, they are likely to respond in kind, and so attack is an elicitor of aggression. Other determinants of aggression do not deal with provocation, but rather teach or encourage ag-gression; these are known as *cultivators* of a general pattern of responding.

Frustration and Aggression

One view of how aggression is elicited is found in the famous "frustra-tion-aggression" hypothesis, first spelled out by John Dollard and his asso-ciates at Yale in 1939. These theorists argued that *frustration,* defined as any blocking of goal-directed activity, naturally leads to aggression. According to the original statement of this hypothesis, aggression was said to be *always* a consequence of frustration and frustration was said to lead *always* to some form of aggression. Such a statement is too strong. In many cases most people, even if severely frustrated, will refrain from showing any direct acts of aggression; speeding drivers will not assault, or even raise their voices to the police officer who has apprehended them. And, as we shall see, factors other than frustration often lead to the occurrence of aggression.

Emotional Arousal and Catharsis

Many parents feel that their children are more likely to become aggres-sive (hitting a younger brother or sister, for example) when they are upset, agitated, or excited. Research has shown that emotional arousal does in-fluence a child's willingness to aggress and that the process operates differ-ently according to the youngster's sex. Boys' overall level of aggression in-creases when they are emotionally aroused, whereas arousal has been found to decrease aggressive behavior in girls (Harris and Siebel, 1976). So-cially learned anxiety about hostile impulses may well account for the pat-tern, inasmuch as females are taught to feel guilty about their aggressive tendencies while males are often led to believe that a willingness to aggress is brave or heroic (see chapter 12).

At one time it was thought that most people could reduce their level of arousal by playing out their aggressive feelings verbally. But research has now shown that this type of *catharsis* does not occur.* Neither children nor adults seem able to "let off steam" by verbally expressing their hostilities (Mallick and McCandless, 1966; Loew, 1967), and permitting a child to speak aggressive words has been shown, for both boys and girls, to *increase* one's willingness to punch another child (Slaby, 1975).

Competition

Do highly competitive situations produce only sporting gamesmanship in children, or can they elicit outright hostility as well? This question was asked in a field experiment conducted by Rocha and Rogers (1976). In their study pairs of kindergarten and first-grade boys competed for a prize by building a tall tower out of blocks. In the high-competition group, few blocks were available; in the low-competition group, blocks were available in abundance. The results clearly showed that high competition bred aggression as measured by interfering with one's partner and taking some of his blocks. More distressing was the fact that boys in the high-competition group often abandoned the relatively practical if distasteful tactics of interference (for example, toppling the other boy's blocks) in favor of out-and-out physical assaults against the opponent. Figure 14–6 indicates that physical aggression was stimulated as much as was interference by introducing the element of high competition into the game. As the authors note:

*The term *catharsis* can be traced to Aristotle, who believed that an audience could be drained of tragic emotions by watching a play. Freud later used the concept to refer to the release of pent-up or repressed feelings.

FIGURE 14–6
Results of Rocha and Rogers's experiment, showing that competitive situations may elicit overt physical aggression between children, as well as encouraging interference with the other child's efforts.

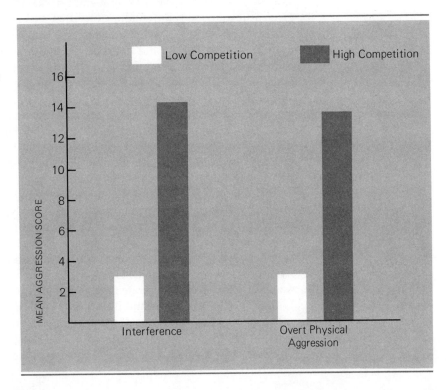

The results of the present experiment clearly supported the hypothesis that competition breeds aggression. Regardless of how aggression was measured, the more competitive the situation, the more aggressively the children behaved. ... It was particularly distressing to discover that [competition] affected physical aggression as well as interference. Toppling the opponent's tower was at least as effective as fighting as an instrumentality to winning the prize, and perhaps a better method since the subject's own tower could be tumbled inadvertently in a brawl. [These and other findings suggest] that competitive situations frequently arouse feelings of rivalry that go beyond merely winning the competition and involve going out of one's way to hurt the other person.

Social Learning of Aggressive Behavior

Although children may be provoked into aggression by irritating or arousing events in their environment, most aggressive acts also can be traced to the child's past learning experiences. Parents or other adults may inadvertently reward aggressive behavior and thus increase its occurrence. Slaby (1977), for example, reports that many teachers provide social reward (attention) to children's verbally aggressive speech, thereby unwittingly strengthening such behavior. In addition to their history of rewards and punishments, youngsters who have been given numerous aggressive models will learn habits that can easily be activated whenever provoking circumstances occur.

In a series of experiments done some years ago, Richard Walters and his associates demonstrated that even rewarding children for "make-believe" aggression in a play situation increases later aggressiveness against other children (Cowan and Walters, 1963; Walters and Brown, 1963, 1964). In the Walters and Brown (1963) experiment, for example, colored marbles were given as rewards to some children, on either a continuous or an intermittent schedule, for hitting a toy Bobo doll similar to the one in Figure 14–7. Children in a control group did not receive these rewards. Two days later the children were put in a potentially frustrating situation and were left to play with another child, who had not received any training in aggression. The degree of aggressive behavior displayed in this situation was the primary measure of the study. The behaviors rated included butting, kneeing, elbowing, kicking, punching and pushing, and pulling by the neck and hair. Children who had been rewarded intermittently for hitting the Bobo doll two days earlier showed significantly more aggression in this game situation than did those in either of the remaining groups.*

In a second experiment by these same investigators (Walters and Brown, 1964) some participants were rewarded only when they hit the Bobo sharply while others were rewarded exclusively for weaker hits. Again, employing measures of aggression in physical contact games, it was found that boys rewarded for the higher magnitude of aggression were more aggressive in this new interpersonal situation than were those who had been rewarded for relatively temperate play.

The studies of Walters and Brown have several striking implications for socialization practices. Consider, for example, the father who enthusias-

---

*The effect of rewarding children intermittently rather than continuously was discussed in chapter 6.

FIGURE 14–7
The "Bobo" doll used
for studying the
influence of reward
on aggressive
behavior in the
Walters experiments.
From Bandura and
Walters, 1963.
Courtesy
Dr. Albert Bandura.

tically encourages his son to roughneck with him in play and to smash away at punching bags, praising the lad for particularly forceful assaults. In addition to building a "real boy," it may be that such training has the unintended effect of promoting aggression in other interpersonal situations. And intermittent reinforcement (which had the greatest effect on children in the Walters experiments) will generally be provided simply because parents or other supervisory adults will not always be present to witness all of the child's aggressive actions. The father who teaches his son to hit a punching bag, for instance, will not necessarily be on the playground to reprimand the child for hitting his friend.

Children also learn aggressive responses as a result of themselves being the *subject* of aggression. Thus parents who physically punish their children are serving as models as well as disciplinary agents. It has been shown, in fact, that parents who punish their children physically tend at the same time to increase the amount of aggression their children display in other situations (Patterson, 1976, 1979).

The role of modeling in the acquisition of aggressive skills and habits was discussed briefly in chapter 6. We saw that children can learn novel ways of behaving aggressively merely by watching the performance of these acts by others, and that this learning takes place even if the aggressive

FIGURE 14–8
Television presents
numerous models of
aggressive behavior.
Strix Pix, Monkmeyer
Press Photo Service.

model is punished for acting out hostilities. More importantly, continual exposure to multiple models who act in a particular way (e.g., aggressively) may induce a general disinhibition so that, beyond imitating particular actions, a widespread tendency to respond aggressively to new situations may develop. At the same time, such exposure may increase the observer's willingness to tolerate aggression directed at others (Drabman and Thomas, 1974; Thomas and Drabman, 1975).

Close-up

Television and Children's Aggressive Behavior

What are the effects upon children of observing violent television programs? The question is one that has been posed continually since the advent of television sets as a common fixture in the American home about three decades ago. Answers to it have ranged from statements that such programs can have an adverse effect on almost anyone to assertions that merely watching entertainment fare can do little to shape children's social behavior.

Early studies by Bandura and his associates showed clearly that youngsters could **learn** novel aggressive responses from television and televisionlike formats. But critics (Halloran, 1964; Klapper, 1968) pointed out that these studies did not prove that the kind of violence found on television or in movies influences the "real-life" social behavior of young observers. In response to the critics, researchers began to ask whether children also would imitate screened aggression against human victims.

In the first study directed toward the answer, four- and five-year-old boys from a Sunday School kindergarten served as subjects (Hanratty, Liebert, Morris, and Fernandez, 1969). Half of them observed a two-and-one-half-minute color sound film in which an adult aggressed against a human clown. The behavior displayed by this symbolic model included sharp and unprovoked verbal insults to the clown, shooting at the clown with a toy machine gun, and beating the clown vigorously with a plastic mallet. Half the group did not see such a film.

Thereafter, half of the subjects in each of these groups were permitted to play in a room where they found a human clown standing idly, as well as a mallet and a toy gun. The remaining children found a plastic Bobo doll rather than a human. The youngsters were left in this situation for ten minutes, during which time their aggressive responses toward the clown, plastic or human, were recorded. Not surprisingly, the brief film increased children's aggression against the inflated Bobo, with **all** the children exhibiting some aggressive action against the toy. In contrast, of those who had not observed the movie, none engaged in any sort of aggressive behavior toward the human clown. There are, of course, strong inhibitions for aggressing against a human being, even one who is attired as a clown, and there was no provocation for doing so. Nonetheless, after observation of the aggressive movie a significant number of physical assaults against the human clown did occur, including at least one swat with the mallet that was hard enough to leave a red mark on the clown's arm for several hours later.

In a second experiment (Hanratty, 1969), it was again found that film of this type, without other provocation, would lead children to physically assault a human victim. Moreover, such aggression was displayed by both boys and girls after viewing films in which either an eight-year-old boy or an adult served as a model. This finding was replicated a third and a fourth time with somewhat older boys (Hanratty, O'Neal, and Sulzer, 1972; Savitsky, Rogers, Izard, and Liebert, 1971). Under some circumstances, then, children will directly imitate filmed aggression against other people.

Still, direct imitative effects require a situation virtually identical to the one observed, and so may be less important from a social point of view than a more general disinhibition (see chapter 6). Considerable research emphasis has more recently been placed on disinhibitory influences.

DISINHIBITORY EFFECTS

Several correlational studies bear directly on the possibility of a relationship between the amount of violence a child observes and the amount of aggressive behavior displayed in naturalistic situations. Uniformly such a relationship has been found, for both elementary (Dominick and Greenberg, 1972) and high-school-age youngsters (McIntyre and Teevan, 1972; McLeod, Atkin, and Chaffee, 1972). McLeod, Atkin, and Chaffee (1972), for example, examined the relationship between viewing televised violence and a variety of measures of aggressive behavior in two relatively large samples of adolescents, one in Maryland and another in Wisconsin. The authors summarized the outcome of these correlational studies as follows:

Our research shows that among both boys and girls at two grade levels [junior high and senior high], the more the child watches violent television fare, the more aggressive he is likely to be as measured by a variety of self-report measures. . . . Partialing out [total] viewing time slightly reduces the positive correlations of violence viewing and aggressive behavior in most cases, but the basic result is the same as for the raw correlations. . . . Similarly, the partialing out of socioeconomic status and school performance does not alter the basic pattern. . . . We may conclude, then, that adolescents viewing high levels of violent content on television tend to have high levels of aggressive behavior, regardless of television viewing time, socioeconomic status or school performance. [pp. 187, 191]

As explained in chapter 2, correlations such as the ones described above are not firm proof of causality; aggressive behavior could be related to viewing violence on television without necessarily being caused by it. One way to increase certainty regarding such possible effects is to conduct a longitudinal study so that change (if any) can be seen directly. Lefkowitz, Eron, Walder, and Huesmann (1972) have done just that. Their report, based on a longitudinal study of the entire population of children of a particular age in a rural New York county, involved approximately nine hundred youngsters. Designed from the outset to relate children's aggressive behavior to various familial, social, and experimental factors that might influence it, these investigators employed a peer measurement technique of aggression, focusing exclusively upon acts that would harm or irritate other persons. The first measures obtained by the investigators showed a significant relationship, for boys, between the amount of television violence that the subjects watched in the third grade, when they were nine years old, and independently assessed peer ratings of how aggressive they were at that time (Eron, 1963).

Lefkowitz and his associates completed the longitudinal phase of their study ten years later by obtaining data from more than four hundred of the youngsters whom they had studied initially. The measures included peer ratings of aggression at this age, self-reports of aggression in an interview, and self-reports of various aspects of television viewing. The results of this ten-year follow-up showed that, for boys, the amount of television violence they watched at age nine was significantly related to how aggressive they were ten years later, at age nineteen. In fact, the strength of this relationship led the

investigators to conclude that a substantial component of overt aggressive behavior at age nineteen was predicted better by the amount of television violence children watched in the third grade than by any other variable measured.

This longitudinal study greatly strengthens the argument that the viewing of television violence causes aggressive behavior, but only true experiments, in which the selection of programs is controlled by the researcher, can put the process to the final test. Numerous experiments have examined the relationship, and the overwhelming majority have found evidence that the causal connection is present (Liebert, Neale, and Davidson, 1973; Liebert and Schwartzberg, 1977).

Leifer and Roberts (1972), for example, obtained information on the subsequent willingness of children and adolescents (kindergartners through twelfth graders) to aggress after they watched television programs that differed in the amount of violent content displayed. The programs were taken directly from the air, without editing. The children were then tested, using a specially designed response hierarchy, on their willingness to aggress. Each child was presented with a series of real-life situations ("You're standing in line for a drink of water. A kid comes along and just pushes you out of line. What do you do?") and asked to choose between a pair of alternative responses. One of the alternatives was typically aggressive ("Push them"), while the other was not ("Go away"). (See Figure 14–9.) These investigators, too, found that the more violent programs reliably produced higher levels of aggressive responding than the less violent ones. It is of further interest that in this experiment understanding the motivations for, and consequences of, violence in a program did **not** relate to a significant degree to the aggression scores. It appears that the instigating effect of viewing is not reduced by an increased understanding of the motivations and consequences that surround it.

Studies of the sort done by Leifer and

"You're walking down the street. Some kid is mad at you and comes up and hits you. What do you do?"

A. HIT THEM OR LEAVE THEM?

D. LEAVE THEM OR CALL THEM "STUPID"?

B. TELL A GROWN-UP OR CALL THEM "STUPID"?

E. HIT THEM OR CALL THEM "STUPID"?

C. LEAVE THEM OR TELL A GROWN-UP?

F. TELL A GROWN-UP OR HIT THEM?

FIGURE 14-9
Sample items from the response hierarchy used by Leifer and Roberts.
Children were shown either slides or pictures of situations such as
these.   From Leifer and Roberts, 1972, by permission. Artist, Jurgen Wolff.

Roberts provide the best source of information about basic processes and causal relationships. However, to ensure generality of such findings to the more complex natural environment, such "laboratory studies" can be supplemented by experimental field research. One such study was conducted by Stein and Friedrich (1972) in a relatively naturalistic situation in order to determine some of the cumulative or longer-range effects of observing television upon children. The subjects were ninety-seven children (fifty-two boys and forty-five girls) between 3½ and 5½ years of age, who were systematically exposed to television programs of differing content during the course of their participation in a summer nursery school.

This carefully designed experiment involved an initial measurement period in which the free play of children in the nursery

school was observed and rated according to a variety of categories; a four-week experimental period in which children were systematically exposed either to aggressive cartoons (**Batman** and **Superman**), neutral television programming (children working on a farm and the like), or prosocial programming (episodes from the program **Mister Rogers' Neighborhood**); and a two-week postviewing period in which effects could be observed and assessed. The children were exposed to the programs for approximately twenty minutes per day three times a week for a four-week period. During this time, and during the two-week postviewing period, the children's behavior was again systematically observed in the naturalistic preschool situation.

Stein and Friedrich found that children who were initially in the upper half of the sample in interpersonal aggression subsequently showed greater interpersonal aggression if they were exposed to the aggressive programming than if they were exposed to either the neutral or the prosocial programming. Thus, aggressive cartoons increased interpersonal aggression significantly for these children despite the fact that they watched television in the nursery school for less than a total of six hours over a four-week period. What is more, as the investigators note:

> [The] effects occurred in naturalistic behavior that was removed both in time and environmental setting from the viewing experience. They occurred with a small amount of exposure, particularly in relation to the amount the children received at home, and they endured during the postviewing period. [P. 247]

PARENTAL REACTIONS AND TELEVISION VIOLENCE

Discussions of the effects of television violence usually consider the possibility that parental reactions may reduce the medium's aggression-proving effects. Grusec (1973) addressed herself to this issue by having five- and ten-year-old children watch an aggressive film with an adult. In one condition the adult was overtly critical of the screen aggressor (for example, by saying "That's awful" when an aggressive act occurred); in the two other conditions the adult either responded neutrally or praised the same hostilities. The critical test came when the children were permitted to play alone after having seen the film under one of these three conditions.

As we might have expected, ten-year-olds who had seen the film with an adult critical of aggression were indeed subsequently less aggressive than their peers who had viewed the film with an accepting or openly approving adult coviewer. More surprising was the behavior of the five-year-olds, who imitated the film's aggressive examples when they were alone regardless of what the adult's stated opinions had been when they had watched together. What is more, there would have been no way for the adult to find out that her criticism had failed to neutralize the film had this not been an experiment. We know this because for all children there was a final phase to Grusec's experiment: A new adult appeared and asked the individual children about each aggressive scene in the film. In this interview situation five-year-olds as well as ten-year-olds were highly critical of the film if they had viewed it originally with a critical adult—considerably more critical than in the other groups. Publicly, then, the five-year-olds seemed to reject the criticized behaviors of the aggressive model, while privately they were imitating most of them.

SUMMARY   The moral sphere includes both moral values and reasoning and actual interpersonal reactions that may help or harm others.

Early analyses of moral development, such as Freud's, stressed the emergence of a unitary moral agent (e.g., the *superego*), but Hartshorne and May's research soon cast doubt on the belief that moral values and behavior are highly consistent. Another approach, Kohlberg's cognitive theory, posits an invariant, universal course of moral development through three levels—*preconventional, conventional,* and *postconventional*—each composed of two differing stages. Kohlberg's theory has been criticized for several reasons. His related conclusions that there are universal moral standards and that development follows the same sequence for everyone have been seriously challenged by recent cross-cultural and longitudinal comparisons.

According to social learning theory, moral development depends on socialization and involves complex interactions between the child and various agents of socialization: parents, siblings, peers, school, church, and mass media.

Prosocial behavior includes cooperation, helping, and sharing. Although these actions generally serve society well, they can also benefit the individual performing them. Contrary to what we might expect, cooperation does not necessarily increase with age. In situations requiring cooperation for success of the individuals, younger children sometimes demonstrate more cooperation than do older ones. Apparently some situations elicit competition in older children that precludes their acting cooperatively. This effect appears stronger in boys than in girls but operates across social class and for both black and white children. In some cultures (e.g., Mexico and the kibbutzim), children are more cooperative than children in the United States, but even here we find that urban settings foster competition. Cooperation can be stimulated, however, by directly reinforcing it, by structuring the situation as a "we" rather than an "I" situation, by exposing children to the benefits of cooperation, and by presenting cooperative models.

Psychologists have addressed themselves to the question of how helping can be elicited or encouraged in children. Exposure to peer models who act out helping in different situations increases subsequent prosocial behavior. Induction, involving pointing out the consequences of helping, apparently does not always increase prosocial behavior. Being "pressured" by verbal lessons to be "good" can have adverse effects in that it makes children oppositional.

Children's willingness to share their possessions with others clearly increases with age. However, many factors are known to influence sharing: emotional state of the potential sharer, reinforcement for sharing, exposure to a powerful model. Forcing children to share is not especially effective; children treated in this manner do not have a strong tendency to share unless they are being watched by others.

Aggression can be provoked by frustration, emotional arousal, and competition. Reinforcement for aggression and exposure to aggressive models are powerful in encouraging such action in children. Extensive investigation of the effects of television aggression has clearly shown that televised models can increase aggression in children. This conclusion is based on correlational and experimental studies and holds across a wide range of children. Parents can modify this effect somewhat by being critical of the screened aggression. However, such criticism does not seem influential for preschoolers; they continue to accept aggression as a way of behaving when they are not with the adult who had been critical.

15 Behavior Problems of Childhood

We have come far in describing and discussing the basic processes of development. With few exceptions—notably mental retardation, genetic disorders, and gender-identity disturbances—our focus has been on normal processes that lead to typical behaviors and attitudes. This chapter, and a portion of chapter 16, will be devoted to a fuller discussion of childhood behavior problems. We will have the opportunity to sample more widely from the array of problems that may arise during youth, portraying the behaviors involved and delineating etiological theories and treatment models. Inasmuch as our aim is to paint a broad developmental picture, the important issue of predicting later problems from early behavior will also be included.

THE CRITERIA FOR IDENTIFYING BEHAVIOR PROBLEMS

Unlike many instances of adult behavior dysfunction, childhood problems are usually not defined by the individual him- or herself. Instead, parents, teachers, and junvenile authorities notice that "something is wrong." Many attempt to remedy the situation for the youngsters, seeking professional help only when their efforts fail or when the disorder appears serious or beyond their understanding. On what bases do adults decide that children have a problem and/or need professional help? There are several, and more than one may operate at any given time.

Behavior is always judged in comparison to *cultural norms*. Action that is deemed quite "regular" and "normal" in one culture or subculture may be judged "abnormal" in another. This criterion is applied to children as well as to adults. Youngsters in the United States, for example, are probably expected to be relatively assertive and aggressive compared to children in some other parts of the world. Then, too, the young are presumed to grow and develop in skills, knowledge, and social behavior at a rate similar to others; their not meeting these *developmental norms* can cause concern in adults. So too may behaviors that are in some way *disturbed in degree:* that occur too frequently or infrequently, are too intense or inadequately intense, endure over too long or short a period of time. For example, it is not atypical for a child to exhibit fear, but the child may be judged to have a problem if he or she is fearful in many situations, has extremely intense reactions, and does not "grow out of" the fears. Concern might also be expressed for the child whose reactions seem *different than previously,* such as the contented youngster who abruptly becomes sullen or morose.

Finally, adults themselves vary in sensitivity, tolerance, and ability to cope with certain kinds of behaviors, and this too influences how a child is perceived and handled. A team of investigators, for example, compared two groups of New York City families and their reporting of child problems (Thomas, Chess, Sillen, and Mendez, 1974). One group consisted of Puerto Rican working-class families, the other of middle- and upper middle-class, predominantly Jewish families. Both groups exhibited high family stability and showed no differences in the prenatal and perinatal complications surrounding the development of the target children. They differed strikingly, though, in both the number and kinds of problems they reported in their children. By the time the children were nine years old, 31 percent of the middle-class as opposed to 10 percent of the working-class children were diagnosed as having behavior disorders. The middle-class parents were interpreted by the investigators as being child-problem oriented and aware of influential theories of child development that emphasized early problems as determinants of later functioning. The working-class parents were concerned about the well-being of their offspring but were not preoccupied with psychological functioning. Their attitude was typified by the remark, "He's a baby—he'll outgrow it." (Thomas et al., 1974, p. 56) Working-class parents also appeared to place less demands on their children to feed and dress themselves and follow through on verbal task directions. Finally, they were less optimistic about obtaining help for their children. Thus, they reported fewer disturbances, but the kinds of problems that they reported were relatively severe.

Shepherd, Oppenheim, and Mitchell (1966) addressed the fascinating issue of parental reporting of childhood problems by contrasting families of children seen in a clinic with families of children who had comparable problems but were not clinic patients. To obtain the sample of nonclinic children questionnaires about behavior problems were sent to teachers and parents of every tenth child listed on school records. The clinic and nonclinic youngsters were then matched according to disorders. Here is a description of one matched pair of boys:*

Clinic Child

M.P., a boy aged 10 yr, was referred to a child-guidance clinic because of refusal to leave his home for the past three months. Previously he had been an energetic boy, good at sport, popular with his school-mates and sufficiently independent to undertake an unescorted coach journey to visit his grandparents. He had begun to complain of feeling "weak and dizzy," stating that his "stomach turned over" if he took food or drink and that his "head wanted to burst out of his skin." He had become very faddy about food. On some days he would eat nothing, though on others he was still capable of taking a good meal. The only liquid he would take was about half a pint of lemon squash daily. He said that he felt too "dizzy" to go to school and, if delivered there forcibly by his father in the car, would cry violently, threaten to jump out of the moving car and, on arrival, either run away or stand sobbing in the cloakroom. He had become very tearful and irritable; he cried and threw things if he were crossed in any way. He took no interest in his friends but would spend his time in the house using his Meccano set or making model aeroplanes.

Nonclinic Child

B.G., a boy aged 10 yr, had suffered from a stream of minor ailments for the previous two years. He had constant sore throats and colds; he had headaches several times a week; and he developed "water blisters" of unknown causation. He had become very anxious about his health. He washed his hands frequently because of "germs"; he gargled; he brushed his teeth frequently; and he made his mother examine his ears and throat every day. He as afraid of dogs; he was afraid to go upstairs by himself, particularly in the dark. He was faddy about food and would not eat fish, eggs or milk. He worried a lot, had bad dreams and occasionally walked in his sleep. He disliked school intensely and would go off in the morning looking very tearful and sometimes "downright ill," so that neighbours had asked if he ought not to be kept at home. Sometimes he

*reprinted with permission from the *Journal of Child Psychology and Psychiatry*, Vol. 7, by Shepard et al. in *Childhood Behavior Disorders and the Child Guidance Clinic.* Copyright 1966, Pergamon Press, Ltd.

vomited in the morning and often refused to eat his breakfast, but unless he had a temperature he was sent to school where he ceased to complain. It was the process of leaving home that he could not bear. He was regarded as backward at school and had been unable to read when he entered Junior School [elementary school] at the age of eight though he had since made progress. He had friends at school but once he had returned home he was unwilling to go out again to play with them. His brothers teased him a lot and he reacted with tears and tantrums; his relationship with his father was poor. (Shepherd, Oppenheim, and Mitchell, 1966, p. 42)

After matching the children, the investigators interviewed the parents. They found that the reactions of clinic mothers differed substantially from those of the nonclinic mothers. Clinic mothers felt helpless and unable to cope with the problems, and they were more worried than the nonclinic mothers about the future welfare and present unhappiness of their children. The nonclinic mothers, in contrast, regarded their children's behavior as temporary difficulties.

Interestingly, the investigators also reinterviewed the families approximately two years later to ascertain how the children had fared. Raters who did not know whether any one child was a clinic or nonclinic client determined that 65 percent of the clinic cases and 61 percent of the nonclinic cases had improved. Although several factors might underlie parental reports of improvement, these figures are consistent with several other studies of improvement rates. Later we shall return to the topic of treatment efficacy. First, though, let us sample from the broad range of behavior problems that are recognized among children, beginning with the most severe dysfunctions.

SEVERE, PERVASIVE DISORDERS

The most severe disturbances of childhood, to which the label *psychoses* has usually been applied, are viewed as distortions in the rate, timing, and sequence of many basic psychological processes such that these processes are qualitatively different than in other children. The major categories, as they generally appear in the literature, are *childhood schizophrenia* and *infantile autism*. Sometimes the two diagnoses are considered to be quite separate, and at other times no distinction is made between them.*

Childhood Schizophrenia

Most broadly, *schizophrenia* is characterized by a defective interaction with reality that displays itself in disturbances in emotion, movement, perception, speech, thought, and social interaction. The schizophrenic child

*These designations are inconsistent even among the major classification systems. In the most recent revision of the American Psychiatric Association's Diagnostic and Statistical Manual of Mental Disorders (DSM-III), childhood schizophrenia no longer appears; instead the more general label *pervasive developmental disorders* includes the child who was once labeled schizophrenic. This change is in recognition that severe childhood disturbance is not simply an early manifestation of schizophrenia as it is described in adulthood. On the other hand, infantile autism is recognized for the first time as a distinct disorder, and is considered a subcategory of pervasive developmental disorders. Our discussion uses the labels childhood schizophrenia and infantile autism to be consistent with most of the present literature.

may thus show a variety of atypical behaviors, such as emotional with-drawal or overdependence, extreme joy and fear, strange mannerisms (fin-ger twiddling, self-destructive head banging, peculiar posture and gait), disorientation in space and time, muteness, idiosyncratic verbalizations, and loose associations in thinking (e.g., Achenbach, 1974; Engel, 1972; Ross, 1974). Some of these disturbances—as well as their severity and pervasiveness—are conveyed in the following case study.

The Case of Jane

The patient, whom I shall call Jane, and her parents were first referred to our hospital when she was 5 years old, from another clinic where the parents had sought aid because of head banging since age 1 year, biting her arms and hands and slapping her face since age 4 years, and never having achieved bowel or bladder training.

Without detailing the parents' background prior to marriage, the development of their individual psychological difficulties and their summation after mar-riage, was apparent. . . . It was during a peak of parental tensions, shortly after the patient had begun to say single words at age 1 year, that her symptom of head banging began. Her development then became arrested and toilet training and learning did not progress significantly.

Physical and neurological examinations, repeated blood counts, blood serology, sedimentation rate, and urinalyses including phenylpyruvic acid testing were negative. Repeated chest x-rays were normal, as were x-rays of the skull. Skele-tal maturation as measured by x-ray was normal. Repeated electroencephalo-grams revealed no abnormalities.

Psychological testing on admission and repeated twice during her hospi-talization indicated that she was grossly retarded and seriously disturbed emo-tionally with marked self-punitive tendencies. Her lack of cooperation precluded any data that would allow conclusions about intellectual capacity.

At admission, the parents described Jane as non-verbal, but vocal, not toilet trained, unable to adequately care for herself, and having difficulties around sleeping and eating. They reported her persistence in hurting herself by in-tense, self-inflicted blows and they pointed out many marks and bruises over her body as evidence of long standing, self-destructive behavior.

During her first eighteen months, the nursing staff reported little significant change, and her attempts to hurt herself were unending. She not only hit her-self with her fists, knees and feet, but bit her arms, hands, lips and tongue, and ground her teeth together. At times it was necessary for two staff members to restrain her self-hurtful behavior, but this proved so exhausting that it became necessary for the staff to rotate their time with her.

Other factors which added to the discomfort of being close to Jane were her habits of regurgitating food, picking at sores on her skin, urinary and inter-mittent fecal incontinence, and her monotonous groaning and wailing.

Meal times were also difficult and messy as Jane shoved food in her mouth with her hands, smearing herself and the surrounding area thoroughly.

Bedtime was another area of stress. From admission on, Jane had been wrapped in a sheet and tucked in bed in order to prevent her self-hurtful attempts. Occa-sionally she spent the night in a side room because of her loud screeching.

The structured activities of school, occupational therapy, picnics and outings also were often just one struggle after another.

Fluctuations in her weekly weight grossly correlated with periods of regression and improvement, since during her more disturbed periods her refusal to eat required hand feeding by the staff. Losses or gains of as much as eight pounds within a week were evident and we found striking correlations between her weight, symptomatology, and factors such as intra-staff tensions, vacations of staff members or her parents, and changes in the assignment of staff working with her. [Gianascol, 1973, pp. 541–543]

Of special note in the case study above is the fact that Jane's development is viewed as being arrested at a particular time, specifically at about one year of age. Development that proceeds normally only to go awry prior to adolescence is frequently taken as a diagnostic sign of childhood schizophrenia.

Infantile Autism

In 1943 Leo Kanner carefully described eleven severely distrubed children whose behavioral patterns, he claimed, could be differentiated from those of other psychotic children. He later (1944) coined a new label for the syndrome—early *infantile autism*—and noted that it encompassed about 10 percent of all severely disturbed children, more boys being affected than girls, as is the case with all psychoses. Kanner originally enumerated several characteristics of infantile autism but reduced them to two necessary symptoms that were evident early in life: extreme aloneness and preoccupation with preservation of sameness in the environment (Eisenberg and Kanner, 1956). In the ensuing years, many, but not all, investigators came to concur with Kanner that infantile autism is a specific syndrome of a severe, pervasive disorder. Today it is widely agreed that autism is characterized by early onset, social isolation, language disorders, and insistence on sameness in the environment (Kessler, 1966; Ritvo, 1976; Rutter, 1978).

Etiology of Severe Disorders

Just as there are diverse definitions of childhood psychoses, so too are there several proposed etiologies. Many investigators tend to believe that organic dysfunction is central. Lauretta Bender, noted for her many years of work with psychotic children, attributes psychotic behavior to physiological defect, reduced competence, and anxiety. Biological disturbance is evidenced, according to Bender, by symptoms such as growth abnormalities, atypical commencement of puberty, excessive flushing and pallor, excessive reactions to infections, and disturbances in eating (cf. Bender, 1947). Bender suggests that the tendency for psychoses is genetically determined but is brought on by some kind of physiological upset.

Bernard Rimland, too, proposes an organic etiology, in this case for autism. In fact, Rimland (1964, 1971, 1974) is one of the researchers who has argued strenuously that autistic children differ from other severely disturbed children. To demonstrate the point he requested that parents complete a specially devised scale describing eighty aspects of their troubled children's characteristics and behavior. One analysis of the data covered 2,218 cases. Table 15-1 shows several items on the scale that distinguishes autistic children from nonautistic psychotic children. For example, larger percentages of parents of autistic youngsters compared to parents of non-autistic psychotic children had suspected deafness in their offspring (pre-

TABLE 15-1
Percentage of Parents of Autistic and Nonautistic Psychotic Children Describing
Their Children in Certain Ways on Rimland's Checklist

| | Autistic | | Nonautistic |
Description of child	Speaking N = 65	Mute N = 53	N = 230
It was suspected at some time that child was nearly deaf.	77	94	54
Child rather stiff and awkward to hold, age 2–5.	90	88	56
Child exceptionally skillful in doing fine work with fingers or play with small objects, age 3–5.	71	75	33
Child fascinated by certain mechanical things, such as the stove or vacuum cleaner, age 3–5.	77	92	56
Child definitely gets upset if certain things he is used to are changed, age 3–5.	87	86	41
Child says "Yes" by repeating the same question he has been asked, age 3–5. (Example: If parent asks, "Shall we go for a walk, Honey?" child says yes by repeating, "Shall we go for a walk, Honey?")	94	12 (item not applicable to mute children)	22

Source: Adapted from Rimland, 1974.

sumably due to social unresponsiveness). Rimland has also argued that autistic children, unlike other severely disturbed children, are unusually attractive and healthy; have parents who rate high in intelligence, education, and occupational status; and come from families in which there is a low incidence of mental dysfunction. From these and other observations Rimland (1964) has suggested that autism is genius gone awry. Specifically, he has proposed that autistic children are predisposed to superior development in such a way that they are also especially susceptible to damage from lack of oxygen. When such anoxia occurs prenatally or at birth, it affects the reticular area of the brain, which, in turn, impairs the ability to associate new stimuli with remembered experience. Thus a change in environment is difficult to interpret, warmth toward caring parents does not develop because parents do not become secondarily reinforcing, and, in general, there is lack of meaning in the world.

The view of Bruno Bettelheim (1966, 1967) stands as an example of a contrasting hypothesis in its emphasis on psychological determinants. Bettelheim believes that autism and/or psychosis is a withdrawal from a world that was traumatically unresponsive during the child's first two years. To protect themselves from the environment upon which they presumably had no effect, autistic children give up the will to act and retreat into a fortress, leaving reality behind. The world that is given up is not necessarily neglectful and depriving of basic physical needs; the child is fed and cared for. Rather, it is a world in which the infant does not matter, is not worthy of interaction and influence. Bettelheim points out that child-rearing practices seemingly as innocuous as scheduled feeding can be destructive in that the environment "robs the infant of the conviction that it was his own wail that resulted in filling his stomach" (Bettelheim, 1967, p. 70). He cautions parents, then, to listen and respond to the young child's smallest contribution just as they would to the messages of older and more articulate offspring.

Several investigators from diverse theoretical viewpoints have, in one way or another, proposed etiologies similar to Bettelheim's in their emphasis on parental behavior (Ferster, 1961, 1966; Goldfarb, 1970). From a behavioral stance, for example, Ferster hypothesized that parents of autistic children fail to provide adequate reinforcement, resulting in an impoverished behavioral repertoire in their children. Such accounts unfortunately have sometimes led to the placing of blame for severe disorders on parents, particularly on mothers. The terms "refrigerator parents" (i.e., cold, mechanical, unresponsive parents) and "schizophrenogenic mother" (i.e., schizophrenia-causing mother) are still too common in discussions of etiology. This is not to discount, however, the possibility that family stress, early trauma, and parental psychopathology may play a role in determining some types of childhood psychoses.

Evidence for Hypothesized Etiologies. Although this discussion cannot do justice to the complexities of etiological issues, a brief summary of evidence for the proposed causes of childhood psychoses is in order. There is growing evidence for the implication of biological factors: support for the inheritance of a predisposition; signs of neurological dysfunction; abnormal EEGs; the presence early in life of autistic symptoms; the severity of symptoms (Davison and Neale, 1978; Folstein and Rutter, 1977). No specific organic hypothesis has firm support, however. The role of parents is also difficult to determine. Parents of children suffering from schizophrenia appear to have higher rates of disorders (schizophrenia, alcoholism, personality problems, and the like) than adults in the population at large (Bender 1974; Goldfarb, Spitzer, and Endicott, 1976). For autism there is little evidence that environmental family factors are critical. It must be remembered that

TABLE 15-2
Percentage of Severely Disturbed Children Falling into Different Outcome Categories Several Years after Initial Contact

Outcome Status*	Middlesex Study	Maudsley Study	Illinois Study
Good	14	14	10
Fair	24	25	16
Poor	14	13	24
Very poor	48	48	50

*For the Middlesex and Maudsley studies, outcome was assessed eight to nine and one-half years after initial contact, when the child ranged in age from 16 to 18 years. Children in the Illinois study were 12 years old at follow-up, and fewer years had elapsed since initial contact.

Source: Adapted from Lotter, 1974.

correlations between parental and child problems cannot be interpreted as causation. Parents of disturbed children, compared to parents of normal children are frequently tense, domineering, inconsistent, and the like; however, this may be the *result* of having a disturbed child. Several studies (e.g., Connerly, 1967, as cited by Ross, 1974) indicate that parents of brain-damaged and retarded children also exhibit more of these behaviors than do parents of normal youngsters, but it is unlikely that they caused the children's difficulties. Finally, it may be that only some psychoses are affected by family factors; some may be the result of an interaction of biological and environmental variables; or perhaps biological deficits make some children more vulnerable to damage from the environment (Cantwell, Baker, and Rutter, 1978).

Prognosis: What Happens to the Severely Disturbed Child?

The occurrence of childhood psychoses is estimated at 4 to 4.5 per 10,000 children (Davison and Neale, 1978; Goldfarb, 1970; Margolies, 1977). What happens to these children later in life? Kanner (1973) reported that of ninety-six autistic children, only eleven were maintaining themselves when they were in their second and third decades of life. Several of these attained a college education; they were employed, for example, as bank teller, accountant, general office worker, and truck-loading supervisor; they had hobbies; most lived alone; few had romantic relationships and personal friendships, although that appeared not to be frustrating.

A later comparison (Lotter, 1974) indicated that for three independent investigations conducted in England and the United States, 62 percent, 61 percent, and 74 percent of the disturbed children were judged as having poor or very poor status several years after initial contact. Table 15-2 shows the considerable consistency in judgments across these investigations. The children rated as having poor and very poor status were considered severely handicapped and unable to lead an independent existence, compared with the minority who were leading normal social lives, functioning satisfactorily in school, or making progress in these areas despite significant behavioral abnormalities. This finding has been confirmed by Lotter (1978) in an analysis of twenty-one reports in which at least some of the children had reached the age of twenty.

Attempts have been made to locate variables that might predict outcome. In trying to account for his "emergers," Kanner was able to point to only two facts: All eleven had been able to speak before the age of five years, and none had been committed to a state institution. Speech capacity, IQ performance, and original severity of the disorder have been shown in several studies to be linked to outcome. Lotter (1978) found that the 50 percent or so most severely affected youngsters in his study remained severely handicapped, whereas the outcome for the others was more varied. It is interesting that adolescence appears to be a time of important transition with some children deteriorating and others improving, particularly in terms of social behavior. Thus, as Lotter noted, studies that follow severely disturbed children at least until their early adult years may increase our understanding of the course and causes of seriously disturbed behavior.

The relatively milder behavior problems of childhood encompass a wide range of difficulties, both quantitatively and qualitatively. They may be so mild and so short-lived that the course of the child's life seems hardly touched—or they may bring about considerable disturbance. Our approach here is to describe several types of well-recognized disorders in order to depict the diversity of difficulties that may arise in development.

Problems in Habits of Elimination

Socialization of the child's habits of elimination is considered important by all developmentalists. As we have already seen, traditional Freudians go so far as to implicate it in the shaping of the entire personality, holding that inevitable conflict exists between the child's desire to freely manipulate expulsion and retention and the parental desire to regulate these functions. Extreme frustration or gratification, it is said, can lead to development of the anal character—that is, the display of orderliness, obstinacy, indecisiveness, and the like (Pollak, 1979). Although theorists of other orientations tend not to foretell of such drastic outcomes, all recognize that toilet training, if not mastered appropriately and at the usual time, can involve conflict and negative consequences for both children and parents. The concern of parents themselves is reflected in a survey showing that of twenty-two categories of possible preschool problems, parents rated difficulties in toilet training as second in importance (Mesibov, Schroeder, and Wesson, 1977).

Attitudes toward toilet training have changed markedly over the years (Walker, 1978). Early and strict training was once advocated. Children who trained easily were considered intellectually superior, and their parents were viewed as exceptional as well. More permissive attitudes eventually prevailed, with many parents simply believing that no effort was necessary—or sufficient—to train the child. The more reasonable middle-of-the-road approach recognizes that toilet control depends upon maturation, but is aided by parental encouragement of practices accepted by society.

Enuresis. In the United States about 50 percent of two-year-olds achieve daytime bladder control; this figure rises to 85 percent for three-year-olds and 90 percent for four-year-olds (Erickson, 1978; Walker, 1978). Nighttime control is achieved more slowly; one investigator reported that it is established by 67 percent of 3-year-olds, 75 percent of 4-year-olds, 80 percent of 5-year-olds, and 90 percent of 8½-year-olds (Harper, cited by Walker, 1978). Figure 15–1 depicts this comparison. Nocturnal enuresis, or nighttime bedwetting, the most frequent clinical complaint regarding elimination, thus is rarely considered a problem before three years of age, may not be reported until school age, and decreases markedly by adolescence. It occurs more frequently in children of low socioeconomic class and from families that have a history of enuresis, and is more than twice as frequent among males as females (Millon, 1969; O'Leary and Wilson, 1975; Tapia, Jekel, and Domke, 1960).

The suspected causes of *enuresis* can be classified as emotional, organic, and learning problems. The psychodynamic view emphasizes emotional

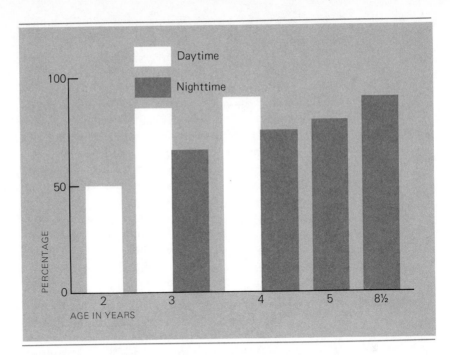

FIGURE 15–1
Percentage of
children at various
ages achieving
daytime and
nighttime bladder
control.

factors. Freud suggested that enuresis is the result of repression of the basic sexual desires and is a form of direct sexual gratification. The view that bedwetting is a symptom of such deep intrapsychic conflict is reflected in descriptions of enuresis as suppressed masturbation or ejaculation and as a cooling of the genitals—a reduction of sexual fire—condemned by the super-ego (Walker, 1978). It also has been interpreted as a weeping through the bladder related to the need for love (O'Leary and Wilson, 1975). Nonetheless, the evidence points to a lack of emotional disturbance in enuretic children aside from a slightly more than usual prevalence of anxiety related to family disruption and situational stress (Walker, 1978). Organic factors such as chronic disease, structural abnormalities, and small functional capacity of the bladder play a role in a small percentage of the cases. The most commonly accepted hypotheses regarding etiology suggest that immaturity of the nervous system and/or a deficit in learning to awake before urination occurs are responsible for most of the cases of enuresis. We shall see later that to a considerable extent the condition is subject to treatment from a learning point of view.

Encopresis. *Encopresis,* a much rarer problem, refers to inappropriate defecation, usually when the child is awake. Estimates of the disorder range from 1.5 percent to 5.6 percent, but reliable data are lacking (Walker, 1978). Although most studies of encopresis have simply been case reports, several organic conditions are known to result in the disorder, including allergies to food, infections of the large intestines, and abnormalities of the intestinal tract. Encopresis frequently is associated with constipation, which, in turn, may be caused by diet, reaction to stress, and the like. Defecation occurs alternately with constipation or the fecal material seeps out. A much smaller number of children suffer from diarrhea, seemingly as a reaction to stressful situations.

As with enuresis, emotional disturbance has been postulated as a cause for encopresis. Both erotic gratification and hostile, aggressive emotions have been implicated by Freudian theorists. The data are insufficient to support these notions or the idea of family disturbance as a cause of encopresis (Walker, 1978). In one of the most extensive investigations, however, it was found that encopretic children fall into two general classes: those for whom original bowel training had been successful but then deteriorated, and those who had never been successfully trained (Anthony, 1957). The youngsters in the two groups differed in an interesting way. The former typically had been subjected to quite coercive toilet-training practices from which they were now apparently rebelling, whereas the latter had experienced a generally neglectful upbringing. In both instances, it appears that teaching parents to toilet train (or retrain) their children can alleviate the problem (Barrett, 1969; Conger, 1970).

Fears and Phobias

Common Fears in Infancy and Childhood. Anyone observing children— or looking back on his or her own childhood—well knows that fearful situations are encountered virtually daily from early in life. The Moro reflex, in which the newborn throws back its head and extends its arms outward in response to sudden noise or loss of support, is considered by many to be an innate fear reaction. Regardless of whether or how this reflex is related to subsequent fear, fearlike behaviors are exhibited during the first year. We have already seen that infants placed on the visual cliff at about six months of age appear frightened of the apparent depth, and fear of strangers occurs by about seven months of age.

Modern psychological research into children's fears is about sixty years old, but we still lack detailed normative information on the nature and incidence of fears (Graziano, DeGiovanni, and Garcia, 1979). In a classic study, Jersild and Holmes (1935) disclosed a number of fears common in infancy and early childhood, revealing an interesting developmental pattern. Figure 15–2, which depicts the fluctuations of fears during the first six years of life, shows a general lessening of fears of concrete objects and situations (i.e., noise and strange objects) and an increase of fears of imaginary situations.

Using the categories developed by Jersild and his associates, Bauer (1976) interviewed kindergarteners, second-, and sixth-grade students about the things they most feared, what they were afraid of when they went to bed, and whether and what kinds of dreams scared them. As Table 15–3 shows, fear of bodily and physical danger increased with age, whereas fear of monsters/ghosts and animals decreased throughout these years.

Fears of boys and girls from age six to sixteen also have been assessed by requesting their parents to complete an eighty-one-item rating scale (Miller, Barrett, Hampe, and Noble, 1972). Three primary dimensions merged from this factor analytic study:

1. fear of *physical injury* related to wars, food poisoning, being kidnapped, and the like, and personal loss through divorce and death.

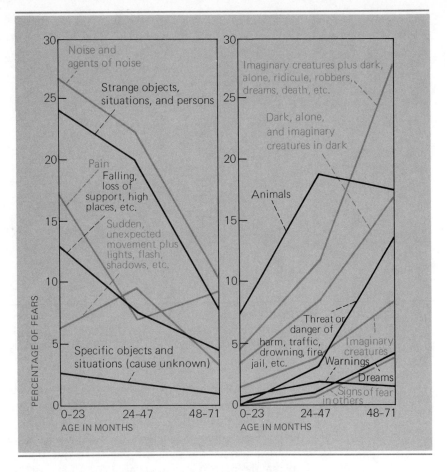

FIGURE 15–2
Relative frequency of
fears in children
during the first six
years of life, as
observed by parents
or teachers or
reported by the
youngsters
themselves.
Adapted from A. T.
Jersild and F. B.
Holmes, Children's
Fears. **Child
Development
Monograph**, 1935,
No. 20. Teachers
College, Columbia
University Bureau of
Publications, by
permission.

Left graph labels (PERCENTAGE OF FEARS vs AGE IN MONTHS, 0–23 / 24–47 / 48–71):
Noise and agents of noise
Strange objects, situations, and persons
Pain
Falling, loss of support, high places, etc.
Sudden, unexpected movement plus lights, flash, shadows, etc.
Specific objects and situations (cause unknown)

Right graph labels (AGE IN MONTHS, 0–23 / 24–47 / 48–71):
Imaginary creatures plus dark, alone, ridicule, robbers, dreams, death, etc.
Dark, alone, and imaginary creatures in dark
Animals
Threat or danger of harm, traffic, drowning, fire, jail, etc.
Imaginary creatures
Warnings
Dreams
Signs of fear in others

2. fear of *natural* events, such as storms and the dark.

3. fear reflecting *psychic stress*, such as fears of exams, social events, making mistakes, being criticized, school, doctors, and dentists.

After comparing their findings with studies of fears of adults the investigators suggested that fear of physical injury and fear involving psychic stress emerge early and continue throughout the life span. On the other

TABLE 15-3
Percentage of Kindergarteners, Second-, and Sixth-Grade Children Reporting Various Kinds of Fears

	Bodily Injury and Physical Danger	Monsters and Ghosts	Animals
Kindergarten	11	74	42
Second grade	53	53	40
Sixth grade	55	5	10

Source: Reprinted with permission from the **Journal of Child Psychology and Psychiatry**, Vol. 17,
Bauer "Percentage of Kinds of Fears." Copyright 1976, Pergamon Press, Ltd.

FIGURE 15-3
Fears can be useful, but excessive fears can cause discomfort and social drawbacks for a child. © Frostie 1978, Woodfin Camp & Associates.

hand, fear of natural events tends to disappear with age or to focus on the dark and loneliness, whereas sexual and moral fears emerge more clearly during adulthood. As fascinating as these developmental trends are, however, present research allows only tentative conclusions to be drawn because much of the data are based on questionnaires, retrospection, and parental reports (Graziano et al., 1979; Wade, 1978).

Excessive Fears. Although fears serve the useful purpose of acting as cues for potentially dangerous situations, in excess they create considerable discomfort and social drawbacks for the child. The scale of positive and negative consequences is decidedly tipped in the latter direction when it comes to persistent phobias, profound and unrealistic fears of specific events, people, or circumstances.

What are the antecedents of phobic behavior? Surely a biological substrate exists, but learning is of paramount importance. Specific trauma was found in one early study to be associated with the first attack of acute anxiety in sixteen out of twenty children suffering from this reaction (Langford, 1937). Recall that Watson and Rayner conditioned fear in the young child, Albert, by pairing a neutral stimulus with noise that already elicited fear (p. 155). Such classical conditioning may play a role in creating apparently irrational phobias. In one study, over half of the fearful undergraduates recalled a specific learning experience that could have accounted for their fears (Rimm, Janda, Lancaster, Nahl, and Dittmar, 1977). Children may also be reinforced for behaving fearfully and may learn fears by observing others react in that fashion. Freudian views of phobias posit that such simple learning experiences are insufficient causes, though; according to psychoanalytic theory, intrapsychic conflict must also be present and somehow related to the phobic situation. For a specific application of these approaches we shall turn to school phobia, the most extensively studied of all childhood fears.

School Phobia. The term *school phobia* seems simple enough to define: It should refer to an irrational, strong fear of the school situation that would lead to resistance to going to or remaining in school. In fact, although the avoidance of school is very much a part of the disorder, the motivation for avoidance is complicated.

It is helpful, to begin with, to distinguish school phobic children from truant children. The former display fear of school; suffer from nausea, abdominal pain, eating disturbances, and anxiety; and have a mutually dependent relationship with their mothers. They remain mostly at home when they are not in school, sometimes for long, continuous periods of time. Truant children, in contrast, tend to be intermittently absent; wander about from their homes; get into trouble by lying and stealing; and experience inconsistent home discipline (Gordon and Young, 1976; Hersov, 1960a; Kennedy, 1965).

Once this distinction has been made, however, and the object of the phobic child's fear is analyzed, fear of leaving the parent has been given as much, if not more, weight than fear of school itself. Eisenberg (1958), for example, has argued that school phobic children and their mothers have developed a mutually dependent relationship in which separation is difficult or disturbing. To the extent that this is the case, school merely represents an occasion that demands separation. Eisenberg supported this contention through his study of eleven preschool children (six boys and five girls) with separation problems. Observation of the mothers and their offspring at the beginning of nursery school attendance showed that the mother contributed at least as much as the child to the separation problem.

> During the first days a typical child would remain close to mother and then begin to oscillate toward and away from the attractions of the play area. As the child began to look less at mother and move away from her, she would take a seat closer to the child and occasionally use a pretext of wiping his nose or checking his toilet needs for intruding into the child's activity. Separation was as difficult for mother as for the child. Similar resistance to separation was shown by the mother when she was required to move to an adjacent room as part of the program for reducing the mutual separation anxiety. [Hetherington and Martin, 1972, p. 59]

Such separation anxiety on the part of both parent and child is viewed as fulfilling basic needs. The child may fear being left alone in the world without support, and may have a concern about death of the parent (Kennedy, 1965). The parent may have ambivalent feelings toward the child but is often overprotective and overindulgent (Gordon and Young, 1976). Psychodynamic theorists, who have contributed heavily to conceptualizing school phobia, emphasize that both child and parent suffer from conflict about dependency.

Social learning theorists, too, acknowledge that fear of losing the mother may be involved in many cases of school phobia. However, they are less likely to focus on intrapsychic conflict. Garvey and Hegrenes (1966), for example, suggest that school becomes a conditioned stimulus for fear by being paired with fear eliciting statements such as, "One of these days when you come home from school, I won't be here." Staying at home reduces fear, and is therefore reinforced. Social learning theorists also take more heavily into account that the school situation may elicit specific and quite understandable fear reactions; one investigation found that 50 percent of the children expressed fear of academic failure and of particular teachers (Hersov, 1960b). Avoidance of school would certainly seem to be profitable in those situations. Moreover, secondary reinforcers such as toys, television, and attention may operate in the home to further strengthen the child's desire to remain there.

It appears that various factors are involved in different cases of school phobias. The child who has strong dependency habits that are encouraged by the parent, who is unhappy in school, and who receives secondary reinforcement for staying at home would seem to be the most vulnerable to this dysfunction.

Psycho-physiological Disorders

Although wide recognition is now being given to the place of psychological factors in all physical illnesses, much attention has historically focused on a particular group of problems, the psychophysiological disorders. These are illnesses that are either caused by or markedly influenced by psychological stress; in children they include asthma, ulcerative colitis, and peptic ulcers (Hetherington and Martin, 1972). For the most part it is thought that psychological or emotional stress brings about detrimental effects in the organ systems of the body, with the exact system being affected dependent upon individual predisposition. Thus, for example, emotional stress will cause ulcers in the stomach or intestines of the person whose gastrointestinal system is particularly vulnerable to react to stress.

Serious consideration has been given to the proposition that certain conflicts are directly related to specific disorders; for example, conflict over dependency and its relation to ulcers. Similarly, a relationship between particular attitudes and psychophysiological dysfunctions has been suggested. Examples are an association between hypertension and vigilance to ward off danger, and duodenal ulcers and desire for revenge. Overall, the evidence for these hypotheses is weak (Davison and Neale, 1978). With regard to psychophysiological disorders in children, investigations have focused simply on demonstrating the existence of psychological factors and in determining their nature, with considerable effort being given to family interactions (Werry, 1972). This can be seen by briefly examining the research on asthma.

Asthma. The physical basis for asthmatic attacks is constriction of the bronchial ducts that supply air to the lungs, resulting in difficulty in breathing and a wheezing sound when the victim exhales. It occurs in about 2 to 5 percent of the population with 60 percent of the victims being under the age of seventeen. During childhood asthma occurs two times as frequently in boys as in girls, but this ratio becomes equal in adulthood (Purcell, 1975).

Asthma may be caused by several factors. Rees (1964) found that allergens (e.g., dust and pollens), respiratory infections (e.g., bronchitis), and emotional reactions (e.g., frustration and anger) were variously implicated. Over half of the studied cases were attributable to some *combination* of these factors. In about 37 percent emotional reactions appeared the dominant cause, in 33 percent they were subsidiary, and in 30 percent they were unimportant. The notion of organic vulnerability has received support from studies that suggest that asthma "runs in families," that familial patterns are consistent with genetic transmission, and that the sympathetic nervous system of asthmatics is unresponsive (Davison and Neale, 1978; Purcell, 1975).

Evidence suggesting the importance of family patterns in the etiology of psychologically induced asthma is found in the fact that some asthmatic children improve markedly when removed from their homes and placed in hospitals (e.g., Long, Lamont, Whipple, Bandler, Blom, Burgin, and Jessner, 1958; Purcell, Brady, Chai, Muser, Molk, Gorden, and Means, 1969). Because one possible reason for this dramatic change is the elimination of particular kinds of dust and other potential allergens in their own households, Long and his associates (1958) controlled for this factor by spraying the hospital rooms of their subjects with dust from their respective homes. Despite the fact that many of these children had previously shown skin sensitivity to house dust, none of them developed asthmatic symptoms in the hospital as a result of exposure to the dust. Other investigations (e.g., Gerard, 1946; Mohr, Taus, Selesnick, and Augerbraun, 1963) have suggested that one specific family pattern associated with asthma is overprotectiveness on the part of the child's mother.

Hyperactivity

Few childhood disorders receive as much attention today as *hyperactivity*. First described in 1845 by a German physician, Henrich Hoffmann (Cantwell, 1975), it was not until the late 1950s that hyperactivity was brought to the fore. At that time concern was growing for children with learning and behavior problems, both of which are frequently displayed by the hyperactive child (Safer and Allen, 1976). Then, in the late 1960s, drug treatment for the disorder commenced, further increasing interest and concern. Today hyperactivity is one of the most commonly recognized childhood problems, occurring in about 5 percent of all elementary school children, with a sex ratio of three to four boys to one girl (O'Leary, 1978a; Safer and Allen, 1976).

What is Hyperactivity? Hyperactive children are excessively and persistently overactive, but especially in structured situations that demand motor control. One investigative team described them this way:

> Hyperactive children seem to be constantly searching for something interesting. In an office they often act as though they are 'turning over rocks' to see

what interesting things may lie below. Unfortunately, this applies to dismantling the dictaphone, turning over the ashtray, and uprooting the rubber plant (Klein and Gittelman-Klein, 1975, p. 53).

In the classroom hyperactive children leave their seats frequently and fidget restlessly. Parents of such children report that their child always seemed unusually energetic, fidgety, and unable to keep his or her hands still. These kinds of behaviors are necessary and sufficient for the diagnosis of hyperactivity.

Other characteristics are widely associated with this atypical activity, however. Based on teacher ratings and school reports, Safer and Allen (1976) concluded that hyperactive children show inattention, have learning problems, and misbehave much more frequently than a cross section of the elementary school population (Table 15–4). These features have been found by many investigators. Still other commonly noted symptoms include distractibility, lability, impulsiveness, low frustration level, and peer conflicts.

One important tool in diagnosing hyperactivity is the use of questionnaires completed by teachers and parents. Figure 15–4 illustrates the abbreviated questionnaire developed by Connors from his original ninety-three-item parent and thirty-nine-item teacher scales (Connors, 1969; Goyette, Connors, and Ulrich, 1978). Connors's questionnaires are among the most widely used and best researched. As the table shows, they require only a simple estimate of the frequency of behaviors commonly noted by researchers. Yet they aid in identifying the hyperactive child and in assessing change in his or her condition.

Several strong controversies surround hyperactivity. Various professional workers recognize the *hyperkinetic* or *hyperactivity syndrome,* a cluster of some of the symptoms mentioned above, particularly learning disabilities and inattention. Others argue that no reliable syndrome exists, that hyperactivity displays itself with or without several other symptoms (Shaffer and Greenhill, 1979). Perhaps even more controversial is the assumption that underlying the proposed syndrome is some kind of central nervous system dysfunction or damage. So deeply ingrained is this supposition that the diagnostic term *minimal brain dysfunction (MBD)* is sometimes used synonymously with hyperactivity.

At present there is little unequivocal evidence for a specific association

TABLE 15-4
Percentage of Hyperactive Children and a Cross Section of Elementary School
Children Displaying Specific Behavioral Characteristics

Characteristic	Hyperactive Children	Elementary School Children
restless; overactive	100	35
inattentive	85	33
learning impairments	78	10
misbehavior: classroom fights or defiance	75	10

Source: Adapted from Safer and Allen, 1976, p. 14. Copyright 1976, University Park Press.

Patient name _____

Teacher's observations
Information obtained _____ by _____
          Month   Day   Year

Observation	Degree of activity			
	Not at all	Just a little	Pretty much	Very much
1. Restless or overactive				
2. Excitable, impulsive				
3. Disturbs other children				
4. Fails to finish things he starts, short attention span				
5. Constantly fidgeting				
6. Inattentive, easily distracted				
7. Demands must be met immediately; easily frustrated				
8. Cries often and easily				
9. Mood changes quickly and drastically				
10. Temper outbursts, explosive and unpredictable behavior				

Other observations of teacher (use reverse side if more space is required)

_____

_____

_____

_____

FIGURE 15–4
Short form of Connors's teacher questionnaire, which is used to evaluate children's hyperactive behaviors.

between brain damage and hyperactivity (Cantwell, 1975; O'Leary, 1978b; Shaffer and Greenhill, 1979). Hyperactive children do not show structural brain defects, and most brain-damaged children are not hyperactive. However, minor physical abnormalities in neonates, histories of pre-, peri-, and postnatal complications, and some evidence for unresponsiveness of the central nervous system have been found (Barkley, 1978; O'Leary, 1978b). Hyperactive children also sometimes show deficient coordination and perceptual problems, both subtle signs of central nervous system dysfunction. The hypothesis of minimal brain dysfunction thus cannot lightly be tossed aside without further research. There is no other satisfactory hypothesis, either. Diet, lead poisoning (from flakes of paint that children ingest), and even exposure to fluorescent lighting have been considered and found wanting as explanations for hyperactivity (although lead poisoning seems to account for some cases). Moreover, learning by reinforcement and imitation is recognized as important in the maintenance of the behavior but is not given a strong place in its origin (O'Leary, 1978b). In all likelihood, several etiological factors are involved.

So far in this chapter we have examined severe childhood disorders, problems of elimination, fears and phobias, psychophysiological dysfunctions, and hyperactivity, all of which are of great concern today. This was not always the case, however. Indeed, it appears that the term *emotional disturbances* was not applied to children until 1932 (Despert, 1965); before then youngsters exhibiting troubled behavior were thought of in terms of moralistic labels such as *possessed, wicked, guilty, insubordinate,* and *incorrigible.* Such views naturally determined the kind of treatment children with behavior problems received. In ancient Greece and Rome they might be left to die; in nineteenth-century London they were imprisoned (O'Leary and O'Leary, 1972).

In the 1930s this began to change. The psychiatric movement, largely inspired by the writings of Freud, gave rise to the appearance of a number of child psychiatric clinics that provided treatment based on traditional psychoanalytic and counseling views of psychotherapy.

Effectiveness of Traditional Psychotherapy

In 1952 Hans J. Eysenck, a British psychologist and researcher, published an article entitled "The Effects of Psychotherapy: An Evaluation." Dealing with the question of whether various types of traditional psychological treatments were actually helpful in treating adult psychological disorders, Eysenck asked about the rate of improvement among those who received treatment. At first blush, the results seemed reasonably promising; approximately two-thirds of those who received treatment showed measurable improvement. However, it is possible, as Eysenck realized, that improvement might occur even if there had been no therapy; a variety of natural experiences in a person's life and the transient nature of certain types of psychological disorders might conspire to produce improvement in some cases. So Eysenck made a comparable study of persons who sought or apparently needed psychotherapy but were unable to receive it. Strikingly, he found that among this group, too, approximately two-thirds showed improvement—despite their receiving no formal therapy whatsoever. It is not surprising, then, that the Eysenck paper stirred a great deal of controversy.

Five years later E. E. Levitt conducted a similar analysis assessing the effects of traditional psychotherapy with children. Examining results of seventeen different studies involving thousands of youngsters, Levitt stated:

> . . . the results, and the conclusions of this paper are markedly similar to those of Eysenck's study. Two-thirds of the patients examined at close of therapy and about three-quarters seen in follow-up have improved. *Approximately the same percentage of improvements are found for comparable groups of untreated children.* [1957, p. 194, italics added]

The findings described above are quite reliable; Levitt reported a further analysis of twenty-two other studies of psychotherapy with children, abstracting his new findings this way: "It must still be concluded that there does not seem to be a sound basis for the contention that psychotherapy facilitates recovery from emotional illness in children" (Levitt, 1963, p. 45). And the pattern has continued. As we saw earlier, a two-year follow-up of children with a variety of disturbances revealed that 65 percent of those who had been seen in a clinic improved, but so had 61 percent of matched control children who had not been seen in a clinic at all (Shepherd, Oppenheim, and Mitchell, 1966).

Partially as a result of the criticism of traditional therapy, there have been attempts to broaden the approaches to treatment. Some of the newer approaches are tied closely to theoretical stances, while others are simply pragmatic. The following discussion touches upon different approaches, including the traditional Freudian view, which, despite criticism, is still adhered to by a number of therapists and counselors.

Psychoanalytic Treatment

Freudian theory postulates that behavioral problems are symptoms of underlying conflict among instinctual demands (id), conscious thoughtful regulation (ego), and self-evaluative thoughts (superego). The conflict is postulated to be unconscious, and treatment is designed to bring it into consciousness, resulting in resolution of the conflict and relief of the symptoms. Therapy focuses on the patient's free verbal associations, dream interpretation, the patient-therapist relationship, and "working through" the conflict.

The application of Freudian theory to the treatment of childhood disorders can be traced to the therapy of Little Hans which was conducted by Hans's father under Freud's supervision. Five-year-old Hans was reported to have an unexplainable and irrational fear of horses, severe enough to prevent his going into the streets. Freud postulated the existence of an underlying Oedipal conflict; that is, that Hans unconsciously desired his mother and felt simultaneous hate, love, and fear toward his father. The fear, however, was projected onto horses, the animals' muzzles and blinders being symbolic representations of the father's mustache and eyeglasses. Treatment consisted of the father interpreting Hans's remarks so as to gradually bring the underlying conflict into consciousness:

> On April 25, 1908, Hans, who had just reached the age of five, was answering some of his father's questions. In a climate of confidence and acceptance, he admitted that he would like to see him dead and marry his mother. This was the culminating point of the therapeutic process, and from that time on, the remnants of the phobia gradually receded: the Oedipus complex had been overcome. [Cited by Ellenberger, 1970, p. 509]

Treatment of children by analytic methods has been carried on extensively by Freud's daughter, Anna, who views its purpose as the liberation of development that has become inhibited or deviant by previous emotional fixations. Consistent with the basic theory, this is accomplished by explorations of inner conflicts, particularly those that are unconscious. But Anna Freud has emphasized that treating children is critically different from treating adults (A. Freud, 1946). One of the major differences is that children do not themselves seek therapy and are not prepared for it. The therapist must therefore take the responsibility of preparing the child by, for example, encouraging insight that a problem exists and establishing a strong child-therapist relationship. A second important difference is that children do not easily enter into free association about their inner lives. Other ways must be found, then, to uncover conflict, such as observing the child at free play, examining the child-parent relationship, and studying the child-therapist relationship. Finally, the therapist must educate the parents as to the child's problems while directly guiding the child in conducting his or her instinctual life. The latter involves determining "what part of the infantile sexual impulses must be suppressed or rejected as unemployable in the cultural world; how much or how little can be allowed gratification" (A. Freud, 1946, p. 45). Such direct guidance and work with parents is not characteristic of several other therapists who nevertheless follow Freudian theory. It is interesting to note that Anna Freud's use of the play setting to diagnose problems differs from that of many analytic therapists in that she does not symbolically interpret the child's actions. For example, while others may interpret the child's throwing a doll across the room as a sign of hatred for the mother, Freud is more likely to view it as a direct expression of anger related to the situation.

Axline's Nondirective Play Therapy

Nondirective play therapy has its basis in the humanistic view of development. Virginia Axline, its foremost proponent, describes the assumptions of the method in this way:

> There seems to be a powerful force within each individual which strives continuously for complete self-realization. This force may be characterized as a drive toward maturity, independence, and self-direction. It goes on relentlessly to achieve consummation, but it needs good "growing ground" to develop a well-balanced structure. Just as a plant needs sun and rain and good rich earth in order to attain its maximum growth, so the individual needs the permissiveness to be himself, the complete acceptance of himself—by himself, as well as by others—and the right to be an individual . . . [1947, p. 10]

Axline points out that when the individual is prevented from achieving complete realization of the self, tension, friction, and resistance occur. Drive for self-realization continues, however, resulting in either an outward fight to establish a self-concept or a struggle confined to an inner world. It is the latter development, manifested by withdrawal, daydreaming, repression, and regression, that is maladjusted behavior. The aim of nondirective therapy is to permit the individual to be him- or herself and to begin to realize the power to think, decide, and mature.

This goal is reached within the context of free play, the child's most natural medium of expression. Play is not used, though, for diagnosis, as it is by Anna Freud, nor is it interpreted symbolically. Rather, it is the background for expressing the insecurity, fear, confusion, aggression, and tension being experienced. Axline provides eight guidelines for conducting therapy:

1. The therapist must develop a warm, friendly relationship with the child.
2. The therapist accepts the child exactly as he or she is.

3. The therapist establishes a feeling of permissiveness in the relationship so that the child feels freedom of expression.

4. The therapist is alert to recognize the feelings of the child and reflect them back, thereby fostering the child's self-insight.

5. The therapist maintains a deep respect for the child's ability to solve problems.

6. The child leads the way; the therapist follows.

7. The therapist does not attempt to hurry the therapy along.

8. The therapist establishes only those limitations that are necessary to anchor the therapy to the world of reality and to make the child aware of his or her responsibility in the relationship. [1947, pp. 73–74]

Children's response to this therapeutic experience, according to Axline, is captured by one seven-year-old boy spontaneously crying out, "Oh, every child just once in his life should have a chance to spill out all over without a 'Don't you dare! Don't you dare! Don't you dare!'" and an eight-year-old girl exclaiming, "In here I turn myself inside out and give myself a shake, shake, shake, and finally I get glad all over that I am me."

Behavior Modification

Of all the innovative approaches that have appeared since Levitt's review of the inefficacy of traditional approaches to children's behavior problems, perhaps none has become as popular as behavior modification.

Within this model, maladaptive behaviors are considered learned ways of dealing with the world that are in themselves the problems. The child's behaviors are not viewed as symptoms of some underlying conflicts. Rather, the focus of therapy is directly on the behavior itself. Critics of behavior modification argue that an approach that ignores deep inner causes will not be effective in the long run because new symptoms of the underlying problem will appear. Investigations into this possibility have been carried out by a number of researchers, many of whom are behavior modifiers. In general,

FIGURE 15–5
In play therapy free play provides a background for a child in which to express the insecurity, fear, confusion, aggression, and tension being experienced.
Sybil Shelton, Monkmeyer Press Photo Service.

The Medical Approach: The Controversial Treatment
of Hyperactivity With Medication

Although our discussion of treatment of behavioral disorders focuses on psychological/educative therapies, the medical approach deserves mention. Based on the assumption that biological dysfunction of the individual is the cause of behavior problems, medical treatment historically has included psychosurgery, electric and chemical shock procedures, physical restraint and confinement, and use of psychoactive drugs. However, psychosurgery was rarely used with children and of the other methods only psychopharmacology continues to be utilized today (Campbell, 1976; Greenberg and Lourie, 1972). Stimulants and antidepressants appear to show the most promise currently, although tranquilizers and sedatives are also used. It should be noted, though, that pediatric psychopharmacology is a relatively new field in which well-controlled research on effectiveness is still largely lacking. Variables that must be examined include the age of the child, individual reactions, side effects, and dosage. The lack of knowledge is no doubt partly responsible for the widely expressed concern over the use of pharmacological treatment for children.

Of all the medication prescribed for children today, the psychostimulants stand at the top of the list. Drugs such as Ritalin, Dexedrine, Benzedrine, and Cylert are commonly used in the treatment of hyperactivity. One estimate places the number of hyperactive children receiving such medication during the school year at between 600 to 700 thousand (O'Leary, 1978a). At first blush psychostimulant drugs would seem inappropriate for the hyperactive child. As it turns out, stimulants have a paradoxical effect on hyperactivity in that they calm behavior rather than excite it. According to one theory, hyperactivity may involve an underaroused

central nervous system that is normalized by stimulants (Cantwell, 1975). In any event, controlled studies demonstrate the power of stimulants to rapidly decrease activity and behavior problems in school, as well as to facilitate concentration (Cantwell and Carlson, 1978; Knopf, 1979; O'Leary, 1978a; Winsberg, Yepes, and Bialer, 1976). Despite this, much concern and anger have been expressed by the public and professionals alike with regard to their use.

In an address entitled "Pills or Skills For Hyperactive Children," psychologist K. Daniel O'Leary (1978a) has summarized several aspects of the controversy surrounding the use of stimulants. Two incidents are of particular interest. In 1970 the **Washington Post** reported that 5 to 10 percent of the school children in Omaha, Nebraska had been given psychostimulant medication for hyperactivity. The report was inaccurate: The percentage applied to children in special classes only, not to the entire school population. Nevertheless, as such it understandably upset many people. Five years later fuel was added to the fire by the book, **The Myth of the Hyperactive Child,** written by journalists Peter Schrag and Diane Divoky. The book can correctly be viewed as an exposé based on the theme that the "illness" of hyperactivity (with accompanying learning disability and brain dysfunction) had been invented so that children's behavior might be controlled by medication and other procedures. In fact, the Schrag and Divoky book is informative, but one cannot help being uncomfortable with its emotional appeal. For example, one edition opens with this blurb from the publisher:

Is conformity a sign of mental health? Is deviance from the norm a sickness? Too many

O'Leary summarized his impressions of **The Myth of the Hyperactive Child** by noting that some of its statements are "clearly exaggerated, and, in certain cases, patently false" (O'Leary, 1978a, p. 2). At the same time, based on several years of working with troubled children, he too questions the appropriateness of widespread treatment with psychostimulants. What are his primary concerns?

First is the lack of evidence for the facilitation of academic achievement. That psychostimulants have an immediate and positive effect on **social behavior** in the classroom and laboratory is not in dispute. It has been assumed that improved behavior and attention would result in improved academic performance. But according to O'Leary, there is no consistent evidence for either short-term or long-term facilitation, and, in fact, long-term studies are still needed. Second, psychostimulants have physical side effects on some children, such as increased blood pressure and heart rate and temporary suppression of growth. Third, the immediate, though fleeting, manageability of hyperactive children when they go on medication leads parents to believe that psychological and educational intervention is unnecessary. For all these reasons, O'Leary leans toward behavior modification programs in which children's behavior is shaped by reinforcement contingencies. Medication then becomes a procedure to fall back on in cases in which the parents cannot maintain a behavioral program or when the child is especially unresponsive to parental and teacher reinforcement. In some of these instances, ongoing assessment could pinpoint the time when medication might be eliminated altogether in favor of behavioral treatment.

they show that new symptoms do *not* occur (e.g., Eysenck, 1960; Lazarus, 1963; Wolpe, 1958). Compellingly, the same conclusion has been reached by Weitzman (1967), a psychoanalytically oriented therapist.

General Characteristics.　At the technique level, behavior modification approaches are characterized by direct observation, systematic manipulation, and repeated assessment (cf. Lovitt, 1970).

Many types of therapy rely on tests of personality or adjustment, or on projective tests to assess the difficulties of individuals seeking help. The behavior modification approach to assessment is quite different as a result of the assumption that specific learning contingencies rather than more general personality problems underlie abnormal behavior. Even when particular behavior patterns occur together, as in the case of autism, the specifics are presumed to be critical information for the therapist to begin treatment. Thus there is considerable reliance on direct observation, and, as necessary, quite individualized assessment of the actual behavior of each youngster for whom treatment is suggested or requested. As Lovitt explains:

> Behavior modifiers agree that before a behavior can be measured, much less changed, it must be directly recorded. If, for example, the target behavior is tantrums, the outbursts are recorded directly; an indirect approach such as an

interview or a standardized adjustment test is not scheduled. If the target behavior is reading, direct measurement on various reading components would be obtained instead of using a standardized reading or achievement test to determine skills. [1970, pp. 87–88]

In part it is obvious that a child's behavior can be altered successfully only if something is done with (or to) him or her: In this sense, of course, manipulation is involved in all types of therapy. We have seen, though, that in traditional therapies intervention is nondirective or global. The behavior modification approach, in contrast, is characterized by a very specific, detailed, and systematic plan for intervention, generally with an eye to altering particular consequences for behaving in certain ways.

Behavior modification is pragmatic in that a manipulation is tried and an immediate effort is made to determine whether the desired changes are occurring. If not, the plan will be changed; that is, a different manipulation will be introduced, and then it too will be evaluated. Thus, repeated assessment, based on regular direct evaluation, is typical of the approach.

The general principles outlined above are usually applied within the framework of one or more of the basic learning paradigms. A concrete understanding of how the approach works can be obtained through actual examples and cases.

A Classical Conditioning Approach to Enuresis. Earlier it was pointed out that the difficulty of enuretic children, viewed in learning terms, is that they have not learned to awaken before bed-wetting occurs. Presumably this is because internal stimulation (i.e., bladder tension) does not arouse them from sleep. Many years ago Mowrer and Mowrer (1938) related the problem to classical conditioning. They reasoned that the desired response could be produced by pairing the ringing of a fairly loud bell (a UCS, or unconditioned stimulus, which would inevitably awaken the child) with bladder stimulation (the CS, or conditioned stimulus). Waking up—an unconditioned response (UCR) to the bell—should then become a conditioned response to the bladder tension alone, permitting the child to reach the toilet in time.

The Mowrers attempted to treat enuretic youngsters accordingly. The children slept on a specially prepared pad made of two pieces of bronze screening separated by a heavy layer of cotton. When urination occurred it invariably would seep through the fabric, close an electrical circuit, and cause the bell to ring. After repeated pairings, bladder tension alone would be expected to waken the child. Thirty children were treated by the Mowrers in this way, for a maximum period of two months, and bed-wetting was successfully eliminated in every case. Additionally:

Personality changes, when they occurred . . . have uniformly been in a favorable direction. In no case has there been any evidence of 'symptom substitution.' Our results, therefore, do not support the assumption, sometimes made, that any attempt to deal directly with the problem of enuresis will necessarily result in the child's developing "something worse." [Mowrer and Mowrer, 1938, p. 451]

The bell and pad apparatus devised by the Mowrers has been successfully used ever since. Approximately 75 percent of the children treated with it have been helped initially; relapses are quite common but many respond to retraining. No other method, behavioral or otherwise, can claim comparable results (Doleys, 1977).

Deconditioning of a Phobia of Loud Noises. Although behavior modification has been extremely successful in eliminating a wide range of phobias in adults, less work has been done with children, perhaps because children's fears are viewed as transitory. Wish, Hasazi, and Jurgela (1973) reported an especially interesting case of an eleven-year-old boy, Steven, in whom a phobia to explosive sounds appeared to be generalizing when he came for treatment. The fear of explosive sounds might have originated with extreme fright of fireworks at the age of two years; it had always been severe, but of small concern because few situations heretofore had elicited fearful responses. The problem became acute when many loud noises began to elicit fear, producing headaches, nausea, and other somatic complaints. Steven's life was increasingly being controlled by the phobia: Thunder and loud street noises sent him hiding under his school desk and family outings were difficult to plan.

The chosen treatment was systematic desensitization. The central goal of systematic desensitization is to pair fear-eliciting stimuli with a response, such as relaxation, that is incompatible with fear, thereby eliminating or markedly reducing the fear. The first step in Steven's treatment was the construction of a fear hierarchy by the therapist, the boy, and his mother. That is, they composed a list of fear-eliciting noises ranging from the least to the most strong. Table 15–5 shows the hierarchy and subjective estimates

TABLE 15-5
Steven's Fear Hierarchy Showing the Subjective Rating of the
Degree of Fear for Each Item

Item	Subjective Rating
fireworks	100
firecrackers	95
thunderstorm	90
sonic boom	80
explosions	70
rocket launcher	65
battle sounds	60
cannon fire	55
21-gun salute	50
machine gun	45
rifle fire	35
pistol shots	30
cork pop	15
balloon pop	10
surf	0

Source: Reprinted with permission from the **Journal of Behavior Therapy and Experimental Psychiatry**, Vol. 4, Wish, Hasazi, and Jurgela, "Steven's fear hierarchy showing the subjective rating of the degree of fear for each item." Copyright © 1973, Pergamon Press, Ltd.

of the degree of fear elicited by each item. The second step of the program involved training Steven to relax. The fear-eliciting noises were then super-imposed on one of Steven's favorite record albums, so that they would be paired with pleasurable music. Beginning with the least fear-eliciting stimulus of surf noise, each noise was presented five times on the album tape. (The noises had been obtained from professional sound effects recordings.)

Finally, Steven self-administered the treatment procedure at home over a period of eight days by listening to the album on earphones while systematically relaxing himself. Session length increased from five minutes on the first day to forty minutes on the eighth day, which was the playing time of the entire album. There were three sessions per day and the volume of the tape was increased each day.

At the end of the eight days Steven was comfortably listening to all of the noises at high volume. When he subsequently was directly exposed to selected sounds from the hierarchy—such as a balloon pop, pistol shots, and explosions—he exhibited no fear. He even refused to leave a fourth of July fireworks display. His parents reported that his peer and family relationships had improved and that he no longer presented problems in the classroom. A check on subjective ratings of the taped noises after nine months strengthened the conclusion that treatment had been effective. Thus, the case provides support for the supposition that systematic desensitization, which is effective with adult phobias, can be beneficial for at least some childhood phobias.

Operant Conditioning and Modeling Applied to Seriously Disturbed Behavior. A combination of operant conditioning and modeling procedures has been applied to extreme behavioral deficiences in children. Notable in this area is the work of O. Ivar Lovaas and his associates (Lovaas, 1968; Stevens-Long and Lovaas, 1974) with autistic children: They found that self-destructive action is reduced by isolating the children, echolalic speech is similarly decreased by nonattention, and normal speech is gradually shaped by food rewards for the imitation of the experimenter's verbalizations (Figure 15–6). Realizing that social reinforcement is typically the cornerstone for building and modifying behavior in the natural environment and that autistic children appear unresponsive to such reinforcement, Lovaas and his associates make a concerted effort to establish the importance of social rewards by pairing them with tangible ones (Lovaas, 1968). For example, when food reinforcement is presented for a particular act, it is paired with the word "good." Later, praise alone may become a reinforcer. (For a discussion of the ethical and practical considerations in the use of tangible rewards in treating behavioral problems, see O'Leary, Poulos, and Devine, 1972.)

A case described by Wiltz and Gordon (1974) illustrates both the use of operant conditioning in behavior modification and the training of parents to deal effectively with their troubled offspring. The child was a nine-year-old boy who had been diagnosed schizophrenic. He refused to attend school and displayed many problem behaviors: lighting matches, taking money from his mother's purse, locking himself in the bathroom, throwing fruit against the wall, and urinating on toilet facilities and the wall. He had spent time in a juvenile detention facility, and his parents were considering returning him because of their failure to manage him in any way.

The investigators thus prepared to train the parents to deal with the child, and they were able to use an innovative method to do so. The entire family, including all the children, moved into a special three-bedroom apartment for five days; one-way mirrors and microphones permitted the investigators to observe the family in the kitchen, living room, and one bedroom. Observations took place continuously from 10:00 a.m. to 7:00 p.m., during which time the mother and children were present continuously and the father was present for the last three hours.

Treatment focused on compliance with commands given by the mother and general appropriate behavior. For several days before the family moved into the treatment residence, and the first two days afterward, a baseline of the boy's behavior was obtained. The parents recorded commands, noncompliance, and destructive acts toward people and property. On the second day of treatment, the parents also completed a programmed text designed to inform them about management of children with behavior modification techniques.

The third day was devoted to training. A reinforcement schedule was put into effect whereby the child earned points for a desired toy based upon his compliance with his mother's commands and generally appropriate behavior. A variable interval schedule was employed, in which reinforcement occurred once during a certain time interval; as the program progressed, the

FIGURE 15-6
The use of positive reinforcement—food and praise—by Lovaas and his associates in the shaping of appropriate social behavior in autistic children.
Photograph by Allan Grant, by permission.

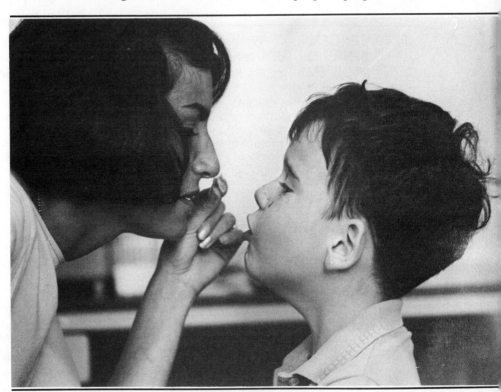

time interval was lengthened and verbal reinforcement was substituted for the points. Thus the child was expected to act in a progressively more acceptable way for less tangible reward. Punishment was also used; whenever the child failed to comply with parental instructions, he was placed on time-out in his bedroom. For each disruption during time-out, additional minutes were added. All of the procedures were modeled by the researchers and rehearsed step by step with the mother and child. The father was brought into the program upon returning to the apartment in the late afternoon.

The final two days of treatment consisted of observations of the implementation of the method, feedback to the participants, and modification of the reinforcement contingencies as just described. The program was continued at home by the family, with telephone supervision from the researchers.

The success of the therapy is evidenced in Figure 15–7 which shows decreases in both noncompliance to parental demands and destructive acts toward other people from the time of pretraining to approximately three weeks after training.

The training of parents to manage their offspring is frequently an important aspect of behavior modification. This study is of particular interest, however, in that it demonstrates the feasibility and advantages of a resident training unit. The effort expended by the family enabled it to obtain intensive therapy over five days, which resulted in rapid beneficial changes at a time when institutionalization was being seriously considered.

PREVALENCE OF BEHAVIOR PROBLEMS

We have already noted the prevalence of several childhood behavior disorders. One way to study their prevalence is to survey cases that arise in clinics, hospitals, schools, and in the offices of various professional workers.

FIGURE 15–7
Rate of (a) noncompliance and (b) destructive acts toward others, before, during, and after training procedures. Reprinted with permission from the *Journal of Behavior Therapy and Experimental Psychiatry*, Vol. 5, Wiltz and Gordon, ''Parental modification of a child's behavior.'' Copyright © 1974, Pergamon Press, Ltd.

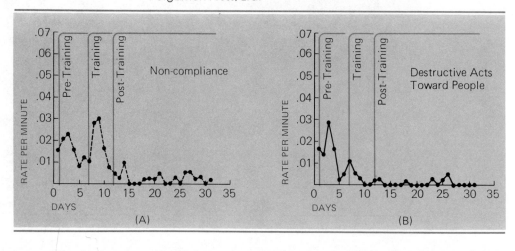

This method is not without its weaknesses. Disorders are defined differently by various workers, many go unreported, and they may be based on differential expectations according to the socioeconomic class and sex of the children being surveyed.

Another way to evaluate prevalence is to ascertain the occurrence of problems by surveying all children in a geographic area or a representative sample of the area. Although this procedure, known as an epidemiological study, also suffers from the above weaknesses, it provides a rough estimate of what might be considered normal childhood problems that are judged tolerable or impermanent. An example is the investigation conducted by Lapouse and Monk (1958) in which almost five hundred mothers in Buffalo, New York, were interviewed about their six- to twelve-year-old youngsters. These mothers reported that 43 percent of the children had seven or more fears and worries, 49 percent were overactive, 48 percent lost their tempers twice weekly, 28 percent experienced nightmares, 27 percent bit their nails, and 10 to 20 percent wet their beds and sucked their thumbs. Many of these figures correspond with information obtained from other studies of the United States and Europe (cf. Anthony, 1970).

From the varied investigations made regarding this issue some general conclusions can be drawn.

1. Although severe disorders (that is, psychoses) are infrequent, the over-all prevalence of less severe behavior disorders in the general child population is quite high.

2. Age is associated with prevalence, with a general tendency for problems to decline in school-age children. Also, specific disorders are age related. As exemplified in Table 15–6, some disorders simply decline or increase over time, whereas others show signs of vacillation.

TABLE 15–6
The Expression of Certain Behavioral Disorders Over Time for Children Studied Longitudinally from 21 Months to 14 Years of Age

Type of Age Trend	Behavioral Item
Symptoms declining with age	Enuresis, encopresis, speech problems, fears, thumbsucking, overeating, temper tantrums, destructiveness
Symptoms increasing with age	Nail biting
Symptoms declining and then increasing with age	Restless sleep, disturbing dreams, timidity, irritability, attention-seeking, dependence, jealousy, food finickiness (boys), somberness
Symptoms increasing and then declining with age	Poor appetite, lying
Symptoms unrelated to age	Oversensitivity

Source: MacFarlane, Allen, and Honzik, 1954.

3. Boys exhibit considerably more deviancy than girls in most categories. For some problems there is a notable sex difference: Boys are more aggressive, acting out antisocial behaviors, while girls are more anxious and inhibited.

4. Many of the less severe problems seem to disappear spontaneously within a few years.

Of these generalizations, speculation about the sex differential abounds. Why should boys show greater prevalence for so many disorders—psychoses, learning difficulties, hyperactivity, bed-wetting, antisocial behavior, and sexual dysfunction? In a review of the literature, Eme (1979) noted that explanations fall into two general types, those that focus on the differential endowment of the sexes and those that locate cause in social variables. With regard to the former, the lack of genes on the Y chromosome is suspect as it is clearly related to some dysfunctions, such as color blindness and hemophilia. Perhaps it is similarly related through subtle enzymatic pathways to behavioral difficulties. Male vulnerability during the pre-, peri-, and postnatal stages, is well established. During infancy 37 percent more males than females die, and throughout life they are more affected by major diseases. Males lag behind females in development, at least early in life, and they also appear more vulnerable to malnutrition and the effects of poverty. The nature and pervasiveness of these facts suggest some biological determination.

But differential socialization seems a reasonable hypothesis, also, especially regarding aggression and anxiety. We must also consider that male deviancy may be reported more frequently. Mothers tend to believe that difficulties with girls are temporary (Shepard, Oppenheim, and Mitchell, 1966), and parents and teachers are less tolerant of male hyperactivity, lack of persistence, distractibility, and disruption (Battle and Lacey, 1972; Chess and Thomas, 1972; Serbin and O'Leary, 1975). Still, this conclusion must be tempered by the possibility that adult tolerance is lower for males because adults generally have experienced a greater difficulty in handling males. In effect, then, biological endowment may interact with socialization and social expectation to create a vicious cycle for the male child.

Finally, how are we to interpret the fact that many behavior problems spontaneously disappear over time? It seems reasonable to assume that many of them represent transient developmental crises. Children are relatively flexible and are, almost by definition, changing. Care should be taken, then, not to overemphasize the importance of behavior problems. At the same time, treatment may be desirable if the child is experiencing immediate discomfort or is being prevented from reaching his or her potential. Furthermore, the complicated relationship between early and later problems must be considered.

THE PREDICTION OF PROBLEM BEHAVIORS

The relationship between early problems and later ones is not only of theoretical importance; it also has practical implications for the treatment of children displaying some sort of psychological dysfunction. If behavior disorders merely disappear or are markedly reduced by the time adulthood is reached, they would be of less concern than if they were highly predictive of later problems. What, then, is known about this issue?

As we have already seen, most severely disturbed children do not escape dysfunction in later life. However, it seems that there has been a tendency to misinterpret the importance of certain childhood problems that are less severe. The point is well illustrated by examining one of what Anthony (1970) has referred to as the "fashionable trends" that have sometimes been involved in defining *abnormal*.

One such trend has been traced by Kanner (1960), following the history of the meaning attributed to children's nail-biting over a twenty-five-year period:

> In 1908, nail biting was regarded as a "stigma of degeneration"; in 1912 it was seen as "an exquisite psychopathic symptom"; in 1931 it was described as "a sign of an unresolved Oedipus complex." Following this, a survey indicated that 66% of school children had been nail-biters at some time or another, which led Kanner to remark that it was "hardly realistic to assume that two-thirds of our youth are degenerate, exquisitely psychopathic or walking around with an unresolved Oedipus complex." [Anthony, 1970, p. 668, citing Kanner, 1960, p. 18]

For the most part, children who display annoying behaviors such as nail-biting, nose-picking, "nervousness," and masturbation grow up to be well-adjusted and productive adults. Fears, irritability, and "nervousness" in childhood fail to predict most adult disorders, and minor sexual deviations in childhood do not relate to deviant adult sex behavior (Robins, 1966). Furthermore, children judged to be shy, withdrawn, or inhibited are no more likely to become neurotic later than are their matched controls (Kohlberg, La Crosse, and Ricks, 1972; Robins, 1966).

Years ago Wickman (1928) compared teachers' and clinicians' views of maladaptive behavior among children. The teachers, he found, viewed aggressive and similar antisocial behavior as considerably "sicker" than social withdrawal and shyness; the clinicians took the opposite view. Through the past decades the "mental health view" that antisocial behavior is the less serious psychological problem has begun to change.

In a major longitudinal study, Robins (1966) followed more than five hundred children, seen in a guidance clinic in the 1920s and 1930s, into adulthood. Referred at the median age of thirteen for antisocial problems, only 16 percent were free of symptoms five years later. When interviewed in their early forties, more than 25 percent were considered antisocial personalities. Eight percent were alcoholics or drug addicts and eleven percent were psychotic. These outcomes are markedly different from those for children referred to the clinic for reasons other than antisocial problems and for a group of normal school children, most of whom were judged "well." Robins (1974) went on to examine twenty-three other studies that followed children who had been diagnosed antisocial in clinics or who had been in trouble in school or with the police. Comparisons with normal children or children suffering from psychoses or less severe disorders showed that only the psychotic children had worse outcomes in adulthood than the antisocial children. In noting that adult antisocial behavior virtually always begins before adulthood, Robins pointed to the obvious negative consequences for society and for the deviant individuals themselves, arguing for better treatment programs.

Recent investigations into the prognosis of hyperactivity also are revealing. Earlier reports seemed to lead to the conclusion that hyperactivity decreased with age. Now it is suggested that although extreme motor activity does lessen with age, restlessness, poor attention span, poor academic achievement, and problems in social functioning persist into adolescence and perhaps into adulthood (Barkley, 1978; Hoy, Weiss, Minde, and Cohen, 1978). Difficulties with peer relationships become central, as do problems in obeying the rules of society. Not all hyperactive children would be expected to follow this pattern, of course, but in summarizing recent evidence Barkley has noted that:

> . . . hyperactivity, despite our best treatment efforts, is a life-long disorder, rather than simply one limited to childhood. No longer can we legitimately inform parents to 'hang in there' until the child reaches adolescence when the disorder ought to disappear. The fact that it does not forces us to . . . approach hyperactivity with the same attitude as we approach developmentally handicapping conditions—as problems to be coped with throughout life . . . (1978, p. 160).

To summarize the issue of prediction of later problems from earlier ones, the current view has shifted from concern about shyness and withdrawn behavior to concern about antisocial, aggressive, and acting-out behavior. Overall, though, prediction from early problems to later ones remains a knotty problem.

The "Iffy" Quality of Predictions

The issue of prediction of behavior is, of course, a central concern to developmentalists, whether normal or deviant behavior is involved. As an example of the "iffy" quality of prediction, let us look again at the Thomas, Chess, and Birch (1970) study that followed 141 children from infancy into adolescence (p. 134). The focus of the investigation was individual temperamental style, with children's temperament categorized into the "difficult child," the "easy child," and the "slow-to-warm-up child" syndromes. The "difficult child" (characterized by biological irregularity, negative mood, high-intensity expression, withdrawal from new stimuli, and slow adaptability) was at greater risk for stressful interaction with the environment and thus for behavior disorders. Seven to ten percent of the sample fit into this category, but these children then provided about half the number of those who developed behavior problems by age five (Chess and Hassibi, 1978). However, it was found that children of any temperamental pattern were vulnerable to difficulties, given certain environmental demands and expectations. Prediction of any one child's development, moreover, was a difficult task (Chess & Thomas, 1977).

SUMMARY

Childhood behavior problems are usually identified by supervisory adults who judge a child's behavior on the basis of cultural and developmental norms. Characteristics of the adults themselves as well as the attitudes they hold are determinants of a child's behavior being judged as a problem.

Childhood psychoses involve severe disturbances in perception, thinking, movement, language, emotions, and social interactions. They can be classified into *childhood schizophrenia* and *infantile autism.*

Kanner first suggested the existence of a unique syndrome of infantile autism that, unlike other childhood psychosis, is present from birth. Today there is fairly wide agreement that autism is characterized by early onset, social isolation, language disorders, and insistence on sameness in the environment. According to Rimland, autistic children differ from other psychotic children in several ways: They are unusually attractive; their families are of high educational, intellectual, and occupational levels; and they manifest particular motor and intellectual abilities, normal EEGs, severe language deficits, and a striking aloneness. Data from Rimland's parental checklist provide some evidence for the coherence of the syndrome.

Several etiologies for psychoses have been proposed. Bender believes that they are genetically predisposed and brought on by physiological upset. Rimland proposes that autism is caused by lack of oxygen (anoxia) before or at birth, which impairs the brain's ability to associate new with old stimuli. Bettelheim argues that the autistic child psychologically withdraws from an unresponsive environment. Ferster focuses on the effects of lack of reinforcement from parents. There is growing evidence for the influence of biological factors.

The prognosis for severe behavior disorders is unfortunately poor: Perhaps 65 to 70 percent of psychotic children remain unable to lead independent adult lives. Speech capacity, IQ, and original severity are related to outcome.

Less severe childhood problems vary greatly in nature: problems in elimination (enuresis and encopresis), fears and phobias (e.g., school phobia), psychophysiological disorders (e.g., asthma), and hyperactivity. Considerable research is being conducted into the prevalence, etiology, and treatment of these disorders.

Various approaches to treatment exist. The *Freudian* approach views behavior problems as symptoms of underlying unconscious conflict, and treatment is aimed at uncovering the conflict. Critics point out that the effectiveness of this approach is questionable. *Nondirective treatment* assumes that individuals have powerful strivings for self-realization, and its purpose is to permit children the freedom to reach this potential. *Behavior modification* is based on the premise that problem behavior is learned and can be modified directly by new learning experiences. Employing direct observation, systematic manipulation, and ongoing evaluation, behavior therapists apply classical and operant conditioning and modeling to treatment.

The prevalence of childhood disorders has been studied by surveys of treatment centers and the general population. Severe disorders are infrequent but the less severe dysfunctions are quite prevalent. There is a general tendency for disorders to decline in school-age children, but specific disorders show different age-related patterns. Boys exhibit more deviancy than girls, notably in acting-out problems. Girls, however, are more anxious and inhibited. Such sex differences may be due to biological tendencies, environmental effects, or a combination of these factors.

The relationship between childhood disorders and adult behavior is a fascinating area of research. Evidence exists that aggressive and antisocial behavior in children is related to antisocial behavior in adulthood. Early hyperactivity seems to be related to later restlessness, poor attention span, poor academic achievement, and problems in social functioning. Overall, though, prediciton from the less severe disorders to later behavior has an "iffy" quality about it.

Road to Maturity

The end of childhood is only one milestone in human development. This final section deals with milestone events that occur during the remainder of the life span.

Chapter 16 is about adolescence and the physical, cognitive, and social changes occurring during the teenage years. Adolescence is viewed as a time of decision-making, when social attachments shift from family to peers and the need to make a vocational choice arises. The chapter also includes examination of three noteworthy problems of adolescence: juvenile delinquency, drug abuse, and adolescent suicide.

Chapter 17 is an overview of later life, including Erik Erikson's classic description of stages of psychosocial development in adulthood and a summary of several ground-breaking empirical investigations of adulthood published in the last few years. The chapter also describes physical, occupational, and social changes that occur in adulthood and during the senior years, ending with an examination of the various ways individuals face impending death.

16

Adolescence

If we were to walk the streets today and ask a random sample of people to define adolescence, chances are that the replies would be marked by enormous agreement. Although the chronological time associated with adolescence varies somewhat, it generally is said to encompass a period ranging from ages eleven or twelve to eighteen or twenty years of age. Sexual maturity—puberty—is usually denoted as the beginning of adolescence, but social roles—commitments to marriage, work, or career training—demark its termination.

Interestingly, adolescence as a stage of life was not always as clearly recognized. We noted in chapter 1 that only in the past few hundred years or so has society viewed childhood as a formative period of life and as distinguishable from adulthood. Adolescence as a separate category emerged even later, during the last two decades of the nineteenth century (Demos and Demos, 1972). It is always difficult to trace all the reasons for such a turn of events. As we shall see, the impetus that came from the excitement of evolutionary theory no doubt played a part. Then, too, as knowledge of development increased, it led to a finer discrimination of the life span, resulting in the formation of more stages. Social conditions may also have helped delineate adolescence.

David Bakan (1971) suggests that adolescence as we know it in the United States is largely associated with urban-industrial life and is a product of several social changes. The United States was dramatically transformed during the late 1800s: The frontier was almost completely gone, the number of cities increased, immigration was high, work shifted from the farm to the factory. There was much concern over property rights, crime and immorality, and the influence of immigrants. This situation, according to Bakan, resulted in three major movements that conspired to strengthen the notion of adolescence. First, compulsory education was established, marking ages sixteen to eighteen years as the cutoff point for this critical life experience. Second, child labor laws, stemming from a need to protect working children and to reduce the labor force surplus, further defined the adolescent period. Finally, juvenile delinquency as a legal category was "invented" in order to remove young people from the punitive consequences of adult criminality. All of these milestones, in Bakan's words, served to transform adolescence from an idea into a social fact. They helped create a stage of life that was to be increasingly studied by psychologists, sociologists, and anthropologists, virtually all of whom viewed it as the transitional period between the worlds of childhood and adulthood.

Although the various disciplines have examined adolescence from different starting points, two themes have been central: adolescence as a period of uniquely dramatic "storm and stress," and adolescence as a search for individual identity. In focusing on these themes we shall have the opportunity to explore some of the major perspectives on adolescence.

G. Stanley Hall, the founder of child study in the United States, was among the first psychologists to investigate and speculate about adolescence. He was particularly influential in propagating the storm and stress view. Hall's ideas, presented in the volumes *Adolescence* (1904, 1905), depended heavily on evolutionary theory and on the related concepts of recapitulation and the inheritance of acquired characteristics. *Recapitulation* is the idea that each individual's development (ontogeny) repeats the development of its species (phylogeny); it is thus often referred to with the phrase *ontogeny recapitulates phylogeny*. A manifestation of recapitulation is found in human prenatal development, in which the growing organism appears to first resemble lower forms of life on the evolutionary scale and then increasingly the higher ones until it reaches human form and function. The *inheritance of acquired characteristics* is the belief that when organisms change in order to adapt to their environments, the change may be passed on to their offspring. Our present knowledge of genetic mechanisms disproves this notion, but Hall was very much in the mold of early evolutionary theorists (Grinder, 1978).

Hall viewed postnatal development, too, as occurring in stages that parallel the development of the human species, moving from the lowest to the highest forms of life. He speculated that from infancy to adolescence the child reflects human history from its apelike ancestry through primitive cave dwelling, hunting, and fishing. Hall believed that adolescence represents the most recent stage of human development, and that environmental influence is especially strong at this time. Adolescence was thus viewed as critically important in introducing change that might then become inherited in the species. Hall hoped that humanity could be improved—that is, made more civilized—by optimal growth and change during the adolescent period (Demos and Demos, 1972). But he also noted that enormous storm and stress occurred due to conflict between impulses such as sensitivity vs. cruelty, selfishness vs. conservatism, and radicalism vs. conservatism. Because Hall's view was based on theory that rapidly became antiquated, it has largely gone by the wayside (Demos and Demos, 1972; Grinder, 1978). However, the idea of storm and stress has been retained by many theorists and the general public as well.

From psychoanalysis came support that upheaval is a necessary and even positive aspect of adolescent development (Blos, 1962; Freud, 1972). We have already seen that according to Freud, the latency period is one of relative calm, when struggles among the psychic structures are minimal. But puberty, with its eruption of sexuality, is bound to bring disturbances. In fact, a lack of disturbance may actually be a sign that normal growth is off its course. Anna Freud spoke directly to this issue with these words:

> We know that the character structure of a child at the end of the latency period represents the outcome of long drawn-out conflicts between id and ego forces. The inner balance achieved . . . is preliminary only and precarious. . . . [I]t has to be abandoned to allow adult sexuality to be integrated into the individual

personality. The so-called adolescent upheavals are no more than the external indications that such internal adjustments are in progress.

... We all know individual children who as late as the age of fourteen, fifteen, or sixteen show no such outer evidence of inner unrest. ... They are, perhaps more than any others, in need of therapeutic help to remove the inner restrictions and clear the path for normal development, however "upsetting" the latter may prove to be. [1972, pp. 317–318]

Bandura's Contribution

Not all investigators are convinced that storm and stress must be an integral part of adolescence. Bandura (1964), of the social learning persuasion, has argued that the inevitability of disturbance is greatly exaggerated. He suggested that the following tendencies have led to overemphasizing the role of disturbance in the lives of young people.

1. *Overinterpretation of adolescent nonconformity and fads.* Whereas faddish group behavior does occur, Bandura argues that adult behavior reflects it as well, as in the fads of dress that men and women adopt almost by dictate of fashion designers. In this sense, adolescents are not all that different.

2. *Mass-media sensationalism.* The adolescent of the media is portrayed as passing through a semidelinquent or neurotic phase, because that character seems so much more fascinating than the run-of-the-mill, relatively undisturbed adolescent.

3. *Overgeneralization from deviant youth.* Descriptions of adolescents often come from mental health professionals who actually come into contact with a biased sample.

4. *Overemphasis on biological determinants of sexual behavior.* This paints the adolescent in the throes of sudden erotic conflict, rather than under the more moderate influence of social learning variables that largely govern human sexuality.

Bandura also proposed that society's expectation that adolescents be rebellious, wild, and unpredictable only increases the chance of just such outcomes. Thus, although adolescence would not be completely problem free in any event, the cultural commitment to the storm and stress hypothesis becomes a self-fulfilling prophecy.

The Anthropologists Benedict and Mead

Finally, anthropological studies have addressed the issue of storm and stress in adolescence. Ruth Benedict, in her classic paper, *"Continuities and discontinuities in cultural conditioning"* (1938), pointed out that humans move from infancy to adulthood in different ways, depending upon their culture. In some instances, cultural habits lend themselves to creating a smooth, continuous pathway; in other cases, discontinuity marks the road to maturity. Our culture, she said:

... goes to great extremes in emphasizing contrasts between the child and the adult. The child is sexless, the adult estimates his virility by his sexual experience; the child must be protected from the ugly facts of life, the adult must meet them without psychic catastrophe; the child must obey, the adult must command this obedience (Benedict, 1938, p. 161).

Mead's (1928) study of adolescence in Samoa serves as a particularly striking example of a culture in which this time of life is characterized by continuity of roles and behavior. Children were permitted, for example, considerable freedom of sexual expression. The transition from obedience to authority also was relatively continuous: From an early age children became authorities for those younger and their power gradually increased. Noting that adolescence in Samoa is a serene period, Mead agreed with Benedict that it is discontinuity in cultural conditioning that creates disturbances in adolescence.

Anthropologists also have emphasized the importance of social rites in bridging discontinuity. In many cultures puberty rites mark the taking on of adult roles. This kind of support may be inadequate in our culture, and adolescents may themselves try to provide rites of passage by engaging in certain activities. It has been suggested, for example, that an important aspect of alcohol consumption by high school students is that society institutionalizes drinking as part of adulthood (Maddox and McCall, 1964). In addition to lack of transitional support, the adolescent period in a technical society is a long one—so long, in fact, that young adulthood is sometimes now described in terms of transition. In short, it is difficult to achieve a sense of stability or of "having arrived."

To the extent that the anthropological analysis is valid, we would anticipate adolescent disturbance in some but not all cultures, and it would display itself in areas in which cultural habits are most discontinuous. It is difficult to precisely test these expectations, although we can ask about the amount and kinds of stress that adolescents do experience.

The Problems of Adolescence

It can be argued that only a small percentage of youth in the United States experience severe turmoil that leads to psychiatric treatment or serious difficulties with the legal system. A study of 6,768 youths representative of the twelve to seventeen-year-old population revealed that 6.3 percent had received some kind of mental health treatment (Vital and Health Statistics, 1974). Parents rated only 4 percent as very nervous, 46 percent as somewhat nervous, and 50 percent as not at all nervous. They also judged that 82 percent of the youth made friends easily, whereas only 1 percent were reported to have a lot of trouble doing so. Overall, parents overwhelmingly rated their offspring as easy to rear (Table 16–1). The problem with the data, of course, is that parents may be biased by social expectation and desirability.

Turning to Offer and Offer's (1975) longitudinal investigation of males, we see that 21 percent experienced substantial crises. Approximately the same number were categorized as traveling a path of continuous growth that smoothly progressed toward a fulfilling adulthood. About 35 percent of the adolescents were said to experience resurgent growth; that is, ups and downs that although troublesome did not ultimately disrupt progression.

FIGURE 16–1
The use of alcoholic beverages appears to serve as a rite of passage into adulthood in our culture.   Mimi Forsyth, Monkmeyer.

Obviously this study is limited in sample, and we have no way of knowing how the results would compare with studies of people at other transitions; for example, the one that is postulated to occur between the ages of thirty-eight and forty-two (about which we will have more to say later).

Our own opinion is that considerably more stability and continuity exist during adolescence than is often recognized (Bandura, 1964; King, 1972). Adolescence does not occur overnight and to a large extent parents and other socializing agents prepare gradually for children's assumption of different roles, interests, behaviors, and status. Still, the many transitions occurring at this time of life probably do somewhat raise the level of discomfort felt by young people.

What are the problem areas? A recent study of 240 randomly chosen high school students from a suburban area isolates some of them for us

TABLE 16–1
Parents' Judgment of How Much Trouble Their Children were to Raise (in Percentage)

None	Just a Little	Some	A lot
59.9	27.2	10.8	2.2

Source: Vital and Health Statistics, Series 11, No. 137. (Rockville, Md.: Department of Health, Education, and Welfare, 1974), p. 17.

TABLE 16-2
Mean Rating of Problem Seriousness by High School Students (Higher Score Indicates More Serious)

Area	All	Male	Female
Physical appearance	2.08	1.86	2.27**
Careers	1.99	1.92	2.07
Grades	1.93	1.77	2.08*
Future schooling	1.68	1.47	1.87*
Present employment	1.57	1.55	1.59
Parents (relationship or conflict)	1.53	1.44	1.60
Independence	1.53	1.39	1.66
Peers	1.38	1.29	1.46
Sexual impulses	1.37	1.54	1.26
Siblings	1.17	1.20	1.19
Alcohol	.98	1.00	.96
Extra-curricula activities	.96	1.20	.90
Smoking	.92	.88	.96
Drugs	.79	.79	.79

*significant sex difference at the .01 level
**significant sex difference at the .001 level
Source: Eme, Maisiak, and Goodale, 1979.

(Eme, Maisiak, and Goodale, 1979). The students were requested to rate fourteen areas according to whether they were of no concern (0), mild concern (1), moderate concern (2), or severe concern (3). Table 16–2 shows the results for all students and then for males and females separately. Concerns about how they looked to others and to themselves, whether they know what career they want and if they will find it, and adequacy of grades were rated of top priority by both sexes. Females were significantly more worried about physical appearance, grades, and future schooling. The investigators also found that college-bound students and those undecided about the future rated grades, future schooling, and extracurricular activities as of greater concern than work-bound students. Freshmen were more worried about physical appearance and sexual impulses than older adolescents, and they shared concern about independence with seniors.

ACHIEVING IDENTITY: THE SEARCH FOR THE SELF

Identity formation has long interested philosophers, but Erik Erikson has been foremost among psychologists to draw attention to it. The word *identity* means sameness, oneness, or the distinguishing attribute of personality of an individual (Webster's New Collegiate Dictionary, 1973). According to Erikson, identity is characterized by the "actually attained but forever to-be-revised sense of the reality of the self within social reality" (1968, p. 211). It is a subjective sense of continuity and sameness. A lifelong process, identity formation is nevertheless considered cardinal during adolescence.

Earlier we noted Erikson's description of the psychosocial stages through which each individual hypothetically passes and the crisis of each stage (pp. 368–371). The crisis of adolescence is *identity vs. role confusion*. The basis of the crisis lies not only in societal demands regarding impending adulthood but also in the physical changes rapidly taking place. Previous trust in one's physical being and bodily functions is now seriously questioned and can be reestablished only by a reevaluation of the self (Maier, 1969). Adolescents seek to discover what they will become.

How does the adolescent achieve this vital identity? Erikson suggests that our culture allows a moratorium during which the rapidly developing child has the opportunity to become integrated into society. A certain amount of experimentation is expected, so that the adolescent may indeed "try on" various commitments and identities much as one tries on new garments before selecting the best fit. This "trying on" is manifested in many ways: endless examination with others of the self, vocations, ideologies; a rich fantasy life involving the taking of a variety of roles; identification with particular individuals, frequently involving a herolike worship. Settling on a vocation is particularly important in this process, and the ability to do so disturbs many young people. "Falling in love," too, can be a means to arrive at a definition of self by seeing oneself reflected and gradually clarified through another (Erikson, 1963).

Most psychologists, whether or not of Erikson's bent for stage theory, agree on the importance of identity formation in adolescence. Thus, Erikson's formulations have generated considerable research during the last two decades.

The most dominant research approach was initiated by Marcia's conceptualization of *identity status* (Bourne, 1978a,b; Marcia, 1966, 1976). Identity statuses are modes of resolution to the identity crisis in late adolescence. They are examined by semistructured interviews about occupation and ideology (politics and religion). The presence or absence of a decision-making process (crisis) and degree of commitment to a position are determined. Marcia proposed that adolescents can be classified into four major statuses: achievement, moratorium, foreclosure, and diffusion. Table 16–3 defines the statuses and also provides a sketch of each derived from research findings. (see p. 518).

Interesting, but not completely consistent, sex differences have been found in identity status (Bourne, 1978a). Among males, those who are of the achievement and moratorium statuses perform better than those of the foreclosure and diffusion statuses on self-esteem, locus of control, interpersonal intimacy, and the like. Females who are of the achievement and foreclosure statuses are more like each other. There is some evidence that they select difficult college majors, are low in anxiety, are less conforming, are more independent, and view themselves as "straight" rather than "hip." It has been speculated that foreclosure in females is adaptive because they are socialized to incorporate parental and conventional standards without crisis and autonomy. As Bourne (1978a) has pointed out, however, the findings are not consistent and, in any event, we might expect that foreclosure is now less adaptive for women than previously. Furthermore, in one recent study, 80 percent of the high-school females were classified as achievers or moratoriums, which are considered the higher statuses (St. Clair and Day, 1979).

If identity formation as Erikson views it is a developmental task, age

TABLE 16-3
Four Identity Statuses and Attributes of Each Derived from Research Findings

Achievement	Moratorium	Foreclosure	Diffusion
CRISIS HAS BEEN EXPERIENCED AND COMMITMENT MADE	ONGOING CRISIS: INDECISION AND STRUGGLE ABOUT ALTERNATIVES	STATIC POSITION WITH MAINTENANCE OF CHILDHOOD VALUES WITHOUT CRISIS	COMMITMENT LACKING: CRISIS MAY OR MAY NOT HAVE OCCURRED
Achievement oriented	High anxiety	High authoritarianism	Withdrawn; lack of intimate relationships
Socially adaptive	High conflict with authority	Close to parents	Somewhat conforming
High levels of intimacy in relationships	Low authoritarianism	High need for social approval	
High levels of moral reasoning, need for complexity, cultural sophistication.	Relate to parents with guilt and ambivalence	Low autonomy	
		Low anxiety	

Source: Adapted from Bourne, 1978b.

changes in status would be anticipated. Meilman's (1979) cross-sectional study of males twelve to twenty-four years of age showed a clear pattern reflecting an increase in achievement status and a decrease in foreclosure and moratorium statuses with age. Nevertheless, two investigations that followed the same individuals for more than three years revealed that no identity status is necessarily stable (Bourne, 1978a). This is, of course, congruous with the idea that identity, at least for some people, is continually reworked as new circumstances are met and incorporated. Dissolution of the old and reconstitution may indeed be crucial in adolescence, but they occur throughout life.

PHYSICAL CHANGES IN ADOLESCENCE

As we have seen, physical appearance is high on the list of adolescent concerns. Although sexual maturation is central, numerous physical changes occur, some being much more obvious than others. Among the obvious and the most easily measured are changes in body size and proportion.

Body Size and Proportion

Height and Weight. Table 16–4 shows the average height and weight attained by a representative sample of twelve to seventeen-year-olds in the United States. Aside from presenting norms, the table is informative in other ways. The columns labeled as 5th and 95th percentiles for each age category are a measure of variability. For example, although the average fifteen-year-old female weighs 124.5 pounds, 5 percent of this age group weighs less than 92.5 pounds and 5 percent weighs more than 174.7 pounds. It is also of interest to compare the data for the sexes. Females who are twelve years old are both taller and heavier than males of the same age,

TABLE 16-4

Mean Height and Weight of U.S. Female and Male Adolescents 12 to 17 Years of Age

| | Age | Height in Inches | | | Weight in Pounds | | |
		Mean	5th Percentile	95th Percentile	Mean	5th Percentile	95th Percentile
F	12	61.1	55.8	65.9	102.7	72.7	141.3
E	13	62.5	57.8	66.9	111.2	80.0	149.8
M	14	63.5	59.6	67.4	119.4	89.1	157.6
A	15	63.9	59.6	68.1	124.5	92.5	174.7
L	16	64.0	59.7	68.1	128.0	98.6	183.7
E	17	64.1	60.0	68.1	126.9	98.2	167.9
	12	60.0	54.6	65.2	94.8	67.5	132.4
M	13	62.9	57.2	68.7	110.2	76.9	156.1
A	14	65.6	59.9	70.7	124.9	86.4	172.1
L	15	67.5	62.4	72.1	135.8	102.1	184.6
E	16	68.6	64.1	73.1	142.9	107.6	187.2
	17	69.1	64.1	73.7	150.0	115.9	200.4

Source: From P. E. Grinder, Adolescence (New York: John Wiley, 1978). Originally from Vital and Health Statistics, Series 11, No. 124 (Rockville, Md.: Department of Health, Education, and Welfare, 1973).

but this pattern reverses itself quite early. Figure 16–2 also shows that from about eleven to thirteen years of age girls tend to be taller than boys.

Increase in height gradually tapers off during childhood, only to dramatically accelerate at approximately eleven to thirteen years in girls and thirteen to fifteen years in boys (Figure 16–3). This adolescent growth spurt

FIGURE 16–2

Differences in height between boys and girls at various ages. Data from E. H. Watson and G. H. Lowrey, **Growth and Development for Children.** Chicago: Year Book Medical Publishers, Inc., 1962, pp. 72–73.

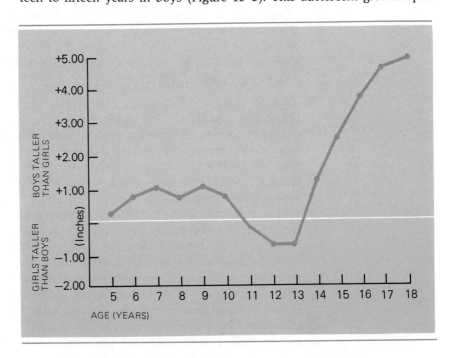

Increase in height for the typical boy and girl, showing the adolescent growth spurt. From Tanner, ''Physical Growth,'' in P. H. Mussen, ed., Carmichael's manual of child psychology, 3rd edition (1970) vol. I, John Wiley & Sons, Inc.

subsequently decreases for both sexes and ceases for most at age seventeen in girls and nineteen in boys. By this time most bones have become ossified so that only 2 percent of total height is still to occur. From about thirty to forty-five years of age stature remains constant; it then begins to decline very slowly (Tanner, 1970).

Other Size Changes. The adolescent growth spurt in height is accompanied by growth of most organs and bodily systems: heart, lungs, pancreas, stomach, intestines, and the reproductive system. Two notable exceptions are the brain, which attains about 90 percent of its size by age eight, and the lymph and thymus tissue, which actually decrease in size during adolescence (Figure 3–15).

The sex differences that emerge by adulthood include a larger heart, lungs, muscle and shoulder width in males, and greater fat and hip width in females. Sex differences in shoulder and hip width become particularly distinguishable at adolescence because cartilage cells in the shoulder region multiply in response to testosterone and those in the pelvis in response to estrogens (Tanner, 1970). In both males and females muscular tissue increases considerably, with males showing more growth. From infancy to adolescence boys have somewhat larger muscles; then, due to their earlier growth spurt, girls actually have larger muscles for about one year. Males subsequently catch up and surpass females. On the other hand, girls have slightly more fat tissue at birth. Both sexes have some fat loss during childhood and this is greater for boys. Just prior to adolescence there may be a gain in fat, but during adolescence fat loss again occurs—and loss is greater in males. Eventually females have a larger proportion of fat tissue.

These and other tissue adjustments bring about changes in body proportion, some of which are not considered attractive for a period of time. For example, the arms and legs become relatively long and the lower jaw may become noticeably large as compared to the rest of the face.

Primary and Secondary Sexual Characteristics

The sequence of development of some of the male primary and secondary sexual characteristics relative to the general growth spurt can be seen in Figure 16–4. The diagram indicates (under each event) the range of ages within which each event may begin or end. Puberty begins with the growth of the testes, followed rapidly by appearance of pubic hair and, within a year, by the growth of the penis. During the next year the first ejaculation may occur. At about the peak of the growth spurt, axillary (underarm) hair appears, as does facial hair. The latter follows a definite pattern: hair first appears at the corners of the upper lip, next along the entire upper lip, then on the cheeks, and finally on the chin area (Tanner, 1970). The growth of the larynx (voicebox), causing a drop in voice pitch and sometimes the embarrassing breaking of the voice, occurs relatively late. Males also show some breast changes; the areola (nipple) widens and enlargement of the breast itself may occur, only to subsequently regress (Tanner, 1970).

In the female, the budding of the breast and appearance of pubic hair are usually the first signs of puberty (Figure 16–5). Menarchy occurs at about thirteen years, normally after the peak of the general growth spurt. It is not a sure sign of reproductive maturity, though; sterility may exist for

FIGURE 16–4

The sequence of adolescent development of some primary and secondary sexual characteristics in males. (The numbers 2–5 for pubic hair refer to specific kinds of changes that have been observed.) From Tanner, 1970, p. 97.

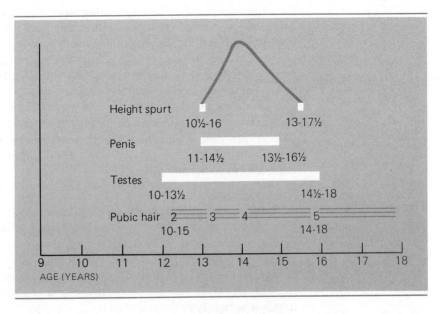

FIGURE 16-5

The sequence of adolescent development of some primary and secondary sexual characteristics in females. (The numbers 2–5 for pubic hair and for breast refer to specific kinds of changes that have been observed.)   From Tanner, 1970, p. 99.

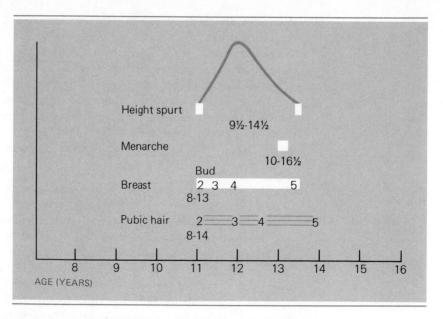

Height spurt
9½-14½

Menarche
10-16½

Breast
Bud
2 3 4   5
8-13

Pubic hair
2 ═══ 3 ══ 4 ═══ 5
8-14

AGE (YEARS)
8   9   10   11   12   13   14   15   16

another twelve to eighteen months. As in males, axillary hair appears about two years after pubic hair. Females, too, show a drop in voice pitch, but it is not nearly as dramatic.

Endocrine Changes

Numerous physiological changes can be traced through adolescence, far too many to be detailed here. To give the scope and flavor, though, they include changes in metabolic rate, blood pressure, respiratory rate, and activation of the oil-producing glands in the skin. Most of these changes are not ordinarily visible.

Also not directly visible are the changes that occur in the functioning of the endocrine glands. The hypothalamus of the brain is said to signal puberty, but, as Tanner (1970) has put it, this does not come out of the blue. Speculation has it that the hypothalamus is held in check by small amounts of the sex hormones that circulate from the beginning of life. For unknown reasons the hypothalamus becomes less sensitive to this hormonal inhibition, setting off secretions in the pituitary and, in turn, in the thyroid and adrenal glands and in the testes and ovaries. The endocrine system is an intricate one, with many feedback loops, and much is still not understood. It is clear, however, that although both sexes secrete male and female hormones, male hormones greatly increase in adolescent boys, and female hormones in adolescent girls.

Effects of Physical Change and Attributes

Adolescents understandably are concerned with the transformations of their physical selves. Not only must they adapt to having their bodies appear and function somewhat differently; they must also acclimate to the change in other people's reaction to them. Aside from obvious sexual changes, they may have to deal with the awkwardness of long limbs, acne, a face that has taken on new proportions, greater size and strength, and perhaps a new beauty or attractiveness.

Although adolescents are criticized for being excessively involved with how they appear to others, physical attributes do indeed influence how others react. It has been shown, for example, that throughout life males are favorably disposed to the mesomorphic body build, that is, the well-muscled, broad-shouldered, narrow-hipped male physique (Lerner and Korn, 1972). And beauty, said to be only skin deep, is correlated with popularity and the ascription of positive personality characteristics (Berscheid and Walster, 1974). Walster and her associates (1966) demonstrated the association of physical attractiveness and how much individuals are liked by setting up a situation in which people were randomly paired at a dance. People were later asked to rate their partners on a variety of intellectual, social, and personality measures, as well as to provide an estimate of how much they liked their partners. Only physical attractiveness was related to liking—and in a positive way. Physically attractive people are also seen by youth as having more desirable personalities (Dion, Berscheid, and Walster, 1972), and attractive children are believed by adults to be less likely to be aggressive (Dion, 1972). Surely, then, physical attributes help shape psychosocial development. So, too, does rate of physical maturation.

The Timing of Maturation. Individuals mature at quite varying rates; Figure 16–6, which shows two adolescent boys and two adolescent girls of the same chronological ages, furnishes a striking example. Such individuality is the result of heredity, diet, health, and other variables. But what are the effects of maturation that deviates from the norm, that is, that occurs early or late? This question has been studied longitudinally in both boys and girls from a middle-class population in California (Eichorn, 1963; Jones, 1965;

FIGURE 16–6
Photographs of adolescents of the same age, illustrating differences in rates of maturation. From J. M. Tanner, in P. H. Mussen, **Carmichael's Manual of Child Psychology,** 3rd. ed., Vo. I. Copyright 1970, reproduced by permission of John Wiley & Sons, Inc., and Dr. James M. Tanner.

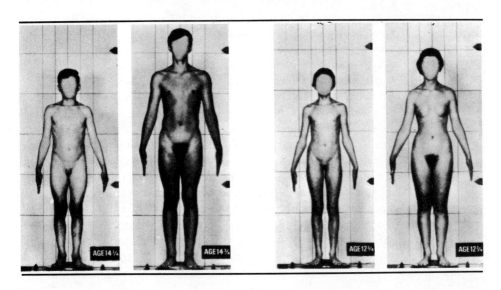

Jones and Bayley, 1950; Mussen and Jones, 1957) yielding a fairly complete picture of the role of rate of maturation on social development.

Early maturation appears to confer distinct advantages on boys. Early maturers are more likely to be elected class officers, have their names in the school newspaper, be rated as attractive, excel in athletics, and be treated as adults. They are less likely to be considered talkative, childish, and restless. On the other hand, late maturers project negative self-concepts. The general pattern of advantage for the early maturers tends to diminish as physical differences disappear, but is not completely lost. As adults they are poised, responsible, and achieving in the conventional way. However, those who mature later are, when in their thirties, relatively more active, exploring, insightful, perceptive, independent, and impulsive. It seems that in coping with being behind their peers, late maturers develop many behaviors that are valued in our society. Overall, though, the early maturing male appears to have an edge over the later maturing male.

What factors account for the advantages that accrue to early-maturing boys? Undoubtedly there are many. They may be given tasks, privileges, and responsibilities usually assigned to older individuals and, providing these challenges are met, may derive personal satisfaction and rewards from others (Eichorn, 1963). Early maturers also have superior physical strength (Carron and Bailey, 1974), a characteristic that along with physical capability is tied closely to the concept of masculinity.

The possible influence of physical capability is demonstrated in a study in which twelve- to fourteen-year-old boys were tested in gym classes and were given either positive or negative feedback about their performance (Ludwig and Maehr, 1967). Positive feedback emphasized that their physical development was quite good for their age level, whereas negative feedback implied that performance was poor for their age level. Both before and after the test, measures were taken of the boys' self-concepts. The results indicated that self-concept improved after positive feedback and declined after negative feedback. Furthermore, feedback influenced the boys' later-stated preferences for physical or nonphysical activity, with the positive feedback group showing increased preference for physical activity and the negative feedback group showing decreased preference.

Turning to females, the effects of the timing of maturation are less clear-cut. Early data from the California Growth Study indicated that late maturers played more prominent roles in school and were rated higher on poise, sociability, cheerfulness, leadership, and expressiveness (Weatherley, 1964). When these adolescents were older (seventeen years of age), however, they showed few differences on projective tests, with a slight advantage to the early maturers (Jones and Mussen, 1958). Other studies indicate that late-maturing females score lower on achievement and ability tests, manifest more anxiety, and are less popular with peers (Douglas and Ross, 1964; Faust, 1960; Weatherley, 1964). On the other hand, in one study sixth-grade girls evaluated their prepubertal female classmates more positively than those who had already matured sexually (Faust, 1960).

Thus, the picture that emerges is complex. Early maturing girls may initially suffer some disadvantage because they are not only larger than their male peers but they also tend to be of stocky build. They may date older males while lacking the adequate emotional and social sophistication necessary to deal with such relationships. They may also be looked on with jealousy by their female peers. Even if this is so, however, the disadvantages appear to vanish rapidly, or perhaps reverse themselves. Moreover, the most consistent result is that the timing of maturation is simply not as powerful a variable for females as for males.

The Secular Trend in Physical Development

One interesting phenomenon especially relevant to adolescence is the so-called *secular growth trend* (*secular* meaning direction over time). There is evidence from many parts of the world that people in general are both taller and heavier than in the past (Muuss, 1972; Tanner, 1970). The armor of medieval knights seems to fit the ten to twelve-year-old boy in the United States today; seats in the La Scala opera house, constructed about 1778, were only thirteen inches wide; and the average height of American sailors in the War of 1812 was purportedly five feet two inches. It was reported from Canada that thirteen to fourteen-year-olds were three inches taller in 1939 than those of the same age in 1892, while a German study found that twelve-year-olds in the 1960s were as large as fifteen-year-olds in 1875. Figure 16–7 illustrates the increase in mean height of boys in the United States from the years 1880 to 1960.

Another aspect of the secular trend is that children grow faster at an earlier age and attain adult size earlier than in the past (Muuss, 1972). Today the average girl reaches her adult height at sixteen to seventeen years of age instead of age eighteen or nineteen, as did females at the turn of the century. Boys in 1880 reached their adult height in their early to mid-twenties; today they do so at eighteen or nineteen years of age.

Given the relationship between general body growth and maturation of the reproductive system, it is not surprising to find a secular decline in the

FIGURE 16–7
Differences between mean height of U.S. boys at varying ages from 1880 to 1960. From Muuss, 1972. In H. V. Meredith, Change in stature and body weight of North American boys during the last eighty years. In L. P. Lipsett and C. C. Spiker (eds.), **Advances in Child Development and Behavior,** Vol. I. New York: Academic Press, 1963, p. 90.

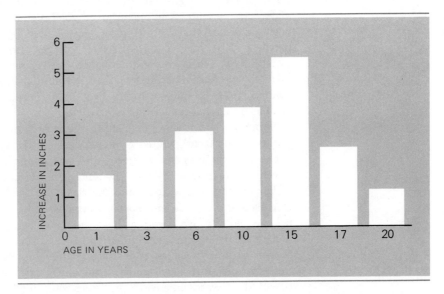

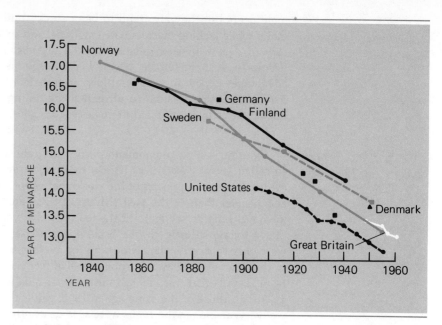

FIGURE 16–8
Secular trend in
average age of
menarche. From
J. M. Tanner, **Growth
at Adolescence.**
Oxford: Blackwell
Scientific Publications,
1962, p. 153.

age of puberty. Figure 16–8 illustrates this overall pattern. Interestingly, there is some evidence that prior to the eighteenth century, perhaps reaching back to 400 B.C., menarche occurred at about thirteen to fifteen years of age (Diers, 1974). It then became delayed so that by 1800 most females in the West experienced menarche at approximately seventeen years of age. The most recent trend, then, seems to be a return to earlier times.

Several reasons for the secular trend in development have been proposed, including artificial lighting and temperature and humidity control (Muuss, 1972). The most obvious ones, however, are better diet and health care. This is supported by the fact that children of the lower socioeconomic classes have been affected by the secular trend more than those of the higher classes who have long enjoyed good diet and health care. It has also been suggested that hybrid vigor plays a role: With increasing mobility people tend to mate outside of their villages, introducing greater genetic variability, which is known to enhance development. In any event, though, there is speculation and data that the secular trend may not continue (Muuss, 1972; Poppleton and Brown, 1966). Perhaps the biological organism has limits that are soon to be reached.

From a psychosocial perspective one may inquire into the implications of the secular trend. Muuss (1972) suggested that we might expect several changes in the interests, attitudes, and social sophistication of today's adolescents compared to those of bygone days. He cited studies that indicate earlier interest in sex, love, and marriage; greater tolerance of others; and increased seriousness and social awareness. The social calendar of youth has seemed to move ahead, as has school curricula—much to the dismay of many parents who remember "when I was a child. . . ." It is not possible, of course, to draw a cause and effect relationship between these facts and trends in physical development. Still, the overall picture is one of a consistent downward extension of adolescence into the years that we previously might have considered childhood.

As children move into their adolescent years they typically continue to perform higher on IQ tests and show increases in language, reading, arithmetic, and other skills. As would be expected, most profit from their formal and informal learning experiences and this continued growth no doubt involves an increased knowledge of the world. But does it also encompass a new cognitive sophistication?

According to Piaget, the answer to this question is a definite *yes*. If you recall from chapter 7, Piaget proposed that at approximately eleven to twelve years of age children begin to develop formal operations. By way of review formal operations is generally characterized by:

> *freedom, mobility,* and *flexibility,* due to the fact that adolescents are able to abstract. They are no longer confined to the concrete, nor to any one idea.
>
> *consideration of all possibilities,* that is, concern about what could be as well as what is.
>
> *control,* which includes taking into account all relevant but not irrelevant premises and information; holding all aspects in mind while considering one; organizing and reflecting on all aspects before drawing conclusions.
>
> *explanation* rather than just description of a phenomenon, which includes relating aspects of the phenomenon. (Smart and Smart, 1978a)

Formal operations require the use of symbolic logic, or to put it in another way, demand that the individual act as a scientist. Indeed, for the most part Piaget's tests involve science related or mathematical problems. Accordingly, the formal operations child should be able to construct all hypothetical solutions, mentally manipulate all combinations of relevant variables, and draw conclusions (see pp. 204–206). Arriving at formal operations is no small accomplishment; in fact, David Elkind (1967), a leading interpreter of Piaget, suggested that a major task of adolescence involves the conquest of thought through formal operations.

There is, indeed, evidence that as children move into adolescence they show a greater ability to solve problems that require formal operations (Keating, 1975; Roberge, 1976). Nevertheless, many individuals do not consistently demonstrate this kind of thinking, even as adults. What factors determine whether formal operations will be acquired? General ability seems to be involved: Those who test higher on measures of verbal and nonverbal intelligence appear to acquire formal operations earlier and more strongly (Cloutier and Goldschmid, 1976; Keating, 1975; Keating and Caramazza, 1975; Keating and Schaefer, 1975). Personality measures have also been implicated in such cognitive performance. Cloutier and Goldschmid (1976) found that ten- to twelve-year-old boys who scored high on tasks involving proportions were active, quick to respond, able to initiate activities when left alone in the classroom, original, somewhat low in discipline, and doubtful of their capacities. These investigators pointed out that activity and initiation are consistent with Piaget's view that cognitive growth involves an active construction of the world. Finally, Piaget (1972) himself has recognized that formal operations may depend upon aptitude and interest.

Acknowledging the individual variation in the attainment of formal operations, Piaget has reasoned that professional specialization causes adolescents to focus on specific domains of fact and knowledge. In turn, it becomes easier to think in some areas. Thus they may demonstrate formal operations in domains of high knowledge and interest but not in others. Specialization and interest mean, of course, that individuals are exposed to and perhaps even trained in thinking in the domain; both of these conditions have been shown to facilitate formal operations (Kuhn and Angelev, 1976; Siegler and Liebert, 1975).

Formal Operations and Egocentrism

The nature of formal operations permits individuals to think about their thinking, to examine their own mental constructions, to reason about their thoughts. They similarly can take the thoughts of others into account. But Elkind (1967) notes that adolescents fail to distinguish between what they and others think about. Because they are concerned primarily with themselves, they believe that others, too, are preoccupied with their appearance and behavior. Elkind refers to this as adolescent egocentrism and noted two consequences: the imaginary audience and the personal fable.

The *imaginary audience* is the belief that one is being observed by others. In turn it plays a role in determining certain behaviors and feelings—for example, self-consciousness, loudness, and faddish dress that frequently characterize adolescents. The *personal fable* involves a belief in the uniqueness of one's feelings and in one's immortality. Thus, Elkind points out, we see lengthy diaries depicting with great drama the special experiences and frustrations of young people, which they presumably regard to be of universal importance. He also suggests that adolescent problems can be attributed partly to the imaginary audience and the personal fable:

> The imaginary audience . . . seems often to play a role in middle-class delinquency. . . . As a case in point, one young man took $1,000 from a golf tournament purse, hid the money, and then promptly revealed himself. It turned out that much of the motivation for this act was derived from the anticipated response of "the audience" to the guttiness of his action. In a similar vein, many young girls become pregnant because, in part at least, their personal fable convinces them that pregnancy will happen to others but never to them. . . . [Elkind, 1967, pp. 1031–1032.]

There is some evidence supporting adolescent belief in an imaginary audience (Elkind and Bowen, 1979; Kissel, 1975; Simmons, Rosenberg and Rosenberg, 1973). Elkind and Bowen (1979), for example, hypothesized that since adolescent egocentrism would be strong during early adolescence, individuals of that age would have a more powerful reaction to the imaginary audience. They tested this preposition by reasoning that self-consciousness, or an unwillingness to reveal oneself to the imaginary audience, would characterize early adolescents. A questionnaire, The Imaginary Audience Scale, was developed to tap two components of the self, the *transient self* and the *abiding self* (Table 16–5). The former consists of momentary appearances and behaviors, such as the condition of the adolescent's clothes and haircut, that are not considered reflections of the true self. The abiding self consists of characteristics that are considered permanent aspects of the self. The

TABLE 16-5
Some of the items on the Imaginary Audience Scale. TS Refers to Transient Self and AS Refers to Abiding Self.

Instructions: Please read the following stories carefully and assume that the events actually happened to you. Place a check next to the answer that best describes what you would do or feel in the real situation.

TS scale   You have looked forward to the most exciting dress up party of the year. You arrive after an hour's drive from home. Just as the party is beginning, you notice a grease spot on your trousers or skirt. (There is no way to borrow clothes from anyone.) Would you stay or go home?
        _____ Go home.
        _____ Stay, even though I'd feel uncomfortable.
        _____ Stay, because the grease spot wouldn't bother me.

AS scale   Let's say some adult visitors came to your school and you were asked to tell them a little bit about yourself.
        _____ I would like that.
        _____ I would not like that.
        _____ I wouldn't care.

TS scale   Your class is supposed to have their picture taken, but you fell the day before and scraped your face. You would like to be in the picture but your cheek is red and swollen. Would you have your picture taken anyway or stay out of the picture?
        _____ Get your picture taken even though you'd be embarrassed.
        _____ Stay out of the picture.
        _____ Get your picture taken and not worry about it.

AS scale   One young person said, "When I'm with people I get nervous because I worry about how much they like me."
        _____ I feel like this often.
        _____ I never feel like this.
        _____ I feel like this sometimes.

Source: From Elkind and Bowen, 1979. Copyright 1979 by the American Psychological Association. Reprinted by permission.

questionnaire was presented to fourth, sixth, eighth, and twelfth-grade girls and boys. As Figure 16–9 indicates, male and female eighth graders (mean age, thirteen years, nine months) were more self-conscious than the others on both the transient and abiding self scales. Females, in general, were more self-conscious than males.

FIGURE 16–9
Mean scores on the Transient Self Scale and the Abiding Self Scale for males and females at several age grade levels. From Elkind and Bowen (1979). Copyright 1979 by the American Psychological Association. Reprinted by permission.

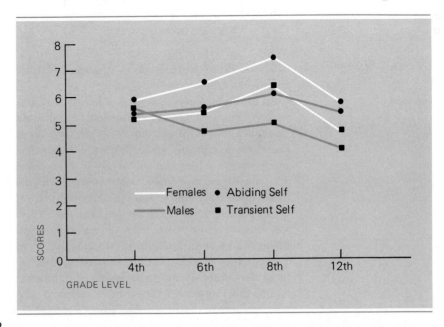

Cognition and Ideology

Adolescence is a time for thinking about and reconsidering one's ideas concerning social, political, and religious frameworks. The specific content of such musings may be related to socioeconomic class, family ideology, and the historical time. Regardless of the content, however, *how* thinking occurs depends upon cognitive level.

As an example of this, we cite a study by Adelson and O'Neil (1966; Adelson, 1975) in which adolescents were given the hypothetical situation that one thousand people had journeyed to a Pacific island to set up a new society. They were asked to describe what they thought the new government and social order should be like. One of the most obvious changes in thinking that occurred with age had to do with abstraction. The younger adolescents dealt with the issues in a personalized, specific way. For example, they tended to refer to the abstract notion of government with the term "he," and spoke of the effects of government on individuals. By fifteen years of age the adolescents viewed government, society, community, and law more abstractly. Law came to function not to coerce individuals to behave positively but to obtain good things for all. Furthermore, laws were not immutable; they could be modified and adapted to fit circumstances. These changes are consistent with cognitive development as proposed by Piaget.

SHIFTING SOCIAL RELATIONSHIPS

Adolescence is almost always viewed as a time of shifting social relationships, characterized by increasing independence from the family and a broadening and strengthening of peer relationships. Parental influence on adolescent behavior and attitudes has been compared to peer influence, and much study has been devoted to the adolescent becoming entrenched in the new generation, one that may seem uniquely different than the preceding one. A sizable number of investigators agree that in general peer influence increases and parental influence decreases (Duncan, 1978). But we shall see that the issues are not simple ones.

The Adolescent and the Family

To examine the transition in social relationships we turn first to the Bowerman and Kinch (1969) study that analyzed the relative orientation toward family or peers among 686 fourth- to tenth-graders in a middle-class school. The youngsters completed questionnaires that permitted conclusions about (1) the extent to which they identified with either family or peers, (2) the group with which they preferred to associate, and (3) the group whose values and norms they considered most like their own.

To assess *identification,* subjects were asked whether family or friends understood them better and whether they would rather become the kind of persons their parents are or the kind their friends presumably would be. For *association orientation,* they were asked which group they most enjoyed doing things with, and which one they would rather spend time with. For the *normative orientation,* subjects were queried as to whose ideas were most like theirs with respect to decisions of right and wrong, things that are fun to do, the importance of school, and what they would do if one group wanted them to do something of which the other did not approve.

TABLE 16-6
Percentage of Fourth- Through Tenth-Graders Demonstrating Family, Peer, or Neutral Orientations

	Grade in School			
	4th	6th	8th	10th
Combined Orientation				
Family	87.1	80.2	41.7	31.6
Neutral	6.9	11.2	18.3	20.2
Peer	5.9	8.6	40.0	48.1
Normative Orientation				
Family	82.2	69.8	33.0	30.4
Neutral	5.9	12.1	14.8	19.0
Peer	11.9	18.1	52.2	50.6
Association Orientation				
Family	75.2	62.1	20.9	15.2
Neutral	15.8	25.0	39.1	29.1
Peer	8.9	12.9	40.0	55.7
Identification				
Family	81.2	77.6	57.4	51.9
Neutral	13.8	18.1	24.3	21.5
Peer	5.0	4.3	18.2	26.6

Source: Adapted from Bowerman and Kinch, 1969.

The youngsters were allowed to choose family, friends, or a neutral response indicating that they felt the same about the two groups. For each of the three types of orientation, subjects were categorized as neutral if there were an equal number of family and peer choices or if choices were neutral; as family-oriented if there were more family than peer choices; and as peer-oriented if the choices were predominantly of friends. A combined orientation rating was made from the three separate orientation ratings.

As Table 16–6 shows, there was a dramatic shift in all aspects of orientation with age; 87.1 percent of fourth-graders but only 31.6 percent of tenth-graders expressed a family orientation on the combined score. It is informative, though, to examine the categories of orientation. Here we see a substantial increase with age in preference to associate with peers rather than family, and in expressed belief that peers hold similar norms. The pattern for identification is somewhat different: Fewer of the older individuals identified with their families, but the shift to peer identification was not as strong as for the other categories. About one-half of the tenth-graders identified with their families, but only about one-quarter with their peers. Since identification involves the preference to be like someone, it is obvious that the family maintains considerable influence.

In discussing the transition of social relationships, Bowerman and Kinch observed:

> ... the nature of family interaction is affected by the decreasing participation and interest of the child in family activities as he becomes more involved in peer association; by the decline of the family as the primary source of affection

with increasing attachment to peers; and by the weakening of authority and control of the parents as the child grows in independence and as norms and values of parents must compete for acceptance with those of peers. These are among the reasons why this transitional period is one of potential increase in parent-child conflict, due not only to the striving of the child to achieve status in two important primary groups with conflicting or competing interests, but also to the difficulties which parents as well as children experience in reacting to the changing situational and interactional characteristics of interpersonal relationships. [P. 137]

Conflict is not inevitable, however; its occurrence depends upon many factors. Other data collected by Bowerman and Kinch suggested that family-peer orientation was affected by the adolescents' opinions as to how well they got along with their family, how their families treated them, whether they received attention from the family, and whether personal problems were discussed in the family. Adolescents also perceive family life as happier when parents discuss family problems and when they respect the opinions of the offspring than when these factors are absent (Slocum, 1958).

The Struggle for Autonomy.   One of the focal points of conflict, when it does occur, is the struggle on the part of young people for autonomy and independence. Dependence and independence do not exist as polar opposites; children may become independent in one area or in relation to some individuals but may increase their dependence in other areas or in relation to other people. Complete independence is not possible and has been described, in a memorable phrase, as "an unnamed form of insanity" (Dewey, 1920). Nevertheless, the desire of adolescents to run their own lives—to decide what they will wear, where they will go, what activities they will engage in, what values they will adopt—frequently runs counter to the established role of authority to which parents are accustomed.

Some parents tend, perhaps simply out of habit, not to want to relinquish decision-making power. Others recognize the need for autonomy for their offspring but are concerned with the speed and circumstances with which it occurs (Campbell, 1969). We saw earlier that parents deal with the development of autonomy in very different ways. Permissive-accepting parents tend to encourage independence, whereas restrictive-accepting parents foster dependence, obedience, compliance, and politeness.

What do adolescents think about their parents' child-rearing practices? In one study seven- through twelfth-graders were asked to rate parental behavior (Elder, 1962). From their answers, seven descriptive categories emerged, ranging from the autocratic parent who allowed little self-regulation by the adolescent, through the democratic parent, to the ignoring parent who took no role in directing the offspring. The students also were asked whether they thought their mothers' and fathers' ideas, rules, or principles were good and reasonable, or wrong and unreasonable. Children from democratic homes were most satisfied with the policies of their par-

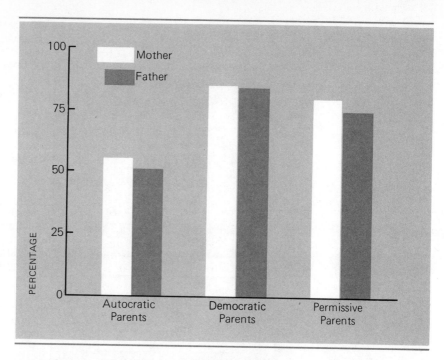

FIGURE 16–10
Percentage of adolescents perceiving their parents as "fair" according to the parents' child-rearing practices. Adapted from Elder, 1962.

ents, whereas children from autocratic homes were least satisfied (Figure 16–10). But at least three-fifths of the students expressed a favorable disposition toward their parents' policies *regardless* of the extent to which they were allowed self-regulation.

Peer Influence   Adolescents relate to each other through informal and formal social groups, such as high school athletic teams, Girl Scouts, fraternities and sororities, and the like. Some of these groups have specific stated goals; the function of a yearbook staff is to produce the yearbook. Nevertheless, even the groups that serve to develop specific skills and knowledge provide a training ground for youth to learn broader lessons in life.

Understanding how informal peer groups operate was furnished by Dunphy's (1963) analysis of Australian youth conducted by actual observation and questionnaires. Dunphy concluded that peers developed into two kinds of social structures, *cliques* and *crowds*, and that a developmental pattern could be traced (Figure 16–11). The clique is a closely knit group of no more than nine members. In early adolescence it is composed of same-sex members. Later, high status boys and girls from unisexual cliques initiate contact with the opposite sex, thereby transforming the cliques into opposite-sex groups. A newly formed heterosexual clique operates in close association with a few other cliques, forming the crowd. A primary purpose of the crowd is the organization of broad social activities, particularly on the weekends. Eventually, though, the crowd gives way to the formation of committed couples.

The Adolescent Subculture.   Adolescent social groups are not, of course, completely independent of the larger society in which they exist. Still, many

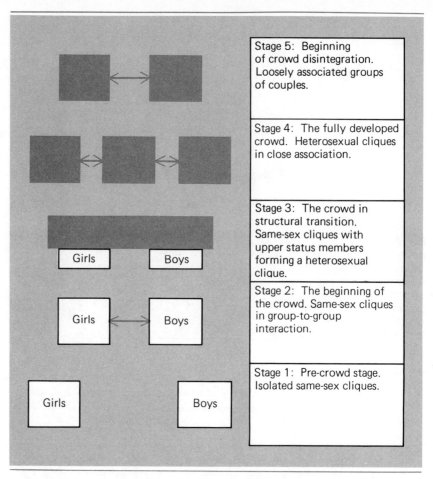

FIGURE 16-11
Dunphy's analysis of clique and crowd formation in adolescence. From Dunphy, 1963.

Stage 5: Beginning of crowd disintegration. Loosely associated groups of couples.

Stage 4: The fully developed crowd. Heterosexual cliques in close association.

Stage 3: The crowd in structural transition. Same-sex cliques with upper status members forming a heterosexual clique.

Stage 2: The beginning of the crowd. Same-sex cliques in group-to-group interaction.

Stage 1: Pre-crowd stage. Isolated same-sex cliques.

adults today are concerned that youth has become excessively cutoff from the adult community and has, in effect, formed its own subculture. James Coleman (1960, 1961) expressed this view after extensively studying high schools. In Coleman's words:

> Industrial society has spawned a peculiar phenomenon, most evident in America but emerging also in other Western societies: adolescent subcultures, with values and activities quite distinct from those of the adult society—subcultures whose members have most of their important associations within and few with adult society. Industrialization, and the rapidity of change itself, has taken out of the hands of the parent the task of training his child, made the parent's skills obsolescent, and put him out of touch with the times—unable to understand, much less inculcate, the standards of a social order which has changed since he was young [1960, p. 337]

Coleman's work has led many to view adults and adolescents as existing in antagonistic, impenetrable, alienated spheres. Although youth has virtually always been considered *alienated* in the sense of becoming autonomous and not subordinate to older generations, the term presently refers to a more dramatic break between adolescents and their families and society. It implies or assumes the disruption of a previous relationship that was positive, desirable, or natural (Cambor, 1973). The term also frequently denotes an overt rejection of the values of the society, and a concomitant construction of a different set of values supported by the youth culture.

Bronfenbrenner (1972), however, has argued that alienated adolescents feel hopeless, powerless, and apathetic because they are discouraged that societal institutions do not achieve the values that the young, in fact, share with the older generation. Bronfenbrenner attributes this state of affairs to the breakdown of the family. He argues that the child is abandoned to the influence of peer groups and the mass media and suffers a crippling dilemma:

> Neither in school, nor in the university, is he given much information or, above all, experience in how to use the institutions of his society—both public and private—to remedy social and political ills. In terms of social action, all he knows is the simplistic, one-shot [demand or destroy] so characteristic of the context in which he has spent so much of his time—the age-segregated peer group and the commercial television screen. For those coming from environments in which the family was still strong, the aggressive impulse is inhibited by early-internalized humanistic values, but there is little knowledge or experience with an alternative course of action for resolving human problems by institutionalized means. [1972, pp. 665-666]

Bronfenbrenner proposes that this situation must be remedied by change in the social institutions, such as modification of work schedules to allow parents to spend more time with their children, an enhancement of the status of women in the home and on the job, reacquaintance of the young with the world of work, and reintegration of the schools with the rest of society (e.g., by having older children actively work with younger ones). In short, it is necessary that adults and youth be provided settings in which they live and grow side by side with opportunity for meaningful communication and sharing.

Not all, however, are disturbed about an adolescent subculture. To begin with, they argue that the distance between the generations is not nearly so severe, that adolescents consider their parents important, show concern about parental disapproval, and conform to parental or peer wishes, depending upon the immediate issue at hand (Douvan and Adelson, 1966; Epperson, 1964; Rosen, 1955). There is also evidence (Costanzo and Shaw, 1966) that the influence of peers is high during early adolescence but then decreases. Still others argue from a different stance that a youth culture, to the extent that it exists, might actually serve in reducing problems during adolescence (e.g., Ausubel, 1954; Campbell, 1969; Eisenstadt, 1956; Matza, 1961). They note the following:

1. In a complex society, the family, with a relatively simple structure of control going from parents to children, cannot provide adequate experience that is relevant to other relationships. Operating within a peer

group allows adolescents to experiment with a greater variety of other situations, thereby preparing them to assume roles of responsibility and authority.

2. The peer group serves both as a standard against which to measure one's accomplishments and as a same-aged group that judges more objectively than family. In this sense, it provides independent status to the adolescent.

3. It provides opportunity for practicing and discussing alternative roles, behaviors, and identities.

4. It sometimes protects adolescents from coercion that adults might impose.

5. Since all adolescents share some of the same experiences, the peer group gives support during transition and decision making concerning social, academic, and occupational matters.

6. It also may lessen the burdens adults would have to bear if they assumed complete responsibility for their offspring.

7. Finally, the peer group actually may decrease the likelihood of deviancy by providing institutionalized forms of behaviors that otherwise might be labeled delinquent.

In short, from this point of view a technological society may profit from strong social groups among the young. At the very least, recognition should be given to the fact that adolescents form not one but many different types of subcultures (Cohen, 1979; Grinder, 1978). Cohen (1979), for example, identified three subcultures among high school youth. The *academic* sub-culture was associated with high interest in studies, aspirations for college, spending time at home, and a relative disinterest in peers and dating. The *delinquent* subculture was associated with frequent dating, an interest in peers, drinking, smoking, spending time away from home, rejection of studies and college, and status regulated by autos and clothes. The *fun* sub-culture was associated with popularity, desirability as a friend or date, athletic ability, and participation in school activities. Interestingly, there was no indication that these subcultures derived from socioeconomic or ethnic groupings. Moreover, Cohen pointed out that they are not antisocial but rather adaptations to the problem of becoming adult. As adult life varies, so too does adolescent life.

Dating and Intimate Relationships

As it has evolved in the United States, dating is a complex social process that takes many forms and serves many functions (Douvan and Adelson, 1966; Grinder, 1978). It is not without its critics. Douvan and Adelson (1966) summarized their reservations about middle-class dating with the following statement.

> There is not much . . . to be cheerful about. The emphasis on the 'dating personality,' in a context of intense sexual and personal competitiveness, can drive the American youngster to displays of emptiness, silliness, artificiality, vanity, vulgarity . . . (pp. 206–207)

FIGURE 16–12
An adolescent's development of intimate relationships and sexuality are important in the achievement of one's identity.   Strix Pix, Monkmeyer Press Photo Service.

Imperfect though it may be, dating serves at least these functions:

1. Recreation, entertainment, social participation
2. Status seeking
3. Sexual gratification
4. Courtship and mate selection
5. Socialization of heterosexual interaction
6. Independence from adult norms (e.g., crossing social-class lines)

Exactly how the dating process is functioning depends upon age and individual needs and desires. But one thing is certain—adolescent steps toward intimate relationships and sexuality are important in the achievement of an identity.

Sexuality.   In this brief discussion of adolescent sexuality two main points are to be considered. The first involves the so-called sexual revolution. There is not complete agreement that a sexual revolution is occurring, and yet the evidence seems to favor the belief that attitudes about sex and sexual behavior itself are more liberal than in previous times. The Sorenson (1973) study of 411 adolescents, thirteen to nineteen-years-old and representative of the larger adolescent population, provides information about youth's sexual behavior and attitudes. Over one-third of the thirteen to fifteen-year-old group and almost two-thirds of the sixteen to nineteen-year-old group reported having had sexual intercourse (Table 16–7). Most of the participants expressed liberal views: They do what they want regardless of societal norms; sexual activities are moral even though society may be opposed to them; and anything two people want to do is moral if it does not hurt either of them. The adolescents considered sex an individual matter, and valued it for its pleasure and intimacy.

TABLE 16-7
Sexual Status of Adolescents: Percent of the Sample

	Total	Girls	Boys	13-15 Years	16-19 Years	White	Nonwhite
Virgins	48	55	41	63	36	55	49
Virgins who have petted	17	19	14	12	21	20	9
Nonvirgins	52	45	59	37	64	45	51
Nonvirgins who had intercourse during the month	31	33	30	15	45	24	31
Nonvirgins having sex with one partner	21	28	15	9	31	19	14

The second point of consideration concerns some of the problems of sexuality, such as increases in venereal disease and early pregnancy (Gordon, 1973). Syphilis and gonorrhea in those under twenty-one years of age are of great concern. Adolescent pregnancy is not necessarily a problem, but physical and mental-health risks are relatively high for women under twenty years of age. Pregnancy complications are four to five times greater than for women in their twenties, and the infant mortality rate is high (Figure 16–13). Furthermore, illegitimacy is high among the young and has been increasing (Gordon, 1973). Often this brings financial, social, and psychological difficulties as well as limitations in educational and vocational growth. Thus, although today's adolescents are frequently viewed as alarmingly sophisticated, the need for sex education is apparent.

FIGURE 16–13
Infant mortality according to age in white and nonwhite mothers.
Reproduced from **Maternal Nutrition and the Course of Pregnancy**, 1973, with the permission of the National Academy of Sciences-National Research Council, Washington, D.C.

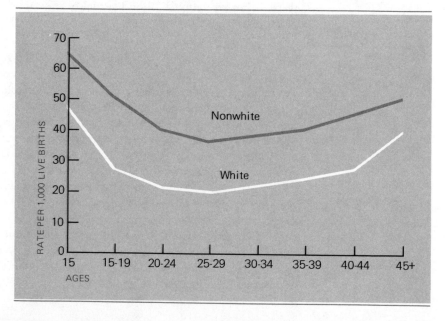

ADOLESCENCE
AS A
VOCATIONAL
CROSSROAD

The Process of
Vocational
Selection

How do individuals come to select a vocation? Ginzberg (1951) and his colleagues have offered one developmental sequence, beginning in childhood. In the *fantasy* period, up to about eleven years of age, children see few restrictions on what they might do when they grow up. (It seems, though, that sex-role limitations operate quite early, as we have mentioned before.) During the *tentative* period, from about eleven to seventeen years of age, they increasingly understand that jobs involve certain activities and require specific training. Thus it becomes clear that one must be matched through training and ability to certain careers. Important, too, is the realization that values play a part in vocational selection. Finally, during the *realistic* period, individuals begin to make plans for choosing a vocation, considering job requirements, talents, opportunity for training, and personal values. Subsequently a commitment is made to a particular vocation. The realistic period was originally viewed by Ginzberg and his associates as culminating at about the mid-twenties. More recently it has been conceptualized as occurring throughout the years of employment (Ginzberg, 1972). People may be forced to change jobs or may desire to do something else, but in either case, adults as well as adolescents may reestablish their identities in the world of work.

Factors Affecting Vocational Choice

Ideally, each of us should have the opportunity to be occupied in a vocation that suits our talents, interests, and personality. It is not a simple matter, even for adults, to assess themselves adequately, to be aware of the wide range of vocations and how to prepare for them, and then to make a realistic "best" choice. For the adolescent, the task is even more difficult and, unfortunately, the ideal is perhaps seldom achieved.

What factors, for good or bad, determine vocational choice? It is possible to conceptualize them broadly into several categories.

FIGURE 16–14
Career decisions are typically made during adolescence.
Mimi Forsyth, Monkmeyer Press Photo Service.

Society's Needs and Rewards. In a very real sense, society sets the limits within which any young person can realistically choose a vocation. Today there is considerably less opportunity for agricultural and unskilled workers than previously because our society has become highly technical. Many recent Ph.D.'s and teachers, too, are having trouble finding positions because society's needs in these areas have shrunk or because too many people have prepared for them. On the other hand, an increasing necessity is anticipated for social-service workers. With the unemployment rate as high as it is, young people try to direct themselves towards areas in which they think the best job opportunities exist. Although this may be a reasonable approach, it's doubtful that employment opportunities can accurately and completely be projected for more than a few decades.

Aside from changing demands, other social determinants come into play (Blau, Gustad, Jessor, Parnes, and Wilcock, 1968). Individuals must meet the functional requirements of any job; that is, they must be trained for any one particular opening. They also must fulfill nonfunctional requirements, such as age, race, and sex, although these are fortunately being reduced. Fi-

FIGURE 16–15

Percentage of adolescents of different socioeconomic classes selecting various occupational aspirations.
Adapted from Karl C. Garrison, **Psychology of Adolescence**, 5th ed., p. 418, © 1956. Reprinted by permission of Prentice-Hall, Inc., Englewood Cliffs, New Jersey. Data of Garrison's text were taken from A. B. Hollingshead, **Elmtown's Youth**. New York: John Wiley & Sons, Inc., 1949. Reproduced by permission of John Wiley & Sons, Inc.

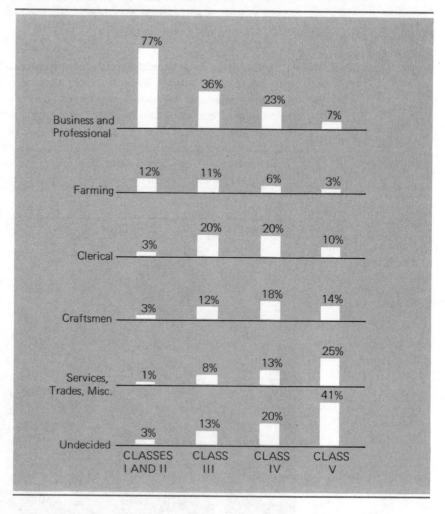

nally, the amount of reward given by society—in terms of financial return, prestige, or freedom—determines which adolescents will enter certain vocations.

Social Class and Attitudes. Vocational aspirations of adolescents are clearly related to their socioeconomic background, with youth from the higher classes selecting the more prestigious vocations (Caro and Pihlblad, 1965; Hollingshead, 1949). This pattern is demonstrated by the results of one study in which adolescents from a small midwestern city listed their preferred future occupations. Of those categorized in Classes I and II, the higher social strata, 77 percent chose business and professional vocations, whereas only 7 percent of those in Class V did so (Figure 16–15). Many of the adolescents of the lower social strata also were undecided about their future.

Although it is possible that adolescents of various social classes hold different values in regard to occupations, other reasons probably exist for this finding. Children often follow in their parents' vocations simply because they are rewarded for doing so. Some lower SES youths may be discouraged from upward job mobility because it is threatening to the older generation, but, for the most part, parents of *all* classes, including the poor, have high aspirations for their offspring. So the problem may be more that lower SES adolescents simply lack the information about how to enter certain vocations, or they may consider aspiring to them unrealistic.

Sex Differences. There are two striking sex differences in vocational selection. The first is that selection itself is considered far more important for the male than for the female. Occupational choice not only potentially defines the social status of the male and his family but is considered intricately tied to his identity as a male and as a person. For many adolescent girls, choosing an occupation means merely picking a job that will serve as a stopgap until they settle down to homemaking. The high percentage of women in the work force belies this notion; however, many working women still do not view their occupations as central to their identity, despite the influence of the women's movement. (For other women, though, occupational choice is highly important.)

The second difference is that females more than males have consistently chosen less professional occupations that are strongly characterized by helping, such as secretary, nurse, teacher, and stewardess (Witty, 1961). In a cross-national survey, male choices varied somewhat depending upon the country, but females from all six nations included in the survey chose minor professional vocations over major ones (Steward and Williamson, 1969). The underlying factor undoubtedly is the sex stereotyping of occupations that has been, and largely still is, rigid. Such stereotyping precludes both males and females from entering certain areas of work, but occupations usually considered male are the more prestigious and valued in society. To opt for them, a female not only must compete with males but also may feel that she is jeopardizing her success as a female.

Horner (1972) postulated that women avoid commitment to certain professional careers because they fear the negative consequences that could accrue: social rejection, failure in personal relationships with males, failure as a parent, being considered cold and aggressive, and the like. She tested this proposition by asking individuals to complete a story that began as follows: "After first-term finals, Anne found herself at the top of her medical-school class . . ." High percentages of females wrote stories that indicated their belief in the negative consequences of career success to women. Although the data collected in subsequent "fear of success" studies have been inconsistent (Zuckerman and Wheeler, 1975), it appears that women's freedom of occupational choice is still precarious.

PROBLEMS OF ADOLESCENCE

Antisocial Behavior in Adolescence: Juvenile Delinquency

Strictly speaking, *juvenile delinquency* refers to acts committed by youths under sixteen to eighteen years of age that are not in keeping with the law. Arrest records provide statistics about juvenile delinquency, but it is difficult to evaluate the actual frequency and seriousness of such behavior. Many delinquent acts are not discovered and others are not recorded. Moreover, it is likely that social class, sex, and age make a substantial difference in what is reported and recorded, and how cases are subsequently handled in the legal system (Empey, 1975; Gibbs and Erickson, 1975). Statistics on juvenile delinquency must therefore be viewed cautiously. It is apparent, though, that *reported* juvenile delinquency has been on the rise for several decades.

Sex Differences. Traditionally, female delinquency has been less frequent and less serious than male delinquency (e.g., Empey, 1975). Sex-role expectations presumably allowed males to act violently and aggressively and encouraged them to display such behavior as a way of demonstrating masculinity. Female delinquency, on the other hand, has usually involved less severe "acting out"—school failure, broken homes, sexual involvement, and the like are examples. Recent studies, however, indicate a change in these patterns: Females are being arrested more frequently and their crimes also are becoming more like those of males (Kratcoski and Kratcoski, 1975; Wise, 1967). For example, the number of violent crimes committed by females under eighteen years of age rose 18 percent from 1970 to 1971 and has continued to increase since then (Kratcoski and Kratcoski, 1975). One explanation for this is the changing female sex role, which may foster independent, assertive behavior that can lead to violence.

Social Class. Even though the frequency of delinquency among lower-class and middle-class youths may not be as discrepant as the reported facts, it stands to reason that the effects of poverty work toward facilitating delinquency. Family disorganization, low standards of living, alienation, and a sense of powerlessness can lead to antisocial acts. Among the poor, street gangs are notoriously associated with delinquency. Perhaps lower-class youths are socialized in ways that counter middle-class norms, and status can be gained by opposing these norms (Empey, 1975). According to

Miller (1958), among gangs of hard-core, lower-class youths being tough and undemonstrative, out-smarting others, and getting into trouble comprise a desirable way of life.

It is not difficult to hypothesize factors underlying delinquency among the poor, but explanations are not as immediately obvious in the case of adolescents who, superficially at least, appear to be growing up in comfortable circumstances. One investigator (Pine, 1966) has offered several hypotheses to account for the phenomenon. He notes, first of all, that the period of adolescence has been extended, particularly for the college-going middle and upper class, from the midteens to at least age twenty-one or twenty-two. The tacking on of additional years to the transition period, Pine suggests, produces an "existential vacuum" for the young; without meaning or purpose, there is an increase in rebellious behavior. And, ironically, adolescents must at the same time contend with the tremendous pressures of society to achieve during the high school and college years. Pine also suggests that changes in middle-class values—particularly with regard to delay of gratification and the work ethic—may contribute to a lessening of discipline and decreased self-control of impulses; with a reduction of both external and internal restrictions, increased delinquency is not a surprising outcome. Finally, Pine notes that successful social mobility is itself a basis for some types of delinquency inasmuch as the adolescent may feel insecure about being accepted in a new environment and may temporarily lose identity, developing a contempt for traditional institutions and beliefs.

Characteristics of Delinquents. Although it is impossible to draw a precise profile of the adolescent delinquent, the classic investigation of William Healy and August Bronner (1936) provides a partial description. They examined families that had at least one delinquent youngster. Among this group they found 105 delinquents who had a nondelinquent sibling (in eight cases, a twin) with whom a comparison could be made. By selecting their subjects in this way, the researchers held socioeconomic and family factors constant. Some remarkable differences were found in the physical health and general developmental history of delinquents as compared with nondelinquents. Some of their findings are listed in Table 16–8 from which it can be seen that there is a uniform and striking pattern of poor physical health among the delinquents compared with the nondelinquents, both through development and at the time of the study. It is not possible, of course, to determine directly any causal relationships from such data. A poor medical history might provide frustrations and impediments in a youngster's life which in turn might lead to delinquent behavior. On the other hand, certain kinds of difficult behavior might be linked to physical defects through some genetic factor.

Perhaps one of the more fascinating outcomes of the Healy and Bronner study is the *lack* of differences between delinquents and nondelinquents in intellectual ability. But the groups were just as surprisingly different on another dimension: hyperactivity. Healy and Bronner found that almost half—fully forty-six—of the delinquent youngsters in their study exhibited hyperactivity, "overrestlessness," and the like, whereas not one of the control

TABLE 16-8

Some Contrasts between 105 Delinquents and Their Nondelinquent Controls from the Same Families

	Number of Cases	
Characteristic	Delinquents	Controls
Developmental History		
Much worried pregnancy	10	3
Very sickly pregnancy	13	6
Very difficult delivery	12	5
Much underweight in early childhood	12	5
Very early bottle fed	10	8
Very late breast fed	7	4
Cross fussy babyhood	14	5
Difficult sphincter training	31	13
Many illnesses or severe illness	28	8
History of distinctly good health	44	75
Physical Conditions at Time of Study		
Weight deviates (more than 10% under or 20% over)	11	10
Retarded sexual development	5	1
Defective vision—more than slight	17	6
Markedly enlarged or diseased tonsils	20	12
Nasal obstruction	6	2
At least some badly carious teeth	27	19
Miscellaneous liabilities	7	3

Source: Adapted from Healy and Bronner, 1936. Copyright © 1936 by Yale University Press.

youngsters from the same family and matched for age could be so characterized. Additionally, they experienced greater feelings of rejection, insecurity, inadequacy, unhappiness, and guilt.

The investigators also sought information as to exactly how delinquent tendencies and behaviors had been acquired; the research was remarkably farsighted. In their evaluation of movies, for example, it was learned that a large percentage of the delinquents (much larger than was true for the controls) attended the movies excessively, several times a week or more often if they were able to, and sometimes stayed to see a performance over and over again. Indeed, a few of the delinquents actually stated that they had patterned their own criminal behavior after material that they had seen in gang and crime motion pictures. Equally important, Healy and Bronner report that what we would now think of as the "social-learning history" of delinquents conspired to produce much of their antisocial behavior. They had been, in the investigators' terms, "loaded with ideas of delinquency" from a mixture of sources, such as the communications and observations of delinquent companions and detective or crime stories and movies.

Many of the Healy and Bronner findings are consistent with later investigations. After years of studying delinquency, Glueck and Glueck (1950; 1974) noted the impulsivity, restlessness, and lack of self-control of such adolescents, as well as their early history of illnesses and accidents. These researchers, however, suggested that delinquency is associated with low intelligence.

A serious problem of any attempt to characterize delinquents is the assumption that all of them are basically alike. In his factor analysis, Quay (1964) found three distinct types:

1. the *unsocialized psychopathic* who was assaultive and defiant of authority
2. the *subcultural socialized* who was involved with bad companions and gangs
3. the *neurotically disturbed* who was timid, shy, and worrisome

Thus, delinquency must be regarded as a heterogeneous category as far as its etiology and treatment are concerned.

Drug Use

Drug use is epidemic among adolescents, if not our entire culture. Use does not automatically imply a drug problem, of course, but the line between use and abuse is a controversial one. At the simplest level, the use of illegal drugs has potential legal consequences. Health, too, must be considered. Although Italy has long been known for its sanctions against drunkenness and its otherwise responsible use of alcohol, it has the second highest rate of cirrhosis due to moderate but continuous alcohol ingestion (Finn, 1979). Tobacco smoking may not seem to be a problem until its association with lung cancer and heart disease is recalled. Beyond this, there is considerable concern about the detrimental effects of drugs: whether they foster crime, cause psychoses, underlie birth defects, lead to increased drug consumption, or can result in physical or psychological dependency. These questions cannot be analyzed across the board but at the very least require examination of the particular drug involved and the degree to which it is used.

With regard to marijuana, evidence suggests that immediate reactions to the usual dosage lead to neither psychotic episodes, crime, nor violence (Abel, 1977). The issue of dependence is less clear, although marijuana is not addictive and does not lead to a need for increased levels. Nevertheless, there are several worldwide reports of its chronic, heavy consumption resulting in decreased conventional motivation and a rise in social indifference (*Marihuana and Health*, 1971). The problem in interpretating these data, however, is the problem of correlation: perhaps individuals who are poorly motivated are especially attracted to the drug. A similar problem of interpretation exists when progression to other drugs is investigated. For example, Blum (1969) found in one student survey that marijuana was associated with the use of other illicit drugs. This fact does not establish a causal link; as he notes, it may point to a general disposition to use psychoactive drugs as a means to alter states of consciousness and social relations.

Reasons and Correlates of Drug Use. There are many reasons why adolescents use drugs (Girdano and Girdano, 1973; Greenspoon, 1971; Nowlis, 1969). In some instances it serves as a rite of passage into adulthood, or at least to indicate to others that one is, indeed, grown up. If peers are using drugs, conformity and imitation can lead to the same behavior. Parental drug consumption, too, is correlated with drug use. Another incentive is to escape misery, whether it is the pain of the ghetto or the anxiety and conflict felt by all people. Nowlis (1969) points out that, for the student, misery may involve the anxiety of being enmeshed in an achieving society, the inability to find an identity, and the lack of meaningful experiences in an environment that is increasingly becoming secular and depersonalized. Temporarily, at least, drugs provide the opportunity simply to escape and drop out from facing these problems. But the escape is not, in all cases, just getting away; rather, it is putting one's self into a situation in which one draws into a personal inner world, frequently sharing the experience with others. Such mind-expanding effects are viewed positively by many drug users.

One way to better understand drug use is to identify patterns of use and nonuse and relate them to the people involved. Kandel and her associates have done this in a fascinating way (Kandel, 1975; Kandel and Faust, 1975; Kandel, Kessler, and Margulies, 1978). Studying high school students, they first established that drug involvement proceeds through three stages: hard liquor, marijuana, and other illicit drugs. Students in one stage do not necessarily move to the next, nor is a causal chain implied. The developmental stages are postulated because most students who used drugs at one stage had also used them at the preceding stage. Kandel and her colleagues (1978) then attempted to determine whether different factors are related to initiation of the three stages. To do so, they observed students from eighteen schools during an academic year, gathering information in the autumn and spring. Both the students and their parents completed questionnaires designed to address parental influence, peer influence, and the influence of individual personal characteristics and behavior. The most serious bias in the study was possible underrepresentation of drug users due to exclusion of school absentees and dropouts. In the sample, 30 percent of those who had not used hard liquor in the autumn did so by spring; 17 percent who had used hard liquor or cigarettes more than twice began smoking marijuana; and 24 percent of those who had used either alcohol or cigarettes and marijuana began to use other illicit drugs.

For initiation into hard liquor, personal prior behaviors were important predictors, namely, participation in minor delinquent acts and use of wine, beer, and tobacco. Personal attitudes and values were relatively unimportant (except for the belief that alcohol is harmful), as were depression, the need to rebel, and psychological problems. The influence of peers and parents were almost equal and primarily involved a modeling effect. Use of hard liquor by these groups rather than their attitudes or the quality of their relationships, predicted adolescent use. The parental attitude that liquor is harmful was a correlate, however.

A different picture emerged regarding initiation into marijuana. Beliefs and attitudes held by the adolescents appeared relatively important, especially the beliefs that marijuana is not harmful and should be legalized. An anticonformist attitude about social values, a liberal political orientation, low grades, class cutting, minor delinquent activities, and the desire to experience the drug were also predictors. Parental influence appeared to be small and did not relate to parental use; rather, the closeness of the relationship and adolescent perception of parental attitudes were factors. In contrast, peer use and attitudes as well as availability of the drug (presumably through peers) were relatively more important than parental influence.

Turning to initiation into other illicit drugs, prior use of marijuana for personal instead of social incentives (e.g., to relieve depression) was the most important personal variable. Major delinquent acts, drug dealing, nonconformity to adult expectations, depression reduction, and increasing self-understanding were predictors. So also were parental use, lack of closeness to parents, parental control, and parental disagreement about discipline. Peer influence was about as strong, with use by a close friend and low intimacy with a best friend being positively correlated with drug use.

In summarizing these results Kandel and her associates suggest that the less serious the drug, the more its use depends upon situational factors. Users of hard liquor may drift into it without conscious decision. Illicit drug use, in contrast, involves a conscious use in response to intrapsychic pressure. Marijuana use falls somewhere in between; values and beliefs are important but personal and family problems are not reported as influential.

Adolescent Suicide

Suicide almost always seems tragic, but it is especially so when it occurs in the young. The suicide rate among adolescents is low compared to that of other age groups but it has been increasing more rapidly. Between 1968 and 1977 suicide rose for all age groups below forty-five years and for those who are sixty-five to seventy-four years of age; the largest increase by far has been for fifteen- to twenty-four-year-olds (Table 16–9). In 1977 suicide was the second leading cause of death in this group, superseded only by accidents (Monthly Vital Statistics Report, 1979), some of which might have been either directly or indirectly the result of self-destruction.

Most theoretical explanations of suicide focus on individual psychological states or on societal conditions (Davison and Neale, 1978; Miller, 1975; Yusin, 1973). The classic psychoanalytic view suggests that the death instinct, Thanatos, is at the root of suicide. Freud also emphasized the complex role that loss of a love object can play. He suggested that to compensate for the loss of a loved one, the individual incorporates the dead love object into the psychic structures. When the love has been ambivalent, hate

TABLE 16-9
Suicide Rate per 100,000 Population For Different Age Groups

Year	5-14	15-24	25-34	35-44	45-54	55-64	65-74	74-85	85+
1977	.5	13.6	17.7	16.8	18.9	19.4	20.1	21.5	17.3
1976	.4	11.7	15.9	16.3	19.2	20.0	19.5	20.8	18.9
1968	.3	7.1	12.0	16.1	19.7	21.5	19.0	21.3	22.1

Source: From Monthly Vital Statistics, Final Mortality Statistics, No. 79, 1120. (Hyattsville, Md.: U.S. Department of Health, Education, and Welfare, 1979).

as well as love are felt toward the incorporated object, leading to depression. Anger, too, may be experienced due to feelings of abandonment. When hate, depression, and anger are strong, they may lead to suicide.

Durkheim's theory is foremost among those that focus on societal causes of suicide (Davison and Neale, 1978; Yusin, 1973). This sociologist proposed three fundamental kinds of self-destruction. *Altruistic* suicide involves a predetermined sacrifice for society, such as the self-immolations that occurred during the Vietnam war. *Anomic* suicide is due to a sense of disorientation that may be caused by a dramatic change in a person's life. *Egoistic* suicide is due to a lack of supportive ties to society and a sense of alienation.

These theoretical formulations, as well as others, have been applied to adolescent suicide. McAnarney (1979), for example, following a sociological analysis, proposed that the United States is becoming less socially cohesive and that adolescents are strongly and adversely affected. Surveying reports from several nations, this investigator found that suicide is correlated with weak family ties, weak formal religion, and high mobility and transition—all of which are apparent in the United States today. Nevertheless, it is likely that both environmental and individual variables interact to bring about suicide.

Empirical studies implicate the following factors in adolescent suicide: loss of a love object, low self-esteem, depression, suggestibility, impulsiveness, aggression turned inward, and a host of environmental stresses including family disorganization and social isolation (Corder, Shorr, and Corder, 1974; Gould, 1965; Jacobs, 1971, Wenz, 1979). In short, many adolescent suicide attempters suffered some psychiatric disturbance and/or environmental deprivation. Among college students, who have a high rate of suicide, self-destruction was correlated with depression and other emotional disturbance, loss of a significant other, low grades, and academic and social pressure (Miller, 1975). Corder, Shorr, and Corder (1974) addressed themselves to determining the variables that might predict suicide among poor, urban youth who suffer various psychiatric disturbances. They compared suicide attempters with nonattempters, all of whom had been admitted to an adolescent unit in a mental health center; the groups were matched on age, sex, IQ and SES. For these adolescents no group differences were found regarding social isolation, absence of strong religious affiliation, recent loss of a significant other, low communication level with significant others, and lack of independent activity. All of the adolescents were characterized by these conditions. Table 16–10 shows the seven variables that did distinguish the groups.

An interesting aspect of adolescent suicide is the disproportion between threatened or attempted suicide and committed suicide (Miller, 1975). Although the ratio varies from study to study, it is substantially greater than for adults. Miller (1975) interprets this as a sign that adolescents, even more than adults, are trying to call attention to their plight and to change it, and often do not actually wish to destroy themselves. As such, suicide attempts and threats can be adaptive, providing that they succeed in rendering help. At the same time, it is a mistake to ignore attempts and threats because they can end in the tragic loss of life.

TABLE 16-10
Variables that Distinguished Suicide Attempters and Nonattempters among Poor,
Urban Adolescents in a Mental Health Unit

History of suicide in an adolescent's family or of other significant people in his or her
  life, or previous threats by the adolescent.
Absence of a warm adult with whom to identify.
Parental conflict and rejection.
Low level of school involvement.
Lack of investment in the future and future goals.
High activity level.
Low impulse control.

Source: From Corder, Shorr, and Corder, 1974.

SUMMARY

Adolescence was first recognized as a stage of life during the latter nineteenth century. The establishment of compulsory education, child labor laws, and the legal concept of juvenile delinquency helped define this period as a transition between childhood and adulthood.

G. Stanley Hall, who drew on evolutionary theory, and Anna Freud, who relied on psychoanalytic theory, both propagated the idea that adolescence is a time of storm and stress. Speaking for the social learning point of view, Bandura has argued that the conflict of adolescence has been exaggerated. The anthropologists Benedict and Mead have pointed out that discontinuity in cultural practices underlies adolescence stress and that cultures vary in the amount of discontinuity that exists. It appears that adolescents in the United States are concerned particularly about physical appearance, future careers, and school grades.

Achieving identity is so central an issue in adolescence that Erikson has cited *identity vs. role confusion* as the primary psychosocial crisis of this stage of life. Adolescents "try on" different commitments and roles and reevaluate themselves as a way of achieving identity. Research into identity status indicates that individuals can be classified into four categories, but possible sex differences and developmental patterns in status are unclear.

Of the many changes occurring, physical growth and sexual development are obvious. Size accelerates rapidly during the *adolescent growth spurt*. Girls advance more rapidly than boys, but there is much individual variation. Boys who mature early appear to have some advantage over late-maturing boys. For girls, the effect of rate of maturation is less clear. The *secular trend* is for people to be taller and heavier than in past times and to attain adult size and sexual maturation earlier in the life span.

During adolescence cognitive development extends to formal operations. Piaget has noted that aptitude and interest may play a part in creating individual differences in the acquisition of formal operations. Adolescent egocentrism may result in the *imaginary audience* and the *personal fable*.

Social relationships shift dramatically during adolescence, with peers becoming more important and family less so. The struggle for autonomy is central to conflict that may occur within the family. Nevertheless, a large percentage of adolescents identify with their parents and accept their parents' policies.

Peers develop into informal cliques and crowds. Some investigators (e.g., Coleman) have emphasized the evolving of a separate youth culture that has values and activities different from those of adult society. The youth culture may serve the adolescent and adults in many ways, providing the young with wider experiences, standards against which to measure themselves, general support, and the like. At the same time, Bronfenbrenner suggests that increased weakening of the family has negative effects, and he argues that the young must be reinstated into the larger society by increased opportunity for adolescents and adults to share and work together.

Dating is a complex social process that serves many functions. Attitudes about sexual behavior may be more liberal than in the past. Of current concern are increases in venereal diseases and the physical and psychological risks of early and illegitimate pregnancies.

Vocational choice is considered a critical aspect of achieving identity. It is influenced by many factors: society's needs, social class, attitudes, and sex roles.

Juvenile delinquency, drug use, and suicide are among the problems of adolescence. It appears that juvenile delinquency has been increasing and that female crime is becoming more similar to male crime. Juvenile delinquency in the poor and middle class has different determinants. Moreover, delinquents cannot be considered a homogenous group.

Society continues to be concerned that drugs foster crime, psychoses, dependency, addiction, and the like. Drugs are used for many reasons, and it is becoming apparent that dichotomizing youth into users and nonusers is an oversimplification. Kandel and her associates have described situational, attitudinal, and intrapsychic determinants of drug use, suggesting that the less serious the drug, the more its use depends on situational factors.

The rate of adolescent suicide is increasing. Psychological and sociological factors have been explored, implicating the loss of a love object, low self-esteem, suggestibility, impulsivity, aggression turned inward, family disorganization, and social isolation.

17 An Overview of Later Life

The adult years are a continuation of much of what has gone before and, as such, frequently have been viewed by developmentalists as more-or-less static. On the contrary, however, adulthood brings physical, social, and psychological changes that are of increasing interest to our society.

Today a growing number of developmental psychologists in the United States are especially interested in the adult years, including those who label themselves life span developmentalists. The study of adulthood includes gerontology and geriatrics. *Gerontology,* which is the study of all facets of aging, barely existed as an academic discipline until the 1960s, but now it is one of the fastest growing fields (Watkins, 1978). It encompasses the work of psychologists, biologists, sociologists, physicians, and urban planners. *Geriatrics* focuses on understanding and treating health problems of the elderly.

An important reason for heightened interest in adulthood and aging is the extended life expectancy of people in the United States. The life span of the average individual has increased dramatically during this century. Figure 17–1 shows the life expectancy for the general population and also for males and females from 1930 to 1977. For the general population in 1930 life expectancy was about 60 years; by 1977 it had risen to 73.2 years. Males born in 1977 are expected to live to 69.3 years, while for females the corresponding figure is 77.1 years (Monthly Vital Statistics Report, 1979).

Another reason for increased concern about the adult years is the alteration in the overall age structure in the United States. After World War II, during the years roughly from 1947 to 1957, 43 million children were born, which is about one-fifth of the present population (Newsweek, 1977). This so-called "baby boom" flooded the schools in the 1950s and 1960s and swelled the labor force in the 1970s. In the 1980s and 1990s a middle-age bulge will exist in the population, and early in the twenty-first century the baby boom generation will be at retirement age. Figure 17–2 depicts this predicted age structure change, which experts feel is unlikely to be altered by another baby boom.

A population that is growing older has different characteristics and

FIGURE 17–1
Life expectancy for the general population and for males and females from 1930 to 1977. From **Monthly Vital Statistics Report,** 1977, Publication No. 79-1120. Hyattsville, Md.: U.S. Department of Health, Education, and Welfare, 1979.

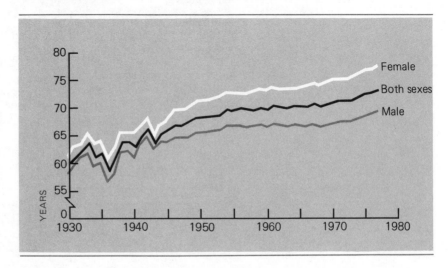

needs than one in which most individuals are young. Bernice Neugarten (1978) has described our society in terms of the emergence of the young-old, people from 55 to 75 years of age. The young-old are retired, relatively healthy and vigorous, fairly well educated and economically comfortable, and socially and politically active. As their number grows, so will their influence. Reflections of the changing age structure are already evident: schools are closing, advertisers are directing themselves to an older market, adults as college students are becoming commonplace, questions are being raised about the adequacy of the Social Security system in future years, and

FIGURE 17–2
The age structure of the United States is expected to shift noticeably in the next decades. (Based on U.S. Census projection, assuming fertility rate of 2.1 children per woman.) Newsweek, February 28, 1977.

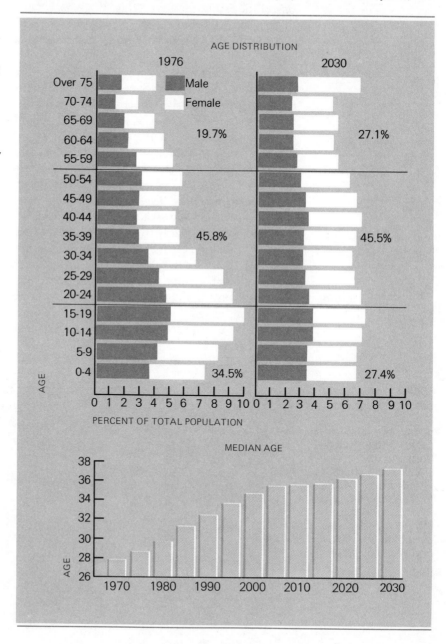

concern is being expressed about the living conditions of the aged. Society might well profit from a better understanding of the changes that accompany movement from the early to middle to later adult years. It is the purpose of this chapter to overview some of these developments. Discussion will begin with a composite view of adulthood and then turn to selected topics, with emphasis on the later years.

A COMPOSITE VIEW OF ADULTHOOD

Several investigators have viewed adulthood broadly, according to some kind of developmental tasks or stages. Their descriptions do not apply to every individual, of course, but serve to depict a commonly occurring life history.

Havighurst's Developmental Tasks

Havighurst (1953) offered one such conceptualization in terms of a variety of tasks that must be mastered during three specific periods of adulthood—early adulthood, middle age, and later maturity (Table 17–1). Although the tasks may be motor, intellectual, emotional, or social, they tend to fall into the realm of psychosocial. According to this scheme, the

TABLE 17–1
Havighurst's Developmental Tasks of Adulthood

Tasks of Early Adulthood	Tasks of Middle Age	Tasks of Later Maturity
1. Selecting a mate.	1. Achieving adult civic and social responsibility.	1. Adjusting to decreasing physical strength and health.
2. Learning to live with a marriage partner.	2. Establishing and maintaining an economic standard of living.	2. Adjusting to retirement and reduced income.
3. Starting a family.	3. Developing adult leisure-time activities.	3. Adjusting to death of spouse.
4. Rearing children.	4. Assisting teenage children to become responsible and happy adults.	4. Establishing an explicit affiliation with one's age group.
5. Managing a home.	5. Relating oneself to one's spouse as a person.	5. Meeting social and civic obligations.
6. Getting started in an occupation.	6. Accepting and adjusting to the physiological changes of middle age.	6. Establishing satisfactory physical living arrangements.
7. Taking on civic responsibility.	7. Adjusting to aging parents.	
8. Finding a congenial social group.		

Source: Copyright 1953 by Longmans, Green, and Co., Inc. From the book Human Development by Robert J. Havighurst. Reprinted by permission of the Davis McKay Co., Inc.

early years must be devoted to selecting a mate, taking on family responsibilities, beginning an occupation, involving oneself in civic duties, and finding a congenial social group. In middle age, civic, social, and economic concerns are great. But individuals also must guide their teenage children, relate to their spouse as a person, and adjust to aging parents, while simultaneously adjusting to their own biological changes. The tasks of the later years require adjustment to declining physical condition, to retirement, and perhaps to the death of a spouse. Older people must also continue to meet social and civic obligations and establish an affiliation with their age group.

Erikson's Psychosocial Stages

Perhaps the best known description of adulthood was provided by Erikson, who, like Havighurst, divided the adult years into three periods. Implicit in Erikson's stages are the tasks of adulthood, but Erikson emphasized the psychosocial conflicts that occur at each stage. Table 17–2 shows these stages and, for the sake of review, also shows the four preceding stages that have been discussed elsewhere in this book.

According to Erikson (1968), the young adult faces the crisis of trying to establish intimate, sharing relationships with others that involve personal commitment. Although these relationships include friendships of various sorts, establishing a special sexual bond is paramount. Such *intimacy* goes beyond an obsessive reduction of sexual tensions to a mutuality of sexual experiences that regulates the differences between the sexes and between individuals. True intimacy means that one is willing to be at least partly defined by one's mate. Erikson notes that intimacy is not possible until the psychosocial conflict of the adolescent stage is resolved; that is, until a sense of identity is achieved. Only when a person is secure in the self can he or she risk fusion with another. Failure to develop intimacy results in what Erikson labels *isolation*, which is characterized by settling for highly stereotyped interpersonal relations. If the historical times favor that kind of interpersonal pattern, Erikson suggests, the individual may seem to prosper, but yet will harbor a painful character disorder in which the self is not realized.

With movement into middle adulthood it is necessary to extend the

TABLE 17–2
Erik Erikson's Stages of Life

Chronological Age	Stage
infancy	basic trust vs. mistrust
1½–3 years (approximately)	autonomy vs. shame, doubt
3–5½ years (approximately)	initiative vs. guilt
5½–12 years (approximately)	industry vs. inferiority
adolescence	identity vs. role confusion
young adulthood	intimacy vs. isolation
adulthood	generativity vs. stagnation
maturity	ego integrity vs. despair

commitment of young adulthood to a wider range of people. The guidance and nurturance of the younger generation is the most obvious example of this extended commitment. Such *generativity* results in an enrichment of the individual through an expansion of interests and investment in others. When generativity is not achieved, a sense of *stagnation*, boredom, and interpersonal impoverishment develops. Individuals who are stagnant may begin to indulge themselves as if they were children, and such self-concern may lead to their becoming physical or psychological invalids. Another very unfortunate result is that the next generation is directly affected by a lack of generativity because it will not receive the guidance required for its proper development.

Finally, in the later years, development focuses on the integration of life's experiences—on embracing these experiences as inevitable aspects of oneself—and in accepting an orderliness in life and death. In Erikson's words *ego integrity* is:

> ... the acceptance of one's one and only life cycle and of the people who have become significant to it as something that had to be and that, by necessity, permitted of no substitutions. It thus means a new and different love of one's parents, free of the wish that they should have been different, and an acceptance of the fact that one's life is one's own responsibility. It is a sense of comradeship with men and women of distant times and of different pursuits who have created orders and objects and sayings conveying human dignity and love. (1968, p. 139)

A meaningful old age, according to Erikson, encompasses an interest in what survives the self and in how the limitations of the self might be transcended. Thus, it tends to involve a detached but active concern with life's traditions and philosophy, bringing to life an accumulated knowledge and mature judgment. The lack of ego integrity in the later years is characterized by *despair* and disgust. There is despair that time is too short to try out alternative paths to integrity, that another life cannot be started. Despair often manifests itself in the display of disgust or a chronic displeasure with institutions and with people.

The Work of Levinson and Gould

Both Havighurst's and Erikson's theories are considered classic descriptions of adulthood. We will now examine the more recent contributions of Daniel J. Levinson and his colleagues and Roger L. Gould, both of whom have studied the course of the adult years.

Levinson and his coworkers (Levinson, Darrow, Klein, Levinson, and Braxton, 1974; Levinson, Darrow, Klein, Levinson, and McKee, 1978) conducted in-depth interviews with men of four occupational groups: blue-and white-collar workers in industry, business executives, academic biologists, and novelists. The researchers met with each man initially from ten to twenty hours and then interviewed the men again two years later. Central to the thinking of the investigators was the concept of the life structure. It refers to the ways in which the individual is plugged into society (roles,

TABLE 17-3
Periods of Development of Men during Early and Middle Adulthood as Delineated by Levinson and His Colleagues

Periods of Development	Ages
Leaving the Family Transition	16–18 to 20–24
effort to establish oneself independent of the family	
Getting Into the Adult World	early 20s to 28
a new home base	
exploration and commitment to adult roles	
fashioning an initial life structure	
Age Thirty Transition	28 to 30
reassessment of life structure	
Settling Down	early 30s to 38
establishing a stable niche	
making it: upward strivings	
becoming one's own man: giving up mentors	
emphasizing parts of the self and repressing others	
The Mid-Life Transition	38 to early 40s
reassessment of life structure	
Restabilization to Middle Adulthood	middle 40s

Source: From Levinson, Darrow, Klein, Levinson, and Braxton, 1974.

memberships, interests, style of living, goals), as well as to the personal meanings, fantasies, and values experienced by the individual.

From the interviews Levinson and his colleagues were able to delineate several developmental periods and transitions occurring from early to middle adulthood (see Table 17–3). The life course that they described consists of relatively stable periods interrupted by transitions that can be calm or chaotic. In either case, though, the transitions involve a crisis of reassessment of one's life and new commitments to the current life structure or to a new structure. If a new life structure is chosen, dramatic shifts in occupation, life style, and marital status may occur. The mid-life transition may be particularly dramatic. This is how the investigators described this transition:

> The Mid-Life Transition occurs whether the individual succeeds or fails in his search for affirmation by society. At 38 he thinks that if he gains the deserved success, he'll be all set. The answer is, he will not. . . . The central issue is not whether he succeeds or fails in achieving his goals. The issue, rather, is what to do with the *experience of disparity* between what he has gained in an inner sense from living within a particular structure and what he wants for himself. . . . To put it differently, it is not a matter of how many rewards one has obtained; it is a matter of the *goodness of fit between the life structure and the self.* (Levinson et al., 1974, p. 254)

Gould's (1972) research method was distinctly different from the work just described. He presented a questionnaire to 524 white, middle-class, educated men and women between the ages of sixteen and sixty. By requesting each participant to rank statements according to importance that he believed relevant to adult development, Gould was able to map certain beliefs and feelings across time. Figure 17–3 shows some of the findings.

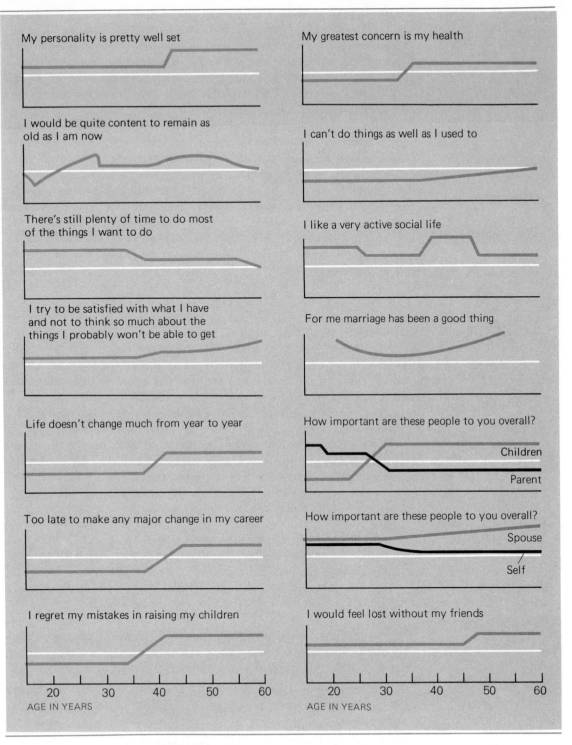

My personality is pretty well set

My greatest concern is my health

I would be quite content to remain as old as I am now

I can't do things as well as I used to

There's still plenty of time to do most of the things I want to do

I like a very active social life

I try to be satisfied with what I have and not to think so much about the things I probably won't be able to get

For me marriage has been a good thing

Life doesn't change much from year to year

How important are these people to you overall?

Children

Parent

Too late to make any major change in my career

How important are these people to you overall?

Spouse

Self

I regret my mistakes in raising my children

I would feel lost without my friends

20   30   40   50   60
AGE IN YEARS

20   30   40   50   60
AGE IN YEARS

FIGURE 17–3

Some of the findings of Gould's study. From R. L. Gould, The phases of adult life: A study in developmental psychology. **American Journal of Psychiatry**, 1972, **129**, 33–43.

From the data Gould was able to profile the adult years. During the middle thirties, for example, people begin to have a sense of time limitation, trying to accept what can be done with their lives, showing an increased interest in offspring, and exhibiting dissatisfaction with marriage. In the early forties, personal discomfort and instability occur, which generally level off in a few years. Marital happiness, interest in friends, and continued interest in one's children characterize the later years.

Gould's work, as well as that of the other investigators who have offered a broad overview of adulthood, sheds light on major themes of development following adolescence. They do not specify the events and timing of each individual's course of life. Rather, they provide a wealth of ideas for general hypotheses. We may ask about the relationship between identity formation and later intimacy, whether Levinson's scheme applies to women, or why some people but not others reject their life structure at mid-life. There is much still to be charted and learned. In the remainder of this chapter we will touch on selected topics that relate to some of the themes we have just encountered.

THE INFLUENCE OF AGE NORMS ON DEVELOPMENT

When age changes and stages are considered, no matter what their content, the role of societal expectations must be taken into account. One of the ways in which society orders itself is through the establishment of age norms: Individuals of different ages are expected to behave differently from those of other ages and to assume different roles. The recognition of age norms is demonstrated in Table 17–4, which shows the high agreement among a middle-class, middle-aged sample as to the appropriateness of certain characteristics or behavior for persons of various ages. To the extent that society places contingencies on age-normative behavior, age norms become a guide or a constraint. People are inclined, then, to "act their age" and establish roles "on time." This, in turn, feeds back to stabilize their own perceptions of themselves as aging organisms (Neugarten, Moore, and Lowe, 1965).

There is some evidence that older people perceive age constraints more strongly than do younger people. Neugarten and her associates (1965) queried different age groups about whether they thought certain behaviors were appropriate at certain ages and whether they approved or disapproved of them. Here are some of the thirty-nine items involved in this survey:

... A woman who feels it's all right at her age to wear a two-piece bathing suit to the beach (when she's 45, 30, 18).

... A woman who decides to have another child (when she's 45, 37, 30).

... A man who's willing to move his family from one town to another to get ahead in his company (when he's 45, 33, 25).

... A man who still prefers living with his parents rather than getting his own apartment (when he's 30, 25, 21).

... A couple who move across the country so they can live near their married children (when they're 40, 55, 70).

TABLE 17-4

Consensus among Middle-Class, Middle-Aged People Regarding the Appropriate Time for Various Characteristics and Behavior

Characteristics or Behavior	Age Range Designated as Appropriate or Expected	Percent Who Agree on the Age Range	
		Men (N = 30)	Women (N = 43)
Best age for a man to marry	20–25	80	90
Best age for a woman to marry	19–24	85	90
When most people should become grandparents	45–50	84	70
Best age for most people to finish school and go to work	20–22	86	82
When most men should be settled on a career	24–26	74	64
When most men hold their top jobs	45–50	71	58
When most people should be ready to retire	60–65	83	86
A young man	18–22	84	83
A middle-aged man	40–50	86	75
An old man	65–75	75	57
A young woman	18–24	89	88
A middle-aged woman	40–50	87	77
An old woman	60–75	83	87
When a man has the most responsibilities	35–50	79	75
When a man accomplishes most	40–50	82	71
The prime of life for a man	35–50	86	80
When a woman has the most responsibilities	25–40	93	91
When a woman accomplishes most	30–45	94	92
A good-looking woman	20–35	92	82

Source: Reprinted from Neugarten, Moore, and Lowe, 1965, by permission of The University of Chicago Press. Copyright © 1965 by The University of Chicago Press.

As Figure 17–4 indicates, the older people evidenced a higher perception of age constraint than did the younger. The investigators interpreted these results in light of the older population's having learned that age is a reasonable criterion by which to evaluate behavior and that to be "offtime" brings negative social and psychological consequences.

The *specific* norms indicated in the Neugarten et al. studies may not exist at the present time as society has witnessed many transitions in recent years. With regard to age, for example, sixty-five years had come to be viewed as "old," partly because mandatory retirement had been set at age sixty-five. Mandatory retirement now has been raised in some cases and we have begun to think of old age as commencing at seventy to seventy-five years. Thus, new norms may indeed be evolving. It is possible, too, that age norms are becoming less restrictive. This is positive in that it allows alternative paths for development. At the same time, however, increased options might also mean increased stress and conflict for many people.

BIOLOGICAL AGING AND HEALTH CHANGES

There is a general biological decline in all humans beginning at about age thirty, but it is gradual and varies greatly in the rate and degree of decrements peculiar to the different organ systems. As shown in Figure 17–5, the speed of nerve conduction, for example, declines little; metabolic rate diminishes less than 20 percent between the ages of thirty and ninety; but

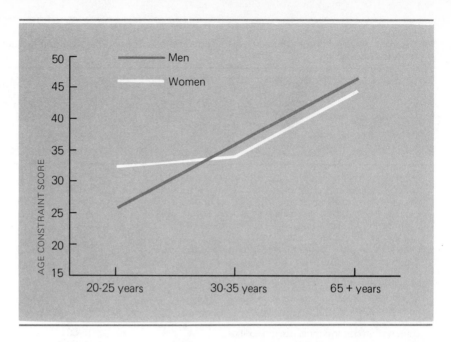

maximum breathing capacity is reduced to less than one-half of its full level. Markedly different patterns are also found for the various sensory systems. Auditory sensitivity begins to decline relatively early (see p. 91), and the decline is often pronounced by age sixty. On the other hand, taste and visual acuity remain quite constant until age fifty and then begin to decline (Corso, 1971). By this time the eyes frequently require more light, though, and the lens have lost elasticity so that focusing on near objects is more difficult. Olfaction may show very little change across the life span (Rovee, Cohen, and Shlapack, 1975).

Individual differences play a significant role in the variability in decline in the biological systems. Most of us have probably observed that some elderly people biologically resemble those many years younger. Research substantiates this picture. For example, in one investigation that compared

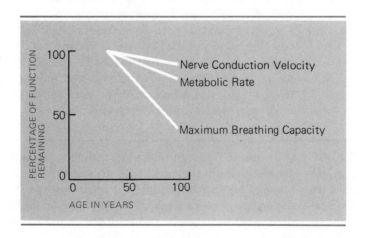

seventy-one-year-old men with younger men, there were few differences between a *subgroup* of very healthy old men and the younger men (Birren, Butler, Greenhouse, Sokoloff, and Yarrow, 1963).

In general, age brings an increasing number of long-term chronic illnesses, with arteriosclerosis being common. By age sixty-five more than one-half of all Americans have some form of heart disease and an almost equal number are afflicted with arthritis. In contrast, the rate of acute or short-term diseases decreases and is lower for those over sixty-five than for members of any other age group. In the course of living, individuals build up a large number of immunities that heighten their resistance to many acute diseases (Estes, 1969).

Throughout adulthood people become aware of and concerned about physical decline and increased health risks. From middle age onward both sexes regret losing the beauty of youth and begin to focus on their health. It is common for men in their forties and fifties to worry about heart attacks, which are associated with stress and competitive strivings (Friedman and Rosenman, 1974). Here, too, however, individual reactions differ markedly to both the prospects and the reality of poor health. Moreover, older people are relatively optimistic in this regard. When Shanas (1968) interviewed twenty-five hundred senior citizens concerning their own estimate of their health, 52 percent stated that they were in good health, 30 percent said their health was fair, and only 18 percent indicated that they were in poor health. Fully 75 percent considered their own health better than that of their contemporaries. It is interesting, too, that no direct relationship exists between age and how the elderly evaluate their health; that is, as many eighty-year-olds as sixty-five-year-olds rate their health as good or fair. Apparently, they take age norms into consideration because infirmities that might lead individuals of age sixty-five to declare their health poor result in very different conclusions in those over eighty (Shanas, 1968).

Theories of
Biological Aging

Interest in the aging process and its causes has been recorded over the centuries, as have the efforts to delay or prevent biological decline. Ponce de Leon's pursuit for the fountain of youth, which resulted in the discovery of Florida in 1512 A.D., serves as a reminder of the continual attempt to eliminate the seemingly irrevocable path to death (Busse, 1977). In present times, scientific research bears the burden of this effort.

One approach to the study of aging is to examine the lives of people who have unusually long life spans. With this in mind, Alexander Leaf (1973) observed remote villages in Ecuador, West Pakistan, and the Soviet Union in which the population lived to older ages than people in the surrounding geographic areas. Life in these villages was not identical, of course, but Leaf noted the strong possibility that genetic factors, a diet low in calories and fats, and physical activity are correlated with longevity. He also suggested the importance of psychological factors. People in these remote places were untouched by the stress and concern of modern life such as the energy crisis and environmental pollution. And the aged themselves had high social status and were expected to be active, contributing members of society (see Figure 17–6, p. 565).

Even though psychological variables are recognized as determinants of aging, enormous interest exists in biological factors. That different species have different life spans argues for the importance of biological factors. Individual cells multiply only to a finite number and, in general, the longer the life span of the species the greater the number of times its cells multiply (Marx, 1974). The role of genetic control is widely accepted: The offspring of parents with long life spans live longer than others (Leaf, 1973), and monozygotic twins have more similar life spans than dizygotic twins (Kallmann and Sander, 1949).

The exact processes of biological aging are being investigated and they encompass a wide range of possibilities (Busse, 1977; Comfort, 1970; Marx, 1974). One general proposal is that cells of the body that can multiply throughout the life span (e.g., white blood cells) increasingly undergo mutation or make errors in copying that render them defective. Another idea is that cells that cannot multiply (e.g., neurons) account for aging as they wear out or become inefficient. It has also been observed that connective tissue (that is, between-the-cells tissue) undergoes change over time that may be primary to aging. Other investigators point to the immunity system, suggesting that it comes to reject or attack parts of the body as well as foreign substances. Whatever the mechanisms of aging, however, it does not seem likely that a fountain of youth will soon be discovered. Meanwhile, humans must contend with the fact that aging and decline in health have implications for virtually all areas of functioning, from motor ability to how people think about themselves.

CHANGES IN INTELLIGENCE, MEMORY, AND PSYCHOMOTOR BEHAVIOR

In chapter 9 age changes on intelligence tests were discussed in detail, and we suggest that the reader review pp. 276–279. It appears that IQ remains relatively stable throughout at least middle age and that later decrement occurs in perceptual-spatial abilities and fluid intelligence rather than in verbal abilities and crystallized intelligence. As we learned, however, these conclusions must be held cautiously due to complex research issues. Moreover, age differences in test performance can be attributed to the actual aging process, generational differences, motivation, and the like.

A considerable amount of research is now being conducted on basic cognitive, motor, and learning abilities throughout the life span. Our discussion here is limited to only two other topics that have broad implications for adult development: memory and psychomotor slowing. The same research and interpretation issues that apply to intelligence test performance are relevant to these basic functions as well.

Memory

A brief review of our earlier discussion of memory (p. 215) will help recall that this cognitive ability consists of three components: a sensory register, short-term storage, and long-term storage. Information is passed from one component to the next and can be retrieved along the way. Memory can be examined by considering the capacity (amount of information that can be handled) and functioning of each component, the processes that facilitate passage of information, and the methods of retrieval. In our society

FIGURE 17–6
Old men in West Pakistan winnow threshed wheat. Ibrihim Shah (right) professes to be eighty years old, while Mohd Ghraib (left) says he is only seventy-five.   1980 John Launois, Black Star.

it is expected that memory will begin to fail as we age (Perlmutter, 1978), but what is less clear are the reasons for this failure. Do we lose the capacity for memory or do the processes associated with storage and retrieval become less effective?

The sensory register receives information from the environment in sensory (e.g., visual, auditory) form and passes it to short-term storage. Although the sensory register has a large capacity, information decays rapidly. There is general agreement, though, that neither capacity nor decay rates change much from childhood onward. However, the time required to clear information out of the sensory register appears to decrease during childhood and to increase during the later years (Baltes, Reese, and Lipsitt, 1980; Elias, Elias, and Elias, 1977). This means that very young children and the elderly lose more information, due to rapid decay, before it can be passed to short-term memory.

Short-term storage is assumed to have limited capacity so that information can be preserved only if it is passed to long-term storage. The capacity of short-term storage seems to remain constant throughout the life span. This conclusion has been reached largely on the basis of memory experiments in which recall of the last items presented, which would be in short-term storage, does not vary significantly with age (Baltes et al., 1980). Much of the experimental testing, however, has been concerned with information processing; that is, the way in which information is put into and passed on from short-term storage. This processing can be examined by investigating how material to be remembered is encoded and retrieved, both of which entail organization of the information. In general, this line of investigation has revealed that older individuals do not process (i.e., organize) information at as high a level or as quickly as younger persons (Elias, Elias, and Elias 1977). However, they can profit from organization provided by the experimenter and from training in organization. With regard to retrieval of information, some loss of function is correlated with age. Simple recognition, which occurs when we are presented with a stimulus and remember we have seen it before, shows less decline with age than free recall, which requires greater organization because there are no cues (Craik, 1977; Perlmutter, 1978).

Long-term storage is considered to be extremely large, if not infinite, in capacity and to be more or less permanent. Relatively little research has been conducted on long-term memory, but it is thought that it is not strongly affected by aging. In fact, one of the stereotypes held about the elderly is that they continually recount experiences of the long past but forget recent events. That crystallized intelligence and verbal abilities (which frequently involve long-term knowledge about the culture) are maintained fairly well by the old supports the belief that information that was stored long ago still exists in memory.

In summary, memory does decline with age and it appears that information processing, not capacity, is affected. Baltes and his colleagues (1980) point out, however, that older adults probably do not practice deliberate memorization, as do younger people who are chronologically closer to the school years or hold jobs that require such skill. Indeed, such memorization, while an asset, may not be critical to the environmental demands placed on the elderly.

Psychomotor Slowing

There is little argument that with middle age comes a slowing of behavior (Birren, 1964, 1974). Psychomotor slowing has been studied with many tasks, but reaction time has been particularly popular. In a simple reaction

FIGURE 17–7
Reaction time to auditory stimuli in relation to age. From J. E. Birren, **The Psychology of Aging.** Englewood Cliffs, N.J.: Prentice-Hall, Inc. Originally from Y. Koga and G. M. Morant, On the degree of association between reaction times in the case of different senses. **Biometrika,** 1923, **15,** 355–359.

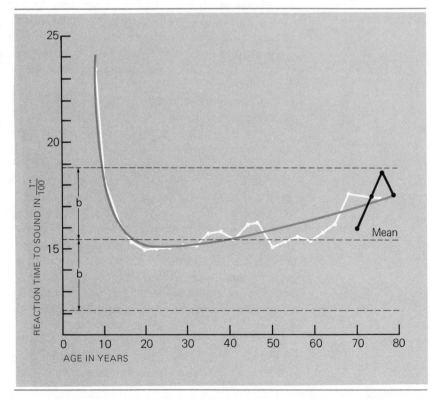

time test some kind of stimulus is presented, such as a flash of light or a noise, and the individual is expected to respond as quickly as possible. Figure 17–7, which shows that reaction time to an auditory stimulus decreases during childhood and then gradually increases after age thirty, represents the general psychomotor slowing that occurs during adulthood.

In a review of the literature pertaining to psychomotor slowing in the elderly, Welford (1977) drew the following conclusions:

1. While there is evidence of slowing of the muscular functions, the speed of the decisions that guide these movements and the time to monitor them are the principle causes for the slowing of reaction time.

2. When movements are simple and can be prepared in advance the changes with age are relatively small.

3. If preparation is not possible, or the movements are to be made rapidly or are complex, there is a greater change with age, often exhibited at the points of decision making.

4. The more complex the signals and responses, the more the age decrement is apparent.

5. Older persons tend to be more cautious in their responses and inspect the signal for a longer period of time. Under certain circumstances this caution translates into greater accuracy of response.

6. Age changes in simple sensorimotor tasks seem largely unrelated to sex, education, or SES.

7. Sensorimotor performance correlates to various extents with intelligence test scores and other measures of cognitive or intellectual functioning.

Decrements in reaction time are sometimes associated with hypertension and poor cardiovascular functioning. Poor reaction time can, in fact, predict cardiovascular impairments (Abrahams and Birren, 1973). This suggests that older individuals who are physically fit should perform better on reaction time tasks than those less physically fit. Botwinick and Thompson (1968) raised this possibility when reviewing the results of a study in which the control group included a number of young athletes. They inquired into the exercise patterns of these young subjects. On the basis of this information the subjects were designated either as athletes or nonathletes and the data were analyzed. The results showed that while the young athletes had significantly shorter reaction times than the older subjects, the nonathletes did not. Spirduso (1975) has further confirmed that physical fitness is associated with faster responding among older people. Performance on four tasks was studied in sixty men classified as older or younger athletes or nonathletes. The older athletes were not only superior to the older nonathletes, but they also surpassed the younger nonathletes on some of the tasks.

There is evidence, too, that practice can lead to improved response speed (Hoyer, Labouvie, and Baltes, 1973; Murrell, 1970). Hoyer and his associates (1973), for example, demonstrated that response speed in elderly females of seventy years could be modified with reinforced or unreinforced practice. On-the-job practice and experience seems to make a difference, too. Studies of on-the-job performance indicate that speed and accuracy improve in workers until ages thirty-five to forty-five, after which accuracy remains high and speed maintains itself or decreases, but at a *slower* rate than experimental studies would predict (Welford, 1977). It is suggested that this retarded rate of slowing is due to experience on the part of older workers.

The general slowing of behavior with age is viewed as an expression of the aging of the nervous system, which involves the loss of neurons, reduced excitability, and changes in transmission of the nerve impulses across the synapses (Birren, 1964, 1974). Although it is subject to individual variation, it affects all persons to some degree. From a functional point of view, we would expect aging people to avoid tasks that require speed, to accomplish less in a specific period of time, and to be less efficient in instances that require speed. This has practical implications. Birren (1974), for example, has noted that with increasing age the accident rate rises because the actual motor response and the ability to make decisions in the face of potential danger are both slowed. He has also suggested that further study of psychomotor slowing is necessary so that we can increase our knowledge of how to structure the environment in ways that are supportive to the older adult.

THE ADULT AND THE FAMILY

Earlier in this text we had occasion to discuss family influences on the child (see especially chapters 10 and 11). Here we view the family from the vantage point of adulthood. Although adult life styles appear more variable now than in the past, most individuals still experience, at some time during their lives, the "traditional" nuclear or extended family. In fact, only a small percentage of adults never marry.

FIGURE 17–8
Learning to plan activities with one's mate is important as one develops the basis for family life.   Freda Leinwand, Monkmeyer Press Photo Service.

In our culture we say that we marry for love; indeed, being in love appears to be a strong motivating force for marrying. But many other factors are involved in selection of a marital partner (Barry, 1970; Brim, 1968). As unromantic as it may be, proximity plays a role: We marry those who live nearby. In general, homogamy (the mating of like with like) is the rule with regard to age, social class, family background, religion, values, and perhaps even personality. Families undoubtedly encourage homogamy, feeling more comfortable with such potential members and perhaps believing that "like with like" stands a better chance of survival than "like with unlike." Finally, readiness for marriage is important. Such a feeling may be based on the age the individual thinks society prescribes for marriage; economic, educational, and occupational circumstances; and psychological needs. In any event, Troll (1975) has noted that historically women have had less power over marital selection than men. Some of the reasons are that women usually cannot directly initiate contact, are in greater supply, and have a shorter age range during which they are considered good candidates for marriage.

Do adults like their marital experiences? The divorce rate in the United States certainly would lead us to answer a resounding "no" to this question. But the majority of divorced people remarry; one study estimated that 80 percent remarry and that 30 percent of all marriages are remarriages (Dean and Gurak, 1978). If Americans are disappointed in marriage, they apparently have not given up trying to find happiness in this relationship. Moreover, there is evidence that married people are happier than the unmarried (Harry, 1976).

Marital happiness depends upon many variables. Couples holding traditional expectations report greater happiness than those holding self-actualizing or expressive expectations (Troll, 1975). The adequacy of performance of marital roles, conformity of one mate to the expectations of the other, and husband's social status and prestige also are important (Chadwick, Albrecht, and Kunz, 1976). There are some data that husbands are more satisfied with marriage than wives and that their satisfaction does not decrease over time as does wives' satisfaction (Troll, 1975). Also, married women appear to suffer more psychological discomfort than single women and married or single men (Bernard, 1973). Marriage may be desired more by women than by men, but this apparently does not mean that they later consider themselves better off in marriage than men.

There is also evidence that marital satisfaction fluctuates over time, although this requires further confirmation. Several studies show a modest curvilinear relationship between the family cycle and satisfaction (Lee, 1978). An example is shown in Figure 17–9, which indicates that the high satisfaction of the beginning years of marriage decreases as offspring grow older, reaching the lowest point when the children are approaching adulthood and moving out. As the couple once again is without children in the home, satisfaction gradually increases into the retirement years. This pattern of marital satisfaction is particularly interesting because, due to smaller family size, earlier departure of the last child from the home, and longer average life span, the length of the postparental years of marriage is increasing (Duvall, 1971; Troll, 1975). Nevertheless, a word of caution is in order.

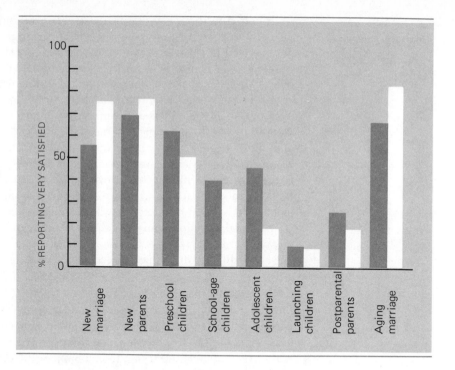

FIGURE 17-9
Percentage of adults reporting that they are very satisfied according to stage of marriage. From B. C. Rollins and H. Feldman, Marital satisfaction over the family life cycle. **Journal of Marriage and the Family,** 1970, 32, 20–28. Copyrighted 1970 by the National Council on Family Relations. Reprinted by permission.

Since virtually all of the studies of marital satisfaction are cross-sectional, generational (cohort) effects cannot be ruled out. Furthermore, the studies may be confounded by the obvious fact that only couples who are still together are queried.

Throughout early and middle adulthood the parental role usually dominates much of the activity and efforts of adults. The birth of the first child can be a time of crisis for the marriage (LeMasters, 1957), but it may be less of a strain than previously thought (Hobbs and Cole, 1976). The arrival of a child also may bring a deepening of commitment and interests. Many parents apparently feel that rearing children is worth the effort; Bernard (1973), for example, reported that between 40 and 50 percent of women cite motherhood as their major satisfaction.

Evidently, the time of launching children into their own relatively independent worlds is especially stressful. The offspring themselves may show uncertainty about leaving and their quest for independence may cause friction. During these middle years, anywhere from the late thirties to the middle fifties, couples are often heavily involved in occupational and civic responsibilities, which may burden the marital relationship. Along with facing the empty nest, both parents also must deal with the beginning signs of biological aging. Thus, the launching process itself is only one of many factors that lead people to rate marital satisfaction as low at this time.

During the postparental years the couple must adjust to being a couple again. If large divergencies in interests and styles of functioning have occurred, the task may be difficult. Nevertheless, many advantages exist: freedom from constant concerns about one's children, privacy previously impossible, increased leisure time, and lessening of financial strain. With health and wealth usually stable, the early postparental years hold the opportunity for newfound enjoyments. For some, these enjoyments include grandparenting. Upon retirement, these postparental couples are the people who Neugarten (1978) has labeled the young-old. Retirement itself may be stressful, of course, and there may be a growing concern for aging parents.

Marital and family ties are considered the primary source of happiness, fulfillment, companionship, and social involvement for the elderly. Lee (1978) examined the association between marital satisfaction and general morale in couples in their late sixties who had been married one time. He found a significant correlation between the measures for both sexes, though it was somewhat stronger for women. Given this association, it is fortunate that older couples assess their marriages positively and report improvement in them (Lee, 1978; Rollins and Feldman, 1970; Stinnett, Carter, and Montgomery, 1972). On the other hand, loss of a mate through death has potentially dire consequences. Several investigations show that widows and widowers are low in life satisfaction and morale, happiness, and adjustment compared to married couples of the same age and also to persons who have never married (Kastenbaum and Costa, 1977; Lee, 1978).

If a couple has had children, it is highly probable that the family has become extended generationally: Among those over sixty-five, 94 percent are grandparents and 46 percent are great-grandparents (Shanas, 1980). Still, most elderly people live alone, and, in fact, this trend for independence has been increasing. Shanas (1980) provides us with some of the relevant statistics. Among the older (sixty-five years and over) unmarried, one of every seven men and one of every three women live alone. In 1975, only 18 percent of all elderly people who had children lived in the same household as one of their children. Thirty-four percent, however, lived apart from their children but within very close proximity to at least one of them. But whether or not the elderly live alone, they are still members of a family, they are generally engaged in its reciprocal helping and support patterns, and they play significant roles in the more subtle interactions involving affectional bonds and transmission of values (Troll, 1971). Due to the longer average life span, the family system increasingly involves four generations. Because this phenomenon was previously rarely seen in the United States, Ethel Shanas refers to four-generation family members as the pioneers in our society.

SEXUAL ACTIVITY AND ATTITUDES

The early adult years is a time of increasing sexual activity, but this pattern reverses itself in the middle thirties and decline is gradual throughout the remainder of life (Martin, 1977). Table 17–5 indicates the frequency of sexual intercourse as reported by almost 500 men and women. Not only does frequency decrease with age, but men reported more activity than women. Much has been written about such findings.

The Climacteric

The *climacteric* is a term that refers to the biological and psychic changes that accompany the termination of the reproductive period in the female and the normal diminution of sexual activity in the male (Rogers, 1979).

TABLE 17-5
Frequency of Sexual Intercourse Reported by Participants in a Cross-Sectional Study

Group	None	Once a Month	Once a Week	2-3 Times a Week	More Than 3 Times a Week
Men					
46–50	0	5	62	26	7
51–55	5	29	49	17	0
56–60	7	38	44	11	0
61–65	20	43	30	7	0
66–71	24	48	26	2	0
Total	12	34	41	12	1
Women					
46–50	14	26	39	21	0
51–55	20	41	32	5	2
56–60	42	27	25	4	2
61–65	61	29	5	5	0
66–71	73	16	11	0	0
Total	44	27	22	6	1

Source: "Sexual Behavior in Middle Life," by E. Pfeiffer, A Verwoerdt, and G. Davis, American Journal of Psychiatry, 1972, **128**, 84.

In males the climacteric is difficult to identify as it is not associated with dramatic change. Aging males do show some sexual performance changes: Erections are not attained as quickly and ejaculations are of less duration and force (Masters and Johnson, 1966). There have been reports of complaints of nervousness, irritability, depression, lack of concentration, and the like (Elias, Elias, and Elias, 1977), but for the most part males do not seem stressed by such symptoms in relationship to a specific climacteric. Furthermore, the differential effects of lowered levels of sex hormones and psychosocial factors are not at all clear. Masters and Johnson (1966) implicate the following psychosocial factors in the lessening of male responsiveness:

1. Monotony associated with a long-standing sexual relationship that may involve lack of interest on the part of the female, loss of attractiveness of the female, and failure of the relationship to develop.
2. Male preoccupation with careers.
3. Physical or mental fatigue.
4. Excessive alcohol consumption.
5. Physical and mental dysfunction of either partner.
6. Fear of failure to perform.

In females the climacteric is commonly known as *menopause.* It is characterized by cessation of the menses, atrophy of the reproductive organs, thinning of the vaginal wall, and decreased vaginal lubrication during sexual stimulation. Hot flashes, insomnia, depression, and crying may occur. Many women do not report these symptoms, however. In one study of the objective records from a general health screening of 329 menopausal women, only 25 percent of the participants had experienced traditional symptoms (Goodman, Stewart, and Gilbert, 1977). Rubin (1968) has estimated that perhaps only 10 to 15 percent of all women seek medical care of menopausal problems. It also appears that menopause usually does not influence sexual activities; in one study, for example, 65 percent of the women voiced the opinion that menopause had no effect on their sexual relations. On the other hand, many women believed that menopause has a negative effect on appearance (Neugarten, 1967).

With the female climacteric comes a drop in estrogen production. Early in the 1960s the use of estrogen replacement therapy became a popular treatment for the control of menopausal symptoms. Now, however, retrospective studies indicate that the chance of uterine cancer is 4.5 to 7.6 times higher in women who received estrogen therapy than in women who were not so treated (Proudfit, 1976). Thus, although estrogen therapy may provide some symptomatic relief, its use is being guardedly watched because of its long-term side effects.

The Later Years

Investigations of the elderly indicate that while there may be a lessening of interest and activity in sexual relations, for many this period of life cannot be described as sexless. One investigation showed, for example, that of 149 men and women between the ages of sixty and ninety-three who were living with their spouses, 54 percent still engaged in sexual relations (Newman and Nichols, 1960). Studying individuals from the time they were sixty-seven until they reached age seventy-seven, another team of researchers reported that their subjects showed no decline in interest in sex (Pfeiffer, Verwoerdt, and Wang, 1969). It is obvious that sexual relations can be important and pleasurable over most of the life span. Moreover, there is agreement that interest in sex during the later years, as well as the capacity to perform, depends on regularity of sexual activity and is correlated with sexual activity during the earlier years (Masters and Johnson, 1966; Rubin, 1968).

One advantage of the aging process in males is that generally the control of ejaculation is better in the fifty to seventy-year-old age group than in the twenty to forty-year-old age group (Masters and Johnson, 1970). Often the older man does not have the specific drive to ejaculate more than every second or third time he has intercourse. With both partners accepting the fact that ejaculation on each ocassion of coitus is not necessary, a more satisfactory sexual relationship may be maintained. Further, the delay in erection coincides with a delay in the lubrication of the vaginal area of the older female partner. Masters and Johnson (1970) suggest that if the male is encouraged to ejaculate on his own demand schedule and to have intercourse as it fits both sexual partners' interest, the average married couple is capable of functioning sexually into their eighties, providing they both enjoy good health.

As mentioned earlier, studies show that men report a greater interest and participation in sexual activity (Pfeiffer, Verwoerdt and Davis, 1972). This must be interpreted within the cultural context of our times. Since women traditionally marry men older than themselves they face periods of being without available sexual partners. In one study (Verwoerdt, Pfeiffer and Wang, 1969) 92 percent of unmarried women reported that sexual activity was continually absent and 45 percent reported that sexual interest was absent as well. Unmarried men did not respond in a similar fashion. Only 18 percent were sexually abstinent and only 15 percent reported no interest in sex. It is possible that future generations of older women will not experience the sexual deprivation reported. Young women today are beginning to be more concerned with sexual fulfillment (Huyck, 1977) and it is likely this concern will continue throughout their lifetime. Future studies of sexual behavior and attitudes in older adults may thus present a changing picture.

OCCUPATIONAL CHANGE

Occupation serves to define individuals in important ways: in social status, economic well-being, life style, and values. Psychologists and sociologists have extensively studied occupational choice and adjustment, stages of occupational development, and social influences on occupational patterns (Whitbourne and Weinstock, 1979). Our discussion will be limited to two topics of special interest, those of mid-career change and retirement.

Mid-career Changes

Mid-career changes are becoming more common in our society, in part due to a middle-life reassessment of life's purpose, an involuntary change of employment that is often caused by automation, and the reentrance of women into the job market after years of child rearing. In defining what constitutes a career change, categories of occupational environments were proposed by Holland (1973) and change was defined as going from one category to another. The typist who advances to secretary does not experience a career change, while the executive who quits the corporate structure to open a restaurant certainly does. Much of the career change literature is anecdotal in nature (Thomas, 1977); however, some studies are based on formal research (Gottfredson, 1977; Wiener and Vaitenas, 1977).

Part of Holland's (1973) career theory suggests that when the job environment runs counter to the personality of the worker mid-career changes are more likely to occur. Wiener and Vaitenas (1977) tested this hypothesis by comparing the personality traits of forty-five mid-career changers all involved originally in enterprising occupations such as management and law with sixty-six vocationally stable controls who were also engaged in enterprising occupations and indicated no desire to change. They predicted that the career changers would score lower on personality tests measuring ascendancy and dominance, since these factors were considered intrinsically necessary for successfully engaging in occupations classified as enterprising. An analysis of the personality test results confirmed their hypothesis, lending support to Holland's theory. Thomas (1977) described similar experiences of career changers who no longer felt compatible with their working environment, either because the initial match of job and personality was poor or because of developmental changes in their values and personality.

Gottfredson (1977), using Holland's occupational classifications, looked at career stability as it is related to age and sex. Data from the Bureau of the Census were analyzed for the years 1965 and 1970 to determine the percentage of persons who changed occupational categories. The analysis indicated that stability of employment within occupational categories was the norm and it tended to increase with age. When shifts did occur for men in the sample it involved changes from technical occupations to primarily managerial, supervisory, or persuasive occupations. However, change was noted in only about 10 percent of the sample and generally this was at younger ages. The older employees changed infrequently because of personal preference and because identification with a specific occupation defined them socially, economically and in regard to potential employment seeking.

We have focused so far on the voluntary mid-life career changers, but workers also must adjust to job change due to circumstances not of their own making. Weinberg (1970) noted that the psychological adjustment to automation is not easy, especially for the older worker. When the worker no longer senses a control over the machine because of its sophistication, he or she often experiences a feeling of personal worthlessness. Also, employees often are faced with the task of relocation without adequate support systems because of layoffs or the complete shutdown of industries. Retraining programs have been shown to offer some relief for the displaced worker. Warr and Lovatt (1977) interviewed 1,655 ex-employees of a steel factory in Great Britain where a program of retraining was offered. They found that the younger employees were more likely to make use of the retraining programs although the older workers had priority. Those employees who engaged in job retraining were more likely to find new employment, but the new jobs tended to pay less, particularly for the older workers.

Perhaps the most dramatic career change currently is that of women re-entering the job market in mid-life. In recent years the number of women in the paid labor force has increased by 12 million (Vriend, 1977), and often these women suffer from "job overload," which is the addition of the employee role to the homemaking role without benefit of good support systems. Such innovations as flexible work schedules, maternity leaves, and day care centers could improve the situation of the working woman, but they are slow in coming. Vriend points out that job choices for the reentering woman are often not adequately thought out and therefore lead to a sense of frustration. Counseling for all career changers certainly would be beneficial, and future emphasis in vocational counseling should be directed to persons in their middle years.

Retirement

Retirement designates the period in life when one's role as a paid worker ceases. It is becoming an increasingly common role adjustment in our society. Retirement originated as a voluntary act or as a way for society to care for people unable to work, but it has become mandatory in many occupations. Interestingly, this policy was never implemented at some of the highest occupational levels, such as those involving Supreme Court Justices and Senators. The capable performance of individuals in their seventies and eighties holding these positions suggests that mandatory retirement policies stem more from an insufficient number of jobs than from the general incapacity of older people to perform in their occupations.

Retirement can be viewed from three perspectives: as a life event, as a process, or as the adopting of a new role (Atchley, 1972). As an *event* retirement is momentary and usually not celebrated in the way that we celebrate noteworthy milestones such as marriage. Even when formally acknowledged, the ritual is likely to involve looking back rather than looking forward. When taken from the *process* perspective, retirement begins with the first acknowledgment that one's employment will someday cease. Atchley (1972) reported that all but 10 percent of adults expect to retire, the majority before the age of sixty. This is not to say that disengagement from paid employment is considered synonymous with the end of a fulfilling and productive life. As younger workers develop a realistic attitude toward retirement and are able to plan for it, the adjustment to "forced" leisure will probably be seen as a more positive experience (Glamser, 1976). Finally, retirement can be viewed as a *social role.* The retiree is expected to cease engaging in work and work-related roles while increasing the time spent with family and friends in leisure and nonwork-related activities.

It has long been proposed that male workers in particular derive much of their identity and satisfaction from employment and that with retirement comes a lowering of morale. Although retirement is undoubtedly difficult for some men, this picture is much too simple. For example, in the first year after retirement a greater percentage of blue- than white-collar retirees actually express a high degree of satisfaction with their circumstances (Stokes and Maddox, 1967). The blue-collar workers may have fallen less far in status, and the leisure of retirement may seem a welcome substitute for their previous occupations. Over time, however, the pattern reverses; white-collar workers retired more than three years appear more contented than their blue-collar counterparts. It has been hypothesized that this is because of the white-collar workers' greater number of outside interests and nonwork activities suited to old age.

Peppers (1976) found that both the quality and quantity of leisure activity of the retired correlated positively with a measure of life satisfaction. Increases in social and physical activities had the strongest positive effect. Interestingly, the retired persons who preferred solitary or sedentary lifestyles had established those patterns well before the age of retirement, suggesting that retirement is a continuation of a life style rather than an abrupt change.

Fillenbaum (1971) proposed that degree of job satisfaction would be inversely related to attitudes toward retirement. She found little to support this idea, however. It appeared instead that the acceptance of retirement as an integral part of the life cycle was a determinant of attitudes toward retirement. The manner in which interests extended beyond the work role also influenced retirement satisfaction. Fillenbaum commented that, "Only when the job is of prime importance as the central organizing factor in a person's life should it affect his retirement attitude" (1971, p. 247).

Financial security also is a determinant of satisfaction in retirees. Kutner, Fanshel, Togo, and Langner (1970), for example, reported that one-half of those rated well-to-do, compared with less than one-fourth of those rated low in socioeconomic status, expressed a high degree of contentment. It is noteworthy, though, that Kutner and his associates also found that, independent of income, elderly citizens who worked indicated higher morale than those who did not. This held true for those earning less than $25 per week, for those earning between $25 and $50, and for those whose incomes exceeded $50 per week. Even though poor health and other indisposing factors may have contributed to the lower morale of those who were not employed, the evidence is nevertheless suggestive that, for those over sixty-five, continuing in some employed capacity may entail rewards above and beyond financial gains, related perhaps to feelings of usefulness and to social interaction.

Older women, a group that constitutes an expanding proportion of retirees, largely have been ignored in the literature (Jaslow, 1976). It has been assumed that the work role has less psychological significance for women. However, in sampling 2,398 women over the age of sixty-five, Jaslow (1976) found that with the exception of the highest economic group morale was highest for those currently employed, next highest for retirees, and lowest for women never having had paid employment. This study suggests the need for the inclusion of females in research on work and retirement.

THE LATER YEARS: DISENGAGEMENT OR ACTIVITY?

Related to the event of retirement is Cumming and Henry's disengagement theory, which is based largely on the study of healthy, economically secure fifty- to ninety-year-olds. These investigators set out to determine what their sample of older people were like, and they did so by several interviews over a period of a few years. Specifically, they wanted to test their observation that aging is an "inevitable mutual withdrawal or disengagement, resulting in decreased interaction between the aging person and others in the social system he belongs to" (1961, p. 14). They were able to trace a decline in interaction by examining such aspects as the number of social roles held by the elderly, the amount of time spent with various other people, and the reactions of the aged to their own lives.

Several of the Cumming and Henry hypotheses or assumptions are provocative. They suggest, for example, that disengagement involves not only the withdrawal from others (except for intimate kin) but also a concomitant preoccupation with the self. An important factor in precipitating this shift is a change in perception of time. The individual begins to measure life in terms of time from death, instead of time from birth, and realizes that the years are too few. Thus, many activities once considered important are put aside as having only *previous* value. The disengaged, according to Cumming and Henry, are tranquil as they gradually loosen or sever their ties with early things. Additionally, these events are considered universal happenings that probably help ease tensions between generations, involving, as they do, the "moving over" of the older for the younger generation.

Although there is little disagreement that people are involved in less social interaction as they become old, disengagement theory has not been well received. It is argued that the source of withdrawal is not the individual's desire but a society that pushes the elderly into inactivity. Furthermore, many behavioral scientists resist the notion that the disengaged person is content and tranquil. In short, it is not at all clear that inactivity and focus on the self is the optimal condition of the aged (cf. Botwinick, 1973).

Several investigations have been addressed to these issues, many of them proposing that *activity* (interpersonal or otherwise), and not disengagement, is positively correlated with high morale. In general, the weight of the evidence seems to support this notion (Botwinick, 1973; Maddox, 1965). Successful aging (as determined by self-report scales and ratings of old people in general) is associated with active daily pursuits by the elderly (Schonfield, 1973). Health, however, remains an important variable, regardless of activity-nonactivity. Personality may also be important. Havighurst, Neugarten, and Tobin (1968) described several "types" of people, some of whom seem to be successful with disengagement. They have high self-concept, are self-directed, and are interested in the world, although not particularly in its interpersonal aspects. Disengagement also may be satisfying to dependent and passive people. Clearly, it is a mistake to stereotype the elderly, thereby ignoring individual needs and desires and forcing them into particular life patterns.

For example, there is considerable discussion about the optimal living conditions of the aged in terms of the impact of living with peers versus living with younger people. Frequently, emphasis is placed on the value of contact with those of the younger generation. However, Rosow (1967) examined the relation between living circumstances and friendship patterns among twelve hundred aged residents of Cleveland; he was especially interested in the effects on those over sixty-five of having few or many age peers living in close proximity. The study's most basic finding was that the greater the concentration of old people, the more friends each resident made. This result was in direct opposition to theories of social integration that stress the importance of older individuals living among younger ones. The density of senior citizens residing in the immediate area was particularly important to working-class individuals; whereas those of higher socioeconomic status were likely to have friends outside of the neighborhood, former blue-collar workers depended almost exclusively on those who lived nearby for extra-familial companionship. The same tendency applied also to those older than seventy-five; they too drew very heavily on their age peers in the immediate neighborhood for friendship.

Nevertheless, individuals exhibited a wide range of attitudes concerning their social lives. Rosow identified four basic themes that seemed common to fairly large groups within the population. He labeled "cosmopolitan" the approximately 30 percent who had little contact with their neighbors and appeared content with the arrangement. The 20 percent who visited infrequently and desired more interpersonal stimulation were termed "isolated." The label "sociable" was applied to the 23 percent who indicated a high degree of social contact and who were satisfied with their social lives; the term "insatiable" was reserved for the 10 percent having a high level of contact and desiring more. It would seem, then, that a relatively active life with interpersonal relationships is optimal for most of the elderly, but that some enjoy a less active existence and, furthermore, that optimal conditions vary a good deal among individuals.

FIGURE 17–10
Conditions of life for elderly people vary remarkably in the United States today.   Photos by Elizabeth Crews and Karen R. Preuss, Jeroboam, and Paul S. Conklin, Monkmeyer.

FACING THE END
OF LIFE

A central fact of adulthood is that with each year after thirty it becomes increasingly likely that death will occur. Not only does death become more probable between ages thirty and ninety, but the rate of increase of its probability also accelerates. The basic trend is present for whites and blacks and for males and females.

Causes of death can be categorized as *extrinsic* and *intrinsic* (e.g., Goldman, 1968). Extrinsic causes are the most commonly cited immediate ones. Heart disease, cancer, other vascular ailments, and accidents accounted for almost 75 percent of all deaths in 1977 (Monthly Vital Statistics Report, 1979). Intrinsic causes are those involving certain general factors: cells wear out and many do not reproduce themselves; the strength of bones and the elasticity of blood vessels decreases; there is also an overall decline in resiliency; injuries take longer to heal; and illnesses are more difficult to shake off. Evidence for the importance of these intrinsic factors has led some experts to conclude that further progress in increasing the life span may depend on finding a way to slow down the overall developmental cycle.

Old age and death have not been favorite topics in our society, which highly values youth and activity. It is frequently pointed out that we have relegated the aged to lonely nursing homes and the dying to isolated hospital rooms (e.g., Dempsey, 1975; Kübler-Ross, 1969; Mitford, 1963). More recently the taboos and negative attitudes have weakened. In the mid-1950s psychology and other disciplines came to view death as a relevant area of investigation (Kastenbaum and Costa, 1977). Perhaps the aging population, threats of wars, and a need to reexamine basic values has played a part in this new trend.

The Dying Process: Kübler-Ross's Work

Kübler-Ross has conducted interviews with terminally ill patients for many years. She has suggested that dying consists of five stages:

1. At first the patient *denies* impending death, perhaps thinking a mistake had been made in the diagnosis. The reality of death is isolated psychologically, and the individual may not want to talk about the seriousness of his or her condition.

2. *Anger and resentment* set in, however, when death as a real event is recognized. Patients may direct these reactions toward anyone available—family, friends, or medical personnel—presumably because their own demise seems unjustified in the face of others' well-being.

3. Some acceptance does occur, however, and the patient begins to *bargain*, to ask, as it were, for time-off in the procession toward death. Thus, he or she may try to take up life's tasks or to plan to live long enough to attend a special event or complete a special task.

4. The next step involves *depression*, which occurs when illness intrudes upon bargaining. Depression may be either a reactive type stemming from shame or guilt at being disfigured by illness, or a preparatory type. The latter has its basis in feelings of loss of the meaningful aspects of one's life—of loved ones, the natural beauty of the world, the cherished book.

5. Finally, though, death is *accepted* as inevitable. The patient frequently is tired, unemotional, and seemingly waiting for the last happening of life.

Kübler-Ross does not maintain that all terminally ill patients progress through all stages because some, for example, may simply continue to deny that they will soon die. She nevertheless suggests that many of the terminally ill experience the five psychological stages. It must be recognized, however, that Kübler-Ross studied a particular group of individuals, those of varying ages who were ill with a terminal disease; in particular, most were cancer patients. It is quite feasible that the elderly do not progress through the proposed stages. Kübler-Ross has made an important contribution by calling attention to the dying process and to the need for compassionate involvement, but the reliability and validity of her specific proposal require further investigation.

The developmental tasks of facing old age and death probably begin relatively early, although they grow more central over time in the ordinary life cycle. Little is known about children's understanding of death. Nagy's (1948, as cited in Kastenbaum and Costa, 1977) study of children from age three to age ten proposed three developmental stages. Children lack an appreciation of death as complete and final until they are about five years old: The dead are considered only less alive to them, and they have a notion that death might be reversible. During this first stage separation is the clearest concept. The second stage is characterized by the view of death as final but not inevitable: One might outwit it. In the final stage, beginning at age nine or ten, finality, inevitability, and personal mortality are comprehended. In their review of death perspectives, Kastenbaum and Costa (1977) noted evidence that cognitive development, rather than chronological age, helps predict children's understanding of death.

Turning to studies of older people, a common finding is that old people are more aware of death than are the young; that is, they report thinking about death more frequently (Jeffers and Verwoerdt, 1969; Cameron, Stewart, and Biber, 1973). But it is not clear, at least for the healthy aged, that such thoughts in any way reduce life's enjoyment or that they can be equated with *concern* about dying. Results of several studies indicate that only 10 to 30 percent of the elderly expressed fear of death (Jeffers and Verwoerdt, 1969). Those expressing fear tended to lack a religious orientation and experienced rejection and depression. More than death, older people feared prolonged illness; pain; loss of social role, self-determination, and dignity; and dependency. They worried about being a burden to others. Some viewed death in positive terms—as the time of meeting dead loved ones, of going home or back to God, or as a reward for living life well.

An individual's attitude towards death may be an extension of attitudes learned early in life. Support for this suggestion is provided by a study in which a number of variables were correlated with anxiety about death (Templer, Ruff, and Franks, 1971). It was found that mothers and fathers within families tended to hold similar views, and that there was a significant correlation between the degree of fear expressed by adolescents and the degree indicated by their same-sex parent. In contrast, no significant correlation was found between age and death anxiety. The finding indicates that fear of death is as great in young as in old people and suggests that parents in some way communicate their views to their children and thereby influence them.

How do the elderly adapt to being old and to impending death? Kastenbaum (1979) has observed that they draw on their past in several ways to adjust to their aging lives and to death.

1. *Validation* involves searching past experiences for competencies. Recalling earlier success can reassure individuals that they are capable of being successful in the present. Such personal validation is of special importance when people in the immediate environment lack knowledge of the older person's past.

2. *Boundary setting* refers to determining the aspects of the past that might better be set aside as belonging only to the past. The house in which children were reared, the shops that were visited, the coworker of many years ago, and memories of a dead spouse must all be dealt with. Is it better to retain them in active memory and meaning—or to set them aside in the service of the present? Kastenbaum believes that whatever the decision, much of the coping effort of old people who are in transition or crisis (e.g., moving to a new home) centers on ferreting out the answer to this question. Moreover, it is an intellectually and emotionally demanding task.

3. *Replaying* refers to the retelling of highly selective, emotionally-laden anecdotes and experiences. Young people, too, appear to replay favorite stories, but perhaps replaying increases with age partly because the wellspring of experience is deeper. Kastenbaum has noted that replaying seems dissociated from time:

> . . . we might compare replaying to a person reaching into a sort of personal juke-box where a few precious records or endless-reel tapes have been chosen from all the music heard over a lifetime. The date the recording was pressed hardly matters any more; it has some other quality that makes it important to the individual. (1979, p. 617)

> Replaying may enable the old person to be independent of scarce gratifications in the immediate environment. And it may serve as an alternative to being oriented to the future where little except death exists.

Butler (1964) has described the process of the *life review*, which consists of reminiscence of the past, particularly of unresolved conflicts. The life review is not an attempt to live in the past but is an effort to integrate experience and bring it into perspective. Butler has suggested that although reviewing life may not be positive for all (e.g., those who are guilt-ridden), it often facilitates an integration of personality and experience. It is perhaps partly through this process that individuals may, to recall Erikson's words, come to affirm their lives as the one and only life they could have had. Perhaps this leads to acceptance of and serenity toward what is yet to come—whether one believes it will be a true afterlife or a spiritual or physical union with the universe.

We think it is fitting to end this book with the story of one woman's death, who, in the eyes of her daughter, "did it exactly the way she had lived, with style and humor and incredible courage" (Williams, 1978, p. 161).

"I Want to Go Home": A Very Old Lady Dies in Style*   Nancy Williams

Anna Grace Péquignot died in 1976, age ninety-six. Nancy Williams wrote this account of her mother's brief final illness and death in a letter to her daughter Christina, who was living overseas.

Dearest Chris,

What I want you to know surely about Grandma is that her death was a triumph of spirit. We wished so much that you had been there so that you could have seen that for yourself. The boys didn't stay at the hospital to be dutiful, they really wanted to be there; nor were any of us depressed at watching her die. She did it exactly the way she had lived, with style and humor and incredible courage. I want to describe those hours to you because you belonged there. If it's too much, darling, just read it in bits.

Mother had the sense to phone me at twelve-thirty on Sunday afternoon, saying in a rather burbly voice that she hadn't been able to dial my number but had had to ask the operator, and that she was the most confused person in Ann Arbor. So we went right over. She was sitting in her chair in the living room and did seem confused and uncomfortable. Her first Grandma-like act was to refuse to let me feed her soup and toast or to have a tray on her lap. After she had eaten she said she needed to go to the bathroom and, thank you, she did not need us to help her with that either.

When she was through she allowed us to help her to bed. Daddy and I have the feeling that from that moment she turned things over to God and to other people; she'd done all she could and now it was up to oth-

ers. During the last month or so she had gradually and oh so reluctantly let go of the last of the duties that made life bearable to her: ironing for me, bringing over to Daddy her business matters, watering her plants. On the other hand, the preceding Friday night she had come over to supper all decked out in her shocking-pink sweater and skirt and matching hair ribbon, to help celebrate Rhys's being accepted into graduate school, and enjoyed her dry martini and shrimp salad and mince pie.

We phoned Dr. Payne to see if there was anything we could do to make Mother more comfortable; neither of us was particularly alarmed, feeling she was just fading a little more. We discussed asking her to come to our house but agreed to hang on as long as possible to everyone's desire to have her be in her own house, since Mother's independence was all-important to her. After Daddy had gone home to do some work, Mother said I should turn off the lights when I left, a typical energy-conserving remark. When I said I was staying, she protested.

I felt uneasy in the living room, so I sat beside her bed. She was able to talk, though with increasing difficulty, and her eyes were mostly closed. She said this prayer: "Dear Jesus, sweet Jesus, forgive me all my sins. Not my will, but thine be done. I'm not afraid to die. Dear God, let me go." Then she thanked Him for her children "and all the kind people who have helped me all my life." Later she seemed to think I'd said something about a "cardinal" when we'd talked of calling a priest. I said if we were going to try for a cardinal, we might as well shoot for the Pope. At which a nice smile went over her face.

Soon Dr. Payne arrived. After checking Mother he told me in his kind, plain way that she was very seriously ill, that she had congestive heart failure, probably renal failure

* From N. Williams, " 'I Want to Go Home': A Very Old Lady Dies in Style," in R. Gross, B. Gross, and S. Seidman (eds.), *The New Old: Struggling for Decent Aging* (Garden City, N.Y.: Anchor Press/Doubleday, 1978).

as well, quite possibly pneumonia. He added, "You know, she will be very mad at us if we bring her back." So I told him that we all wanted Mother to do what she most wanted now, to die as soon as possible, and that we wanted her to be comfortable. We decided that it wasn't feasible for me to try to care for her at home (her home), that nurses at the hospital would be able to move her, change her (renal failure), administer oxygen. After Dr. Payne had called an ambulance and left, I sat by Mother and she roused herself to say another prayer: "If I were to make my last statement, it would go like this. This is what it would be like. 'Dear Jesus, not my will but thine be done. Forgive me for my sins. And please, **please**, don't let me be too much trouble.' " At which, needless to say, I nearly dissolved, and kissed her and said she had never been a trouble. She looked at me and said, "Is this it?" I wish now I'd said that perhaps it was. I think I told her that I didn't know but I thought everything was going to be all right.

Rhys and young Lloyd arrived just before the ambulance. The five or six young men who came with the ambulance were just darling with Mother. They called her "Anna," which she might not have appreciated if she'd been her old self, one of them, "Anna dear," and they each described to her what they were about to do. I thought Mother by then did not hear or care much. I was wrong. She told the ambulance squad not to make too much commotion and alarm the other apartment dwellers, and not to use the siren, because there was enough noise pollution around already.

Then began the final eight hours. We got to the hospital at 6:25 P.M. Sunday, and Mother died at about one-fifty the next morning. As the four of us sat by Mother's bed, nurses administered oxygen and tried to make her a little more comfortable. She kept the plastic gizmo around her head and in her nostrils for an hour, maybe, then decided that was enough; every time any of us or a nurse would try to reinsert it, she would firmly, very firmly, remove it. About eight or

so, Dr. Payne came and said to forget it if she felt so strongly. Rhys holds that it wasn't just the discomfort, that she didn't want any delaying tactics.

One of the most wondrous moments was when the boys returned from making phone calls and I said, "Mother, Lloyd and Rhys are here now." She opened her eyes and said, "Thank you for coming to help me die." At which point Lloyd knelt down by her bed and kissed her hand and said, "I love you, Granny," and Rhys stood on the other side and held her other hand. And Mother smiled, quite fleetingly, but she smiled.

During Dr. Payne's visit, he sat by her bed, and she tried to talk to him. What finally came out after laborious minutes was, "I'll give up smoking if. . . ." Dr. Payne just sat there quietly, his chin on the bedrail, waiting, not trying to interpret, just waiting. Mother never did finish her sentence, but Dr. Payne told me the next day that he knew beyond a doubt that what she was trying to say was, "I'll stop smoking if you don't stop me from dying." A long and fond admirer of my mother in all her stubborn independence, he observed that he didn't consider her offer a very good bargain under the circumstances.

Then there was the time when Mother opened her eyes and said, "Am I dead?" And I said, "Not yet, Mom." At which point she said, with fierce intensity, "Oh, God." The boys both thought she looked beautiful. I think they hadn't seen her hair down in a long time; it was indeed very long. They said she looked like an American Indian and were especially moved when she asked whether she was dead, because an old Indian man in the movie **Little Big Man** had said just those words and looked just like her when he was dying and the rain had fallen on his face and roused him. Rhys told Mother how pretty she looked. Again that fleeting smile went across her face, and she blew him two kisses, that familiar ironic gesture of hers when somebody paid her a compliment.

When we made these little jokes we were pleased when Mother understood and smiled. But after a while I think we all sensed that perhaps we were pulling her back to life in the same way as the oxygen and that we needed to let her go. Afterward Lloyd quoted Ram Dass to the effect that when a person is dying it's important for him to know it's all right to let go, that he doesn't have to hang on.

A splendid episode: Mother had had the bedpan, but almost immediately afterward needed it again. She tried to tell us she wanted it by making the letter "p" with her index finger and thumb and the index finger of her other hand (either for "pot" or "pee"). When we didn't get it, she pointed to her crotch, and when we still didn't understand, she finally managed to really spit out, "P, as in Piss!" And when the nurses were putting the bedpan under her, she pulled down her hospital gown and whispered, "Modesty, you know." The boys loved that.

I guess the last little joke we had was when a nurse wiped Mother's lips with a cool cloth. She grimaced and drew back and my husband said quickly, "That's a dry martini, Bobby." The little smile appeared.

There isn't much more to tell. From time to time Mother would say, "Oh, God," as though pleading with him. At one point she said, "I want to go home." When I made

some feeble explanation about the hospital's greater comforts, she shook her head impatiently. And I belatedly knew what home she was talking about. Hallelujah! We all held her hands and stroked her hair and said, "Hi, Granny." About midnight the nurses moved her to a private room. About one o'clock Daddy and the boys left, to get some sleep before work the next day. I lay down on some put-together chairs, relieved that Mother seemed to be really resting for the first time. I could hear a little breath once in a while. After a few minutes a nurse came in, checked Mother's pulse, and said, "I think she's gone."

I just stayed there a bit, saying good-by. When a very brisk young night nurse appeared, I said, "What will you do with my mother's body tonight?" She replied, "The eye man will be here in fifteen minutes to remove her cornea and then we'll put her in the cooler till morning." Can you imagine? She should be held for a witness, as my mother used to say. I just packed up my things, pulled the sheet up around Mother (saying to myself that it was so damn hot in that hospital she'd probably enjoy being in the cooler), and went out.

SUMMARY   The study of adulthood is undergoing enormous expansion today in the disciplines of psychology, biology, sociology, medicine, and urban planning. *Gerontology* is the study of all facets of aging, while *geriatrics* focuses on the health problems of the elderly. A primary reason for the expansion of interest in adulthood and aging is the changing age structure of our society. Due to the lengthening of the average life span and the post-World War II baby boom, the average age of the population will continue to increase over the next decades.

Adulthood has frequently been cast in developmental stages or tasks. Havighurst's developmental tasks and Erikson's psychosocial stages are classic descriptions of adulthood. Drawing on their more recent research, Levinson and his colleagues and Gould have offered overviews of the adult years. In considering any of the changes that occur with age, the influence of *age norms* should be taken into account. The expectations society places on individuals on the basis of age act as guidelines for behavior and attitudes.

Biological decline begins at about thirty years of age but varies greatly with the different systems—for example, breathing capacity drops off relatively rapidly, whereas nerve conduction does not. Acute diseases decrease, but chronic ones increase. Individual variation is striking, as is the fact that the elderly are fairly optimistic about their health. Psychological factors undoubtedly play a role in the aging process, but much attention is being given to biological determinants.

Research is being conducted on age changes in basic intellectual, cognitive, motor, and learning abilities. Decrements in memory have been documented and appear to be caused by decline in information processing rather than in capacity of the sensory register, short-term, or long-term components of memory. Another well-documented age change is psychomotor slowing. Older people appear to require more time to make decisions and monitor motor movements, especially when the situation is complex and there is little time to prepare. Psychomotor slowing is less evident in those who are physically fit and have the opportunity to practice, whether in the laboratory or on the job. With our aging population, there is a great need to better understand age decrements in basic functioning.

Although we may marry for love in our culture, proximity and homogamy are influential in the selection of a mate. The divorce rate is high, but so is the rate at which remarriage occurs. Traditional expectation for marriage, adequate performance of marital roles, conformity of one mate to the other's expectations, and husband's status affect marital satisfaction. Satisfaction with marriage also fluctuates over time. Satisfaction appears high in the beginning years, gradually decreases until after the children have been launched, and then increases into the later years. Marital and family ties are particularly important to the elderly. Although many old people live alone today, they are connected to the web of family life.

The *climacteric* refers to changes that accompany the termination of the reproductive period in the female and the diminution of sexual activity in the male. It is not dramatic in males, although the time required for erections increases while the duration and force of ejaculation decreases. Several psychological variables have been implicated in male unresponsiveness. In females the climacteric, known as *menopause,* involves cessation of the menses and other biological change. Distress such as hot flashes and depression are reported in a minority of women. Estrogen therapy, which had been used widely is now used with caution. Studies indicate that sexual activity declines from early adulthood, but for many the late years of life are not sexless. In fact, biological change can be advantageous to the quality of sexual experience.

Mid-career changes occur among a small number of people. One of the factors in voluntary change is a poor match between personality and the job. Involuntary career change and reentrance of women into the workforce are other kinds of mid-career changes. Retirement can be viewed as an event, process, or social role. Variables important in people's reaction to retirement include the quality and quantity of leisure activities, attitudes toward retirement, and financial security.

Related to retirement is the question of optimal living conditions for the elderly. Cumming and Henry proposed that the elderly voluntarily withdraw from the social system, being preoccupied with themselves and feeling content with this situation. While not refuting the fact of withdrawal, others argue that it is forced upon the elderly and is not optimal. This contention is generally supported, but some people (i.e., those in poor health or those who have a history of dependency and passivity) may prefer disengagement. The same individual preference is displayed toward actual living conditions, and hard-and-fast rules cannot be made.

Although more people are living longer today than previously, death in adulthood becomes increasingly probable after thirty years, due to both intrinsic and extrinsic factors. According to Kübler-Ross, many terminally ill patients experience death in five stages: denial, anger, bargaining, depression, and acceptance. Little is known about childrens' understanding of death, although one investigator has suggested three stages of comprehension. Healthy old people tend to think more about death than do the young, but they are not necessarily concerned with or fearful of it. They appear to be more concerned with illness, pain, and dependency. Some view death positively. The elderly often draw on their past when trying to adapt to the last years of life, using techniques such as validity seeking, boundary setting, replaying, and and the life review.

Glossary

A

acceptance-rejection A dimension of parental behavior that refers to the respect and love, or lack of both of them, that parents feel for their children.

accommodation Piaget's term for the act of improving one's cognitive model of the world by adjusting it to external reality.

achievement Any action directed at gaining approval or avoiding disapproval from oneself or from others for competence in performance where public standards of excellence are applicable.

afterbirth The placental membranes, which are discharged after the fetus has emerged from the uterus.

aggression Action that brings, or has the potential to cause, discomfort to someone else. The type of aggression a person displays and his or her ability to control such action change in important ways with age and experience.

allele Each member of a gene pair is called an allele.

altruism Unselfish action that is not motivated by self-interest.

amnion A thin membrane that forms a sac around the embryo.

androgyny Exhibiting both stereotypic masculine and feminine behaviors.

anoxia A lack of oxygen, occurring at birth if the umbilical cord fails to provide oxygen until the newborn begins to use his or her lungs.

assimilation Piaget's term for the interpretation of reality in terms of one's internal model of the world constructed from previous knowledge.

attachment The affectionate, reciprocal relationship that is formed between one individual and another.

B

blastocyst The hollow ball of cells that is the result of the zygote multiplying by mitosis. The inner mass of the blastocyst is the developing individual, while its outer layer will develop into the support system of the fetus.

breech position An abnormal birth position, with the fetus's buttocks emerging first instead of the normal head first delivery.

C

Caesarean section The surgical removal of the fetus through the uterine and abdominal walls.

case study The systematic description of the behavior of a single individual.

cephalocaudal growth Early development that starts from the cephalic (head) region and proceeds to the caudal (tail) region.

chorion The outer embryonic membrane that is associated with the formation of the placenta.

classical conditioning A learning process whereby an individual begins to respond to a stimulus (CS) that had not previously elicited a response, as a result of repeated pairing with a stimulus (UCS) that does produce the response.

climacteric The biological and psychic changes that accompany the termination of the reproductive period in the female and the normal diminution of sexual activity in the male.

conception The union of ovum and sperm resulting in the creation of the zygote.

correlation Pertains to the relationship between two or more factors or variables.

correlational method A method used to investigate the existing relationship between two or more events or variables. This method does not permit causal inferences to be drawn directly, and events or experiences are not manipulated.

critical period A very short span of time in the early life of an organism during which the organism may be especially sensitive to specific influence.

cross-sectional study A study of a group of individuals of various ages at a specific point in time to determine developmental changes.

crystallized intelligence The ability to understand relationships, make jugements, and solve problems based on cultural information and skills.

cultural norms Standards of a culture by which behaviors are judged.

D

dependent variable A measurable aspect of the subject's behavior that may change as the independent variable is altered.

developmental norms The standards by which the development of skills, knowledge, and social behavior among children is judged.

differentiation The progressive refinement of motor development, usually in reference to infants or young children.

discrimination The process by which a person learns to respond to a specific stimulus and not to other, similar ones.

dishabituation The recovery of a reflexive response to an original stimulus after a new stimulus has been presented is called dishabituation.

dizygotic twins Twins that result when two ova are released and fertilized by two sperm at approximately the same time.

DNA (Deoxyribonucleic Acid) DNA carries genetic information in chromosomes from generation to generation.

dominant gene The dominant gene will display itself in an offspring when paired with a dissimilar form for a particular characteristic.

Down's syndrome A chromosomal aberration resulting in moderate to severe retardation. It occurs in about one in every 500–600 births. Most Down syndrome victims have an extra, free-floating #21 chromosome.

E

ego One of Freud's three structures of personality, the ego appears during the first year of life in response to the infant not being able to have everything he or she wants, and is the practical, rational component of personality.

encopresis Inappropriate defecation.

enuresis An inability to control one's bladder functions; bedwetting.

erythroblastosis A condition occurring when there is Rh incompatibility between a mother and her offspring. It is the actual destruction of the offspring's red blood cells by antibodies produced in the mother's system in reaction to the foreign protein (Rh factor) that is threatening her system.

ethology The study of animal behavior, often aimed at developing an understanding of social behavior. Its basic premise is that all animals, including humans, possess species-wide characteristics that are the foundation for the development of social behaviors.

experimental method A method of developmental research, it involves the manipulation of various treatments, circumstances, or events to which a person is exposed, allowing inferences as to causal relationships between such manipulations and subsequent behavior.

extinction The gradual diminution of a conditioned response, resulting in the eventual elimination of the response.

F

fetal alcohol syndrome The pattern of congenital malformation of the fetus due to daily consumption of three or more drinks by the mother during pregnancy. The greatest risk occurs during the twelfth to the eighteenth weeks of pregnancy and also during the last trimester.

fetus The name assigned to the organism created by the union of a sperm and an ovum from about the eighth week after conception until birth.

fixation Freud used this term to describe a child's inability to move from one stage of development to the next. He posited that frustration, overindulgence, or a combination of the two result in fixation.

fluid intelligence The capacity to perceive relationships and strategies; to have the capacity to deal with any problem.

G

gametes The reproductive cells; the ova in the female, the sperm in the male.

gene Genes, composed of DNA, are centrally involved in protein synthesis and act as blueprints for development.

generalization A situation in which one stimulus can be substituted for another and still produce the same response.

genotype The entire genetic endowment of an individual.

grammar The study of the rules followed in producing "permissible language constructions."

geriatrics The field of study that focuses on understanding and treating problems of the elderly.

gerontology The study of all facets of aging.

H

habituation After repeated presentation of the same stimulus the initial reflexive response will diminish and eventually disappear. This adjustment to a stimulus is known as habituation.

handedness Also known as laterality, this term refers to the preference for using one hand over the other.

heterozygous This term is used to describe gene pairs whose alleles are different.

hierarchic integration As a result of differentiation, an infant is able to integrate individual actions into more complex and sophisticated patterns of behavior; this process is known as hierarchic integration.

homozygous A term used to describe gene pairs whose alleles are the same.

hyperactivity Excessive and persistent overactivity, especially in structured situations that demand more control.

I

id One of three structures of personality as set forth by Freud. He defined the id as a reservoir of primitive instincts and drives that is present at birth. It is the force that presses for immediate gratification of bodily needs and wants.

identity Sameness, oneness, or the distinguishing attribute of personality of an individual. A subjective sense of continuity and sameness.

imprinting An innate, instinctual form of learning that takes place during a critical period in the individual's life. It often refers to the following response in animals.

inbreeding Used in animal studies, it refers to the mating of related animals with the intent, over generations, of producing a ''pure'' strain in which the animals are genetically alike.

independent variable In an experimental situation the independent variable is a condition created by the experimenter or a manipulation of the subject by the experimenter.

infantile autism A psychosis among children that is characterized by extreme aloneness and a preoccupation of sameness in the environment.

intelligence quotient (IQ) A number representing intellectual ability. The ratio of an individual's mental age to his or her chronological age, multiplied by 100. It is often calculated by statistical computation.

intersensory behavior The interaction of two or more sensory systems.

introversion Introversion and extroversion are directly opposite approaches to the social environment. An introvert is extremely shy and anxious in novel social situations and is always ready to withdraw from people. An extrovert is friendly, at ease among people, and is ready to seek out others in social situations.

J

juvenile delinquency Acts committed by youth, under sixteen or eighteen years of age, that are not in keeping with the law.

K

Kleinfelter's syndrome A chromosomal aberration found exclusively in phenotypic males. Such males generally have an additional X chromosome (although some have more than one additional X chromosome), and suffer from atypical sexual development and skeletomuscular abnormalities. About 25 percent are of below normal intelligence.

L

labor The process by which the fetus is expelled from its mother's uterus, occurring within a few hours to a few weeks after lightening.

learning This term refers to all those processes by which an activity originates or is changed through reacting to an encountered situation.

lightening The beginning of the biological preparation for birth. Toward the end of gestation the head of the fetus turns down, relieving the pressure against the mother's diaphragm.

longitudinal study The process of observing or testing an individual or individuals at different points in their lives, noting stability and change in their behavior and characteristics over time.

M

maturation The changes that take place more or less inevitably in all normal members of a species so long as they are provided with an environment suitable to the species.

meiosis The specialized cell division of the reproductive cells that occurs during cell maturation resulting in the gametes having half of the number of chromosomes as other cells.

mental age (MA) An individual's mental age is equivalent to the chronological age of those whose performance that he or she equals.

mental retardation Significantly subaverage general intellectual functioning existing concurrently with deficits in adaptive behavior.

mitosis Typical cell division in which chromosomes in each cell duplicate before the cell divides into two identical daughter cells.

monozygotic twins   Twins created by the joining of one ovum and one sperm, with the resulting mass then dividing into two zygotes.

morphology   The study of the formation of words.

N

neonate   The name given to a newborn from birth to about one month of age.

O

observational learning   Such learning is the result of viewing the behavior of others, presented both live and symbolically.

öogenesis   The maturation of ova.

operant conditioning   This type of learning focuses on the consequences (rewards or punishments) that follow behavior.

ova   Egg cells produced in the ovaries that combine with sperm to produce the zygote.

P

parturition   The technical term for birth.

perception   The integration of impulses from the different sense organs and the comparison of these impulses with previous input; the selection, organization, and modification of specific input by the brain.

permissiveness-restrictiveness   A dimension of parental behavior that describes the range to which parents permit their offspring autonomy and freedom in their actions.

phenotype   The outward manifestation of one's genetic makeup.

phonemes   Single sounds grouped together; the raw materials of speech.

placenta   A structure that develops in the uterus following conception through which nutrients and wastes are exchanged between mother and fetus.

preferential looking   The preference an infant might exhibit for one object over another when two or more objects are presented. Preference is displayed by looking at one object and not the other, or by looking for a longer period of time at one than the other.

preformation   An archaic theory that assumed the adult was preformed in the gametes.

premature   A birth is considered premature when it occurs before thirty-seven weeks of gestation.

proximodistal growth   Growth that occurs from the center axis outward. It is exemplified in pre-

natal development by the growth of the chest, trunk, and internal organs before the growth of the limbs, fingers, and toes.

psychosis   Severely disturbed behavior in which distortions in the rate, timing, and sequence of many basic psychological processes are evident.

R

range of reaction   The broadest possible expression of a genotype. The range of reaction may be broad or narrow, depending on the particular genotype and the environment.

recapitulation   The belief that each individual's development (ontogeny) repeats the development of its species (phylogeny).

recessive gene   When dissimilar genes for a characteristic have been transmitted to an offspring, the recessive form will not be displayed. A recessive trait will only appear in an offspring if both parents have transmitted it.

reflex action   Unlearned and automatic specific responses to specific stimulation. Close to 100 reflexes have been identified.

reliability   This term refers to the consistency of a test.

representative sample   A group that accurately and proportionately displays the characteristics to which generalizations are to be made.

Rh factor   This protein, named after the Rhesus monkey in which it was first discovered, is found in the blood and is inherited by 85 percent of the general population. If a mother and offspring display Rh incompatibility, complications can develop.

rhogam   A substance that can prevent erythroblastosis formation in the mother.

S

scheme   For Piaget, a scheme is the mental structure underlying a sequence of behaviors.

schizophrenia   A psychosis that is characterized by disturbances in reality relationships and concept formations, as well as affective, behavioral, and intellectual deficits. Schizophrenics may experience delusions and hallucinations, communicate in a disorganized way, and display inappropriate emotions.

secular growth trend   Refers to the trend for people to be larger and to mature earlier than they did in former eras.

self-control   Self-control has been characterized as one's ability to rise above the immediate pressures of a situation and to be able to avoid succumbing to an immediate impulse.

semantics The study of the relationship of language to meaning.

sensation Sensation involves stimulation of the sensory receptors by physical energies from the internal and external environment.

sex identity A self-awareness of being of one sex; an internal experience.

sex role The behaviors and roles that society prescribes for the sexes.

socialization The processes by which individuals acquire the knowledge, skills, attitudes, and values of the society or subgroups of the society to which they belong.

society A group of people who live together and share common institutions, traditions, activities, behaviors, interests, beliefs, and values.

socioeconomic status (SES) This is indicated by occupation, income, and education; such characteristics define our stratified society.

spermatogenesis The maturation of the sperm.

superego The personality component, posited by Freud, emerging during the third or fourth year of life. It is the ''moral agent,'' which develops as the child identifies with its same-sex parent and begins to absorb society's standards of right and wrong.

syntax The aspect of grammar that concerns itself with how words are combined into phrases and sentences.

T

teratology The name given to the study of malformations and other deviations from normal prenatal development.

Turner's syndrome Sex chromosome aberration occurring in phenotypic females. Most frequently the female has a single X chromosome (XO). Mental deficiencies occur in about 20 percent of the cases. Other abnormalities include a lack of ovarian tissue, failure to develop secondary sex characteristics, short stature, and deformity of the neck and forearm.

U

umbilical cord The ''lifeline'' comprised of arteries and veins that serves as a transport system between the developing child and his or her mother.

V

validity The degree to which a test actually measures what it purports to measure.

visual acuity The relative ability of individuals to detect both small stimuli and small details of large visual patterns.

visual constancy The phenomenon of seeing certain aspects of the environment as constant despite changes that may occur at the retina.

visual fixation Visual fixation is determined by whether or not an infant will look at an object presented to him or her, and has been used to measure whether or not the infant sees the stimulus.

Z

zygote The cell mass that is the result of the union of an ovum and a sperm.

References

Abel, E. L. The relationship between cannabis and violence: A review. *Psychological Bulletin,* 1977, **84,** 193–211.

Abel, E. L. Fetal alcohol syndrome: Behavioral teratology. *Psychological Bulletin,* 1980, **87,** 29–50.

Abrahams, J. P., & Birren, J. E. Reaction time as a function of age and behavioral predisposition to coronary heart disease. *Journal of Gerontology,* 1973, **28,** 471–478.

Abravanel, E. Developmental changes in the inter-sensory patterning of space. *Proceedings of the 75th Annual Convention of the American Psychological Association,* 1967, **2,** 161–162.

Achenbach, T. *Developmental psychopathology.* New York: Ronald Press, 1974.

Adelson, J. The development of ideology in adolescence. In D. E. Dragastin and G. H. Elder, Jr., eds., *Adolescence in the life cycle: Psychological change and social context.* New York: John Wiley, 1975.

Adelson, J., & O'Neil, R. The development of political thought in adolescence: A sense of community. *Journal of Personality and Social Psychology,* 1966, **4,** 295–308.

Adesso, V. J., Vargas, J. M., & Siddall, J. W. The role of awareness in reducing nail-biting behavior. *Behavior Therapy,* 1979, **10,** 148–154.

Aiken, L. R. Verbal factors and mathematics: A review of research. *Journal for Research in Mathematics Education,* 1971, **2,** 304–313.

Aiken, L. R. Biodata correlates of attitudes towards mathematics in three age and two sex groups. *School Science and Mathematics,* 1972, **72,** 386–395.

Ainsworth, M. D. S. Further research into the adverse effects of maternal deprivation. In J. Bowlby, ed., *Child care and the growth of love.* Baltimore: Penguin, 1965.

Ainsworth, M. D. S. *Infancy in Uganda.* Baltimore, Johns Hopkins Press, 1967.

Ainsworth, M. D. S. Infant development and mother-infant interaction among Ganda and American families. In P. H. Leiderman, S. R. Tulkin, and A. Rosenfeld, eds., *Culture and infancy: Variations in the human experience.* New York: Academic Press, 1977, pp. 119–149.

Ainsworth, M. D. S., & Bell, S. M. Some contemporary patterns of mother-infant interaction in the feeding situation. In J. A. Ambrose, ed., *Stimulation in early infancy.* London: Academic Press, 1969.

Ainsworth, M. D. S., & Bell, S. M. Attachment, exploration, and separation: Illustrated by the behavior of one-year-olds in a strange situation. *Child Development,* 1970. **41,** 49–67.

Ainsworth, M. D. S., & Bell, S. M. Mother-infant interaction and the development of competence. In K. Connolly and J. Bruner eds., *The growth of competence.* London: Academic Press, 1974.

Ainsworth, M. D. S., Bell, S. M., & Stayton, D. J. Infant-mother attachment and social development: 'Socialisation' as a product of reciprocal responsiveness to signals. In M. P. M. Richards, ed., *The integration of a child into a social world.* New York: Cambridge University Press, 1974.

Ainsworth, M. D. S., & Wittig, B. A. Attachment and exploratory behavior of one-year-olds in a strange situation. In B. M. Foss, ed., *Determinants of infant behavior.* London: Methuen, 1969, pp. 111–136.

Albert, R. S. Toward a behavioral definition of genius. *American Psychologist,* 1975, **30,** 140–151.

Aldous, J. The search for alternatives: Parental behaviors and children's original problem solutions. *Journal of Marriage and the Family,* 1975, **37,** 711–722.

Aleksandrowicz, M. K., & Aleksandrowicz, D. R. Obstetrical pain-relieving drugs as predictors of infant behavior variability. *Child Development,* 1974, **45,** 935–945.

All about that baby. *Newsweek,* August 7, 1978.

Alpern, G. D. The failure of a nursery school enrichment program for culturally disadvantaged children. *American Journal of Orthopsychiatry,* 1966, **36,** 244–245.

Altus, W. D. Birth order and its sequele. *Science,* 1965, **151,** 44–49.

Ames, L. B. Predictive value of infant behavior examination. In J. Hellmuth, ed., *Exceptional infant.* New York: Brunner/Mazel, 1967, pp. 207–239.

Amsterdam, B. Mirror self-image reactions before age two. *Developmental Psychobiology,* 1972, **5,** 297–305.

Anastasi, A. Heredity, environment, and the question "How?" *Psychological Review,* 1958, **65,** 197–208.

Anastasi, A. *Psychological testing.* New York: Macmillan, 1968.

Anderson, L. D. The predictive value of infant tests in relation to intelligence at 5 years. *Child Development,* 1939, **10,** 202–212.

Anderson, R. C., & Anderson, R. M. Transfer of originality training. *Journal of Educational Psychology,* 1963, **54,** 300–304.

Anthony, E. J. An experimental approach to the psychopathology of childhood: Encopresis. *British Journal of Medical Psychology,* 1957, **30,** 146–175.

Anthony, E. J.   The behavior disorders of childhood. In P. H. Mussen, ed., *Carmichael's manual of child psychology.* New York: John Wiley, 1970, **2**, pp. 667–764.

Antonovsky, A.   Class and the chance for life. In L. Rainwater, ed., *Social problems and public policy.* Chicago: Aldine, 1974, pp. 170–179.

Arasteh, J. D.   Creativity and related processes in the young child: A review of the literature. *Journal of Genetic Psychology,* 1968, **112**, 77–108.

Aries, P.   *Centuries of childhood,* trans. R. Baldick. New York: Knopf, 1962.

Armentrout, J. A., & Burger, G. K.   Children's reports of parental child-rearing behaviors at five grade levels. *Developmental Psychology,* 1972, **7**, 44–48.

Aronfreed, J.   *Conduct and conscience.* New York: Academic Press, 1968.

Aronson, E., & Rosenbloom, S.   Space perception in early infancy: Perception within a common auditory-visual space. *Science,* 1971, **172**, 1161–1163.

Asher, R. A.   The influence of sampling and comparison processes on the development of communication effectiveness. Paper given at meeting of American Psychological Association, September, 1972.

Ashton, B. G.   *Genes, chromosomes and evolution.* London: Longsman, Green, & Co., 1967.

Ashton, P. T.   The role of the attachment bond in effective parenting. In J. H. Stevens Jr. and M. Mathews, eds., *Mother/child, father/child relationships.* Washington, D.C.: The National Association for the Education of Young Children, 1978, pp. 31–50.

Ashton, R.   The state variable in neonatal research: A review. *Merrill-Palmer Quarterly,* 1973, **19**, 3–20.

Ashton, R.   Infant states and stimulation. *Developmental Psychology,* 1976, **12**, 569–570.

Aslin, R. N. & Banks, M. S.   Early visual experience in humans: Evidence for a critical period in the development of binocular vision. In H. L. Pick, H. W. Leibowitz, J. E. Singer, A. Steinschneider, and H. W. Stevenson, eds., *Psychology: From research to practice.* New York: Plenum, 1978.

Atchley, R. C.   *The social forces in later life.* Belmont, Ca.: Wadsworth, 1972.

Ausubel, D. P.   *Theory and problems of adolescent development.* New York: Grune & Stratton, 1954.

Ausubel, F., Beckwith, J., & Janssen, K.   The politics of genetic engineering: Who decides who's defective? *Psychology Today,* June, 1974, 30–43.

Aviram, A., & Milgram, R. M.   Dogmatism, locus of control and creativity in children educated in the Soviet Union, the United States, and Israel. *Psychological Reports,* 1977, **40**, 27–34.

Axline, V. M.   *Play therapy.* Boston: Houghton Mifflin, 1947.

Azrin, N. H., & Lindsley, O. R.   The reinforcement of cooperation between children. *Journal of Abnormal and Social Psychology,* 1956, **52**, 100–102.

Bach, G.   Father fantasies and father typing in father-separated children. *Child Development,* 1946, **17**, 63–80.

Bachrach, R., Huesmann, L. R., & Peterson, R. A.   The relation between locus of control and the development of moral judgment. *Child Development,* 1977, **48**, 1340–1352.

Badaines, J.   Identification, imitation, and sex role preference in father-present and father-absent black and chicano boys. *Journal of Psychology,* 1976, **92**, 15–24.

Badger, E.   The infant stimulation/mother training project. In B. M. Caldwell and S. J. Steadman, eds., *Infant education: A guide for helping handicapped children in the first three years.* New York: Walker, 1977.

Baer, D. M., Peterson, R. F., & Sherman, J. A.   The development of imitation by reinforcing behavioral similarity to a model. *Journal of the Experimental Analysis of Behavior,* 1967, **10**, 405–416.

Baer, D. M., Rowbury, T. G., & Goetz, E. M.   Behavioral traps in the preschool: A proposal for research. In A. D. Pick, ed., *Minnesota symposia on child psychology,* **10**. Minneapolis: University of Minnesota Press, 1976, 3–27.

Baer, D. M., & Sherman, J. A.   Reinforcement control of generalized imitation in young children. *Journal of Experimental Child Psychology,* 1964, **1**, 37–49.

Bakan, D.   Adolescence in America: From idea to social fact. *Daedalus,* 1971, **100**, 979–995.

Baldwin, A. L.   *Theories of child development.* New York: John Wiley, 1967.

Baldwin, A. L., Kalhorn, J., & Breese, F. H.   Patterns of parent behavior. *Psychological Monographs,* 1945, **58**, No. 3.

Baltes, P. B., Reese, H. W., & Lipsitt, L. P.   Life-span developmental psychology. *Annual Review of Psychology,* 1980, **31**, 65–110.

Baltes, P. B., & Schaie, K. W.   Aging and IQ: The myth of the twilight years. *Psychology Today,* March, 1974, 35–38, 40.

Baltes, P. B., & Schaie, K. W.   On the plasticity of intelligence in adulthood and old age; Where Horn and Donaldson fail. *American Psychologist,* 1976, **31**, 720–725.

Bandura. A.   The stormy decade: Fact or fiction? *Psychology in the schools,* 1964, **1**, 224–231.

Bandura, A.   Influence of models' reinforcement contingencies on the acquisition of imitative responses. *Journal of Personality and Social Psychology,* 1965, **1**, 589–595.

Bandura, A.   Social-learning theory of identificatory processes. In D. A. Goslin, ed., *Handbook of socialization theory and research,* Chicago: Rand McNally, 1969, pp. 213–262.

Bandura, A.   *Social learning theory.* Englewood Cliffs, N.J.: Prentice-Hall, Inc., 1977.

Bandura, A., & Mischel, W.   Modification of self-imposed delay of reward through exposure to live and symbolic models. *Journal of Personality and Social Psychology,* 1965, **2**, 698–705.

Bandura, A., & Perloff, B.   Relative efficacy of self-monitored and externally imposed reinforcement systems. *Journal of Personality and Social Psychology,* 1967, **7**, 111–116.

Bandura, A., & Walters, R. H.   *Adolescent aggression.* New York: Ronald Press, 1959.

Bandura, A., & Walters, R. H.   *Social learning and personality development.* New York: Holt, Rinehart & Winston, 1963.

Banks, M. S., Aslin, R. N., & Letson, R. D.   Sensitive period for the development of human binocular vision. *Science,* 1975, **190**, 675–677.

Bardwick, J. M.   *In transition.* New York: Holt, Rinehart and Winston, 1979.

Barkley, R. A.   Recent developments in research on hyperactive children. *Journal of Pediatric Psychology,* 1978, **3**, 158–163.

Barnett, C. R., Leiderman, P. H., Grobstein, R., & Klaus, M.

Neonatal separation: The maternal side of interactional deprivation. *Pediatrics*, 1970, **45**, 197–205.

Barrett, B. H. Behavior modification in the home: Parents adapt laboratory-developed tactics to bowel-train a 5½ year-old. *Psychotherapy: Theory, Research, and Practice*, 1969, **6**, 172–176.

Barry, W. A. Marriage research and conflict: An integrative review. *Psychological Bulletin*, 1970, **73**, 41–54.

Bateson, P. P. G. Imprinting and the development of preferences. In A. Ambrose, ed., *Stimulation in early infancy*. New York: Academic Press, 1969.

Battle, E., & Lacey, B. A. Context for hyperactivity in children over time. *Child Development*, 1972, **43**, 757–772.

Bauer, D. H. An exploratory study of developmental changes in children's fears. *Journal of Child Psychology and Psychiatry*, 1976, **17**, 69–74.

Bauer, E. E. Suggested curriculum for educable mentally retarded children. Unpublished paper, Indiana University, 1967.

Bayley, N. On the growth of intelligence. *American Psychologist*, 1955, **10**, 805–818.

Bayley, N. Research in child development: A longitudinal perspective. *Merrill-Palmer Quarterly of Behavior and Development*, 1965, **11**, 184–190.

Bayley, N. Development of mental abilities. In P. H. Mussen, ed., *Carmichael's manual of child psychology*. New York: John Wiley, 1970, **1**, 1163–1209.

Bayley, N., & Schaefer, E. S. Correlations of maternal and child behaviors with the development of mental abilities: Data from the Berkeley Growth Study. *Monographs of the Society for Research in Child Development*, 1964, **29** (6, Whole No. 97).

Beaman, A. L., Klentz, B., Diener, E., & Svanum, S. Self-awareness and transgression in children: Two field studies. *Journal of Personality and Social Psychology*, 1980.

Becker, W. C. Consequences of parental discipline. In M. L. Hoffman and L. W. Hoffman, eds., *Review of child development research*, Vol. 1. New York: Russell Sage Foundation, 1964.

Becker, W. C. Teaching reading and language to the disadvantaged—What we have learned from field research. *Harvard Educational Review*, 1977, **47**, 518–543.

Beckwith, L. Relationships between infants' social behavior and their mothers' behavior. *Child Development*, 1972, **43**, 397–411.

Beeghley, L. *Social stratification in America*. Santa Monica, Ca.: Goodyear, 1978.

Beilin, H. Learning and operational convergence in logical thought development. *Journal of Experimental Child Psychology*, 1965, **2**, 317–339.

Beintema, D. J., & Prechtl, H. F. R. A neurological study of newborn infants. Clinics in Developmental Medicine, No. 28. Spastics International Medical Publications in association with William Heinemann Medical Books Ltd., London, 1968.

Bell, R. Q. Stimulus control of parent or caretaker behavior by offspring. *Developmental Psychology*, 1971, **4**, 63–72.

Bell, S. M., & Ainsworth, M. D. S. Infant crying and maternal responsiveness. *Child Development*, 1972, **43**, 1171–1190.

Belmont, L., & Marolla, F. A. Birth order, family size, and intelligence. *Science*, 1973, **182**, 1096–1101.

Bem, S. L. The measurement of psychological androgyny. *Journal of Consulting and Clinical Psychology*, 1974, **42**, 155–162.

Bem, S. L. On the utility of alternative procedures for assessing psychological androgyny. *Journal of Consulting and Clinical Psychology*, 1977, **45**, 196–205.

Bench, J., & Vass, A. Fetal audiometry. *Lancet*, 1970, **1**, 91–92.

Benda, C. E., Squires, N. D., Ogonik, N. J., & Wise, R. Personality factors in mild mental retardation: Part I. Family background and sociocultural patterns. *American Journal of Mental Deficiency*, 1963, **68**, 24–40.

Bender, L. Childhood schizophrenia: Clinical study of one hundred schizophrenic children. *American Journal of Orthopsychiatry*, 1947, **17**, 40–46.

Bender, L. The family patterns of 100 schizophrenic children observed at Bellevue, 1935–1952. *Journal of Autism and Childhood Schizophrenia*, 1974, **4**, 279–292.

Benedict, R. Continuities and discontinuities in cultural conditioning. *Psychiatry*, 1938, **1**, 161–167.

Bereiter, C., & Engelmann, S. *Teaching disadvantaged children in the preschool.* Englewood Cliffs, N.J.: Prentice-Hall, Inc., 1966.

Berko, J., & Brown, R. Psycholinguistic research methods. In P. H. Mussen, ed., *Handbook of research methods in child development*. New York: John Wiley, 1960, pp. 517–557.

Berkowitz, L., & Connor, W. H. Success, failure and social responsibility. *Journal of Personality and Social Psychology*, 1966, **4**, 664–669.

Berlyne, D. E. Children's reasoning and thinking. In P. H. Mussen, ed., *Carmichael's manual of child psychology*. New York: John Wiley, 1970, **1**, 939–981.

Bernard, G., & Sontag, L. W. Foetal reactivity to tonal stimulation: A preliminary report. *Journal of Genetic Psychology*, 1947, **70**, 205–210.

Bernard, J. *The future of marriage.* New York: Bantam, 1973.

Bernstein, B. Linguistic codes, hesitation phenomena and intelligence. *Language and Speech*, 1962, **5**, 31–46. (a)

Bernstein, B. Social class, linguistic codes and grammatical elements. *Language and Speech*, 1962, **5**, 221–240. (b)

Berscheid, E., & Walster, E. Physical attractiveness. In L. Berkowitz, ed., *Advances in experimental social psychology*. New York: Academic Press, 1974.

Bettelheim, B. *The empty fortress.* New York: Macmillan, 1966.

Bettelheim, B. Where self begins. *New York Times*, February 12, 1967.

Bettelheim, B. *The children of the dream: Communal childrearing and American education.* New York: Macmillan, 1969.

Bijou, S. W., & Baer, D. M. *Child development* (Vol. 2). New York: Appleton-Century-Crofts, 1965.

Bijou, S. W., Birnbrauer, J. S., Kidder, J. D., & Tague, C. Programmed instruction as an approach to teaching reading, writing, and arithmetic to retarded children. *Psychological Record*, 1966, **16**, 505–522.

Biller, H. B. A note on father absence and masculine development in lower class Negro and white boys. *Child Development*, 1968, **39**, 1003–1006.

Biller, H. B. Father dominance and sex-role development in kindergarten age boys. *Developmental Psychology*, 1969, **1**, 87–94.

Biller, H. B. Paternal and sex-role factors in cognitive and academic functioning. In *Nebraska Symposium of Motivation*, J. K. Cole and R. Dienstbier, eds., Lincoln, Neb.: University of Nebraska Press, 1974.

Birch, H. G., & Belmont, L. Auditory-visual integration, intelligence and reading ability in school children. *Perceptual and Motor Skills*, 1965, **20**, 295–305.

Birch, H. G., & Lefford, A. Intersensory development in children. *Monographs of the Society for Research in Child Development*, 1963, **28**, Whole No. 89.

Birch, H. G., & Lefford, A. Visual differentiation, intersensory integration and voluntary motor control. *Monographs of the Society for Research in Child Development*, 1967, **32**, Serial No. 110.

Birns, B. Individual differences in human neonates' responses to stimulation. *Child Development*, 1965, **36**, 249–256.

Birns, B. The emergence and socialization of sex differences in the earliest years. *Merrill-Palmer Quarterly*, 1976, **22**, 229–254.

Birns, B., Blank, M., Bridger W. H., & Escalona, S. Behavioral inhibition in neonates produced by auditory stimuli. *Child Development*, 1965, **36**, 639–645.

Birren, J. E. *The psychology of aging*. Englewood Cliffs, N.J.: Prentice-Hall, Inc., 1964.

Birren, J. E. Translation in gerontology—from lab to life, psychophysiology and speed of response. *American Psychologist*, 1974, **29**, 808–815.

Birren, J. E., Butler, R. N., Greenhouse, S. W., Sokoloff, L., & Yarrow, M., eds., *Human aging: A biological and behavioral study*. Public Health Service Publication No. 986. Washington, D.C.: U.S. Government Printing Office, 1963.

Blanchard, R., & Biller, H. B. Father availability and academic performance among third-grade boys. *Developmental Psychology*, 1971, **4**, 301–305.

Blau, P. M., Gustad, J. W., Jessor, R., Parnes, H. S., & Wilcock, R. C. Occupational choice: A conceptual framework. In D. G. Zytowski, ed., *Vocational behavior: Reading in theory and research*. New York: Holt, Rinehart and Winston, 1968, pp. 358–370.

Blau, T. H. Torque and schizophrenic vulnerability. *American Psychologist*, 1977, **32**, 997–1005.

Blehar, M. C., Lieberman, A. F., Ainsworth, M. D. S. Early face-to-face interaction and its relation to later infant-mother attachment. *Child Development*, 1977, **48**, 182–194.

Block, J. Debatable conclusions about sex differences. *Contemporary Psychology*, 1976, **21**, 517–522.

Block, J. H. Conceptions of sex role: Some cross-cultural and longitudinal perspectives. *American Psychologist*, 1973, **28**, 512–526.

Bloom, K., & Esposito, A. Social conditioning and its proper control procedures. *Journal of Experimental Child Psychology*, 1975, **19**, 209–222.

Bloom, L. M. *Language development: Form and function in emerging grammars*. Cambridge, Mass.: M.I.T. Press, 1970.

Bloom, L. M. *One word at a time: The use of single word utterances before syntax*. The Hague: Mouton Publishers, 1973.

Bloom, L. M., Lightbown, P., & Hood, L. Structure and variation in child language. *Monographs of the Society for Research in Child Development*, 1975, **40** (Serial No. 160).

Blos, P. *On adolescence*. New York: Free Press, 1962.

Blum, J. E., Jarvik, L. F., & Clark, E. T. Rate of change on selective tests of intelligence: A twenty year longitudinal study. *Journal of Gerontology*, 1970, **25**, 171–176.

Blum, L. Educating college women in mathematics. Paper presented at the conference "Educating Women for Science: A Continuous Spectrum," Mills College, 1976.

Blum, R. H. & Associates. *Students and drugs*. San Francisco: Jossey-Bass, 1969, **2**.

Blumberg, M. L. Psychopathology of the abusing parent. *American Journal of Psychotherapy*, 1974, **28**, 21–29.

Bond, E. K. Perception of form by the human infant. *Psychological Bulletin*, 1972, **77**, 225–245.

Bornstein, M. H., Kessen, W., & Weiskopf, S. Color vision and hue categorization in young human infants. *Science*, 1975, **191**, 201–202.

Botwinick, J. *Aging and behavior*. New York: Springer, 1973.

Botwinick, J., & Thompson, L. W. Age difference in reaction time: An artifact? *The Gerontologist*, 1968, **8**, 25–28.

Bourne, E. The state of research on ego identity: A review and appraisal. Part I. *Journal of Youth and Adolescence*, 1978, **7**, 223–251. (a)

Bourne, E. The state of research on ego identity: A review and appraisal. Part II. *Journal of Youth and Adolescence*, 1978, **7**, 371–392. (b)

Bower, T. G. R. Slant perception and shape constancy in infants. *Science*, 1966, **151**, 832–834. (a)

Bower, T. G. R. The visual world of infants. *Scientific American*, 1966, **215**, 80–92. (b)

Bower, T. G. R. The development of the object concept. In J. Mehler, ed., *Handbook of cognitive psychology*. Englewood Cliffs, N.J.: Prentice-Hall, Inc., 1970.

Bower, T. G. R. *Development in infancy*. San Francisco: W. H. Freeman, 1974.

Bower, T. G. R. *The perceptual world of the child*. Cambridge, Mass.: Harvard University Press, 1977.

Bowerman, C. E., & Kinch, J. W. Changes in family and peer orientation of children between the fourth and tenth grades. In M. Gold and E. Douvan, eds., *Adolescent development*. Boston: Allyn & Bacon, 1969, pp. 137–141.

Bowerman, M. *Early syntactic development: A cross-linguistic study with special reference to Finnish*. Cambridge, Mass.: Cambridge University Press, 1973.

Bowerman, M. Semantic factors in the acquisition of rules for word use and sentence construction. In D. M. Morehead and A. E. Morehead, eds., *Normal and deficient child language*. Baltimore: University Park Press, 1976, pp. 99–179.

Bowlby, J. Maternal care and mental health. *World Health Organization Monographs*, No. 2, 1951.

Bowlby, J. Some pathological processes set in train by early mother-child separation. *Journal of Mental Science*, 1953, **99**, 265–267.

Bowlby, J. The nature of the child's tie to his mother. *International Journal of Psychoanalysis*, 1958, **39**, 1–24.

Bowlby, J. *Attachment and loss*, Vol. I: *Attachment*. London: Hogarth; New York: Basic Books, 1969.

Brack, D. C. Displaced—the midwife by the male physician. *Women & Health,* 1976, **1,** 18–24.

Brackbill, Y. Extinction of the smiling response in infants as a function of reinforcement schedule. *Child Development,* 1958, **29,** 115–124.

Braine, M. D. S. The ontogeny of English phrase structure: The first phase. *Language,* 1963, **39,** 1–13.

Braine, M. D. S. Children's first word combinations. *Monographs of the Society for Research in Child Development,* 1976, **41** (Serial No. 164).

Braine, M. D. S., & Shanks, B. L. The development of conservation of size. *Journal of Verbal Learning and Verbal Behavior,* 1965, **4,** 227–242.

Brazelton, T. B. *Infants and mothers; Differences in development.* New York: Dell Pub. Co., Inc., 1969.

Brazelton, T. B. Effect of prenatal drugs on the behavior of the neonate. *American Journal of Psychiatry,* 1970, **126,** 1261–1266.

Brazelton, T. B. Neonatal behavioral assessment scale. Clinics in Developmental Medicine, No. 50. Spastics International Medical Publications in association with William Heinemann Medical Books Ltd., London, 1973.

Brennan, W. M., Ames, E. W., & Moore, R. W. Age differences in infants' attention to patterns of different complexities. *Science,* 1966, **151,** 354–356.

Brim, O. G. Family structure and sex role learning by children. *Sociometry,* 1958, **21,** 1–16.

Brim, O. G. Adult socialization. In J. Clausen, ed., *Socialization and society.* Boston: Little, Brown, 1968.

Broadhurst, P. L. Studies in psychogenetics: The quantitative inheritance of behavior in rats investigated by selective and cross-breeding. *Bulletin of the British Psychological Society,* 1958, **34,** 2A (Abstract).

Brockman, L. M., & Ricciuti, H. N. Severe protein-calorie malnutrition and cognitive development in infancy and early childhood. *Developmental Psychology,* 1971, **4,** 312–319.

Brodzinsky, D., Jackson, J., & Overton, W. Effects of perceptual shielding in the development of spatial perspectives. *Child Development,* 1972, **43,** 1041–1046.

Bromley, D. B. *The psychology of human aging.* Baltimore: Penguin Books, 1966.

Bronfenbrenner, U. Socialization and social class through time and space. In E. E. Macoby, T. M. Newcomb, and E. L. Hartley, eds., *Readings in social psychology.* New York: Holt, 1958.

Bronfenbrenner, U. *Two worlds of childhood: U.S. and U.S.S.R.* New York: Russell Sage Foundation, 1970.

Bronfenbrenner, U. The roots of alienation. In U. Bronfenbrenner, ed., *Influences on human development.* Hinsdale, Ill.: Dryden Press, 1972, pp. 658–677.

Bronfenbrenner, U. *A report on longitudinal evaluations of preschool programs, Volume II: Is early intervention effective?* Washington, D.C.: Department of Health, Education, and Welfare, 1974.

Bronfenbrenner, U. Who needs parent education? *Teachers College Record,* 1978, **79,** 766–787.

Bronson, G. The postnatal growth of visual capacity. *Child Development,* 1974, **45,** 873–890.

Bronson, W. C. Mother-toddler interaction. *Merrill-Palmer Quarterly,* 1974, **20,** 275–301.

Brookhart, J., & Hock, E. The effects of experimental context and experiential background on infants' behavior toward their mother and a stranger. *Child Development,* 1976, **47,** 333–340.

Brophy, J. E., & Good, T. L. Teachers' communication of differential expectations for children's classroom performance: Some behavioral data. *Journal of Educational Psychology,* 1970, **61,** 365–374.

Broverman, I. K., Broverman, D. M., Clarkson, F., Rosenkrantz, P. S., & Vogel, S. R. Sex-role stereotypes and clinical judgments of mental health. *Journal of Consulting and Clinical Psychology,* 1970, **34,** 1–7.

Broverman, I. K., Vogel, S. R., Broverman, D. M., Clarkson, F. E., & Rosenkrantz, P. S. Sex-role stereotypes: A current appraisal. *Journal of Social Issues,* 1972, **28,** 59–78.

Browder, F. E. The relevance of mathematics. *The American Mathematical Monthly,* 1976, **83,** 249–254.

Brown, J. L. States in newborn infants. *Merrill-Palmer Quarterly,* 1964, **10,** 313–327.

Brown, M. Why genetic defects may be a thing of the past. *New York Magazine,* September 18, 1978.

Brown, R. How shall a thing be called? *Psychological Review,* 1958, **65,** 14–21.

Brown, R. *Social psychology.* New York: Free Press, 1965.

Brown, R. The first sentences of child and chimpanzee. In *Psycholinguistics: Selected papers of Roger Brown.* New York: Free Press, 1970.

Brown, R. *A first language: The early stages.* Cambridge, Mass.: Harvard University Press, 1973.

Brown, R., & Bellugi, U. Three processes in the child's acquisition of syntax. *Harvard Educational Review,* 1964, **34,** 133–151.

Brown, R., Cazden, C. B., & Bellugi-Klima, U. The child's grammar from I to III. In J. P. Hill, ed., *Minnesota symposia on child psychology.* Minneapolis: The University of Minnesota Press, 1969, **2,** 28–73.

Bruner, J. S. The ontogenesis of speech acts. *Journal of Child Language,* 1975, **2,** 1–19.

Bryan, J. H. Children's reactions to helpers: Their money isn't where their mouths are. In J. Macaulay & L. Berkowitz, eds., *Altruism and helping behavior.* New York: Academic Press, 1970, pp. 61–73.

Bryant, P. E., Jones, P., Claxton, V., & Perkins, G. M. Recognition of shapes across modalities by infants. *Nature,* 1972, **240,** 303–304.

Burchard, J. D., & Barrera, F. An analysis of timeout and response cost in a programmed environment. *Journal of Applied Behavior Analysis,* 1972, **5,** 271–282.

Burger, G. K., Lamp, R. E., & Rogers, D. Developmental trends in children's perceptions of parental child-rearing behavior. *Developmental Psychology,* 1975, **11,** 391.

Burgess, J. K. The single-parent family: A social and sociological problem. *Family Coordinator,* 1970, **19,** 137–144.

Burt, C. The genetic determination of differences in intelligence: A study of monozygotic twins reared together and apart. *British Journal of Psychology,* 1966, **57,** 137–153.

Burt, C. Inheritance of general intelligence. *American Psychologist,* 1972, **27,** 175–190.

Burton, D. Birth order and intelligence. *Journal of Social Psychology,* 1968, **76,** 199–206.

Burton, R. V.   Generality of honesty reconsidered. *Psychological Review*, 1963, **70**, 481–499.

Burton, R. V. Maccoby, F., & Allinsmith, W.   Antecedents of resistance to temptation in four-year-old children. *Child Development*, 1961, **32**, 689–710.

Buss, A., & Plomin, R.   *A temperament theory of personality development*. Wiley-Interscience, 1975.

Buss, A. H., Plomin, R., & Willerman, L.   The inheritance of temperament. *Journal of Personality*, 1973, **41**, 513–524.

Busse, E. W.   Theories of aging. In E. W. Busse and E. Pfeiffer, eds., *Behavior and adaptation in late life*. Boston: Little, Brown, 1977.

Busse, T. V.   Child rearing antecedents of flexible thinking. *Developmental Psychology*, 1969, **1**, 585–591.

Butler, R. N.   The life review: An interpretation of reminiscence in the aged. In R. Kastenbaum, ed., *New thoughts on old age*. New York: Springer, 1964.

Butterworth, G., & Castillo, M.   Coordination of auditory and visual space in newborn infants. *Perception*, 1976, **5**, 155–161.

Caldwell, B. M.   The usefulness of the critical period hypothesis in the study of filiative behavior. *Merrill-Palmer Quarterly of Behavior and Development*, 1962, **8**, 229–242.

Caldwell, B. M., Bradley, R. H., & Elardo, R.   Early stimulation. In J. Wortis, ed., *Mental retardation and developmental disabilities: An annual review*. New York: Brunner/Mazel, 1975, pp. 152–194.

Caldwell, B. M., & Richmond, J. B.   The impact of theories of child development. *Children*, 1962, **9**, 73–78.

Caldwell, B. M., Wright, C. M., Honig, A. S., Tannenbaum, J.   Infant day care and attachment. *American Journal of Orthopsychiatry*, 1970, **40**, 397–412.

Cambor, C. G.   Adolescent alienation syndrome. In J. C. Schoolar, ed., *Current issues in adolescent psychiatry*. New York: Brunner/Mazel, 1973, pp. 101–117.

Cameron, P., Stewart, L., & Biber, H.   Consciousness of death across the life span. *Journal of Gerontology*, 1973, **28**, 189–196.

Campbell, E. Q.   Adolescent socialization. In D. A. Goslin, ed., *Handbook of socialization theory and research*. Chicago: Rand McNally, 1969, pp. 821–859.

Campbell, M.   Biological intervention in psychoses of childhood. In E. Schopler and R. J. Reichler eds., *Psychopathology and child development*. New York: Plenum, 1976, pp. 243–270.

Campos, J. J., Langer, A., & Krowitz, A.   Cardiac response on the visual cliff in prelocomotor human infants. *Science*, 1970, **170**, 196–197.

Cantwell, D. P.   Psychiatric illness in the families of hyperactive children. *Archives of General Psychiatry*, 1972, **27**, 414–417.

Cantwell, D. P.   *The hyperactive child*. New York: Spectrum Publ., 1975.

Cantwell, D. P., Baker, L., & Rutter, M.   Family factors. In M. Rutter and E. Schopler, eds., *Autism: A reappraisal of concepts and treatment*. New York: Plenum, 1978, pp. 269–296.

Cantwell, D. P., & Carlson, G. A.   Stimulants. In J. S. Werry, ed., *Pediatric psychopharmacology: The use of behavior modifying drugs on children*. New York: Brunner/Mazel, 1978.

Capute, A. J., Accardo, P. J., Vining, E. P. G., Rubenstein, J. E., & Harryman, S.   *Primitive reflex profile*. Baltimore: University Park Press, 1978.

Caputo, D. V., & Mandell, W.   Consequences of low birth weight. *Developmental Psychology*, 1970, **3**, 363–383.

Carey, W. B., Lipton, W. L., & Myers, R. A.   Temperament in adopted and foster babies. *Child Welfare*, 1974, **53**, 352–359.

Carlsmith, L.   Effects of early father absence on scholastic aptitude. *Harvard Educational Review*, 1964, **34**, 3–21.

Carmichael, L.   Onset and early development of behavior. In P. H. Mussen, ed., *Carmichael's manual of child psychology* (3rd ed.). New York: John Wiley, 1970, Vol. I, pp. 447–563.

Caro, F. G., & Pihlblad, C. T.   Aspirations and expectations: A reexamination of the basis for social class differences in the occupational orientation of male high school students. *Sociology and Social Research*, 1965, **49**, 465–475.

Caron, A. J., Caron, R. F., & Carleson, V. R.   Do infants see objects or retinal images? Shape constancy revisited. Paper presented at the meeting of the Society for Research in Child Development, New Orleans, 1977.

Carpenter, G.   Mother's face and the newborn. In R. Lewin, ed., *Child Alive*. New York: Doubleday, 1975.

Carroll, J. B.   Language and thought. Englewood Cliffs, N.J.: Prentice-Hall, Inc., 1964.

Carroll, J. B., & Casagrande, J. B.   The function of language classifications in behavior. In E. Maccoby, ed., *Readings in social psychology*. New York: Holt, Rinehart & Winston, 1958, pp. 18–31.

Carron, A. V., & Bailey, D. A.   Strength development in boys from 10 through 16 years. *Monographs of the Society for Research in Child Development*, 1974, **39**, (4), Serial No. 157, 1–37.

Carter, A. L.   Development of the presyntactic communication system: A case study. *Journal of Child Language*, 1975, **2**, 233–250.

Carter, C. O.   The genetics of common malformations. In *Congenital malformations: Papers and discussions presented at the second international conference on congenital malformations*. New York: The International Medical Congress, 1964, pp. 306–313.

Casler, L.   Maternal deprivation: A critical review of the literature. *Monographs of the Society for Research in Child Development*, 1961, **26**, No. 2.

Cattell, R. B.   Theory of fluid and crystallized intelligence: A critical experiment. *Journal of Educational Psychology*, 1963, **54**, 1–22.

Cattell, R. B.   *The scientific analysis of personality*. Baltimore: Penguin, 1965.

Caudill, W., & Frost, L.   A comparison of maternal care and infant behavior in Japanese-American, American, and Japanese families. In U. Bronfenbrenner and M. A. Mahoney, eds., *Influences on human development*. Hinsdale, Ill.: Dryden Press, 1975, pp. 139–150.

Caudill, W., & Weinstein, H.   Maternal care and infant behavior in Japan and America. *Psychiatry*, 1969, **32**, 12–43.

Cazden, C. B.   Subcultural differences in child language: An interdisciplinary review. *Merrill-Palmer Quarterly*, 1966, **12**, 185–219.

Cazden, C. B.   The acquisition of noun and verb inflections. *Child Development*, 1968, **39**, 433–448.

Chabon, I. *Awake and aware.* New York: Delacorte Press, 1966.

Chadwick, B. A., Albrecht, S. L. & Kunz, P. R. Marital and family role satisfaction. *Journal of Marriage and the Family,* 1976, **38,** 431–440.

Chen, H. P., & Irwin, O. C. Infant speech vowel and consonant types. *Journal of Speech Disorders,* 1964, **11,** 27–29.

Chernoff, G. F. The fetal alcohol syndrome in mice: An animal model. *Teratology,* 1977, **15,** 223–229.

Chess S. The influence of defect on development in children with congenital rubella. *Merrill-Palmer Quarterly,* 1974, **20,** 255–274.

Chess, S., & Hassibi, M. *Principles and practice of child psychiatry.* New York: Plenum, 1978.

Chess, S., & Thomas, A. Differences in outcome with early intervention in children with behavior disorders. In M. Roff, L. Robins, and M. Pollack, eds., *Life history research in psychopathology,* Vol. 2. Minneapolis: University of Minnesota Press, 1972.

Chess, S., & Thomas, A. Temperamental individuality from childhood to adolescence. *Journal of the American Academy of Child Psychiatry,* 1977, **16,** 218–226.

Cheyne, J. A. Behavioral and physiological reactions to punishment: Attention, anxiety and the timing of punishment hypothesis. Paper presented at the Biennial Meeting of the Society for Research in Child Development, Santa Monica, 1969.

Chilman, C. S. Child-rearing and family relationship patterns of the very poor. *Welfare in Review,* 1965, 9–19.

Chomsky, C. *The acquisition of syntax in children from 5 to 10.* Cambridge, Mass.: M.I.T. Press, 1969.

Claren, S. K., & Smith, D. W. The fetal alcohol syndrome. *New England Journal of Medicine,* 1978, **298,** 1063–1067.

Clark, E. V. What's in a word? On the child's acquisition of semantics in his first language. In T. E. Moore, ed., *Cognitive development and the acquisition of language.* New York: Academic Press, 1973.

Clark, H. H., & Clark, E. V. *Psychology and language.* New York: Harcourt Brace Jovanovich, Inc. 1977.

Clark, H. H., & Haviland, S. E. Comprehension and the given-new contract. In R. O. Freedle, ed., *Discourse production and comprehension.* Norwood, N.J.: Ablex Publishing, 1977, pp. 1–40.

Clark, H. K. Emmy noether. *The American Mathematical Monthly,* 1972, **79,** 136–149.

Clarke, A. D. B., & Clarke, A. M. Prospects for prevention and amelioration of mental retardation: A guest editorial. *American Journal of Mental Retardation,* 1977, **81,** 1–123.

Clarke-Stewart, K. A. Interactions between mothers and their young children: Characteristics and consequences. *Monographs of the Society for Research in Child Development,* 1973, **38,** (6–7, Whole No. 153).

Clarke-Stewart, K. A. And daddy makes three: The father's impact on mother and young child. *Child Development,* 1978, **49,** 466–478.

Clausen, J. A. Family structure. Socialization and personality. In L. W. Hoffman and M. L. Hoffman, eds., *Review of child development research.* Vol. 2. New York: Russell Sage Foundation, 1966, pp. 1–54.

Clifton, R. K.,, Graham, F. K., & Hatton, H. M. Newborn heart rate response and response habituation as a function of stimulus duration. *Journal of Experimental Child Psychology,* 1968, **6,** 265–278.

Cloutier, R., & Goldschmid, M. L. Individual differences in the development of formal reasoning. *Child Development,* 1976, **47,** 1097–1102.

Coates, B., Anderson, E. P., & Hartup, W. W. Interrelations in the attachment behavior of human infants. *Developmental Psychology,* 1972, **6,** 218–230. (*a*)

Coates, B., Anderson, E. P., & Hartup, W. W. The stability of attachment behaviors in the human infant. *Developmental Psychology,* 1972, **6,** 231–237. (*b*)

Coates, B., & Hartup, W. W. Age and verbalization in observational learning. *Developmental Psychology,* 1969, **1,** 556–562.

Cohen, J. High school subcultures and the adult world. *Adolescence,* 1979, **14,** 491–502.

Cohen, L. B. Concept acquisition in the human infant. Paper presented at the meeting of the Society for Research in Child Development, New Orleans, 1977.

Cohen, L. B., DeLoache, J. S., & Pearl, R. An examination of interference effects in infants' memory for faces. *Child Development,* 1977, **48,** 88–96.

Cohen, L. B., DeLoache, J. S., & Strauss, M. S. Infant visual perception. In J. Osofsky, ed., *Handbook of infancy.* New York: John Wiley, 1978.

Cohen, L. J., & Campos, J. J. Father, mother and stranger as elicitors of attachment behaviors in infancy. *Developmental Psychology,* 1974, **10,** 146–154.

Coleman, J. S. The adolescent subculture and academic achievement. *The American Journal of Sociology,* 1960, **65,** 337–347.

Coleman, J. S. *The adolescent society.* New York: Free Press, 1961.

Coleman, J. S., Campbell, E. Q., Hobson, C. J., McPartland, J., Mood, A. M., Weinfeld, F. D., & York, R. L. *Equality of educational opportunity.* Report from Office of Education, Washington, D.C.: U.S. Government Printing Office, 1966.

Collins, W. A., & Getz, S. K. Children's social responses following model reactions to provocation: Pro-social effects of television drama. *Journal of Personality,* 1976, **44,** 499–500.

Collis, G. M. Visual co-orientation and maternal speech. In H. R. Schaffer ed., *Studies in mother-infant interaction.* London: Academic Press, 1977.

Comfort, A. Biological theories of aging. *Human Development,* 1970, **13,** 127–139.

Committee on the Infant and Preschool Child. Statement on day care. *Pediatrics,* 1957, **56,** 484.

Condry, J., & Condry, S. Sex differences: A study of the eye of the beholder. *Child Development,* 1976, **47,** 812–819.

Conger, J. C. The treatment of encopresis by the management of social consequences. *Behavior Therapy,* 1970, **1,** 389–390.

Connors, C. K. A teacher rating scale for use in drug studies with children. *American Journal of Psychiatry,* 1969, **126,** 884–888.

Copans, S. A. Human prenatal effects: Methodological problems and some suggested solutions. *Merrill-Palmer Quarterly,* 1974, **20,** 43–52.

Copobianco, R. J., & Cole, D. A. Social behavior of mentally retarded children. *American Journal of Mental Deficiency*, 1960, **64**, 638–651.

Corder, B. F., Shorr, W., & Corder, R. F. A study of social and psychological characteristics of adolescent suicide attempters in an urban, disadvantaged area. *Adolescence*, 1974, **9**, 1–5.

Corman, L., & Gottlieb, J. Mainstreaming mentally retarded children: A review of research. In N. R. Ellis, ed., *International review of research in mental retardation*. Vol. 9. New York: Academic Press, 1978, pp. 251–275.

Cornell, E. H., & Gottfried, A. W. Intervention with premature human infants. *Child Development*, 1976, **47**, 32–39.

Corso, J. F. Sensory processes and age effects in normal adults. *Journal of Gerontology*, 1971, **26**, 90–105.

Costanzo, P. R., & Shaw, M. E. Conformity as a function of age level. *Child Development*, 1966, **37**, 967–975.

Cowan, P. A. & Walters, R. H. Studies of reinforcement of aggression, Part I: Effects of scheduling. *Child Development*, 1963, **34**, 543–552.

Craik, F. I. M. Age differences in human memory. In J. E. Birren and K. W. Schaie, eds., *Handbook of the psychology of aging*. New York: Van Nostrand Reinhold, 1977.

Crandall, V. Parents as identification models and reinforcers of children's achievement behavior. Progress report, NIMH Grant M-2238, January 1961.

Crandall, V. Achievement behavior in young children. In *The young child: Reviews of research*. Washington, D.C.: National Association for the Education of Young Children, 1967.

Crandall, V. Differences in parental antecedents of internal-external control in children and in young adulthood. Paper presented at the meeting of the *American Psychological Association*, Montreal, August 1973.

Crandall, V., Dewey, R., Katkovsky, W., & Preston, A. Parents' attiudes and behaviors and grade-school children's academic achievements. *Journal of Genetic Psychology*, 1964, **104**, 53–66.

Crandall, V., Katkovsky, W., & Crandall, V. J. Children's beliefs in their own control of reinforcements in intellectual-academic achievement situations. *Child Development*, 1965, **36**, 90–109.

Crandall, V., Katkovsky, W., & Preston, A. A conceptual formulation for some research on children's achievement development. *Child Development*, 1960, **31**, 787–797. (*a*)

Crandall, V., Katkovsky, W., & Preston, A. Parent behavior and children's achievement development. Paper read at the meeting of *American Psychological Association*, Chicago, 1960. (*b*)

Crandall, V., Katkovsky, W., & Preston, A. Motivational ability determinants of young children's intellectual achievement behaviors. *Child Development*, 1962, **33**, 643–661.

Crandall, V., Preston, A., & Rabson, A. Maternal reactions and the development of independence and achievement behavior in young children. *Child Development*, 1960, **31**, 243–251.

Crawley, S. B., Rogers, P. P., Friedman, S., Iacobbo, M., Criticos, A., Richardson, L., & Thompson, M. Developmental changes in the structure of mother-infant play. *Developmental Psychology*, 1978, **14**, 30–36.

Crites, J. O. Parental identification in relation to vocational interest development. *Journal of Educational Psychology*, 1962, **53**, 262–270.

Cromwell, R. L. A social learning approach to mental retardation. In N. R. Ellis, ed., *Handbook of mental deficiency*. New York: McGraw-Hill, 1963, pp. 41–91.

Cronbach, L. J. *Essentials of psychological testing*. 2nd ed. New York: Harper & Row, Pub., 1960.

Cronbach, L. J. Five decades of public controversy over mental testing. *American Psychologist*, 1975, **30**, 1–14.

Cruttenden, A. An experiment involving comprehension of intonation in children from 7 to 10. *Journal of Child Language*, 1974, **1**, 221–231.

Csapo, M. The effect of self-recording and social reinforcement components of parent training programs. *Journal of Experimental Child Psychology*, 1979, **27**, 479–488.

Cumming, E., & Henry, W. E. *Growing old: The process of disengagement*. New York: Basic Books, 1961.

Dalby, J. T. Environmental effects on prenatal development. *Journal of Pediatric Psychology*, 1978, **3**, 105–109.

Dale, P. S. *Language development*. Hinsdale, Ill.: Dryden, 1972.

D'Andrade, R. G. Sex differences and cultural institutions. In E. E. Maccoby, ed., *The development of sex differences*. Stanford, CA: Stanford University Press, 1966.

Darley, J. M., & Latane, B. Bystander intervention in emergencies: Diffusion of responsibility. *Journal of Personality and Social Psychology*, 1968, **8**, 377–383.

Davis, B. D. Prospects for genetic intervention in man. *Science*, 1970, **170**, 1279–1283.

Davis, K. Final note on a case of extreme isolation. *American Journal of Sociology*, 1947, **57**, 432–457.

Davison, G. C., & Neale, J. M. *Abnormal psychology*. New York: John Wiley, 1978.

Day, M. C. Developmental trends in visual scanning. In H. W. Reese, ed., *Advances in child development and behavior*, Vol. 10. New York: Academic Press, 1975, pp. 153–193.

Dean, G., & Gurak, D. T. Marital homogamy the second time around. *Journal of Marriage and the Family*, 1978, **40**, 559–570.

DeFries, J. C. & Plomin, R. Behavioral genetics. *Annual Review of Psychology*, 1978, **29**, 473–515.

DeHaan, R. F., & Havighurst, R. J. *Educating gifted children*. Chicago: University of Chicago Press, 1957.

Dehaene, P. H. Le syndrome d'alcoolisone foetal dans le nord de la france. *Revue de l'Alcoolisme*, 1977, **23**, 145–158.

De Hirsch, K., Jansky, J., & Langford, W. S. Comparisons between prematurely and maturely born children at three age levels. *American Journal of Orthopsychiatry*, 1966, **36**, 616–628.

Demos, J., & Demos, V. Adolescence in historical perspective. In D. Rogers, ed., *Issues in adolescent psychology*. Englewood Cliffs, N.J.: Prentice-Hall, Inc., 1972.

Dempsey, D. *The way we die*. New York: McGraw-Hill, 1975.

Denney, N. W., & Acito, M. A. Classification training in two- and three-year-old children. *Journal of Experimental Child Psychology*, 1974, **17**, 37–48.

Dennis, W. Goodenough scores, art experience, and modernization. *Journal of Social Psychology*, 1966, **68**, 211–228.

Dennis, W., & Dennis, M. G. The effects of cradling practices upon the onset of walking in Hopi children. *Journal of Genetic Psychology*, 1940, **56**, 77–86.

Despert, J. L. *The emotionally disturbed child—then and now.* New York: Vantage, 1965.

Deutsch. M., Katz, I., & Jensen, A. R. *Social class, race, and psychological development.* New York: Holt, Rinehart and Winston, 1968.

DeVries, R. Relationship among Piagetian, IQ and achievement assessments. *Child Development*, 1974, **45**, 746–756.

Dewey, J. *Reconstruction in philosophy.* New York: Holt and Co., 1920.

Dick-Read, G. *Childbirth without fear.* New York: Dell Pub. Co., Inc., 1944.

Diers, C. J. Historical trends in the age at menarche and menopause. *Psychology Reports*, 1974, **34**, 931–937.

Dion, K. Physical attractiveness and evaluations of children's transgressions. *Journal of Personality and Social Psychology*, 1972, **24**, 207–213.

Dion, K., Berscheid, E., & Walster, E. What is beautiful is good. *Journal of Personality and Social Psychology*, 1972, **24**, 285–290.

Dlugokinski, E. L., & Firestone, J. J. Congruence among four methods of measuring other centeredness, *Child Development*, 1973, **44**, 304–308.

Dobbing, J. Undernutrition and the developing brain. In W. Hinwich, ed., *Developmental neurobiology.* Springfield, Ill.: Charles C. Thomas, 1970.

Dobson, V., & Teller, D. Y. Visual acuity in human infants: A review and comparison of behavioral and electrophysiological studies. *Vision Research*, 1978, **18**, 1469–1484.

Doleys, D. M. Behavioral treatments for nocturnal enuresis in children: A review of the recent literature. *Psychological Bulletin*, 1977, **84**, 30–54.

Dominick, J. R., & Greenberg, B. S. Attitudes toward violence: The interaction of television exposure, family attitudes, and social class. In G. A. Comstock and E. A. Rubinstein, eds., *Television and social behavior*, Vol. III. *Television and adolescent aggressiveness.* Washington, D.C.: U.S. Government Printing Office, 1972, pp. 314–335.

Domino, G. Maternal personality correlates of sons' creativity. *Journal of Consulting and Clinical Psychology*, 1969, **33**, 180–183.

Donagher, P. C., Poulos, R. W., Liebert, R. M., & Davidson, E. E. Race, sex, and social example: An analysis of character portrayals on interracial television entertainment. *Psychological Reports*, 1976, **38**, 3–14.

Donaldson, M., & Wales, R. J. On the acquisition of some relational terms. In J. R. Hayes, ed., *Cognition and the development of language.* New York: John Wiley, 1970, pp. 235–268.

Dorfman, D. D. The Cyril Burt question: New findings. *Science*, 1978, **201**, 1177–1186.

Douglas, J. W. B., & Ross, J. M. Age of puberty related to educational ability, attainment and school leaving age. *Journal of Child Psychology and Psychiatry*, 1964, **5**, 185–196.

Douvan, E., & Adelson, J. *The adolescent experience.* New York: John Wiley, 1966.

Dreger, R. M., & Miller, K. S. Comparative psychological studies on Negroes and whites in the United States. *Psychological Bulletin*, 1960, **57**, 361–402.

Drillien, C. M. The incidence of mental and physical handicaps in school-age children of very low birthweight. *Pediatrics*, 1961, **17**, 452–464.

Duberman, L. *Social inequality: Class and caste.* Philadelphia: Lippincott, 1976.

Duke, M. P., & Fenhagen, E. Self-parental alienation and locus of control in delinquent girls. *Journal of Genetic Psychology*, 1975, **27**, 103–107.

Duncan, D. F. Measuring the generation gap: Attitudes toward parents and other adults. *Adolescence*, 1978, **13**, 77–81.

Dunford, R. E. The genetic development of cutaneous localization. *Journal of Genetic Psychology*, 1930, **37**, 499–513.

Dunn, L. M. Special education for the mildly retarded: Is much of it justified? *Exceptional Children*, 1968, **35**, 5–22.

Dunphy, D. C. The social structure of urban adolescent peer groups. *Sociometry*, 1963, **26**, 230–246.

Duvall, E. M. *Family development.* Philadelphia: Lippincott, 1971.

Earl, H. G. 10,000 children battered and starved. In J. Leavitt, ed., *The battered child*, General Learning Corporation, 1974, pp. x–xv.

Earn, A. A. Mental concentration—a new and effective psychological tool for the abolition of suffering childbirth. *American Journal of Obstetrics and Gynecology*, 1962, **83**, 29.

Eckert, H. M. Age changes in motor skills. In G. L. Rarick, ed., *Physical activity.* New York: Academic Press, 1973.

Edwards, C. P. Societal complexity and moral development: A Kenyan study. *Ethos*, 1975, **3**, 505–527.

Eells, K. Some implications for school practice of the Chicago studies of cultural bias in intelligence tests. *Harvard Educational Review*, 1953, **23**, 284–297.

Eells, K., Davis, A., Havighurst, R. J., Herrick, V. E., & Tyler, R. W. *Intelligence and cultural differences.* Chicago: University of Chicago Press, 1951.

Ehri, L. C. Sentence contexts as facilitators of noun pair learning in children. *Journal of Experimental Child Psychology*, 1972, **14**, 242–256.

Eibl-Eibesfeldt, I. *Ethology: The biology of behavior.* New York: Holt, Rinehart & Winston, 1970.

Eichorn, D. H. Biological correlates of behavior. In H. W. Stevenson, ed., *Child psychology.* Chicago: The University of Chicago Press, 1963, **1**, 4–61.

Eimas, P. D. Speech perception in early infancy. In L.B. Cohen and P. Salapatek, eds., *Infant perception: From sensation to cognition* (Vol. 2). New York: Academic Press, 1975, pp. 193–231.

Eimas, P. D., Siqueland, E. R., Jusczyk, P., & Vigorito, Speech perception in infants. *Science*, 1971, **171**, 303–306.

Eisenberg, L. School phobia: A study in the communication of anxiety. *American Journal of Psychiatry*, 1958, **114**, 712–718.

Eisenberg, L., & Kanner, L. Early infantile autism, 1943–1955. *American Journal of Orthopsychiatry*, 1956, **26**, 556–566.

Eisenberg, R. B. Auditory behavior in the human neonate. I. Methodological problems and the logical design of research procedures. *Journal of Auditory Research*, 1965, **5**, 159–177.

Eisenberg, R. B. *Auditory competence in early life.* Baltimore: University Park Press, 1976.

Eisenberger, R. Is there a deprivation-satiation function for social approval? *Psychological Bulletin*, 1970, **74**, 255–275.

Eisenstadt, S. N. *From generation to generation.* New York: Free Press, 1956.

Elder, G. H. Structural variations in the child rearing relationship. *Sociometry*, 1962, **25**, 241–262.

Elias, M. F., Elias, P. K., & Elias, J. W. *Basic processes in adult developmental psychology.* St. Louis: C. V. Mosby, 1977.

Elkind, D. Egocentrism in adolescence. *Child Development*, 1967, **38**, 1025–1034.

Elkind, D., & Bowen, R. Imaginary audience behavior in children and adolescence. *Developmental Psychology*, 1979, **15**, 38–44.

Ellenberger, H. F. *The discovery of the unconscious.* New York: Basic Books, 1970.

Eme, R. F. Sex differences in childhood psychopathology: A review. *Psychological Bulletin*, 1979, **86**, 574–595.

Eme, R., Maisiak, R., & Goodale, W. Seriousness of adolescent problems. *Adolescence*, 1979, **14**, 93–99.

Emery, A. E. H. *Elements of medical genetics.* New York: Churchill Livingston, 1979.

Empey, L. T. Delinquency theory and recent research. In R. E. Grinder, ed., *Studies in adolescence.* New York: Macmillan, 1975.

Engel, M. *Psychopathology in childhood.* New York: Harcourt Brace Jovanovich, Inc., 1972.

Engen, T., Lipsitt, L. P., & Kaye, H. Olfactory responses and adaptation in the human neonate. *Journal of Comparative and Physiological Psychology*, 1963, **56**, 73–77.

English, D. S., ed. *Genetic and reproductive engineering.* New York: MSS Information Service, 1974.

English, H. B., & English, A. C. *A comprehensive dictionary of psychological and psychoanalytical terms.* New York: Longman, 1958.

Epperson, D. C. A reassessment of indices of parental influence in "the adolescent society." *American Sociological Review*, 1964, **29**, 93–96.

Epstein, A. S., & Radin, N. Motivational components related to father bet and cognitive functioning in preschoolers. *Child Development*, 1975, **46**, 83.

Erickson, M. *Child psychopathology.* Englewood Cliffs, N.J.: Prentice-Hall, Inc., 1978.

Erikson, E. H. *Childhood and society.* New York: W. W. Norton & Co., Inc., 1963.

Erikson, E. H. *Identity: Youth and crisis.* New York: W. W. Norton & Co., Inc., 1968.

Erlenmeyer-Kimling, L., & Jarvik, L. S. Genetics and intelligence: A review. *Science*, 1963, **142**, 1477–1479.

Ernest, J. Mathematics and sex. *The American Mathematical Monthly*, 1976, **83**, 595–614.

Eron, L. D. Relationship of TV viewing habits and aggressive behavior in children. *Journal of Abnormal and Social Psychology*, 1963, **67**, 193–196.

Ervin-Tripp, S. Discourse agreement: How children answer questions. In J. R. Hayes, ed., *Cognition and the development of language.* New York: John Wiley, 1970, pp. 79–107.

Escalona, S. K. Basic modes of social interaction: Their emergence and patterning during the first two years of life. *Merrill-Palmer Quarterly*, 1973, **19**, 205–232.

Esposito, N. J. Review of discrimination shift learning in young children. *Psychological Bulletin*, 1975, **82**, 432–455.

Estes, E. H. Health experience in the elderly. In E. W. Busse and E. Pfeiffer, eds., *Behavior and adaptation in later life.* Boston: Little, Brown, 1969.

Etzel, B., & Gewirtz, J. L. Experimental modification of caretaker-maintained high rate operant crying in a 6- and 20-week-old infant (*Infans tyrannotearus*): Extinction of crying with reinforcement of eye contact and smiling. *Journal of Experimental Child Psychology*, 1967, **5**, 303–317.

Eysenck, H. J. The inheritance of extraversion-introversion. *Acta Psychologica*, 1956, **12**, 95–110.

Eysenck, H. J., ed., *Behavior therapy and the neuroses.* London: Pergamon Press, 1960.

Fagan, J. F. Infant color perception. *Science*, 1974, **183**, 973–975.

Fantz, R. L. Depth discrimination in dark-hatched chicks. *Perceptual and Motor Skills*, 1958, **8**, 47–50. (*a*)

Fantz, R. L. Pattern vision in young infants. *Psychological Record*, 1958, **8**, 43–47. (*b*)

Fantz, R. L. The origin of form perception. *Scientific American*. 1961, **204**, 66–72.

Fantz, R. L. Pattern vision in newborn infants. *Science*, 1963, **140**, 296–297.

Fantz, R. L. Studying visual perception and the effects of visual exposure in early infancy. In D. Gelfand, ed., *Social learning in childhood.* Belmont, CA: Brooks/Cole, 1969, pp. 46–56.

Fantz, R. L., Fagan, J. F., & Miranda, S. Early vision selectivity. In L. B. Cohen and P. Salapatek, eds., *Infant perception: From sensation to cognition: Basic visual processes.* Vol. 1. New York: Academic Press, 1975, pp. 249–341.

Fantz, R. L., Ordy, J. M., & Udelf, M. S. Maturation of pattern vision in infants during the first 6 months. *Journal of Comparative & Physiological Psychology*, 1962, **55**, 907–917.

Faust, M. S. Developmental maturity as a determinant in prestige of adolescent girls. *Child Development*, 1960, **31**, 173–184.

Fein, G. G., & Clarke-Stewart, A. *Day care in context.* New York: John Wiley, 1973.

Feingold, B. D., & Mahoney, M. J. Reinforcement effects on intrinsic interest: undermining the overjustification hypothesis. *Behavior Therapy*, 1975, **6**, 367–377.

Feld, S. Need achievement and test anxiety in children and maternal attitudes and behaviors toward independent accomplishments: A longitudinal study. Paper read at the meeting of American Psychological Association, Cincinnati, 1959.

Feldman, D. H., & Bratton, J. C. Relativity and giftedness: Implications for equality of educational opportunity. *Exceptional Children*, 1972, **38**, 491–492.

Felixbrod, J. J., & O'Leary, K. D. Effects of reinforcement on children's academic behavior as a function of self-determined and externally imposed contingencies. *Journal of Applied Behavior Analysis*, 1973, **6**, 241–250.

Ferguson, C. A. Absence of copula and the notion of simplicity: A study of normal speech, baby talk, foreigner talk, and pidgins. In D. Hymes, ed., *Pidginization and creolization of languages.* Cambridge: Cambridge University Press, 1971, pp. 141–150.

Ferguson, C. A., & Farwell, C. B. Words and sounds in early language acquisition. *Language*, 1975, **51**, 419–439.

Ferreira, A. J. *Prenatal environment.* Springfield, Ill.: Charles C Thomas, 1969.

Ferster, C. B. Positive reinforcement and behavioral deficits of autistic children. *Child Development*, 1961, **32**, 437–456.

Ferster, C. B. The repertoire of the autistic child in relation to principles of reinforcement. In L. Gottschalk and A. H. Auerback, eds., *Methods of research in psychotherapy.* New York: Appleton-Century-Crofts, 1966.

Field, T. Interaction behaviors of primary versus secondary caretaker fathers. *Developmental Psychology*, 1978, **14**, 183–184.

Fillenbaum, G. G. On the relation between attitude to work and attitude to retirement. *Journal of Gerontology*, 1971, **26**, 244–248.

Finley, C. J. Arithmetic achievement in mentally retarded children: The effect of presenting the problem in different contexts. *American Journal of Mental Deficiency*, 1962, **67**, 281–286.

Finn, P. Teenage drunkenness: Warning signal, transient boisterousness, or symptom of social change? *Adolescence*, 1979, **14**, 817–834.

Fischer, J. L., & Fischer, A. The New Englanders of Orchard Town, U.S.A. In B. B. Whiting, ed., *Six cultures.* New York: John Wiley, 1963, pp. 869–1010.

Fischer, W. F. Sharing in preschool children as a function of amount and type of reinforcement. *Genetic Psychology Monographs*, 1963, **68**, 215–245.

Fisher, R. A. The correlation between relatives on the supposition of Mendelian inheritance. *Transactions of the Royal Society of Edinburgh*, 1918, **52**, 399–433.

Flavell, J. H. *The developmental psychology of Jean Piaget.* New York: Van Nostrand, 1963.

Flavell, J. H. Concept development. In P. Mussen, ed., *Carmichael's manual of child psychology*, 3rd ed. New York: John Wiley, 1970.

Flavell, J. H. The development of inferences about others. In T. Mischel, ed., *Understanding about persons.* Oxford: Blackwell, Basil, & Mott, 1974.

Flavell, J. H. *Cognitive development.* Englewood Cliffs, N.J.: Prentice-Hall, Inc., 1977.

Flavell, J. H., Botkin, P. T., Fry, C. L., Wright, J. C., Jarvis, P. E. *The development of role-taking and communication skills in children.* New York: John Wiley, 1968.

Flavell, J. H., & Wellman, H. M. Metamemory. In R. V. Kail and J. W. Hagen, eds., *Memory in cognitive development.* Hillsdale, N.J.: Lawrence Erlbaum Associates, 1976.

Floyd, J. M. K. Effects of amount of reward and friendship status of the other on the frequency of sharing in children. Unpublished doctoral thesis, University of Minnesota, 1964.

Folstein, S., & Rutter, M. Infantile autism: A genetic study of 21 twin pairs. *Journal of Child Psychology and Psychiatry*, 1977, **18**, 297–321.

Fontana, V. *Somewhere a child is crying: Maltreatment—causes and prevention.* New York: Macmillan, 1973.

Forbes, H. S. & Forbes, H. B. Total sense reaction: Hearing. *Journal of Comparative Psychology*, 1927, **7**, 353–356.

Forssman, H. Epilepsy in an XYY man. *Lancet*, 1967, **1**, 1389.

Fox, L. H. Facilitating educational development of mathematically precocious youth, in J. C. Stanley, D. P. Keating, and L. H. Fox, eds., *Mathematical talent.* Baltimore: Johns Hopkins University Press, 1974, pp. 23–46.

Fox, L. H. Women and the career relevance of mathematics and science. *School Science and Mathematics*, 1976, **76**, 347–353.

Franklin, A. W., ed. *The challenge of child abuse.* New York: Academic Press, 1977.

Frazier, T. M., Davis, G. H., Goldstein, H., & Goldberg, I. D. Cigarette smoking and prematurity: A prospective study. *American Journal of Obstetrics and Gynecology*, 1961, **81**, 988–996.

Freedman, D. G. Behavioral assessment in infancy. In G. B. A. Stoelinga and J. J. Van Der Werff Ten Bosch, eds., *Normal and abnormal development of brain and behavior.* Leiden: Leiden University Press, 1971.

Freedman, D. G., & Keller, B. Inheritance of behavior in infants. *Science*, 1963, **10**, 196–198.

Freud, A. *The psycho-analytical treatment of children.* New York: International Universities Press, Inc., 1946.

Freud, A. Adolescence. In J. F. Rosenblith, W. Alinsmith, and J. P. Williams, eds., *The causes of behavior.* Boston: Allyn & Bacon, 1972, pp. 317–323.

Freud, A., & Dann, S. An experiment in group upbringing. In *The psychoanalytic study of the child.* Vol. 6. New York: International Universities Press, 1951.

Freud, S. *An outline of psycho-analysis.* Translated and newly edited by J. Strachey. New York: W. W. Norton & Co., Inc., 1949.

Freud, S. Some psychical consequences of the anatomical distinction between the sexes. In P. C. Lee and R. S. Stewart, eds., *Sex differences: Cultural and developmental dimensions.* New York: Urizen Books, 1976.

Friedman, M., & Rosenman, R. H. *Type A behavior and your heart.* New York: Knopf, 1974.

Friedrich, W. N., & Boriskin, J. A. The role of the child in abuse: A review of the literature. *American Journal of Orthopsychiatry*, 1976, **46**, 580–590.

Frijda, N. H. Simulation of human long-term memory. *Psychological Bulletin*, 1972, **77**, 1–31.

Frodi, A. M., Lamb, M. E., Leavitt, L. A., and Donovan, W. L. Fathers' and mothers' responses to infant smiles and cries. *Infant Behavior and Development*, 1978, **1**.

Frodi, A. M., Lamb, M. E., Leavitt, L. A., Donovan, W. L., Neff, C., & Sherry, D. Fathers' and mothers' responses to the faces and cries of normal and premature infants. *Developmental Psychology*, 1978, **14**, 490–498.

Fry, P. S. Affect and resistance to temptation. *Developmental Psychology*, 1975, **11**, 466–472.

Gagne, E. The effects of locus of control and goal setting on persistence at a learning task. *Child Study Journal*, 1975, **5**, 193–199.

Gallagher, B. J. III. An empirical analysis of attitude differences between three kin-related generations. *Youth and Society*, 1974, **5**, 327–349.

Gallagher, B. J. III Attitude differences across three generations: Class and sex components. *Adolescence*, 1979, **14**, 501–516.

Garcia, J., & Koelling, R. A. Relation of cue to consequence in avoidance learning. *Psychonomic Science*, 1966, **4**, 123–124.

Gardner, R. A., & Gardner, B. T. Teaching sign language to a chimpanzee. *Science*, 1969, **165**, 664–672.

Garmezy, N. Vulnerability research and the issue of primary intervention. *American Journal of Orthopsychiatry,* 1971, **41,** 101–116.

Garmezy, N. Children at risk: The search for the antecedents of schizophrenia. Part I. Conceptual models and research methods. *Schizophrenia Bulletin,* 1974, **8,** 14–90.

Garnica, O. K. Some characteristics of prosoaic input to young children. Unpublished doctoral dissertation, Stanford University, 1975.

Garvey, W. P., & Hegrenes, J. P. Desensitization techniques in the treatment of school phobia. *American Journal of Orthopsychiatry,* 1966, **36,** 147–152.

Gelles, R. J. Child abuse as psychopathology: A sociological critique and reformulation. *American Journal of Orthopsychiatry,* 1973, **43,** 611–621.

Gelles, R. J. Violence toward children in the United States. In R. Bourne & E. H. Newberger, eds., *Critical perspectives on child abuse.* Lexington, MA: Lexington Books, D.C. Heath, 1979.

Gelman, R. Conservation acquisition: A problem of learning to attend to relevant attributes. *Journal of Experimental Child Psychology,* 1969, **7,** 167–187.

Gelman, R. Cognitive development. *Annual Review of Psychology,* 1978, **29,** 297–332.

Gelman, R. & Shatz, M. Listener-dependent adjustments in the speech of 4-year-olds. Paper given at meeting of the Psychonomic Society, 1972.

Gerard, M. W. Bronchial asthma in children. *Nervous Child,* 1946, **5,** 327–331.

Gesell, A. The stability of mental-growth careers. *39th Yearbook of the National Society for the Study of Education,* 1940, Part II, 149–159.

Gesell, A., & Ames, L. B. The development of handedness. *Journal of Genetic Psychology,* 1947, **70,** 155–175.

Gesell, A., Halverson, H. M., Thompson, H., Ilg, F. L., Castner, B. M., Ames, L. B., & Amatruda, C. S. *The first five years of life: A guide to the study of the preschool child.* New York: Harper & Row, 1940.

Gesell, A., & Thompson, H. Learning and growth in identical twins. *Genetic Psychology Monographs,* 1929, **6,** 1–124.

Getzels, J. W., & Dillon, J. T. The nature of giftedness and the education of the gifted. In R. M. W. Travers, ed., *Second handbook on teaching.* Chicago: Rand McNally, 1973.

Getzels, J. W., & Jackson, P. W. The meaning of "giftedness"—an examination of an expanding concept. In W. B. Barbe and J. S. Renzulli, eds., *Psychology and education of the gifted.* New York: Halsted Press, 1975. pp. 56–60.

Gewirtz, J. L. The role of stimulation in models for child development. In L. L. Dittmann, ed., *Early child care: The new perspective.* New York: Atherton Press, 1968.

Gewirtz, J. L. Attachment, dependence, and a distinction in terms of stimulus control. In J. L. Gewirtz, ed., *Attachment and dependency.* Washington, D. C.; V. H. Winston & Sons, 1972.

Gholson, B., & Danziger, S. Effects of two levels of stimulus complexity upon hypothesis sampling systems among second and sixth grade children. *Journal of Experimental Child Psychology,* 1975, **20,** 105–118.

Gholson, B., Levine, M., & Phillips, S. Hypotheses, strategies, and stereotypes in discrimination learning. *Journal of Experimental Child Psychology,* 1972, **13,** 423–446.

Gianascola, A. J. Experiences in the psychotherapy of a non-verbal, self-destructive, psychotic child. In S. A. Szurek and I. N. Berlin, eds., *Clinical studies in childhood psychoses.* New York: Brunner/Mazel, 1973, pp. 540–550.

Gibbs, J. C. Kohlberg's stages of moral judgment: A constructive critique. *Harvard Educational Review,* 1977, **47,** 43–61.

Gibbs, J. P., & Erickson, M. L. Major developments in the sociological study of deviance. *Annual Review of Sociology,* 1975, 21–42.

Gibson, E. J., *Principles of perceptual learning and development.* Englewood Cliffs, N.J.: Prentice-Hall, Inc., 1969.

Gibson, E. J., & Walk, R. D. The "visual cliff." *Scientific American,* 1960, **202,** 64–71.

Gil, D. G. *Violence against children.* Cambridge, MA: Harvard University Press, 1970.

Gil, D. G. Unraveling child abuse. In R. Bourne & E. H. Newberger, eds., *Critical perspectives on child abuse.* Lexington, MA: Lexington Books, Heath, 1979, pp. 69–79.

Ginzberg, E. Toward a theory of occupational choice: A restatement. *Vocational Guidance Quarterly,* 1972, **20,** 169–176.

Ginzberg, E., Ginzberg, S. W., Axelrad, S., & Herma, J. L. *Occupational choice.* New York: Columbia University Press, 1951.

Ginzburg, H., & Opper, S. *Piaget's theory of intellectual development: An introduction.* Englewood Cliffs, NJ: Prentice-Hall, Inc., 1969.

Giovannoni, J. M., & Billingsley, A. Child neglect among the poor: A study of parental adequacy in families of three ethnic groups. In S. Chess and A. Thomas, eds., *Annual progress in child psychiatry and child development.* New York: Brunner/Mazel, 1971, pp. 323–334.

Girdano, D. D., & Girdano, D. A. *Drugs—a factual account.* Reading, MA: Addison-Wesley, 1973.

Gladston, R. Observations on children who have been physically abused and their parents. *American Journal of Psychiatry,* 1965, **122,** 440–443.

Glamser, F. D. Determinants of a positive attitude toward retirement. *Journal of Gerontology,* 1976, **31,** 104–107.

Gliner, C. R. Tactual discrimination thresholds for shape and texture in young children. *Journal of Experimental Child Psychology,* 1967, **5,** 536–547.

Glucksberg, S., Hay, A., & Danks, J. H. Words in utterance contexts: Young children do not confuse the meanings of *same* and *different. Child Development,* 1976, **47,** 737–741.

Glucksberg, S., & Kim, N. Unpublished study, 1969.

Glucksberg, S., & Krauss, R. M. What do people say after they have learned to talk? Studies of the development of referential communication. *Merrill-Palmer Quarterly,* 1967, **13,** 309–316.

Glucksberg, S., Krauss, R. M., & Higgins, E. T. The development of referential communication skills. In F. D. Horowitz, ed., *Review of Child Development Research.* Chicago: University of Chicago Press, 1975, **4,** 305–345.

Glucksberg, S., Krauss, R. M., & Weisberg, R. Referential communication in nursery school children: Method and some preliminary findings. *Journal of Experimental Child Psychology,* 1966, **3,** 333–342.

Glueck, S., & Glueck, E. *Unraveling juvenile delinquency.* New York: The Commonwealth Fund, 1950.

Glueck, S., & Glueck, E. *Of delinquency and crime.* Springfield, IL: Charles C Thomas, 1974.

Goetz, E. M., & Baer, D. M. Social control of form diversity and the emergence of new forms in children's blockbuilding. *Journal of Applied Behavior Analysis*, 1973, **6**, 209–217.

Goldberg, S. Prematurity: Effects on parents-infant interaction. *Journal of Pediatric Psychology*, 1978, **3**, 137–144.

Golden, N. L., Sokol, R. J., & Rubin, I. L. Angel dust: Possible effects on the fetus. *Pediatrics*, 1980, **65**, 18–20.

Goldfarb, W. Infant rearing and problem behavior. *American Journal of Orthopsychiatry*, 1943, **13**, 249–265.

Goldfarb, W. Childhood psychosis. In P. H. Mussen, ed., *Carmichael's manual of child psychology.* New York: John Wiley, 1970, **2**, 765–830.

Goldfarb, W., Spitzer, R. L., & Endicott, J. A study of psychopathology of parents of psychotic children by structured interview. *Journal of Autism and Childhood Schizophrenia*, 1976, **6**, 327–338.

Goldman, G. Clinical perspectives. In A. Simon and L. J. Epstein, eds., *Aging in modern society.* Washington, D.C.: American Psychiatric Association, 1968.

Goldstein, H., Moss, J. W., & Jordan, L. J. The efficacy of special class training on the development of mentally retarded children. Cooperative Research Project No. 619. Washington, D.C.: U.S. Office of Education, 1965.

Goldstein, K. M., Caputo, D. B., & Taub, H. B. The effects of prenatal and perinatal complications on development at one year of age. *Child Development*, 1976, **47**, 613–621.

Goodman, H., Gottlieb, J., & Harrison, R. H. Social acceptance of EMRs integrated into a non-graded elementary school. *American Journal of Mental Deficiency*, 1972, **76**, 412–417.

Goodman, M. J., Stewart, C. J. & Gilbert, F. Pattern of menopause. *Journal of Gerontology*, 1977, **32**, 291–298.

Gordon, D. A. & Young, R. D. School phobia: A discussion of etiology, treatment, and evaluation. *Psychological Reports*, 1976, **39**, 783–804.

Gordon, S. *The sexual adolescent.* Belmont, CA.: Wadsworth, 1973.

Goren, C. Form perception, innate form preferences and usually-mediated head turning in human newborns. Paper presented at the meeting of the Society for Research in Child Development, Denver, 1975.

Gottesman, I. I. Heritability of personality. *Psychological Monographs*, 1963, **77**, 1–21.

Gottesman, I. I. Genetic variance in adaptive personality traits. *Journal of Child Psychology, Psychiatry, and Allied Disciplines*, 1966, **7**, 199–208.

Gottfredson, G. D. Career stability and redirection in adulthood. *Journal of Applied Psychology*, 1977, **62**, 436–445.

Gottfried, A. W. Intellectual consequences of perinatal anoxia. *Psychological Bulletin*, 1973, **80**, 231–242.

Gottlieb, J., & Budoff, M. Social acceptability of retarded children in nongraded schools differing in architecture. *American Journal of Mental Deficiency*, 1973, **78**, 15–19.

Gottlieb, J., & Davis, J. E. Social acceptance of EMR children during overt behavioral interactions. *American Journal of Mental Deficiency*, 1973, **78**, 141–143.

Gould, R. E. Suicide problems in children and adolescents. *American Journal of Psychotherapy*, 1965, **9**, 228–246.

Gould, R. L. The phases of adult life: A study in developmental psychology. *American Journal of Psychiatry*, 1972, **129**, 33–43.

Goulet, L. R., & Barclay, A. The Vineland Social Maturity Scale: Utility in assessment of Binet MA. *American Journal of Mental Deficiency*, 1963, **67**, 916–921.

Goyette, C. H., Conners, C. K., & Ulrich, R. F. Normative data on revised Conners parent and teacher rating scales. *Journal of Abnormal Child Psychology*, 1978, **6**, 221–236.

Granat, K., & Granat, S. Below-average intelligence and mental retardation. *American Journal of Mental Deficiency*, 1973, **78**, 27–32.

Gray, M. Women in mathematics. *The American Mathematical Monthly*, 1972, **79**, 475–479.

Graziano. A. M., DeGiovanni, I. S., & Garcia, K. Behavioral treatment of children's fears: A review. *Psychological Bulletin*, 1979, **86**, 804–830.

Green, J. American women in mathematics—the first Ph.D.'s. Paper presented at the 84th annual meeting of the American Mathematical Society. Atlanta, January, 1978.

Green, R. Age-intelligence relationship between ages sixteen and sixty-four: A rising trend. *Developmental Psychology*, 1969, **1**, 618–627.

Greenberg, D. J., & O'Donnell, W. J. Infancy and the optional level of stimulation. *Child Development*, 1972, **43**, 639–645.

Greenberg, L. M., & Lourie, R. S. Physiochemical treatment methods. In B. B. Wolman, ed., *Manual of child psychopathology.* New York: McGraw-Hill, 1972, pp. 1010–1031.

Greenfield, P. M., & Smith, J. H. *The structure of communication in early language development.* New York: Academic Press, 1976.

Greenspoon, L. *Marihuana reconsidered.* Cambridge, MA: Harvard University Press, 1971.

Grimm, H. Analysis of short-term dialogues in 5–7 year olds: Encoding of intentions and modifications of speech acts as a function of negative feedback. Paper presented at the Third International Child Language Symposium, London, September 1975.

Grinder, R. E. *A history of genetic psychology.* New York: John Wiley, 1967.

Grinder, R. E. *Adolescence.* New York: John Wiley, 1978.

Grossman, H. J. ed., *Manual on terminology and classification in mental retardation, 1973 revision.* Washington, D.C.: American Association on Mental Deficiency, 1973.

Grotevant, H. D., Scarr, S., & Weinberg, R. A. Intellectual development in family constellations with adopted and natural children: A test of the Zajonc and Markus Model. *Child Development*, 1977, **48**, 1699–1703.

Grusec, J. E. Power and the internalization of self-denial. *Child Development*, 1971, **42**, 93–105.

Grusec, J. E. Effects of co-observer evaluations on imitation: A developmental study. *Developmental Psychology*, 1973, **8**, 141.

Guilford, J. P. Creative abilities in the arts. *Psychological Review*, 1957, **64**, 110–118.

Guilford, J. P. Intelligence: 1965 model. *American Psychologist*, 1966, **21**, 20–26.

Gunzburg, H. C. A "finishing school" for the mentally subnormal. *Medical Officer*, 1965, **114**, 99–102.

Haaf, R. A.   Complexity and facial resemblance as determinants of response to facelike stimuli by 5- and 10-week-old infants. *Journal of Experimental Child Psychology,* 1974, **18,** 480–487.

Haaf, R. A., & Bell, R. Q.   A facial dimension in visual discrimination by human infants. *Child Development,* 1967, **38,** 893–899.

Hagen, J. W., & Hale, G. A.   The development of attention in children. In A. D. Pick, ed., *Minnesota symposium on child psychology,* Minneapolis: University of Minnesota Press, 1973, 7.

Haith, M. M.   The response of the human newborn to visual movement. *Journal of Experimental Child Psychology,* 1966, **3,** 235–243.

Hall, G. S.   *Adolescence,* I. New York: Appleton, 1904.

Hall, G. S.   *Adolescence,* II. New York: Appleton, 1905.

Halloran, J. D.   Television and violence. *The Twentieth Century,* 1964, **174,** 61–72.

Halverson, H. M.   An experimental study of prehension in infants by means of systematic cinema records. *Genetic Psychology Monographs,* 1931, **10,** 107–286.

Halverson, H. M.   Complications of the early grasping reactions. *Genetic Psychology Monographs,* 1936, **47,** 47–63.

Hamburg, B. A.   The psychology of sex differences: An evolutionary perspective. In R. C. Friedman, R. N. Richart, & R. L. Vande Wiele, eds., *Sex differences in behavior.* New York: John Wiley, 1974.

Handlon, J., & Gross, P.   The development of sharing behavior. *Journal of Abnormal and Social Psychology,* 1959, **59,** 425–428.

Hanratty, M. A.   Imitation of film-mediated aggression against live and inanimate victims. Unpublished master's thesis. Vanderbilt University, 1969.

Hanratty, M. A., Liebert, R. M., Morris, L. W., & Fernandez, L. E.   Imitation of film-mediated aggression against live and inanimate victims. Proceedings of the 77th Annual Convention of the American Psychological Association, 1969, **4.** 457–458 (Summary).

Hanratty, M. A., O'Neal, E., & Sulzer, J. L.   The effect of frustration upon imitation of aggression. *Journal of Personality and Social Psychology,* 1972, **21,** 30–34.

Hansen, R., & Neujahr, J.   Career development of males and females gifted in science. *The Journal of Educational Research,* 1974, **68,** 43–45.

Hardyck, C., & Petrinovich, L. F.   Left-handedness. *Psychological Bulletin,* 1977, **84,** 385–404.

Harlow, H.   The formation of learning sets. *Psychological Review,* 1949, **56,** 51–65.

Harlow, H.   The nature of love. *American Psychologist,* 1958, **13,** 673–685.

Harlow, H.   *Learning to Love.* New York: Ballantine, 1971.

Harlow, H. F., & Harlow, M. K.   Learning to think. *Scientific American,* 1949, **181,** 36–39.

Harlow, H. F., & Harlow, M. K.   The young monkeys. In P. Cramer, ed., *Readings in developmental psychology today.* Del Mar, CA: CRM Books, 1970, pp. 58–63.

Harlow, H. F., & Zimmerman, R. R.   Affectional responses in the infant monkey. *Science,* 1959, **130,** 431–432.

Harmon, L. R.   The development of a criterion of scientific competence. In C. W. Taylor and F. Barron, eds., *Scientific creativity: Its recognition and development.* New York: John Wiley, 1963.

Harris, M. B., & Siebel, C. E.   Affect, aggression, and altruism. *Developmental Psychology,* 1976, **11,** 623–627.

Harris, M. B., & Trujillo, A. E.   Improving study habits of junior high school students: A comparison of self-management and group discussion approaches. *Journal of Counseling Psychology,* 1975.

Harry, J.   Evolving sources of happiness for men over the life cycle: A structural analysis. *Journal of Marriage and the Family,* 1976, **38,** 289–296.

Harter, S.   The effects of social reinforcement and task difficulty level on the pleasure derived by normal and retarded children from cognitive challenge and mastery. *Journal of Experimental Child Psychology,* 1977.

Harter, S.   Pleasure derived from challenge and the effects of receiving grades on children's difficulty level choices. Unpublished manuscript, University of Denver, 1980.

Harter, S.   Effectance motivation reconsidered: Toward a developmental model. In press, 1979. Publication outlet unspecified.

Hartig, M., & Kanfer, F. H.   The role of verbal self-instructions in children's resistance to temptation. *Journal of Personality and Social Psychology,* 1973, **25,** 259–267.

Hartmann, D. P., Gelfand, D. M., Smith, C. L., Paul, S. C., Cromer, C. C., & Lebenta, D. V.   Help or else: The effects of avoidance training procedures on children's altruistic behavior. Paper presented at meeting of Western Psychological Association, San Francisco, April 1974.

Hartmann, D. P., Gelfand, D. M., Smith, C. L., Paul, S. C Page, B. C., & Lebenta, D. V.   Factors affecting the acquisition and elimination of children's donating behavior. *Journal of Experimental Child Psychology,* 1976, **21,** 328–338.

Hartshorne, H., May, M. A., & Shuttleworth, F. K.   *Studies in the nature of character, Studies in deceit.* New York: Macmillan, 1928, 1.

Hartshorne, H., May, M. A., & Shuttleworth, F. K.   *Studies in the nature of character, Studies in the organization of character.* New York: Macmillan, 1930, 3.

Haven, E. W.   Factors associated with the selection of advanced academic mathematics courses by girls in high school. Research Bulletin 72-12. Princeton: N.J. Educational Testing Service, 1972.

Havighurst, R. J.   *Human development and education.* New York: Longmans Green, 1953.

Havighurst, R. J.   *The public schools of Chicago.* Chicago: The Board of Education of the City of Chicago, 1964.

Havighurst, R. J.   Minority subcultures and the law of effect. In F. F. Korten, S. W. Cook, and J. I. Lacey, eds., *Psychology and the problem of society.* Washington, D.C.: American Psychological Association, 1970, pp. 275–288.

Havighurst, R. J., Neugarten, B. L., & Tobin, S. S.   Disengagement and patterns of aging. In B. L. Neugarten, ed., *Middle age and aging.* Chicago: University of Chicago Press, 1968, pp. 161–172.

Havighurst, R. J., & Taba, H., eds.,   *Adolescent character and personality.* New York: John Wiley, 1949.

Hayes, C.   *The ape in our house.* New York: Harper & Row, Pub., 1951.

Hayes, H., White, B. L. and Held, R. Visual accommodation in human infants. *Science*, 1965, **148**, 528–530.

Healy, W., & Bronner, A. F. *New light on delinquency and its treatment.* New Haven: Yale University Press, 1936.

Heber, R. Research in prevention of socio-cultural mental retardation. In D. G. Forgays, ed., *Primary Prevention of Psychopathology.* Vol. 2: *Environmental Influences,* Hanover, NH: Univ. Press of New England, 39–62.

Heber, R., Garber, H., Harrington, S., Hoffman, C., & Falender, C. *Rehabilitation of Families at Risk for Mental Retardation.* Madison: Rehabil. Res. Train. Cent. Ment. Retard., Univ. Wisconsin, 1972.

Helson, R. Women mathematicians and the creative personality. *Journal of Consulting and Clinical Psychology, 1971,* **36,** 210–220.

Helson, R., & Crutchfield, R. S. Mathematicians: The creative researcher and the average Ph.D. *Journal of Consulting and Clinical Psychology, 1970,* **34,** 250–257.

Herbert, E. W., Gelfand, D. M., and Hartmann, D. Imitation and self-esteem as determinants of self-critical behavior. *Child Development,* 1969, **40,** 421–430.

Hershenson, M. Visual discrimination in the human newborn. *Journal of Comparative & Physiological Psychology,* 1964, **58,** 270–276.

Hersov, L. A. Persistent non-attendance at school. *Journal of Child Psychology and Psychiatry,* 1960, **1,** 130–136. (*a*)

Hersov, L. A. Refusal to go to school. *Journal of Child Psychology and Psychiatry,* 1960, **1,** 137–145. (*b*)

Herzog, E., & Sudia, C. E. Children in fatherless families. In B. M. Caldwell and H. N. Ricciuti, eds., *Review of child development literature.* Chicago: University of Chicago Press, 1973, 3.

Hess, E. H. Imprinting. *Science,* 1959, **130,** 133–141.

Hess, R. D. Social class and ethnic influences on socialization. In P. H. Mussen, ed., *Carmichael's manual of child psychology,* New York: John Wiley, 1970, **2,** 457–557.

Hess, R. D., & Shipman, V. C. Early experience and the socialization of cognitive modes in children. *Child Development,* 1965, **36,** 869–888.

Hess, R. D., & Shipman, V. C. Maternal attitudes toward the school and the role of the pupil: Some social class comparisons. In A. H. Passow, ed., *Developing programs for the educationally disadvantages.* New York: Teachers College, Columbia University, 1968.

Heston, L. L. Psychiatric disorders in foster home reared children of schizophrenic mothers. *British Journal of Psychiatry,* 1966, **112,** 819–825.

Hetherington, E. M. Effects of paternal absence on sex-typed behaviors in negro and white preadolescent males. *Journal of Personality and Social Psychology,* 1966, **4,** 87–91.

Hetherington, E. M. The effects of familial variables on sex typing, on parent-child similarity and on imitation in children. In J. P. Hill, ed., *Minnesota symposia on child psychology.* Minneapolis: University of Minnesota Press, 1967, 1.

Hetherington, E. M. Sex typing, dependency, and aggression. In T. D. Spencer and N. Kass, eds., *Perspectives in child psychology; Research and review.* New York: McGraw-Hill, 1970, pp. 193–231.

Hetherington, E. M. Effects of father absence on personal-ity development in adolescent daughters. *Developmental Psychology,* 1972, **7,** 313–326.

Hetherington, E. M., & McIntyre, C. W. Developmental psychology. In M. R. Rosenzweig and L. W. Porter, eds., *Annual review of psychology,* Palo Alto, CA: Annual Reviews, Inc., 1975, **26,** pp. 97–136.

Hetherington, E. M., & Martin, B. Family interaction and psychopathology in children. In H. C. Quay and J. S. Werry, eds., *Psychopathological disorders of childhood.* New York: John Wiley, 1972, pp. 30–82.

Higgins, E. T. A social and developmental comparison of oral and written communication skills. Doctoral dissertation, Columbia University, 1973.

Higgins, E. T. Social class differences in verbal communication accuracy, *Psychological Bulletin,* 1976, **83,** 695–714.

Hilgard, E. R., & Bower, G. H. *Theories of learning.* New York: Appleton-Century-Crofts, 1966.

Hobbs, D. F., & Cole, S. P. Transition to parenthood: A decade replication. *Journal of Marriage and the Family,* 1976, **38,** 723–731.

Hobbs, N. Helping disturbed children: Ecological and psychological strategies. *American Psychologist,* 1966, **21,** 1105–1115.

Hoffman, L. W. Effects of maternal employment on the child—A review of the research. *Developmental Psychology,* 1974, **10,** 204–228.

Hoffman, M. L. Identification and conscience development. *Child Development,* 1971, **42,** 1071–1082.

Hoffman, M. L. Altruistic behavior and the parent-child relationship. Report #36, Developmental Program, Department of Psychology, University of Michigan, August 1973. (mimeo)

Hoffman, M. L. Moral internalization, parental power, and the nature of parent-child interaction. *Developmental Psychology,* 1975, **11,** 228–239.

Hoffman, M. L. Sex differences in empathy and related behaviors. *Psychological Bulletin,* 1977, **84,** 712–722.

Hoffman, L. W. Effects on children: Summary and discussion. In F. I. Nye & L. W. Hoffman, eds., *The employed mother in America.* Chicago, Rand McNally, 1963. (*a*)

Hoffman, L. W. Mother's enjoyment of work and effects on the child. In F. I. Nye & L. W. Hoffman, eds., *The employed mother in America.* Chicago: Rand McNally, 1963. (*b*)

Holland, J. L. *Making vocational choices: A theory of careers.* Englewood Cliffs, N.J.: Prentice-Hall, Inc., 1973.

Holland, V. M., & Palermo, D. C. On learning "less": Language and cognitive development. *Development,* 1975, **46,** 437–43.

Hollinger, C. S., & Jones, R. L. Community attitudes toward slow learners and mental retardates: What's in a name? *Mental Retardation,* 1970, **8,** 19–23.

Hollingshead, A. B. *Elmtown's youth: The impact of social classes on youth.* New York: John Wiley, 1949.

Hollingworth, L. S. *Children above 180 IQ.* New York: World Book Co., 1942, pp. 300–302.

Holmes, F. B. An experimental study of children's fears. In A. T. Jersild, & F. B. Holmes, eds., *Children's Fears.* New York: Columbia Univ. Teachers College, 1935, p. 167–296.

Holmes, L. B. Genetic counseling for the older pregnant woman: New data and questions. *The New England Journal of Medicine*, 1978, **298**, 1419–1421.

Holstein, C. B. Irreversible, stepwise sequence in the development of moral judgment: A longitudinal study of males and females. *Child Development*, 1976, **47**, 51–61.

Holtzman, W. H. The changing world of mental measurement and its social significance. *American Psychologist*, 1971, **26**, 546–553.

Homme, L. E., C'De Baca, P., Devine, J. R., Steinhorst, R., & Rickert, E. J. Use of the Premack principle in controlling the behavior of nursery school children. *Journal of the Experimental Analysis of Behavior*, 1963, **6**, 544.

Honzik, M. P. Environmental correlates of mental growth: Prediction from the family setting at 21 months. *Child Development*, 1967, **38**, 337–364.

Honzik, M. P., MacFarland, J. W., & Allen, L. The stability of mental test performance between 2 and 18 years. *Journal of Experimental Education*, 1948, **17**, 309–324.

Horn, J. L. Organization of data on life-span development of human abilities. In L. R. Goulet and P. B. Baltes, eds., *Lifespan developmental psychology: Research and theory*. New York: Academic Press, 1970, pp. 423–466.

Horn, J. L., & Cattell, R. B. Age differences in primary mental ability factors. *Journal of Gerontology*, 1966, **21**, 210–220.

Horn, J. L., & Donaldson, G. On the myth of intellectual decline in adulthood. *American Psychologist*, 1976, **31**, 701–719.

Horn, J. M., Plomin, R., & Rosenman, R. Heritability of personality traits in adult male twins. *Behavior Genetics*, 1976, **6**, 17–30.

Horner, M. S. Toward an understanding of achievement related conflicts in women. *Journal of Social Issues*, 1972, **28**, 157–176.

Horner, M. S. A psychological barrier to achievement in women: The motive to avoid success. In D. C. McClelland and R. S. Steele, eds., *Human motivation: a book of readings*. Morristown, N.J.: General Learning Press, 1973.

Horney, K. The flight from womanhood: The masculinity-complex as viewed by men and women. *International Journal of Psychoanalysis*, 1926, **7**, 324–329.

Horowitz, F. D. ed. Visual attention, auditory stimulation, and language discrimination in young infants. *Monographs of the Society for Research In Child Development*, 1974, **39** (5, Serial No. 158).

Hoy, E. Predicting another's visual perspective: A unitary skill? *Developmental Psychology*, 1974, **10**, 462.

Hoy, E. Measurement of egocentrism in children's communication. *Developmental Psychology*, 1975, **11**, 392.

Hoy, E., Weiss, G., Minde, K., & Cohen, N. The hyperactive child at adolescence: Cognitive, emotional and social functioning. *Journal of Abnormal Child Psychology*, 1978, **6**, 311–324.

Hoyer, W. J., Labouvie, G. V. & Baltes, P.B. Modification of response speed deficits and intellectual performance in the elderly. *Human Development*, 1973, **16**, 233–242.

Hubel, D. H. & Wiesel, T. N. Binocular interaction in striate cortex of kittens reared with artificial squint. *Journal of Neurophysiology*, 1965, **28**, 1041–1059.

Hubel, D. H. & Wiesel, T. N. The period of susceptibility to the physiological effects of unilateral eye closure in kittens. *Journal of Physiology*, 1970, **206**, 419–436.

Hughes, C. C., Tremblay, M., Rapoport, R. N., & Leighton, A. H. *People of cove and woodlot: Communities from the viewpoint of social psychiatry*. New York: Basic Books, 1960.

Hulsebus, R. C. Operant conditioning in infant behavior: a review. In H. W. Reese, ed., *Advances in child development and behavior*. New York: Academic Press, vol. 8, 1973.

Hunt, J. McV. *Intelligence and experience*. New York: The Ronald Press, 1961.

Hunt, J. McV. Psychological development: Early experience. *Annual Review of Psychology*, 1979, **30**, 103–43.

Hunt, J. McV., Mohandessi, K., Ghodssi, M., Akiyama, M. The psychological development of orphan-age-reared infants: Interventions with outcomes. Tehran: *Genetic Psychology Monograph*, 1976, **94**, 177–226.

Hunt, J. McV., & Quay, H. C. Early vibratory experience and the question of innate reinforcement value of vibration and other stimuli: A limitation on the discrepancy (burnt soup) principle in motivation. *Psychological Review*, 1961, **68**, 149–56.

Hunt, M. *Sexual behavior in the 1970s*. Chicago, IL: Playboy Press, 1974.

Hunter, I. M. L. Tactile-kinesthetic perception of straightness in blind and sighted humans. *Quarterly Journal of Experimental Psychology*, 1954, **6**, 149–154.

Husén, T. ed. *International study of achievement in mathematics. A comparison of twelve countries*. N.Y.: John Wiley, 1967, Vol. I, II.

Hutt, C., & Hutt, S. J. The neonatal evoked heart rate response and the law of initial value. *Psychophysiology*, 1970, **6**, 661–668.

Huttenlocher, J., Eisenberg, K., & Strauss, S. Comprehension: Relation between perceived actor and logical subject. *Journal of Verbal Learning and Verbal Behavior*, 1968, **7**, 527–530.

Huyck, M. H. Sex and the older woman. In L. Troll, J. Isreal and K. Isreal, eds., *Looking ahead: A woman's guide to the problems and joys of growing older*. Englewood Cliffs, N.J.: Prentice Hall, Inc., 1977.

Illingworth, R. S. Predictive value of developmental tests in the 1st year. *Journal of Child Psychology and Psychiatry*, 1961, **2**, 210–215.

Infant Mortality Rates: Socioeconomic Factors. Vital and Health Statistics, Series 22, Number 14. U.S. Department of Health, Education, and Welfare. Rockville, MD, 1972.

Inhelder, B. *The diagnosing of reasoning in the mentally retarded*. New York: John Day Co., 1968.

Isen, A. M., Horn, N., & Rosenhan, D. L. Effects of success and failure on children's generosity. *Journal of Personality and Social Psychology*, 1973, **27**, 239–247.

Jackson, D. *The etiology of schizophrenia*. New York: Basic Books, 1960.

Jackson, P. W. & Messick, D. Creativity. In P. London and D. Rosenhan, eds., *Foundations of abnormal psychology*. New York: Holt, Rinehart, & Winston, 1968, pp. 226–250.

Jacobs, B. S., & Moss, H. A. Birth order and sex of sibling as determinants of mother-infant interaction. *Child Development*, 1976, **47**, 315–322.

Jacobs, J. *Adolescent suicide*. New York: John Wiley, 1971.

Jacobs, P. A., Brunton, M., & Melville, M. M. Aggressive behavior, mental subnormality and the XYY male. *Nature*, 1965, **208**, 1351–1352.

Jakobson, R. Why "mama and papa"? In *Selected writings of Roman Jakobson.* The Hague: Mouton, 1962, pp. 538–545.

Jaslow, P. Employment, retirement, and morale among older women. *Journal of Gerontology,* 1976, **31,** 212–218.

Jeffers, F. C., & Verwoerdt, A. How the old face death. In E. W. Busse and E. Pfeiffer, eds., *Behavior and adaptation in late life.* Boston: Little, Brown, 1969, 163–181.

Jencks, C., Smith, M., Acland, H., Bane, M., Cohen, D., Gintis, H., Heyns, B., & Michelson, S. *Inequality: A reassessment of the effect of family and schooling in America.* New York: Basic Books, 1972.

Jensen, A. R. How much can we boost IQ and scholastic achievement? *Harvard Educational Review,* 1969, **39,** 1–123.

Jensen, A. R. Level I and Level II abilities in three ethnic groups. *American Educational Research Journal,* 1973, **10,** 263–276.

Jensen, A. R. Cumulative deficit: A testable hypothesis? *Developmental Psychology,* 1974, **10,** 996–1019. (a)

Jensen, A. R. Interaction of Level I and Level II abilities with race and socioeconomic status. *Journal of Educational Psychology,* 1974, **66,** 99–111. (b)

Jensen, A. R. Cumulative deficit in IQ of blacks in the rural south. *Developmental Psychology,* 1977, **13,** 184–191.

Jensen, A. R. Sir Cyril Burt in perspective. *American Psychologist,* 1978, **33,** 499–503.

Jensen, A. R., and Figueroa, R. A. Forward and backward digit span interaction with race and IQ: Predictions from Jensen's theory. *Journal of Educational Psychology,* 1975, **67,** 882–893.

Jensen, G. D. Mother-infant relationship in the monkey *Macaca nemestrina:* Development of specificity of maternal response to own infant. *Journal of Comparative and Physiological Psychology,* 1965, **59,** 305–308.

Jersild, A. T. *Child psychology* (6th ed.) Englewood Cliffs, NJ: Prentice-Hall, Inc., 1968.

Jersild, A. T., & Holmes, F. B. *Children's fears.* New York: Bureau of Publications, Teacher's College, Columbia University, 1935.

Jesperson, J. O. *Language: Its nature, development, and origin.* London: Allen and Unwin, 1922.

Joffe, J. M. *Prenatal determinants of behavior.* Oxford, England: Pergamon, 1969.

Johnston, A., DeLuca, D., Murtaugh, K., & Diener, E. Validation of a laboratory play measure of child aggression. *Child Development,* 1977, **48,** 324–327.

Jones, M. C. Psychological correlates of somatic development. *Child Development,* 1965, **36,** 899–911.

Jones, M. C., & Bayley, N. Physical maturing among boys as related to behavior. *Journal of Educational Psychology,* 1950, **41,** 129–148.

Jones, M. C., & Mussen, P. H. Self-conceptions, motivations, and interpersonal attitudes of early and late maturing girls. *Child Development,* 1958, **29,** 491–501.

Kagan, J., Kearsley, R. B., and Zelazo, P. R. The Effects of Infant Day Care on Psychological Development. Paper presented at the American Association for the Advancement of Science meeting, Boston, February 1975. (ERIC Document Reproduction Service No. ED 122 946.)

Kagan, J., & Klein, R. E. Cross cultural perspectives on early development. *American Psychologist,* 1973, **28,** 947–961.

Kagan, S., & Madsen, M. C. Cooperation and competition of Mexican, Mexican-American, and Anglo-American children of two ages and four instructional sets. *Developmental Psychology,* 1971, **5,** 32–39.

Kagan, S., & Madsen, M. C. Experimental analyses of cooperation and competition of Anglo-American and Mexican children. *Developmental Psychology,* 1972, **6,** 49–59. (a)

Kagan, S., & Madsen, M. C. Rivalry in Anglo-American and Mexican children of two ages. *Journal of Personality and Social Psychology,* 1972, **24,** 214–220. (b)

Kalil, K., Youssef, Z., & Lerner, R. M. Class-inclusion failure: Cognitive deficit or misleading reference? *Child Development,* 1974, **45,** 1122–1125.

Kallmann, F. J. *The genetics of schizophrenia.* Locust Valley, NY: J. J. Augustin, Publisher, 1938.

Kallmann, F. J., & Sander, G. Twin studies on senescence. *American Journal of Psychiatry,* 1949, **106,** 29–36.

Kamin, L. Heredity, intelligence, politics, and psychology. Unpublished mimeo, Princeton University, 1974. (a)

Kamin, L. *The science and politics of IQ.* Potomac, Md.: Eribaum, 1974. (b)

Kandel, D. Stages in adolescent involvement in drug use. *Science,* 1975, **190,** 912–914.

Kandel, D., & Faust, R. Sequence and stages in patterns of adolescent drug use. *Archives of General Psychiatry,* 1975, **32,** 923–932.

Kandel, D. B., Kessler, R. C., & Margulies, R. Z. Antecedents of adolescent initiation into stages of drug use: A developmental analysis. *Journal of Youth and Adolescence,* 1978, **7,** 13–40.

Kandel, D. B., & Lesser, G. S. *Youths in two worlds.* San Francisco: Jossey Bass, 1972.

Kanner, L. Autistic disturbances of affective contact. *Nervous Child,* 1943, **2,** 217–250.

Kanner, L. Early infantile autism. *Journal of Pediatrics,* 1944, **25,** 211–217.

Kanner, L. Do behavior symptoms always indicate psychopathology? *Journal of Child Psychology and Psychiatry,* 1960, **1,** 17–25.

Kaplan, A. G., & Bean, J. P. *Beyond sex-role stereotypes: Readings toward a psychology of androgyny.* Boston: Little, Brown, 1976.

Kaplan, B. J. Malnutrition and mental deficiency. *Psychological Bulletin,* 1972, **78,** 321–334.

Karmel, B. Z. The effect of age, complexity, and amount of contour on pattern preferences in human infants. *Journal of Experimental Child Psychology,* 1969, **7,** 339–354.

Karmel, B. Z. Contour effects and pattern preferences in infants: A reply to Greenberg and O'Donnell (1972). *Child Development,* 1974, **45,** 196–199.

Karmel, B. Z., Hoffman, R. F. & Fegy, M. J. Processing of contour information by human infants evidenced by pattern-dependent potentials, *Child Development,* 1974, **45,** 39–48.

Karp, L. E. *Genetic engineering: Threat or promise?* Chicago: Nelson-Hall, 1976.

Kasatkin, N. I. First conditioned responses and the beginnings of the learning process in the human infant. In G. Newton & A. H. Riesen, eds., *Advances in psychobiology,* New York: John Wiley, 1972, 1.

Kasatkin, N. I., & Levikova, A. M.   On the development of early conditioned reflexes and differentiations of auditory stimuli in infants. *Journal of Experimental Psychology*, 1935, **18**, 1–19.

Kastenbaum, R.   *Humans developing.* Boston: Allyn & Bacon, 1979.

Kastenbaum, R., & Costa, P. T.   Psychological perspectives on death. *Annual Review of Psychology*, 1977, **28**, 225–249.

Katkovsky, W., Crandall, V. C., and Good, S.   Parental antecedents of children's beliefs in internal-external control of reinforcement in intellectual achievement situations. *Child Development*, 1967, **38**, 765–776.

Keating, D. P.   Precocious cognitive development at the level of formal operation. *Child Development*, 1975, **46**, 276–280.

Keating, D. P., & Caramazza, A.   Effects of age and ability on syllogistic reasoning in early adolescence. *Developmental Psychology*, 1975, **11**, 837–842.

Keating, D. P., & Schaefer, R. A.   Ability and sex differences in the acquisition of formal operations. *Developmental Psychology*, 1975, **11**, 531–532.

Keen, R. E.   Effects of auditory stimuli on sucking behavior in the human neonate. *Journal of Experimental Child Psychology*, 1964, **1**, 348–354.

Kellogg, W. N., & Kellogg, L. A.   *The ape and the child: A study of environmental influence upon early behavior.* New York: McGraw-Hill, 1933.

Kempe, C. H., Silverman, F. N., Steele, B. F., Droegemueller, W., & Silver, H. K.   The battered-child syndrome. *Journal of American Medical Association*, 1962, **181**, 17–24.

Kempler, B.   Stimulus correlates of area judgments: A psychophysical developmental study. *Developmental Psychology*, 1971, **4**, 158–163.

Kendler, T. S.   Development of mediating responses in children. In J. C. Wright and J. Kagan, eds., *Basic cognitive processes in children. Monographs of the Society for Research in Child Development*, 1963, **28**, 33–51.

Kendler, T. S.   The effect of training and stimulus variables on the reversal-shift ontogeny. *Journal of Experimental Child Psychology*, 1974, **17**, 87–106.

Kendler, T. S., Kendler, H. H., & Learnard, B.   Mediated responses to size and brightness as a function of age. *American Journal of Psychology*, 1962, **75**, 571–586.

Kennedy, W. A.   School phobia: Rapid treatment of fifty cases. *Journal of Abnormal Psychology*, 1965, **70**, 285–289.

Kennedy, W. A.   A follow-up normative study of Negro intelligence and achievement. *Monographs of the Society for Research in Child Development*, 1969, **34**, Serial No. 126.

Kennedy, W. A., Van de Riet, V., & White, J. C., Jr.   A normative sample of intelligence and achievement of Negro elementary school children in the southeastern United States. *Monographs of the Society for Research in Child Development*, 1963, **28**, No. 6.

Kent, N., & Davis, D. R.   Discipline in the home and intellectual development. *British Journal of Medical Psychology*, 1957, **30**, 27–33.

Kessen, W.   *The child.* New York: John Wiley, 1965.

Kessen, W., Haith, M. M., & Salapatek, P. H.   Infancy. In P. H. Mussen, ed., *Carmichael's manual of child psychology*, New York: John Wiley, 1970, **1**, pp. 287–445.

Kessler, J. W.   *Psychopathology of childhood.* Englewood Cliffs, NJ: Prentice-Hall, Inc., 1966.

Kety, S. S., Rosenthal, D., Wender, P. H., & Schulsinger, F.   The types and prevalence of mental illness in the biological and adoptive families of adopted schizophrenics. In Rosenthal and Kety, eds., *The transmission of schizophrenia*, 1968, pp. 345–362.

King, L. M.   Social and cultural influences on psychopathology. In M. R. Rosenzweig & L. W. Porter, eds., *Annual Review of Psychology*, 1978, **29**, 405–433.

King, S. H.   Coping and growth in adolescence. *Seminars in Psychiatry*, 1972, **4**, 343–353.

Kingsley, R. C., & Hall, V.   Training conservation through the use of learning sets. *Child Development*, 1967, **38**, 111–126.

Kirk, S. A.   *Educating exceptional children.* 2nd ed. Boston: Houghton-Mifflin, 1972.

Kissel, S.   A study in childhood egocentricity. *Journal of Clinical Psychology*, 1975, **31**, 646–648.

Kistiakowsky, V.   Women in engineering, medicine, and science. Conference on Women in Science and Engineering, National Research Council, 1973.

Klapper, J. T.   The impact of viewing "aggression": Studies and problems of extrapolation. In O. N. Larsen, ed., *Violence and the mass media.* New York: Harper & Row, Inc., 1968.

Klaus, M. H. and Kennell, J. H.   Parent-to-infant attachment. In J. H. Stevens, Jr. & M. Mathews, eds., *Mother/child, father/child relationships.* Washington, D.C., The National Association for the Education of Young Children, 1978, 5–29.

Klein, D. F., & Gittelman-Klein, R.   Problems in the diagnosis of minimal brain dysfunction and the hyperkinetic syndrome. In R. Gittelman-Klein, ed., *Recent advances in child psychopharmacology.* New York: Human Sciences Press, 1975, pp. 47–63.

Kluger, R.   *Simple justice.* New York; Knopf, 1976.

Knobloch, H., & Pasamanick, B.   Seasonal variations in the births of the mentally deficient. *American Journal of Public Health*, 1958, **48**, 1201–1208.

Knobloch, H., & Pasamanick, B.   *Gesell and Amatruda's developmental diagnosis.* New York: Harper & Row, 1974.

Knopf, I. J.   *Childhood psychopathology: A developmental approach.* Englewood Cliffs, N.J.: Prentice-Hall, Inc., 1979.

Knox, D. H.   Conceptions of love at three developmental levels. *The Family Coordinator*, 1970, **19**, 151–157.

Knox, D. H., & Sporakowski, M. J.   Attitudes of college students toward love. *Journal of Marriage and the Family*, 1968, **30**, 638–642.

Koch, H. L.   The relation of primary mental abilities in five- and six-year-olds to sex of child and characteristics of his siblings. *Child Development*, 1954, **25**, 209–223.

Koch, H. L.   Sibling influence on children's speech. *Journal of Speech Disorder*, 1956, **21**, 322–328.

Kogan, N., & Pankove, E.   Creative ability over a five year span. *Child Development*, 1972, **43**, 427–442.

Kohlberg, L.   The development of children's orientations toward a moral order: I. Sequence in the development of moral thought. *Vita Humana*, 1963, **6**, 11–33.

Kohlberg, L.   A cognitive-developmental analysis of children's sex-role concepts and attitudes. In E. E. Maccoby, ed., *The development of sex differences.* Stanford: Stanford University Press, 1966, 82–173.

Kohlberg, L. Moral and religious education and the public schools: A developmental view. In T. Sizer, ed., *Religion and public education*. Boston: Houghton-Mifflin, 1967.

Kohlberg, L. Stage and sequence: The cognitive-developmental approach to socialization. In D. A. Goslin, ed., *Handbook of socialization theory and research*. Chicago: Rand McNally, 1969, 347–480.

Kohlberg, L. From is to ought: How to commit the naturalistic fallacy and get away with it in the study of moral development. In T. Mischel, ed., *Cognitive development and epistemology*. New York: Academic Press, 1971, pp. 151–235.

Kohlberg, L. The claim to moral adequacy of a highest stage of moral judgment. *Journal of Philosophy*, 1973, **70**, 630–646.

Kohlberg, L. Moral stages and moralization: The cognitive-developmental approach. In T. Lickona, ed., *Moral development and behavior: Theory, research, and social issues*. New York: Holt, Rinehart, & Winston, 1976.

Kohlberg, L., & Kramer, R. Continuities and discontinuities in childhood and adult moral development. *Human Development*, 1969; **12**, 93–120.

Kohlberg, L., La Crosse, J., & Ricks, D. The predictability of adult mental health from childhood behavior. In B. Wolman, ed., *Manual of child psychopathology*. New York: McGraw-Hill, 1972, pp. 1217–1283.

Kohlberg, L., & Ullian, D. Z. Stages in the development of psychosexual concepts and attitudes. In R. C. Friedman, R. M. Richart, & R. L. Van Wiele, eds., *Sex differences in behavior*. New York: John Wiley, 1974.

Kohn, M. L. Social class and parent-child relationships: An interpretation. *American Journal of Sociology*, 1963, **68**, 471–480.

Kolata, G. B. Behavioral teratology: Birth defects of the mind. *Science*, 1978, **202**, 732–734. (a)

Kolata, G. B. In vitro fertilization: Is it safe and repeatable? *Science*, 1978, **201**, 698–699. (b)

Komarovsky, M. Cultural contradictions and sex-roles: The masculine case. *American Journal of Sociology*, 1973, **78**, 783–884.

Korslund, M. K., & Eppright, E. S. Taste sensitivity and eating behavior of preschool children. *Journal of Home Economics*, 1967, **59**, 168–170.

Kotelchuck, M. The nature of a child's tie to his father. Unpublished doctoral dissertation, Harvard University, 1972.

Kotelchuck, M. The infant's relationship to the father: experimental evidence. In M. E. Lamb, ed., *The Role of the Father in Child Development*. New York: John Wiley, 1976.

Kotelchuck, M., Zelazo, P., Kagan, J., and Spelke, E. Infant reaction to parental separations when left with familiar and unfamiliar adults. *Journal of Genetic Psychology*, 1975, **126**, 255–262.

Kratcoski, P. C., & Kratcoski, J. E. Changing patterns in the delinquent activities of boys and girls: A self-reported delinquency analysis. *Adolescence*, 1975, **10**, 83–91.

Krauss, R. M., & Weinheimer, S. Changes in reference phrases as a function of frequency of usage in social interaction: A preliminary study. *Psychonomic Science*, 1964, **1**, 343–346.

Kreutzer, M. A., Leonard, C., & Flavell, J. H. An interview study of children's knowledge about memory. *Monographs of the Society for Research in Child Development*, 1975, **40**, (1, Serial No. 159).

Kron, R. E., Stein, M., & Goddard, K. E. A method of measuring sucking behavior of newborn infants. *Psychosomatic Medicine*, 1963, **25**, 181.

Kübler-Ross, E. *On death and dying*. New York: Macmillan, 1969.

Kuhn, K., & Angelev, J. An experimental study of the development of formal operational thought. *Child Development*, 1976, **47**, 697–706.

Kundsin, R. B., ed., *Women and success*. N.Y.: Morrow, 1974.

Kurke, M. The role of motor experience in the visual discrimination of depth in the chick. *Journal of Genetic Psychology*, 1955, **86**, 191–196.

Kurtines, W., & Greif, E. B. The development of moral thought: Review and evaluation of Kohlberg's approach. *Psychological Bulletin*, 1974, **81**, 453–470.

Kutner, B., Fanshel, D., Togo, A., & Langner, T. S. Factors related to adjustment in old age. In R. G. Kuhlen and G. G. Thompson, eds., *Psychological studies of human development*. Englewood Cliffs, NJ: Prentice Hall, Inc., 1970, pp. 583–595.

Labov, W. The logic of nonstandard English. In F. Williams, ed., *Language and poverty: Perspectives on a theme*. Chicago: Markham Publishing Co., 1970.

Labov, W., Cohen, P., Robins, C., & Lewis, J. *A study of the non-standard English of Negro and Puerto Rican speakers in New York City*. 2 vols. Final Report, U.S. Office of Education Cooperative Research Project No. 3288. New York: Columbia University, 1968. (Mimeographed.)

Lagerspetz, K. Genetics and social causes of aggressive behavior in mice. *Scandinavian Journal of Psychology*, 1961, **2**, 167–173.

Laird, M. D., & Hogan, M. An elective program of preparation for childbirth at the Sloan Hospital for Women. *American Journal of Obstetrics and Gynecology*, 1956, **72**, 647.

Lamaze, F. *Painless childbirth*. Chicago: Henry Regnery Co., 1970.

Lamb, M. E. The relationships between infants and their mothers and fathers. Doctoral dissertation, Yale University, 1975.

Lamb, M. E. Effects of stress and cohort on mother- and father-infant interaction. *Developmental Psychology*, 1976, **12**, 435–443. (a)

Lamb, M. E. Interactions between eight-month-old children and their fathers and mothers. In M. E. Lamb, ed., *The role of the father in child development*. New York: John Wiley, 1976. (b)

Lamb. M. E. Interactions between two-year-olds and their mothers and fathers. *Psychological Reports*, 1976, **38**, 447–450. (c)

Lamb. M. E. The one-year-old's interaction with its parents. Paper presented at the Eastern Psychological Association meeting, New York, April 1976. (d)

Lamb. M. E. The role of the father: An overview. In M. E. Lamb, ed., *The role of the father in child development*. New York: John Wiley, 1976. (e)

Lamb, M. E. Father-infant and mother-infant interaction in the first year of life. *Child Development*, 1977, **48**, 167–181. (a)

Lamb, M. E. The development of mother-infant and father-infant attachments in the second year of life. *Development Psychology*, 1977, **13**, 637–648. (b)

Lamb, M. E. The father's role in the infant's social world. In J. H. Stevens, Jr., & M. Mathews, eds., *Mother/child, father/*

child relationship. Washington, D.C., The National Association for the Education of Young Children, 1978, 87–108.

Landreth, C. *Early childhood: Behavior and learning.* New York: Knopf, 1967.

Lane, H. *The wild boy of Aveyron.* Cambridge, MA: Harvard University Press, 1976.

Lange-Eichbaum, W. *The problem of genius.* New York: Macmillan, 1932.

Langford, W. Anxiety attacks in children. *American Journal of Orthopsychiatry,* 1937, **7,** 210–219.

Lapouse, R., & Monk, M. An epidemiologic study of behavior characteristics in children. *American Journal of Public Health,* 1958, **48,** 1134–1144.

Lappé, M., & Morison, R. S., eds., Ethical and scientific issues posed by human uses of molecular genetics. *Annals of the New York Academy of Science,* 1976, **265.**

Lashley, K. S., & Russell, J. T. The mechanism of vision: XI. A preliminary test of innate organization. *Journal of Genetic Psychology,* 1934, **45,** 136–144.

Latané, B., & Rodin, J. A lady in distress: inhibiting effects of friends and strangers on bystander intervention. *Journal of Experimental Social Psychology,* 1969, **5,** 189–203.

Lawrence, W., & Kartye, J. Extinction of social competency skills in severely and profoundly retarded females. *American Journal of Mental Deficiency,* 1971, **75,** 630–634.

Lazarus, A. The result of behavior therapy in 126 cases of severe neuroses. *Behavior Research and Therapy,* 1963, **1,** 69–79.

Leaf, A. Getting old. *Scientific American,* September, 1973.

Leary, M. E. Children who are tested in an alien language: Mentally retarded? *The New Republic,* 1970, **162,** 17–18.

Leboyer, F. *Birth without violence.* New York: Knopf, 1975.

Lee, G. R. Marriage and morale in later life. *Journal of Marriage and the Family,* 1978, **40,** 131–139.

Leff, R. Effects of punishment intensity and consistency on the internalization of behavioral suppression in children. *Developmental Psychology,* 1969, **1,** 27–56.

Lefkowitz, M. M., Eron, L. D., Walder, L. O., & Huesmann, L. R. Television violence and child aggression: A followup study. In G. A. Comstock and E. A. Rubinstein, eds., *Television and social behavior,* Vol. III: *Television and adolescent aggressiveness.* Washington, D.C.: U.S. Government Printing Office, 1972, 35–135.

Lefkowitz, M. M., Eron, L. D., Walder, L. O., Huesmann, L. R. *Growing up to be violent: A longitudinal study of the development of aggression.* N.Y.: Pergamon Press, 1977.

Leifer, A., Leiderman, P., Barnett, C., & Williams, J. Effects of mother-infant separation on maternal attachment behavior. *Child Development,* 1972, **43,** 1203–1218.

Leifer, A. D., & Roberts, D. F. Children's responses to television violence. In J. P. Murray, E. A. Rubinstein, and G. A. Comstock, eds., *Television and social behavior,* Vol. II: *Television and social learning.* Washington, D.C.: U.S. Government Printing Office, 1972, 43–180.

Leizer, J. I., & Rogers, R. W. Effects of method of discipline, timing of punishment, and timing of test on resistance to temptation. *Child Development,* 1974, **45,** 790–793.

LeMasters, E. E. Parenthood as crisis. *Marrige and family living,* November, 1957.

Lenneberg, E. H. *Biological foundations of language.* New York: John Wiley, 1967.

Lennox, W. G., Gibbs, E. L., & Gibbs, F. A. Inheritance of cerebral dysrhythmia and epilepsy. *Archives of Neurological Psychiatry,* 1940, **44,** 1155.

Leonard, L. B. The role of nonlinguistic stimuli and semantic relations in children's acquisition of grammatical utterances. *Journal of Experimental Child Psychology,* 1975, **19,** 346–367.

Lepper, M. R., Greene, D., & Nisbett, R. E. Undermining children's intrinsic interest with extrinsic reward: A test of the "overjustification" hypothesis. *Journal of Personality and Social Psychology,* 1973, **28,** 129–137.

Lerner, R. M., & Knapp, J. R. Actual and perceived intrafamilial attitudes of late adolescents and their parents. *Journal of Youth and Adolescence,* 1975, **4,** 17–36.

Lerner, R. M., & Korn, S. J. The development of body build stereotypes in males. *Child Development,* 1972, **43,** 908–920.

Lesser, G. Problems in the analysis of pattern abilities: A reply. *Child Development,* 1973, **44,** 19–20.

Lesser, G., Fifer, G., & Clark, D. H. Mental abilities of children from different social-class and cultural groups. *Monographs of the Society for Research in Child Development,* 1965, **30,** (4, Whole No. 102).

Lester, B. M. Cardiac habituation of the orienting response to an auditory signal in infants of varying nutritional status. *Developmental Psychology,* 1975, **11,** 432–442.

Levenstein, P. Cognitive growth in preschoolers through verbal interaction with mothers. *American Journal of Orthopsychiatry,* 1970, **40,** 426–432.

Levenstein, P. VIP children reach school: Latest chapter. Verbal Interaction Project. Progress Report, 1974.

Levenstein, P. A message from home: findings from a program for nonretarded, low-income preschoolers. In M. J. Begab, and S. B. Richardson, eds., *The mentally retarded and society: A social science perspective.* Baltimore: University Park Press, 1975.

Levenstein, P. The mother-child home program. In *The Preschool in Action,* M. C. Day & R. K. Parker, eds., Boston: Allyn & Bacon, 1976. 2nd ed.

Leventhal, A. S., & Lipsitt, L. P. Adaptation, pitch discrimination, and sound localization in the neonate. *Child Development,* 1964, **35,** 759–767.

Levine, F., & Fasnecht, B. Token rewards may lead to token learning. *American Psychologist,* 1974, **29,** 816–820.

Levine, M. The development of hypothesis testing. In Liebert, R. M., Poulos, R. W., & Strauss, G. D., *Developmental psychology.* Englewood Cliffs, NJ: Prentice-Hall, Inc., 1974.

LeVine, R. A. Cross-cultural study in child psychology. In P. H. Mussen, ed., *Carmichael's manual of child psychology,* New York: John Wiley, 1970, **2,** 559–612.

LeVine, R. A. Parental goals: A cross-cultural view. *Teachers College Record,* 1974, **76,** 226–239.

Levinson, D. J., Darrow, C. M., Klein, E. B., Levinson, M. H., & Braxton, M. The psychosocial development of men in early adulthood and the mid-life crisis. In D. F. Ricks, A. Thomas, and M. Roff, eds., *Life history research in psychopathology,* Minneapolis: University of Minnesota Press, 1974, **3,** 243–258.

Levinson, D. J., Darrow, C. M., Klein, E. B., Levinson, M. H., & McKee, B. *The seasons of a man's life.* New York: Knopf, 1978.

Levitt, E. E. The results of psychotherapy with children: An evaluation. *Journal of Consulting Psychology,* 1957, **21**, 189–196.

Levitt, E. E. Psychotherapy with children: A further evaluation. *Behavior Research and Therapy,* 1963, **1**, 45–51.

Lewis, M., ed. *Origins of intelligence: Infancy and early childhood,* New York: Plenum, 1976.

Lewis, M., & Weintraub, M. Sex of parents X sex of child: Socioemotional development. In R. C. Friedman, R. M. Richart, & R. L. Van Wiele, eds., *Sex differences in behavior.* New York: John Wiley, 1974.

Liberty, C., & Ornstein, P. A. Age differences in organization and recall: The effects of training in categorization. *Journal of Experimental Child Psychology,* 1973, **15**, 169–186.

Liebert, R. M. Effects of an available therapeutic activity on reactions to failure. Unpublished doctoral dissertation, Stanford University, 1966.

Liebert, R. M. Television and social learning: Some relationships between viewing violence and behaving aggressively. In J. P. Murray, E. A. Rubinstein, and G. A. Comstock, eds., *Television and social behavior,* Vol. II: *Television and social learning.* Washington, D.C.: U.S. Government Printing Office, 1972, 1–43.

Liebert, R. M. Moral development: A theoretical and empirical analysis. In G. J. Whitehurst, and B. Zimmerman, eds., *The functions of language and cognition.* New York: Academic Press, 1979.

Liebert, R. M., & Fernandez, L. E. Effects of vicarious consequences on imitative performance. *Child Development,* 1970, **41**, 847–852.

Liebert, R. M., Neale, J. M., & Davidson, E. S. *The early window: Effects of television on children and youth.* New York: Pergamon Press Inc., 1973.

Liebert, R. M., & Ora, J. P. Children's adoption of self-reward patterns: Incentive level and method of transmission. *Child Development,* 1968, **39**, 537–544.

Liebert, R. M., & Poulos, R. W. Television and personality development: socializing effects of an entertainment medium. In A. Davids, ed., *Personality development and psychopathology: Current topics,* New York: John Wiley, 1975, **2**, 61–97.

Liebert, R. M., & Schwartzberg, N. S. Effects of mass media. *Annual Review of Psychology,* 1977, **28**, 141–173.

Liebert, R. M., Sobol, M. P., & Copemann, C. D. Effects of vicarious consequences and race of model upon imitative performance by black children. *Developmental Psychology,* 1972, **6**, 453–456.

Liebert, R. M., Speigler, M. D., & Hall, M. Effects of the value of contingent self-administered and noncontingent externally imposed reward on children's behavioral productivity. *Psychonomic Science,* 1970, **18**, 245–246.

Liebert, R. M., Sprafkin, J. N., & Poulos, R. W. Selling cooperation to children. In W. S. Hale, ed., *Proceedings of the 20th Annual Conference of the Advertising Research Foundation.* New York: Advertising Research Foundation, Inc., 1975, 54–57.

Liebman, R., Minuchin, S., & Baker, L. The use of structural family therapy in the treatment of intractable asthma. *American Journal of Psychiatry,* 1974, **131**, 535–540.

Lifshitz, M., & Ramot, L. Toward a framework for developing children's locus of control: Implications from the kibbutz system. *Child Development,* 1978, **49**, 85–95.

Light, R. J. Abused and neglected children in America: A study of alternative policies. *Harvard Educational Review,* 1973, **43**, 556–598.

Lind, J. 1973: personal communication, as cited by Klaus, M. H., and Kennell, J. H. Parent-to-infant attachment, in J. H. Stevens, Jr., & M. Matthews, eds., *Mother/child, father/child relationships.* Washington, D.C., The National Association for the Education of Young Children, 1978.

Lipsitt, L. P., Engen, T., & Kaye, H. Developmental changes in the olfactory threshold of the neonate. *Child Development,* 1963, **34**, 371–376.

Lipsitt, L. P., & Levy, N. Electrotactual threshold in the neonate. *Child Development,* 1959, **30**, 547–554.

Loehlin, J. C., & Nichols, R. C. *Heredity, environment and personality.* Austin: University of Texas Press, 1976.

Loew, C. A. Acquisition of a hostile attitude and its relationship to aggressive behavior. *Journal of Personality and Social Psychology,* 1967, **5**, 335–341.

London, P., & Hemphill, B. M. The motivations of blood donors. *Transfusion,* 1965, **5**, 559–568.

Long, R. T., Lamont, J. H., Whipple, B., Bandler, L., Blom, G. E., Burgin, L., & Jessner, L. A psychosomatic study of allergic and emotional factors in children with asthma. *American Journal of Psychiatry,* 1958, **114**, 890–899.

Longstreth, L. E. Incentive stimuli as determinants of instrumental response strength in children. *Journal of Comparative and Physiological Psychology,* 1962, **55**, 398–401.

Lotter, V. Social adjustment and placement of autistic children in Middlesex: A follow-up study. *Journal of Autism and Childhood Schizophrenia,* 1974, **4**, 1, 11–32.

Lotter, V. Follow-up studies. In M. Rutter and E. Schopler, eds., *Autism: A reappraisal of concepts and treatment.* New York: Plenum, 1978, 475–495.

Lovaas, O. I. Some studies in the treatment of childhood schizophrenia. In J. M. Schlien, ed., *Research in psychotherapy: Proceedings of the third conference.* Washington, D.C.: American Psychological Association, 1968, 103–121.

Lovitt, T. Behavior modification: The current scene. *Exceptional children,* 1970, **37**, 85–91.

Loye, D., Gorney, R., & Steele, G. Effects of television: An experimental field study. *Journal of Communication,* 1977, **27** (3), 206–216.

Lubchenco, L. O., Horner, F. A., Reed, L. H., Hix, I. E., Metcalf, D., Cohig, R., Elliott, H. C., & Bourg, M. Sequelae of premature birth. *American Journal of Diseases of Children,* 1963, **106**, 101–115.

Ludwig, D. J., & Maehr, M. L. Changes in self concept and stated behavioral preferences. *Child Development,* 1967, **38**, 453–467.

Lynn, D. B. *The father: His role in child development.* Monterey, CA: Brooks/Cole, 1974.

Lytton, H., Martin, N. G., & Eaves L. Environmental and genetical causes of variation in ethological aspects of behavior in two-year-old boys. *Social Biology,* 1977, **24**, 200–211.

McAnarney, E. Adolescent and young adult suicide in the U.S.—A reflection of societal unrest? *Adolescence,* 1979, **14**, 765–774.

McArthur, L. Z., & Eisen, S. V. Achievements of male and female storybook characters as determinants of achievement behavior by boys and girls. *Journal of Personality and Social Psychology,* 1975.

McAskie, M. Carelessness or fraud in Sir Cyril Burt's kinship data? A critique of Jensen's analysis. *American Psychologist*, 1978, **33**, 496–498.

McCall, J. N., & Johnson, O. G. The independence of intelligence from family size and birth order. *Journal of Genetic Psychology*, 1972, **121**, 207–213.

McCall, R. B., Applebaum, M. I., & Hogarty, P. S. Developmental changes in mental performance. *Monographs of the Society for Research in Child Development*, 1973, **38**, Whole No. 150.

McCall, R. B., & Melson, W. H. Complexity, contour, and area as determinants of attention in infants. *Developmental Psychology*, 1970, **3**, 343–349.

McCartney, W. *Olfaction and odours.* New York: Springer-Verlag, 1968.

McClearn, G. E. Genetic influences on behavior and development. In P. H. Mussen, ed., *Carmichael's manual of child psychology*, 3rd ed. New York: Wiley, 1970, 39–76.

McClelland, D. C. The importance of early learning in the formation of motives. In J. Atkinson, ed., *Motives in fantasy, action and society.* Princeton: D. Van Nostrand, 1958.

McClelland, D. C. *The achieving society.* Princeton, N.J.: D. Van Nostrand, 1961.

McClelland, D. C., Atkinson, I. W., Clark, R., & Lowell, E. *The achievement motive.* New York: Appleton-Century-Crofts, 1953.

Maccoby, E., & Feldman, S. Mother-attachment and stranger-reactions in the third year of life. *Monographs of the Society for Research in Child Development*, 1972, **37**, (no. 1, serial no. 146).

Maccoby, E. E., & Hagen, J. W. Effects of distraction upon central versus incidental recall: developmental trends. *Journal of Experimental Child Psychology*, 1965, **2**, 280–289.

Maccoby, E. E., & Jacklin, C. N. *The psychology of sex differences.* Stanford, CA: Stanford University Press, 1974.

McCrae, J., & Herbert-Jackson, E. Are behavioral effects of infant day care programs specific? *Developmental Psychology*, 1976, **12**, 269–270.

MacFarland, J. W., Allen, L., & Honzik, M. P. *A developmental study of the behavior problems of normal children.* Berkeley: University of California Press, 1954.

McGurk, H., & Lewis, M. Space perception in early infancy: Perception within a common auditory-visual space? *Science*, 1974, **186**, 649–50.

McIntyre, J. J., & Teevan, J. J. Television violence and deviant behavior. In G. A. Comstock and E. A. Rubinstein, eds., *Television and social behavior*, Vol. III: *Television and adolescent aggressiveness.* Washington, D.C.: U.S. Government Printing Office, 1972, pp. 383–435.

MacKinnon, D. W. The nature and nurture of creative talent. *American Psychologist*, 1962, **17**, 484–495.

MacKinnon, D. W. Selecting students with creative potential. In P. Heist, ed., *The creative college student: An unmet challenge.* San Francisco: Jossey-Bass, 1968.

Mackworth, J. F. Development of attention. In V. Hamilton and M. D. Vernon, eds., *The development of cognitive processes.* New York: Academic Press, 1976.

McLeod, J. M., Atkin, C. K., & Chaffee, S. H. Adolescents, parents, and television use: Adolescent self-report measures from Maryland and Wisconsin samples. In G. A. Comstock and E. A. Rubinstein, eds., *Television and social behavior*, Vol. III: *Television and adolescent aggressiveness.* Washington, DC: U.S. Government Printing Office, 1972, pp. 173–238.

McNeil, E. B. *The concept of human development.* Belmont, CA: Wadsworth, 1966.

McNeill, D. *The acquisition of language.* New York: Harper & Row, Pub., 1970. (*a*)

McNeill, D. The development of language. In P. Mussen, ed., *Carmichael's manual of child psychology.* New York: John Wiley, 1970, pp. 1061–1161. (*b*)

McNemar, Q. *The revision of the Stanford-Binet Scale: An analysis of the standardization data.* Boston: Houghton-Mifflin, 1942.

MacRae, J. M. Retests of children given mental tests as infants. *Journal of Genetic Psychology*, 1955, **87**, 111–119.

Maddox, G. L. Fact and artifact: Evidence bearing on disengagement theory from the Duke Geriatrics Project. *Human Development*, 1965, **8**, 117–130.

Maddox, G. L., & McCall, B. C. *Drinking among teen-agers.* New Brunswick, NJ: Rutgers Center of Alcohol Studies, 1964.

Madsen, C. H., Becker, W. C., Thomas, D. R., Koser, L., & Plager, E. An analysis of the reinforcing function of "sit down" commands. In R. K. Parker, ed., *Readings in Educational Psychology.* Boston: Allyn & Bacon, 1968.

Madsen, M. C. Developmental and cross-cultural differences in the cooperative and competitive behavior of young children. *Journal of Cross-Cultural Psychology*, 1971, **2**, 365–371.

Madsen, M. C., & Shapira, A. Cooperative and competitive behavior of urban Afro-American, Anglo-American, Mexican-American, and Mexican village children. *Developmental Psychology*, 1970, **3**, 16–20.

Magenis, R. E., Overton, K. M., Chamberlin, J., Brady, T., & Lovrien, E. Parental origin of the extra chromosome in Down's syndrome. *Human Genetics*, 1977, **37**, 7–16.

Maier, H. W. *Three theories of child development.* New York: Harper & Row, Pub., 1969.

Malinowski, B. *Sex and repression in savage society.* New York: Harcourt Brace Jovanovich, Inc., 1927.

Mallick, S. K., & McCandless, B. A study of catharsis of aggression. *Journal of Personality and Social Psychology*, 1966, **4**, 591–596.

Mandler, G. Organization and recognition. In E. Tulving and W. Donaldson, eds., *Organization of Memory*, New York: Academic Press, 1972.

Marcia, J. E. Development and validation of ego identity status. *Journal of Personality and Social Psychology*, 1966, **3**, 551–558.

Marcia, J. E. Identity six years after: A follow-up study. *Journal of Youth and Adolescence*, 1976, **5**, 145–160.

Marg, E., Freeman, D. N., Peltzman, P., & Goldstein, P. Visual acuity development in human infants: Evoked potential measurements. *Investigative Opthamology*, 1976, **15**, 150–153.

Margolies, P. J. Behavioral approaches to the treatment of early infantile autism: A review. *Psychological Bulletin*, 1977, **84**, 249–264.

Marihuana and health. Department of Health, Education, and Welfare, Washington, D.C.: U.S. Government Printing Office, 1971.

Markman, E. M., & Siebert, J. Classes and collections: Internal organization and resulting holistic properties. *Cognitive Psychology,* 1976, **8,** 561–577.

Martin, B. Parent-child relations. In F. Horowitz, ed., *Review of child development literature.* Chicago: University of Chicago Press, 1975, **4,** pp. 463–470.

Martin, C. E. Sexual activity in the aging male. In J. Money, & H. Mousafh, eds., *Handbook of sexology.* Amsterdam: ASP Biol. Med. Press, 1977.

Martinson, R. A. *Educational programs for gifted children.* Sacramento: California State Department of Public Instruction, 1961.

Martinson, R. A. Analysis of problems and priorities: Advocate survey and statistical sources. Appendix B. In Marland, 1971, pp. B1–B35.

Martinson, R. A., Hermanson, D., & Banks, G. An independent study-seminar for the gifted. *Exceptional Children,* 1972, **38,** 421–426.

Marvin, R. S., Greenberg, M. T. & Mossler, D. G. The early development of conceptual perspective taking: Distinguishing among multiple perspectives. *Child Development,* 1976, **47,** 511–514.

Marx, J. L. Aging research: Cellular theories of senescence. *Science,* 1974, 240–242.

Marx, J. L. Restriction enzymes: Prenatal diagnosis of genetic disease. *Science,* 1978, **202,** 1068–1069.

Masangkay, Z., McClusky, K., McIntyre, C., Sims-Knight, J., Vaughn, B., & Flavell, J. The early development of inferences about the visual percepts of others. *Child development,* 1974, **45,** 357–366.

Masters, W. H., & Johnson, V. E. *Human sexual response.* Boston: Little, Brown, 1966.

Masters, W. H., & Johnson, V. E. *Human sexual inadequacy.* Boston: Little, Brown, 1970.

Matheny, A. P., Wilson, R. S., Dolan, A. B. Relations between twins' similarity of appearance and behavioral similarity: Testing an assumption. *Behavior Genetics,* 1976, **6,** 343–351.

Matza, D. Subterranean traditions of youth. *The Annals of the American Academy of Political and Social Sciences,* 1961, **338,** 102–118.

Maurer, D., & Salapatik, P. Developmental changes in the scanning of faces by young infants. *Child Development,* 1976, **77,** 523–527.

Mead, M. *Coming of age in Samoa.* New York: Morrow, 1928.

Mead, M. *Sex and temperament in three primitive societies.* New York: Morrow, 1935.

Mednick, M. T. Research creativity in psychology graduate students. *Journal of Consulting Psychology,* 1963, **23,** 827–830.

Mednick, S. A. A learning theory approach to research in schizophrenia. *Psychological Bulletin,* 1958, **55,** 316–327.

Mednick, S. A. Breakdown of individuals at high risk for schizophrenia: Possible predispositional perinatal factors. *Mental Hygiene,* 1970, **54,** 50–63.

Mednick, S. A., & Schulsinger, F. Some premorbid characteristics related to breakdown in children with schizophrenic mothers. In D. Rosenthal and S. S. Kety, eds., *The transmission of schizophrenia.* Elmsford, NY: Pergamon Press, 1968.

Meichenbaum, D. Theoretical and treatment implications of developmental research on verbal control of behavior. *Canadian Psychological Review,* 1975, **16,** 22–27.

Meichenbaum, D., & Goodman, J. Training impulsive children to talk to themselves: A means of developing self-control. *Journal of Abnormal Psychology,* 1971, **77,** 115–126.

Meilman, P. W. Cross-sectional age changes in ego identity status during adolescence. *Developmental Psychology,* 1979, **15,** 230–231.

Mendel, G. Experiments in plant-hybridization, 1865. Reprinted in J. A. Peters, ed., *Classic papers in genetics.* Englewood Cliffs, NJ: Prentice-Hall, Inc., 1959, pp. 1–20.

Menig-Peterson, C. L. The modification of communicative behavior in preschool-aged children as a function of the listener's perspective. *Child Development,* 1975, **46,** 1015–1018.

Menn, L. *Pattern, control, and contrast in beginning speech: A case study in the development of word form and word function.* Unpublished doctoral dissertation, University of Illinois, 1976.

Mesibov, G. B., Schroeder, C. S., & Wesson, L. Parental concerns about their children. *Journal of Pediatric Psychology,* 1977, **2,** 13–17.

Miller, D. T., Weinstein, S. M., & Karniol. R. Effects of age and self-verbalization on children's ability to delay gratification. *Developmental Psychology,* 1978, **14,** 569–570.

Miller, G. A. The magical number seven, plus or minus two: Some limits on our capacity for processing information. *Psychological Review,* 1956, **63** (2), 81–97.

Miller, J. P. Suicide and adolescence. *Adolescence,* 1975, **10,** 11–24.

Miller, L. C., Barrett, C. L., Hampe E., & Noble, H. Factor structure of childhood fears. *Journal of Consulting and Clinical Psychology,* 1972, **39,** 264–268.

Miller, N. E., & Dollard, J. *Social learning and imitation.* New Haven: Yale University Press, 1941, 1953.

Miller, R. W. Susceptibility of the fetus and child to chemical pollutants. *Science,* 1974, **184,** 812–813.

Miller, W., & Ervin, S. The development of grammar in child language. In U. Bellugi and R. Brown, eds., *The acquisition of language. Monographs of the Society for Research in Child Development,* 1964, **29,** (1, whole No. 92), 9–34.

Miller, W. A., & Erbe, R. W. Prenatal diagnosis of genetic disorders. *Southern Medical Journal,* 1978, **71,** 201–207.

Miller, W. B. Lower class culture as a generating milieu of gang delinquency. *Journal of Social Issues,* 1958, **14,** 5–19.

Millon, T. *Modern psychopathology: A biosocial approach to maladaptive learning and functioning.* Philadelphia: Saunders, 1969.

Mischel, W. Preference for delayed reinforcement: An experimental study of a cultural observation. *Journal of Abnormal and Social Psychology,* 1958, **56,** 57–61.

Mischel, W. A social-learning view of sex differences in behavior. In E. E. Maccoby, ed., *The development of sex differences.* Stanford, CA: Stanford University Press, 1966.

Mischel, W. *Personality and assessment.* New York: John Wiley, 1968.

Mischel, W. Sex-typing and socialization. In P. H. Mussen, ed. *Carmichaels' Manual of child psychology,* New York: John Wiley, 1970, **2.**

Mischel, W. *Introduction to personality.* New York: Holt, Rinehart, & Winston, 1971.

Mischel, W. Processes in delay of gratification. In L. Berkowitz, ed., *Advances in Experimental Psychology,* New York: Academic Press, 1974, **7,** 249–292.

Mischel, W., & Ebbesen, E. Attention in delay of gratification. *Journal of Personality and Social Psychology*, 1970, **16**, 329–337.

Mischel, W., Ebbesen, E., & Raskoff, A. Cognitive and attentional mechanisms in delay of gratification. Unpublished manuscript, Stanford University, 1971.

Mischel, W., & Liebert, R. M. Effects of discrepancies between observed and imposed reward criteria on their acquisition and transmission. *Journal of Personality and Social Psychology*, 1966, **3**, 45–53.

Mischel, W., & Metzner, R. Preference for delayed reward as a function of age, intelligence, and length of delay interval. *Journal of Abnormal and Social Psychology*, 1962, **64**, 1425–431.

Mischel, W., & Patterson, C. J. Substantive and structural elements of effective plans for self-control. *Journal of Personality and Social Psychology*, 1976, **34**, 942–950.

Mischel, W., & Staub, E. Effects of expectancy on waiting and working for larger rewards. *Journal of Personality and Social Psychology*, 1965, **2**, 625–633.

Mitford, J. *The American way of death.* New York: Simon & Schuster, 1963.

Moely, B. E., Olson, F. A., Halwes, T. G., & Flavell, J. H. Production deficiency in young children's clustered recall. *Developmental Psychology*, 1969, **1**, 25–34.

Mohr, G. J., Taus, H., Selesnick, S. & Augenbraun, B. Studies of eczema and asthma in the pre-school child. *Journal of American Academic Child Psychiatry*, 1963, **2**, 271–291.

Money, J., & Ehrhardt, A. *Man and woman; boy and girl.* Baltimore: Johns Hopkins University Press, 1972.

Money, J., & Nurcombe, B. Ability tests and cultural heritage: The Draw-a-Person and Bender tests in aboriginal Australia. *Journal of Learning Disabilities*, 1974, **7**, 297–303.

Montagu, M. F. A. *Prenatal influences.* Springfield, IL: Chas C Thomas, 1962.

Montagu, M. F. A. *Life before birth.* New York: Signet, 1965.

Monthly Vital Statistics Report, Final Mortality Statistics, 1977, No. 79-1120. Hyattsville, MD: National Center For Health Statistics, H.E.W., 1979.

Moore, B. S., Underwood, B., & Rosenhan, D. L. Affect and altruism. *Developmental Psychology*, 1973, **8**, 99–104.

Moore, T. Children of full-time and part-time mothers. *International Journal of Social Psychiatry*, 1964, **2**, 1–10.

Moore, T. Stress in normal childhood. *Human Relations*, 1969, **22**, 235–250.

Morrison, J. R., & Stewart, M. A. A family study of the hyperactive child syndrome. *Biological Psychiatry*, 1971, **3**, 189–195.

Morse, P. A. The discrimination of speech and nonspeech stimuli in early infancy. *Journal of Experimental Child Psychology*, 1972, **14**, 477–492.

Moss, H. A. Sex, age and state as determinants of mother-infant interaction. *Merrill-Palmer Quarterly*, 1967, **13**, 19–36.

Moss, H. A., Robson, K. S., and Pedersen, F. Determinants of maternal stimulation of infants and consequences of treatment for later reactions to strangers. *Developmental Psychology*, 1969, **1**, 239–246.

Mowrer, O. H. The meaning and management of crying, *Child Study*, Jan. 1–5, 1938.

Mowrer, O. H., & Mowrer, W. M. Enuresis: A method for

its study and treatment. *American Journal of Orthopsychiatry*, 1938, **8**, 436–447.

Moynihan, D. P. *The Negro family: The case for national action.* Washington, D.C.: Office of Policy Planning and Research, Department of Labor, 1965.

Mozans, H. J. *Woman in science.* Cambridge, MA: MIT Press, 1974.

Mueller, E. The maintenance of verbal exchanges between young children. *Child Development*, 1972, **43**, 930–938.

Munn, N. L. *Psychology: The fundamentals of human adjustment.* Boston: Houghton Mifflin, 1946.

Munsinger, H. Children's resemblance to their biological and adopting parents in two ethnic groups. *Behavior Genetics*, 1975, **5**, 239–254.

Murphy, G. *Psychological thought from Pythagoras to Freud.* New York: Harcourt Brace Jovanovich, Inc., 1968.

Murray, J. P., & Ahammer, T. M. *Kindness in the kindergarten: A multi-dimensional program for facilitating altruism.* Paper presented to the biennial meeting of the Society for Research in Child Development, New Orleans, March 1977.

Murrell, F. H. The effect of extensive practice on age differences in reaction time. *Journal of Gerontology*, 1970, **25**, 268–274.

Mussen, P. H., & Jones, M. C. Self-conceptions, motivations, and interpersonal attitudes of early and late maturing boys. *Child Development*, 1957, **28**, 243–256.

Muuss, R. E. Adolescent development and the secular trent. In D. Rogers, ed., *Issues in adolescent development.* New York: Appleton-Century-Crofts, 1972.

Naeye, R. L., personal communication, 1979.

Nash, J. Historical and social changes in the perception of the role of the father. In M. E. Lamb, ed., *The role of the father in child development.* New York: Wiley, 1976.

Neale, J. M., & Liebert, R. M. *Science and behavior, second edition.* Englewood Cliffs, NJ: Prentice-Hall, Inc., 1980.

Neale, J. M. & Oltmanns, T. F. *Schizophrenia.* New York; John Wiley, 1980.

Nealey, S. M., & Edwards, B. J. "Depth perception" in rats without pattern vision experience. *Journal of Comparative and Physiological Psychology*, 1960, **53**, 468–469.

Neimark, E. D. Model for a thinking machine: An information-processing framework for the study of cognitive development, *Merrill-Palmer Quarterly*, 1970, **16**, 345–68.

Neimark, E. D. Intellectual development during adolescence. In F. D. Horowitz, ed., *Review of child development research.* Chicago: University of Chicago Press, 1975, **4**. (a)

Neimark, E. D. Longitudinal development of formal operations thought. *Genetic Psychology Monographs*, 1975, **91**, 171–225. (b)

Neimark, E. D., Slotnick, N. S., & Ulrich, T. Development of memorization strategies. *Developmental Psychology*, 1971, **5**, 427–432.

Nelson, K. Structure and strategy in learning to talk. *Monograph of the Society for Research in Child Development*, 1973, **38**, No. 149.

Nelson, K. Concept, word, and sentence: Interrelations in acquisition and development. *Psychological Review*, 1974, **81**, 267–285.

Nelson, L., & Madsen, M. C. Cooperation and competition

in four-year-olds as a function of reward contingency and subculture. *Developmental Psychology,* 1969, **1,** 340–344.

Nelson, M. M., Asling, C. W., & Evans, H. M. Production of multiple congenital abnormalities in young by pteroylglutamic acid deficiency during gestation. *Journal of Nutrition,* 1952, **48,** 61–80.

Neugarten, B. L. A new look at menopause. *Psychology Today,* December, 1967.

Neugarten, B. L. Age groups in American society and the rise of the young-old. *Annals of the American Academy,* September 1974, 187–198.

Neugarten, B. L. The rise of the young-old. In Gross, R., Gross, B., & Seidman, S., eds., *The new old: Struggling for decent aging.* Garden City, New York: Doubleday, 1978.

Neugarten, B., Moore, J. W., & Lowe, J. C. Age norms, age constraints, and adult socialization. *The American Journal of Sociology,* 1965, **70,** 710–717.

Newberger, E. H. The myth of the battered child syndrome. In R. Bourne and E. H. Newberger, eds., *Critical perspectives on child abuse.* Lexington, MA: Heath, 1979.

Newell, K. M. & Kennedy, J. A. Knowledge of results and children's motor learning. *Developmental Psychology,* 1978, **14,** 531–536.

Newman, G., & Nichols, C. R. Sexual activities and attitudes in older persons. *Journal of the American Medical Association,* 1960, **173,** 521–530.

Newman, H. H., Freeman, F. N., & Holzinger, K. J. *Twins: A study of heredity and environment.* Chicago: University of Chicago Press, 1937.

Newsweek, February 28, 1977.

Newton, N. The effect of psychological environment on childbirth: Combined cross-cultural and experimental approach. *Journal of Cross-Cultural Psychology,* 1970, **1,** 85–90.

New York Times. Family ponders its rare, fatal hereditary disease. September 30, 1975.

1975 Handbook on Women Workers. Washington, D.C.
1975 Bureau, US Department of Labor, Bulletin 297.

Nissen, H. W., Chow, K. L., & Semmes, J. Effects of restricted opportunity for tactile, kinaesthetic and manipulative experience on the behavior of a chimpanzee. *American Journal of Psychology,* 1951, **64,** 485–507.

Nowlis, H. H. *Drugs on the college campus.* New York: Doubleday, 1969.

Nuckolls, K. B., Cassell, M. D., & Kaplan, B. H. Psychosocial assets, life crisis, and the prognosis of pregnancy. *American Journal of Epidemiology,* 1972, **95,** 431–441.

Nunnally, J. C., & Lemond, L. C. Exploratory behavior and human development. In H. W. Reese, ed., *Advances in child development and behavior,* Vol. 8. New York: Academic Press, 1973, 59–109.

O'Bryan, K. G., & Boersma, F. J. Eye movements, perceptual activity, and conservation development. *Journal of Experimental Child Psychology,* 1971, **12,** 157–169.

O'Connor, K., Mann, D., & Bardwick, J. M. Relationships between self-ratings of individual and stereotypical sex-role identification and self-esteem in an upper class adult population. *Journal of Consulting and Clinical Psychology,* 1978, **46.**

Offer, D., & Offer, J. *From teenage to young manhood: A psychological study.* New York: Basic Books, 1975.

O'Leary, K. D. Pills or skills for hyperactive children. Manuscript based on Presidential address, Clinical Division, Section III, Experimental-Behavioral Science, American Psychological Association, Toronto, Canada, August 1978. (*a*)

O'Leary, K. D. The etiology of hyperactivity. Paper presented at the Second Annual Italian Behavior Therapy Association Meeting, Venice, Italy, June 1978. (*b*)

O'Leary, K. D., & O'Leary, S. G. *Classroom management.* New York: Pergamon Press, 1972.

O'Leary, K. D., Poulos, R. W., & Devine, V. T. Tangible reinforcers: Bonuses or bribes? *Journal of Consulting and Clinical Psychology,* 1972, **38,** 1–8.

O'Leary, D. C. & Wilson, G. T. *Behavior therapy: Application and outcome.* Englewood Cliffs, N.J.: Prentice Hall, Inc., 1975.

Olson, G. M. An information processing analysis of visual memory and habituation in infants. In T. J. Tighe and R. N. Leaton, eds., *Habituation: Perspectives from child development, animal behavior, and neurophysiology.* Hillsdale, NJ: Lawrence Erlbaum Associates, 1976.

Ornstein, P. A. Memory development in children. In R. M. Liebert, R. W. Poulos, and G. S. Marmor, *Developmental psychology, 2nd Ed.* Englewood Cliffs, NJ: Prentice-Hall, Inc., 1977.

Ornstein, P. A., Hale, G. A., & Morgan, J. S. Developmental differences in recall and output organization. *Bulletin of the Psychonomic Society,* 1977, **9,** 29–32.

Ornstein, P. A., Naus, M. J., & Liberty, C. Rehearsal and organizational processes in children's memory. *Child Development,* 1975, **46,** 818–830.

Osen, L. M. *Women in mathematics.* Cambridge, MA: MIT Press, 1974.

Palme, O. The emancipation of man. In M. S. Mednick and S. S. Tangri, eds., New perspectives on women. *Journal of Social Issues,* 1972, **28,** No. 2.

Palmer, F. H. Inferences to the socialization of the child from animal studies: A view from the bridge. In D. A. Goslin, ed., *Handbook of socialization theory and research.* Chicago: Rand McNally, 1969, pp. 25–55.

Palmer, F. H., & Semlear, T. Early intervention as compensatory education. In Liebert, R. M., Poulos, R. W., & Marmor, G. S. *Developmental psychology,* 2nd ed. Englewood Cliffs, NJ: Prentice-Hall, Inc., 1977.

Paloutzian, R. F., Hasazi, J., Streifel, J., & Edgar, C. L. Promotion of positive social interaction in severely retarded young children. *American Journal of Mental Deficiency,* 1971, **75,** 519–524.

Parikh, B. S. *Moral judgment and its relation to family environmental factors in Indian and American urban upper middle class families.* Unpublished doctoral dissertation, Boston University, 1975.

Parke, R. D., & Collmer, C. W. Child abuse: An interdisciplinary analysis. In E. M. Hetherington, ed., *Review of child development research.* Chicago: University of Chicago Press, 1975, **5.**

Parke, R. D., & O'Leary, S. Father-mother-infant interaction in the newborn period: Some findings, some observations, and some unresolved issues. In K. F. Riegel and J. Meacham, eds., *The developing individual in a changing world,* The Hague: Mouton, 1975, **2.**

Parke, R. D., & Swain. D. B. The father's role in infancy: A reevaluation. *The Family Coordinator,* 1976, **25,** 365–371.

Parke, R. D., & Swain, D. B.   The family in early infancy: Social interactional and attitudinal analyses. Paper presented at the Society for Research in Child Development meeting, New Orleans, March 1977.

Parsons, T., & Bales, R. F.   *Family, socialization, and interaction process.* Glencoe, Il.: Free Press, 1955.

Pasamanick, B., Rogers, M. E., & Lilienfeld, A. M. Pregnancy experience and the development of behavior disorder in children. *American Journal of Psychiatry,* 1956, **112,** 613–618.

Passman, R., & Weisberg, P.   Mother and "security" blankets as familiarization objects for children's play behavior (The Linus phenomenon is real). Paper presented at the meeting of the Eastern Psychological Association, Boston, April 1972.

Patterson, G. R.   The aggressive child: Victim & architect of a coercive system. In E. J. Mack, L. A. Harmmerlynk, & L. C. Handy, eds., *Behavior modification in families.* New York: Brunner/Mazel, 1976.

Patterson, G. R.   A performance theory for coercive family interaction. In R. R. Cairns, ed., *Social interaction: Analysis & Illustration.* Hillsdale, NJ: Lawrence Erlbaum, 1979.

Pease, D., Wolens, L., & Stockdale, D. F.   Relationship and prediction of infant tests. *Journal of Genetic Psychology,* 1973, **122,** 31–35.

Pedersen, F. A., & Robson, K. S.   Father participation in infancy. *American Journal of Orthopsychiatry,* 1969, **39,** 466–472.

Peiper, A.   Sinnesempfindungen des Kindes vor seiner. *Geburt. Wschr. Kinderheilk,* 1925, **29,** 236–241.

Perlmutter, M.   What is memory aging the aging of? *Developmental Psychology,* 1978, **14,** 330–345.

Peppers, L. G.   Patterns of leisure and adjustment to retirement. *Gerontologist,* 1976, **16,** 441–446.

Perry, D. G., & Garrow, H.   The "social deprivation-satiation effect": An outcome of frequency or perceived contingency? *Developmental Psychology,* 1975, **11,** 681–688.

Peterson, C. L., Danner, F. W., & Flavell, J. H. Developmental changes in children's response to three indications of communicative failure. *Child Development,* 1972, **43,** 1463–1468.

Pfeiffer, E. Verwoerdt. A., & Davis, G.   Sexual behavior in middle life. *American Journal of Psychiatry,* 1972, **128,** 82–87.

Pfeiffer, E. Verwoerdt. A., & Wang, H.   The natural history of sexual behavior in a biologically advantaged group of aged individuals. *Journal of Gerontology,* 1969, **24,** 193–198.

Phillips, S., King, S., & DuBois, L.   Spontaneous activities of female versus male newborns. *Child Development,* 1978, **49,** 590–597.

Phillips, S., & Levine, M.   Probing for hypotheses with adults and children: Blank trials and introtacts. *Journal of Experimental Psychology: General,* 1975, **104,** 327–354.

Piaget, J.   *The language and thought of the child.* New York: Harcourt Brace Jovanovich, Inc., 1926.

Piaget, J.   *The origins of intelligence in children.* New York: International Universities Press, 1952.

Piaget, J.   *The moral judgment of the child.* New York: Collier, 1962.

Piaget, J.   Intellectual evolution from adolescence to adulthood. *Human Development,* 1972, **15,** 1–12.

Piaget, J., & Inhelder, B.   *Le développement des quantités chez l'enfant.* Neuchâtel: Delachaux and Niestle, 1941.

Piaget, J., & Inhelder, B.   *The child's conception of space.* Boston: Routledge & Kegan Paul, 1956.

Piaget, J., & Inhelder, B.   *The psychology of the child.* New York: Basic Books, 1969.

Piaget, J., & Inhelder, B.   *Memory and intelligence.* New York: Basic Books, 1973.

Pick, A. D., Frankel, D. G., & Hess, V. L.   Children's attention: The development of selectivity. In E. M. Hetherington, ed., *Review of child development research,* **5,** 1975.

Pick, H. L.   Research on taste in the Soviet Union. In M. R. Kare and B. P. Halpern, eds., *Physiological and behavioral aspects of taste.* Chicago: University of Chicago Press, 1961.

Pick, H. L., & Pick, A. D.   Sensory and perceptual development. In P. H. Mussen, ed., *Carmichael's manual of child psychology.* New York: John Wiley, 1970, **1,** 773–847.

Pietrinferno, G.   The development of comparison processes in children's communication. Doctoral dissertation, Princeton University, 1973.

Pine, G. J.   The affluent delinquent. *Phi Delta Kappan,* 1966, **48,** (4), 138–143.

Plomin, R., & DeFries, J. C.   Genetics and intelligence: Recent data. *Intelligence,* 1980, **4,** 15–24.

Plomin, R., & DeFries, J. C.   Multivariate behavioral genetic analysis of twin data on scholastic abilities. *Behavior Genetics,* 1979, **9,** 505–517.

Plomin, R., DeFries, J. C., & Loehlin, J. C.   Genotype-environment interaction and correlation in the analysis of human behavior. *Psychological Bulletin,* 1977, **84,** 309–322.

Plomin, R., DeFries, J. C., & McClearn, G. E.   *Behavioral genetics: A primer.* San Francisco: Freeman, 1980.

Plomin, R., & Foch, T. T.   A twin study of objectively assessed personality in childhood. *Journal of Personality and Social Psychology,* 1980, in press.

Plomin, R., Foch, T. T., & Rowe, D. C.   Aggression in late childhood: Environment, not genes. *Journal of Research in Personality,* 1980, in press.

Plomin, R., & Rowe, D. C.   A twin study of temperament in young children. *The Journal of Psychology,* 1977, **97,** 197–213.

Plomin, R., & Rowe, D. C.   Genetic and environmental etiology of social behavior in infancy. *Developmental Psychology,* 1979, **15,** 62–72.

Pollak, J. M.   Obsessive-compulsive personality: A review. *Psychological Bulletin,* 1979, **86,** 225–241.

Poppleton, P. K., & Brown, P. E.   The secular trend in puberty: Has stability been achieved? *British Journal of Educational Psychology,* 1966, **36,** 97–101.

Posner, M.   *Cognition: An introduction.* Glenview, IL: Scott, Foresman, 1973.

Poulos, R. W., & Liebert, R. M.   Influence of modeling, exhortative verbalization, and surveillance on children's sharing. *Developmental Psychology,* 1972, **6,** 402–408.

Powell, L. F.   The effects of extra stimulation and maternal involvement on the development of low-birth-weight infants and on maternal behavior. *Child Development,* 1974, **45,** 106–113.

Pratt, K. C.   The neonate. In L. Carmichael, ed., *Manual of child psychology.* 2nd ed. New York: John Wiley, 1954, pp. 215–291.

Premack, D. Reinforcement theory. In D. Levine, ed., *Nebraska Symposium on Motivation*. Lincoln: University of Nebraska Press, 1965, **13.**

President's Task Force on Manpower Conservation. *One-third of a nation.* Washington, D.C.: U.S. Government Printing Office, 1964.

Price, W. H., & Whatmore, P. B. Criminal behaviour and the XYY male. *Nature,* 1967, **213,** 815.

Priddle, R. E., & Rubin, K. H. A comparison of two methods for the training of spatial cognition. *Merrill-Palmer Quarterly,* 1977, **23,** 57–65.

Proshansky, H. The development of intergroup attitudes. In I. W. Hoffman, and M. L. Hoffman, eds., *Review of child development research.* New York: Russell Sage Foundation, 1966, **2.**

Proshansky, H., & Newton, P. The nature and meaning of Negro self-identity. In M. Deutsch, I. Katz, & A. R. Jensen, eds., *Social class, race, and psychological development.* New York: Holt, Rinehart, & Winston, 1968.

Proudfit, C. M. Estrogens and menopause. *Journal of the American Medical Association,* 1976, **236,** 939–940.

Purcell, K. Childhood asthma: The role of family relationships, personality, and emotions. In A. Davids, ed., *Child personality and psychology.* New York: Wiley Interscience, 1975, **2,** 101–135.

Purcell, K., Brady, K., Chai, H., Muser, J., Molk, L., Gorden, N., & Means, J. The effect on asthma in children of experimental separation from the family. *Psychosomatic Medicine,* 1969, **31,** 144–164.

Quay, H. C. Personality dimensions in delinquent males as inferred from the factor analysis of behavior ratings. *Journal of Research on Crime and Delinquency,* 1964, **1,** 33–37.

Rabinowitz, R. G. Internal-external control expectancies in black children of differing socioeconomic status. *Psychological Reports,* 1978, **42,** 1339–1345.

Radin, N. Father-child interaction and the intellectual functioning in four year old boys. *Developmental Psychology,* 1972, **6,** 353–361.

Radin, N. Observed paternal behaviors as antecedents of intellectual functioning in young boys. *Developmental Psychology,* 1973, **8,** 369–376.

Radin, N. The role of the father in cognitive, academic and intellectual development. In M. E. Lamb, ed., *The role of the father in child development.* New York: John Wiley, 1976.

Rainwater, L. The lower class: Health, illness, and medical institutions. In Rainwater, L., ed., *Social problems and public policy.* Chicago: Aldine, 1974, 179–187.

Rappaport, J. *Community psychology.* New York: Holt, Rinehart, & Winston, 1977.

Raskin, P. A. Sex-role development in young children: A review and integration of current models. Unpublished manuscript, State University of New York at Albany, 1979.

Reed, E. W. Genetic anomalies in development. In F. D. Horowitz, ed., *Review of child development research.* Chicago: University of Chicago Press, 1975, 59–99.

Rees, L. The importance of psychological, allergic and infective factors in childhood asthma. *Journal of Psychosomatic Research,* 1964, **7,** 253–262.

Reese, H. W., & Parnes, S. J. Programming creative behavior. *Child Development,* 1970, **41,** *1413–423.*

Reese, H. W., & Porges, S. W. Development of learning processes. In V. Hamilton & M. D. Vernon, eds., *The development of cognitive processes.* New York: Academic Press, 1976.

Reis, M. & Gold, D. Relation of paternal availability to problem solving and sex role orientation in young boys. *Psychological Reports,* 1977, **40,** 823–829.

Renshaw, S. The errors of cutaneous localization and the effect of practice on the localization movement in children and adults. *Journal of Genetic Psychology,* 1930, **28,** 223–238.

Rest, J. Development hierarchy in preference and comprehension of moral judgment. Unpublished doctoral dissertation, University of Chicago, 1968.

Reynolds, G. S. *A primer of operant conditioning.* Glenview, IL: Scott, Foresman, 1968.

Rheingold, H. L. The effect of environmental stimulation upon social and exploratory behavior in the human infant. In B. M. Foss, ed., *Determinants of Infant Behavior.* New York: John Wiley, 1961, 143–171.

Rheingold, H. L., & Eckerman, C. O. The infant separates himself from his mother. *Science,* 1970, **168,** 78–83.

Rheingold, H. L., Gewirtz, J. L., & Ross, H. W. Social conditioning of vocalizations in the infant. *Journal of Comparative and Physiological Psychology,* 1959, **52,** 68–73.

Rice, H. E., & Grusec, J. Saying and doing: Effects on observer performance. Journal of Personality and Social Psychology, 1975, **32,** 584–593.

Riegel, K. F., & Riegel, R. M. Development, drop, and death. *Developmental Psychology,* 1972, **6,** 306–319.

Riesen, A. H. Arrested vision. In R. S. Daniel, ed., *Contemporary readings in general psychology.* Boston: Houghton Mifflin, 1965, pp. 76–79.

Rimland, B. *Infantile autism: The syndrome and its implications for a neural theory of behavior.* New York: Appleton-Century-Crofts, 1964.

Rimland, B. The differentiation of childhood psychoses: An analysis of checklists for 2,218 psychotic children. *Journal of Autism and Childhood Schizophrenia,* 1971, **1,** 161–174.

Rimland, B. Infantile autism: Status and research. In A. Davids, ed., *Child personality and psychopathology: Current topics,* New York: Wiley Interscience, 1974, **1,** 137–167.

Rimm, D., Janda, L. H., Lancaster, D. W., Nahl, M., & Dittmar, K. An exploratory investigation of the origin and maintenance of phobias. *Behaviour Research and Therapy,* 1977, **15,** 231–238.

Rimm, D. C., & Masters, J. C. *Behavior therapy.* New York: Academic Press, 1979.

Rist, R. C. Student social class and teacher expectations: The self-fulfilling prophecy in ghetto education. *Harvard Educational Review,* 1970, **40,** 411–451.

Ritvo, E. R. Autism: From adjective to noun. In E. R. Ritvo, ed., *Autism: Diagnosis, current research and management.* New York: Spectrum Publ., 1976, pp. 3–6.

Roberge, J. J. Developmental analyses of two formal operational structures: Combinatorial thinking and conditional reasoning. *Developmental Psychology,* 1976, **12,** 563–564.

Robin, A. L., Armel, S., & O'Leary, K. D. The effects of self-instruction on writing deficiencies. *Behavior Therapy,* 1975, **6,** 178–187.

Robins, L. N. Deviant children grown up: A sociological

and psychiatric study of sociopathic personality. Baltimore: Williams and Wilkins, 1966.

Robins, L. N. Antisocial behavior disturbances of childhood: Prevalence, prognosis, and prospects. In E. J. Anthony, ed., *The child in his family,* New York: John Wiley, 1974, **3,** 447–460.

Robinson, H. B. *Social-cultural deprivation as a form of child abuse.* Governor's Council on Child Abuse. Raleigh: North Carolina State Board of Health, 1967.

Robinson, H. B., & Robinson, N. M. *The mentally retarded child: A psychological approach.* New York: McGraw-Hill, 1965.

Robinson, H. B., & Robinson, N. M. Mental retardation. In P. H. Mussen, ed., *Carmichael's Manual of Child Psychology.* New York: John Wiley, 1970, **2,** 615–658.

Robinson, N. M., & Robinson, H. B. A follow-up study of children of low birthweight and control children at school age. *Pediatrics,* 1965, **35,** 425–433.

Robinson, N. M., & Robinson, H. B. *The mentally retarded child: A psychological approach.* New York: McGraw-Hill, 1976.

Robinson, W. P. The elaborated code in working class language. *Language and Speech,* 1965, **8,** 243–252.

Robson, K. S., & Moss, H. A. Bethesda, Maryland: Child Research branch, NIMH. Unpublished findings as cited in H. F. Harlow, 1971.

Robson, K. S., Pedersen, F. A., and Moss, H. A. "Developmental Observations of Dyadic Gazing in Relation to the Fear of Strangers and Social Approach Behavior." *Child Development* 40, no. 2 (1969): 619–627.

Rocha, R. F., & Rogers, R. W. Ares and Babbitt in the classroom: Effects of competition and reward on children's aggression. *Journal of Personality and Social Psychology,* 1976, **33,** 588–593.

Rogers, D. *The adult years, and introduction to aging.* Englewood Cliffs, N.J.: Prentice Hall, Inc., 1979.

Rollins, B. C., & Feldman, H. Marital satisfaction over the family life cycle. *Journal of Marriage and the Family,* 1970, **32,** 20–28.

Rosen, B. C. The reference group approach to the parental factor in attitude and behavior formation. *Social Forces,* 1955, **34,** 137–144.

Rosen, B. C., & D'Andrade, R. The psychological origins of achievement motivation. *Sociometry,* 1959, **22,** 185–218.

Rosenbaum, M. S., & Drabman, R. S. Self-control training in the classroom: A review and critique. *Journal of Applied Behavior Analysis,* 1980, in press.

Rosenberg, B. G., & Sutton-Smith, B. Ordinal position and sex-role identification. *Genetic Psychology Monographs,* 1964, **70,** 297–328.

Rosenberg, M. *Society and the adolescent self-image.* Princeton: Princeton University Press, 1965.

Rosenhan, D., & White, G. M. Observation and rehearsal as determinants of prosocial behavior, *Journal of Personality and Social Psychology,* 1967, **5,** 424–431.

Rosenthal, D. *Genetic theory and abnormal behavior.* New York: McGraw-Hill, 1970.

Rosenthal, D., & Kety, S. S., eds. *The transmission of schizophrenia.* London: Pergamon Press, 1968.

Rosenzweig, M. R. Environmental complexity, cerebral change, and behavior. *American Psychologist,* 1966, **21,** 321–332.

Rosenzweig, M. R., Bennett, E. L., & Diamond, M. C. Brain changes in response to experience. *Scientific American,* 1972 (Feb.), **226,** 22–29.

Rosow, I. *Social integration of the aged.* New York: Free Press, 1967.

Rosow, I. Status and role change through the life span. In R. H. Binstock and E. Shanas, eds., *Handbook of aging and the social sciences.* New York: Van Nostrand Reinhold, 1976.

Ross, A. O. *Behavior disorders of children.* New York: General Learning Press, 1971.

Ross, A. O. *Psychological disorders of children: A behavioral approach to theory, research, and therapy.* New York: McGraw-Hill, 1974.

Ross, G., Kagan, J., Zelazo, P., & Kotelchuck, M. Separation protest in infants in home and laboratory, *Developmental Psychology,* 1975, **11,** 256–257.

Rothenberg, B. B., & Orost, J. H. The training of conservation of number in young children. *Child Development,* 1969, **40** (3), 707–726.

Rovee, C. K., Cohen, R. Y., & Shlapack, W. Life-span stability in olfactory sensitivity. *Developmental Psychology,* 1975, **11,** 311–318.

Rubin, I. Sex and aging man and woman. In C. E. Vincent, ed., *Human sexuality in medical education and practice.* Springfield, IL: Chas C Thomas, 1968.

Rubin, K. H., & Schneider, F. W. The relationship between moral judgment, egocentric, and altruistic behavior. *Child Development,* 1973, **44,** 661–665.

Rubin, R. A., & Balow, B. Measures of infant development and socioeconomic status as predictors of later intelligence and school achievement. *Developmental Psychology,* 1979, **15,** 225–227.

Rudnick, M., Sterritt, G. M., & Flax, M. Auditory and visual rhythm perception and reading ability. *Child Development,* 1967, **38,** 581–588.

Ruff, H. A. Infant recognition of the invariant form of objects. *Child Development,* 1978, **49** (2), 343–366.

Rugh, R., & Shettles, L. B. *From conception to birth.* New York: Harper & Row, Pub., 1971.

Rushton, J. P. Generosity in children: Immediate and long-term effects of modeling, preaching, and moral judgment. *Journal of Personality & Social Psychology,* 1975, **31,** 459–466.

Rushton, J. P. Socialization and the altruistic behavior of children. *Psychological Bulletin,* 1976, **83,** 898–913.

Rushton, J. P., & Owen, D. Immediate and delayed effects of television modeling and preaching on children's generosity. *British Journal of Social and Clinical Psychology,* 1975, **14,** 309–310.

Rushton, J. P., & Weiner, J. Altruism and cognitive development in children. *British Journal of Social and Clinical Psychology,* 1975, **14,** 341–349.

Rutter, M. Psychological development: Predictors from infancy. *Journal of Child Psychology and Psychiatry,* 1970, **11,** 49–62.

Rutter, M. Diagnosis and definition. In M. Rutter and E. Schopler, eds., *Autism: A reappraisal of concepts and treatment.* New York: Plenum, 1978, pp. 1–25.

Ryder, V. P. A docent program in science for gifted elementary pupils. *Exceptional Children,* 1972, **38,** 629–631.

Sachs, J. S., Brown, R., & Salerno, R. A.   Adults speech to children. In W. van Raffler Engel, & Y. LeBrun, eds., *Baby talk and infant speech (Neurolinguistics 5)*. Amsterdam: Swets & Zeitlinger, 1976, pp. 240–245.

Safer, D. J., & Allen, R. P.   *Hyperactive children. Diagnosis and management.* Baltimore: University Park Press, 1976.

Saint-Anne Dargassies, S.   Part V: Neurological maturation of the premature infant of 28 to 41 weeks gestational age. In F. Falkner, ed., *Human development*. Philadelphia: W. B. Saunders, 1966, pp. 306–326.

St. Clair, K. L.   Neonatal assessment procedures: A historical review. *Child Development*, 1978, **49**, 280–292.

St. Clair, S., & Day, H. D.   Ego identity status and values among high school females. *Journal of Youth and Adolescence*, 1979, **8**, 317–326.

Salapatek, P.   Pattern perception in early infants. In L. B. Cohen & P. Salapatek, eds., *Infant perception: From sensation to cognition*. New York: Academic Press, 1975, **1**.

Salapatek, P., & Banks, M. S.   Infant sensory assessment vision. In F. D. Minifie & L. L. Lloyd, eds., *Communicative and cognitive abilities—early behavioral assessment*. Baltimore: University Park Press, 1977.

Salapatek, P., Bechtold, A. G., & Bushnell, E. W.   Infant visual acuity as a function of viewing distance. *Child Development*, 1976, **47**, 860–863.

Salapatek, P., & Kessen, W.   Visual scanning of triangles by the human newborn. *Journal of Experimental Child Psychology*, 1966, **3**, 155–167.

Sameroff, A. J.   Early influences on development: Fact or fancy? *Merrill-Palmer Quarterly*, 1975, **21**, 267–294.

Sampson, E. E.   Study of ordinal position: Antecedents and outcomes. In B. Maher, ed., *Progress in experimental personality research*. New York: Academic Press, 1965, **2**, 175–228.

Sanger, M. D.   Language learning in infancy: A review of the autistic hypothesis and an observational study of infants. Unpublished Ed.D. Thesis, Harvard University, 1955.

Santrock, J. W.   Paternal absence, sex-typing, and identification. *Developmental Psychology*, 1970, **2**, 264–272.

Saunders, P. S.   An experimental analysis of egocentrism in children's communication. Doctoral dissertation. Rutgers University, 1969.

Savitsky, J. C., Rogers, R. W., Izard, C. E., & Liebert, R. M.   The role of frustration and anger in the imitation of filmed aggression against a human victim. *Psychological Reports*, 1971, **29**, 807–810.

Scarr, S.   Genetic factors in activity motivation. *Child Development*, 1966, **37**, 663–673.

Scarr, S.   Social introversion-extroversion as a heritable response. *Child Development*, 1969, **40**, 823–832.

Scarr, S., & Weinberg, R. A.   The IQ performance of black children adopted by white families. *American Psychologist*, 1976, **31**, 726–739.

Scarr-Salapatek, S.   Genetics and the development of intelligence. In F. D. Horowitz, ed., *Review of child development research*. Chicago; University of Chicago Press, 1975, **4**, 1–57.

Scarr-Salapatek, S., & Williams, M. L.   The effects of early stimulation on low-birth-weight infants. *Child Development*, 1973, **44**, 94–101.

Schachter, S.   The psychology of affiliation. Palo Alto: Stanford University Press, 1959.

Schaefer, E. S.   A circumplex model for maternal behavior. *Journal of Abnormal and Social Psychology*, 1959, **59**, 226–235.

Schaefer, E. S.   Children's reports of parental behavior: An inventory. *Child Development*, 1965, **36**, 413–424.

Schaefer, W. S., & Bayley, N.   Maternal behavior, child behavior and their intercorrelations from infancy through adolescence. *Monographs of the Society for Research in Child Development*, 1963, **28**, 1–27.

Schaffer, H. R.   The multivariate approach to early learning. In R. A. Hinde & J. Stevenson-Hinde, eds., *Constraints in learning*. Englewood Cliffs, N.J.: Prentice-Hall, Inc., 1973.

Schaffer, H. R., & Emerson, P. E.   The development of social attachments in infancy. *Monographs of the Society for Research in Child Development*, 1964, **29**, No. 3. (a)

Schaffer, H. R., & Emerson, P. E.   Patterns of response to physical contact in early human development. *Journal of Child Psychology and Psychiatry*, 1964, **5**, 1–13. (b)

Scheerenberger, R. C.   Mental retardation: Definition, classification, and prevalence. *Mental Retardation Abstract*, 1964, **1**, 432–441.

Scheinfeld, A.   *Twins and supertwins*. Baltimore: Penguin Books, 1973.

Schiff, I. & Wilson, E.   Clinical aspects of aging of the female reproductive system. In E. L. Schneider, ed., *The aging reproductive system*, New York: Raven Press, 1978.

Schneider, D. M., & Smith, R. T.   *Class differences and sex roles in American kinship and family structure*. Englewood Cliffs, N.J.: Prentice-Hall, Inc., 1973.

Schneirla, T. C., & Rosenblatt, J. S.   Behavioral organization and genesis of the social bond in insects and mammals. *American Journal of Orthopsychiatry*, 1961, **31**, 223–253.

Schonfield, D.   Further commitments and successful aging: I. The random sample. *Journal of Gerontology*, 1973, **28**, 189–196.

Schrag, P., & Divoky, D.   *The myth of the hyperactive child.* New York: Dell Pub. Co., Inc., 1975.

Schulman, C. A.   Effects of auditory stimulation on heart rate in premature infants as a function of level of arousal, probability of CNS damage, and conceptional age. *Developmental Psychobiology*, 1970, **2**, 172–183.

Scollon, R. T.   *One child's language from one to two: The origins of construction*. Unpublished doctoral dissertation, University of Hawaii, 1974.

Sears, R. R.   *Your ancients revisited: A history of child development*. Chicago: University of Chicago Press, 1975.

Sears, R. R., Maccoby, E. E., & Levin, H.   *Patterns of child rearing*. Evanston, IL: Row Peterson, 1957.

Seligman, M. E.   On the generality of the laws of learning. *Psychological Review*, 1970, **77**, 406–418.

Sells, L.   High school mathematics as the critical filter in the job market. Paper from the Wellesley-Wesleyan Math Project, 1976–77.

Serbin, L., & O'Leary, K. D.   How nursery schools teach girls to shut up. *Psychology Today*, December, 1975, 57–58.

Severy, L. J., & Davis, K. E.   Helping behavior among normal and retarded children. *Child Development*, 1971, **42**, 1017–1031.

Shaffer, D., & Greenhill, L.   A critical note on the predictive validity of "The Hyperkenetic Syndrome." *Journal of Child Psychology and Psychiatry*, 1979, **20**, 61–72.

Shanas, E. The aged report on their health problems. In A. Simon and L. J. Epstein, eds., *Aging in modern society*, Washington, D.C.: American Psychiatric Association, 1968.

Shanas, E. Older people and their families: The new pioneers. *Journal of Marriage and the Family*, 1980, **42**, 9–15.

Shantz, C., & Sigel, I. Logical operations and concepts of conservation in children. Report to Office of Education, U.S. Department of Health, Education & Welfare, June 1967.

Shantz, C., & Wason, J. Assessment of spatial egocentrism through expectancy violation. *Psychonomic Science*, 1970, **18**, (2), 93–94.

Shapira, A., & Madsen, M. C. Between- and within-group cooperation and competition among kibbutz and nonkibbutz children. *Developmental Psychology*, 1974, **10**, 140–145.

Shatz, M. The comprehension of indirect directives: Can two-year-olds shut the door? Paper presented at the Summer Meeting of the Linguistic Society of America, Amherst, MA, July 1974.

Sheingold, K. Developmental differences in intake and storage of visual information. *Journal of Experimental Child Psychology*, 1973, **16**, 1–11.

Shepherd, M., Oppenheim, A. N., & Mitchell, S. Childhood behavior disorders and the child guidance clinic: An epidemiological study. *Journal of Psychology and Psychiatry*, 1966, **7**, 39–52.

Sherman, J. A., & Bushell, D. Behavior modification as an educational technique. In F. D. Horowitz, ed., *Review of Child Development Research*. Chicago: University of Chicago Press, 1975, **4**.

Sherman, M., & Key, C. B. The intelligence of isolated mountain children. *Child Development*, 1932, **3**, 279–290.

Sherman, M., & Sherman, J. C. Sensorimotor responses in infants. *Journal of Comparative Psychology*, 1925, **5**, 53–68.

Sherman, M., Sherman, J. C., & Flory, C. D. Infant behavior. *Comparative Psychology Monographs*, 1936, **12** (4).

Sherman, S. Patterns of contacts for residents of age-segregated and age-integrated housing. *Journal of Gerontology*, 1975, **30**, 103–107.

Shields, J. *Monozygotic twins brought up apart and brought up together*. London: Oxford University Press, 1962.

Shinn, M. Father absence and children's cognitive development. *Psychological Bulletin*, 1978, **85**, 295–324.

Shirley, M. M. The first two years: A study of twenty-five babies. *Intellectual development*. Institute of Child Welfare Monograph Series No. 7. Minneapolis: University of Minnesota Press, 1933, 1961.

Shuey, A. M. *The testing of Negro intelligence*. 2nd ed. Lynchburg, VA: Bell, 1966.

Siegelman, M. Parent behavior correlates of personality traits related to creativity in sons and daughters. *Journal of Consulting and Clinical Psychology*, 1973, **40**, 43–47.

Siegler, I. C. The terminal drop hypothesis: Fact or artifact? *Experimental Aging Research*, 1975, **1**, 169.

Siegler, R. S. Stages as decision rules. Paper presented at the Annual Meeting of the Jean Piaget Society, Philadelphia, 1975.

Siegler, R. S., & Atlas, M. Acquisition of formal scientific reasoning by 10- and 13-year-olds: Detecting interactional patterns in data. Complex Information Processing Paper #308, Carnegie-Mellon University, 1975.

Siegler, R. S., Liebert, D. E., & Liebert, R. M. Inhelder and Piaget's pendulum problem: Teaching preadolescents to act as scientists. *Developmental Psychology*, 1973, **9**, 97–101.

Siegler, R. S., & Liebert, R. M. Effects of presenting relevant rules and complete feedback on the conservation of liquid quantity task. *Developmental Psychology*, 1972, **7**, 133–138. (*a*)

Siegler, R. S., & Liebert, R. M. Learning of liquid quantity relationships as a function of rules and feedback, number of training problems, and age of subject. *Proceedings of the 80th Annual Convention of the American Psychological Association*, 1972, **7**, 117–118. (*b*)

Siegler, R. S., & Liebert, R. M. Acquisition of formal scientific reasoning by 10- and 13-year-olds: Designing a factorial experiment. *Developmental Psychology*, 1975, **11**, 401–402.

Sigel, I., Roeper, A., & Hooper, F. A training procedure for acquisition of Piaget's conservation of quantity: A pilot study and its replication. In I. Sigel & F. Hooper, eds., *Logical thinking in children: Research based on Piaget's theory*. New York: Holt, Rinehart, and Winston, 1968.

Simmons, R., Rosenberg, F., & Rosenberg, M. Disturbance in the self image in adolescence. *American Sociological Review*, 1973. **38**, 553–568.

Simpson, E. L. Moral development research: A case study of scientific cultural bias. *Human Development*, 1974, **17**, 81–106.

Simpson, G. G., Pittendrigh, C. S., & Tiffany, L. H. *Life. An introduction to biology*. New York: Harcourt Brace Jovanovich Inc., 1957.

Simpson, R. L. Parental influence, anticipatory socialization, and social mobility. *American Sociological Review*, 1962, **27**, 517–522.

Singer, J. L., & Singer, D. G. Fostering imaginative play in preschool children: effects of television viewing and direct adult modeling. Paper presented at the Annual Meeting of the American Psychological Association, New Orleans, LA, 1974.

Singer, R. N. Motor learning as a function of age and sex. In G. L. Rarick, ed., *Physical activity*, New York: Academic Press, 1973.

Sinnot, E. W., Dunn, L. C., & Dobzhansky, T. *Principles of genetics*. New York: McGraw-Hill, 1958.

Siqueland, E. R., & DeLucia, C. A. Visual reinforcement of non-nutritive sucking in human infants. *Science*, 1969, **165**, 1144–1146.

Skeels, H. M. Adult status of children with contrasting early life experiences: A follow-up study. *Monographs of the Society for Research in Child Development*, 1966, **31**, No. 3.

Skinner, B. F. *Walden two*. London: Macmillan, 1948.

Skinner, B. F. *Verbal behavior*. New York: Appleton-Century-Crofts, 1957.

Skodak, M., & Skeels, H. M. A final follow-up study of 100 adopted children. *Journal of Genetic Psychology*, 1949, **75**, 85–125.

Slaby, R. G. Verbal regulation of aggression and altruism. In W. Hartup & J. De Wit, eds., *Determinants and origins of aggressive behavior*. The Hague: Mouton, 1975, pp. 199–205.

Slaby, R. G., & Frey, K. S. Development of gender constancy and selective attention to same-sex models. *Child Development*, 1975, **46**, 849–856.

Slaby, R. G., & Parke, R. D.   Effect on resistance to deviation of observing a model's affective reaction to response consequences. *Developmental Psychology*, 1971, **5**, 40–47.

Slobin, D. I.   Universals of grammatical development in children. In G. B. Flores d'Arcais & W. J. M. Levelt, eds., *Advances in psycholinguistics*. Amsterdam: North-Holland Publishing, 1970, pp. 174–186.

Slocum, W. C.   Some factors associated with happiness in unbroken homes. *Family Life Coordination*, 1958, **6**, 35–39.

Smart, M. S., & Smart, R. C.   *Adolescents: Development and relationships*. New York: Macmillan, 1978. (*a*)

Smart, M. S., & Smart, R. C.   *Infants: Developments and relationships* (2nd Ed). New York: Macmillan, 1978. (*b*)

Smith, N. V.   *The acquisition of phonology: A case study*. Cambridge: Cambridge University Press, 1973.

Smith, R. T.   A comparison of socioenvironmental factors in monozygotic and dizygotic twins, testing an assumption. In S. G. Vandenberg, ed., *Methods and goals in human behavior genetics*. New York: Academic Press, 1965.

Snow, C. E.   Mothers' speech to children learning language. *Child Development*, 1972, **43**, 549–565.

Snow, C. E.   The development of conversation between mothers and babies. *Journal of Child Language*, 1977, **4**, 1–22.

Sontag, L. W.   Differences in modifiability of fetal behavior and psychology. *Psychosomatic Medicine*, 1944, **6**, 151–154.

Sontag, L. W., Baker, C. T., & Nelson, V. L.   Mental growth and personality development: A longitudinal study. *Monographs for Society for Research in Child Development*, 1958, **23**, No. 68.

Sorenson, R. C.   *Adolescent sexuality in contemporary America*. New York: World Publishing Co., 1973.

Sostek, A. M.   Infant scales in the pediatric setting: The Brazelton neonatal behavioral assessment scale and the Carey infant temperament questionnaire. *Journal of Pediatric Psychology*, 1978, **3**, 113–121.

Spelke, E., Zelazo, P., Kagan, J., & Kotelchuck, M.   Father interaction and separation protest. *Developmental psychology*, 1973, **9**, 83–90.

Spence, J. T.   Verbal reinforcement combinations and concept-identification learning: The role of reinforcement. *Journal of Experimental Psychology*, 1970, **85**, 321–329.

Spence, J. T., Helmreich, R., & Stapp, J.   Ratings of self and peers and sex-role attributes and their relation to self-esteem and conceptions of masculinity and femininity. *Journal of Personality*, 1975, **32**, 29–39.

Spirduso, W. W.   Reaction and movement time as a function of age and physical activity level. *Journal of Gerontology*, 1975, **30**, 435–440.

Spitz, R. A.   The role of ecological factors in emotional development in infancy. *Child Development*, 1949, **20**, 145–155.

Spitz, R. A.   Unhappy and fatal outcomes of emotional deprivation and stress in infancy. In I. Galdston, ed., *Beyond the Germ Theory*. Health Education Council, 1954, pp. 120–131.

Stanley, J. C.   Intellectual precocity. In J. C. Stanley, D. P. Keating, & L. H. Fox, eds., *Mathematical talent*. Baltimore: Johns Hopkins University Press, 1974. pp. 1–22.

Stanley, J. C., Keating, D. P., & Fox, L. H.   *Mathematical talent*. Baltimore: Johns Hopkins University Press, 1974.

Staples, F. R.   The responses of infants to color. *Journal of Experimental Psychology*, 1937, **15**, 119–141.

Staub, E.   The use of role playing and induction in children's learning of helping and sharing behavior. *Child Development*, 1971, **42**, 805–816.

Staub, E., & Sherk, L.   Need for approval, children's sharing behavior, and reciprocity in sharing. *Child Development*, 1970, **41**, 243–252.

Stechler, G.   Newborn attention as affected by medication during labor. *Science*, 1964, **144**, 315–317.

Stechler, G., Bradford, S., & Levy, L.   Attention in the newborn: Effect on motility and skin potential. *Science*, 1966, **151**, 1246–1248.

Steele, B. F., & Pollock, D. A.   A psychiatry study of parents who abuse infants and small children. In R. E. Helfer, and C. H. Kempe, eds., *The battered child*. Chicago: University of Chicago Press, 1968.

Stein, A. H., & Friedrich, L. K.   Television content and young children's behavior. In J. P. Murray, E. A. Rubinstein, and G. A. Comstock, eds., *Television and social behavior*, Vol. II: *Television and social learning*. Washington, D.C.: U.S. Government Printing Office, 1972, 202–317.

Stein, A. H., & Friedrich, L. K.   Impact of television on children & youth. In E. M. Hetherington, ed., *Review of Child Development Research*. Chicago: University of Chicago Press, 1975, **5**.

Stephens, W. B., Miller, C. K., & McLaughlin, J. A.   The development of moral conduct in retardates and normals. Paper presented at the meeting of the Society for Research in Child Development, Santa Monica, 1969.

Stevens-Long & Lovaas, I. O.   Research and treatment with autistic children in a program of behavior therapy. In A. Davids, ed., *Child personality and psychopathology: Current topics*, Vol. 1. New York: Wiley Interscience, 1974.

Stevenson, H. W.   Developmental psychology. In D. Sills, ed., *International encyclopedia of the social sciences*. New York: Macmillan, 1968.

Stevenson, H. W., & Zigler, E.   Probability learning in children. *Journal of Experimental Psychology*, 1958, **56**, 185–192.

Steward, G. H., & Williamson, R. C.   A cross-national study of adolescent professional goals. *Human Development*, 1969, **12**, 248–254.

Stewart, R. S.   Psychoanalysis and sex differences: Freud and beyond Freud. In P. C. Lee & R. S. Stewart, *Sex differences: Cultural and developmental dimensions*. New York: Urz, 1976.

Stinnett, N., Carter, L. M., & Montgomery, J. E.   Older persons' perceptions of their marriages. *Journal of Marriage and the Family*, 1972, **34**, 665–670.

Stokes, R. G., & Maddox, G. L.   Some social factors in retirement adaptation. *Journal of Gerontology*, 1967, **22**, 329–333.

Stone, L. J., Smith, H. T., & Murphy, L. B.   *The competent infant*. New York: Basic Books, 1973.

Stott, L. H., & Ball, R. S.   Infant and preschool mental tests: Review and evaluation. *Monographs of the Society for Research in Child Development*, 1965, **30**, (No. 3).

Strohner, H., & Nelson, K. E.   The young child's development of sentence comprehension: Influence of event probability, nonverbal context, syntactic form, and strategies. *Child Development*, 1974, **45**, 567–576.

Strupp, H. H.   *An introduction to Freud and modern psychoanalysis*. Woodbury, N.Y.: Barron's Educational Series, 1967.

Suomi, S. J., & Harlow, H. F. Social rehabilitation of isolate-reared monkeys. *Developmental Psychology*, 1972, **6**, 487–496.

Sussman, M. B. The family today. *Children Today*. March–April, 1978.

Sutton-Smith, B., & Rosenberg, B. G. *The sibling*. New York: Holt, Rinehart, and Winston, 1970.

Symonds, P. M. The Psychology of Parent-Child Relationships. New York: Appleton-Century-Crofts, 1939.

Talkington, L. W. Response-chain learning of mentally retarded adolescents under four conditions of reinforcement. *American Journal of Mental Deficiency*, 1971, **76**, 337–340.

Tanner, J. M. The regulation of human growth. *Child Development*, 1963, **34**, 816–847.

Tanner, J. M. Physical growth. In P. H. Mussen, ed., *Carmichael's manual of child psychology* (3rd. ed.). New York: John Wiley 1970, **1**, 77–155.

Tanner, J. M. Physical growth. In P. H. Mussen, ed., *Carmichael's manual of child psychology* (3rd. ed.). New York: John Wiley 1970, **1**, 77–155.

Tapia, F., Jekel, J., & Domke, H. Enuresis: An emotional symptom? *Journal of Nervous and Mental Disease*, 1960, **130**, 61–66.

Tate, B. G., & Baroff, G. S. Aversive control of self-injurious behavior in a psychotic boy. *Behavior Research and Therapy*, 1966, **4**, 281–287.

Taylor, R. Psychosocial development among black children and youth: A reexamination. *American Journal of Orthopsychiatry*, 1976, **46**, 4–19.

Telford, C. W., & Sawrey, J. M. *The exceptional individual*. Englewood Cliffs, N.J.: Prentice-Hall, Inc., 1972.

Templer, D. I., Ruff, C. F., & Franks, C. M. Death anxiety: Age, sex, and parental resemblance in diverse populations. *Developmental Psychology*, 1971, **4**, 108.

Teplin, L. A. A comparison of racial/ethnic preferences among Anglo, Black, and Latino children. *American Journal of Orthopsychiatry*, 1976, **46**, 702–709.

Terman, L. M. A preliminary study in the psychology and pedagogy of leadership. *Pedagogical Seminar*, 1904, **11**, 413–451.

Terman, L. M. Genius and stupidity: A study of some of the intellectual processes of seven "bright" and seven "dull" boys. *Pedagogical Seminar*, 1906, **13**, 307–373.

Terman, L. M. Mental and physical traits of a thousand gifted children. In L. M. Terman, ed., *Genetic studies of genius*. Stanford: Stanford University Press, 1925, **1**.

Terman, L. M. Scientists and nonscientists in a group of 800 gifted men. *Psychological Monographs*, 1954, **68**, 1–44.

Thomas, A., & Chess, S. Development in middle childhood. *Seminars in Psychiatry*, 1972, **4**, 331–341.

Thomas, A., & Chess, S. Evolution of behavior disorders into adolescence. *American Journal of Psychiatry*, 1976, **133**, 539–542.

Thomas, A., Chess, S., & Birch, H. G. *Temperament and behavior disorders in children*. New York: New York University Press, 1968.

Thomas, A., Chess, S., & Birch, H. G. The origin of personality. *Scientific American*, 1970, **223**, 102–109.

Thomas, A., Chess, S., Sillen, J., & Mendez, O. Cross-cultural study of behavior in children with special vulnerabilities to stress. In D. F. Ricks, A. Thomas, & M. Roff, eds., *Life history research in psychopathology*, Minneapolis: University of Minnesota Press, 1974, **3**, 53–67.

Thomas, L. E. Mid-career changes: Self-selected or externally mandated? *Vocational Guidance Quarterly*, 1977, **25**, 320–328.

Thomas, M. Visual fixation responses of infants to stimuli of varying complexity. *Child Development*, 1965, **36**, 629–638.

Thomas, M., & Jones-Molfese, V. Infants and I scale: Inferring change from the ordinal stimulus selections of infants for configural stimuli. *Journal of Experimental Child Psychology*, 1977, **23**(2), 329–339.

Thompson, W. R. The inheritance and development of intelligence. *Research Publications of the Association for Research in Nervous and Mental Diseases*, 1954, **33**, 209–331.

Thompson, W. R., & Grusec, J. E. Studies of early experience. In P. H. Mussen, ed., *Carmichael's manual of child psychology*. New York: John Wiley, 1970, **1**, 565–654.

Thompson, W. R., & Melzack, R. Early environment. *Scientific American*, 1956, **114**, 38–42.

Thurstone, L. L., & Thurstone, T. G. Factorial studies of intelligence. *Psychometric Monograph*, 1941, No. 2.

Time, April, 1978.

Tolor, B., & Blumin, S. S. Self-concept and locus of control in primary grade children identified as requiring special educational programming. *Psychological Reports*, 1977, **40**, 43–49.

Toner, I. J., & Smith, R. A. Age and verbalization in delay maintenance behavior in children. *Journal of Experimental Child Psychology*, 1977, **24**, 123–128.

Tresemer, D., & Pleck, J. Sex-role boundaries and resistance to sex-role change. *Women's Studies*, 1974, **2**, 61–78.

Troll, L. E. The family of later life: A decade review. *Journal of Marriage and the Family*, 1971, **33**, 263–290.

Troll, L. E. *Early and middle adulthood*. Monterey, CA.: Brooks/Cole, 1975.

Troll, L. E., Neugarten, B. L., & Kraines, R. J. Similarities in values and other personality characteristics in college students and their parents. *Merrill-Palmer Quarterly*, 1969, **15**, 323–336.

Tulving, E. Episodic and semantic memory. In E. Tulving & W. Donaldson, eds., *Organization of memory*. New York: Academic Press, 1972.

Tulving, E., & Pearlstone, Z. Availability versus accessibility of information in memory for words. *Journal of Verbal Learning and Verbal Behavior*, 1966, **5**, 381–391.

Turnbull, C. *The forest people*. New York: Simon & Schuster, 1961.

Tyler, F. B., Rafferty, J., & Tyler, B. Relationships among motivations of parents and their children. *Journal of Genetic Psychology*, 1962, **101**, 69–81.

Ugurel-Semin, R. Moral behavior and moral judgment of children. *Journal of Abnormal and Social Psychology*, 1952, **47**, 463–474.

U.S. Bureau of the Census, Statistical Abstract of the U.S., 1977. Washington, D.C., 1977.

Updegraff, R. The visual perception of distance in young children and adults: A comparative study. *University of Iowa Studies of Child Welfare*, 1930, **4** (No. 40).

Urberg, K. A., & Labouvie-Vief, G. Conceptualizations of

sex roles: A life span developmental study. *Developmental Psychology,* 1976, **12,** 15–23.

Uzgiris, I. C. Patterns of vocal and gestural imitation in infants. In F. J. Monks, W. W. Hartup, & V. DeWit, eds., *Determinants of Behavioral Development.* New York: Academic Press, 1972.

Vandenberg, S. G. Contributions to twin research in psychology. *Psychological Bulletin,* 1966, **66,** 327–352.

Vandenberg, S. G. Hereditary factors in normal personality traits (as measured by inventories). In J. Wortis, ed., *Recent advances in biological psychiatry,* New York: Plenum, 1967, **9.**

Velandia, W., Grandon, G. M., & Page, E. B. Family size, birth order, and intelligence in a large South American sample. *American Educational Research Journal,* 1978, **15,** 399–416.

Verwoerdt, A., Pfeiffer, E., & Wang, H. Sexual behavior in senescence: II. Patterns of sexual activity and interest. *Geriatrics,* 1969, **24,** 137–154.

Vital and Health Statistics. *Infant Mortality rates: Socioeconomic factors.* Series 22, No. 14. Rockville, MD.: U S Department of Health, Education, and Welfare, 1972.

Vital and Health Statistics. *Parent ratings of behavioral patterns of youths 12–17 years.* Series 11, No. 137. Rockville, MD.: Department of Health, Education, and Welfare, 1974.

Vriend, T. J. The case for women. *Vocational Guidance Quarterly,* 1977, **25,** 329–331.

Waddington, C. H. *The strategy of the genes.* London: Allen and Unwin, 1957.

Wade, T. C. Factor analytic approaches to the investigation of common fears: A critical appraisal and reanalysis. *Behavior Therapy,* 1978, **9,** 923–935.

Wahler, R. G. Oppositional children: a quest for parental reinforcement control. *Journal of Applied Behavior Analysis,* 1969, **2,** 159–170.

Waite, W. W., & Osborne, J. G. Sustained behavioral contrast in children. *Journal of the Experimental Analysis of Behavior,* 1972, **18,** 113–117.

Walk, R. D., & Gibson, E. J. A comparative and analytical study of visual depth perception. *Psychological Monographs,* 1961, **75,** (15, Whole No. 519).

Walker, C. E. Toilet training, enuresis, and encopresis. In P. R. Magrab, ed., *Psychological management of pediatric problems,* Baltimore: University Park Press, 1978, **1.**

Wallace, A. R. On the tendencies of varieties to depart indefinitely from the original type. Linnean Society Papers, 1858. In P. Appleman, ed., *Darwin, a Norton critical edition.* New York: W. W. Norton & Co., Inc., 1970.

Wallach, M. A., & Kogan, N. *Modes of thinking in young children: A study of the creativity-intelligence distinction.* New York: Holt, Rinehart, & Winston, 1965.

Wallach, M. A., & Wing, C. W. *The talented student: A validation of the creativity-intelligence distinction.* New York: Holt, Rinehart, & Winston, 1969.

Walster, E., Aronson, V, Abrahams, D., & Rottmann, L. Importance of physical attractiveness in dating behavior, *Journal of Personality and Social Psychology,* 1966, **18,** 508–516.

Walters, R. H., & Brown, M. Studies of reinforcement of aggression. Part III: Transfer of responses to an interpersonal situation. *Child Development,* 1963, **34,** 563–572.

Walters, R. H., & Brown, M. A test of the high-magnitude

theory of aggression. *Journal of Experimental Child Psychology,* 1964, **1,** 376–387.

Walters, R. H., Leat, M., & Mezei, H. Response inhibition and disinhibition through empathic learning. *Canadian Journal of Psychology,* 1963, **17,** 235–243.

Ward, I. L. Sexual behavior differentiation: Prenatal hormonal and environmental control. In R. C. Friedman, R. N. Richart, & R. L. Van de Wiele, eds., *Sex differences in behavior,* New York: John Wiley, 1974.

Ward, W. C., Kogan, N., & Pankove, E. Incentive effects in children's creativity. *Child Development,* 1972, **43,** 669–676.

Warden, D. A. The influence of context on children's use of identifying expressions and references. *British Journal of Psychology,* 1976, **67,** 101–112.

Warr, P. & Lovatt, J. Retraining and other factors associated with job finding after redundancy. *Journal of Occupational Psychology,* 1977, **50,** 67–84.

Watkins, B. T. Gerontology comes of age. In R. Gross, B. Gross, & S. Seidman, eds., *The new old: Struggling for decent aging.* Garden City, N.Y.: Doubleday, 1978.

Watson, J. B. Psychology as the behaviorist views it. *Psychological Review,* 1913, **20,** 158–177.

Weatherley, D. Self-perceived rate of physical maturation and personality in late adolescence. *Child Development,* 1964, **35,** 1197–1210.

Webster's New Collegiate Dictionary. Springfield, MA.: Merriam Co., 1973.

Weikart, D. P. Relationship of curriculum, teaching, and learning in preschool education. In J. C. Stanley, ed., *Preschool programs for the disadvantaged.* Baltimore: Johns Hopkins University Press, 1972, pp. 22–66.

Weinberg, J. Individual adaptation to automation. In H. T. Blumenthal, ed., *Interdisciplinary topics in gerontology: Age, work, and automation.* New York: S. Karger, 1970.

Weiner, B., & Kun, A. The development of causal attributions and the growth of achievement and social motivation. In S. Feldman & D. Bush, eds., *Cognitive development and social development.* New York: Erlbaum Press, 1976.

Weinraub, M. Fatherhood!! The myth of the second-class parent. In J. H. Stevens Jr., & M. Mathews, eds., *Mother/child, father/child relationships.* Washington, D.C.: The National Association for the Education of Young Children, 1978, pp. 109–113.

Weinraub, M., & Frankel, J. Sex differences in parent-infant interaction during free play, departure, and separation. *Child Development,* 1977, **48,** 1240–1249.

Weinstein, L. Project Re-ED schools for emotionally disturbed children: Effectiveness as viewed by referring agencies, parents, and teachers. *Exceptional Children,* 1969, **35,** 703–711.

Weinstein, L. The evaluation research: The effectiveness of the Re-ED intervention. Unpublished manuscript, George Peabody College for Teachers, 1971.

Weir, M. W. Development changes in problem solving strategies. *Psychological Review,* 1964, **71,** 473–490.

Weir, R. H. *Language in the crib.* The Hague: Mouton, 1962.

Weir, R. H. Questions on the learning of phonology. In F. Smith, & G. A. Miller, eds., *The genesis of language: A psycholinguistic approach.* Cambridge, Mass.: M.I.T. Press, 1966, pp. 153–168.

Weisberg, P. Social and nonsocial conditioning of infant vocalizations. *Child Development*, 1963, **34**, 377–388.

Weisz, J. R., & Zigler, E. Cognitive development in retarded and nonretarded persons: Piagetian tests of the similar sequence hypothesis. *Psychological Bulletin*, 1979, **86**, 831–851.

Weitzman, B. Behavior therapy and psychotherapy. *Psychological Review*, 1967, **74**(4), 300–317.

Welford, A. T. Motor performance. In J. E. Birren and K. W. Schaie, eds., *Handbook of the psychology of aging*. New York: Van Nostrand Reinhold, 1977.

Wellesley-Wesleyan Math Project, 1976–77. Description and materials obtained from S. Tobias, The Math Clinic, Wesleyan University, Middletown, CT.

Wellman, B. L. Some new bases for interpretation of the IQ. *Journal of Genetic Psychology*, 1932, **41**, 116–126. (*a*)

Wellman, B. L. The effects of preschool attendance upon the IQ. *Journal of Experimental Education*, 1932, **1**, 48–49. (*b*)

Wellman, H. M., Ritter, K., & Flavell, J. H. Deliberate memory behavior in the delayed reactions of very young children. *Developmental Psychology*, 1975, **11**, 780–787.

Wender, P. H., Rosenthal, D., Kety, S. S., Schulsinger, S., & Welner, J. Cross-fostering: A research strategy for clarifying the role of genetic and experiential factors in the etiology of schizophrenia. *Archives of General Psychiatry*, 1974, **30**, 121–128.

Wender, P. H., Rosenthal, D., Rainer, J. D., Greenhill, L., & Sarlin, B. Schizophrenics' adopting parents. *Archives of General Psychiatry*, 1977, **34**, 777–784.

Wenz, F. V. Sociological correlates of alienation among adolescent suicide attempts. *Adolescence*, 1979, **14**, 19–30.

Werner, H. *Comparative psychology of mental development*. Chicago: Follet, 1948.

Werner, H., & Kaplan, B. *Symbol formation*. New York: John Wiley, 1964.

Werry, J. S. Psychosomatic disorders (with a note on anesthesia, surgery, and hospitalization). In H. C. Quay, & J. S. Werry, eds., *Psychopathological disorders in children*. New York: John Wiley, 1972, pp. 122–163.

Whitbourne, S. K., & Weinstock, C. S. *Adult development*. New York: Holt, Rinehart and Winston, 1979.

White, B., & Held, R. Plasticity of sensorimotor development in the human infant. In J. F. Rosenblith and W. Allinsmith, eds., *The causes of behavior*. 2nd ed. Boston: Allyn and Bacon, 1966, pp. 60–71.

White, B. L. *The first three years of life*. Englewood Cliffs, NJ: Prentice-Hall, 1975.

White, G. M. Immediate and deferred effects of model observation and guided and unguided rehearsal on donating and stealing. *Journal of Personality and Social Psychology*, 1972, **21**, 139–148.

White, S. H. Evidence for a hierarchial arrangement of learning processes. In L. P. Lipsitt & C. C. Spiker, eds., *Advances in child development and behavior*. New York: Academic Press, 1965, **2**, pp. 187–220.

Whitehurst, G. Production of novel and grammatical utterances by young children. *Journal of Experimental Child Psychology*, 1972, **13**, 502–515.

Whitehurst, G. J. Discrimination learning as a function of reinforcement condition, task complexity and chronological age. *Journal of Experimental Child Psychology*, 1969, **7**, 314–325.

Whitehurst, G. J., & Vasta, R. *Child behavior*. Boston: Houghton Mifflin, 1977.

Whiting, J. W. M., & Child, I. L. *Child training and personality: A cross-cultural study*. New Haven: Yale University Press, 1953.

Whorf, B. L. *Language, thought & reality*. Cambridge: M.I.T. Press, 1956.

Wichern, F., & Nowicki, S. Independence training practices and locus of control orientation in children and adolescents. *Developmental Psychology*, 1976, **12**, 77.

Wickelgren, W. A. *Learning and memory*. Englewood Cliffs, N.J.: Prentice, Hall, 1977.

Wickman, E. K. *Children's behavior and teacher's attitudes*. New York: Commonwealth Fund, 1928.

Wieman, L. A. Stress patterns of early child language. *Journal of Child Language*, 1976, **3**, 283–286.

Wiener, G. Scholastic achievement at age 12–13 of prematurely born infants. *Journal of Special Education*, 1968, **2**, 237–250.

Wiener, G., Rider, R. V., Oppel, W. C., Fischer, L. K., & Harper, P. A. Correlates of low birthweight: Psychological status of 6–7 years of age. *Pediatrics*, 1965, **35**, 434–444.

Wiener, Y., & Vaitenas, R. Personality correlates of voluntary midcareer change in enterprising occupations. *Journal of Applied Psychology*, 1977, **62**, 706–712.

Willerman, L. Activity level and hyperactivity in twins. *Child Development*, 1973, **44**, 288–293.

Willerman, L., & Churchill, J. A. Intelligence and birthweight in identical twins. *Child Development*, 1967, **38**, 623–629.

Willerman, L., & Fiedler, M. F. Infant performance and intellectual precocity. *Child Development*, 1974, **45**, 483–486.

Willerman, L., & Plomin, R. Activity level in children and their parents. *Child Development*, 1973, **44**, 854–858.

Willerman, L., & Stafford, R. E. Maternal effects on intellectual functioning. *Behavior Genetics*, 1972, **2**, 321–325.

Williams, F. Some preliminaries and prospects. In F. Williams, ed., *Language and poverty: Perspectives on a theme*. Chicago: Markham, 1970.

Williams, J. E., Bennett, S. M., & Best, D. L. Awareness and expression of sex stereotypes in young children. *Developmental Psychology*, 1975, **11**, 635–642.

Williams, N. I want to go home: A very old lady dies in style. In R. Gross, B. Gross, and S. Seidman, eds., *The new old: Struggling for decent aging*. Garden City, N.Y.: Doubleday, 1978.

Williams, R. J. *The human frontier*. New York: Harcourt Brace Jovanovich, Inc., 1946.

Willie, C. V. The black family and social class. *American Journal of Orthopsychiatry*, 1974, **44**, 50–60.

Wilson, R. S. Synchronies in mental development: An epigenetic perspective. *Science*, 1978, **202**, 939–948.

Wiltz, N. A., & Gordon, S. B. Parental modification of a child's behavior in an experimental residence. *Journal of Behavior Therapy and Experimental Psychiatry*, 1974, **5**, 107–109.

Windle, W. F., ed. *Neurological and psychological deficits of asphyxia neonatorum*. Springfield, IL: Charles C Thomas, 1958.

Winick, M., Brasel, J., & Valasco, E. G. Effects of prenatal nutrition upon pregnancy risk. *Clinical Obstetrics and Gynecology*, 1973, **16**, 184–198.

Winsberg, B. G., Yepes, L. E., & Bialer, I. Pharmacologic management of children with hyperactive/aggressive/inattentive behavior disorders. *Clinical Pediatrics*, 1976, **15**, 471–477.

Winterbottom, M. R. The relation of childhood training in independence to achievement motivation. Unpublished doctoral dissertation, University of Michigan, 1953.

Wise, N. J. Delinquency among middle-class girls. In E. Vaz, ed., *Middle class juvenile delinquency*. New York: Harper & Row, Pub., 1967.

Wish, P. A., Hasazi, J. E., & Jurgela, A. R. Automated direct deconditioning of a childhood phobia. *Journal of Behavior Therapy and Experimental Psychiatry*, 1973, **4**, 279–283.

Witkin, H. A., Mednick, S. A., Schulsinger, F., Bakkeström, E., Christiansen, K. O., Goodenough, D. R., Hirschhorn, K., Lundsteen, C., Owen, D. R., Philip, J., Rubin, D. B., & Stocking, M. Criminality in XYY and XXY men. *Science*, 1976, **193**, 547–555.

Witty, P. A study of pupil's interests, grades 9, 10, 11, 12. *Education*, 1961, **82**, 169–174.

Wolff, P. H. The development of attention in young infants. *Annals of the New York Academy of Science*, 1965, **118**, 815–830.

Wolff, P. H. The causes, controls, and organization of behavior in the neonate. *Psychological Issues*, 1966, **5**(1), Monograph 17, 1–105.

Wolpe, J. *Psychotherapy by reciprocal inhibition*. Stanford: Stanford University Press, 1958.

Women and Minorities in Science and Engineering. National Science Foundation, NSF 77–304, 1977.

Wood-Gush, D. G. M. A study of sex drive of two strains of cockerels through three generations. *Animal Behavior*, 1960, **8**, 43–53.

Yang, R. K., Zweig, A. R., Douthitt, T. C., & Federman, E. J. Successive relationships between maternal attitudes during pregnancy, analgesic medication during labor and delivery, and newborn behavior. *Developmental Psychology*, 1976, **12**, 6–14.

Yarrow, L. J. Attachment and dependency. In J. L. Gewirtz, ed., *Attachment and dependency*. New York: V. H. Winston & Sons, 1972, pp. 81–95.

Yarrow, L. J., & Goodwin, M. S. The immediate impact of separation: Reactions of infants to a change in mother figures. In L. J. Stone, H. T. Smith, and L. B. Murphy, eds., *The competent infant: Research and commentary*. New York: Basic Books, 1973, 1032–1039.

Yarrow, L. J., Goodwin, M. S., Manheimer, H., & Milowe, I. D. Infant experiences and cognitive and personality development at ten years. Paper presented at the annual meeting of the American Orthopsychiatric Association, Washington, D.C., March 1971.

Yarrow, L. J., & Pedersen, F. A. Attachment: its origins and course. In *The Young Child: Reviews of Research, Vol. II*. Washington, D.C.: National Association for the Education of Young Children, 1972, pp. 302–311.

Yarrow, M. R., Campbell, J. D., & Burton, R. V. Recollections of childhood: A study of the retrospective method. *Monographs of the Society for Research in Child Development*, 1970, **35**(5), Serial No. 138.

Yerushalmy, J. The relationship of parents' smoking to outcome of pregnancy: Implications as to the problem of inferring causation from observed effects. *American Journal of Epidemiology*, 1971, **93**, 443–456.

Yerushalmy, J. Infants with low birth weight born before their mothers started to smoke cigarettes. *American Journal of Obstetrics and Gynecology*, 1972, **112**, 277–284.

Yonge, G. D. Structure of experience and functional fixedness. *Journal of Educational Psychology*, 1966, **57**, 115–120.

Young, E. R., & Parish, T. S. Impact of father absence during childhood on the psychological adjustment of college females. *Sex Roles*, 1977, **3**, 217–227.

Yurchenco, H. *A mighty hard road: The Woody Guthrie story*. New York: McGraw-Hill, 1970.

Yusin, A. S. Attempted suicide in an adolescent—the resolution of an anxiety state. *Adolescence*, 1973, **8**, 17–28.

Zajonc, R. B. Family configuration and intelligence. *Science*, 1976, **192**, 227–236.

Zajonc, R. B., & Markus, G. B. Birth order and intellectual development. *Psychological Bulletin*, 1975, **82**, 74–88.

Zaporozhets, A. V. The development of perception in the preschool child. In P. H. Mussen, ed., *European research in cognitive development: Monographs of the Society for Research in Child Development*, 1965, **30** (2, Whole No. 100), 82–101.

Zelazo, P. R., Zelazo, N., & Kolb, S. "Walking" in the newborn. *Science*, 1972, **176**, 314–315.

Zigler, E. Motivational and emotional factors in the behavior of the retarded. *Connecticut Medicine*, August 1968, pp. 584–592.

Zigler, E. The effectiveness of Head Start: Another look. *Educational Psychologist*, 1978, **13**, 71–77.

Zigler, E., & Balla, D. Developmental cause of responsiveness to social reinforcement in normal children and institutionalized retarded children. *Developmental Psychology*, 1972, **6**, 66–73.

Zigler, E., & de Labry, J. Concept-switching in middle-class, lower-class, and retarded children. *Journal of Abnormal Social Psychology*, 1962, **65**, 267–272.

Zimmerman, B. J., & Rosenthal, T. L. Observational learning of rule-governed behavior by children. *Psychological Bulletin*, 1974, **81**, 29–42.

Zuckerman, M., & Wheeler, L. To dispel fantasies about the fantasy-based measure of fear of success. *Psychological Bulletin*, 1975, **82**, 932–946.

Chapter Opening Photo Credits

Name Index

A

Abel, E. L., 58, 545
Abrahams, J. P. 567
Abravanel, E., 103
Accardo, P. J., 69
Achenbach, T., 475
Acito, M. A., 210
Acland, H., 129
Adelson, J., 530, 535, 536
Adesso, V. J., 424
Ahammer, T. M., 456
Ainsworth, M. D. S., 333, 372, 375, 382, 385
Akiyama, M., 385
Albert, R. S., 301
Albrecht, S. L., 569
Aldous, J., 336
Aleksandrowicz, D. R., 65
Aleksandrowicz, M. K., 65
Allen, L., 274, 280
Allen, R. P., 487, 488
Allinsmith, W., 416
Altus, W. D., 343
Amatruda, C. S., 82
Ames, E. W., 96
Ames, L. B., 82, 83, 275
Amsterdam, B., 195
Anastasi, A., 10, 291
Anderson, E. P., 375
Anderson, L. D., 274
Anderson, R. C., 311
Anderson, R. M., 311
Angélév, J., 528
Anthony, E. J., 482, 501, 502–3
Antonovsky, A., 351
Apgar, Virginia, 68
Appelbaum, M. I., 280
Appleton, 111
Arasteh, J. D., 311
Archimedes, 203
Ariès, Philippe, 5
Aristotle, 170, 301, 461 fn
Armentrout, J. A., 342
Aronfried, J., 168–69, 418, 457
Aronson, E., 104
Asher, R. A., 257
Ashton, B. G., 112, 114
Ashton, P. T., 391

Ashton, R., 71, 72
Aslin, R. N., 105
Asling, C. W., 54
Atchley, R. C., 576
Atkin, C. K., 465
Atkinson, I. W., 434
Atkinson, R. C., 217
Atlas, M., 206
Augenbraun, B., 487
Ausubel, D. P., 535
Ausubel, F., 145
Axline, Virginia M., 492–93
Azrin, N. H., 450

B

Bachrach, R., 439
Badger, E., 385
Baer, Donald M., 172, 312–13, 376
Bailey, D. A., 524
Baken, David, 511
Baker, C. T., 280, 286
Baker, L., 479
Baldwin, A. L., 211, 212, 286, 367
Bales, R. F., 334
Ball, R. S., 281
Balla, D., 298
Baltes, P. B., 34, 278, 565, 566, 567
Bandler, L., 487
Bandura, Albert, 17, 130 fn, 170, 172–73, 174, 407–8, 411, 424, 425–26, 432, 464, 513, 515, 549
Bane, M., 129
Banks, M. S., 105
Barclay, A., 300
Bardwick, J. M., 401, 411
Barkley, R. A., 498, 504
Barnett, C. R., 383
Baroff, G. S., 32, 39
Barrera, F., 170
Barrett, B. H., 482
Barrett, C. L., 482
Barry, W. A., 569
Bartsch, T. W., 34
Battle, E., 502
Bauer, D. H., 483

Bayley, N., 133, 273, 274, 275, 286, 288, 303, 378, 524
Beaman, A. L., 423
Bean, J. P., 411
Becker, W. C., 159, 336, 338
Beckwith, J., 145
Beckwith, L., 382
Beeghley, L., 349
Beilin, H., 200
Beintema, D. J., 71
Bell, R. Q., 97
Bell, S. M., 333, 382
Bellows, George, 6 fig.
Bellugi, U., 234
Bellugi-Klima, U., 236, 238–39
Belmont, L., 104, 284
Bem, S. L., 411
Bench, J., 90
Benda, C. E., 298
Bender, Lauretta, 476, 478, 505
Benedict, Ruth, 513–14, 549
Bennett, E. L., 106
Bennett, S. M., 396
Berko, J., 229, 243
Berkowitz, L., 457
Berlyne, D. E., 176
Bernard, G., 90
Bernard, J., 569, 570
Bernstein, Basil, 354
Berscheid, E., 523
Best, D. L., 396
Bettelheim, Bruno, 324, 477–78, 505
Bialer, I., 494
Biber, H., 581
Bijou, S. W., 163, 376–77
Biller, H. B., 336
Billingsley, A., 356
Binet, Alfred, 8, 19, 270, 302, 315
Birch, H. G., 103, 104, 134, 504
Birns, B., 73, 90, 135, 400, 404, 408
Birren, J. E., 563, 566, 568, 569
Blanchard, R., 336
Blank, M., 90
Blau, P. M., 540
Blau, T. H., 83
Blehar, M. C., 385, 391
Block, J., 399, 411
Blom, G. E., 487
Bloom, K., 225

Friedman, S., 81
Friedrich, L. K., 467
Friedrich, W. N., 399
Frijda, N. H., 215
Frodi, A. M., 67, 383
Frost, L., 325
Fry, P. S., 422, 423

G

Gagne, E., 438
Galton, Sir Francis, 126, 136, 145, 302
Garber, H., 392
Garcia, J., 156
Garcia, K., 482
Gardner, B. T., 226
Gardner, R. A., 226
Garnica, O. K., 238
Garrow, H., 165
Garvey, W. P., 486
Gelfand, D. M., 458
Gelles, Richard J., 340, 341
Gelman, Rachel, 200, 201, 202, 221, 258
Genevese, Kitty, 454
Gerard, M. W., 487
Gesell, Arnold, 14 fig., 15, 80, 81, 82, 83
Getz, S. K., 456
Getzels, J. W., 305
Gewirtz, J. L., 225, 376, 377
Ghodssi, M., 385
Gholson, B., 182, 183
Gianascol, A. J., 476
Gibbs, E. L., 121
Gibbs, F. A., 121
Gibbs, J. C., 447, 448
Gibbs, J. B., 542
Gibson, E. J., 98–100, 105, 108
Gil, David G., 339, 341, 342
Gilbert, F., 573
Gill, L., 457
Ginsburg, H., 190
Gintis, H., 129
Ginzberg, E., 539
Giovannoni, J. M., 356
Girdano, D. A., 545
Girdano, D. D., 545
Gittelman-Klein, R., 488
Gladston, R., 340
Glamser, F. D., 576
Gleitman, L. R., 236
Gliner, C. R., 89
Glucksberg, S., 251, 252, 254, 256, 257, 258
Glueck, E., 544
Glueck, S., 544
Goddard, Henry, 121
Goddard, K. E., 65
Goethe, J. W. von, 301
Goetz, E. M., 312–13
Gold, D., 287
Goldberg, I. D., 58

Goldberg, S., 67
Golden, N. L., 59
Goldfarb, W., 282, 478, 479
Goldman, G., 579
Goldschmid, M. L., 527
Goldstein, H., 58
Goldstein, K. M., 64
Goldstein, P., 94
Good, T. L., 352
Goodale, W., 516
Goodman, J., 419
Goodman, M. J., 573
Goodwin, M. S., 388, 389
Gorden, N., 487
Gordon, D. A., 485
Gordon, S., 54, 538
Gordon, S. B., 498
Goren, C., 97
Gorney, R., 456
Gottesman, I. L., 118, 133, 135
Gottfredson, G. D., 574, 575
Gottfried, A. W., 64, 67
Gould, R. E., 548
Gould, Roger L., 557, 558, 560, 585
Goulet, L. R., 300
Goyette, C. H., 488
Graham, F. K., 90
Granat, K., 293
Granat, S., 293
Grandon, G. M., 285
Graziano, A. M., 482, 484
Green, R., 276–77
Greenberg, B. S., 465
Greenberg, D. J., 96
Greenberg, L. M., 494
Greenberg, M. T., 202
Greenfield, P. M., 233, 259
Greenhill, L., 132, 488, 489
Greenhouse, S. W., 563
Greenspoon, L., 545
Greif, E. B., 447
Grimm, H., 261
Grinder, R. E., 44, 512, 536
Grobstein, R., 383
Gross, P., 457
Grossman, H. J., 293
Grotevant, H. D., 136
Grusec, J. E., 54, 55, 60, 459, 468
Guilford, J. P., 266, 307
Gurak, D. T., 569
Guthrie, Woody, 115
Gustad, J. W., 540

H

Haaf, R. A., 97
Hagen, J. W., 214, 215
Haith, M. M., 69, 92, 96
Hale, G. A., 214
Hall, G. Stanley, 8, 9, 512, 549
Hall, M., 432
Hall, V., 200
Halloran, J. D., 464

Halverson, H. M., 82
Halwes, T. G., 218
Hamburg, B. A., 401
Hampe, E., 482
Handlon, J., 457
Hanratty, M. A., 465
Hardyck, C., 83
Harlow, Harry F., 176, 177, 178, 185, 200, 215, 374, 381, 385, 386, 387, 392, 393
Harlow, M. K., 176, 178, 386, 387
Harmon, L. R., 305
Harper, P. A., 66
Harrington, S., 392
Harris, M. B., 432, 460
Harry, J., 569
Harryman, S., 69
Harter, S., 435–36
Hartig, M., 419–21
Hartmann, D. P., 458
Hartshorn, H., 444, 445, 468
Hartup, W. W., 22, 23, 24, 25, 33, 375
Hasazi, J. E., 301, 497
Hassibi, M., 504
Hatton, H. M., 90
Havighurst, R. J., 291, 348, 349, 458, 555, 556, 557, 578, 582
Haviland, S. E., 259
Hay, A., 251
Hayes, C., 226
Healy, William, 543–44
Hebb, D. O., 106
Heber, R., 392
Hegrenes, J. P., 486
Held, R., 106
Helmreich, R., 411
Helson, R., 305
Hemphill, B. M., 457
Henry, W. E., 577, 586
Herbert-Jackson, E., 391
Hershenson, M., 97
Hersov, L. A., 485, 486
Herzog, E., 346, 347
Hess, E. H., 376
Hess, Robert D., 357, 358
Hess, V. L., 214
Heston, L. L., 131–32
Hetherington, E. M., 336, 343, 346, 399, 485, 486
Heynes, B., 129
Higgins, E. T., 254, 354
Hilgard, E. R., 152
Hix, I. E., 66
Hobbs, D. F., 570
Hock, E., 392
Hoffman, C., 392
Hoffman, M. L., 399, 418, 443, 459
Hoffmann, Henrich, 487
Hoffmann, Lois, 344
Hogan, M., 63
Hogarty, P. S., 280
Holland, J. L., 574, 575
Holland, V. M., 198
Hollinger, C. S., 294

Hollingshead, A. B., 541
Holmes, F. B., 392, 482
Holmes, L. B., 142
Holstein, C. B., 448
Holtzman, W. H., 268
Holzinger, K. J., 127
Homer, Winslow, 6 *fig.*
Homme, L. E., 165
Honig, A. S., 391
Honzik, M. P., 274, 280, 286, 287
Hood, L., 242
Hooper, F., 199
Horn, J. L., 267, 277, 278, 279
Horn, J. M., 138
Horn, N., 457
Horner, F. A., 66
Horner, M. S., 438, 541
Horowitz, F. D., 192
Hoy, E., 196, 256, 504
Hoyer, W. J., 567
Hubel, D. H., 105
Huesmann, L. R., 439, 466
Hughes, C. C., 425
Hull, Clark, 17
Hulsebus, R. C., 157
Hunt, J. McV., 266, 283, 376, 382, 383,
    385, 392
Hunter, I. M. L., 89
Hutt, C., 90
Hutt, S. J., 90
Huttenlocher, J., 249
Huyck, M. H., 574

I

Iacobbo, M., 81
Ilg, F. L., 82
Illingworth, R. S., 275
Inhelder, Bärbel, 192, 195, 197, 204,
    205, 206, 216, 297
Irwin, O. C., 228
Isard, S., 250
Isen, A. M., 457
Izard, C. E., 465

J

Jacklin, C. N., 399, 400, 402, 412–13
Jackson, D., 131
Jackson, J., 196
Jackson, P. W., 305, 307
Jacobs, B. S., 343
Jacobs, J., 548
Jacobs, P. A., 143–44
Jakobson, R., 231
Janda, L. H., 484
Jansky, J., 65
Janssen, K., 145
Jarvik, L. F., 278
Jarvik, L. S., 127
Jaslow, P., 577
Jeffers, F. C., 581

Jekel, J., 480
Jencks, C., 129
Jensen, Arthur R., 128, 129, 284,
    288–89, 293, 353
Jensen, G. D., 385
Jersild, A. T., 387, 482
Jespersen, J. O., 228
Jessner, L., 487
Jessor, R., 540
Joffe, J. M., 54, 61
Johnson, O. G., 284
Johnson, V. E., 572, 573
Johnston, A., 140
Joncich, G. M., 157
Jones, Mary Cover, 155, 523, 524
Jones, P., 103
Jones, R. L., 294
Jones-Molfese, V., 97
Jurgela, A. R., 497
Jusczyk, P., 226

K

Kagan, J., 324, 328, 380, 381, 390–91
Kagan, S., 452
Kalhorn, J., 286
Kalil, K., 253
Kallikak, Martin, 121
Kallman, Franz J., 131, 564
Kamin, Leon, 128–29
Kandel, D. B., 546, 547, 550
Kanfer, F. H., 419–21, 422–23
Kanner, Leo, 476, 479, 503, 505
Kaplan, A. G., 411
Kaplan, B. H., 55
Kaplan, B. J., 54
Karmel, B. Z., 96
Karniol, R., 429
Karp, L. E., 144, 145
Kartye, J., 301
Kasatkin, N. I., 90, 155
Kastenbaum, R., 571, 580, 581, 582,
    583
Katkovsky, W., 336, 433, 436, 439
Katz, I., 353
Kaye, H., 89
Kearsley, R. B., 390–91
Keating, D. P., 527
Keen, R. E., 90
Keller, B., 133
Kellogg, L. A., 226
Kellogg, W. N., 226
Kempe, C. H., 339, 340
Kempler, B., 198
Kendler, Howard H., 178, 180, 183,
    185, 200, 215
Kendler, Tracy S., 178, 180, 183, 185,
    200, 215
Kennedy, J. A., 81
Kennedy, W. A., 289, 485
Kennell, J. H., 383, 385
Kenney, H. J., 209
Kent, N., 286

Kessen, W., 5, 8, 69, 96, 101
Kessler, R. C., 546
Kety, S. S., 132
Key, C. B., 288
Kim, N., 257
Kinch, J. W., 530, 531–32
King, L. M., 350
King, S., 404
King, S. H., 515
Kingsley, R. C., 200
Kissel, S., 528
Klapper, J. T., 464
Klaus, M. H., 383, 385
Klein, D. F., 488
Klein, E. B., 557
Klein, R. E., 324, 328
Klentz, B., 423
Klineberg, Otto, 288
Kluger, R., 353
Knobloch, H., 54, 64, 275
Knopf, I. J., 494
Koch, H. L., 343
Koelling, R. A., 156
Kogan, N., 306, 307, 309, 311
Kohlberg, Laurence, 409, 411, 445–49,
    468, 503
Köhler, Wolfgang, 176
Kohn, M. L., 357
Kolata, G. B., 44, 58, 60, 61, 65
Kolb, S., 79
Koltsova, M. M., 155
Komarovsky, M., 412
Korn, S. J., 523
Korslund, M. K., 89
Koser, L., 159
Kotelchuck, M., 380, 381
Kramer, R., 448
Kratcoski, J. E., 542
Kratcoski, P. C., 542
Krauss, R. M., 254, 256, 257, 258
Kreutzer, M. A., 220
Kron, R. E., 65
Krowitz, A., 100
Kübler-Ross, E., 580, 587
Kuhn, K., 528
Kun, A., 434
Kunz, P. R., 569
Kurke, M., 105
Kurtines, W., 447
Kutner, B., 576, 577

L

Labouvie, E. W., 34
Labouvie, G. V., 567
Labouvie-Vief, G., 396
Labov, W., 354–55
Lacey, B. A., 502
La Cross, J., 503
Lagerspetz, K., 119
Laird, M. D., 63
Lamaze, Fernand, 63

R

Rabinowitz, R. G., 439
Rabson, A., 434, 436
Radin, N., 286, 287, 336
Rafferty, J., 434
Rainer, J. D., 132
Rainwater, L., 351
Ramot, L., 439
Rapoport, R. N., 425
Raskin, P. A., 408
Raskoff, A., 429
Rayner, R., 155, 484
Reed, E. W., 142, 143
Reed, L. H., 66
Rees, L., 487
Reese, H. W., 153, 155, 313, 565
Reis, M., 287
Renshaw, S., 103
Reynolds, G. S., 165
Rheingold, H. L., 225, 382
Rice, H. E., 459
Richardson, L., 81
Richmond, J. B., 14
Rickert, E. J., 165
Ricks, D., 503
Rider, R. V., 66
Riegel, K. F., 278
Riegel, R. M., 278
Riesen, A. H., 105–6
Rimland, Bernard, 476–77, 505
Rimm, D., 424, 484
Rist, R. C., 352, 354, 360
Ritter, K., 218
Roberge, J. J., 527
Roberts, D. F., 466
Robins, C., 354
Robins, L. N., 503
Robinson, H. B., 66, 143, 266, 293, 297, 298
Robinson, N. M., 66, 143, 266, 293, 297, 298
Robinson, W. P., 354
Robson, K. S., 375, 383, 385
Rocha, R. F., 461
Rockwell, Norman, 6 *fig.*
Rodin, J., 454
Roeper, A., 199
Rogers, D., 342, 571
Rogers, L. W., 418, 419
Rogers, M. E., 66
Rogers, P. P., 81
Rogers, R. W., 461, 465
Rollins, B. C., 571
Rosen, B. C., 436, 535
Rosenbaum, M. S., 432
Rosenberg, B. G., 343
Rosenberg, F., 528
Rosenberg, M., 353, 528
Rosenbloom, S., 104
Rosenhan, D. L., 457, 459
Rosenkrantz, P. S., 396
Rosenman, R., 138
Rosenman, R. H., 563

Rosenthal, D., 125, 130, 131, 132, 143
Rosenthal, T. L., 240
Rosenzweig, M. R., 106
Rosow, I., 578
Ross, A. O., 421, 475, 479
Ross, G., 381
Ross, H. W., 225
Ross, J. M., 524
Rothenberg, B. B., 200
Rousseau, Jean-Jacques, 5
Rovee, C. K., 89, 562
Rowbury, T. G., 312
Rowe, D. C., 138, 140
Rubenstein, J. E., 69
Rubin, I., 573
Rubin, I. L., 59
Rubin, K. H., 202, 460
Rudnick, M., 104
Ruff, C. F., 581
Ruff, H. A., 101
Rugh, R., 52, 56, 57, 58, 60
Rushton, J. P., 455, 459, 460
Russell, J. T., 105
Rutter, M., 478, 479

S

Sachs, J. S., 238
Safer, D. J., 487, 488
Saint-Anne Dargassies, S., 89
St. Clair, K. L., 68
St. Clair, S., 517
Salapatek, P., 69, 96, 97, 105, 191
Salerno, R. A., 238
Sander, G., 564
Sarlin, B., 132
Saunders, P. S., 257
Savitsky, J. C., 465
Sawrey, J. M., 296
Scarr, S., 130, 133, 136
Scarr-Salapatek, S., 67, 117
Schacter, S., 343
Schaefer, E. S., 286, 288, 337, 338
Schaefer, R. A., 527
Schaefer, W. S., 133
Schaffer, H. R., 73–74, 135, 152, 380, 381, 383
Schaie, K. W., 278
Scheerenberger, R. C., 293
Scheinfeld, A., 47, 123
Schneider, D. M., 355
Schneider, F. W., 460
Schonfield, D., 578
Schrag, Peter, 494–95
Schroeder, C. S., 480
Schulman, C. A., 90
Schulsinger, F., 132
Schwartzberg, N. S., 466
Scollon, R. T., 259
Sears, R. R., 167, 322, 336, 343
Selesnick, S., 487
Seligman, M. E., 156
Semmes, J., 105

Serbin, L., 502
Severy, L. J., 300
Shaffer, D., 488, 489
Shanas, Ethel, 563, 571, 586
Shanks, B. L., 198
Shantz, C., 196, 199
Shapira, A., 452
Shatz, M., 258, 261
Shaw, M. E., 535
Sheingold, K., 217
Shepherd, M., 473–74, 491, 502
Sherk, L., 457
Sherman, J. A., 170, 172
Sherman, J. C., 89, 92
Sherman, J. G., 160
Sherman, M., 89, 92, 288
Sherry, D., 67
Shettles, L. B., 52, 56, 57, 58, 60
Shields, J., 127
Shiffrin, R. M., 217
Shinn, M., 346
Shipley, E. F., 236
Shipman, Virginia C., 357, 358
Shirley, Mary M., 8, 81, 228
Shlapack, W., 89, 562
Shorr, W., 548
Shuey, A. M., 289
Shuttleworth, F. K., 444
Siddall, J. W., 424
Siebel, C. E., 460
Siebert, J., 253
Siegelman, M., 311
Siegler, I. C., 278
Siegler, R. S., 200, 202, 206, 528
Sigel, I., 199, 200
Sillen, J., 472
Silver, H. K., 339
Silverman, F. N., 339
Simmons, R., 528
Simon, Theophile, 270, 315
Simpson, E. L., 448
Simpson, G. G., 44, 58
Sims-Knight, J., 196
Singer, D. G., 456
Singer, J. L., 456
Singer, R. N., 81
Sinnott, E. W., 45
Siqueland, E. R., 157, 226
Skeels, Harold M., 130, 282–83, 315
Skinner, B. F., 16 *fig.*, 17, 163, 240, 262, 424, 426
Skodak, M., 130
Slaby, R. G., 409, 422, 461, 462
Slobin, D. I., 242
Slocum, W. C., 532
Slotnik, N. S., 218
Smith, C. L., 458
Smith, C. S., 236
Smith, D. W., 58
Smith, H. T., 72
Smith, J. H., 233, 259
Smith, M., 129
Smith, N. V., 235
Smith, R. A., 429

Subject Index

A

Appearance
  and liking, 523
  of neonate, 68
Appropriateness, and creativity, 307
Arapesh, 404
Arousal, and aggression, 460–61
Assimilation, cognitive, 189–90, 212
Asthma, 486–87
Attachment, 372–86
  critical and sensitive periods, 376
  defined, 372
  determinants, 382–83
  ethological view, 372–76
  feeding vs. comfort study, 373–74
  five steps in development, 377–80
  learning theory, 376–77
  objects of, 380–82
  of parents, 383–86
  psychoanalytic view, 372
Attention
  and habituation, 152
  as reinforcer, 159
  selective, 214–15
  visual, changes in, 97
Australia, 533
Australian aboriginals, 292
Autism. *See* Infantile autism
Autoclitic frames, 240–41
Autonomy
  adolescent struggle for, 532–33
  Erikson's theory, 370
  psychological, 338
Avoidance learning, 167

B

Babbling, 226–27
Babinsky reflex, 69 *table*, 70, 89
Babkin reflex, 69 *table*
Bayley Scales of Infant Development,
    273, 275
Bedwetting, 480–81, 496–97
Behavior
  and cultural experiences, 328
  genetic influences, 117–18
  intersensory, 102–4
  and moral values, 444–45
  multiple determined, 28
  norms, 472
  preverbal, 226–28, 231
Behavioral theory, of language
    development, 225
Behavior chaining, 160
Behavior genetics
  defined, 118–19
  methods of study, 119–25
  personality studies, 136–41
  temperament study, 135
  usefulness, 140–41
Behaviorism, vs. cognitive theories,
    12–13
Behavior modification, 493–500. *See*
    also Classical conditioning;
    Operant conditioning

for enuresis, 496–97
  general characteristics, 495–96
  for noise phobia, 497–98
Behavior problems, 472–506
  childhood schizophrenia, 474–76
  criteria for identifying, 472–74
  elimination disturbances, 480–82
  etiology and prognosis of severe
      disorders, 476–79
  fashionable trends, 503
  fears and phobias, 482–86
  genetic determinants, 130–33
  hyperactivity, 487–89
  infantile autism, 476
  prediction of, 502–4
  prevalence, 500–02
  psychophysiological disorders,
      486–87
  treatment methods, 490–500
Behavior shaping, 160–61
Bible, 83
Binet-Simon Metrical Scale of
    Intelligence, 270
Birth, 61–68
  and attachment, 383–85
  cultural variations, 62
  perinatal complication, 61, 63–65
  prematurity, 65–67. *See also*
      Premature birth
  recent trends, 62–63
  stages, 61
Birth defects, 53, 54–61
Birthing centers, 384
Birth order
  and IQ, 136, 284–85
  and social development, 342–43
Birthweight, 65–67
Blacks
  family structure, 355
  IQ scores, 128, 288–90, 292, 293
  language differences, 354
  poverty among, 349
  school performance, 349
  self-esteem, 353
  sickle cell trait, 115, 146
  teacher expectancy study, 352–53
Blastocyst, 48, 50
Blindness, 89
Body size
  adolescent changes, 518–21
  growth patterns, 74–75
Boundary setting, and dying, 581–82
Brain
  changes in adolescence, 520
  and reflexes, 71, 79
  sensation vs. perception, 88
Brain damage
  and hyperactivity, 488–89
  and mental retardation, 296
Brazelton Neonatal Assessment Scale,
    68
Breasts, at puberty, 521
Breech birth, 63
Brightness, perception of, 92
Brown v. Board of Education, 353

C

Caesarean section, 64
California Growth Study, 523–24
California Personality Inventory, 135
Canada, 48
Career. *See* Occupation
Case study research, 22, 29–31
Castration complex, 407
Catharsis, and aggression, 460–61
Cattell Intelligence Tests, 273
Centration, 197–98, 214
Cephalocaudal growth, 75–76
Chaining behavior, 160
Child abuse, 339–42
Childbirth. *See* Birth
Childbirth Without Fear (Dick-Read), 60
Child Guidance Study, 280
Childhood schizophrenia
  behavior modification therapy,
      498–500
  characteristics, 474–76
  etiology, 478
Child psychology, 4
Child rearing. *See also* Parents;
    Parenting
  and achievement striving, 436
  cultural differences, 322–27
  goals of parenting, 331–32
  satisfaction from, 570
  and socioeconomic status, 355–59
Children
  auditory perception, 91
  changing views of, 5–8
  creative, 306, 307–9
  in institutions, 387, 389
  intelligence tests for, 270–73, 275–76
  intersensory behavior, 103, 104
  motor development, 77–83
  physical growth, 74–77
  punishment by adults, 168–69
  selective attention, 214–15
  taste sense, 88–89
  view of death, 581
Children's Hospital Medical Center
    (Boston), 340
Chitling Test, 291
Chorion, 48
Chromosomal aberrations
  causes and incidence, 142
  Down's syndrome, 142
  genetic screening, 144–46
  and mental retardation, 296
  of sex chromosomes, 143–44
Chromosomes
  aberrant. *See* Chromosomal
      aberrations
  and conception, 45–46, 48
  and sex identity, 405
  sex-linked traits, 116
  and species variability, 112–13
Cigarette smoking
  by adolescents, 545, 546
  and olfaction, 90
  during pregnancy, 58

Memory, 215–21
  components, 217
  effects of aging, 564–66
  of mentally retarded, 297
  metamemory, 220–21
  operations, 218–20
  types, 216
Menarche, 521, 526
Menopause, 572–73
Menstrual cycle, and fertilization, 46
Mental age (MA), 270
Mental representation
  Piaget's theory, 195, 207–8
  three modes (Bruner), 208–10
Mental retardation, 293–301
  chromosomal aberrations, 142, 143,
    144
  cognitive defects, 296–98
  and cooperative behavior, 452
  and cultural bias, 292
  defined, 293
  etiology, 296
  familial, 296
  levels and measurement, 294–96
  due to PKU, 125–26
  social and emotional factors,
    298–300
  social skills, 300–301
Mesoderm, 50
Metamemory, 220–21
Methadone, prenatal effects, 61
Mexican-Americans, 452
Midwifery, 63
Minimal brain dysfunction (MBO),
    488–89. *See also*
    Hyperactivity
Mistrust, 370
Mitosis, 48, 142
Modeling
  of aggression, 464
  of cooperation, 453
  of delay of gratification, 425–26
  of helping behavior, 456
  as observational learning, 172–74
  and resistance to temptation, 421–22
  sex differences, 422
  and sex-role learning, 408–9
  of sharing behavior, 458–60
  to treat behavior problems, 498–500
Mood. *See also* Emotions
  and resistance to temptation, 422–23
  and sharing behavior, 457
Mongolism, 142. *See also* Down's
    syndrome
Monogamous families, 330
Monozygotic twins, 47–48
  behavior genetic studies, 122–23
  chromosomal aberrations, 142, 143
Moral development, 443–50
  and behavior, 444–45
  cognitive stages, 445–50
  psychoanalytic theory, 443–44
Moratorium status, 517–18

Moro reflex, 69 *table,* 70–71
  and fear, 482–83
Morphology, 230, 242–47
Mothers. *See also* Parents
  age of, and chromosomal
    aberrations, 142, 143, 144
  age of, and prenatal development,
    54
  effect on child's IQ, 286, 287
  employed, 343–46
  family role, 333–36
  fear of leaving, 485
  food provider vs. comforter role,
    372–73
  formation of attachment to infant,
    383–85
  neglectful, 355–56
  as object of infant attachment,
    374–75, 378–81
  overprotective, 487
  of premature infants, 67
  prenatal influences, 54–60
  sensitivity to infants, 382–83
  separation of infant from, 387–89
Motivation, for achievement, 434–36
Motor development, 77–83
  course of, 78–80
  locomotion, 81–82
  manual skills, 82–83
  maturation and learning influences,
    80–81
Movement
  of fetus, 52
  reflexive vs. voluntary, 79–80
  visual perception of, 92
Multiple conceptions, 47–48
Mundugumor, 404
Muscles, in adolescence, 520–21
Myth of the Hyperactive Child, The
    (Schrag and Divoky),
    494–95

N

Narcotics, effect of prenatal
    development, 58. *See also*
    Drugs
National Genetics Foundation, 145
National Health Center, 350
National Merit Scholarship
    Qualifying Test, 135
Nature-nurture controversy, 10
  and intelligence, 266
  issues, 117–18
  and personality development, 364
  Piaget's theory, 188
Navaho, 213
Negative punishment, 159, 170
Negative reinforcement, 159, 167
Neonates, 68–72. *See also* Infants; Birth
  attachment factors, 383–85
  auditory perception, 90–91
  habituation, 152–53

intersensory behavior, 102, 104
  olfaction, 89
  physical condition, 68
  PKU screening, 125
  reflexes, 69–71
  sensorimotor period, 191
  sensory capacity, 71
  sex differences, 404
  states of consciousness, 71–72
  taste, 88
  touch sensation, 89
  vision, 92–94, 96, 97
Nervous system
  aging, 568
  growth, 75
Netherlands, 284
New England, 324
New York City
  behavior study, 472
  child abuse, 339
  day care, 392
  Genovese murder, 453–54
Nigeria, 331
Nonreversal shifts, 179–80
Nova Scotia, 424–26
Nuclear families, 330
Nutrition, and prenatal development,
    54

O

Object permanence, 210–12
Observation
  in developmental research, 22
  passive, 22–23
Observational learning, 170–76. *See
    also* Modeling
  defined, 170
  developmental trends, 170–71
  direct imitative effects, 174
  and grammar acquisition, 239–40
  importance of imitation, 172
  inhibitory and disinhibitory effects,
    174–76
  modeling, 172–74
  three steps, 175
Occupation
  and child rearing, 357
  choosing, 539–42
  mid-career changes, 574–75
  retirement, 575–77
Occupational status, 349
Oedipal conflict, 333, 371, 443
Old age, adjustment to, 581–82. *See
    also* Aging
Olfaction, 89–90
  and aging, 562
  conditioning experiments, 156
Oogenesis, 46
Operant conditioning, 156–70
  and attachment, 377
  developmental trends, 157–58
  generalization, 162

Sex chromosomes
  aberrations, 143–44
  traits linked to, 116
  gender determination, 45–46
Sex differences
  aggression, 460
  asthma, 487
  behavior problems, 501–2
  biological determinants, 401–3
  cooperation, 452
  enuresis, 480
  expectation of success, 437–38
  extent of, 399–400
  identity status, 517
  hyperactivity, 487
  juvenile delinquency, 542
  moral development, 445
  mythical, 398 *table*, 399
  physiological, 399, 520–21
  social and cultural influences, 404
  vocational choice, 541–42
Sex hormones, 402, 405
Sex identity, 404–11
  cognitive development theory,
    409–10, 411
  defined, 405
  evaluation of theories and genders,
    410–11
  Money and Ehrhardt's model,
    405–6
  psychoanalytic theory, 407, 410–11
  social learning theory, 407–9, 411
Sex-linked inheritance, 116
Sex roles, 396–413
  changes in, 411–10
  defined, 405
  and sex identity, 404–11. *See also* Sex
    identity
Sex stereotypes, 396–99
  and occupational choice, 541
Sexual gratification, and bedwetting,
    481
Sexuality
  of adolescents, 537–38
  and aging, 571–74
Shame, vs. autonomy, 370
Shaping behavior
  and language development, 237–38
  technique, 160–61
Sharing, 456–60
Short-term memory, 217
  and aging, 565
Siblings, and socialization, 342–43. *See
    also* Birth order
Sickle cell anemia, 114–15
  genetic screening, 144, 146
Significates, 207
Signifiers, 207, 208
Sign language, 226
Signs, 208, 209
Single-subject research, 31–33
Siriono Indians, 62, 323–24
Sleep, of neonate, 71
Smell. *See* Olfaction

Social behavior, inheritance studies,
    133–41
Social conversation, 235–39
Social deprivation, 386–90
  after childbirth, 383–84
Social development, 322–61
  aggression, 460–68
  cultural context, 322–32
  in the family, 333–48
  prosocial behavior, 450–60
  socioeconomic factors, 348–59
Social isolation, 386–87
Socialization
  defined, 322
  and moral development, 449
  and sex differences, 404
  and sex stereotypes, 397
Social learning, and modeling, 172–74
Social Learning and Imitation (Miller and
    Dollard), 172
Social learning theory, 16–18
  of adolescence, 513
  of attachment, 376–77
  of parent-child interaction, 334
  of school phobia, 486
  of sex identity development, 407–9,
    411
Social relationships
  in adolescence, 530–38
  of elderly, 578
Social skills, of mentally retarded,
    300–301
Society
  defined, 322
  ecology of, 328–30
Society for the Prevention of Cruelty
    to Children, 338
Socioeconomic status (SES), 348–59
  and behavior norms, 472–73
  and child rearing, 355–59
  the disadvantaged, 348–50
  and enuresis, 480
  expectancy studies, 351–52
  and family structure, 355
  and health and longevity, 350–51
  and IQ scores, 287–89, 291, 293
  and juvenile delinquency, 542–43
  language difference, 354–55
  and locus on control, 439
  and self-esteem, 353
  and vocational choice, 541
Soviet Union, 324–25, 563
Sperm
  and conception, 44, 45, 46, 47
  damage to, 61
  formation, 113
Spermatogenesis, 46
Stagnation, vs. generativity, 557
Stanford-Binet intelligence tests
  black scores, 289
  constancy of scores, 280
  content, 271–72
  correlation of scores with tests in
    infancy, 274

  scoring, 270–71, 273
  socioeconomic factors, 287
  twin studies, 127
  validity, 269
Startle reflex, 152
Stimulus
  conditioned, 153, 154
  discriminative, 162
  unconditioned, 153, 154
Stimulus control, 162–63
Stress
  of adolescence, 512–13
  and child abuse, 341
  and fear, 483
  of mother, and prenatal
    development, 54–55
  physiological disorders, 486
  due to poverty, 355–56
Striving, *See* Achievement striving
Structural genes, 117
Success, fear of, 541–42
Sucking reflex, 69 *table*
Suicide, in adolescence, 547–49
Superego
  defined, 365
  and moral development, 443
  and sex identity, 407, 410
Suppression, via punishment, 167
Supreme Court, 353
Symbol
  Bruner's theory, 209
  Piaget's theory, 208
Symbolic mode, 208–9, 210
Syntax, 229–30
  combining with semantic
    information, 249–53
  observational learning, 240
  transformational grammar theory,
    246–47
  of two-word sentence, 240–42
Syphilis, 55, 56

T

Taste, 88–89
  aversive conditioning, 156
  effects of aging, 562
Tay Sachs disease, 146
Tchambuli, 404
Telegraphic communication, 235–36
Television, and aggression, 38, 464–68
Temperament
  and behavior problems, 504
  and infant test scores, 275
  inheritance studies, 134–35
Temptation, resistance to, 416–24
  and discipline, 416–21
  and emotional state, 422–23
  and objective self-awareness,
    423–24
  situational factors, 421–22
Teratogens, 53–54, 55–61
Terotology, 53–54